Double-Take

Aaron Douglas, cover of *Fire!!* November 1926

Double-Take

A Revisionist Harlem Renaissance Anthology

Edited by
VENETRIA K. PATTON
and
MAUREEN HONEY

Rutgers University Press
New Brunswick, New Jersey, and London

ABL 7900
2-20-2002
ωω
$ 60⁰⁰

Library of Congress Cataloging-in-Publication Data

Double-take : a revisionist Harlem Renaissance anthology / edited by Venetria K. Patton
and Maureen Honey.
    p.   cm.
    Includes bibliographical references and indexes.
    ISBN 0-8135-2929-8 (cloth : alk. paper) — ISBN 0-8135-2930-1 (pbk. : alk. paper)
      1. American literature—Afro-American authors. 2. American literature—New York
(State)—New York. 3. Harlem (New York, N.Y.)—Intellectual life. 4. Afro-Americans—
Literary collections. 5. American literature—20th century. 6. Afro-American arts.
7. Harlem Renaissance.   I. Patton, Venetria K., 1968–   II. Honey, Maureen, 1945–

PS509.N4 D68 2001
810.8'0896073'09041—dc21

                                                 00-045897

British Cataloging-in-Publication data for this book is available from the British Library.

Manufactured in the United States of America

For my late husband, Rogers J. Druhet III—our time was too short.

—Venetria K. Patton

CONTENTS

CREATIVE WRITING

ILLUSTRATIONS AND SONG LYRICS

Illustrations

Song Lyrics

ACKNOWLEDGMENTS

We would like to thank those who provided financial, intellectual, and emotional support for this project. We benefited immensely from grants to assist with permission fees and research expenses provided by the University of Nebraska Research Council and the University of Nebraska Humanities Center, headed by Steve Hilliard. The English department graduate program, headed by Barbara Di Bernard, also provided us with a generous amount of research support. We greatly appreciate the hard work of our assistants, Mary Curran and Stephanie Gustafson, who helped us in the initial stages of our research, and especially that of Michael Medwick, who went above and beyond the call of duty to bring this project to completion and who functioned as our "third arm." We must also thank our editor, Leslie Mitchner, for recognizing the value of our project and generously extending our deadline in order for us to do our best work. We thank as well Robin Du Blanc, copyeditor; Theresa Liu, editorial assistant; Tricia Politi, production coordinator; and Marilyn Campbell, director of the prepress department, who made this a better work. We wish to extend special thanks to the NAACP and the National Urban League for their generous permission to reprint material from *The Crisis* and *Opportunity.* These journals form the backbone of our study, and without the generosity of their publishers, we could not have produced this volume.

We have also benefited from the hard work and valuable insights of our colleagues in the area of Harlem Renaissance studies. This anthology is an outgrowth of tremendous groundbreaking work by Houston Baker, Robert Bone, Sterling Brown, Thadious Davis, Henry Louis Gates, Jr., Hugh Gloster, Nathan Irvin Huggins, Gloria Hull, David Levering Lewis, Deborah McDowell, Nellie Y. McKay, Arnold Rampersad, Ruth Elizabeth Randolph, Lorraine Elena Roses, Amritjit Siingh, Claudia Tate, Mary Helen Washington, Cheryl Wall, and others. We greatly appreciate the kind assistance of our colleagues in English at UNL as well, particularly Kenneth Price, Ralph Grajeda, and Oyekan Owomoyela. Ronald Jemal Stephens at the University of Nebraska read numerous drafts of the proposal and sections of the manuscript, while Jennifer DeVere Brody at the University of

Illinois at Chicago pointed us toward important sources that helped us to provide a fuller picture of the Renaissance. We also appreciated the thoughtful comments of our manuscript reviewers, which helped us better articulate our vision of the period.

We would be remiss if we did not also recognize the support of our families and friends. Special thanks go to Christopher Barker for initially suggesting this project. Venetria would also like to thank Ronald Stephens for his encouragement, her son Hollis Druhet for letting Mommy work when he would rather play, and her friend Andreaus Boise for always being there and keeping her sane. She must also thank Maureen for being a wonderful collaborator, great mentor, and a dedicated friend. Maureen would like to acknowledge warmly the support of her partner, Tom Kiefer, as she worked the long hours necessary to make this book a reality. She, above all, thanks Venetria, to whom great credit is due for conceiving this anthology, for the wise decisions that she made on its contents, and for being the best colleague and friend one could possibly have.

INTRODUCTION

On March 21, 1924, almost all of the future stars of the Harlem Renaissance gathered at Manhattan's Civic Club to inaugurate what would become known as the New Negro Movement of the 1920s and 1930s. This event was a dinner arranged to honor Jessie Fauset for the publication of her first novel, *There Is Confusion,* just published by Boni and Liveright. Poet Gwendolyn Bennett wrote her poem "To Usward" especially for the occasion and recited it that evening. In the audience receiving a round of applause was the most famous black woman poet of her day, Georgia Douglas Johnson, author of two recent books of poetry: *The Heart of a Woman* (1918) and *Bronze* (1922).

Despite the reason for this gathering, Fauset's prominent role as literary editor of *The Crisis,* the leading African American periodical in the nation, and the spotlighted presence of Bennett and Johnson, the evening was dominated by men. Most notably, the absent Jean Toomer, whose astonishing experimental novel *Cane* (1923) had also recently been published by Boni and Liveright, and Walter White, whose first novel, *The Fire in the Flint* (1924), would soon appear from Alfred A. Knopf, were praised effusively by the stream of male speakers who made up the program. Bennett's single poem was eclipsed by the evening's literary centerpiece, a poetry reading by rising star Countee Cullen. The most influential black power broker of the era, Alain Locke, was master of ceremonies—and known for his cultivation of male writers.

Cross-Currents of Gender, Genre, and Sexuality

The overshadowing of women at the Civic Club dinner (now known as the official beginning of the Harlem Renaissance) emblematizes the gender imbalance in the period. Although most of the male writers present at this event have come down to us in history as heart and soul of the New Negro Movement, the women who were there have been rediscovered only within the last ten or fifteen years. These women and their sister writers dropped out of sight, while their male colleagues' work continued to be read, studied, and debated. Anthologies of the Harlem Renaissance that followed the era were dominated by male writers; only a handful of contributions by women were included. Even now, with the vast amount of scholarship being done on their works, the prominent role of women in the movement continues to be overshadowed by male-authored texts. Although recent collections on the Harlem Renaissance include the names of Angelina Weld Grimké, Helene Johnson, Jessie Fauset, Dorothy West, Nella Larsen, Georgia Douglas Johnson, Anne Spencer, and others, the gender ratio is still nearly two to one—or greater—in favor of selections by men. With the exception of novelist Zora Neale Hurston (and perhaps Nella Larsen), women continue to be classified among the movement's minor writers.

This anthology attempts to redress the ongoing historical emphasis on male writers from the last century's first flowering of modern literature by African Americans. By including nearly equal numbers of male and female contributors as well as roughly equal contributions by men and women, we hope to restore and underline the importance of women's writings to our understanding of a literary awakening whose primary metaphors were female-centered: fertility, gestation, and birth. In doing so, we realize we are not representing the actual numbers of essays, poetry and short story collections, or novels published by men and women during the era—rather, we try to even out the disadvantages of gender that kept black women from publishing books as widely as their male peers. We emphasize instead the era's periodicals and anthologies as sources for our volume: in these venues, which largely fueled the Harlem Renaissance, women enjoyed greater success.

We intend to foster conversations about women's historically marginalized relationship to the Harlem Renaissance by including noncanonical selections as well as those considered within the canon. By emphasizing multiple genres through the inclusion of drama, song, and visual art, we call attention to the participation of women in all of the period's artistic venues, not just to the poetry for which they were best known. We also illustrate the cross-fertilization that occurred as writers tried their hand at various genres and the conversations that took place among them. By providing biographical sketches of the creative writers anthologized here, we try to suggest ways that gender, class, and sexual orientation informed the careers and writings of Harlem Renaissance participants as a way of extending our understanding of its racial politics.

By including texts with homoerotic themes, such as those by Richard Bruce Nugent, Countee Cullen, Angelina Weld Grimké, Mae Cowdery, and others, we invite attention to the interface between race and same-sex love that existed during the Renaissance. Often these are texts that are left out of Harlem Renaissance anthologies because they do not always conform to the period's focus on race and because the formal models in which they took shape were quite often traditional. Yet same-sex love was an important subject for many of these writers, and the traditional aesthetic framing can be interpreted as a veil covering gay or lesbian subtext.

Some of the questions arising from this gender and genre inclusivity are: To what degree were men and women of the Harlem Renaissance animated by the same racial subjects and concerns, to what degree by the specifics of gender? How does our inclusion of women, gay men, and lesbians as full partners in construction of the movement complicate and extend our notion of the Renaissance—both its weaknesses and its strengths? Is it a distortion of the historical literary record or an instructive corrective of it to devote equal time to women writers when they were overshadowed by men in their own time? Is it a distortion of history or a truer picture of it to consider as gay or lesbian texts the writings of people who did not openly identify themselves as such, especially those, like Langston Hughes, whose sexual orientation is the subject of continued debate? Can we speak of an overarching African American aesthetic that serves as an umbrella for male and female, gay, bisexual, and straight writers of the Renaissance, or are there separate literary traditions based on gender or sexual orientation running through it?

One thing is clear: when we pay attention to gender issues attached to the Harlem Renaissance, we notice interesting things. One of these is how many women's texts appeared at groundbreaking moments. Georgia Douglas Johnson's poetry collection *The Heart of a Woman,* with its introductory praise from the best-known African American poetry critic of his day, William Stanley Braithwaite, helped begin a new era of self-revelation for black poets. Published in 1918, Johnson's collection of lyric verse departed dramatically from the dialect poems of Paul Laurence Dunbar and Joseph Cotter, Sr., heralding a claim made by African American writers of the twenties to the full range of poetic expression from which they had previously been discouraged. Jessie Fauset's *There Is Confusion* (1924) was arguably the first significant novel of the Harlem Renaissance, if one considers *Cane* a prose poem. It too opened the door to new ways of thinking about black literature and life with its focus on middle-class characters and the absence of the folk vernacular so characteristic of the previous generation. Nella Larsen's novels *Quicksand* (1928) and *Passing* (1929) explored a new psychological territory in African American fiction, and she became the first black woman to win a Guggenheim Fellowship for creative writing. Angelina Weld Grimké's play *Rachel* (1916) was the first serious drama by an African American playwright to be produced on stage and not to be written in dialect. Its characters, like Fauset's, were middle class, urban, northern, college educated, and portrayed in a warm domestic atmosphere. It marked a startling departure from the musicals, comedies, pageants, and minstrel shows depicting happy-go-lucky black people that had preceded it.

All of these female-authored texts were lauded by the black press when they appeared, and three of these women, Johnson, Fauset, and Grimké, would go on to extensive publication in the journals and anthologies of the Harlem Renaissance. They in fact would become some of its most notable figures, for their key roles in the movement as well as for their writing—Johnson for her Saturday night literary gatherings at her home in Washington, D.C., Fauset for her discovery of major black talent in her job as literary editor of *The Crisis* from 1919 to 1926, and Grimké for her anti-lynching organizing and her influence on many young Renaissance writers as a teacher at D.C.'s Dunbar High School. Their pioneering works, along with Larsen's, would be supplanted by the innovative literature of writers experimenting with urban working-class subjects and a new black aesthetic based on African motifs, but they signaled the creative independence and assault on demeaning stereotypes with which the Harlem Renaissance first identified itself. This pathbreaking role was only dimly outlined in subsequent anthologies, however, which emphasized male-authored texts and New Negro militance.

Another aspect of the Renaissance one notices is how many of its participants are now under discussion as gay, lesbian, or bisexual. New research by Gloria Hull, David Levering Lewis, Arnold Rampersad, Henry Louis Gates, Jr., Deborah McDowell, Steven Watson, and others focuses on the same-sex liaisons and/or literary subtexts of Countee Cullen, Angelina Weld Grimké, Alice Dunbar-Nelson, Langston Hughes, Claude McKay, Wallace Thurman, Richard Bruce Nugent, Mae Cowdery, Gladys Casely Hayford, and Nella Larsen.[1] Social histories of the period indicate that Harlem was a major center of gay life in the 1920s and 1930s, with its gay cabarets and drag balls attended by thousands, its lesbian blues singers such as Gladys Bentley, Bessie Smith, and Ma Rainey, its gay or bisexual power brokers Alain Locke and Carl Van Vechten, and its proximity to Greenwich Village's own center of gay/lesbian life. A'Lelia Walker's famed parties at her Harlem address in the late twenties were frequented by gays and lesbians. Anthologies of the period have yet to highlight this historical context, however, or the significance of same-sex love poetry, blues lyrics, and fictional representations in the Renaissance. To help do so, we include texts by these writers with possible gay or lesbian subtexts that have been largely left out of the major anthologies: Dunbar-Nelson's "*You! Inez!*"; Grimké's "El Beso," "The Want of You," and "A Mona Lisa"; McKay's "To O.E.A."; Hughes's "Desire" and "Poem [2]"; Cullen's "Sacrament," "Little Sonnet to Little Friends," and the frequently reprinted "Tableau"; Hayford's "Rainy Season Love Song" and "The Serving Girl"; Nugent's "Shadow," "Sahdji," and his well-known "Smoke, Lilies, and Jade!"; and Cowdery's "Dusk," "Insatiate," and "Poem . . . for a Lover."

Recurring Themes

Placing the texts of men and women, minor and major writers, lesser known and canonized selections, multiple genres, and homoerotic texts side by side, this anthology opens opportunities for new understandings of the Harlem Renaissance. The movement is traditionally viewed as one characterized by generational splits (rear guard vs. vanguard) or divides based on the debate over art versus propaganda; on the contrary, we have made selections that point to the connections shared by this diverse set of writers. Although

1. Gloria Hull, *Color, Sex, and Poetry: Three Women Writers of the Harlem Renaissance* (Bloomington: Indiana University Press, 1987); David Levering Lewis, *When Harlem Was in Vogue* (New York: Alfred A. Knopf, 1981); Arnold Rampersad, *The Life of Langston Hughes* (New York: Oxford University Press, 1986); Henry Louis Gates, Jr., "The Black Man's Burden," in *Fear of a Queer Planet: Queer Politics and Social Theory,* ed. Michel Warner (Minneapolis: University of Minnesota Press, 1993); Deborah McDowell, *The Changing Same: Black Women's Literature, Criticism, and Theory* (Bloomington: Indiana University Press, 1995); and Steven Watson, *The Harlem Renaissance: Hub of African-American Culture, 1920–1930* (New York: Pantheon Books, 1995).

women poets are associated with nature poetry, Langston Hughes wrote about nature too, for instance, and Georgia Douglas Johnson, like many male writers, used folk vernacular in her prose. A poem ignored by anthologies, such as Hughes's "Lullaby" (*The Crisis,* 1926), can suggest linkages to women who wrote about babies or motherhood. Similarly, Claude McKay's "Like a Strong Tree" (*Survey Graphic* and *The New Negro,* 1925) echoes Angelina Weld Grimké's often anthologized "The Black Finger" (*Opportunity,* 1923). An aesthetically flawed poem by gifted writer Zora Neale Hurston, "Passion" (*Negro World,* 1922), can illustrate the period's early focus on traditional love lyrics. By including the poetry, prose, or drama not often anthologized or associated with particular writers, we hope to illustrate the multidimensional commonalities that characterize the Harlem Renaissance.

Sterling Brown and others have identified certain themes that reappear despite the gender and generational differences so often commented upon: Africa is a source of race pride, black American heroes or heroines are apotheosized, racial political propaganda is considered essential, the black folk tradition is affirmed, and candid self-revelation is on display.[2] Nathan Huggins adds to this list an emphasis on the urbanity of the New Negro and joy of discovering both the variety and unity of black people. Much of the literature sought to define this "New Negro" or in some way addressed the issue of identity, according to Huggins: "What did Africa mean? What did the slave and peasant past mean? What could a folk tradition mean to the 'New Negro'? What was color, itself? Blackness, clearly, was not only a color, it was a state of mind. So, what of the mulatto, and what of 'passing'?"[3] Huggins and David Levering Lewis point to questions about the important role of art in the Renaissance. These questions are reflected in the debate about art and propaganda, but are also related to the issue of artistic integrity—could black artists avoid mimicking European forms and still produce great art? Other themes that critics have noted in relation to the movement are the prominent role of the Christian church in this very secular artistic movement, anger at racism, and an indictment of Western culture.

In addition to these themes, we have noticed recurring discussions across both genders of migration, domestic servitude, motherhood, children, nature, and passionate love. Because of the new urban identity of the New Negro, discussions of migration from the South or other rural areas are quite frequent. Washerwomen are another frequent subject for both genders, perhaps because they symbolized the exploitation of black labor as a whole and because white soap suds were an apt metaphor for white supremacy. Motherhood was a site of artistic production because it encompassed the past rape of black women by white masters during slavery and because black mothers represented the anticipated better future of the race. The validation of mothers present in the dominant culture had been denied African American women, whose representation as

2. Watson, *Harlem Renaissance.*

3. Nathan Huggins, *Voices from the Harlem Renaissance* (New York: Oxford University Press, 1976), 9. See also David Levering Lewis, ed., *The Portable Harlem Renaissance Reader* (New York: Viking, 1994).

mammies caring for white people was a familiar stereotype. Writers of the Harlem Renaissance addressed this erasure by creating images of black women as maternal figures and centered their concept of artistic awakening on birth. Nature was a central source of imagery for both genders as well. Images of night, shadow, trees, dawn, dusk, earth stood for black pride, resilience, awakening, or protection. Finally, love and sensuality were important subjects for all of these writers. As Bernard Bell has noted, African Americans were dehumanized by a racist culture as incapable of romantic love, denied positive identities as sensual beings.[4] Participating in a larger cultural rebellion against Victorian prudery, writers of the Renaissance proclaimed themselves fully human followers of the heart, celebrants of the flesh.

There are key differences between male and female writers, however. As Cheryl Wall, Gloria Hull, Deborah McDowell, Claudia Tate, and others have pointed out, the system of patronage operating during the Harlem Renaissance privileged men.[5] As a result, it was harder for most women to get the financial and professional support they needed to get into print. While many of them had work published in the period's journals and anthologies, relatively few collections of poetry or short stories were published by women, and not as many of their plays were produced.

Critics also point to women's avoidance of the urban vernacular and "primitivism," particularly in their poetry (with the important exception of the blues singers). This vernacular and associations with "the primitive" of Africa resonated with sexuality, problematic terrain for black women at the time, who were burdened with a stereotype of themselves as prostitutes in the larger culture. To claim their humanity, intelligence, and artistic creativity, therefore, they tended to turn to middle-class subjects and traditional poetic forms even when celebrating their African roots. This tendency was fostered by the fact that most of them came from middle-class backgrounds, even though they were financially strapped. When women did dip into the vernacular, they tended to recuperate the folk dialect of the generation preceding them, a safer discourse in terms of its association with rural family life.

Women addressed gender oppression in their writing as well as racism. Essays by women frequently emphasized gender issues and the double burden of being female and black. Cheryl Wall notes that images of rooms, a symbol of confinement, reappear in women's texts, and allusions to journeys abound. Restricted in their ability to travel, they took imaginative flights instead. Women, like men, wrote about nature, but they infused these natural images with a feminist subtext. Pastoral settings dominated by female allusions are often contrasted with alien manmade urban spaces, for example, or nature is portrayed as a liberating force for women's spirits. Birds and flowers appear as representations of women's imprisonment or freedom. In these ways, women of the Harlem

---

4. Bernard Bell, *The Afro-American Novel and Its Tradition* (Amherst: University of Massachusetts Press, 1987).

5. Cheryl Wall, *Women of the Harlem Renaissance* (Bloomington: Indiana University Press, 1995); McDowell, *Changing Same;* and Claudia Tate, ed., *Georgia Douglas Johnson: The Selected Works* (New York: G.K. Hall, 1997).

Renaissance responded to the feminist stirrings that resulted in gaining female suffrage in 1920, but they grappled uneasily with the sometimes conflicting imperatives of racial solidarity and feminist revolt.

Contested Periodization

Another issue highlighted by gender awareness, as we will explicate later, is the contested nature of periodization. While there is general agreement about the significance of the Harlem Renaissance, there is less accord on when the movement begins and ends, since it is not marked by a consistent set of aesthetics or recognizable style. Literature from the period covered a wide range of forms from classic sonnets to modernist verse to blues and jazz aesthetics to folklore. The movement is associated with the 1920s, the Jazz Age, but just when it emerged and disappeared is a source of debate. In fact, Nathan Huggins refers to the Harlem Renaissance as a "convenient fiction,"[6] because there is no clear demarcation separating the old from the "New Negro." Despite this lack of clarity, writers and scholars have sought to impose order and meaning on this rather organic surge in artistic creativity; a brief review of this debate helps define this anthology's contribution.

In *The Harlem Renaissance Remembered,* Arna Bontemps divides the period into two phases: black propaganda (1921–1924) and connection of black writers to the white intelligentsia and publishing establishment (1924–1931), ending with the Depression of the 1930s. Nathan Huggins, in *Voices from the Harlem Renaissance,* follows Bontemps's lead by dating the era's beginnings to the end of World War I and its demise to the Depression. The editors of the more recent *Call and Response* echo these assessments in their preference for two distinct terms: "Harlem Renaissance" and the "Reformation," the latter referring to the post-Renaissance aftermath of the thirties and forties.

However, for others, including ourselves, the 1930s are merely an extension of the Harlem Renaissance. For example, Alain Locke describes the thirties as the "second and truly sound phase of the cultural development of the Negro in American literature and art."[7] This extension of the movement into the 1930s is embraced by *The Norton Anthology of African American Literature,* edited by Henry Louis Gates, Jr., and Nellie Y. McKay. According to its time line, 1919–1940, the years of the Harlem Renaissance traverse two full decades. David Levering Lewis also uses a more comprehensive time frame. In *The Portable Harlem Renaissance Reader,* he ascribes the years 1917–1935 to the movement, from the opening of American theater to black actors with the Broadway productions of Ridgely Torrence in 1917 to the Harlem Riot of 1935, and he places a great deal of importance on World War I and the race riots of 1919 as watershed events ushering in the concept of the New Negro.

---

6. Huggins, *Voices from the Harlem Renaissance,* 9.
7. Quoted in Patricia Liggins Hill et al., *Call and Response: The Riverside Anthology of the African American Literary Tradition* (Boston: Houghton Mifflin, 1998), 791.

Despite general agreement that the 1920s represent its zenith, then, periodization of the Harlem Renaissance is clearly an issue of some debate. Our anthology contributes to that conversation by heeding the observation of Cheryl Wall and Gloria Hull that narrower time and geographical parameters for the Harlem Renaissance work against women, most of whom published in a scattered way across a continuum of time and from regions outside Harlem. In that spirit, we are attaching the movement's parameters to two landmark works, neither of which was written in Harlem nor in the 1920s: the production of Angelina Weld Grimké's play *Rachel* (1916) and the publication of Zora Neale Hurston's novel *Their Eyes Were Watching God* (1937). Bracketing the Renaissance with these two texts not only opens up debates about gender and the movement's vast literary range, it pins the period to African American–authored creative literature rather than to political events, economic events, expository prose, or texts generated by whites: all areas dominated by men. Our parameters also underscore the importance of women to the movement, despite the handicaps of gender that limited their ability to get into print.

Although flawed aesthetically and outside the militant and vernacular discourse that has come to be identified with the Harlem Renaissance, there are sound reasons for tracing the period's beginnings to *Rachel* and for scrutinizing Grimké's play more carefully than we have done in the past. The play's groundbreaking nature is rooted in the fact that it was the first serious drama by an African American playwright to be performed on stage with an African American cast. It was performed in both Washington, D.C., and in New York. Subtitled "A Play of Protest," *Rachel* anticipated Du Bois's call to combine art with propaganda since the play centers on the evils of racism and lynching. It was seeing *Rachel* that persuaded the Renaissance's premier playwright, Willis Richardson, to devote his creative life to drama and directly led to his first play, *The Chip Woman's Fortune* (1923), the first serious African American–authored play to be produced on Broadway. We can see in *Rachel*'s foregrounding of racism's devastating impact on mothers and children glimpses of a major theme of women in the Harlem Renaissance: the equation of motherlessness with protest against racism. Finally, we see in this play some of the seeds about racism and family life sown for contemporary women writers, particularly Toni Morrison in her novels *The Bluest Eye* (1970) and *Beloved* (1991).

Hailed in its own day as the first drama to portray black people positively, a corrective to ubiquitous plantation stereotypes, *Rachel* was produced by the NAACP as a counter-narrative to D. W. Griffith's blockbuster film *The Birth of a Nation* (1915). Griffith's racist narrative glorified the Ku Klux Klan at a time when record numbers of black people were being lynched (by some estimates nearly two thousand in the century's first three decades alone). The propaganda function of *Rachel* was overtly theorized by Grimké, who aimed it at a white audience to gain support for anti-lynching legislation, although it was actually seen by mainly African American audiences. This was in part why it eschewed the folk vernacular that would become a hallmark of much Renaissance writing.

More importantly, *Rachel*'s urban and middle-class characters constituted a dramatic change from the minstrel stereotypes to which American audiences were accustomed, and its language was a departure from the dialect art forms of Paul Laurence Dunbar, Joseph Cotter, Sr., and Charles Chesnutt, who had dominated the first decades of the twentieth century. In this way Grimké's play was an important step toward expanding the limited forms in which black artists were trapped. It inaugurated the literature from Georgia Douglas Johnson, Countee Cullen, Jessie Fauset, Claude McKay, and others that would illustrate Du Bois's contention that African Americans should lay claim to the high art forms of the dominant culture in order to advance their acceptance as first-class American citizens and end segregation.

Ending the Harlem Renaissance with Hurston's *Their Eyes Were Watching God* (1937) conforms to critical consensus about the death of the movement, which is anywhere from 1935 to 1940. It also signals the devastating impact of the Depression on publishing opportunities for black writers and points to the coming ascendancy of urban realism and naturalism in African American letters with the publication of Richard Wright's *Black Boy* (1939) and *Native Son* (1940). Indeed, it was Wright's highly critical review of Hurston's novel in *New Masses* that helped bury the Renaissance. Wright's perspective sounded the death knell for rural folk vernacular as the basis of an authentic African American aesthetic and for women writers of the Harlem Renaissance—even the gifted Hurston, whose now-acclaimed novel went out of print for thirty years after its first run.

Drama Ushers in the Harlem Renaissance

While Zora Neale Hurston has been revived as a major writer of the twentieth century and *Their Eyes Were Watching God* as one of its most beautiful novels, *Rachel* continues to be largely ignored. This is in part due to its dated sensibility, but it also stems from the fact that drama of the Harlem Renaissance is overshadowed by the genres of poetry, fiction, and expository prose in contemporary anthologies. Yet drama was an important part of this era, and we include plays here to underline that historical significance. The period did not produce nearly as much good drama as it did poetry and fiction, but in many ways, plays ushered in the movement, and many writers specializing in other genres wrote plays. In addition to the impact of *Rachel,* produced in 1916 and published in 1920, it was the success of white writer Ridgely Torrence's *Three Plays for a Negro Theatre* that propelled mainstream interest in African American life. Produced in the fall of 1917 by Torrence's wife, Emily Hapgood, at the Garden Street Theatre, *The Rider of Dreams, Simon the Cyrenian,* and *Granny Maumee* were considered daring for the time not only because the cast was all black, but the parts were dignified. These successful plays were followed by several dramas, musicals, and novels about African Americans throughout the following decade.

Notable among these was Richardson's 1923 production of *The Chip Woman's Fortune,* the astounding Broadway run of *Harlem* (1929), coauthored by Wallace Thurman and white writer William Jourdan Rapp, and the 1921 musical *Shuffle Along,* written by African Americans Aubry Lyles and Flournoy Miller with songs by Eubie Blake and Noble Sissle. The first all-black musical, *Shuffle Along,* had an immediate and long-lasting impact on the Harlem Renaissance; its imitators helped to promote the "Talented Tenth"[8] notion of the arts as a new approach to race relations. The era's most famous black star, Josephine Baker, was in the play along with the celebrated Florence Mills. Tellingly, song-writer Eubie Blake composed the musical's central number, "Love Will Find a Way," with some trepidation, because he feared white audiences would not accept a romantic lyric sung by black actors. Yet he was determined to break out of the buffoon straitjacket of minstrel shows and to portray African Americans as capable of operating within the full range of dominant culture art forms.

Many key figures of the Harlem Renaissance were involved in the production and promotion of drama. For example, Langston Hughes was among *Shuffle Along*'s many admirers and said he came to Harlem in large part to see the production. He became seriously involved with drama during the 1930s; his record-breaking *Mulatto* was performed on Broadway in 1935, enjoying the longest run of any African American–authored serious play. Demonstrating the importance he attached to the stage, Hughes established several people's theaters: the Suitcase Theatre in Harlem, the Negro Theatre of Los Angeles, and the Skyloft Players in Chicago. In 1926 Du Bois originated the Krigwa Little Theatre movement in response to the lack of serious drama in New York about blacks, with its four principles of "About us, By us, For us, and Near us." Montgomery Gregory, a drama professor at Howard University, established the first National Negro Theatre in the United States when he organized the Department of Dramatic Arts at Howard University in 1921, which brought national attention to the Howard Players. Du Bois advocated "race" or "propaganda plays" on the order of Grimké's *Rachel,* while Gregory and Locke promoted "folk plays" such as Richardson's *The Chip Woman's Fortune* or Georgia Douglas Johnson's prize-winning *Plumes* (1927).

We have tried to indicate the important role of drama in creating the Renaissance by including dramatic pieces that are typically included only in specialized drama collections. The work of important dramatists Willis Richardson, Eulalie Spence, and May Miller are represented as well as the plays of writers who are better known for other genres, such as Hurston, Hughes, Johnson, and of course Grimké herself. The centrality of drama to African American artistic and social advancement during the Harlem Renaissance can best be appreciated, we feel, by placing dramatic texts alongside the more familiar works of poetry and prose.

Music and Visual Art: Neglected Genres

Two other neglected genres we include in this collection are music and visual art, although music is gaining ground with the inclusion of lyrics in *The Norton Anthology,*

---

8. The phrase "Talented Tenth" first appeared in W.E.B. Du Bois's *The Negro Problem* (1903). This concept espoused by Du Bois emphasized the importance of higher education, particularly in the liberal arts, for the most able ten percent of African Americans. Du Bois feared the overemphasis on industrial training advocated by Booker T. Washington and exemplified by the Tuskegee Institute would permanently confine African Americans to second-class citizenship. A percentage of the population would have to be educated to uplift the race.

Call and Response, and other recent anthologies. Some argue that music was at the heart of the Renaissance, particularly blues and jazz. Certainly it functioned as social glue to the movement's movers and shakers in cabarets and speakeasies while providing inspiration for the most innovative poets of the era. The blues of the Harlem Renaissance grew out of the spirituals and work songs of the South, borrowing their harmonic and structural devices and vocal techniques. Unlike these earlier forms, however, blues were sung by a single person and played on one or more instruments, rather than emerging from a chorus. The blues were also secular. There was no promise of heaven—only complaints about earthly troubles with an occasional promise of a good time or fine loving. During the Great Migration of African Americans from the South to cities of the North from 1910 to 1930, the blues evolved from country blues to classic city blues. By 1920 the recording industry in Tin Pan Alley in New York City made blues the latest craze, replacing ragtime. For example, Mamie Smith's "Crazy Blues" sold 75,000 copies in one month in 1920. Most of the city blues were sung by women, with Mamie Smith, Ma Rainey, Gladys Bentley, and Bessie Smith being the most well known.

Jazz was another music idiom that had a tremendous effect on both blacks and whites during the Renaissance. Jazz was a blending of the rhythm and melodies of Africa with the harmonic forms of Europe. Joel A. Rogers describes jazz as African Americans' "explosive attempt to cast off the blues and be happy, carefree happy, even in the midst of sordidness and sorrow" (see "Jazz at Home" in the essay section). Rogers describes jazz as "atavistically African. . . . In its barbaric rhythm and exuberance there is something of the bamboula, a wild, abandoned dance of the West African and the Haytian Negro." African American jazz differed from African music in that it was faster and more complex: "With its cowbells, auto horns, calliopes, rattles, dinner gongs, kitchen utensils, cymbals, screams, crashes, clankings and monotonous rhythm it bears all the marks of a nerve-strung, strident, mechanized civilization." Jazz and blues, as well as their predecessor, ragtime, came to be considered quintessentially American music, and the genesis of all three was African American. We have sought to indicate the influence of this music on writers of the Harlem Renaissance by including sample lyrics from such popular performers as W. C. Handy, Jelly Roll Morton, Bessie Smith, and Ma Rainey, as well as poems reflecting its rhythms.

The central role of visual art in writings of the Harlem Renaissance is another consideration of this multigenre anthology. Its importance is revealed by the large number of photographs of African art and illustrations inspired by it dispersed throughout the pages of periodicals and anthologies of the period; several of the latter we include here. One of the reigning influences of art was what African intellectual Léopold Senghor termed "Negritude," the "soulful and artistic qualities of native peoples."[9] This was a concept that described the impact of African sculpture on abstract impressionist European artists, such as Picasso and Matisse, in a movement that came to be known as "primitivism." In his 1925 essay "The Legacy of the Ancestral Arts" (see the essay section), Alain

9. Quoted in Huggins, *Voices from the Harlem Renaissance,* 7.

Locke articulates the connection as follows: "The African art object, a half generation ago the most neglected of ethnological curios, is now universally recognized as a 'notable instance of plastic representation,' a genuine work of art, masterful over its material in a powerful simplicity of conception, design and effect." He then links the new respect for African art with the need to develop an African American art aesthetic, as does painter, poet, and *Opportunity* art editor Gwendolyn Bennett in her essay, "The American Negro Paints" (see the essay section). To illustrate the new direction of this art, we have included these essays and artwork by Aaron Douglas, Richard Bruce Nugent, Charles Cullen, and James Lesesne Wells, whose drawings were integrated into the era's major journals and anthologies.

In an effort to make visible the activities of women in all the art forms of the Harlem Renaissance, including visual art, we have reprinted original illustrations by Gwendolyn Bennett, Laura Wheeler (Waring), Louise Latimer, and Vivian Schuyler (Key) from *The Crisis.* Their work was formally conservative, in keeping with the tendency of women to avoid associations with the "primitivist" aesthetic, but it is representative of the eclectic images run in the magazine. Gwendolyn Bennett, whose training at the Pratt Institute and Paris led to her position as professor of fine art at Howard University and her editorship at *Opportunity,* was a well-known illustrator of the period, in addition to her roles as writer and editor. Although they never achieved the heights of the period's superstar, Aaron Douglas, Wheeler and Schuyler contributed much cover art to *The Crisis,* and Wheeler in particular was an important artist. She was a graduate of the Pennsylvania Academy of Fine Arts as well as Académie la Grande-Chaumière in Paris, and her work was included in exhibitions of African American artists and alluded to by critics like Locke and Bennett in their discussions of directions for black art. Her black-and-white silhouettes of African settings drew on the Art Deco movement for their aesthetic. Vivian Schuyler graduated from the Pratt Institute of Fine Arts, and her cover design for the November 1927 issue of *The Crisis,* James Weldon Johnson's classic, "Lift Every Voice and Sing," won the Amy Spingarn Prize that year. Schuyler's work was representational and thus out of touch with the abstract African motifs of Douglas and others that broke new ground, but it centered on positive portrayals of black women and appeared frequently in *The Crisis.*

The Pan-Africanist Nature of the Harlem Renaissance

Our discussion of the Harlem Renaissance remains grounded in the United States, but we hope our selections point to the larger arena of the New Negro Movement. Even though Harlem is the place most closely associated with this movement, London and Paris were also centers for black emigrants from the British Empire, Martinique, Haiti, and Senegal. The cultural growth of all these cities was propelled by emigration of blacks from the West Indies and Africa after World War I dislodged them from their homelands, helping to foster a Pan-Africanist dream of worldwide black unity. The era of the New Negro was not just an African American concept, in other words, but a wordwide expression of black self-assertion. This grew out of the atrocities of World War I, which undermined Western society's claim to a higher standard of civilization and encouraged people of African descent to reject a white supremacist ideology. We have included diasporic writers such as the Jamaican-born Claude McKay, Eric Walrond, of Barbadian and Guyanese parentage, and Sierra Leone resident Gladys May Casely Hayford (a k a Aquah Laluah) to emphasize this global aspect. We have also included the back-to-Africa writing of Jamaicans Marcus Garvey and W. A. Domingo, as well as Jessie Fauset's reflections on the Second Pan-African Congress of 1921 organized by W.E.B. Du Bois.

Despite the global nature of the New Negro movement and the variety of locations inhabited by its writers, particularly the women, we are in accord with other anthologies that have identified Harlem as its ideological center. The Great Migration between 1910 and1930 entailed massive population shifts as southern blacks migrated North in hopes of better social and economic opportunities—most of them came to Harlem, where housing was relatively good. By 1930 one million African Americans were believed to have left the South, but only 333,000 were shown to have migrated to places other than Harlem, and by the end of the 1920s it was the most densely populated black area in the world. Thus, according to Patricia Liggins Hill, "Harlem became both center and symbol of black culture and thought."[10]

The Arts as Civil Rights

Because of the large and growing black population and the city's history of African American excellence in the arts, New York was a natural center for the Harlem Renaissance. New York was America's cultural capital, and it was the center of publishing, drama, music, and painting. It was also the headquarters of the three biggest civil rights organizations: the NAACP (National Association for the Advancement of Colored People) founded by W.E.B. Du Bois (publisher of *The Crisis*) in 1909; the NUL (National Urban League) founded by Charles S. Johnson (publisher of *Opportunity*) in 1910; and the UNIA (Universal Negro Improvement Association) founded by Marcus Garvey (publisher of *Negro World*) in 1914.

These periodicals played a significant role in the development of the Harlem Renaissance because the organizations to which they were attached viewed support of the arts as the primary means to access civil rights. As David Levering Lewis notes: "The Harlem Renaissance was a somewhat forced phenomenon, a cultural nationalism of the parlor, institutionally encouraged and directed by leaders of the national Civil Rights Establishment for the paramount purpose of improving race relations."[11] Leaders of the movement believed that whites would be persuaded to accept the humanity of African Americans if blacks could achieve artistic equality and that such equality would lead to

10. Hill et al., *Call and Response*, 773.
11. Lewis, *Portable Harlem Renaissance Reader,* xv.

the achievement of civil rights. The NAACP and the NUL sought to encourage interracial collaboration between liberal whites and Du Bois's "Talented Tenth," the best and brightest of African American artists and intellectuals. They worked actively to connect black writers with white publishers.

The relative paucity of African American literature produced before the launching of the Harlem Renaissance pointed to the lack of a cultural agenda for African Americans, in the view of civil rights leaders. According to David Levering Lewis, between 1908 and 1923 only a handful of significant literary works by black writers appeared: Sutton Griggs's *Pointing the Way* (1908), W.E.B. Du Bois's *The Quest of the Silver Fleece* (1911), James Weldon Johnson's *The Autobiography of an Ex-Colored Man* (1912), Du Bois's *Darkwater* (1920), McKay's *Harlem Shadows* (1922), and Jean Toomer's *Cane* (1923). We would add to that list Angelina Weld Grimké's *Rachel* (1916), Willis Richardson's *The Chip Woman's Fortune* (1923), Georgia Douglas Johnson's two books of poetry published in 1918 and 1922, and Joseph Cotter, Jr.'s, poetry collection, *The Band of Gideon* (1918). Leaders like Du Bois and Locke felt there was an opportunity to convince white America that African American writing was worthy of publication and that the race had the intellectual fortitude necessary to create such work. According to Du Bois, "until the art of black folk compels recognition they will not be regarded as human."[12] James Weldon Johnson also argued that the arts were a useful means for asserting the cultural dignity of African Americans: "No people that has produced great literature and art has ever been looked upon by the world as distinctly inferior. . . . And nothing will do more to change the mental attitude and raise his status than a demonstration of intellectual parity by the Negro through the production of literature and art."[13] These were the core beliefs that fueled the Harlem Renaissance.

The NAACP membership rolls included a number of scholarly writers who contributed frequently to *The Crisis*. Foremost among these were James Weldon Johnson, whose landmark anthology, *The Book of American Negro Poetry* (1922), brought many new writers to the fore; editor Du Bois; field organizer and novelist Walter White; and Jessie Redmon Fauset. In 1919 Du Bois appointed Fauset as literary editor because he wanted to nurture the best African American talent in the nation. Fauset was not only an excellent editor, but a talented writer in her own right, whose exceptional literary career flourished during the 1920s. Fauset has been frequently described as midwife to the Harlem Renaissance because she discovered and encouraged so many new writers: Gwendolyn Bennett, Countee Cullen, Langston Hughes, Georgia Douglas Johnson, Claude McKay, and Jean Toomer. Fauset mined this talent in such a way as to make *The Crisis* the premier African American magazine of the era. As early as 1919, its circulation had reached 104,000, whereas the circulation of *Opportunity*, the closest competitor, reached only 11,000 by 1928.

12. Quoted in Lewis, *Portable Harlem Renaissance Reader,* xvi.

13. James Weldon Johnson, ed., *The Book of American Negro Poetry* (New York: Harcourt, Brace & Company, 1922), vii.

Although *Opportunity* did not enjoy the same level of success as *The Crisis*, its editor, Charles S. Johnson, was another key figure of the Harlem Renaissance. According to Langston Hughes, Johnson "did more to encourage and develop Negro writers during the 1920s than anyone else."[14] This point is affirmed by Zora Neale Hurston, who believed that the Renaissance was Johnson's doing, but "his hush-mouth nature has caused it to be attributed to many others."[15] Johnson was particularly frustrated by the lack of respect and visibility accorded to black writers who did not write in dialect, and he used *Opportunity* to break down the stereotypes that confined African American writers to that form. According to Robert Hemenway, Johnson "single-handedly made *Opportunity* an expression of 'New Negro' thought, and 'New Negroes' made it clear that they would not accept a subordinate role in American society."[16] However, Johnson needed the proper means of getting this point across; it was not sufficient merely to bring these great artists to a black audience.

This was the motivation behind Johnson's organization of the March 21, 1924, Civic Club dinner to celebrate Jessie Fauset's new novel, although it was Regina Anderson of the 134th Street Branch of the New York Public Library in Harlem and Georgia Douglas Johnson who had urged him to honor her. He wanted to bring white literary giants shoulder to shoulder with black writers. The dinner proved to be a tremendous success, with black artists securing financial support or the promise of future support. Among the carefully selected white editors, writers, and publishers whom Johnson invited was Paul Kellogg, editor of *Survey Graphic*. Kellogg was so impressed with what he saw that he decided to commission a special issue devoted to Harlem and selected as editor Alain Locke, whom Johnson hailed as "dean" of the New Negro movement. This special issue was later revised and expanded into Locke's landmark anthology, *The New Negro* (1925).

Shortly after this momentous dinner, *The Crisis* and *Opportunity* instituted award ceremonies to recognize black artists, which also helped solidify collaboration between them and the white publishing industry. In 1924 *The Crisis* announced the Amy Einstein Spingarn Prizes in Literature and Art. Amy Spingarn, wife of NAACP board member Joel Elias Spingarn, funded the program. She also served as a judge along with a racially integrated group of popular writers: Edward Bok, Witter Bynner, Charles Waddell Chesnutt, Sinclair Lewis, Robert Morss Lovett, Van Wyck Brooks, Carl Van Doren, Zona Gale, James Weldon Johnson, and Eugene O'Neill. The first *Opportunity* prizes were dispersed in May 1925 at an elaborate ceremony with approximately three hundred participants. The prizes were funded by the wife of National Urban League board chairman and Fisk University trustee, L. Hollingsworth Wood. A week after the ceremony *The New York Herald Tribune* predicted that the country was "on the edge, if not already in the midst of, what might

---

14. Quoted in Arna Bontemps, ed., *The Harlem Renaissance Remembered* (New York: Dodd, Mead, 1972), 215.

15. Quoted in Bontemps, *Harlem Renaissance Remembered*, 215.

16. Robert E. Hemenway, *Zora Neale Hurston: A Literary Biography* (Champaign-Urbana: University of Illinois Press, 1977), 9.

not improperly be called a Negro renaissance."[17] A second *Opportunity* awards banquet was followed by donations for future prizes and the establishment of other prizes related to African American arts and letters.

It is this interracial cooperation that sparked the influential anthology *The New Negro* in 1925 which grew out of the special issue of *Survey Graphic,* "Harlem: Mecca of the New Negro." Reaching a record number of 42,000 readers, the issue's sales persuaded Albert and Charles Boni to publish a revised and expanded collection of its poetry and prose, along with winners of the first *Opportunity* contest. In his foreword to the anthology, Locke set the terms that have come to be identified with the Harlem Renaissance: "There is a renewed race-spirit that consciously and proudly sets itself apart. Justifiably then, we speak of the offerings of this book embodying these ripening forces as culled from the first fruits of the Negro Renaissance." In the collection's first essay, his own "The New Negro," he sought to define this spirit: "[T]he younger generation is vibrant with a new psychology; the new spirit is awake in the masses."

Despite its limitations, *The New Negro* continues to hold a place of significance because it both alerted the world to the emergence of an international cultural revolution and attempted to define it. Although the text was held in high regard by its original audience, it is important to note the controversy surrounding it, strains of which run through the material here. Hailed as a definitive anthology, it was at the same time immediately critiqued by some contributors and even repudiated by others. These different responses appear to be rooted in Locke's attempts to smooth over important differences between the writers brought together in the collection, who differed in terms of ideology and aesthetics. For example, Jean Toomer would later write that Locke "tricked and misused" him because he did not consider himself a black writer despite his African American ancestry,[18] while Bruce Nugent was at least as concerned with his sexual identity as with his racial one. Langston Hughes and Countee Cullen were at opposite ends of the aesthetic spectrum, with Hughes preferring jazz- and blues-inspired poems over Cullen's lyrical verse. In fact, Cullen would later be the object of a veiled attack in Hughes's "The Negro Artist and the Racial Mountain" (1926) in which Hughes disparaged him for wishing to be known as a poet who "happened to be Negro," not as a "Negro poet" (see the essay section).

The New Negro did not address these important differences regarding aesthetics, politics, sexuality, and other pertinent issues dividing the younger and older generations of the movement. Indeed, Locke sought to gloss over these tensions. He omitted some of socialist Claude McKay's most militant poems, such as "If We Must Die" (see the creative writing section) and "Mulatto," and toned down a McKay poem he did include, "The White House," by changing the title to "White Houses," something McKay bitterly

17. Quoted in Lewis, *Portable Harlem Renaissance Reader,* xxviii. According to Lewis, this statement gave the movement its name.

18. Quoted in Arnold Rampersad, introduction to *The New Negro: Voices of the Harlem Renaissance,* ed. Alain Locke (New York: Athenaeum, 1992), xxii.

denounced. Despite A. Philip Randolph and Chandler Owen's important contribution to the movement through their editing of *The Messenger,* they were not included. Locke also ignored Garveyism, which has been characterized as the most important mass movement in black America of the 1920s. Garvey's *Negro World,* with a circulation of 200,000 at its peak, made literature readily available to the black masses. However, Locke's exclusion of Garveyism was probably in deference to Du Bois, whose integrationist philosophy clashed with Garvey's more radical separatism. Locke's rather conservative and elitist view of culture seems to stem from what Lewis describes as his Eurocentric definition of culture, a limitation that has since come to be blamed for many of the Renaissance's failures.[19]

The ideological and artistic differences that Locke attempted to minimize in his anthology could not be contained. This is particularly true of the very public ongoing debate between Locke and Du Bois regarding the role of literature and whether black writing should be art or propaganda, a debate worth summarizing here. Locke had spent his career developing a particular theory of African American art, which he articulated and defended through the duration of the Harlem Renaissance. As literary critic for *Opportunity,* he urged black writers to make their work "universally" relevant. In an early essay, "The Colonial Literature of France" (1923), he argued that the black artist should embrace "art for its own sake, combined with that stark cult of veracity—the truth whether it hurts or not."[20] Thus, in editing *The New Negro,* he sought to show that the new Renaissance writers should create "art for art's sake," which distinguished them from the previous wave of African American writers, like Grimké and Fauset, who addressed social issues in their creative work, explicitly using it as a propaganda tool.

This distinction did not sit well with many members of the civil rights establishment, particularly Du Bois, who was not only a writer, but a sociologist and political leader. Although he and Locke both looked at literature as a way to advance the race, they differed sharply over what constituted propaganda: "Mr. Locke has newly been seized with the idea that Beauty rather than propaganda should be the object of Negro literature and art. His book proves the falseness of this thesis. . . . If Mr. Locke's thesis is insisted upon too much, it is going to turn the Negro Renaissance into decadence. It is the fight for Life and Liberty that is giving birth to Negro literature and art today and when turning from the fight or ignoring it, the young Negro tries to do pretty things or things that catch the passing fancy of the really unimportant critics and publishers about him, he will find that he has killed the soul of Beauty in art."[21] Locke responded by arguing that art as propaganda perpetuated notions of black inferiority.[22]

Although Du Bois and Locke were the primary figures in this debate, they were outdone by a group of young writers who took Locke's position much further than he had

---

19. See Lewis, *When Harlem Was in Vogue.*
20. Quoted in Hill et al., *Call and Response,* 788.
21. Quoted in Hill et al., *Call and Response,* 789.
22. See Hill et al., *Call and Response,* 790.

intended. Langston Hughes spoke for them in his 1926 essay, "The Negro Artist and the Racial Mountain" (see the essay section), which appeared in *The Nation:* "We younger Negro artists who create now intend to express our individual dark-skinned selves without fear or shame. If white people are pleased we are glad. If they are not, it doesn't matter. We know we are beautiful. And ugly too. The tom-tom cries and the tom-tom laughs. If colored people are pleased we are glad. If they are not, their displeasure doesn't matter either. We build our temples for tomorrow, strong as we know how, and we stand on top of the mountain, free within ourselves."

Following this manifesto of artistic freedom, Hughes and Richard Bruce Nugent envisioned a new magazine, which they named *Fire!!* They, along with Zora Neale Hurston, Gwendolyn Bennett, Aaron Douglas, and John Davis, selected the multitalented writer Wallace Thurman as editor. The editorial board members were determined to express their own sensibilities and to break free of the notion of art as politics to express instead the multiple dimensions of being African American. *Fire!!* promised "to burn up a lot of old, dead conventional Negro-white ideas of the past." The foreword to the first and only issue of November 1926 proclaimed to weave "vivid, hot designs upon an ebon bordered loom and . . . satisfy pagan thirst for beauty unadorned." In other words, this would be a daring and controversial journal. In fact, in order to underline its radical nature, Thurman decided that they needed to include at least one piece on homosexuality and another on prostitution. He and Nugent flipped a coin to determine who would write which story. Nugent's "Smoke, Lilies, and Jade!" about homoerotic attraction, and Thurman's "Cordelia the Crude," about a young prostitute, were the result (see the creative writing section).

Both pieces outraged middle-class African American sensibilities. Rean Graves of the *Baltimore Afro-American* was incensed by the magazine and wrote in his review, "I have just tossed the first issue of *Fire!!* into the fire." Benjamin Brawley went so far as to say that if the U.S. Post Office found out about Thurman's "Cordelia the Crude," the magazine might be barred from the mail.[23] Locke, although more balanced in his review, disapproved of the "effete echoes of contemporary decadence" he found throughout the issue.[24] For a time the writers associated with the project were ostracized by the black community. However, the real source of the magazine's demise was financial. The magazine was expensive to buy (one dollar), expensive to produce (one thousand dollars), lacked institutional support, and was poorly distributed. Ironically, hundreds of unsold copies burned in an actual apartment fire.

In many ways *Fire!!* was the antithesis of *The New Negro*, and it is telling that Alain Locke was not among its nine editors. Less than a year after appearing in his anthology, the younger writers had moved on without Locke. Symbolizing their upstart independence from the NAACP and NUL was Zora Neale Hurston's impudent dubbing of the influ-

---

23. Quoted in Trudier Harris and Thadious M. Davis, eds., *Afro-American Writers from the Harlem Renaissance to 1940*, vol. 51 of *Dictionary of Literary Biography* (Detroit: Gale, 1987), 263.

24. Quoted in Harris and Davis, *Afro-American Writers*, 220.

ential whites that supported their contests and attended their parties as "Negrotarians," and her referral to prominent Harlem writers as the "Niggerati." In hopes of ironing out the differences between the younger and older generations, in late 1926 Du Bois organized a symposium entitled, "The Criteria of Negro Art" (see essay of the same name in the essay section). He feared that politics were disappearing from the Renaissance and that whites would point to the success of a handful of writers as evidence that there was no color line. However, the fissure remained, and the rebelling younger artists gained momentum, particularly with the publication of Claude McKay's *Home to Harlem* in 1928. This first bestseller of the Renaissance embodied the values of the younger generation.

Presenting and Assessing the Harlem Renaissance

The tensions surrounding issues of art and politics during the Harlem Renaissance point to continuing fault lines in the presentation of the Harlem Renaissance: How should it be assessed? What lessons can we draw from its meteoric heights and rapid descent? Did African American writers escape the ghetto of plantation dialect and the colonization of Eurocentric art forms only to fall into another trap of essentialized Western fantasies about primitive sensual Africa? Were black women betrayed by their male mentors and colleagues? Which texts should we privilege for study—those considered artistically superior, those advancing positive images of black people, or those representing concerns of the time? How do we sort out the thorny tangle of aesthetics and voice when it comes to women's texts and those by gay, lesbian, or bisexual writers? Should we dispense with the categories of "major" and "minor" writers? If not, how do we judge the accomplishments of black women in an era when so many opportunities were unavailable because of the double disadvantages they faced?

These are some of the questions we hope an anthology of this sort can raise. In constructing it, we began with Alain Locke's touchstone text *The New Negro* as an important reflection of the ideology of the movement. However, we recognized the limitations of relying solely on Locke's interpretation, particularly since he included only one essay by a woman, Elise Johnson McDougald's "The Task of Negro Womanhood" (see the essay section). Although critics have commented on the representativeness of Locke's contributors—whites, blacks, men, women, older and younger artists and intellectuals were included—the volume is bound by his philosophy of racial cooperation and the celebration of art for art's sake as well as marred by a degree of sexism, elitism, and political conservatism. Although women were included in the volume, they are outnumbered almost three to one, for instance, and the male writers had far more pieces included than the women, a gender imbalance that was repeated in succeeding anthologies. Locke's conservatism is reflected in his appeal to a white audience, his hopes that whites would gain a new understanding of black humanity through the display of the race's intelligence and artistic talents. He hoped to generate social change, but he did not want to ruffle too many feathers and avoided including radical social protest or material with a socialistic bent. Locke's elitism is evident in his favoring of the spirituals over the blues and his distancing himself from the largely working-class Marcus Garvey movement.[25] Locke's "New Negro," in other words, was clearly a proper middle-class African American, most often male.

Thus, to round out our picture of the movement, we have turned to the periodical literature of the period. We relied heavily on the *The Crisis* and *Opportunity,* as these journals and their contests honed much of the talent of the Harlem Renaissance, and their editors, W.E.B. Du Bois and Charles S. Johnson, were initially quite welcoming to women. Even in the later part of the 1920s, after Jessie Fauset had left *The Crisis* in 1926 and Gwendolyn Bennett had departed *Opportunity* in 1928, these two journals continued to publish large numbers of poems and stories by women. We have also looked to such journals as A. Philip Randolph and Chandler Owen's *The Messenger,* Marcus Garvey's *Negro World,* Max Eastman's *The Liberator,* Dorothy West's *Challenge,* and of course the single issue of Wallace Thurman's *Fire!!* as important venues for African American writers. Along with central anthologies of the period, such as James Weldon Johnson's *The Book of American Negro Poetry* (1922), Countee Cullen's *Caroling Dusk* (1927), and Charles S. Johnson's *Ebony and Topaz* (1927), we have utilized a variety of sources to provide a sense of what was published during the 1916–1937 period covered by our anthology. Cullen's volume was especially significant because it included roughly equal numbers of poems by women and men.

Despite the contested nature of the movement, there are writers who are repeatedly anthologized in collections such as ours and who constitute a nucleus of the Harlem Renaissance: Alain Locke, W.E.B. Du Bois, Langston Hughes, Zora Neale Hurston, Countee Cullen, Claude McKay, Jean Toomer, and Nella Larsen are clearly canonical writers of the period. There are also signature literary pieces that are wedded to the era and are thus also included here: McKay's "If We Must Die," Hughes's "The Negro Speaks of Rivers," Cullen's "Heritage," Hurston's story "Sweat," and sections of Toomer's *Cane* among them. Thus, despite disagreements regarding aspects of the Harlem Renaissance, there is a nucleus of agreed upon texts and writers.

It is time, however, to consider the next group of core texts and writers. Perhaps Bruce Nugent's "Sahdji," the first African American–authored story with a homoerotic subtext, or his "Smoke, Lilies, and Jade!" the first openly gay prose text penned by an African American and an astonishing example of modernist literature, should be elevated to the Harlem Renaissance canon. The poetry of Angelina Weld Grimké furnishes other possible

25. Marcus Mosiah Garvey (1887–1940), a native of St. Ann's Bay, Jamaica, in the British West Indies, founded the first important Pan-Africanist nationalist movement, the Universal Negro Improvement Association (UNIA). He established UNIA in Jamaica in 1914, moving the headquarters to Harlem in 1916. The movement flourished after he began publication of the newspaper *Negro World.* He used the newspaper to spread his message of racial pride, economic self-sufficiency, and black nationalism. He founded the Black Star Line, a steamship company, to allow blacks to move to Liberia. Garvey is generally associated with the phrase "Back to Africa"; however, his company did not actually transport anyone back to Africa. In 1923, in a thinly veiled move by the U.S. government to nullify his impact, he was indicted for mail fraud in connection with a mail campaign to sell stock in his fledgling Black Star Line. Garvey served two years of his five-year sentence before President Calvin Coolidge commuted his sentence and had him deported. Garvey moved his headquarters to London but was never able to revive the movement.

texts for inclusion, particularly the lesbian sensibility and subtle race pride evident in poems like "El Beso" or "Dusk." The cerebral verse of Anne Spencer is another possibility, with its complex nature analogues to gender and race issues. Jessie Fauset's *Plum Bun* (1928) (although not included here), when viewed against the context of her uphill battle to be editor, mentor, teacher, and writer with few supports, shimmers with unexpected force, and the impressive prose of her many essays is only now being reviewed. Georgia Douglas Johnson's short but luminously spare and haunting play *Plumes* is yet another overlooked text of lasting value.

By bringing these and other frequently omitted texts into dialogue with the more familiar nucleus of Harlem Renaissance writings, we hope to encourage not only a more gender-balanced view of this remarkable literary awakening, but to emphasize its continual unfolding. Indeed, excavation of lost literature from the period is still taking place. We have included, for instance, unreprinted stories by Dorothy West ("The Black Dress"), Gwendolyn Bennett ("Tokens"), and Anita Scott Coleman ("Two Old Women A-Shopping Go!"), as well as unreprinted poems by Georgia Douglas Johnson, Jessie Fauset, John F. Matheus, Joseph S. Cotter, Jr., Wallace Thurman, and Richard Bruce Nugent. Overshadowed by texts that have made it into the canon, those often considered minor or left to languish in the period's journals can come to life when viewed within the contexts of sexism, homophobia, and racism. Whether major or minor, female- or male-authored, texts of the Harlem Renaissance enrich our understanding of African American history and culture. These texts served as inspiring, pathbreaking trails—away from silence, against all odds, toward futures their creators only dimly perceived.

A NOTE ON THE TEXT

All texts are as they were when originally published, and source identifications are by the earliest appearance of the pieces. Typographical errors in the originals have been silently corrected. Since this anthology is designed to accompany a selection of novels, we decided to avoid novel excerpts, with the exception of Wallace Thurman's "Emma Lou" from *The Blacker the Berry* and Jean Toomer's "Blood-Burning Moon" from *Cane.* In a few cases, we deleted sections of long plays or essays and have indicated the deletions by ellipses. Creative writing is arranged by author to provide a sense of individual style or interest and to link the texts to the lives of the writers. We put the writers in chronological order by date of birth to provide a sense of literary lineage. Within each author entry, the creative works are grouped by genre: poetry first, arranged in chronological order, followed by short stories, then plays where applicable. Rejecting a thematic arrangement, we selected a neutral organization to give readers maximum freedom to locate themes for themselves. To foster a sense that male and female writers shared many concerns and aesthetic choices, we have not separated them by gender. Since we wanted to contextualize the creative writing with ideological currents sweeping through the Harlem Renaissance, we set the essays apart and arranged them by subject so that readers can get a sense of the dialogues that occurred. Illustrations are dispersed throughout the volume in much the same way they were in anthologies and periodicals of the day. Where possible, we have paired illustrations and the pieces with which they originally appeared. Song lyrics are inserted throughout the volume to give a sense of the interplay of themes and aesthetics that existed between writers and musicians. We hope that the inclusion of lyrics and illustrations will give a better sense of the period's artistic vitality.

CHRONOLOGY

1916   Angelina Weld Grimké's *Rachel* is performed (it is published in 1920). Fenton Johnson publishes his third poetry collection, *Songs of the Soil.*

1917   Ridgely Torrence's *The Rider of Dreams, Simon the Cyrenian,* and *Granny Maumee* are performed with all-black casts. James Weldon Johnson's *Fifty Years and Other Poems* is published.

1918   Joseph S. Cotter, Jr.'s *The Band of Gideon and Other Lyrics* and Georgia Douglas Johnson's *The Heart of a Woman and Other Poems* are published.

1919   Claude McKay's poem "If We Must Die" is published in *The Liberator.*

1920   Eugene O'Neill's *Emperor Jones* is performed starring African American Charles Gilpin in the lead role.

1921   *Shuffle Along* is written and performed by African Americans.

1922   *Shuffle Along* becomes the first all-black Broadway production. Georgia Douglas Johnson's *Bronze: A Book of Verse,* James Weldon Johnson's *Book of American Negro Poetry,* and Claude McKay's *Harlem Shadows* are published.

1923   Jean Toomer's *Cane* and Robert Kerlin's *Negro Poets and Their Poems* are published. Willis Richardson's *The Chip Woman's Fortune* is the first nonmusical by an African American to be produced on Broadway.

1924   Jessie Fauset's *There Is Confusion* and Walter White's *The Fire in the Flint* are published. Charles S. Johnson hosts Civic Club dinner in March. Zora Neale Hurston's first story, "Drenched in Light," is published in *Opportunity.*

1925   First *Opportunity* awards banquet held in May. First *Crisis* awards dinner held in November at Harlem's Renaissance Casino. Countee Cullen's first poetry collection, *Color,* Alain Locke's *The New Negro,* and a special issue of *Survey Graphic,* also edited by Locke, are published.

1926   The first and only issue of *Fire!!,* edited by Wallace Thurman, is published, containing the first African American homoerotic prose text, "Smoke, Lilies, and

Jade!" by Richard Bruce Nugent. Langston Hughes's *The Weary Blues*, Carl Van Vechten's *Nigger Heaven*, Eric Walrond's *Tropic Death*, and Walter White's *Flight* are published. Countee Cullen edits an all-black issue of *Palms*.

1927   Countée Cullen's *Copper Sun* and *The Ballad of the Brown Girl*, James Weldon Johnson's *God's Trombones*, Langston Hughes's *Fine Clothes to the Jew*, Cullen's *Caroling Dusk* poetry anthology, Charles S. Johnson's anthology, *Ebony and Topaz*, and Alain Locke and Gregory Montgomery's drama collection, *Plays of Negro Life*, are published. James Weldon Johnson's *Autobiography of an Ex-Coloured Man* (1912) is reprinted with his name given as the author.

1928   W.E.B. Du Bois's *Dark Princess*, Jessie Fauset's *Plum Bun*, Rudolph Fisher's *The Walls of Jericho*, Nella Larsen's *Quicksand*, and Claude McKay's *Home to Harlem* are published. Georgia Douglas Johnson publishes her third poetry collection, *An Autumn Love Cycle*. In November, Wallace Thurman edits *Harlem*, a journal that lasts only one issue.

1929   Claude McKay's *Banjo: A Story without a Plot*, Nella Larsen's *Passing*, Wallace Thurman's *The Blacker the Berry*, and Countee Cullen's poetry collection *The Black Christ* are published. Thurman's play *Harlem*, cowritten with William Jourdan Rapp, is a hit production on Broadway.

1930   Langston Hughes's *Not without Laughter* and Willis Richardson's drama collection, *Plays and Pageants from the Life of the Negro*, are published. Marc Connelly's play *The Green Pastures* opens on Broadway in February.

1931   Arna Bontemps's *God Sends Sunday*, Jessie Fauset's *The Chinaberry Tree*, George Schuyler's *Black No More*, and James Weldon Johnson's history, *Black Manhattan*, are published. Johnson's *Book of American Negro Poetry* is reprinted.

1932   Sterling A. Brown's poetry collection *Southern Road*, Claude McKay's collection *Gingertown and Other Stories*, Countee Cullen's novel *One Way to Heaven*, Rudolph Fisher's second novel, *The Conjure-Man Dies*, and Wallace Thurman's second novel, *Infants of the Spring*, are published.

1933   James Weldon Johnson publishes the autobiographical *Along This Way*. Claude McKay publishes his third novel, *Banana Bottom*, and Jessie Fauset publishes her last novel, *Comedy, American Style*.

1934   Nancy Cunard edits *Negro: An Anthology*. Langston Hughes publishes his short story collection, *The Ways of White Folks*, and Zora Neale Hurston publishes her first novel, *Jonah's Gourd Vine*. Dorothy West founds *Challenge* magazine.

1935   Zora Neale Hurston publishes a folklore collection, *Mules and Men*. Langston Hughes's play *Mulatto* becomes the longest-running black-authored drama on Broadway.

1936   Arna Bontemps's novel *Black Thunder* and Mae V. Cowdery's collection, *We Lift Our Voices and Other Poems*, are published.

1937   Zora Neale Hurston publishes the last novel of the Harlem Renaissance, *Their Eyes Were Watching God*. Dorothy West edits one issue of *New Challenge*.

ESSAYS

"The New Negro," cover of *The Messenger,* May 1923

Alain Locke

The New Negro

In the last decade something beyond the watch and guard of statistics has happened in the life of the American Negro and the three norns[1] who have traditionally presided over the Negro problem have a changeling in their laps. The Sociologist, the Philanthropist, the Race-leader are not unaware of the New Negro, but they are at a loss to account for him. He simply cannot be swathed in their formulae. For the younger generation is vibrant with a new psychology; the new spirit is awake in the masses, and under the very eyes of the professional observers is transforming what has been a perennial problem into the progressive phases of contemporary Negro life.

Could such a metamorphosis have taken place as suddenly as it has appeared to? The answer is no; not because the New Negro is not here, but because the Old Negro had long become more of a myth than a man. The Old Negro, we must remember, was a creature of moral debate and historical controversy. His has been a stock figure perpetuated as an historical fiction partly in innocent sentimentalism, partly in deliberate reactionism. The Negro himself has contributed his share to this through a sort of protective social mimicry forced upon him by the adverse circumstances of dependence. So for generations in the mind of America, the Negro has been more of a formula than a human being—a something to be argued about, condemned or defended, to be "kept down," or "in his place," or "helped up," to be worried with or worried over, harassed or patronized, a social bogey or a social burden. The thinking Negro even has been induced to share this same general attitude, to focus his attention on controversial issues, to see himself in the distorted perspective of a social problem. His shadow, so to speak, has been more real to him than his personality. Through having had to appeal from the unjust stereotypes of his oppressors and traducers to those of his liberators, friends and benefactors, he has

1. The three norns are Norse goddesses of fate.

The New Negro, 1925.

had to subscribe to the traditional positions from which his case has been viewed. Little true social or self-understanding has or could come from such a situation.

But while the minds of most of us, black and white, have thus burrowed in the trenches of the Civil War and Reconstruction, the actual march of development has simply flanked these positions, necessitating a sudden reorientation of view. We have not been watching in the right direction; set North and South on a sectional axis, we have not noticed the East till the sun has us blinking. . . .

There is, of course, a warrantably comfortable feeling in being on the right side of the country's professed ideals. We realize that we cannot be undone without America's undoing. It is within the gamut of this attitude that the thinking Negro faces America, but with variations of mood that are if anything more significant than the attitude itself. Sometimes we have it taken with the defiant ironic challenge of McKay:

> Mine is the future grinding down to-day
> Like a great landslip moving to the sea,
> Bearing its freight of debris far away
> While the green hungry waters restlessly
> Heave mammoth pyramids, and break and roar
> Their eerie challenge to the crumbling shore.

Sometimes, perhaps more frequently yet, it is taken in the fervent and almost filial appeal and counsel of Weldon Johnson's:

> O Southland, dear Southland!
> Then why do you still cling
> To an idle age and a musty page,
> To a dead and useless thing?

But between defiance and appeal, midway almost between cynicism and hope, the prevailing mind stands in the mood of the same author's "To America," an attitude of sober query and stoical challenge:

> How would you have us, as we are?
>   Or sinking 'neath the load we bear,
> Our eyes fixed forward on a star,
>   Or gazing empty at despair?

> Rising or falling? Men or things?
>   With dragging pace or footsteps fleet?
> Strong, willing sinews in your wings,
>   Or tightening chains about your feet?

More and more, however, an intelligent realization of the great discrepancy between the American social creed and the American social practice forces upon the Negro the taking of the moral advantage that is his. Only the steadying and sobering effect of a truly characteristic gentleness of spirit prevents the rapid rise of a definite cynicism and counter-hate and a defiant superiority feeling. Human as this reaction would be, the majority still deprecate its advent, and would gladly see it forestalled by the speedy amelioration of its causes. We wish our race pride to be a healthier, more positive achievement than a feeling based upon a realization of the shortcomings of others. But all paths toward the attainment of a sound social attitude have been difficult; only a relatively few enlightened minds have been able, as the phrase puts it, "to rise above" prejudice. The ordinary man has had until recently only a hard choice between the alternatives of supine and humiliating submission and stimulating but hurtful counter-prejudice. Fortunately from some inner, desperate resourcefulness has recently sprung up the simple expedient of fighting prejudice by mental passive resistance, in other words by trying to ignore it. For the few, this manna may perhaps be effective, but the masses cannot thrive upon it.

Fortunately there are constructive channels opening out into which the balked social feelings of the American Negro can flow freely.

Without them there would be much more pressure and danger than there is. These compensating interests are racial but in a new and enlarged way. One is the consciousness of acting as the advance-guard of the African peoples in their contact with Twentieth Century civilization; the other, the sense of a mission of rehabilitating the race in world esteem from that loss of prestige for which the fate and conditions of slavery have so largely been responsible. Harlem, as we shall see, is the center of both these movements; she is the home of the Negro's "Zionism." The pulse of the Negro world has begun to beat in Harlem. A Negro newspaper carrying news material in English, French and Spanish, gathered from all quarters of America, the West Indies and Africa has maintained itself in Harlem for over five years. Two important magazines, both edited from New York, maintain their news and circulation consistently on a cosmopolitan scale. Under American auspices and backing, three Pan-African congresses have been held abroad for the discussion of common interests, colonial questions and the future co-operative development of Africa. In terms of the race question as a world problem, the Negro mind has leapt, so to speak, upon the parapets of prejudice and extended its cramped horizons. In so doing it has linked up with the growing group consciousness of the dark-peoples and is gradually learning their common interests. As one of our writers has recently put it: "It is imperative that we understand the white world in its relations to the non-white world." As with the Jew, persecution is making the Negro international.

As a world phenomenon this wider race consciousness is a different thing from the much asserted rising tide of color. Its inevitable causes are not of our making. The consequences are not necessarily damaging to the best interests of civilization. Whether it actually brings into being new armadas of conflict or argosies of cultural exchange and enlightenment can only be decided by the attitude of the dominant races in an era of critical change. With the American Negro, his new internationalism is primarily an effort to recapture contact with the scattered peoples of African derivation. Garveyism may be a transient, if spectacular, phenomenon, but the possible rôle of the American Negro in the future development of Africa is one of the most constructive and universally helpful missions that any modern people can lay claim to.

Constructive participation in such causes cannot help giving the Negro valuable group incentives, as well as increased prestige at home and abroad. Our greatest rehabilitation may possibly come through such channels, but for the present, more immediate hope rests in the revaluation by white and black alike of the Negro in terms of his artistic endowments and cultural contributions, past and prospective. It must be increasingly recognized that the Negro has already made very substantial contributions, not only in his folk-art, music especially, which has always found appreciation, but in larger, though humbler and less acknowledged ways. For generations the Negro has been the peasant matrix of that section of America which has most undervalued him, and here he has contributed not only materially in labor and in social patience, but spiritually as well. The South has unconsciously absorbed the gift of his folk-temperament. In less than half a generation it will be easier to recognize this, but the fact remains that a leaven of humor, sentiment, imagination and tropic nonchalance has gone into the making of the South from a humble, unacknowledged source. A second crop of the Negro's gifts promises still more largely. He now becomes a conscious contributor and lays aside the status of a beneficiary and ward for that of a collaborator and participant in American civilization. The great social gain in this is the releasing of our talented group from the arid fields of controversy and debate to the productive fields of creative expression. The especially cultural recognition they win should in turn prove the key to that revaluation of the Negro which must precede or accompany any considerable further betterment of race relationships. But whatever the general effect, the present generation will have added the motives of self-expression and spiritual development to the old and still unfinished task of making material headway and progress. No one who understandingly faces the situation with its substantial accomplishment or views the new scene with its still more abundant promise can be entirely without hope. And certainly, if in our lifetime the Negro should not be able to celebrate his full initiation into American democracy, he can at least, on the warrant of these things, celebrate the attainment of a significant and satisfying new phase of group development, and with it a spiritual Coming of Age.

A. Philip Randolph and Chandler Owen

The New Negro—What Is He?

Our title was the subject of an editorial in *The New York Age* which formed the basis of an extensive symposium. Most of the replies, however, have been vague and nebulous. *The Messenger,* therefore, undertakes to supply *The New York Age* and the general public with a definite and clear portrayal of the New Negro.

It is well nigh axiomatic that the most accurate test of what a man or institution or a movement is, is first, what its aims are; second, what its methods are, or how it expects to achieve its aims; and third, its general relations to current movements.

Now, what are the aims of the New Negro? The answer to this question will fall under three general heads, namely, political, economic, and social.

In politics, the New Negro, unlike the Old Negro, cannot be lulled into a false sense of security with political spoils and patronage. A job is not the price of his vote. He will not continue to accept political promisory notes from a political debtor, who has already had the power, but who has refused to satisfy his political obligations. The New Negro demands political equality. He recognizes the necessity of selective as well as elective representation. He realizes that so long as the Negro votes for the Republican or Democratic party, he will have only the right and privilege to elect but not to select his representatives. And he who selects the representatives controls the representatives. The New Negro stands for universal suffrage.

A word about the economic aims of the New Negro. Here, as a worker, he demands the full product of his toil. His immediate aim is more wages, shorter hours and better working conditions. As a consumer, he seeks to buy, in the market, commodities at the lowest possible price.

The social aims of the New Negro are decidedly different from those of the Old Negro. Here he stands for absolute and unequivocal "*social equality.*" He realizes that there cannot be any qualified equality. He insists that a society which is based upon justice can

The Messenger, August 1920.

only be a society composed of *"social equals."* He insists upon [equality] of social treatment. With respect to intermarriage, he maintains that it is the only logical, sound and correct aim for the Negro to entertain. He realizes that the acceptance of laws against intermarriage is tantamount to the acceptance of the stigma of inferiority. Besides, laws against intermarriage expose Negro women to sexual exploitation, and deprive their offspring, by white men, of the right to inherit the property of their father. Statistics show that there are nearly four million mulattoes in America as a result of miscegenation.

So much then for the aims of the New Negro. A word now about his methods. It is with respect to methods that the essential difference between the New and the Old Negro relates.

First, the methods by which the New Negro expects to realize his political aims are radical. He would repudiate and discard both of the old parties—Republican and Democratic. His knowledge of political science enables him to see that a political organization must have an economic foundation. A party whose money comes from working people must and will represent working people. Now, everybody concedes that the Negro is essentially a worker. There are no big capitalists among them. There are a few petit bourgeoisie,[1] but the process of money concentration is destined to weed them out and drop them down into the ranks of the working class. In fact, the interests of all Negroes are tied up with the workers. Therefore, the Negro should support a working class political party. He is a fool or insane, who opposes his best interests by supporting his enemy. As workers, Negroes have nothing in common with their employers. The Negro wants high wages; the employer wants to pay low wages. The Negro wants to work short hours; the employer wants to work him long hours. Since this is true, it follows as a logical corollary that the Negro should not support the party of the employing class. Now, it is a question of fact that the Republican and Democratic parties are parties of the employing or capitalist class.

On the economic field, the New Negro advocates that the Negro join the labor unions. Wherever white unions discriminate against the Negro worker, then the only sensible thing to do is to form independent unions to fight both the white capitalists for more wages and shorter hours, on the one hand, and white labor unions for justice, on the other. It is folly for the Negro to fight labor organization because some white unions ignorantly ignore or oppose him. It is about as logical and wise as to repudiate and condemn writing on the ground that it is used by some crooks for forgery. As a consumer, he would organize cooperative societies to reduce the high cost of living.

The social methods are: education and physical action in self defense. That education must constitute the basis of all action, is beyond the realm of question. And to fight back in self defense, should be accepted as a matter of course. No one who will not fight to protect his life is fit to live. Self defense is recognized as a legitimate weapon in all civilized countries. Yet the Old Crowd Negroes have counseled the doctrine of non-resistance.

1. Small business owners; a Marxist economic category.

As to current movements, the Negro would accept, praise and support that which his enemies reject, condemn and oppose. He is tolerant. He would restore free speech, a free press and freedom of assemblage. He would release Debs. He would recognize the right of Russia to self determination. He is opposed to the Treaty and the League of Nations. Yet, he rejects Lodge's reservations.[2] He knows that neither will help the people. As to Negro leaders, his object is to destroy them all and build up new ones.

Finally, the New Negro arrived upon the scene at the time of all other forward progressive groups and movements—after the great world war. He is the product of the same world wide forces that have brought into being the great liberal and radical movements that are now seizing the reins of political, economic and social power in all of the civilized countries of the world.

His presence is inevitable in these times of economic chaos, political upheaval and social distress. Yes, there is a New Negro. And it is he who will pilot the Negro through this terrible hour of storm and stress.

---

2. Eugene V. Debs, labor organizer and five-time Socialist Party candidate for U.S. president between 1900 and 1920, was convicted and imprisoned for sedition in violation of the 1917 Espionage Act. He was released in 1921 by presidential order but did not regain his citizenship until 1976. Henry Cabot Lodge, U.S. senator (1893–1924), led the successful congressional opposition to U.S. participation in the League of Nations following World War I. He opposed the Treaty of Versailles, which included the creation of the League of Nations. Lodge introduced several amendments—Lodge reservations—that would have required the approval of Congress before the U.S. would be bound by League decisions. President Woodrow Wilson rejected the reservations because they would have destroyed the intent of the League; however, the treaty was defeated in the Senate.

William Stanley Braithwaite

The Negro in American Literature

True to his origin on this continent, the Negro was projected into literature by an over-mastering and exploiting hand. In the generations that he has been so voluminously written and talked about he has been accorded as little artistic justice as social justice. Ante-bellum literature imposed the distortions of moralistic controversy and made the Negro a wax-figure of the market place: post-bellum literature retaliated with the condescending reactions of sentiment and caricature, and made the Negro a *genre* stereotype. Sustained, serious or deep study of Negro life and character has thus been entirely below the horizons of our national art. Only gradually, through the dull purgatory of the Age of Discussion, has Negro life eventually issued forth to an Age of Expression.

Perhaps I ought to qualify this last statement that the Negro was *in* American literature generations before he was part of it as a creator. From his very beginning in this country the Negro has been, without the formal recognition of literature and art, creative. During more than two centuries of an enslaved peasantry, the race has been giving evidence, in song and story lore, of an artistic temperament and psychology precious for itself as well as for its potential use and promise in the sophisticated forms of cultural expression. Expressing itself with poignancy and a symbolic imagery unsurpassed, indeed, often unmatched, by any folk-group, the race in servitude was at the same time the finest national expression of emotion and imagination and the most precious mass of raw material for literature America was producing. Quoting these stanzas of James Weldon Johnson's "O Black and Unknown Bards," I want you to catch the real point of its assertion of the Negro's way into the domain of art:

> O black and unknown bards of long ago,
>   How came your lips to touch the sacred fire?
> How, in your darkness, did you come to know
>   The power and beauty of the minstrel's lyre?

The New Negro, 1925.

Who first from midst his bonds lifted his eyes?
    Who first from out the still watch, lone and long,
Feeling the ancient faith of prophets rise
    Within his dark-kept soul, burst into song?

There is a wide, wide wonder in it all,
    That from degraded rest and servile toil
The fiery spirit of the seer should call
    These simple children of the sun and soil.
O black slave singers, gone, forgot, unfamed,
    You—you, alone, of all the long, long line
Of those who've sung untaught, unknown, unnamed,
    Have stretched out upward, seeking the divine.

How misdirected was the American imagination, how blinded by the dust of controversy and the pall of social hatred and oppression, not to have found it irresistibly urgent to make literary use of the imagination and emotion it possessed in such abundance. . . .

———————

I shall have to run back over the years to where I began to survey the achievement of Negro authorship. The Negro as a creator in American literature is of comparatively recent importance. All that was accomplished between Phillis Wheatley and Paul Laurence Dunbar, considered by critical standards, is negligible, and of historical interest only. Historically it is a great tribute to the race to have produced in Phillis Wheatley not only the slave poetess in eighteenth century Colonial America, but to know she was as good, if not a better, poetess than Ann Bradstreet, whom literary historians give the honor of being the first person of her sex to win fame as a poet in America.

Negro authorship may, for clearer statement, be classified into three main activities: Poetry, Fiction, and the Essay, with an occasional excursion into other branches. In the drama, until very recently, practically nothing worth while has been achieved, with the exception of Angelina Grimké's *Rachel* [see the creative writing section], notable for its sombre craftsmanship. Biography has given us a notable life story, told by himself, of Booker T. Washington. Frederick Douglass's story of his life is eloquent as a human document, but not in the graces of narration and psychologic portraiture, which has definitely put this form of literature in the domain of the fine arts. Indeed, we may well believe that the efforts of controversy, of the huge amount of discursive and polemical articles dealing chiefly with the race problem that have been necessary in breaking and clearing the impeded pathway of racial progress, have absorbed and in a way dissipated the literary energy of many able Negro writers.

Let us survey briefly the advance of the Negro in poetry. Behind Dunbar, there is nothing that can stand the critical test. We shall always have a sentimental and historical interest in those forlorn and pathetic figures who cried in the wilderness of their ignorance and oppression. With Dunbar we have our first authentic lyric utterance, an utterance more authentic, I should say, for its faithful rendition of Negro life and character than for any rare or subtle artistry of expression. When Mr. Howells, in his famous introduction to the *Lyrics of Lowly Life,* remarked that Dunbar was the first black man to express the life of his people lyrically, he summed up Dunbar's achievement and transported him to a place beside the peasant poet of Scotland, not for his art, but precisely because he made a people articulate in verse.

The two chief qualities in Dunbar's work are, however, pathos and humor, and in these he expresses that dilemma of soul that characterized the race between the Civil War and the end of the nineteenth century. The poetry of Dunbar is true to the life of the Negro and expresses characteristically what he felt and knew to be the temper and condition of his people. But its moods reflect chiefly those of the era of Reconstruction and just a little beyond—the limited experience of a transitional period, the rather helpless and subservient era of testing freedom and reaching out through the difficulties of life to the emotional compensations of laughter and tears. It is the poetry of the happy peasant and the plaintive minstrel. Occasionally, as in the sonnet to "Robert Gould Shaw" and the "Ode to Ethiopia," there broke through Dunbar, as through the crevices of his spirit, a burning and brooding aspiration, an awakening and virile consciousness of race. But for the most part, his dreams were anchored to the minor whimsies; his deepest poetic inspiration was sentiment. He expressed a folk temperament, but not a race soul. Dunbar was the end of a régime, and not the beginning of a tradition, as so many careless critics, both white and colored, seem to think.

After Dunbar many versifiers appeared—all largely dominated by his successful dialect work. I cannot parade them here for tag or comment, except to say that few have equalled Dunbar in this vein of expression, and none have deepened it as an expression of Negro life. Dunbar himself had clear notions of its limitations—to a friend in a letter from London, March 15, 1897, he says: "I see now very clearly that Mr. Howells has done me irrevocable harm in the dictum he laid down regarding my dialect verse." Not until James W. Johnson published his "Fiftieth Anniversary Ode" on the emancipation in 1913, did a poet of the race disengage himself from the background of mediocrity into which the imitation of Dunbar snared Negro poetry. Mr. Johnson's work is based upon a broader contemplation of life, life that is not wholly confined within any racial experience, but through the racial he made articulate that universality of the emotions felt by all mankind. His verse possesses a vigor which definitely breaks away from the brooding minor undercurrents of feeling which have previously characterized the verse of Negro poets. Mr. Johnson brought, indeed, the first intellectual substance to the content of our poetry, and a craftsmanship which, less spontaneous than that of Dunbar's, was more balanced and precise.

Here a new literary generation begins; poetry that is racial in substance, but with the universal note, and consciously the background of the full heritage of English poetry. With each new figure somehow the gamut broadens and the technical control improves. The brilliant succession and maturing powers of Fenton Johnson, Leslie Pinckney Hill, Everett Hawkins, Lucien Watkins, Charles Bertram Johnson, Joseph Cotter, Georgia Douglas Johnson, Roscoe Jameson and Anne Spencer bring us at last to Claude

McKay and the poets of the younger generation and a poetry of the masterful accent and high distinction. Too significantly for mere coincidence, it was the stirring year of 1917 that heard the first real masterful accent in Negro poetry. In the September *Crisis* of that year, Roscoe Jameson's "Negro Soldiers" appeared:

> These truly are the Brave,
> These men who cast aside
> Old memories to walk the bloodstained pave
> Of Sacrifice, joining the solemn tide
> That moves away, to suffer and to die
> For Freedom—when their own is yet denied!
> O Pride! O Prejudice! When they pass by
> Hail them, the Brave, for you now crucified.

The very next month, under the pen name of Eli Edwards, Claude McKay printed ["The Harlem Dancer"; see the creative writing section] in *The Seven Arts*. . . .

With Georgia Johnson, Anne Spencer and Angelina Grimké, the Negro woman poet significantly appears. Mrs. Johnson especially has voiced in true poetic spirit the lyric cry of Negro womanhood. In spite of lapses into the sentimental and the platitudinous, she has an authentic gift. Anne Spencer, more sophisticated, more cryptic but also more universal, reveals quite another aspect of poetic genius. Indeed, it is interesting to notice how today Negro poets waver between the racial and the universal notes.

Claude McKay, the poet who leads his generation, is a genius meshed in this dilemma. His work is caught between the currents of the poetry of protest and the poetry of expression; he is in turn the violent and strident propagandist, using his poetic gifts to clothe arrogant and defiant thoughts, and then the pure lyric dreamer, contemplating life and nature with a wistful sympathetic passion. When the mood of "Spring in New Hampshire" or the sonnet "The Harlem Dancer" possesses him, he is full of that spirit and power of beauty that flowers above any and all men's harming. How different, in spite of the admirable spirit of courage and defiance, are his poems of which the sonnet "If We Must Die" [see the creative writing section] is a typical example. Negro poetic expression hovers for the moment, pardonably perhaps, over the race problem, but its highest allegiance is to Poetry—it must soar.

Let me refer briefly to a type of literature in which there have been many pens, but a single mind. Dr. Du Bois is the most variously gifted writer which the race has produced. Poet, novelist, sociologist, historian and essayist, he has produced books in all these fields with the exception, I believe, of a formal book of poems, and has given to each the distinction of his clear and exact thinking, and of his sensitive imagination and passionate vision. *The Souls of Black Folk* was the book of an era; it was a painful book, a book of tortured dreams woven into the fabric of the sociologist's document. This book has more profoundly influenced the spiritual temper of the race than any other written in its generation. It is only through the intense, passionate idealism of such substance as makes *The Souls of Black Folk* such a quivering rhapsody of wrongs endured and hopes to be fulfilled that the poets of the race with compelling artistry can lift the Negro into the only full and complete nationalism he knows—that of the American democracy. No other book has more clearly revealed to the nation at large the true idealism and high aspiration of the American Negro.

In this book, as well as in many of Dr. Du Bois's essays, it is often my personal feeling that I am witnessing the birth of a poet, phoenix-like, out of a scholar. Between *The Souls of Black Folk* and *Darkwater*, published four years ago, Dr. Du Bois has written a number of books, none more notable, in my opinion, than his novel *The Quest of the Silver Fleece*, in which he made Cotton the great protagonist of fate in the lives of the Southern people, both white and black. I only know of one other such attempt and accomplishment in American fiction—that of Frank Norris[1]—and I am somehow of the opinion that when the great epic novel of the South is written this book will prove to have been its forerunner. Indeed, the Negro novel is one of the great potentialities of American literature. Must it be written by a Negro? To refer to [a recent article in *The Independent*]:

> The white writer seems to stand baffled before the enigma and so he expends all his energies on dialect and in general on the Negro's minstrel characteristics. . . . We shall have to look to the Negro himself to go all the way. It is quite likely that no white man can do it. It is reasonable to suppose that his white psychology will always be in his way. I am not thinking at all about a Negro novelist who shall arouse the world to the horror of the deliberate killings by white mobs, to the wrongs that condemn a free people to political serfdom. I am not thinking at all of the propaganda novel, although there is enough horror and enough drama in the bald statistics of each one of the annual Moton letters to keep the whole army of writers busy. But the Negro novelist, if he ever comes, must reveal to us much more than what a Negro thinks about when he is being tied to a stake and the torch is being applied to his living flesh; much more than what he feels when he is being crowded off the sidewalk by a drunken rowdy who may be his intellectual inferior by a thousand leagues. Such a writer, to succeed in a big sense, would have to forget that there are white readers; he would have to lose self-consciousness and forget that his work would be placed before a white jury. He would have to be careless as to what the white critic might think of it; he would need the self-assurance to be his own critic. He would have to forget for the time being, at least, that any white man ever attempted to dissect the soul of a Negro.

What I here quote is both an inquiry and a challenge! Well informed as the writer is, he does not seem to detect the forces which are surely gathering to produce what he longs for.

The development of fiction among Negro authors has been, I might almost say, one of the repressed activities of our literary life. A fair start was made the last decade of the nineteenth century when Chesnutt and Dunbar were turning out both short stories and novels. In Dunbar's case, had he lived, I think his literary growth would have been in the evolution of the Race novel as indicated in *The Uncalled* and *The Sport of the Gods*. The former was, I think, the most ambitious literary effort of Dunbar; the latter was his

---

1. Frank Norris (1870–1902) was an American writer known for his critical portrayals of corporate exploitation and ruthlessness.

most significant; significant because, thrown against the background of New York City, it displayed the life of the race as a unit, swayed by currents of existence, of which it was and was not a part. The story was touched with that shadow of destiny which gave to it a purpose more important than the mere racial machinery of its plot. But Dunbar in his fiction dealt only successfully with the same world that gave him the inspiration for his dialect poems; though his ambition was to "write a novel that will deal with the educated class of my own people." Later he writes of *The Fanatics:* "You do not know how my hopes were planted in that book, but it has utterly disappointed me." His contemporary, Charles W. Chesnutt, was concerned more primarily with the fiction of the Color Line and the contacts and conflicts of its two worlds. He was in a way more successful. In the five volumes to his credit, he has revealed himself as a fiction writer of a very high order. But after all Mr. Chesnutt is a story-teller of genius transformed by racial earnestness into the novelist of talent. His natural gift would have found freer vent in a flow of short stories like Bret Harte's, to judge from the facility and power of his two volumes of short stories, *The Wife of His Youth and Other Stories* and *The Conjure Woman.* But Mr. Chesnutt's serious effort was in the field of the novel, where he made a brave and partially successful effort to correct the distortions of Reconstruction fiction and offset the school of Page and Cable. Two of these novels, *The Marrow of Tradition* and *The House Behind the Cedars,* must be reckoned among the representative period novels of their time. But the situation was not ripe for the great Negro novelist. The American public preferred spurious values to the genuine; the coinage of the Confederacy was at literary par. Where Dunbar, the sentimentalist, was welcome, Chesnutt, the realist, was barred. In 1905 Mr. Chesnutt wrote *The Colonel's Dream,* and thereafter silence fell upon him.

From this date until the past year, with the exception of *The Quest of the Silver Fleece,* which was published in 1911, there has been no fiction of importance by Negro authors. But then suddenly there comes a series of books, which seems to promise at least a new phase of race fiction, and possibly the era of the major novelists. Mr. Walter White's novel *The Fire in the Flint* is a swift moving straightforward story of the contemporary conflicts of black manhood in the South. Coming from the experienced observation of the author, himself an investigator of many lynchings and riots, it is a social document story of first-hand significance and importance; too vital to be labelled and dismissed as propaganda, yet for the same reason too unvarnished and realistic a story to be great art. Nearer to the requirements of art comes Miss Jessie Fauset's novel *There Is Confusion.* Its distinction is to have created an entirely new milieu in the treatment of the race in fiction. She has taken a class within the race of established social standing, tradition and culture, and given in the rather complex family story of *The Marshalls* a social document of unique and refreshing value. In such a story, race fiction, detaching itself from the limitations of propaganda on the one hand and genre fiction on the other, emerges from the color line and is incorporated into the body of general and universal art.

Finally, in Jean Toomer, the author of *Cane* [see "Blood-Burning Moon" in the creative writing section], we come upon the very first artist of the race, who with all an artist's passion and sympathy for life, its hurts, its sympathies, its desires, its joys, its defeats and strange yearnings, can write about the Negro without the surrender or compromise of the artist's vision. So objective is it, that we feel that it is a mere accident that birth or association has thrown him into contact with the life he has written about. He would write just as well, just as poignantly, just as transmutingly, about the peasants of Russia, or the peasants of Ireland, had experience brought him in touch with their existence. *Cane* is a book of gold and bronze, of dusk and flame, of ecstasy and pain, and Jean Toomer is a bright morning star of a new day of the race in literature.

Ruth Whitehead Whaley

Closed Doors: A Study in Segregation

In proportion as men differ in race, characteristics or ideas, just so much do they distrust, dislike and abuse each other. The more unlike the more disliked. The natural tendency of two unlike groups is to fear, hate and exterminate the other. The stronger or better trained group becomes the dominant power. It cries aloud its superiority. Any indignity heaped upon the other group is justified in the name of their inferiority. Inferiority is an old misnomer for injustice. It is not the unique product of present day conditions. Centuries ago the Romans justified their world plunder by calling their victims barbarians. The nobility of Europe looks down upon the peasant who feeds them. The Norman called the Saxon inferior. Of this inferiority complex the Negro in America has been and is the chief sufferer. He is called inferior because he is of a different race, different color, as an excuse for the indignity heaped upon him, a balm for irritated consciences. When two different groups are living side by side there arise animosities and prejudices born of their ignorance each of the other. They have a mutual desire to exploit and exterminate. By the dominant group the dominated is called a problem or menace. Thus in America the Negro Problem—where to relegate this Black People, in what manner best to quell each noble impulse of theirs, how to feed each base inclination—the solution of this problem has been the chief pursuit of a vast majority of white America.

The first solution attempted was slavery. But the economic advantage of unpaid free labor in the South over hired labor in the North was too great. Thus slavery was ended and, incidentally and as collateral to the main issue, the Negro was free.

The second solution suggested was colonization in some possession of the United States or in Africa. It was never accomplished. The South was never willing to give up the easily exploited Negro labor. The second solution was cast aside. The third solution

The Messenger, July 1923.

attempted is segregation (not the voluntary collecting of Negroes as the word might denote, rather, the closed door). Thus far and no farther shalt thou come.

Segregation! Volumes might be written about it. It is the Negro's nemesis. The evil of segregation lies not alone in being excluded or relegated, it goes far deeper—the heritage of thinking black, the segregated atmosphere, the reaction upon the dominant group. If segregation consisted in nothing more than separate schools, churches, housing districts, etc., that alone, as despicable and undesirable as it would be, could not constitute the menace we now face. The most insidious weapon of segregation is the atmosphere it carries. This separating and setting apart is the most virulent expression of vaunted superiority. The dividing line is so visible until, being constantly seen, it nurtures a particular train of thought, a distinct psychological reaction. Segregation is the chief exponent of "divine right of race." The tendency is for the dominant group to excuse and justify the segregation with false and illogical reasoning. They finally believe it. The segregated group becomes over-race-conscious, hates bitterly and loses the value of inter-relation. The justification offered for segregation is the inferiority of the Negro. The blight of segregation is the belief in his inferiority it engenders in both groups. It colors the treatment which the dominant group gives the segregated. It has an unwholesome effect upon the oppressed.

The "Negro's place" has usually been applied to him socially, industrially or educationally. But in recent years this place means also his residence. Segregation ordinances began to flourish in 1911. He must not live in certain restricted areas. To be more exact, he must not own homes or reside in certain restricted white districts. No one objects if he lives in the same house as servant with his employer. But to live in his own house next door—the proximity was too great. The real reason seemed to be fear of social equality. The mere proximity was not dreaded but the character of the proximity. If as servant—no objection. If as owner, as resident—it couldn't be. It doesn't follow that segregation of the Negro in residential quarters will in any manner solve the "race problem." The knowledge of the average white person concerning the Negro whom he dislikes is meagre and usually based on hearsay, or knowledge of the servant class only. If they are to be forever separated by iron bars he will learn little more about him than he already knows. The acquaintance of one intelligent Negro would give him a different view of them perhaps. Why relegate the Negro to certain sections if his taste and purse lead him elsewhere, so long as he conducts himself properly? Industry segregates the Negro—the reason he is shiftless. Remember that where the Negro has been given fair opportunity he has proven these charges false. Segregation in industry begins in the Labor Unions—the irony of it—certain jobs are gladly given him: "that's his place." But many jobs are closed to him: of these we speak. When segregation does not flourish, the Negro's good record is excused as being exceptional in the particular instance referred to. Educational segregation is not a myth, for even yet there is a prevalent idea that classical and professional education should be denied Negroes generally. That in spite of the record of hundreds and thousands of Negro college and professional graduates. One underlying objection to higher education is the knowledge that the educated Negroes will not be so easily exploited. Having been trained in the same arts and sciences, there will be a closer consciousness between educated Negroes and educated whites, and Banquo's ghost—social equality—might become a reality. For it is folly to give persons the same advantages and contact during formative periods, then ask them to forget it all and accept benighted dogmas again. But social equality does not of necessity mean wholesale inter-marriage, or race amalgamation. It does mean that each person will have the right to choose any other person for social intercourse, friendship or marriage. And why not? In some sections the Negro has been barred from any part in political affairs through various ingenious schemes. Where he has been allowed free use of the ballot he has in most places until recently segregated himself. As in all other cases of segregation it has proved detrimental to him.

In the Negro world there is one figure who is the victim of a two-fold segregation and discrimination—the New Negro Woman. Woman's emancipation is strangely parallel with the Negro's struggle. Inferiority is the reason given for her oppression. She has been considered as a mere chattel, cowed and subdued, taught that she, like children, must be seen and not heard. Petted as an ornament of the home, a plaything for the male, producer of a line of warriors and race builders. Lacking all chance for development, she is called inferior because she hasn't developed. The Negro woman falls heir to all these prejudices, and to add injury to distress she is a Negro. If there is any one person against whom the doors have been closed it is the New Negro Woman. As a woman she was outside her sphere. As a Negro woman she was impossible. In industry, education and politics she is gradually coming into her own. But remember her closed doors are of the thickness of two—she is first a woman, then a Negro. May the fates be kind to her!

A fair and thoughtful view of segregation leads one to believe that it is a futile gesture of the white man to the Negro. An expiring death groan ere the inevitable happens. It is impossible to stop the upward striving of the Negro by segregation; their progress may be retarded. But Time, the great winnower and sifter of truth, will aid them. The great mass of "exceptional Negroes," who have attained far more than Negroes are supposed to attain, are now to be reckoned with. Closer association of the races in cities of the North and East produces both good and bad results. Seeing more Negroes, they of necessity see more "bad Negroes," also more intelligent and ambitious Negroes than ever before. Theories are slowly and reluctantly being revised. The result is sometimes more segregation, sometimes less dependent upon the innate justice and honesty of that particular group.

But segregation, as terrible as it is, the curse of segregated atmosphere as blighting as it is, will not forever be. The Egyptians and Babylonians once were supreme in power. They also enslaved and segregated. They are now a memory of history only. The ancestors of Horace and Socrates have so lost in prestige until Macaulay says of them: "Their people have degenerated into timid slaves and their language into a barbarous jargon."[1]

---

1. Thomas Babington Macaulay (1800–1859) was an eminent nineteenth-century British historian and statesman.

The barbarians, of whom Aristotle said: "It is impossible for them to count beyond their fingers," did subsequently produce a Shakespeare and Newton. In the cycle of the years, the evolution and revolution of ideas and civilizations, the segregated Negro will also come into his own. He will lose his "inferiority" when and as he loses its mate, injustice. Finally the shadow will be lifted. The closed door swings ajar.

James Weldon Johnson

Harlem: The Culture Capital

In the history of New York, the significance of the name Harlem has changed from Dutch to Irish to Jewish to Negro. Of these changes, the last has come most swiftly. Throughout colored America, from Massachusetts to Mississippi, and across the continent to Los Angeles and Seattle, its name, which as late as fifteen years ago had scarcely been heard, now stands for the Negro metropolis. Harlem is indeed the great Mecca for the sight-seer, the pleasure-seeker, the curious, the adventurous, the enterprising, the ambitious and the talented of the whole Negro world; for the lure of it has reached down to every island of the Carib Sea and has penetrated even into Africa.

In the make-up of New York, Harlem is not merely a Negro colony or community, it is a city within a city, the greatest Negro city in the world. It is not a slum or a fringe, it is located in the heart of Manhattan and occupies one of the most beautiful and healthful sections of the city. It is not a "quarter" of dilapidated tenements, but is made up of new-law apartments and handsome dwellings, with well-paved and well-lighted streets. It has its own churches, social and civic centers, shops, theaters and other places of amusement. And it contains more Negroes to the square mile than any other spot on earth. A stranger who rides up magnificent Seventh Avenue on a bus or in an automobile must be struck with surprise at the transformation which takes place after he crosses One Hundred and Twenty-fifth Street. Beginning there, the population suddenly darkens and he rides through twenty-five solid blocks where the passers-by, the shoppers, those sitting in restaurants, coming out of theaters, standing in doorways and looking out of windows are practically all Negroes; and then he emerges where the population as suddenly becomes white again. There is nothing just like it in any other city in the country, for there is no preparation for it; no change in the character of the houses and streets; no change, indeed, in the appearance of the people, except their color.

The New Negro, 1925.

Negro Harlem is practically a development of the past decade, but the story behind it goes back a long way. There have always been colored people in New York. In the middle of the last century they lived in the vicinity of Lispenard, Broome and Spring Streets. When Washington Square and lower Fifth Avenue were the center of aristocratic life, the colored people, whose chief occupation was domestic service in the homes of the rich, lived in a fringe and were scattered in nests to the south, east and west of the square. As late as the '80's the major part of the colored population lived in Sullivan, Thompson, Bleecker, Grove, Minetta Lane and adjacent streets. It is curious to note that some of these nests still persist. In a number of the blocks of Greenwich Village and Little Italy may be found small groups of Negroes who have never lived in any other section of the city. By about 1890 the center of colored population had shifted to the upper Twenties and lower Thirties west of Sixth Avenue. Ten years later another considerable shift northward had been made to West Fifty-third Street.

The West Fifty-third Street settlement deserves some special mention because it ushered in a new phase of life among colored New Yorkers. Three rather well-appointed hotels were opened in the street and they quickly became the centers of a sort of fashionable life that hitherto had not existed. On Sunday evenings these hotels served dinner to music and attracted crowds of well-dressed diners. One of these hotels, the Marshall, became famous as the headquarters of Negro talent. There gathered the actors, the musicians, the composers, the writers, the singers, dancers and vaudevillians. There one went to get a close-up of Williams and Walker, Cole and Johnson, Ernest Hogan, Will Marion Cook, Jim Europe, Aida Overton, and of others equally and less known. Paul Laurence Dunbar was frequently there whenever he was in New York. Numbers of those who love to shine by the light reflected from celebrities were always to be found. The first modern jazz band ever heard in New York, or perhaps anywhere, was organized at the Marshall. It was a playing-singing-dancing orchestra, making the first dominant use of banjos, saxophones, clarinets and trap drums in combination, and was called the Memphis Students. Jim Europe was a member of that band, and out of it grew the famous Clef Club, of which he was the noted leader, and which for a long time monopolized the business of "entertaining" private parties and furnishing music for the new dance craze. Also in the Clef Club was "Buddy" Gilmore, who originated trap drumming as it is now practised, and set hundreds of white men to juggling their sticks and doing acrobatic stunts while they manipulated a dozen other noise-making devices aside from their drums. A good many well-known white performers frequented the Marshall and for seven or eight years the place was one of the sights of New York.

The move to Fifty-third Street was the result of the opportunity to get into newer and better houses. About 1900 the move to Harlem began, and for the same reason. Harlem had been overbuilt with large, new-law apartment houses, but rapid transportation to that section was very inadequate—the Lenox Avenue Subway had not yet been built—and landlords were finding difficulty in keeping houses on the east side of the section filled. Residents along and near Seventh Avenue were fairly well served by the Eighth Avenue Elevated. A colored man in the real estate business at this time, Philip

A. Payton, approached several of these landlords with the proposition that he would fill their empty or partially empty houses with steady colored tenants. The suggestion was accepted, and one or two houses on One Hundred and Thirty-fourth Street east of Lenox Avenue were taken over. Gradually other houses were filled. The whites paid little attention to the movement until it began to spread west of Lenox Avenue; they then took steps to check it. They proposed through a financial organization, the Hudson Realty Company, to buy all properties occupied by colored people and evict the tenants. The Negroes countered by similar methods. Payton formed the Afro-American Realty Company, a Negro corporation organized for the purpose of buying and leasing houses for occupancy by colored people. Under this counter stroke the opposition subsided for several years.

But the continually increasing pressure of colored people to the west over the Lenox Avenue dead line caused the opposition to break out again, but in a new and more menacing form. Several white men undertook to organize all the white people of the community for the purpose of inducing financial institutions not to lend money or renew mortgages on properties occupied by colored people. In this effort they had considerable success, and created a situation which has not yet been completely overcome, a situation which is one of the hardest and most unjustifiable the Negro property owner in Harlem has to contend with. The Afro-American Realty Company was now defunct, but two or three colored men of means stepped into the breach. Philip A. Payton and J. C. Thomas bought two five-story apartments, dispossessed the white tenants and put in colored. J. B. Nail bought a row of five apartments and did the same thing. St. Philip's Church bought a row of thirteen apartment houses on One Hundred and Thirty-fifth Street, running from Seventh Avenue almost to Lenox.

The situation now resolved itself into an actual contest. Negroes not only continued to occupy available apartment houses, but began to purchase private dwellings between Lenox and Seventh Avenues. Then the whole movement, in the eyes of the whites, took on the aspect of an "invasion"; they became panic-stricken and began fleeing as from a plague. The presence of one colored family in a block, no matter how well bred and orderly, was sufficient to precipitate a flight. House after house and block after block was actually deserted. It was a great demonstration of human beings running amuck. None of them stopped to reason why they were doing it or what would happen if they didn't. The banks and lending companies holding mortgages on these deserted houses were compelled to take them over. For some time they held these houses vacant; preferring to do that and carry the charges than to rent or sell them to colored people. But values dropped and continued to drop until at the outbreak of the war in Europe, property in the northern part of Harlem had reached the nadir.

In the meantime the Negro colony was becoming more stable; the churches were being moved from the lower part of the city; social and civic centers were being formed; and gradually a community was being evolved. Following the outbreak of the war in Europe, Negro Harlem received a new and tremendous impetus. Because of the war thousands of aliens in the United States rushed back to their native lands to join the colors and immigration practically ceased.[1] The result was a critical shortage in labor. This short-age was rapidly increased as the United States went more and more largely into the busi-ness of furnishing munitions and supplies to the warring countries. To help meet this shortage of common labor, Negroes were brought up from the South. The government itself took the first steps, following the practice in vogue in Germany of shifting labor according to the supply and demand in various parts of the country. The example of the government was promptly taken up by the big industrial concerns, which sent hundreds, perhaps thousands, of labor agents into the South, who recruited Negroes by wholesale. I was in Jacksonville, Fla., for a while at that time, and I sat one day and watched the stream of migrants passing to take the train. For hours they passed steadily, carrying flimsy suit cases, new and shiny, rusty old ones, bursting at the seams, boxes and bundles and imped-imenta of all sorts, including banjos, guitars, birds in cages and what not. Similar scenes were being enacted in cities and towns all over that region. The first wave of the great exodus of Negroes from the South was on. Great numbers of these migrants headed for New York or eventually got there, and naturally the majority went up into Harlem. But the Negro population of Harlem was not swollen by migrants from the South alone; the opportunity for Negro labor exerted its pull upon the Negroes of the West Indies, and those islanders in the course of time poured into Harlem to the number of twenty-five thousand or more.

These new-comers did not have to look for work; work looked for them, and at wages of which they had never even dreamed. And here is where the unlooked for, the unprece-dented, the miraculous happened. According to all preconceived notions, these Negroes suddenly earning large sums of money for the first time in their lives should have had their heads turned; they should have squandered it in the most silly and absurd man-ners imaginable. Later, after the United States had entered the war and even Negroes in the South were making money fast, many stories in accord with the tradition came out of that section. There was the one about the colored man who went into a general store and on hearing a phonograph for the first time promptly ordered six of them, one for each child in the house. I shall not stop to discuss whether Negroes in the South did that sort of thing or not, but I do know that those who got to New York didn't. The Negroes of Harlem, for the greater part, worked and saved their money. Nobody knew how much they had saved until congestion made expansion necessary for tenants and ownership profitable for landlords, and they began to buy property. Persons who would never be suspected of having money bought property. The Rev. W. W. Brown, pastor of the Met-ropolitan Baptist Church, repeatedly made "Buy Property" the text of his sermons. A large part of his congregation carried out the injunction. The church itself set an example by purchasing a magnificent brownstone church building on Seventh Avenue from a white congregation. Buying property became a fever. At the height of this activity, that is, 1920–21, it was not an uncommon thing for a colored washerwoman or cook to go into a real estate office and lay down from one thousand to five thousand dollars on a

---

1. That is, they enlisted in the armies of their home countries in Europe.

house. "Pig Foot Mary" is a character in Harlem. Everybody who knows the corner of Lenox Avenue and One Hundred and Thirty-fifth Street knows "Mary" and her stand, and has been tempted by the smell of her pigsfeet, fried chicken and hot corn, even if he has not been a customer. "Mary," whose real name is Mrs. Mary Dean, bought the five-story apartment house at the corner of Seventh Avenue and One Hundred and Thirty-seventh Street at a price of $42,000. Later she sold it to the Y.W.C.A. for dormitory purposes. The Y.W.C.A. sold it recently to Adolph Howell, a leading colored undertaker, the price given being $72,000. Often companies of a half dozen men combined to buy a house—these combinations were and still are generally made up of West Indians—and would produce five or ten thousand dollars to put through the deal.

When the buying activity began to make itself felt, the lending companies that had been holding vacant the handsome dwellings on and abutting Seventh Avenue decided to put them on the market. The values on these houses had dropped to the lowest mark possible and they were put up at astonishingly low prices. Houses that had been bought at from $15,000 to $20,000 were sold at one-third those figures. They were quickly gobbled up. The Equitable Life Assurance Company held 106 model private houses that were designed by Stanford White. They are built with courts running straight through the block and closed off by wrought-iron gates. Every one of these houses was sold within eleven months at an aggregate price of about two million dollars. Today they are probably worth about 100 per cent more. And not only have private dwellings and similar apartments been bought but big elevator apartments have been taken over. Corporations have been organized for this purpose. Two of these, the Antillian Realty Company, composed of West Indian Negroes, and the Sphinx Securities Company, composed of American and West Indian Negroes, represent holdings amounting to approximately $750,000. Individual Negroes and companies in the South have invested in Harlem real estate. About two years ago a Negro institution of Savannah, Ga., bought a parcel for $115,000 which it sold a month or so ago at a profit of $110,000.

I am informed by John E. Nail, a successful colored real estate dealer of Harlem and a reliable authority, that the total value of property in Harlem owned and controlled by colored people would at a conservative estimate amount to more than sixty million dollars. These figures are amazing, especially when we take into account the short time in which they have been piled up. Twenty years ago Negroes were begging for the privilege of renting a flat in Harlem. Fifteen years ago barely a half dozen colored men owned real property in all Manhattan. And down to ten years ago the amount that had been acquired in Harlem was comparatively negligible. Today Negro Harlem is practically owned by Negroes.

The question naturally arises, "Are the Negroes going to be able to hold Harlem?" If they have been steadily driven northward for the past hundred years and out of less desirable sections, can they hold this choice bit of Manhattan Island? It is hardly probable that Negroes will hold Harlem indefinitely, but when they are forced out it will not be for the same reasons that forced them out of former quarters in New York City. The situation is entirely different and without precedent. When colored people do leave Harlem, their homes, their churches, their investments and their businesses, it will be because the land has become so valuable they can no longer afford to live on it. But the date of another move northward is very far in the future. What will Harlem be and become in the meantime? Is there danger that the Negro may lose his economic status in New York and be unable to hold his property? Will Harlem become merely a famous ghetto, or will it be a center of intellectual, cultural and economic forces exerting an influence throughout the world, especially upon Negro peoples? Will it become a point of friction between the races in New York?

I think there is less danger to the Negroes of New York of losing out economically and industrially than to the Negroes of any large city in the North. In most of the big industrial centers Negroes are engaged in gang labor. They are employed by thousands in the stockyards in Chicago, by thousands in the automobile plants in Detroit; and in those cities they are likely to be the first to be let go, and in thousands, with every business depression. In New York there is hardly such a thing as gang labor among Negroes, except among the longshoremen, and it is in the longshoremen's unions, above all others, that Negroes stand on an equal footing. Employment among Negroes in New York is highly diversified; in the main they are employed more as individuals than as nonintegral parts of a gang. Furthermore, Harlem is gradually becoming more and more a self-supporting community. Negroes there are steadily branching out into new businesses and enterprises in which Negroes are employed. So the danger of great numbers of Negroes being thrown out of work at once, with a resulting economic crisis among them, is less in New York than in most of the large cities of the North to which Southern migrants have come.

These facts have an effect which goes beyond the economic and industrial situation. They have a direct bearing on the future character of Harlem and on the question as to whether Harlem will be a point of friction between the races in New York. It is true that Harlem is a Negro community, well defined and stable; anchored to its fixed homes, churches, institutions, business and amusement places; having its own working, business and professional classes. It is experiencing a constant growth of group consciousness and community feeling. Harlem is, therefore, in many respects, typically Negro. It has many unique characteristics. It has movement, color, gayety, singing, dancing, boisterous laughter and loud talk. One of its outstanding features is brass band parades. Hardly a Sunday passes but that there are several of these parades of which many are gorgeous with regalia and insignia. Almost any excuse will do—the death of an humble member of the Elks, the laying of a cornerstone, the "turning out" of the order of this or that. In many of these characteristics it is similar to the Italian colony. But withal, Harlem grows more metropolitan and more a part of New York all the while. Why is it then that its tendency is not to become a mere "quarter"?

I shall give three reasons that seem to me to be important in their order. First, the language of Harlem is not alien; it is not Italian or Yiddish; it is English. Harlem talks American, reads American, thinks American. Second, Harlem is not physically a "quarter." It is not a section cut off. It is merely a zone through which four main arteries of the city run. Third, the fact that there is little or no gang labor gives Harlem Negroes the opportunity for individual expansion and individual contacts with the life and spirit of New York. A thousand Negroes from Mississippi put to work as a gang in a Pittsburgh steel mill will for a long time remain a thousand Negroes from Mississippi. Under the conditions that prevail in New York they would all within six months become New Yorkers. The rapidity with which Negroes become good New Yorkers is one of the marvels to observers.

These three reasons form a single reason why there is small probability that Harlem will ever be a point of race friction between the races in New York. One of the principal factors in the race riot in Chicago in 1919 was the fact that at that time there were 12,000 Negroes employed in gangs in the stockyards. There was considerable race feeling in Harlem at the time of the hegira of white residents due to the "invasion," but that feeling, of course, is no more. Indeed, a number of the old white residents who didn't go or could not get away before the housing shortage struck New York are now living peacefully side by side with colored residents. In fact, in some cases white and colored tenants occupy apartments in the same house. Many white merchants still do business in thickest Harlem. On the whole, I know of no place in the country where the feeling between the races is so cordial and at the same time so matter-of-fact and taken for granted. One of the surest safeguards against an outbreak in New York such as took place in so many Northern cities in the summer of 1919 is the large proportion of Negro police on duty in Harlem.

To my mind, Harlem is more than a Negro community; it is a large scale laboratory experiment in the race problem. The statement has often been made that if Negroes were transported to the North in large numbers the race problem with all of its acuteness and with new aspects would be transferred with them. Well, 175,000 Negroes live closely together in Harlem, in the heart of New York—75,000 more than live in any Southern city— and do so without any race friction. Nor is there any unusual record of crime. I once heard a captain of the 38th Police Precinct (the Harlem precinct) say that on the whole it was the most law-abiding precinct in the city. New York guarantees its Negro citizens the fundamental rights of American citizenship and protects them in the exercise of those rights. In return the Negro loves New York and is proud of it, and contributes in his way to its greatness. He still meets with discriminations, but possessing the basic rights, he knows that these discriminations will be abolished.

I believe that the Negro's advantages and opportunities are greater in Harlem than in any other place in the country, and that Harlem will become the intellectual, the cultural and financial center for Negroes of the United States, and will exert a vital influence upon all Negro peoples.

Brenda Ray Moryck

A Point of View:
An Opportunity Dinner Reaction

"Irvin Cobb and Octavus Roy Cohen[1]—recognized experts in the field of the short story of ebony hue and chocolate flavor? Why, I thought they were white men!"

"I thought so too."

"But they can't be!"

"Why not?"

"Because they write Negro stories."

"Well—suppose they do."

"Then they must be Negroes themselves. We are told that people can only write very well of their own race because they know that race best."

"Indeed."

The foregoing bit of conversation was recently overheard in a Southern city.

And there you have it—the Caucasian, with his facile pen, sketching life, wherever he finds it, excelling in any field to which he turns his art, while he recommends with sincerest sophistry that his darker brother keep within the narrow and prescribed area of his own racial precincts.

A paradox—a white man may be an expert in his treatment of a theme on black folk, but a colored man, and I say "colored" advisedly, is not to be encouraged to emulate his example by reciprocation. Strange, too, when colored people always have known, and always will know, as long as white people continue to depend upon them for the most intimate personal services one human being can render another, far more about them individually and collectively than they will ever know about the black race.

Yet one of the most popular arguments advanced by modern critics to convince the Negro writer of the wisdom of curtailing whatever free play he might care to allow his

1. Irvin Cobb and Octavius Roy Cohen were white writers who achieved success in prominent magazines like the *Saturday Evening Post* with comical stories based on minstrel stereotypes and caricatures of black people.

Opportunity, August 1925.

imagination in the treatment of any and all themes, is the one which states that he knows best about his own people. Granted that he does, is it not possible that in the range of his varied experiences he may not, through intimate contact with other peoples, come to know them equally as well, even as Thomas Nelson Page, Ruth McEnery Stuart, Joel Chandler Harris and others,[2] not omitting the estimable Messrs. Cobb and Cohen, have come to know and understand a certain type of Negro? I venture to say that a Negro writer living North could excel some of his present peers in the handling of an Irish or Jewish or Italian or Polish or even upper-class Caucasian theme if he were to try, for living and attending school for the most part, as he does, among the heterogeneous type of Americans, native, or foreign-born, contemptuously classed as "poor white trash," and either working for or with—no matter which, so the daily contact is there—better class Caucasians from clerks to royalty, he runs the gamut of the social scale in his daily existence and may be presumed to have direct knowledge of all classes of white people.

Then, too, his schooling, whether little or much, if academic training is as valuable as it is purported to be, should have contributed vastly to his understanding of white people. Whether or not the Negro writer has attended mixed schools or colored schools, been tutored by white or colored instructors, or by both, is of scant importance. The essential point is that his entire history and literature courses have been built up almost exclusively about the genealogy, character, growth, development and achievements of the Caucasian race. Where more than a passing reference to Negroes or Mongolians has been made in a school text, it has been by way of some dry-as-dust anthropological treatise intended to draw the attention of an esoteric few. The daily newspapers, with exception of those few Afro-American sheets which recently became so popular with both blacks and whites, are journals of Caucasian customs, manners, habits, pursuits, enterprises and engagements. The intelligent Negro lives in a white world perforce, for since he is outnumbered ten to one according to the census count, he cannot ward off this daily enlightenment as to how the other nine-tenths live, even if he would. He begins the a b c of knowledge of the white race with his first academic studies, and does not take his final degree in "Caucasianology" until the hour of his death, frequently being ministered to by a white physician during his passing, by which time he merits every award given for high attainment and proficiency in a prescribed course. His natural endowment of curiosity renders him an apt pupil in the school of life.

If, then, familiarity with the subject is the first requisite for intelligent writing about it, the educated Negro possesses the proper basic material in a pre-eminent degree. Pause but a moment and think of the beautiful and appealing love lyrics of the Negro *poet*—on his haunting and wistful nature poems, so devoid of any reference to color, so charmingly free of all race consciousness. Consider "Fog," as a prose example, the story which took first prize in a recent literary contest inaugurated to discover Negro talent [see the creative writing section for John F. Matheus's story]. With a masterly and impersonal stroke, the author has handled varied classes, types and races of people—

2. All the writers mentioned are white.

the Negro element in his theme, sketched in evidently to make it conform to the rules of competition, being the weakest part. The Negro poet has long since discarded the bonds of Negro dialect as the sole vehicle of his expression and gloriously transcended themes purely subjective in character. His fancy wanders where it lists. Why not the Negro writer of fiction?

I am not, however, advocating that he direct his talent to delineating Caucasian character to the utter exclusion of his interest in his own race. My intention is merely to point out his ability to write freely on any subject, should he elect to do so, contrary to the advice of his well-wishers and critics.

There is a danger, it seems to me, in confining a writer to certain limits. His vision is narrowed, his imagination is dwarfed and warped, and his theme is robbed of its universality of appeal if he must forever be bound to the task of depicting racial reactions peculiar to the Negro. The Negro race as a whole now differs from the white race in externals only. "Death and the mysteries of life, the pain and the grief that flesh and souls are heirs to, the eternal problems that address themselves to all generations and races, produce in the soul of the Negro the same reactions as in any other individual," says Robert T. Kerlin in his essay on "Contemporary Poetry of the Negro." Granted that intrinsically the Negro of pure African stock is more emotional, has greater depth of feeling, larger capacity for enjoyment, vaster appreciation for sensuous beauty than his white brother—is essentially more of the artist, more of the poet—and also more of the buffoon, still he exhibits his atavistic traits after three hundred years of cultivation and adulteration only in proportion as he is removed from modern civilized culture. The individual differences so avidly hit upon by contemporary writers are found only in a certain type of Negro—a very captivating colorful creature of swiftly changing moods, and unexpected humorous or sad reactions it is true, but one type only, nevertheless.

The writer who wishes to confine either his realism or his imagination to the still primitive groups, groups whose precinct is Seventh Street or Seventh Avenue [in Harlem,] Chicago or Alabama, will find an unfailing wealth of marketable material whose novel appeal cannot be denied. And the author who would make the prose literature of his race cannot afford to discount the valuable contribution which a study of any people still in the elementary stages of American civilization furnishes. Myra Kelly has given us those charming stories, "Little Citizens" and "Little Aliens"; Kathleen Norris, with her delightful gift for portraying Irish humor and Irish pathos, still paints the Americanized descendants of Ireland's emigrants; O. Henry offered us young America of the gutter and the curbstone; and I am told upon excellent authority that "Little Afro-Americans" is now in the process of being manuscripted.[3]

Further still, the Negro writer must delve into the past and steep himself in all the tragic lore of the South prior to the Civil War, adding to his present invaluable memory-store of slave history and slave legend those poignant episodes of Negro life so replete

---

3. These are all white writers who were well regarded at the time for their depictions of ordinary Americans.

with the very essence of reality, and with his native capacity for relishing the dramatic—the sad as well as the gay—interpret them for the World, as only he can, if he would complete and enrich the racial literature which will some day be held precious. But when he has finished this task of painting tragic history, albeit history embellished by the imagination—when he wearies of the grotesque and the humorous in his race, when his pen lags over the delineation of those superstitions and credulous characters once so numerous in the South but now fast disappearing; when he is done with slush and maudlin sentimentality, to what shall he turn his attention?

There still remains a rich unexplored field if he must continue the study of his own race—the vast domain of the colored *hoi polloi,* the middle-class Negro, neither unintelligent nor yet cultured, and the realm of the highly cultivated few, few not in numbers, but by comparison. Jessie Fauset, in *There Is Confusion,* has sketched both classes, and Walter White, with another motive than that of pure entertainment, has presented us the problems and difficulties daily faced by the ambitious, educated groups of Negroes in his book *The Fire in the Flint.* Other writers may follow their lead with similar works, but such stories, estimable though they are, do not represent purely creative art. They are both, more or less, propaganda novels, conceived for the purpose of presenting to a white audience certain facts and conditions concerning Negroes. They are not the charming impersonal themes so ably handled by many of the best Caucasian writers, and not always the best either, but the most widely read.

Let the young writer try his hand at this sort of writing for the sole purpose of entertaining. He will discover before very long, when he writes of life as he finds it, and so will his audience and his critics, that he is writing not of Negroes but of just people—people no different in standards, customs, habits and culture from any other enlightened American groups—merely American people. I say American, because the Negro is now American, thoroughly so, having through amalgamation of blood—there is no denying it when one views the ever increasing Nordic features and coloring appearing among the so-called blacks—through assimilation of ideas and ideals, and conscious and unconscious imitation, absorbed every iota of the good and bad in American life.

Undoubtedly, if he had been allowed to remain in his native land, Africa, and his black blood had never known the taint of many nations diffused through it in honorable and dishonorable ways, he would still have been as distinctly different in character as the Mongolian or Jew alienated from other peoples either by physical, political, or racial barriers, and developing in isolation a distinct race consciousness. Or if, having been brought to America, he had been huddled into a pale or ghetto, there to develop solely among his own kind, we should still see among all classes, traits and characteristics peculiarly individual to him. We should then probably have had a black Tolstoi writing of a dusky Anna Karenina.

But the Negro, for a large part, is no longer a Negro. He is an American, or living abroad, an Englishman, a Frenchman, or a German, according to his present place of abode with *sometimes* a dark skin and sometimes a skin not so dark. Contrary to the premise submitted by many so-called scientists that one drop of Negro blood makes a man a Negro, the black blood is not strong, but weak, and when once permeated by the Caucasian complex, the Negro becomes a Caucasian in all but his physique and frequently even in that. He sheds his peculiarly different African heritage with the ease with which a chameleon changes its colors and dons a new garment which, in the fifth and sixth generation of American civilization, the heritage which many Negroes can now boast, has become his skin.

How long has the Jew or any other immigrant remained racially different once he has become a part of America? Only so long as he has been forced to keep to himself and has not been assimilated in the great melting pot. Once he has acquired money and grappled to himself those advantages which he came seeking, he emerges from racedom, just as an American citizen. Witness the upper class Jew in any community or study the high-born Mongolians numerous in diplomatic circles in Washington or on the Pacific Coast. Seldom, if ever, are their reactions in any way peculiarly racial once they have become Americanized. They differ only as any other people differ according to birth and breeding. That too when both races have carefully preserved their racial integrity.

In any untutored people, we find emotionalism, unrestraint and novel and unexpected responses to the experiences of life, hence the naiveté of the masses of Negroes, who have long fascinated the white public and recently have begun to charm their own people. In any peoples just emerging from a long period of subjugation to a dominant group, we find greater depth of feeling, more intense religious fervor, a more serious and challenging outlook on life, than in the chosen few, who are the lords of the earth. The ordinary Negro is but a part of the great human family.

Likewise does he run true to form in the upper strata of society. He has on the one hand, all the airs, graces, superficialities and hypocrisies of the white race; all the shallowness, the meanness, the irreverence for holy things, the insatiable thirst for pleasure, the irritation at restraint, the envy, the jealousy; the contempt for the weak, the repudiation of the idea that he is his brother's keeper and the rejection of the Golden Rule which have ever characterized the over-sophisticated and too successful since the days of Babylon's glory, while on the other hand, he possesses in the same degree as all other representatives of a high degree of civilization—the tampering of his white forbears is responsible for the present degree—noble ideals, lofty thought, keen intellect, sane philosophy, sound judgment, hunger for knowledge, and a craving for all that is finest and best in life.

Prejudice against his color, when he shows any, has greatly hampered his progress as far as his material desires are concerned, but in spite of Fate, the mass Negro, the financially successful Negro and the cultured Negro as a whole, parallel their Caucasian complements in all but monetary wealth.

A story of any one of these types can be worked up into a purely Negro theme, of course, by depicting the tragedies and disappointments wrought by discrimination, and injustice—common occurrences in the daily lives of colored people—but at best such works are morbid. Yet any other attempt to portray the normal, ordinary pursuits of the classes of Negroes just described, unless spattered with constantly repeated references to color or to race, becomes at once simply an account of individuals, not of Negroes as such.

Konrad Bercovici, in a recent article published in the Harlem number of the *Survey Graphic,* argues that the Negro should preserve his racial heritage even as the Jew has held fast to his. The cases are not analogous, even in the instances where Jews are found to be true to the original type. Their ranks were closed against all modifying and assimilating influences of their religion. Now that their orthodoxy is somewhat weakening in this country, even they are becoming more and more like any other Americans. "The Good Provider," an undeniably true picture of prosperous American Jewish life, gives patent evidence of that fact. "Humoresque," likewise a gripping portrait of the Jew, represents his gradual change in character in proportion to his contact with the broadening influences of life. The high-class young Jews found in private schools and colleges are exactly the prototype of other American youth.

Granted, however, that the Negro should wish to emulate the Jew in his earlier stages of development in America, it is too late. He was robbed forever of his opportunity of remaining a distinct group of people long, long ago by his white ancestors. He is now from one-sixteenth to nine-tenths Caucasian and if he preserves any racial characteristics at all they must be of a Janus nature.

Mr. Bercovici likewise points out that in his study of Negro groups gleaned from intimate Harlem contacts with all classes of colored Americans, he found among them distinct differences of character and thought, peculiarly individual to the Negro.

I beg to differ with his findings.

Because I have discovered so few people whose opinions I value to agree with me on this subject, and can quote no significant authorities, I must be intensely personal in what follows, offering my own experiences and those of others well known to me to support my contention. I therefore ask my readers' indulgence.

If Mr. Bercovici were to leave off his exquisite word-painting of gypsy and Roumanian life and write a story of his colored friends—a certain well-known Negro actor[4] and his clever wife, a chemist of recognized ability in her line—would he find, I wonder, when that comedian had doffed the robes of the "Emperor Jones" or when Mrs. "Emperor Jones" had returned to her tiny New York apartment, or any of the others of the little Harlem group, anything especially different in their habits of life or manner of thought which would be a startling revelation to a jaded world fast learning how the other half lives? I think not.

Yet, not alone, either, are Konrad Bercovici and the other Caucasian critics in staunchly advocating the idea that a Negro writer must forever write of Negroes, first because he lacks the necessary knowledge for any other sort of writing and second, because portrayal of the Negro character offers something new and refreshing. They are warmly seconded by many of the ablest men of letters of the darker race. At a dinner

4. A reference to Charles Patrick Gilpin, who performed the part of the Emperor Jones in Eugene O'Neill's play of the same name in 1920.

not so long ago, I heard a prominent Negro, distinguished in a certain field of literature, eloquently argue for this same prescribed idea—he—a man of distinctly Caucasian features, and soft, straight hair, whose only identity with the race is his color and his wish, whose wife is a highly cultivated young woman, charming and beautiful after the Spanish pattern, whose fair-skinned babies—four of them, two of them fair-haired also, gambol about their inviting play-room, just as any babies do, scrapping, hitting, pounding, banging, crying, only to don quickly their company manners and smile and curtsey adorably or offer a pink-dimpled hand when guests appear, just as any other well-bred infants do the world over, exhibiting in no-wise those peculiarly different characteristics attributed to the Negro and argued for by their father.

For pastime, I recently wrote an intimate study of an eminent Negro author and his lovely wife and submitted it to a number of personal friends for their diversion. Except for the use of names and a passing reference to the color and features of a child, no one recognized it as a "colored story." There was nothing in the scholarly elegance of the man nor in the gracious charm of the woman nor in the cunning capers of the three children to brand them as Negroes, although in reality this couple very ardently and energetically identifies itself with the black race.

These are but a few examples. A panoramic view of cultured American Negro life will reveal many, many others of the same cast all over the country. The colored schools are filled with children of such parents, the large southern cities abound in their number—not always with quite the same cultural attainment as the very privileged few, but with a background as fitting and an outlook as sane and devoid of emotion as any of their compatriots of the same level of society, whose ancestors have enjoyed some little education and certain additional advantages.

Without stressing the unpleasant and dismal element of race-prejudice and its cursed results, it would be impossible to construct a Negro theme as such from the daily tragedies and joys and ordinary pursuits of colored people, except of those belonging to the untrained and inexperienced groups, who through continued lack of enlightenment and contact with refining influences have reverted or remained true to the African type, which I frankly and readily admit is peculiarly different from all other race types.

Above that class, the Negro becomes just a person, differing from all other persons in color, according to the amount of Negro blood in his veins, in dress, tastes and habits, according to the degree of his cultivation, in manner of living, according to wealth. Proof of this fact may be found in the thousands of so-called colored people who yearly sever themselves with such ease from the race to which the laws of Virginia and South Carolina and a few other states, grown hysterical over what they once started and cannot now control, have assigned them, to become lost in the milieu of an immigrant crowded white world. If he were inherently different, the peculiar racial characteristics supposedly his would be as apparent in the white-skinned Negro as in the black.

If then, a survey of colored American life reveals the fact that people are people, white or black, the Negro prose writer with safe assurance may invade with his pen any world he desires, for by merely knowing his own race people, he knows in addition all other people of his country not alone through study and observation but *per se.* Freedom of range of idea, unhampered by race consciousness or smothered by race pride, he as well as the poet must have, if the latent gift of creative art recently uncovered to the public is to reach the ripe fulfilment of its rich promise.

Not only then will he produce a great Negro literature, but beyond that in time, he too will be added to that list of honored men, which bears the names of the makers of the creative literature of the world.

George S. Schuyler

The Negro-Art Hokum

Negro Art "made in America" is as non-existent as the widely advertised profundity of Cal Coolidge, the "seven years of progress" of Mayor Hylan, or the reported sophistication of New Yorkers. Negro art there has been, is, and will be among the numerous black nations of Africa; but to suggest the possibility of any such development among the ten million colored people in this republic is self-evident foolishness. Eager apostles from Greenwich Village, Harlem, and environs proclaimed a great renaissance of Negro art just around the corner waiting to be ushered on the scene by those whose hobby is taking races, nations, peoples and movements under their wing. New art forms expressing the "peculiar" psychology of the Negro were about to flood the market. In short, the art of Homo Africanus was about to electrify the waiting world. Skeptics patiently waited. They still wait.

True, from dark-skinned sources have come those slave songs based on Protestant hymns and Biblical texts known as the spirituals, work songs and secular songs of sorrow and tough luck known as the blues, that outgrowth of ragtime known as jazz (in the development of which whites have assisted), and the Charleston, an eccentric dance invented by the gamins around the public market-place in Charleston, S.C. No one can or does deny this. But these are contributions of a caste in a certain section of the country. They are foreign to Northern Negroes, West Indian Negroes, and African Negroes. They are no more expressive or characteristic of the Negro race than the music and dancing of the Appalachian highlanders or the Dalmatian peasantry are expressive or characteristic of the Caucasian race. If one wishes to speak of the musical contributions of the peasantry of the South, very well. Any group under similar circumstances would have produced something similar. It is merely a coincidence that this peasant class happens to be of a darker hue than the other inhabitants of the land. One recalls the remarkable likeness of the minor strains of the Russian mujiks to those of the Southern Negro.

The Nation, June 1926.

As for the literature, painting and sculpture of Aframericans—such as there is—it is identical in kind with the literature, painting, and sculpture of white Americans: that is, it shows more or less evidence of European influence. In the field of drama little of any merit has been written by and about Negroes that could not have been written by whites. The dean of the Aframerican literati is W.E.B. Du Bois, a product of Harvard and German universities; the foremost Aframerican sculptor is Meta Warwick Fuller, a graduate of leading American art schools and former student of Rodin; while the most noted Aframerican painter, Henry Ossawa Tanner, is dean of American painters in Paris and has been decorated by the French Government. Now the work of these artists is no more "expressive of the Negro soul"—as the gushers put it—than are the scribblings of [white writers] Octavus Cohen or Hugh Wiley.

This, of course, is easily understood if one stops to realize that the Aframerican is merely a lampblacked Anglo-Saxon. If the European immigrant after two or three generations of exposure to our schools, politics, advertising, moral crusades, and restaurants becomes indistinguishable from the mass of Americans of the older stock (despite the influence of the foreign-language press), how much truer must it be of the sons of Ham who have been subjected to what the uplifters call Americanism for the last three hundred years. Aside from his color, which ranges from very dark brown to pink, your American Negro is just plain American. Negroes and whites from the same localities in this country talk, think, and act about the same. Because a few writers with a paucity of themes have seized upon imbecilities of the Negro rustics and clowns and palmed them off as authentic and characteristic Aframerican behavior, the common notion that the black American is so "different" from his white neighbor has gained wide currency. The mention of the word "Negro" conjures up in the average white American's mind a composite stereotype of Bert Williams, Aunt Jemima, Uncle Tom, Jack Johnson, Florian Slappey, and the various monstrosities scrawled by the cartoonists.[1] Your average Aframerican no more resembles this stereotype than the average American resembles a composite of Andy Gump, Jim Jeffries, and a cartoon by Rube Goldberg.[2]

Again, the Africamerican is subject to the same economic and social forces that mold the actions and thoughts of the white Americans. He is not living in a different world as some whites and a few Negroes would have us believe. When the jangling of his Connecticut alarm clock gets him out of his Grand Rapids bed to a breakfast similar to that eaten by his white brother across the street; when he toils at the same or similar work in the mills, mines, factories, and commerce alongside the descendants of Spartacus, Robin Hood, and Eric the Red; when he wears similar clothing and speaks the same language with the same degree of perfection; when he reads the same Bible and belongs to the

1. Bert Williams was a popular African American entertainer who performed before black and white audiences wearing blackface makeup. Jack Johnson was the first African American heavyweight boxing champion of the world. Florian Slappey was a fictional creation of Octavus Cohen.

2. Andy Gump was a cartoon character created by Robert Sidney Smith and others. Jim Jeffries was a white champion boxer who lost to Jack Johnson. Rube Goldberg drew "Crazy Inventions," cartoons of complicated inventions designed to perform simple operations.

Baptist, Methodist, Episcopal, or Catholic church; when his fraternal affiliations also include the Elks, Masons, and Knights of Pythias; when he gets the same or similar schooling, lives in the same kind of houses, owns the same makes of cars (or rides in them), and nightly sees the same Hollywood version of life on the screen; when he smokes the same brands of tobacco, and avidly peruses the same puerile periodicals; in short, when he responds to the same political, social, moral, and economic stimuli in precisely the same manner as his white neighbor, it is sheer nonsense to talk about "racial differences" as between the American black man and the American white man. Glance over a Negro newspaper (it is printed in good Americanese) and you will find the usual quota of crime news, scandal, personals, and uplift to be found in the average white newspaper—which, by the way, is more widely read by the Negroes than is the Negro press. In order to satisfy the cravings of an inferiority complex engendered by the colorphobia of the mob, the readers of the Negro newspapers are given a slight dash of racialistic seasoning. In the homes of the black and white Americans of the same cultural and economic level one finds similar furniture, literature, and conversation. How, then, can the black American be expected to produce art and literature dissimilar to that of the white American?

Consider Coleridge-Taylor, Edward Wilmot Blyden, and Claude McKay, the Englishmen; Pushkin, the Russian; Bridgewater, the Pole; Antar, the Arabian; Latino, the Spaniard; Dumas, *père* and *fils,* the Frenchmen; and Paul Laurence Dunbar, Charles W. Chesnutt, and James Weldon Johnson, the Americans.[3] All Negroes; yet their work shows the impress of nationality rather than race. They all reveal the psychology and culture of their environment—their color is incidental. Why should Negro artists of America vary from the national artistic norm when Negro artists in other countries have not done so? If we can foresee what kind of white citizens will inhabit this neck of the woods in the next generation by studying the sort of education and environment the children are exposed to now, it should not be difficult to reaon that the adults of today are what they are because of the education and environment they were exposed to a generation ago. And that education and environment were about the same for blacks and whites. One contemplates the popularity of the Negro-art hokum and murmurs, "How come?"

This nonsense is probably the last stand of the old myth palmed off by Negrophobists for all these many years, and recently rehashed by the sainted Harding,[4] that there are "fundamental, eternal, and inescapable differences" between white and black Americans. That there are Negroes who will lend this myth a helping hand need occasion no surprise. It has been broadcast all over the world by the vociferous scions of slaveholders,

---

3. This is a listing of artists of African ancestry: Samuel Coleridge-Taylor, composer; Edward Wilmot Blyden, educator and journalist; Claude McKay, Jamaican-born poet, featured in this anthology; Alexander Pushkin, author of verse novels; George Augustus Polgreen Bridgewater, concert violinist; Antar-bin Shedad, Egyptian poet; Juan Latino, African-born poet and professor; Alexandre Dumas *père,* author of *The Three Musketeers;* Alexandre Dumas *fils,* author of *The Lady of Camellias;* Paul Laurence Dunbar, foremost African American poet at the turn of the century; Charles Chesnutt, African American author; James Weldon Johnson, African American writer and civil rights leader featured in this anthology.

4. Warren G. Harding was the twenty-ninth U.S. president.

"scientists" like Madison Grant and Lothrop Stoddard,[5] and the patriots who flood the treasury of the Ku Klux Klan; and is believed, even today, by the majority of free, white citizens. On this baseless premise, so flattering to the white mob, that the blackamoor is inferior and fundamentally different, is erected the postulate that he must needs be peculiar; and when he attempts to portray life though the medium of art, it must of necessity be a peculiar art. While such reasoning may seem conclusive to the majority of Americans, it must be rejected with a loud guffaw by intelligent people.

5. Madison Grant and Lothrop Stoddard were white supremacist writers.

Langston Hughes

The Negro Artist and the Racial Mountain

One of the most promising of the young Negro poets[1] said to me once, "I want to be a poet—not a Negro poet," meaning, I believe, "I want to write like a white poet"; meaning subconsciously, "I would like to be a white poet," meaning behind that, "I would like to be white." And I was sorry the young man said that, for no great poet has ever been afraid of being himself. And I doubted then that, with his desire to run away spiritually from his race, this boy would ever be a great poet. But this is the mountain standing in the way of any true Negro art in America—this urge within the race toward whiteness, the desire to pour racial individuality into the mold of American standardization, and to be as little Negro and as much American as possible.

But let us look at the immediate background of this young poet. His family is of what I suppose one would call the Negro middle class: people who are by no means rich yet never uncomfortable nor hungry—smug, contented, respectable folk, members of the Baptist church. The father goes to work every morning. He is a chief steward at a large white club. The mother sometimes does fancy sewing or supervises parties for the rich families of the town. The children go to a mixed school. In the home they read white papers and magazines. And the mother often says, "Don't be like niggers" when the children are bad. A frequent phrase from the father is, "Look how well a white man does things." And so the word white comes to be unconsciously a symbol of all virtues. It holds for the children beauty, morality, and money. The whisper of "I want to be white" runs silently through their minds. This young poet's home is, I believe, a fairly typical home of the colored middle class. One sees immediately how difficult it would be for an artist born in such a home to interest himself in interpreting the beauty of his own people. He is never taught to see that beauty. He is taught rather not to see it, or if he does, to be ashamed of it when it is not according to Caucasian patterns.

1. This is a reference to Countee Cullen.

The Nation, June 1926.

For racial culture the home of a self-styled "high-class" Negro has nothing better to offer. Instead there will perhaps be more aping of things white than in a less cultured or less wealthy home. The father is perhaps a doctor, lawyer, landowner, or politician. The mother may be a social worker, or a teacher, or she may do nothing and have a maid. Father is often dark but he has usually married the lightest woman he could find. The family attend a fashionable church where few really colored faces are to be found. And they themselves draw a color line. In the North they go to white theatres and white movies. And in the South they have at least two cars and [a] house "like white folks." Nordic manners, Nordic faces, Nordic hair, Nordic art (if any), and an Episcopal heaven. A very high mountain indeed for the would-be racial artist to climb in order to discover himself and his people.

But then there are the low-down folks, the so-called common element, and they are the majority—may the Lord be praised! The people who have their hip of gin on Saturday nights and are not too important to themselves or the community, or too well fed, or too learned to watch the lazy world go round. They live on Seventh Street in Washington or State Street in Chicago and they do not particularly care whether they are like white folks or anybody else. Their joy runs, bang! into ecstasy. Their religion soars to a shout. Work may be a little today, rest a little tomorrow. Play awhile. Sing awhile. O, let's dance! These common people are not afraid of spirituals, as for a long time their more intellectual brethren were, and jazz is their child. They furnish a wealth of colorful, distinctive material for any artist because they still hold their own individuality in the face of American standardizations. And perhaps these common people will give to the world its truly great Negro artist, the one who is not afraid to be himself. Whereas the better-class Negro would tell the artist what to do, the people at least let him alone when he does appear. And they are not ashamed of him—if they know he exists at all. And they accept what beauty is their own without question.

Certainly there is, for the American Negro artist who can escape the restrictions the more advanced among his own group would put upon him, a great field of unused material ready for his art. Without going outside his race, and even among the better classes with their "white" culture and conscious American manners, but still Negro enough to be different, there is sufficient matter to furnish a black artist with a lifetime of creative work. And when he chooses to touch on the relations between Negroes and whites in this country with their innumerable overtones and undertones, surely, and especially for literature and the drama, there is an inexhaustible supply of themes at hand. To these the Negro artist can give his racial individuality, his heritage of rhythm and warmth, and his incongruous humor that so often, as in the blues, becomes ironic laughter mixed with tears. But let us look again at the mountain.

A prominent Negro clubwoman in Philadelphia paid eleven dollars to hear Raquel Meller sing Andalusian popular songs. But she told me a few weeks before she would not think of going to hear "that woman," Clara Smith, a great black artist, sing Negro folksongs. And many an upper-class Negro church, even now, would not dream of employing a spiritual in its services. The drab melodies in white folks' hymnbooks are much to be preferred. "We want to worship the Lord correctly and quietly. We don't believe in 'shouting.' Let's be dull like the Nordics," they say, in effect.

The road for the serious black artist, then, who would produce a racial art is most certainly rocky and the mountain is high. Until recently he received almost no encouragement for his work from either white or colored people. The fine novels of Chesnutt go out of print with neither race noticing their passing. The quaint charm and humor of Dunbar's dialect verse brought to him, in his day, largely the same kind of encouragement one would give a sideshow freak (A colored man writing poetry! How odd!) or a clown (How amusing!).

The present vogue in things Negro, although it may do as much real harm as good for the budding colored artist, has at least done this: it has brought him forcibly to the attention of his own people among whom for so long, unless the other race had noticed him beforehand, he was a prophet with little honor. I understand that Charles Gilpin acted for years in Negro theatres without any special acclaim from his own, but when Broadway gave him eight curtain calls, Negroes, too, began to beat a tin pan in his honor. I know a young colored writer,[2] a manual worker by day, who had been writing well for the colored magazines for some years, but it was not until he recently broke into the white publications and his first book was accepted by a prominent New York publisher that the "best" Negroes in his city took the trouble to discover that he lived there. Then almost immediately they decided to give a grand dinner for him. But the society ladies were careful to whisper to his mother that perhaps she'd better not come. They were not sure she would have an evening gown.

The Negro artist works against an undertow of sharp criticism and misunderstanding from his own group and unintentional bribes from the whites. "Oh, be respectable, write about nice people, show how good we are," say the Negroes. "Be stereotyped, don't go too far, don't shatter our illusions about you, don't amuse us too seriously. We will pay you," say the whites. Both would have told Jean Toomer not to write *Cane* [see "Blood-Burning Moon" in the creative writing section]. The colored people did not praise it. The white people did not buy it. Most of the colored people who did read *Cane* hate it. They are afraid of it. Although the critics gave it good reviews the public remained indifferent. Yet (excepting the work of Du Bois) *Cane* contains the finest prose written by a Negro in America. And like the singing of Robeson,[3] it is truly racial.

But in spite of the Nordicized Negro intelligentsia and the desires of some white editors we have an honest American Negro literature already with us. Now I await the rise of the Negro theatre. Our folk music, having achieved world-wide fame, offers itself to the genius of the great individual American composer who is to come. And within the next decade I expect to see the work of a growing school of colored artists who paint and model the beauty of dark faces and create with new technique the expressions of

---

2. Hughes is referring to himself. He relates this event, which happened in 1925, in his autobiography, *The Big Sea* (1940).

3. Paul Robeson, the notable African American bass singer and actor.

their own soul-world. And the Negro dancers who will dance like flame and the singers who will continue to carry our songs to all who listen—they will be with us in even greater numbers tomorrow.

Most of my own poems are racial in theme and treatment, derived from the life I know. In many of them I try to grasp and hold some of the meanings and rhythms of jazz. I am as sincere as I know how to be in these poems and yet after every reading I answer questions like these from my own people: Do you think Negroes should always write about Negroes? I wish you wouldn't read some of your poems to white folks. How do you find anything interesting in a place like a cabaret? Why do you write about black people? You aren't black. What makes you do so many jazz poems?

But jazz to me is one of the inherent expressions of Negro life in America; the eternal tom-tom beating in the Negro soul—the tom-tom of revolt against weariness in a white world, a world of subway trains, and work, work, work; the tom-tom of joy and laughter, and pain swallowed in a smile. Yet the Philadelphia clubwoman is ashamed to say that her race created it and she does not like me to write about it. The old subconscious "white is best" runs through her mind. Years of study under white teachers, a lifetime of white books, pictures, and papers, and white manners, morals, and Puritan standards made her dislike the spirituals. And now she turns up her nose at jazz and all its manifestations—likewise almost everything else distinctly racial. She doesn't care for the Winold Reiss portraits of Negroes because they are "too Negro."[4] She does not want a true picture of herself from anybody. She wants the artist to flatter her, to make the white world believe that all Negroes are as smug and as near white in soul as she wants to be. But, to my mind, it is the duty of the younger Negro artist, if he accepts any duties at all from outsiders, to change through the force of his art that old whispering "I want to be white," hidden in the aspirations of his people, to "Why should I want to be white? I am a Negro—and beautiful!"

So I am ashamed for the black poet who says, "I want to be a poet, not a Negro poet," as though his own racial world were not as interesting as any other world. I am ashamed, too, for the colored artist who runs from the painting of Negro faces to the painting of sunsets after the manner of the academicians because he fears the strange un-whiteness of his own features. An artist must be free to choose what he does, certainly, but he must also never be afraid to do what he might choose.

Let the blare of Negro jazz bands and the bellowing voice of Bessie Smith singing blues penetrate the closed ears of the colored near-intellectuals until they listen and perhaps understand. Let Paul Robeson singing "Water Boy," and Rudolph Fisher writing about the streets of Harlem, and Jean Toomer holding the heart of Georgia in his hands, and Aaron Douglas drawing strange black fantasies cause the smug Negro middle class to turn from their white, respectable, ordinary books and papers to catch a glimmer of their own beauty. We younger Negro artists who create now intend to express our individual

---

4. Winold Reiss (1887–1953) was a Bavarian portrait painter who provided many of the illustrations for *The New Negro* (1925).

dark-skinned selves without fear or shame. If white people are pleased we are glad. If they are not, it doesn't matter. We know we are beautiful. And ugly too. The tom-tom cries and the tom-tom laughs. If colored people are pleased we are glad. If they are not, their displeasure doesn't matter either. We build our temples for tomorrow, strong as we know how, and we stand on top of the mountain, free within ourselves.

Amy Jacques Garvey

On Langston Hughes:
I Am a Negro—and Beautiful

Too much cannot be said in denouncing the class of "want-to-be-white" Negroes one finds everywhere. This race destroying group are dissatisfied with their mothers and with their creator—mother is too dark "to pass" and God made a mistake when he made black people. With this fallacy uppermost in their minds, they peel their skins off, and straighten their hair, in a mad effort to look like their ideal type. To what end, one asks? To the end that they may be admitted to better jobs, moneyed circles, and in short, share the blessings of the prosperous white race. They are too lazy to help build a prosperous Negro race, but choose the easier route—crossing the racial border. It is the way of the weakling, and in their ignorance and stupidity they advise others to do likewise. As if 400,000,000 Negroes could change their skins overnight. And if they could, would they? Seeing that the bulk of Negroes are to be found on the great continent of Africa, and they, thank Heaven, are proud of their black skins and curly hair. The "would-be-white" few are fast disappearing in the Western world, as the entire race, through the preachments of Marcus Garvey [see "Africa for the Africans" in the essay section], has found its soul, and is out to acquire for itself and its posterity all that makes other races honored and respected.

This urge for whiteness is not just a mental gesture. It is a slavish complex, the remnant of slavery, to look like "Massa," to speak like him, even to cuss and drink like him. In last week's issue of *The Nation* magazine, Langston Hughes, a poet, wrote a splendid article on the difficulties facing the Negro artist [see "The Negro Artist and the Racial Mountain" in the essay section], in which he described the racial state of mind of a Philadelphia club woman, which is typical of the group under discussion. He states: "The old subconscious 'white is best' runs through her mind. Years of study under white teachers, a lifetime of white books, pictures, and papers, and white manners, morals, and Puritan standards made her dislike the spirituals. And now she turns up her nose at jazz and

Negro World, 1926.

all its manifestations—likewise almost everything else distinctly racial. She doesn't care for the Winold Reiss portraits of Negroes because they are 'too Negro.'[1] She does not want a true picture of herself from anybody. She wants the artist to flatter her, to make the white world believe that all Negroes are as smug and as near white in soul as she wants to be."

We are delighted with the frank statement of Mr. Hughes in a white magazine; we do not know if he is a registered member of the Universal Negro Improvement Association; in any event his closing [paragraphs mark] him as a keen student of Garveyism, and with stamina enough to express its ideals: "[T]o my mind, it is the duty of the younger Negro artist, if he accepts any duties at all from outsiders, to change through the force of his art that old whispering 'I want to be white,' hidden in the aspirations of his people, to 'Why should I want to be white? I am a Negro—and beautiful!'. . . We younger Negro artists who create now intend to express our individual dark-skinned selves without fear or shame. If white people are pleased we are glad. If they are not, it doesn't matter."

Bravo, Mr. Hughes! From now on under your leadership we expect our artists to express their real souls, and give us art that is colorful, full of ecstasy, dulcent and even tragic; for has it not been admitted by those who would undervalue us that the Negro is a born artist? Then let the canvas come to life with dark faces; let poetry charm the muses with the hopes and aspirations of our race; let the musicians drown our sorrows with the merry jazz; while a race is in the making, and steadily moving on to nationhood and to power.

Play up, boys, and let the world know "we are Negroes and beautiful."

---

1. Winold Reiss (1887–1953) was a Bavarian portrait painter who provided many of the illustrations for *The New Negro* (1925).

W.E.B. Du Bois

Criteria of Negro Art

The question comes next as to the interpretation of these new stirrings, of this new spirit: Of what is the colored artist capable? We have had on the part of both colored and white people singular unanimity of judgment in the past. Colored people have said: "This work must be inferior because it comes from colored people." White people have said: "It is inferior because it is done by colored people." But today there is coming to both the realization that the work of the black man is not always inferior. Interesting stories come to us. A professor in the University of Chicago read to a class that had studied literature a passage of poetry and asked them to guess the author. They guessed a goodly company, from Shelley and Robert Browning down to Tennyson and Masefield. The author was Countee Cullen. Or again, the English critic John Drinkwater went down to a Southern seminary, one of the sort which finishes young white women of the South. The students sat with their wooden faces while he tried to get some response out of them. Finally he said, "Name me some of your Southern poets." They hesitated. He said finally, "I'll start out with your best: Paul Laurence Dunbar!"

With the growing recognition of Negro artists in spite of the severe handicaps, one comforting thing is occurring to both white and black. They are whispering, "Here is a way out. Here is the real solution of the color problem. The recognition accorded Cullen, Hughes, Fauset, White and others shows there is no real color line. Keep quiet! Don't complain! Work! All will be well!"

I will not say that already this chorus amounts to a conspiracy. Perhaps I am naturally too suspicious. But I will say that there are today a surprising number of white people who are getting great satisfaction out of these younger Negro writers because they think it is going to stop agitation of the Negro question. They say, "What is the use of your fighting and complaining; do the great thing and the reward is there." And many colored people are all too eager to follow this advice; especially those who weary of the eternal struggle

The Crisis, October 1926.

along the color line, who are afraid to fight and to whom the money of philanthropists and the alluring publicity are subtle and deadly bribes. They say, "What is the use of fighting? Why not show simply what we deserve and let the reward come to us?"

And it is right here that the National Association for the Advancement of Colored People comes upon the field, comes with its great call to a new battle, a new fight and new things to fight before the old things are wholly won; and to say that the beauty of truth and freedom which shall some day be our heritage and the heritage of all civilized men is not in our hands yet and that we ourselves must not fail to realize.

There is in New York tonight a black woman molding clay by herself in a little bare room, because there is not a single school of sculpture in New York where she is welcome. Surely there are doors she might burst through, but when God makes a sculptor, He does not always make the pushing sort of person who beats his way through doors thrust in his face. This girl is working her hands off to get out of this country so that she can get some sort of training.

There was Richard Brown. If he had been white he would have been alive today instead of dead of neglect. Many helped him when he asked but he was not the kind of boy that always asks. He was simply one who made colors sing.

There is a colored woman in Chicago who is a great musician. She thought she would like to study at Fontainebleau this summer where Walter Damrosch and a score of leaders of art have an American school of music. But the application blank of this school says: "I am a white American and I apply for admission to the school."

We can go on the stage; we can be just as funny as white Americans wish us to be; we can play all the sordid parts that America likes to assign to Negroes; but for anything else there is still small place for us.

And so I might go on. But let me sum up with this: Suppose the only Negro who survived some centuries hence was the Negro painted by white Americans in the novels and essays they have written. What would people in a hundred years say of black Americans? Now turn it around. Suppose you were to write a story and put in it the kind of people you know and like and imagine. You might get it published and you might not. And the "might not" is still far bigger than the "might." The white publishers catering to white folk would say, "It is not interesting"—to white folk, naturally not. They want Uncle Toms, Topsies, good "darkies" and clowns. I have in my office a story with all the earmarks of truth. A young man says that he started out to write and had his stories accepted. Then he began to write about the things he knew best about, that is, about his own people. He submitted a story to a magazine, which said, "We are sorry, but we cannot take it." "I sat down and revised my story, changing the color of the characters and the locale and sent it under an assumed name with a change of address and it was accepted by the same magazine that had refused it, the editor promising to take anything else I might send in providing it was good enough."

We have, to be sure, a few recognized and successful Negro artists; but they are not all those fit to survive or even a good minority. They are but the remnants of that ability and genius among us whom the accidents of education and opportunity have raised on the tidal waves of chance. We black folk are not altogether peculiar in this. After all, in the world at large, it is only the accident, the remnant, that gets the chance to make the most of itself; but if this is true of the white world it is infinitely more true of the colored world. It is not simply the great clear tenor of Roland Hayes that opened the ears of America. We have had many voices of all kinds as fine as his and America was and is as deaf as she was for years to him. Then a foreign land heard Hayes and put its imprint on him and immediately America with all its imitative snobbery woke up. We approved Hayes because London, Paris, and Berlin approved him and not simply because he was a great singer.

Thus it is the bounden duty of black America to begin this great work of the creation of beauty, of the preservation of the realization of beauty, and we must use in this work all the methods that men have used before. And what have been the tools of the artist in times gone by? First of all, he has used the truth—not for the sake of truth, not as a scientist seeking truth, but as one upon whom truth eternally thrusts itself as the highest handmaid of imagination, as the one great vehicle of universal understanding. Again artists have used goodness—goodness in all its aspects of justice, honor, and right—not for sake of an ethical sanction but as the one true method of gaining sympathy and human interest.

The apostle of beauty thus becomes the apostle of truth and right not by choice but by inner and outer compulsion. Free he is but his freedom is ever bounded by truth and justice; and slavery only dogs him when he is denied the right to tell the truth or recognize an ideal of justice.

Thus all art is propaganda and ever must be, despite the wailing of the purists. I stand in utter shamelessness and say that whatever art I have for writing has been used always for propaganda for gaining the right of black folk to love and enjoy. I do not care a damn for any art that is not used for propaganda. But I do care when propaganda is confined to one side while the other is stripped and silent.

In New York we have two plays: *White Cargo* and *Congo*. In *White Cargo* there is a fallen woman. She is black. In *Congo* the fallen woman is white. In *White Cargo* the black woman goes down further and further and in *Congo* the white woman begins with degradation but in the end is one of the angels of the Lord.

You know the current magazine story: a young white man goes down to Central America and the most beautiful colored woman there falls in love with him. She crawls across the whole isthmus to get to him. The white man says nobly, "No." He goes back to his white sweetheart in New York.[1]

In such cases, it is not the positive propaganda of people who believe white blood divine, infallible, and holy to which I object. It is the denial of a similar right of propaganda to those who believe black blood human, lovable, and inspired with new ideals for the world. White artists themselves suffer from this narrowing of their field. They

---

1. This story was made into a film, *Flying Down to Rio* (1933), which starred Dolores Del Rio, Fred Astaire, and Ginger Rogers.

cry for freedom in dealing with Negroes because they have so little freedom in dealing with whites. DuBose Heyward writes *Porgy* and writes beautifully of the black Charleston underworld.[2] But why does he do this? Because he cannot do a similar thing for the white people of Charleston, or they would run him out of town. The only chance he had to tell the truth of human degradation was to tell it of colored people. I should not be surprised if Octavus Roy Cohen had approached *The Saturday Evening Post* and asked permission to write about a different kind of colored folk than the monstrosities he has created;[3] but if he has, the *Post* has replied, "No. You are getting paid to write about the kind of colored people you are writing about."

In other words, the white public today demands from its artists, literary and pictorial, racial pre-judgment which deliberately distorts truth and justice, as far as colored races are concerned, and it will pay for no other.

On the other hand, the young and slowly growing black public still wants its prophets almost equally unfree. We are bound by all sorts of customs that have come down as second-hand soul clothes of white patrons. We are ashamed of sex and we lower our eyes when people will talk of it. Our religion holds us in superstition. Our worst side has been so shamelessly emphasized that we are denying we have or ever had a worst side. In all sorts of ways we are hemmed in and our new young artists have got to fight their way to freedom.

The ultimate judge has got to be you and you have got to build yourselves up into that wide judgment, that catholicity of temper which is going to enable the artist to have his widest chance for freedom. We can afford the truth. White folk today cannot. As it is now we are handing everything over to a white jury. If a colored man wants to publish a book, he has got to get a white publisher and a white newspaper to say it is great; and then you and I say so. We must come to the place where the work of art when it appears is reviewed and acclaimed by our own free and unfettered judgment. And we are going to have a real and valuable and eternal judgment only as we make ourselves free of mind, proud of body and just of soul to all men.

And then do you know what will be said? It is already [being said]. Just as soon as true art emerges; just as soon as the black artist appears, someone touches the race on the shoulder and says, "He did that because he was an American, not because he was a Negro; he was born here; he was trained here; he is not a Negro—what is a Negro anyhow? He is just human; it is the kind of thing you ought to expect."

I do not doubt that the ultimate art coming from black folk is going to be just as beautiful, and beautiful largely in the same ways, as the art that comes from white folk, or yellow, or red; but the point today is that until the art of the black folk compels recognition they will not be rated as human. And when through art they compel recognition then let the world discover if it will that their art is as new as it is old and as old as new.

2. *Porgy* (1925) was the first novel by DuBose Heyward, an American novelist, dramatist, and poet. *Porgy* was the basis for a successful play (1927), opera (*Porgy and Bess* 1935), and film (1959).

3. Octavus Roy Cohen was a humorist who capitalized on stereotypes of African Americans in his work.

I had a classmate once who did three beautiful things and died. One of them was a story of a folk who found fire and then went wandering in the gloom of night seeking again the stars they had once known and lost; suddenly out of blackness they looked up and there loomed the heavens; and what was it they said? They raised a mighty cry: "It is the stars, it is the ancient stars, it is the young and everlasting stars!"

Richard Wright

Blueprint for Negro Writing

(1) The Role of Negro Writing: Two Definitions

Generally speaking, Negro writing in the past has been confined to humble novels, poems, and plays, prim and decorous ambassadors who went a-begging to white America. They entered the Court of American Public Opinion dressed in the knee-pants of servility, curtsying to show that the Negro was not inferior, that he was human, and that he had a life comparable to that of other people. For the most part these artistic ambassadors were received as though they were French poodles who do clever tricks.

White America never offered these Negro writers any serious criticism. The mere fact that a Negro could write was astonishing. Nor was there any deep concern on the part of white America with the role Negro writing should play in American culture; and the role it did play grew out of accident rather than intent or design. Either it crept in through the kitchen in the form of jokes; or it was the fruits of that foul soil which was the result of a liaison between inferiority-complexed Negro "geniuses" and burnt-out white Bohemians with money.

On the other hand, these often technically brilliant performances by Negro writers were looked upon by the majority of literate Negroes as something to be proud of. At best, Negro writing has been something external to the lives of educated Negroes themselves. That the productions of their writers should have been something of a guide in their daily living is a matter which seems never to have been raised seriously.

Under these conditions Negro writing assumed two general aspects: (1) It became a sort of conspicuous ornamentation, the hallmark of "achievement." (2) It became the voice of the educated Negro pleading with white America for justice.

Rarely was the best of this writing addressed to the Negro himself, his needs, his sufferings, his aspirations. Through misdirection, Negro writers have been far better to

The New Challenge, 1937.

others than they have been to themselves. And the mere recognition of this places the whole question of Negro writing in a new light and raises a doubt as to the validity of its present direction.

(2) *The Minority Outlook*

Somewhere in his writings Lenin makes the observation that oppressed minorities often reflect the techniques of the bourgeoisie more brilliantly than some sections of the bourgeoisie themselves.[1] The psychological importance of this becomes meaningful when it is recalled that oppressed minorities, and especially the petty bourgeois sections of oppressed minorities, strive to assimilate the virtues of the bourgeoisie in the assumption that by doing so they can lift themselves into a higher social sphere. But not only among the oppressed petty bourgeoisie does this occur. The workers of a minority people, chafing under exploitation, forge organizational forms of struggle to better their lot. Lacking the handicaps of false ambition and property, they have access to a wide social vision and a deep social consciousness. They display a greater freedom and initiative in pushing their claims upon civilization than even do the petty bourgeoisie. Their organizations show greater strength, adaptability, and efficiency than any other group or class in society.

That Negro workers, propelled by the harsh conditions of their lives, have demonstrated this consciousness and mobility for economic and political action there can be no doubt. But has this consciousness been reflected in the work of Negro writers to the same degree as it has in the Negro workers' struggle to free Herndon and the Scottsboro Boys,[2] in the drive toward unionism, in the fight against lynching? Have they as creative writers taken advantage of their unique minority position?

The answer decidedly is *no.* Negro writers have lagged sadly and as time passes the gap widens between them and their people.

How can this hiatus be bridged? How can the enervating effects of this long standing split be eliminated?

In presenting questions of this sort an attitude of self-consciousness and self-criticism is far more likely to be a fruitful point of departure than a mere recounting of past achievements. An emphasis upon tendency and experiment, a view of society as something becoming rather than as something fixed and admired is the one which

1. V. I. Lenin (1870–1924), architect of the Bolshevik Revolution in 1917 and first leader of Russia's Communist Party. Wright was a leftist himself and involved with the American Communist Party in the 1930s.

2. Angelo Herndon was a member of the Communist Party convicted in 1933 of inciting insurrection. He was sentenced to twenty years in prison, but the U.S. Supreme Court reversed the decision in 1937. The Scottsboro boys were nine black youths charged with raping two white women in Scottsboro, Alabama, in 1931. Despite testimony by doctors that the women had not been raped, the all-white jury convicted them; they were all sentenced to death except the youngest—who was twelve at the time. The U.S. Supreme Court reversed the convictions in 1932 and again in 1935. Further trials led to more reconvictions and successful appeals until the state, under pressure from citizens' groups, dropped the remaining charges and paroled all but one of the convicted youths. The case was championed by the Communist Party, which fought the NAACP for the right to represent the defendants.

points the way for Negro writers to stand shoulder to shoulder with Negro workers in mood and outlook.

(3) A Whole Culture

There is, however, a culture of the Negro which is his and has been addressed to him; a culture which has, for good or ill, helped to clarify his consciousness and create emotional attitudes which are conducive to action. This culture has stemmed mainly from two sources: (1) the Negro church; (2) and the folklore of the Negro people.

It was through the portals of the church that the American Negro first entered the shrine of western culture. Living under slave conditions of life, bereft of his African heritage, the Negroes' struggle for religion on the plantations between 1820–60 assumed the form of a struggle for human rights. It remained a relatively revolutionary struggle until religion began to serve as an antidote for suffering and denial. But even today there are millions of American Negroes whose only sense of a whole universe, whose only relation to society and man, and whose only guide to personal dignity comes through the archaic morphology of Christian salvation.

It was, however, in a folklore moulded out of rigorous and inhuman conditions of life that the Negro achieved his most indigenous and complete expression. Blues, spirituals, and folk tales recounted from mouth to mouth; the whispered words of a black mother to her black daughter on the ways of men; the confidential wisdom of a black father to his black son; the swapping of sex experiences on street corners from boy to boy in the deepest vernacular; work songs sung under blazing suns—all these formed the channels through which the racial wisdom flowed.

One would have thought that Negro writers in the last century of striving at expression would have continued and deepened this folk tradition, would have tried to create a more intimate and yet a more profoundly social system of artistic communication between them and their people. But the illusion that they could escape through individual achievement the harsh lot of their race swung Negro writers away from any such path. Two separate cultures sprang up: one for the Negro masses, unwritten and unrecognized; and the other for the sons and daughters of a rising Negro bourgeoisie, parasitic and mannered.

Today the question is: Shall Negro writing be for the Negro masses, moulding the lives and consciousness of those masses toward new goals, or shall it continue begging the question of the Negroes' humanity?

(4) The Problem of Nationalism in Negro Writing

In stressing the difference between the role Negro writing failed to play in the lives of the Negro people, and the role it should play in the future if it is to serve its historic function; in pointing out the fact that Negro writing has been addressed in the main to a small white audience rather than to a Negro one, it should be stated that no attempt is being made here to propagate a specious and blatant nationalism. Yet the nationalistic character of the Negro people is unmistakable. Psychologically this nationalism is reflected in the whole of Negro culture, and especially in folklore.

In the absence of fixed and nourishing forms of culture, the Negro has a folklore which embodies the memories and hopes of his struggle for freedom. Not yet caught in paint or stone, and as yet but feebly depicted in the poem and novel, the Negroes' most powerful images of hope and despair still remain in the fluid state of daily speech. How many John Henrys have lived and died on the lips of these black people?[3] How many mythical heroes in embryo have been allowed to perish for lack of husbanding by alert intelligence?

Negro folklore contains, in a measure that puts to shame more deliberate forms of Negro expression, the collective sense of Negro life in America. Let those who shy at the nationalist implications of Negro life look at this body of folklore, living and powerful, which rose out of a unified sense of a common life and a common fate. Here are those vital beginnings of a recognition of value in life as it is *lived,* a recognition that marks the emergence of a new culture in the shell of the old. And at the moment this process starts, at the moment when a people begin to realize a *meaning* in their suffering, the civilization that engenders that suffering is doomed.

The nationalist aspects of Negro life are as sharply manifest in the social institutions of Negro people as in folklore. There is a Negro church, a Negro press, a Negro social world, a Negro sporting world, a Negro business world, a Negro school system, Negro professions; in short, a Negro way of life in America. The Negro people did not ask for this, and deep down, though they express themselves through their institutions and adhere to this special way of life, they do not want it now. This special existence was forced upon them from without by lynch rope, bayonet and mob rule. They accepted these negative conditions with the inevitability of a tree which must live or perish in whatever soil it finds itself.

The few crumbs of American civilization which the Negro has got from the tables of capitalism have been through these segregated channels. Many Negro institutions are cowardly and incompetent; but they are all that the Negro has. And, in the main, any move, whether for progress or reaction, must come through these institutions for the simple reason that all other channels are closed. Negro writers who seek to mould or influence the consciousness of the Negro people must address their messages to them through the ideologies and attitudes fostered in this warping way of life.

(5) The Basis and Meaning of Nationalism in Negro Writing

The social institutions of the Negro are imprisoned in the Jim Crow political system of the South, and this Jim Crow political system is in turn built upon a plantation-feudal

---

3. John Henry is a mythological folk hero, a black steel driver commemorated in the song "John Henry."

economy. Hence it can be seen that the emotional expression of group-feeling which puzzles so many whites and leads them to deplore what they call "black chauvinism" is not a morbidly inherent trait of the Negro, but rather the reflex expression of a life whose roots are imbedded deeply in Southern soil.

Negro writers must accept the nationalist implications of their lives, not in order to encourage them, but in order to change and transcend them. They must accept the concept of nationalism because, in order to transcend it, they must *possess* and *understand* it. And a nationalist spirit in Negro writing means a nationalism carrying the highest possible pitch of social consciousness. It means a nationalism that knows its origins, its limitations; that is aware of the dangers of its position; that knows its ultimate aims are unrealizable within the framework of capitalist America; a nationalism whose reason for being lies in the simple fact of self-possession and in the consciousness of the interdependence of people in modern society.

For purposes of creative expression it means that the Negro writer must realize within the area of his own personal experience those impulses which, when prefigured in terms of broad social movements, constitute the stuff of nationalism.

For Negro writers even more so than for Negro politicians, nationalism is a bewildering and vexing question, the full ramifications of which cannot be dealt with here. But among Negro workers and the Negro middle class the spirit of nationalism is rife in a hundred devious forms; and a simple literary realism which seeks to depict the lives of these people devoid of wider social connotations, devoid of the revolutionary significance of these nationalistic tendencies, must of necessity do a rank injustice to the Negro people and alienate their possible allies in the struggle for freedom.

(6) Social Consciousness and Responsibility

The Negro writer who seeks to function within his race as a purposeful agent has a serious responsibility. In order to do justice to his subject matter, in order to depict Negro life in all of its manifold and intricate relationships, a deep, informed, and complex consciousness is necessary; a consciousness which draws for its strength upon the fluid lore of a great people, and moulds this lore with the concepts that move and direct the forces of history today.

With the gradual decline of the moral authority of the Negro church, and with the increasing irresolution which is paralyzing Negro middle class leadership, a new role is devolving upon the Negro writer. He is being called upon to do no less than create values by which his race is to struggle, live and die.

By his ability to fuse and make articulate the experiences of men, because his writing possesses the potential cunning to steal into the inmost recesses of the human heart, because he can create the myths and symbols that inspire a faith in life, he may expect either to be consigned to oblivion, or to be recognized for the valued agent he is.

This raises the question of the personality of the writer. It means that in the lives of Negro writers must be found those materials and experiences which will create a meaningful picture of the world today. Many young writers have grown to believe that a Marxist analysis of society presents such a picture. It creates a picture which, when placed before the eyes of the writer, should unify his personality, organize his emotions, buttress him with a tense and obdurate will to change the world.

And, in turn, this changed world will dialectically change the writer. Hence, it is through a Marxist conception of reality and society that the maximum degree of freedom in thought and feeling can be gained for the Negro writer. Further, this dramatic Marxist vision, when consciously grasped, endows the writer with a sense of dignity which no other vision can give. Ultimately, it restores to the writer his lost heritage, that is, his role as a creator of the world in which he lives, and as a creator of himself.

Yet, for the Negro writer, Marxism is but the starting point. No theory of life can take the place of life. After Marxism has laid bare the skeleton of society, there remains the task of the writer to plant flesh upon those bones out of his will to live. He may, with disgust and revulsion, say *no* and depict the horrors of capitalism encroaching upon the human being. Or he may, with hope and passion, say *yes* and depict the faint stirrings of a new and emerging life. But in whatever social voice he chooses to speak, whether positive or negative, there should always be heard or *over*-heard his faith, his necessity, his judgment.

His vision need not be simple or rendered in primer-like terms; for the life of the Negro people is not simple. The presentation of their lives should be simple, yes; but all the complexity, the strangeness, the magic wonder of life that plays like a bright sheen over the most sordid existence, should be there. To borrow a phrase from the Russians, it should have a *complex simplicity.* Eliot, Stein, Joyce, Proust, Hemingway, and Anderson; Gorky, Barbusse, Nexo, and Jack London no less than the folklore of the Negro himself should form the heritage of the Negro writer.[4] Every iota of gain in human thought and sensibility should be ready grist for his mill, no matter how far-fetched they may seem in their immediate implications.

(7) The Problem of Perspective

What vision must Negro writers have before their eyes in order to feel the impelling necessity for an about face? What angle of vision can show them all the forces of modern society in process, all the lines of economic development converging toward a distant point of hope? Must they believe in some "ism"?

They may feel that only dupes believe in "isms"; they feel with some measure of justification that another commitment means only another disillusionment. But anyone destitute of a theory about the meaning, structure and direction of modern society is a lost victim in a world he cannot understand or control.

4. T. S. Eliot (1888–1965), Gertrude Stein (1874–1946), James Joyce (1882–1941), Marcel Proust (1871–1922), Ernest Hemingway (1898–1961), Sherwood Anderson (1876–1941), Maxim Gorky (1868–1936), Henri Barbusse (1873–1935), Martin Nexo (1869–1954), and Jack London (1876–1916) were all white writers.

But even if Negro writers found themselves through some "ism," how would that influence their writing? Are they being called upon to "preach"? To be "salesmen"? To "prostitute" their writing? Must they "sully" themselves? Must they write "propaganda"?

No; it is a question of awareness, of consciousness; it is, above all, a question of perspective.

Perspective is that part of a poem, novel, or play which a writer never puts directly upon paper. It is that fixed point in intellectual space where a writer stands to view the struggles, hopes, and sufferings of his people. There are times when he may stand too close and the result is a blurred vision. Or he may stand too far away and the result is a neglect of important things.

Of all the problems faced by writers who as a whole have never allied themselves with world movements, perspective is the most difficult of achievement. At its best, perspective is a pre-conscious assumption, something which a writer takes for granted, something which he wins through his living.

A Spanish writer recently spoke of living in the heights of one's time. Surely, perspective means just *that*.

It means that a Negro writer must learn to view the life of a Negro living in New York's Harlem or Chicago's South Side with the consciousness that one-sixth of the earth's surface belongs to the working class. It means that a Negro writer must create in his readers' minds a relationship between a Negro woman hoeing cotton in the South and the men who loll in swivel chairs in Wall Street and take the fruits of her toil.

Perspective for Negro writers will come when they have looked and brooded so hard and long upon the harsh lot of their race and compared it with the hopes and struggles of minority peoples everywhere that the cold facts have begun to tell them something.

(8) The Problem of Theme

This does not mean that a Negro writer's sole concern must be with rendering the social scene; but if his conception of the life of his people is broad and deep enough, if the sense of the *whole* life he is seeking is vivid and strong in him, then his writing will embrace all those social, political, and economic forms under which the life of his people is manifest.

In speaking of theme one must necessarily be general and abstract; the temperament of each writer moulds and colors the world he sees: Negro life may be approached from a thousand angles, with no limit to technical and stylistic freedom.

Negro writers spring from a family, a clan, a class, and a nation; and the social units in which they are bound have a story, a record. Sense of theme will emerge in Negro writing when Negro writers try to fix this story about some pole of meaning, remembering as they do so that in the creative process meaning proceeds *equally* as much from the contemplation of the subject matter as from the hopes and apprehensions that rage in the heart of the writer.

Reduced to its simplest and in most general terms, theme for Negro writers will rise from understanding the meaning of their being transplanted from a "savage" to a "civilized" culture in all of its social, political, economic, and emotional implications. It means that Negro writers must have in their consciousness the fore-shortened picture of the *whole,* nourishing culture from which they were torn in Africa, and of the long, complex (and for the most part, unconscious) struggle to regain in some form and under alien conditions of life a *whole* culture again.

It is not only this picture they must have, but also a knowledge of the social and emotional milieu that gives it tone and solidity of detail. Theme for Negro writers will emerge when they have begun to feel the meaning of the history of their race as though they in one life time had lived it themselves throughout all the long centuries.

(9) Autonomy of Craft

For the Negro writer to depict this new reality requires a greater discipline and consciousness than was necessary for the so-called Harlem school of expression. Not only is the subject matter dealt with far more meaningful and complex, but the new role of the writer is qualitatively different. The Negro writer's new position demands a sharper definition of the status of his craft, and a sharper emphasis upon its functional autonomy.

Negro writers should seek through the medium of their craft to play as meaningful a role in the affairs of men as do other professionals. But if their writing is demanded to perform the social office of other professions then the autonomy of craft is lost and writing detrimentally fused with other interests. The limitations of the craft constitute some of its greatest virtues. If the sensory vehicle of imaginative writing is required to carry too great a load of didactic material, the artistic sense is submerged.

The relationship between reality and the artistic image is not always direct and simple. The imaginative conception of a historical period will not be a carbon copy of reality. Image and emotion possess a logic of their own. A vulgarized simplicity constitutes the greatest danger in tracing the reciprocal interplay between the writer and his environment.

Writing has its professional autonomy; it should complement other professions, but it should not supplant them or be swamped by them.

(10) The Necessity for Collective Work

It goes without saying that these things cannot be gained by Negro writers if their present mode of isolated writing and living continues. This isolation exists *among* Negro writers as well as *between* Negro and white writers. The Negro writers' lack of thorough integration with the American scene, their lack of a clear realization among themselves of their possible role, have bred generation after generation of embittered and defeated literati.

Barred for decades from the theater and publishing houses, Negro writers have been *made* to feel a sense of difference. So deep has this white-hot iron of exclusion been burnt into their hearts that thousands have all but lost the desire to become identified with American civilization. The Negro writers' acceptance of this enforced isolation and their attempt to justify it is but a defense-reflex of the whole special way of life which has been rammed down their throats.

This problem, by its very nature, is one which must be approached contemporaneously from *two* points of view. The ideological unity of Negro writers and the alliance of that unity with all the progressive ideas of our day [are] the primary pre-requisite[s] for collective work. On the shoulders of white writers and Negro writers alike rest[s] the responsibility of ending this mistrust and isolation.

By placing cultural health above narrow sectional prejudices, liberal writers of all races can help to break the stony soil of aggrandizement out of which the stunted plants of Negro nationalism grow. And, simultaneously, Negro writers can help to weed out these choking growths of reactionary nationalism and replace them with hardier and sturdier types.

These tasks are imperative in the light of the fact that we live in a time when the majority of the most basic assumptions of life can no longer be taken for granted. Tradition is no longer a guide. The world has grown huge and cold. Surely this is the moment to ask questions, to theorize, to speculate, to wonder out of what materials can a human world be built.

Each step along this unknown path should be taken with thought, care, self-consciousness, and deliberation. When Negro writers think they have arrived at something which smacks of truth, humanity, they should want to test it with others, feel it with a degree of passion and strength that will enable them to communicate it to millions who are groping like themselves.

Writers faced with such tasks can have no possible time for malice or jealousy. The conditions for the growth of each writer depend too much upon the good work of other writers. Every first rate novel, poem, or play lifts the level of consciousness higher.

Zora Neale Hurston

Characteristics of Negro Expression

Drama

The Negro's universal mimicry is not so much a thing in itself as an evidence of something that permeates his entire self. And that thing is drama.

His very words are action words. His interpretation of the English language is in terms of pictures. One act described in terms of another. Hence the rich metaphor and simile.

The metaphor is of course very primitive. It is easier to illustrate than it is to explain because action came before speech. Let us make a parallel. Language is like money. In primitive communities actual goods, however bulky, are bartered for what one wants. This finally evolves into coin, the coin being not real wealth but a symbol of wealth. Still later even coin is abandoned for legal tender, and still later for cheques in certain usages.

Every phase of Negro life is highly dramatised. No matter how joyful or how sad the case there is sufficient poise for drama. Everything is acted out. Unconsciously for the most part of course. There is an impromptu ceremony always ready for every hour of life. No little moment passes unadorned.

Now the people with highly developed languages have words for detached ideas. That is legal tender. "That-which-we-squat-on" has become "chair." "Groan-causer" has evolved into "spear" and so on. Some individuals even conceive of the equivalent of cheque words, like "ideation" and "pleonastic." Perhaps we might say that *Paradise Lost* and *Sartor Resartus* are written in cheque words.

The primitive man exchanges descriptive words. His terms are all close fitting. Frequently the Negro, even with detached words in his vocabulary—not evolved in him but transplanted on his tongue by contact—must add action to it to make it do. So we have "chop-axe," "sitting-chair," "cook-pot" and the like because the speaker has in his mind the picture of the object in use. Action. Everything illustrated. So we can say the white

Negro: An Anthology, 1935.

man thinks in a written language and the Negro thinks in hieroglyphics.

A bit of Negro drama familiar to all is the frequent meeting of two opponents who threaten to do atrocious murder one upon the other.

Who has not observed a robust young Negro chap posing upon a street corner, possessed of nothing but his clothing, his strength and his youth? Does he bear himself like a pauper? No, Louis XIV could be no more insolent in his assurance. His eyes say plainly "Female, halt!" His posture exults "Ah, female, I am the eternal mate, the giver of life. Behold in my hot flesh all the delights of this world. Salute me, I am strength." All this with a languid posture; there is no mistaking his meaning.

A Negro girl strolls past the corner lounger. Her whole body panging[1] and posing. A slight shoulder movement that calls attention to her bust, that is all of a dare. A hippy undulation below the waist that is a sheaf of promises tied with conscious power. She is acting out "I'm a darned sweet woman and you know it."

These little plays by strolling players are acted out daily in a dozen streets in a thousand cities, and no one ever mistakes the meaning.

Will to Adorn

The will to adorn is the second most notable characteristic in Negro expression. Perhaps his idea of ornament does not attempt to meet conventional standards, but it satisfies the soul of its creator.

In this respect the American Negro has done wonders to the English language. It has often been stated by etymologists that the Negro has introduced no African words to the language. This is true, but it is equally true that he has made over a great part of the tongue to his liking and has his revision accepted by the ruling class. No one listening to a Southern white man talk could deny this. Not only has he softened and toned down strongly consonanted words like "aren't" to "aint" and the like, he has made new force words out of old feeble elements. Examples of this are "hamshanked," "battle-hammed," "double-teen," "bodaciously," "mufflejawed."

But the Negro's greatest contribution to the language is: (1) the use of metaphor and simile; (2) the use of the double descriptive; (3) the use of verbal nouns.

1. Metaphor and Simile

One at a time, like lawyers going to heaven.	That's a lynch.
Yo sho is propaganda.	That's a rope.
Sobbing hearted.	Cloakers—deceivers.
I'll beat you till: (*a*) a rope like okra,	Regular as pig-tracks.
(*b*) slack like lime, (*c*) smell like onions.	Mule blood—black molasses.
Fatal for naked.	Syndicating—gossiping.
Kyting along.	Flambeaux—cheap cafe (lighted by
	flambeaux).
	To put yo'self on de ladder.

1. Yearning, responding.

2. The Double Descriptive

High-tall.

Little-tee-ninchy (tiny).

Low-down.

Top-superior.

Sham-polish.

Lady-people.

Kill-dead.

Hot-boiling.

Chop-ax.

Sitting-chairs.

De watch wall.

Speedy-hurry.

More great and more better.

3. Verbal Nouns

She features somebody I know.

Funeralize.

Sense me into it.

Puts the shamery on him.

'Taint everybody you kin confidence.

I wouldn't friend with her.

Jooking—playing piano or guitar as it is done in Jook-houses (houses of ill-fame).

Uglying away.

I wouldn't scorn my name all upon you.

Bookooing (*beaucoup*)[2] around—showing off.

4. Nouns from Verbs

Won't stand a broke.

She won't take a listen.

He won't stand straightening.

That is such a compliment.

That's a lynch.

The stark, trimmed phrases of the Occident seem too bare for the voluptuous child of the sun, hence the adornment. It arises out of the same impulse as the wearing of jewelry and the making of sculpture—the urge to adorn.

On the walls of the homes of the average Negro one always finds a glut of gaudy calendars, wall pockets and advertising lithographs. The sophisticated white man or Negro would tolerate none of these, even if they bore a likeness to the Mona Lisa. No commercial art for decoration. Nor the calendar nor the advertisement spoils the picture for this lowly man. He sees the beauty in spite of the declaration of the Portland Cement Works or the butcher's announcement. I saw in Mobile a room in which there was an over-stuffed mohair living-room suite, an imitation mahogany bed and chifferobe, a console victrola. The walls were gaily papered with Sunday supplements of *The Mobile Register*. There were seven calendars and three wall pockets. One of them was decorated with a lace doily. The mantel-shelf was covered with a scarf of deep home-made lace, looped up with a huge bow of pink crêpe paper. Over the door was a huge lithograph showing the Treaty of Versailles being signed with a Waterman fountain pen.

It was grotesque, yes. But it indicated the desire for beauty. And decorating a decoration, as in the case of the doily on the gaudy wall pocket, did not seem out of place

2. This is a translation from the French *beaucoup,* meaning "very much." Hurston most likely found this French-derived slang in Louisiana, which was settled by the French.

to the hostess. The feeling back of such an act is that there can never be enough of beauty, let alone too much. Perhaps she is right. We each have our standards of art, and thus are we all interested parties and so unfit to pass judgment upon the art concepts of others.

Whatever the Negro does of his own volition he embellishes. His religious service is for the greater part excellent prose poetry. Both prayers and sermons are tooled and polished until they are true works of art. The supplication is forgotten in the frenzy of creation. The prayer of the white man is considered humorous in its bleakness. The beauty of the Old Testament does not exceed that of a Negro prayer.

Angularity

After adornment the next most striking manifestation of the Negro is Angularity. Everything that he touches becomes angular. In all African sculpture and doctrine of any sort we find the same thing.

Anyone watching Negro dancers will be struck by the same phenomenon. Every posture is another angle. Pleasing, yes. But an effect achieved by the very means which a European strives to avoid.

The pictures on the walls are hung at deep angles. Furniture is always set at an angle. I have instances of a piece of furniture in the *middle* of a wall being set with one end nearer the wall than the other to avoid the simple straight line.

Asymmetry

Asymmetry is a definite feature of Negro art. I have no samples of true Negro painting unless we count the African shields, but the sculpture and carvings are full of this beauty and lack of symmetry.

It is present in the literature, both prose and verse. I offer an example of this quality in verse from Langston Hughes:[3]

> I aint gonna mistreat ma good gal any more.
> I'm just gonna kill her next time she makes me sore.
>
> I treats her kind but she don't do me right.
> She fights an' quarrels most ever night.
>
> I can't have no woman's got such low-down ways,
> Cause a blue-gummed[4] woman aint de style now'days.
>
> I brought her from de South an' she's goin' on back
> Else I'll use her head for a carpet tack.

3. This extract is taken from Hughes's poem "Evil Woman," which appeared in *Fine Clothes to the Jew* (1927). The line breaks Hurston uses are different, but otherwise the poem is as Hughes wrote it.
4. "Blue-gum" is slang for dark gums.

It is the lack of symmetry which makes Negro dancing so difficult for white dancers to learn. The abrupt and unexpected changes. The frequent change of key and time are evidences of this quality in music (note the *St. Louis Blues*).

The dancing of the justly famous Bo-Jangles and Snake Hips are excellent examples.[5]

The presence of rhythm and lack of symmetry are paradoxical, but there they are. Both are present to a marked degree. There is always rhythm, but it is the rhythm of segments. Each unit has a rhythm of its own, but when the whole is assembled it is lacking in symmetry. But easily workable to a Negro who is accustomed to the break in going from one part to another, so that he adjusts himself to the new tempo.

Dancing

Negro dancing is dynamic suggestion. No matter how violent it may appear to the beholder, every posture gives the impression that the dancer will do much more. For example, the performer flexes one knee sharply, assumes a ferocious face mask, thrusts the upper part of the body forward with clenched fists, elbows taut as in hard running or grasping a thrusting blade. That is all. But the spectator himself adds the picture of ferocious assault, hears the drums and finds himself keeping time with the music and tensing himself for the struggle. It is compelling insinuation. That is the very reason the spectator is held so rapt. He is participating in the performance himself—carrying out the suggestions of the performer.

The difference in the two arts is: the white dancer attempts to express fully; the Negro is restrained, but succeeds in gripping the beholder by forcing him to finish the action the performer suggests. Since no art ever can express all the variations conceivable, the Negro must be considered the greater artist, his dancing is realistic suggestion, and that is about all a great artist can do.

Negro Folklore

Negro folklore is not a thing of the past. It is still in the making. Its great variety shows the adaptability of the black man: nothing is too old or too new, domestic or foreign, high or low, for his use. God and the Devil are paired, and are treated no more reverently than Rockefeller and Ford. Both of these men are prominent in folklore, Ford being particularly strong, and they talk and act like good-natured stevedores or mill-hands. Ole Massa is sometimes a smart man and often a fool. The automobile is ranged alongside of the oxcart. The angels and the apostles walk and talk like section hands. And through it all walks Jack, the greatest culture hero of the South; Jack beats them all—even the Devil, who is often smarter than God.

---

5. Bill "Bo-Jangles" Robinson (1876–1949) and Earl "Snake Hips" Tucker (1905–1937) were well-known African American dancers of the era.

Culture Heroes

The Devil is next after Jack as a culture hero. He can out-smart everyone but Jack. God is absolutely no match for him. He is good-natured and full of humour. The sort of person one may count on to help out in any difficulty.

Peter the Apostle is the third in importance. One need not look far for the explanation. The Negro is not a Christian really. The primitive gods are not deities of too subtle inner reflection; they are hard-working bodies who serve their devotees just as laboriously as the suppliant serves them. Gods of physical violence, stopping at nothing to serve their followers. Now of all the apostles Peter is the most active. When the other ten fell back trembling in the garden, Peter wielded the blade on the posse. Peter first and foremost in all action. The gods of no peoples have been philosophic until the people themselves have approached that state.

The rabbit, the bear, the lion, the buzzard, the fox are culture heroes from the animal world. The rabbit is far in the lead of all the others and is blood brother to Jack. In short, the trickster-hero of West Africa has been transplanted to America.

John Henry is a culture hero in song, but no more so than Stacker Lee, Smokey Joe or Bad Lazarus. There are many, many Negroes who have never heard of any of the song heroes, but none who do not know John (Jack) and the rabbit.

Examples of Folklore and the Modern Culture Hero

Why de Porpoise's Tail Is on Crosswise

Now, I want to tell you 'bout de porpoise. God had done made de world and everything. He set de moon and de stars in de sky. He got de fishes of de sea, and de fowls of de air completed.

He made de Sun and hung it up. Then He made a nice gold track for it to run on. Then He said, "Now, Sun, I got everything made but Time. That's up to you. I want you to start out and go round de world on dis track just as fast as you kin make it. And de time it takes you to go and come, I'm going to call day and night." De Sun went zoomin' on cross de elements. Now, de porpoise was hanging round there and heard God what he told de Sun, so he decided he'd take dat trip round de world hisself. He looked up and saw de Sun kytin' along, so he lit out too, him and dat Sun!

So de porpoise beat de Sun round de world by one hour and three minutes. So God said, "Aw naw, this aint gointer do! I didn't mean for nothin' to be faster than de Sun!" So God run dat porpoise for three days before he run him down and caught him, and took his tail off and put it on crossways to slow him up. Still he's de fastest thing in de water.

And dat's why de porpoise got his tail on crossways.

Rockefeller and Ford

Once John D. Rockefeller and Henry Ford was woofing at each other. Rockefeller told Henry Ford he could build a solid gold road round the world. Henry Ford told him if he would he would look at it and see if he liked it, and if he did he would buy it and put one of his tin lizzies on it.

Originality

It has been said so often that the Negro is lacking in originality that it has almost become a gospel. Outward signs seem to bear this out. But if one looks closely its falsity is immediately evident.

It is obvious that to get back to original sources is much too difficult for any group to claim very much as a certainty. What we really mean by originality is the modification of ideas. The most ardent admirer of the great Shakespeare cannot claim first source even for him. It is his treatment of the borrowed material.

So if we look at it squarely, the Negro is a very original being. While he lives and moves in the midst of a white civilization, everything that he touches is re-interpreted for his own use. He has modified the language, mode of food preparation, practice of medicine, and most certainly the religion of his new country, just as he adapted to suit himself the Sheik haircut made famous by Rudolph Valentino.

Everyone is familiar with the Negro's modification of the whites' musical instruments, so that his interpretation has been adopted by the white man himself and then re-interpreted. In so many words, Paul Whiteman is giving an imitation of a Negro orchestra making use of white-invented musical instruments in a Negro way. Thus has arisen a new art in the civilised world, and thus has our so-called civilisation come. The exchange and re-exchange of ideas between groups.

Imitation

The Negro, the world over, is famous as a mimic. But this in no way damages his standing as an original. Mimicry is an art in itself. If it is not, then all art must fall by the same blow that strikes it down. When sculpture, painting, dancing, literature neither reflect nor suggest anything in nature or human experience we turn away with a dull wonder in our hearts at why the thing was done. Moreover, the contention that the Negro imitates from a feeling of inferiority is incorrect. He mimics for the love of it. The group of Negroes who slavishly imitate is small. The average Negro glories in his ways. The highly educated Negro the same. The self-despisement lies in a middle class who scorns to do or be anything Negro. "That's just like a Nigger" is the most terrible rebuke one can lay upon this kind. He wears drab clothing, sits through a boresome church service, pretends to have no interest in the community, holds beauty contests, and otherwise apes all the mediocrities of the white brother. The truly cultured Negro scorns him, and the Negro "farthest down" is too busy "spreading his junk" in his own way to see or care. He likes his own things best. Even the group who are not Negroes but belong to the "sixth race,"[6] buy such records as "Shake Dat Thing" and "Tight Lak Dat." They really enjoy hearing a good bible-beater preach, but wild horses could drag no such admission from them. Their ready-made expression is: "We

---

6. Hurston may be referring here to mulattoes.

done got away from all that now." Some refuse to countenance Negro music on the grounds that it is niggerism, and for that reason should be done away with. Roland Hayes was thoroughly denounced for singing spirituals until he was accepted by white audiences. Langston Hughes is not considered a poet by this group because he writes of the man in the ditch, who is more numerous and real among us than any other.

But, this group aside, let us say that the art of mimicry is better developed in the Negro than in other racial groups. He does it as the mocking-bird does it, for the love of it, and not because he wishes to be like the one imitated. I saw a group of small Negro boys imitating a cat defecating and the subsequent toilet of the cat. It was very realistic, and they enjoyed it as much as if they had been imitating a coronation ceremony. The dances are full of imitations of various animals. The buzzard lope, walking the dog, the pig's hind legs, holding the mule, elephant squat, pigeon's wing, falling off the log, seabord (imitation of an engine starting), and the like.

Absence of the Concept of Privacy

It is said that Negroes keep nothing secret, that they have no reserve. This ought not to seem strange when one considers that we are an outdoor people accustomed to communal life. Add this to all-permeating drama and you have the explanation.

There is no privacy in an African village. Loves, fights, possessions are, to misquote Woodrow Wilson, "Open disagreements openly arrived at." The community is given the benefit of a good fight as well as a good wedding. An audience is a necessary part of any drama. We merely go with nature rather than against it.

Discord is more natural than accord. If we accept the doctrine of the survival of the fittest there are more fighting honors than there are honors for other achievements. Humanity places premiums on all things necessary to its well-being, and a valiant and good fighter is valuable in any community. So why hide the light under a bushel? Moreover, intimidation is a recognised part of warfare the world over, and threats certainly must be listed under that head. So that a great threatener must certainly be considered an aid to the fighting machine. So then if a man or woman is a facile hurler of threats, why should he or she not show their wares to the community? Hence the holding of all quarrels and fights in the open. One relieves one's pent-up anger and at the same time earns laurels in intimidation. Besides, one does the community a service. There is nothing so exhilarating as watching well-matched opponents go into action. The entire world likes action, for that matter. Hence prize-fighters become millionaires.

Likewise love-making is a biological necessity the world over and an art among Negroes. So that a man or woman who is proficient sees no reason why the fact should not be moot. He swaggers. She struts hippily about. Songs are built on the power to charm beneath the bed-clothes. Here again we have individuals striving to excel in what the community considers an art. Then if all of his world is seeking a great lover, why should he not speak right out loud?

It is all in a view-point. Love-making and fighting in all their branches are high arts, other things are arts among other groups where they brag about their proficiency just as brazenly as we do about these things that others consider matters for conversation behind closed doors. At any rate, the white man is despised by Negroes as a very poor fighter individually, and a very poor lover. One Negro, speaking of white men, said, "White folks is alright when dey gits in de bank and on de law bench, but dey sho 'kin lie about wimmen folks."

I pressed him to explain. "Well you see, while mens makes out they marries wimmen to look at they eyes, and they know they gits em for just what us gits em for. 'Nother thing, white mens say they goes clear round de world and wins all de wimmen folks way from they men folks. Dat's a lie too. They don't win nothin, they buys em. Now de way I figgers it, if a woman don't want me enough to be wid me, 'thout I got to pay her, she kin rock right on, but these here white men don't know what do wid a woman when they gits her—dat's how come they gives they wimmen so much. They got to. Us wimmen works jus as hard as us does an come home an sleep wid us every night. They own wouldn't do it and its de mens fault. Dese white men done fooled theyself bout dese wimmen.

"Now me, I keeps me some wimmens all de time. Dat's whut dey wuz put here for—us mens to use. Dat's right now, Miss. Y'll wuz put here so us mens could have some pleasure. Course I don't run round like heap uh men folks. But if my ole lady go way from me and stay more'n two weeks, I got to git me somebody, aint I?"

The Jook

Jook is the word for a Negro pleasure house. It may mean a bawdy house. It may mean the house set apart on public works where the men and women dance, drink and gamble. Often it is a combination of all these.

In past generations the music was furnished by "boxes," another word for guitars. One guitar was enough for a dance; to have two was considered excellent. Where two were playing one man played the lead and the other seconded him. The first player was "picking" and the second was "framming," that is, playing chords while the lead carried the melody by dexterous finger work. Sometimes a third player was added, and he played a tom-tom effect on the low strings. Believe it or not, this is excellent dance music.

Pianos soon came to take the place of the boxes, and now player-pianos and victrolas are in all of the Jooks.

Musically speaking, the Jook is the most important place in America. For in its smelly, shoddy confines has been born the secular music known as blues, and on blues has been founded jazz. The singing and playing in the true Negro style is called "jooking."

The songs grow by incremental repetition as they travel from mouth to mouth and from Jook to Jook for years before they reach outside ears. Hence the great variety of subject-matter in each song.

The Negro dances circulated over the world were also conceived inside the Jooks. They too make the round of Jooks and public works before going into the outside world.

In this respect it is interesting to mention the Black Bottom.[7] I have read several false accounts of its origin and name. One writer claimed that it got its name from the black sticky mud on the bottom of the Mississippi river. Other equally absurd statements gummed the press. Now the dance really originated in the Jook section of Nashville, Tennessee, around Fourth Avenue. This is a tough neighbourhood known as Black Bottom—hence the name.

The Charleston is perhaps forty years old, and was danced up and down the Atlantic seaboard from North Carolina to Key West, Florida.

The Negro social dance is slow and sensuous. The idea in the Jook is to gain sensation, and not so much exercise. So that just enough foot movement is added to keep the dancers on the floor. A tremendous sex stimulation is gained from this. But who is trying to avoid it? The man, the woman, the time and the place have met. Rather, little intimate names are indulged in to heap fire on fire.

These too have spread to all the world.

The Negro theatre, as built up by the Negro, is based on Jook situations, with women, gambling, fighting, drinking. Shows like *Dixie to Broadway* are only Negro in cast, and could just as well have come from pre-Soviet Russia.

Another interesting thing—Negro shows before being tampered with did not specialise in octoroon chorus girls.[8] The girl who could hoist a Jook song from her belly and lam it against the front door of the theatre was the lead, even if she were as black as the hinges of hell. The question was "Can she jook?" She must also have a good belly wobble, and her hips must, to quote a popular work song, "Shake like jelly all over and be so broad, Lawd, Lawd, and be so broad." So that the bleached chorus is the result of a white demand and not the Negro's.

The woman in the Jook may be nappy headed and black, but if she is a good lover she gets there just the same. A favorite Jook song of the past has this to say:

> *Singer:* It aint good looks dat takes you through dis world.
> *Audience:* What is it, good mama?
> *Singer:* Elgin movements in your hips. Twenty years guarantee.[9]

And it always brought down the house too.

> Oh de white gal rides in a Cadillac,
> De yaller gal rides de same,
> Black gal rides in a rusty Ford
> But she gits dere just de same.

7. This was a popular dance step.

8. "Octoroon" is a term no longer in use. It referred to a person who was one-eighth African American. "Octoroon chorus girls" alludes to the light-skinned women dancers favored by Harlem nightclubs and Broadway musical producers.

9. Elgin was a company that made elegant watches with a twenty-year guarantee.

The sort of woman her men idealise is the type that is put forth in the theatre. The art-creating Negro prefers a not too thin woman who can shake like jelly all over as she dances and sings, and that is the type he put forth on the stage. She has been banished by the white producer and the Negro who takes his cue from the white.

Of course a black woman is never the wife of the upper class Negro in the North. This state of affairs does not obtain in the South, however. I have noted numerous cases where the wife was considerably darker than the husband. People of some substance, too.

This scornful attitude towards black women receives mouth sanction by the mud-sills.

Even on the works and in the Jooks the black man sings disparagingly of black women. They say that she is evil. That she sleeps with her fists doubled up and ready for action. All over they are making a little drama of waking up a yaller[10] wife and a black one.

A man is lying beside his yaller wife and wakes her up. She says to him, "Darling, do you know what I was dreaming when you woke me up?" He says, "No honey, what was you dreaming?" She says, "I dreamt I had done cooked you a big, fine dinner and we was setting down to eat out de same plate and I was setting on yo' lap jus huggin you and kissin you and you was so sweet."

Wake up a black woman, and before you kin git any sense into her she be done up and lammed you over the head four or five times. When you git her quiet she'll say, "Nigger, know whut I was dreamin when you woke me up?"

You say, "No honey, what was you dreamin?" She says, "I dreamt you shook yo' rusty fist under my nose and I split yo' head open wid a axe."

But in spite of disparaging fictitious drama, in real life the black girl is drawing on his account at the commissary. Down in the Cypress Swamp as he swings his axe he chants:

> Dat ole black gal, she keep on grumblin,
> New pair shoes, new pair shoes,
> I'm goint to buy her shoes and stockings
> Slippers too, slippers too.

Then adds aside: "Blacker de berry, sweeter de juice."[11]

To be sure the black gal is still in power, men are still cutting and shooting their way to her pillow. To the queen of the Jook!

Speaking of the influence of the Jook, I noted that Mae West in *Sex* had much more flavor of the turpentine quarters than she did of the white bawd. I know that the piece she played on the piano is a very old Jook composition. "Honey let yo' drawers hang low" had been played and sung in every Jook in the South for at least thirty-five years. It has always puzzled me why she thought it likely to be played in a Canadian bawdy house.

10. "Yaller" is dialect for "yellow," i.e., a light-skinned African American.
11. It is from this saying that Wallace Thurman drew the title of his novel, *The Blacker the Berry* (1929).

Speaking of the use of Negro material by white performers, it is astonishing that so many are trying it, and I have never seen one yet entirely realistic. They often have all the elements of the song, dance, or expression, but they are misplaced or distorted by the accent falling on the wrong element. Every one seems to think that the Negro is easily imitated when nothing is further from the truth. Without exception I wonder why the black-face comedians *are* black-face; it is a puzzle—good comedians, but darn poor niggers. Gershwin and the other "Negro" rhapsodists come under this same axe. Just about as Negro as caviar or Ann Pennington's athletic Black Bottom. When the Negroes who knew the Black Bottom in its cradle saw the Broadway version they asked each other, "Is you learnt dat *new* Black Bottom yet?" Proof that it was not *their* dance.

And God only knows what the world has suffered from the white damsels who try to sing blues.

The Negroes themselves have sinned also in this respect. In spite of the goings up and down on the earth, from the original Fisk Jubilee Singers down to the present,[12] there has been no genuine presentation of Negro songs to white audiences. The spirituals that have been sung around the world are Negroid to be sure, but so full of musicians' tricks that Negro congregations are highly entertained when they hear their old songs so changed. They never use the new style songs, and these are never heard unless perchance some daughter or son has been off to college and returns with one of the old songs with its face lifted, so to speak.

I am of the opinion that this trick style of delivery was originated by the Fisk Singers; Tuskegee and Hampton followed suit and have helped spread this misconception of Negro spirituals.[13] This Glee Club style has gone on so long and become so fixed among concert singers that it is considered quite authentic. But I say again, that not one concert singer in the world is singing the songs as the Negro song-makers sing them.

If anyone wishes to prove the truth of this let him step into some unfashionable Negro church and hear for himself.

To those who want to institute the Negro theatre, let me say it is already established. It is lacking in wealth, so it is not seen in the high places. A creature with a white head and Negro feet struts the Metropolitan boards. The real Negro theatre is in the Jooks and the cabarets. Self-conscious individuals may turn away the eye and say, "Let us search elsewhere for our dramatic art." Let 'em search. They certainly won't find it. Butter Beans and Susie,[14] Bo-Jangles and Snake Hips are the only performers of the real Negro school it has ever been my pleasure to behold in New York.

12. The Fisk Jubilee Singers were the preeminent touring African American choral group of the era. They came from Fisk University, the oldest historically black college in the nation, located in Nashville, Tennessee.

13. Tuskegee Institute in Alabama was established by Booker T. Washington. Hampton Normal and Agricultural Institute in Hampton, Virginia, was founded by Samuel Chapman Armstrong to educate freed slaves.

14. Butter Beans and Susie were African American entertainers.

Dialect

If we are to believe the majority of writers of Negro dialect and the burnt-cork artists, Negro speech is a weird thing, full of "ams" and "Ises." Fortunately we don't have to believe them. We may go directly to the Negro and let him speak for himself.

I know that I run the risk of being damned as an infidel for declaring that nowhere can be found the Negro who asks "am it?" nor yet his brother who announces "Ise uh gwinter." He exists only for a certain type of writers and performers.

Very few Negroes, educated or not, use a clear clipped "I." It verges more or less upon "Ah." I think the lip form is responsible for this to a great extent. By experiment the reader will find that a sharp "I" is very much easier with a thin taut lip than with a full soft lip. Like tightening violin strings.

If one listens closely one will note too that a word is slurred in one position in the sentence but clearly pronounced in another. This is particularly true of the pronouns. A pronoun as a subject is likely to be clearly enunciated, but slurred as an object. For example: "You better not let me ketch yuh."

There is a tendency in some localities to add the "h" to "it" and pronounce it "hit." Probably a vestige of old English. In some localities "if" is "ef."

In story telling "so" is universally the connective. It is used even as an introductory word, at the very beginning of a story. In religious expression "and" is used. The trend in stories is to state conclusions; in religion, to enumerate.

I am mentioning only the most general rules in dialect because there are so many quirks that belong only to certain localities that nothing less than a volume would be adequate.

> Now He told me, He said: "You got the three witnesses. One is water, one is spirit, and one is blood. And these three correspond with the three in heben—Father, Son and Holy Ghost."
>
> Now I ast Him about this lyin in sin and He give me a handful of seeds and He tole me to sow 'em in a bed and He tole me: "I want you to watch them seeds." The seeds come up about in places and He said: "Those seeds that come up, they died in the heart of the earth and quickened and come up and brought forth fruit. But those seeds that didn't come up, they died in the heart of the earth and rotten.
>
> "And a soul that dies and quickens through my spirit they will live forever, but those that dont never pray, they are lost forever." (Rev. Jessie Jefferson)

Laura Wheeler, "Africa in America," cover of *The Crisis,* June 1924

Jessie Redmon Fauset

Impressions of the
Second Pan-African Congress

I

The dream of a Pan-African Congress had already come true in 1919. Yet it was with hearts half wondering, half fearful that we ventured to realize it afresh in 1921. So tenuous, so delicate had been its beginnings. Had the black world, although once stirred by the terrific rumblings of the Great War, relapsed into its lethargy? Then out of Africa just before it was time to cross the Atlantic came a letter, one of many, but this the most appealing word from the Egyptian Sudan: "Sir: We cannot come but we are sending you this small sum ($17.32), to help toward the expenses of the Pan-African Congress. Oh Sir, we are looking to you for we need help sorely!"

So with this in mind we crossed the seas not knowing just what would be the plan of action for the Congress, for would not its members come from the four corners of the earth and must there not of necessity be a diversity of opinion, of thought, of project? But the main thing, the great thing, was that Ethiopia's sons through delegates were stretching out their hands from all over the black and yearning world.

II

Then one day, the 27th of August, we met in London in Central Hall, under the shadow of Westminster Abbey. Many significant happenings had those cloisters looked down on, but surely on none more significant than this group of men and women of African descent, so different in rearing and tradition and yet so similar in purpose. The rod of the common oppressor had made them feel their own community of blood, of necessity, of problem.

Men from strange and diverse lands came together. We were all of us foreigners. South Africa was represented, the Gold Coast, Sierra Leone and Lagos, Grenada, the United States of America, Martinique, Liberia. No natives of Morocco or of East Africa came, yet men

The Crisis, December 1921.

who had lived there presented and discussed their problems. British Guiana and Jamaica were there and the men and women of African blood [who] were at that time resident in London.

That was a wonderful meeting. I think that at first we did not realize how wonderful. The first day Dr. Alcindor of London and Rev. Jernagin of Washington presided; the second day Dr. Du Bois and Mr. Archer, ex-Mayor of Battersea, London. Of necessity those first meetings had to be occasions for getting acquainted, for bestowing confidences for opening up our hearts. Native African and native American stood side by side and said, "Brother, this is my lot; tell me what is yours!"

Mr. H. A. Hunt of Fort Valley, Ga., Mr. R. P. Sims of Bluefield, W. Va., Dr. Wilberforce Williams of Chicago, Mrs. Hart Felton of Americus, Ga., Professor Hutto of Bainbridge, Ga., Rev. W. H. Jernagin of Washington, D.C., Dr. H. R. Butler of Atlanta, Mr. Nelson of Kentucky, Dr. Du Bois, Mr. White, Mrs. Kelley and Miss Fauset—all these told of America. And in return Dr. Olaribigbee and Mr. Thomas of West Africa, Mr. Augusto of Lagos, Mrs. Davis of South Africa, Mr. Marryshow of Grenada, Mr. Norman Leys, a white Englishman who knew East Africa well, Mr. Arnold, also white, who knew Morocco, Mr. Varma and Mr. Satkalavara of India told the tale of Africa and of other countries of which the Americans knew little or nothing.

We listened well. What can be more fascinating than learning at first hand that the stranger across the seas, however different in phrase or expression, yet knows no difference of heart? We were all one family in London. What small divergences of opinion, slight suspicions, doubtful glances there may have been at first were all quickly dissipated. We felt our common blood with almost unbelievable unanimity.

Out of the flood of talk emerged real fact and purpose for the American delegate. First, that West Africa had practically no problems concerning the expropriation of land but had imminent something else, the problem of political power and the heavy and insulting problem of segregation. The East African, on the other hand, and also the South African had no vestige of a vote (save in Natal), had been utterly despoiled of the best portions of his land, nor could he buy it back. In addition to this the East African had to consider the influx of the East Indian who might prove a friend, or might prove as harsh a taskmaster as the European despoiler.

Through the interplay of speech and description and idea, two propositions flashed out—one, the proposition of Mr. Augusto, a splendid, fearless speaker from Lagos, that the Pan-African Congress should accomplish something very concrete. He urged that we start with the material in hand and advance to better things. First of all let us begin by financing the Liberian loan. Liberia is a Negro Independency already founded. "Let us," pleaded Mr. Augusto, "lend the solid weight of the newly-conscious black world toward its development."

The other proposition was that of Mr. Marryshow, of Grenada, and of Professor Hutto of Georgia. "We must remember," both of them pointed out, "that not words but actions are needed. We must be prepared to put our hands in our pockets; we must make sacrifices to help each other." "Tell us what to do," said Mr. Hutto, "and the Knights of Pythias of Georgia stand ready, 80,000 strong, to do their part."

Those were fine, constructive words. Then at the last meeting we listened to the resolutions which Dr. Du Bois had drawn up. Bold and glorious resolutions they were, couched
in winged, unambiguous words. Without a single dissenting vote the members of the Congress accepted them. We clasped hands with our newly found brethren and departed,
feeling that it was good to be alive, and most wonderful to be colored. Not one of us but
envisaged in his heart the dawn of a day of new and perfect African brotherhood.

III

Down to Dover we flew, up the English Channel to Ostend, and thence to Brussels.

Brussels was different. How shall I explain it? The city was like most other large cities,
alive and bustling, with its share of noise. All about us were beautiful, large buildings
and commodious stores, except in the public squares where the ancient structures, the
town hall and the like, centuries old, recalled the splendor and dignity of other days.
But over Brussels hung the shadow of monarchical government. True, London is the heart
of a monarchy, too, but the stranger does not feel it unless he is passing Buckingham
Palace or watching the London Horse Guards change.

At first it was not so noticeable.

We had been invited by Paul Otlet and Senator LaFontaine and had been helped greatly
by M. Paul Panda, a native of the Belgian Congo who had been educated in Belgium. The
Congress itself was held in the marvellous Palais Mondial, the World Palace situated in
the Cinquantenaire Park. We could not have asked for a better setting. But there *was* a
difference. In the first place, there were many more white than colored people—there
are not many of us in Brussels—and it was not long before we realized that their interest was deeper, more immediately significant than that of the white people we had found
elsewhere. Many of Belgium's economic and material interests centre in Africa in the Belgian Congo. Any interference with the natives might result in an interference with the
sources from which so many Belgian capitalists drew their prosperity.

After all, who were these dark strangers speaking another tongue and introducing
Heaven only knew what ideas to be carried into the Congo? Once when speaking of the
strides which colored America had made in education I suggested to M. Panda that perhaps some American colored teachers might be induced to visit the Congo and help with
the instruction of the natives.

"Oh, no, no, no!" he exclaimed, and added the naive explanation, "Belgium would never
permit that, the colored Americans are too *malins* (clever)."

After we had visited the Congo Museum we were better able to understand the unspoken determination of the Belgians to let nothing interfere with their dominion in the
Congo. Such treasures! Such illimitable riches! What a store-house it must plainly be for
them. For the first time in my life I was able to envisage what Africa means to Europe,
depleted as she has become through the ages by war and famine and plague. In the
museum were the seeds of hundreds of edible plants; there was wood—great trunks of
dense, fine-grained mahogany as thick as a man's body is wide and as long as half a New
York block. Elephants' tusks gleamed, white and shapely, seven feet long from tip to base

without allowing for the curve, and as broad through as a man's arm. All the wealth of the world—skins and furs, gold and copper—would seem to center in the Congo.

Nor was this all. Around us in the spacious rooms were the expression of an earlier but well developed art, wood-carvings showing beyond the shadow of a doubt the inherent artistry of the African. Dearest of all, yet somehow least surprising to us, was the number of musical instruments. There is not a single musical instrument in the world, I would venture to say, of which the Congo cannot furnish a prototype.

Native wealth, native art lay about us in profusion even in the museum. Small wonder that the Belgian men and women watched us with careful eyes.

The program in Brussels was naturally different from that in London. We undertook to learn something of the culture which colored people had achieved in the different parts of the world, but we hoped also to hear of actual native conditions as we had heard of them in the first conference. M. Panda spoke of the general development of the Congo, Madame Sarolea of the Congolese woman. Miss Fauset told of the colored graduates in the United States and showed the pictures of the first women who had obtained the degree of Doctor of Philosophy. Bishop Phillips of Nashville and Bishop Hurst of Baltimore greeted the assembly. Mrs. Curtis told of Liberia, the presiding officer of the Conference, M. Diagne, and his white colleague M. Barthelemy from the Pas de Calais, in the French Chamber of Deputies, ably assisted.

Belgian officialdom was well represented. General Sorelas of Spain spoke of the problem of the mixed race. Another General, a Belgian, splendid in ribbons and orders, was on the platform, and two members of the Belgian Colonial Office were present, "unofficially."

There was no doubt but that our assembly was noted. A fine, fresh-faced youth from the International University gave us a welcome from students of all nations; we were invited to a reception at the Hôtel de Ville (City Hall) in the ancient public square, and on the last day General Sorelas and his beautiful wife and daughters received us all in their home.

And yet the shadow of Colonial dominion governed. Always the careful Belgian eye watched and peered, the Belgian ear listened. For three days we listened to pleasant generalities without a word of criticism of Colonial Governments, without a murmur of complaint of Black Africa, without a suggestion that this was an international Congress called to define and make intelligible the greatest set of wrongs against human beings that the modern world has known. We realized of course how delicate the Belgian situation was and how sensitive a conscience the nation had because of the atrocities of the Leopold regime.[1] We knew the tremendous power of capital organized to exploit the Congo; but despite this we proposed before the Congress was over to voice the wrongs of Negroes temperately but clearly. We assumed of course that this was what Belgium expected, but

1. This is a reference to Leopold II, who became king of Belgium in 1865. He organized the exploration of the Congo and in 1885 was recognized as sovereign ruler of the Congo Free State. He viewed the state as his personal property and exploited it in order to recover his expenses. However, in 1908 expenses and international criticism forced him to turn the state over to Belgium for annexation as a colony.

we reckoned without our hosts in a very literal sense. Indeed as we afterward found, we were reckoning without our own presiding officer, for without doubt M. Diagne on account of his high position in the French Government had undoubtedly felt called on to assure the Belgian Government that no "radical" step would be taken by the Congress. He sponsored therefore a mild resolution suggested by the secretaries of the Palais Mondial stating that Negroes were "susceptible" of education and pledging cooperation of the Pan-African Congress with the international movement in Belgium. When the London resolutions (which are published this month as our leading editorial) were read, M. Diagne was greatly alarmed, and our Belgian visitors were excited. The American delegates were firm and for a while it looked as though the main session of the Pan-African Congress was destined to end in a rather disgraceful row. It was here, however, that the American delegates under the leadership of Dr. Du Bois, showed themselves the real masters of the situation. With only formal and dignified protest, they allowed M. Diagne to "jam through" his resolutions and adjourn the session; but they kept their own resolutions in place before the Congress to come up for final consideration in Paris, and they maintained the closing of the session in Brussels in order and unity. I suppose the white world of Europe has never seen a finer example of unity and trust on the part of Negroes toward a Negro leader.

But we left Belgium in a thoughtful and puzzled mood. How great was this smothering power which made it impossible for men even in a scientific Congress to be frank and to express their inmost desires? Not one word, for instance, had been said during the whole Congress by Belgian, white or black, or French presiding officer which would lead one to suspect that Leopold and his tribe had ever been other than the Congo's tutelary angels. Apparently not even an improvement could be hinted at. And the few Africans who were present said nothing. But at that last meeting just before we left, a Congolese came forward and fastened the button of the Congo Union in Dr. Du Bois' coat.

What lay behind that impassive face?

IV

At last Paris!

Between Brussels and the queen city of the world we saw blasted town, ravaged village and plain, ruined in a war whose basic motif had been the rape of Africa. What should we learn of the black man in France?

Already we had realized that the black colonial's problem, while the same intrinsically, wore on the face of it a different aspect from that of the black Americans. Or was it that we had learned more quickly and better than they the value of organization, of frankness, of freedom of speech? We wondered then and we wonder still though Heaven knows in all humility.

But Paris at last, with its glow and its lights and its indefinable attraction!

We met in the Salle des Ingénieurs (Engineers' Hall) in little Rue Blanche back of the Opera. Logan was there, Béton and Dr. Jackson, men who had worked faithfully and well for us even before we had come to Paris. And around us were more strange faces—new types to us—from Senegal, from the French Congo, from Madagascar, from Annam. I looked at that sea of dark faces and my heart was moved within me. However their white over-lords or *their* minions might plot and plan and thwart, nothing could dislodge from the minds of all of them the knowledge that black was at last stretching out to black, hands of hope and the promise of unity though seas and armies divided.

On the platform was, I suppose, the intellectual efflorescence of the Negro race. To American eyes and, according to the papers, to many others, Dr. Du Bois loomed first, for he had first envisaged this moment and many of us knew how gigantically he had toiled. Then there was M. Bellegarde, the Haitian minister to France and Haitian delegate to the assembly of the League of Nations. Beside him sat the grave and dignified delegate from the Liga Africana of Lisbon, Portugal, and on the other side the presiding officer, M. Diagne, and his colleague M. Candace, French deputy from Guadeloupe. A little to one side sat the American Rayford Logan, assistant secretary of the Pan-African Congress at Paris and our interpreter. His translations, made off-hand without a moment's preparation, were a remarkable exhibition.

In the audience besides those faithful American delegates who had followed us from London on, were other friends, Henry O. Tanner, Captain and Mrs. Napoleon Marshall, who had joined us in Paris, Bishop and Mrs. Hurst, who had come back from Brussels to Paris with us, Captain and Mrs. Arthur Springarn, white delegates from America, who had attended the conferences regularly and had laughed and worked with us in between whiles.

The situation in Paris was less tense, one felt the difference between monarchy and republic. But again the American was temporarily puzzled. Even allowing for natural differences of training and tradition, it seemed absurd to have the floor given repeatedly to speakers who dwelt on the glories of France and the honor of being a black Frenchman, when what we and most of those humble delegates wanted to learn was about *us*.

The contrast between the speakers of the Eastern and Western hemispheres with but two exceptions was most striking. Messieurs Diagne and Candace gave us fine oratory, magnificent gestures—but platitudes. But the speeches of Dr. Du Bois, of Edward Frazier, of Walter White, of Dr. Jackson, of a young and fiery Jamaican and of M. Bellegarde, gave facts and food for thought. The exceptions were the speeches of M. Challaye, a white member of the Society for the Defense of African Natives, and those of the grave and courtly Portuguese, Messieurs Magalhaens and Santos-Pinto.

But this audience was different from that in Brussels. To begin with, its members were mainly black and being black, had suffered. More than one man, to whom the unusually autocratic presiding officer had not given the right to speak said to me after hearing Dr. Du Bois' exposition of the meaning and purpose of the Pan-African Congress, "Do you think I could get a chance to speak to Dr. Du Bois? There is much I would tell him."

France is a colonial power but France is a republic. And so, when our resolutions were presented once more to this the final session of the Pan-African Congress, that audience felt that here at last was the fearless voicing of the long stifled desires of their hearts, here was comprehension, here was the translation of hitherto unsyllabled, unuttered

prayers. The few paragraphs about capitalism M. Diagne postponed "for the consideration of the next Pan-African Congress." But the rest that yearning, groping audience
accepted with their souls.

The last session of the last day was over. It was midnight and spent and happy we
found our way home through the streets of Paris, which never sleeps.

V

Yet after all the real task was at Geneva. The city struck us dumb at first with its beauty
of sky and water—the blue and white of the September heavens above, Lake Geneva and
the Rhône River gliding green and transparent under stone bridges, black and white swans,
red-beaked, floating lazily about green baby islands, and above and beyond all in the far
distance Mont Blanc rising hoary, serene and majestic. In the sunset it looked like bur-
nished silver.

But scant time we had for looking at that! The Assembly of the League of Nations
was on. A thousand petitions and resolutions were in process of being presented. Delegates from many nations were here and men of international name and fame were presiding. How were we to gain audience?

Fortunately for us Dr. Du Bois' name and reputation proved the open sesame. He had
not been in the city two hours before invitations and requests for interviews poured in.
One of our staunchest helpers was an English woman, Lady Cecelia, wife of that Mr. Roberts
who had worked with Montague in India. She presided at meals at a long table in the dining room of the Hôtel des Familles and here Dr. Du Bois was made a welcome guest
throughout his whole stay. Here came to meet and confer with him on our cause Mr.
Roberts himself, Mr. Lief-Jones, M.P., Professor Gilbert Murray (representing South Africa
at the Assembly of the League of Nations), and John H. Harris of the Anti-Slavery and Abo-
rigines' Protection Society. M. Bellegarde, Haitian Minister to France and delegate to the
Assembly, was also at that hotel and gave us generously of his aid and assistance.

On Monday night, September 13, Dr. Du Bois addressed the English Club of Geneva
and conveyed to them some idea of what the black world was thinking, feeling and doing
with regard to the Negro problem. I am sure that many of that group of people, thinkers
and students though they were, had never dreamed before that there might even be a
black point of view. But they took their instruction bravely and afterwards thanked Dr.
Du Bois with shining eyes and warm hand clasps.

Besides meeting and conferring with these distinguished personages Dr. Du Bois had
luncheon conferences with René Claparède of the executive committee of the Société Inter-
nationale pour la Protection des Indigènes and with William Rappard, head of the Mandates Commission of the League of Nations, a dinner conference with G. Spiller, former
secretary of the Races Congress, and an interview with Albert Thomas, head of the International Bureau of Labor.

At the end of a week of steady driving, by dint of interviewing, of copying, of
translating, of recopying, we were ready to present and did present to Sir Eric Drummond,

secretary of the League of Nations, a copy in French and English of the resolutions entitled *To the World* and of the manifesto. Mr. Thomas and M. Rappard, who both heartily endorsed the appointment of a "man of Negro descent" to the Mandates Commission, Professor Gilbert Murray, and M. Bellegarde also received copies.

And between whiles we listened to the world striving to right its wrongs at the Assembly of the League of Nations.

Of course we were at a disadvantage because America, not being in the League of Nations, had no delegate. But Professor Murray suggested to M. Bellegarde, the Haitian delegate, that he state the second resolution during the debate on Mandates. This he did, as Professor Murray writes us, with "quite remarkable success" and "I think that next year it may be quite suitable to put it down as a resolution."

VI

Results are hard to define. But I must strive to point out a few. First then, out of these two preliminary conferences of 1919 and 1921, a definite organization has been evolved, to be known as the Pan-African Congress. There will be more of this in these pages. Naturally, working with people from all over the world, with the necessity for using at least two languages, with the limited detailed knowledge which the black foreigner is permitted to get of Africa and with the pressure brought to bear on many Africans to prevent them from frank speech—action must be slow and very careful. It will take years for an institution of this sort to function. But it is on its own feet now and the burden no longer is on black America. It must stand or fall by its own merits.

We have gained proof that organization on our part arrests the attention of the world. We had no need to seek publicity. If we had wanted to we could not have escaped it. The press was with us always. The white world is feverishly anxious to know of our thoughts, our hopes, our dreams. Organization is our strongest weapon.

It was especially arresting to notice that the Pan-African Congress and the Assembly of the League of Nations differed not a whit in essential methods. Neither attempted a hard and fast program. Lumbering and slow were the wheels of both activities. There had to be much talk, many explanations, an infinity of time and patience and then talk again. Neither the wrongs of Africa nor of the world, can be righted in a day nor in a decade. We can only make beginnings.

The most important result was our realization that there is an immensity of work ahead of all of us. We have got to learn everything—facts about Africa, the difference between her colonial governments, one foreign language at least (French or Spanish), new points of view, generosity of ideal and of act. All the possibilities of all black men are needed to weld together the black men of the world against the day when black and white meet to do battle.

God grant that when that day comes we shall be so powerful that the enemy will say, "But behold! these men are our brothers."

Marcus Garvey

Africa for the Africans

For five years the Universal Negro Improvement Association has been advocating the cause of Africa for the Africans—that is, that the Negro peoples of the world should concentrate upon the object of building up for themselves a great nation in Africa.

When we started our propaganda toward this end several of the so-called intellectual Negroes who have been bamboozling the race for over half a century said that we were crazy, that the Negro peoples of the western world were not interested in Africa and could not live in Africa. One editor and leader went so far as to say at his so-called Pan-African Congress that American Negroes could not live in Africa, because the climate was too hot. All kinds of arguments have been adduced by these Negro intellectuals against the colonization of Africa by the black race. Some said that the black man would ultimately work out his existence alongside of the white man in countries founded and established by the latter. Therefore, it was not necessary for Negroes to seek an independent nationality of their own. The old time stories of "African fever," "African bad climate," "African mosquitos," "African savages," have been repeated by these "brainless intellectuals" of ours as a scare against our people in America and the West Indies taking a kindly interest in the new program of building a racial empire of our own in our Motherland. Now that years have rolled by and the Universal Negro Improvement Association has made the circuit of the world with its propaganda, we find eminent statesmen, and leaders of the white race coming out boldly advocating the cause of colonizing Africa with the Negroes of the western world. A year ago ago Senator McCullum of the Mississippi Legislature introduced a resolution in the House for the purpose of petitioning the Congress of the United States of America and the President to use their good influence in securing from the Allies sufficient territory in Africa in liquidation of the war debt, which territory should be used for the establishing of an independent nation for American Negroes. About the same time Senator France of Maryland gave expression to a similar

The Messenger, September 1920.

desire in the Senate of the United States. During a speech on the "Soldiers' Bonus." He said: "We owe a big debt to Africa and one which we have too long ignored. I need not enlarge upon our peculiar interest in the obligation to the people of Africa. Thousands of Americans have for years been contributing to the missionary work which has been carried out by the noble men and women who have been sent out in that field by the churches of America."

This reveals a real change on the part of prominent statesmen in their attitude on the African question. Then comes another suggestion from Germany, for which Dr. Heinrich Schnee, a former Governor of German East Africa, is author. This German statesman suggests in an interview given out in Berlin, and published in New York, that America takes over the mandatories of Great Britain and France in Africa for the colonization of American Negroes. Speaking on the matter, he says, "As regards the attempt to colonize Africa with the surplus American colored population, this would in a long way settle the vexed problem, and under the plan such as Senator France has outlined, might enable France and Great Britain to discharge their duties to the United States, and simultaneously ease the burden of German reparations which is paralyzing economic life."

With expressions as above quoted from prominent world statesmen, and from the demands made by such men as Senators France and McCullum, it is clear that the question of African nationality is not a far-fetched one, but is as reasonable and feasible as was the idea of an American nationality.

A "Program" at Last

I trust that the Negro peoples of the world are now convinced that the work of the Universal Negro Improvement Association is not a visionary one, but very practical, and that it is not so far fetched, but can be realized in a short while if the entire race will only co-operate and work toward the desired end. Now that the work of our organization has started to bear fruit we find that some of these "doubting Thomases" of three and four years ago are endeavoring to mix themselves up with the popular idea of rehabilitating Africa in the interest of the Negro. They are now advancing spurious "programs" and in a short while will endeavor to force themselves upon the public as advocates and leaders of the African idea.

It is felt that those who have followed the career of the Universal Negro Improvement Association will not allow themselves to be deceived by these Negro opportunists who have always sought to live off the ideas of other people.

The Dream of a Negro Empire

It is only a question of a few more years when Africa will be completely colonized by Negroes, as Europe is by the white race. What we want is an independent African nationality, and if America is to help the Negro peoples of the world establish such a nationality, then we welcome the assistance.

It is hoped that when the time comes for American and West Indian Negroes to settle in Africa, they will realize their responsibility and their duty. It will not be to go to Africa for the purpose of exercising an over-lordship over the natives, but it shall be the purpose of the Universal Negro Improvement Association to have established in Africa that brotherly co-operation which will make the interests of the African native and the American and West Indian Negro one and the same, that is to say, we shall enter into a common partnership to build up Africa in the interests of our race.

Oneness of Interests

Everybody knows that there is absolutely no difference between the native-African and the American and West Indian Negroes, in that we are descendants from one common family stock. It is only a matter of accident that we have been divided and kept apart for over three hundred years, but it is felt that when the time has come for us to get back together, we shall do so in the spirit of brotherly love, and any Negro who expects that he will be assisted here, there or anywhere by the Universal Negro Improvement Association to exercise a haughty superiority over the fellows of his own race makes a tremendous mistake. Such men had better remain where they are and not attempt to become in any way interested in the higher development of Africa.

The Negro has had enough of the vaunted practice of race superiority as inflicted upon him by others, therefore he is not prepared to tolerate a similar assumption on the part of his own people. In America and the West Indies, we have Negroes who believe themselves so much above their fellows as to cause them to think that any readjustment in the affairs of the race should be placed in their hands for them to exercise a kind of an autocratic and despotic control as others have done to us for centuries. Again I say, it would be advisable for such Negroes to take their hands and minds off the now popular idea of colonizing Africa in the interest of the Negro race, because their being identified with this new program will not in any way help us because of the existing feeling among Negroes everywhere not to tolerate the infliction of race or class superiority upon them, as is the desire of the self-appointed and self-created race leadership that we have been having for the last fifty years.

The Basis of an African Aristocracy

The masses of Negroes in America, the West Indies, South and Central America are in sympathetic accord with the aspirations of the native Africans. We desire to help them build up Africa as a Negro Empire, where every black man, whether he was born in Africa or the Western world, will have the opportunity to develop on his own lines under the protection of the most favorable democratic institutions.

It will be useless, as before stated, for bombastic Negroes to leave America and the West Indies to go to Africa, thinking that they will have privileged positions to inflict upon the race that bastard aristocracy that they have tried to maintain in this Western world at the expense of the masses. Africa shall develop an aristocracy of its own, but it shall be based upon service and loyalty to race. Let all Negroes work toward that end. I feel that it is only a question of a few more years before our program will be accepted not only by the few statesmen of America who are now interested in it, but by the strong statesmen of the world, as the only solution to the great race problem. There is no other way to avoid the threatening war of the races that is bound to engulf all mankind, which has been prophesied by the world's greatest thinkers; there is no better method than by apportioning every race to its own habitat.

The time has really come for the Asiatics to govern themselves in Asia, as the Europeans are in Europe and the Western world, and also it is wise for the Africans to govern themselves at home, and thereby bring peace and satisfaction to the entire human family.

The Future as I See It

It comes to the individual, the race, the nation, once in a lifetime, to decide upon the course to be pursued as a career. The hour has now struck for the individual Negro as well as the entire race to decide the course that will be pursued in the interest of our own liberty.

We who make up the Universal Negro Improvement Association have decided that we shall go forward, upward and onward toward the great goal of human liberty. We have determined among ourselves that all barriers placed in the way of our progress must be removed, must be cleared away for we desire to see the light of a brighter day.

The Negro Is Ready

The Universal Negro Improvement Association for five years has been proclaiming to the world the readiness of the Negro to carve out a pathway for himself in the course of life. Men of other races and nations have become alarmed at this attitude of the Negro in his desire to do things for himself and by himself. This alarm has become so universal that organizations have been brought into being here, there and everywhere for the purpose of deterring and obstructing this forward move of our race. Propaganda has been waged here, there and everywhere for the purpose of misrepresenting the intention of this organization; some have said that this organization seeks to create discord and discontent among the races; some say we are organized for the purpose of hating other people. Every sensible, sane and honest-minded person knows that the Universal Negro Improvement Association has no such intention. We are organized for the absolute purpose of bettering our condition, industrially, commercially, socially, religiously and politically. We are organized not to hate other men, but to lift ourselves, and to demand respect of all humanity. We have a program that we believe to be righteous; we believe it to be just, and we have made up our minds to lay down ourselves on the altar of sacrifice for the realization of this great hope of ours, based upon the foundation of righteousness. We declare to the world that Africa must be free, that the entire Negro race must be emancipated from industrial bondage, peonage and serfdom; we make no compromise, we make no apology in this our declaration. We do not desire to create offense on the part of other races, but we are determined that we shall be heard, that we shall be given the rights to which we are entitled.

The Propaganda of Our Enemies

For the purpose of creating doubts about the work of the Universal Negro Improvement Association, many attempts have been made to cast shadow and gloom over our work. They have even written the most uncharitable things about our organization; they have spoken so unkindly of our effort, but what do we care? They spoke unkindly and uncharitably about all the reform movements that have helped in the betterment of humanity. They maligned the great movement of the Christian religion; they maligned the great liberation movements of America, of France, of England, of Russia; can we expect, then, to escape being maligned in this, our desire for the liberation of Africa and the freedom of four hundred million Negroes of the world?

We have unscrupulous men and organizations working in opposition to us. Some are trying to capitalize the new spirit that has come to the Negro to make profit out of it to their own selfish benefit; some are trying to set back the Negro from seeing the hope of his own liberty, and thereby poisoning our people's mind against the motives of our organization; but every sensible far-seeing Negro in this enlightened age knows what propaganda means. It is the medium of discrediting that which you are opposed to, so that the propaganda of our enemies will be of little avail as soon as we are rendered able to carry to our peoples scattered throughout the world the true message of our great organization.

"Crocodiles" as Friends

Men of the Negro race, let me say to you that a greater future is in store for us; we have no cause to lose hope, to become faint-hearted. We must realize that upon ourselves depend our destiny, our future; we must carve out that future, that destiny, and we who make up the Universal Negro Improvement Association have pledged ourselves that nothing in the world shall stand in our way, nothing in the world shall discourage us, but opposition shall make us work harder, shall bring us closer together so that as one man the millions of us will march on toward the goal that we have set for ourselves. The new Negro shall not be deceived. The new Negro refuses to take advice from anyone who has not felt with him, and suffered with him. We have suffered for three hundred years, therefore we feel that the time has come when only those who have suffered with us can interpret our feelings and our spirit. It takes the slave to interpret the feelings of the slave; it takes the unfortunate man to interpret the spirit of his unfortunate brother; and so it takes the suffering Negro to interpret the spirit of his comrade. It is strange that so many people are interested in the Negro now, willing to advise him how to act, and what organizations he should join, yet nobody was interested in the Negro to the extent of not making him a slave for two hundred and fifty years, reducing him to industrial peonage and serfdom after he was freed; it is strange that the same people can be so interested in the Negro now, as to tell him what organization he should follow and what leader he should support.

Whilst we are bordering on a future of brighter things, we are also at our danger period, when we must either accept the right philosophy, or go down by following deceptive propaganda which has hemmed us in for many centuries.

Deceiving the People

There is many a leader of our race who tells us that everything is well, and that all things will work out themselves and that a better day is coming. Yes, all of us know that a better day is coming; we all know that one day we will go home to Paradise, but whilst we are hoping by our Christian virtues to have an entry into Paradise we also realize that we are living on earth, and that the things that are practiced in Paradise are not practiced here. You have to treat this world as the world treats you; we are living in a temporal, material age, an age of activity, an age of racial, national selfishness. What else can you expect but to give back to the world what the world gives you, and we are calling upon the four hundred million Negroes of the world to take a decided stand, a determined stand, that we shall occupy a firm position; that position shall be an emancipated race and a free nation of our own. We are determined that we shall have a free country; we are determined that we shall have a flag; we are determined that we shall have a government second to none in the world.

An Eye for an Eye

Men may spurn the idea, they may scoff at it; the metropolitan press of this country may deride us; yes, white men may laugh at the idea of Negroes talking about government; but let me tell you there is going to be a government, and let me say to you also that whatsoever you give, in like measure it shall be returned to you. The world is sinful, and therefore man believes in the doctrine of an eye for an eye, a tooth for a tooth. Everybody believes that revenge is God's, but at the same time we are men, and revenge sometimes springs up, even in the most Christian heart.

Why should man write down a history that will react against him? Why should man perpetrate deeds of wickedness upon his brother which will return to him in like measure? Yes, the Germans maltreated the French in the Franco-Prussian war of 1870, but the French got even with the Germans in 1918. It is history, and history will repeat itself. Beat the Negro, brutalize the Negro, kill the Negro, burn the Negro, imprison the Negro, scoff at the Negro, deride the Negro, it may come back to you one of these fine days, because the supreme destiny of man is in the hands of God. God is no respecter of persons, whether that person be white, yellow or black. Today the one race is up, tomorrow it has fallen; today the Negro seems to be the footstool of the other races and nations of the world; tomorrow the Negro may occupy the highest rung of the great human ladder.

But, when we come to consider the history of man, was not the Negro a power, was he not great once? Yes, honest students of history can recall the day when Egypt, Ethiopia and Timbuctoo towered in their civilizations, towered above Europe, towered above Asia. When Europe was inhabited by a race of cannibals, a race of savages, naked men, heathens and pagans, Africa was peopled with a race of cultured black men, who were masters in art, science and literature; men who were cultured and refined; men who, it was said, were like the gods. Even the great poets of old sang in beautiful sonnets of the delight it afforded the gods to be in companionship with the Ethiopians. Why, then, should we lose hope? Black men, you were once great; you shall be great again. Lose not courage, lose not faith, go forward. The thing to do is to get organized; keep separated and you will be exploited, you will be robbed, you will be killed. Get organized, and you will compel the world to respect you. If the world fails to give you consideration, because you are black men, because you are Negroes, four hundred millions of you shall, through organization, shake the pillars of the universe and bring down creation, even as Samson brought down the temple upon his head and upon the heads of the Philistines.

An Inspiring Vision

So Negroes, I say, through the Universal Negro Improvement Association, that there is much to live for. I have a vision of the future, and I see before me a picture of a redeemed Africa, with her dotted cities, with her beautiful civilization, with her millions of happy children, going to and fro. Why should I lose hope, why should I give up and take a back place in this age of progress? Remember that you are men, that God created you Lords of this creation. Lift up yourselves, men, take yourselves out of the mire and hitch your hopes to the stars; yes, rise as high as the very stars themselves. Let no man pull you down, let no man destroy your ambition, because man is but your companion, your equal; man is your brother; he is not your lord; he is not your sovereign master.

We of the Universal Negro Improvement Association feel happy; we are cheerful. Let them connive to destroy us; let them organize to destroy us; we shall fight the more. Ask me personally the cause of my success, and I say opposition; oppose me, and I fight the more, and if you want to find out the sterling worth of the Negro, oppose him, and under the leadership of the Universal Negro Improvement Association he shall fight his way to victory, and in the days to come, and I believe not far distant, Africa shall reflect a splendid demonstration of the worth of the Negro, of the determination of the Negro, to set himself free and to establish a government of his own.

W. A. Domingo

Gift of the Black Tropics

Almost unobserved, America plays her usual role in the meeting, mixing and welding of the colored peoples of the earth. A dusky tribe of destiny seekers, these brown and black and yellow folk, eyes filled with visions of an alien heritage—palm-fringed seashores, murmuring streams, luxuriant hills and vales—have made an epical march from the far corners of the earth to the Port of New York and America. They bring the gift of the black tropics to America and to their kinsmen. With them come vestiges of a quaint folk life, other social traditions, and as for the first time in their lives, colored people of Spanish, French, Dutch, Arabian, Danish, Portuguese, British and native African ancestry meet and move together, there comes into Negro life the stir and leavening that is uniquely American. Despite his inconsiderable numbers, the black foreigner is a considerable factor and figure. It is not merely his picturesqueness that he brings, his lean, sun-burnt features, quaint manners and speech, his tropical incongruities, these as with all folkways rub off in less than a generation—it is his spirit that counts and has counted in the interplay of his life with the native population.

According to the census for 1920 there were in the United States 73,803 foreign-born Negroes; of that number 36,613, or approximately 50 per cent, lived in New York City, 28,184 of them in the Borough of Manhattan. They formed slightly less than 20 per cent of the total Negro population of New York.

Here they have their first contact with each other, with large numbers of American Negroes, and with the American brand of race prejudice. Divided by tradition, culture, historical background and group perspective, these diverse peoples are gradually hammered into a loose unit by the impersonal force of congested residential segregation. Unlike others of the foreign-born, black immigrants find it impossible to segregate themselves into colonies; too dark of complexion to pose as Cubans or some other Negroid but alien-tongued foreigners, they are inevitably swallowed up in black Harlem. Their

The New Negro, 1925.

situation requires an adjustment unlike that of any other class of the immigrant population; and but for the assistance of their kinsfolk they would be capsized almost on the very shores of their haven.

From 1920 to 1923 the foreign-born Negro population of the United States was increased nearly 40 per cent through the entry of 30,849 Africans (black). In 1921 the high-water mark of 9,873 was registered. This increase was not permanent, for in 1923 there was an exit of 1,525 against an entry of 7,554. If the 20 per cent that left that year is an index of the proportion leaving annually, it is safe to estimate a net increase of about 24,000 between 1920 and 1923. If the newcomers are distributed throughout the country in the same proportion as their predecessors, the present foreign-born Negro population of Harlem is about 35,000. These people are therefore a formidable minority whose presence cannot be ignored or discounted. It is this large body of foreign-born who contribute those qualities that make New York so unlike Pittsburgh, Washington, Chicago and other cities with large aggregations of American Negroes.

The largest number come from the British West Indies and are attracted to America mainly by economic reasons: though considerable numbers of the younger generation come for the purposes of education. The next largest group consists of Spanish-speaking Negroes from Latin America. Distinct because of their language, and sufficiently numerous to maintain themselves as a cultural unit, the Spanish element has but little contact with the English-speaking majority. For the most part they keep to themselves and follow in the main certain definite occupational lines. A smaller group, French-speaking, have emigrated from Haiti and the French West Indies. There are also a few Africans, a batch of voluntary pilgrims over the old track of the slave-traders.

Among the English-speaking West Indian population of Harlem are some 8,000 natives of the American Virgin Islands. A considerable part of these people were forced to migrate to the mainland as a consequence of the operation of the Volstead Act which destroyed the lucrative rum industry and helped to reduce the number of foreign vessels that used to call at the former free port of Charlotte Amalie for various stores. Despite their long Danish connection these people are culturally and linguistically English, rather than Danish. Unlike the British Negroes in New York, the Virgin Islanders take an intelligent and aggressive interest in the affairs of their former home, and are organized to co-operate with their brothers there who are valiantly struggling to substitute civil government for the present naval administration of the islands.

To the average American Negro, all English-speaking black foreigners are West Indians, and by that is usually meant British subjects. There is a general assumption that there is everything in common among West Indians, though nothing can be further from the truth. West Indians regard themselves as Antiguans or Jamaicans as the case might be, and a glance at the map will quickly reveal the physical obstacles that militate against homogeneity of population; separations of many sorts, geographical, political and cultural, tend everywhere to make and crystallize local characteristics.

This undiscriminating attitude on the part of native Negroes, as well as the friction generated from contact between the two groups, has created an artificial and defensive unity among the islanders which reveals itself in an instinctive closing of their ranks when attacked by outsiders; but among themselves organization along insular lines is the general rule. Their social grouping, however, does not follow insular precedents. Social gradation is determined in the islands by family connections, education, wealth and position. As each island is a complete society in itself, Negroes occupy from the lowliest to the most exalted positions. The barrier separating the colored aristocrat from the laboring class of the same color is as difficult to surmount as a similar barrier between Englishmen. Most of the islanders in New York are from the middle, artisan and laboring classes. Arriving in a country whose every influence is calculated to democratize their race and destroy the distinctions they had been accustomed to, even those West Indians whose stations in life have been of the lowest soon lose whatever servility they brought with them. In its place they substitute all of the self-assertiveness of the classes they formerly paid deference to.

West Indians have been coming to the United States for over a century. The part they have played in Negro progress is conceded to be important. As early as 1827 a Jamaican, John Brown Russwurm, one of the founders of Liberia, was the first colored man to be graduated from an American college and to publish a newspaper in this country; sixteen years later his fellow countryman, Peter Ogden, organized in New York City the first Odd-Fellows Lodge for Negroes. Prior to the Civil War, West Indian contribution to American Negro life was so great that Dr. W.E.B. Du Bois, in his *Souls of Black Folk,* credits them with main responsibility for the manhood program presented by the race in the early decades of the last century. Indicative of their tendency to blaze new paths is the achievement of John W. A. Shaw of Antigua who, in the early '90's of the last century, passed the civil service tests and became deputy commissioner of taxes for the County of Queens.

It is probably not realized, indeed, to what extent West Indian Negroes have contributed to the wealth, power and prestige of the United States. Major-General Goethals, chief engineer and builder of the Panama Canal, has testified in glowing language to the fact that when all other labor was tried and failed it was the black men of the Caribbean whose intelligence, skill, muscle and endurance made the union of the Pacific and the Atlantic a reality.

Coming to the United States from countries in which they had experienced no legalized social or occupational disabilities, West Indians very naturally have found it difficult to adapt themselves to the tasks that are, by custom, reserved for Negroes in the North. Skilled at various trades and having a contempt for body service and menial work, many of the immigrants apply for positions that the average American Negro has been schooled to regard as restricted to white men only, with the result that through their persistence and doggedness in fighting white labor, West Indians have in many cases been pioneers and shock troops to open a way for Negroes into new fields of employment.

This freedom from spiritual inertia characterizes the women no less than the men, for it is largely through them that the occupational field has been broadened for colored women in New York. By their determination, sometimes reinforced by a dexterous use of their hatpins, these women have made it possible for members of their race to enter the needle trades freely.

It is safe to say that West Indian representation in the skilled trades is relatively large; this is also true of the professions, especially medicine and dentistry. Like the Jew, they are forever launching out in business, and such retail businesses as are in the hands of Negroes in Harlem are largely in the control of the foreign-born. While American Negroes predominate in forms of business like barber shops and pool rooms in which there is no competition from white men, West Indians turn their efforts almost invariably to fields like grocery stores, tailor shops, jewelry stores and fruit vending in which they meet the fiercest kind of competition. In some of these fields they are the pioneers or the only surviving competitors of white business concerns. In more ambitious business enterprises like real estate and insurance they are relatively numerous. The only Casino and moving picture theatre operated by Negroes in Harlem is in the hands of a native of one of the small islands. On Seventh Avenue a West Indian woman conducts a millinery store that would be a credit to Fifth Avenue.

The analogy between the West Indian and the Jew may be carried farther; they are both ambitious, eager for education, willing to engage in business, argumentative, aggressive and possessed of great proselytizing zeal for any cause they espouse. West Indians are great contenders for their rights and because of their respect for law are inclined to be litigious. In addition, they are, as a whole, home-loving, hard-working and frugal. Like their English exemplars they are fond of sport, lack a sense of humor (yet the greatest black comedian of America, Bert Williams, was from the Bahamas) and are very serious and intense in their attitude toward life. They save their earnings and are mindful of their folk in the homeland, as the volume of business of the Money Order and Postal Savings Departments of College Station Post Office will attest.

Ten years ago it was possible to distinguish the West Indian in Harlem, especially during the summer months. Accustomed to wearing cool, light-colored garments in the tropics, he would stroll along Lenox Avenue on a hot day resplendent in white shoes and flannel pants, the butt of many a jest from his American brothers who, today, have adopted the styles that they formerly derided. This trait of non-conformity manifested by the foreign-born has irritated American Negroes, who resent the implied self-sufficiency, and as a result there is a considerable amount of prejudice against West Indians. It is claimed that they are proud and arrogant; that they think themselves superior to the natives. And although educated Negroes of New York are loudest in publicly decrying the hostility between the two groups, it is nevertheless true that feelings against West Indians are strongest among members of that class. This is explainable on the ground of professional jealousy and competition for leadership. As the islanders press forward and upward they meet the same kind of opposition from the native Negro that the Jew and other ambitious white aliens receive from white Americans. Naturalized West Indians have found from experience that American Negroes are reluctant to concede them the right to political leadership even when qualified intellectually. Unlike their American brothers, the islanders are free from those traditions that bind them to any party and, as a consequence, are independent to the point of being radical. Indeed, it is they who largely compose the few political and economic radicals in Harlem; without them the genuinely radical movement among New York Negroes would be unworthy of attention.

There is a diametrical difference between American and West Indian Negroes in their worship. While large sections of the former are inclined to indulge in displays of emotionalism that border on hysteria, the latter, in their Wesleyan Methodist and Baptist churches maintain in the face of the assumption that people from the tropics are necessarily emotional, all the punctilious emotional restraint characteristic of their English background. In religious radicalism the foreign-born are again pioneers and propagandists. The only modernist church among the thousands of Negroes in New York (and perhaps the country) is led by a West Indian, Rev. E. Ethelred Brown, an ordained Unitarian minister, and is largely supported by his fellow islanders.

In facing the problem of race prejudice, foreign-born Negroes, and West Indians in particular, are forced to undergo considerable adjustment. Forming a racial majority in their own countries and not being accustomed to discrimination expressly felt as racial, they rebel against the "color line" as they find it in America. For while color and caste lines tend to converge in the islands, it is nevertheless true that because of the ratio of population, historical background and traditions of rebellions before and since their emancipation, West Indians of color do not have their activities, social, occupational and otherwise, determined by their race. Color plays a part but it is not the prime determinant of advancement; hence, the deep feeling of resentment when the "color line," legal or customary, is met and found to be a barrier to individual progress. For this reason the West Indian has thrown himself wholeheartedly into the fight against lynching, discrimination and the other disabilities from which Negroes in America suffer.

It must be remembered that the foreign-born black men and women, more so even than other groups of immigrants, are the hardiest and most venturesome of their folk. They were dissatisfied at home, and it is to be expected that they would not be altogether satisfied with limitation of opportunity here when they have staked so much to gain enlargement of opportunity. They do not suffer from the local anesthesia of custom and pride which makes otherwise intolerable situations bearable for the home-staying majorities.

Just as the West Indian has been a sort of leaven in the American loaf, so the American Negro is beginning to play a reciprocal role in the life of the foreign Negro communities, as for instance the recent championing of the rights of Haiti and Liberia and the Virgin Islands, as well as the growing resentment at the treatment of natives in the African colonial dependencies. This world-wide reaction of the darker races to their common as well as local grievances is one of the most significant facts of recent development. Exchange of views and sympathy, extension and co-operation of race organizations beyond American boundaries, principally in terms of economic and educational projects, but also to a limited extent in political affairs, are bound to develop on a considerable scale in the near future. Formerly, ties have been almost solely through the medium of church missionary enterprises.

It has been asserted that the movement headed by the most advertised of all West Indians, Marcus Garvey, absentee "president" of the continent of Africa, represents the attempt of West Indian peasants to solve the American race problem. This is no more true than it would be to say that the editorial attitude of *The Crisis* during the war reflected the spirit of American Negroes respecting their grievances or that the late Booker T. Washington successfully delimited the educational aspirations of his people. The support given Garvey by a certain type of his countrymen is partly explained by their group reaction to attacks made upon him because of his nationality. On the other hand, the earliest and most persistent exposures of Garvey's multitudinous schemes were initiated by West Indians in New York like Cyril Briggs and the writer.

Prejudice against West Indians is in direct ratio to their number; hence its strength in New York where they are heavily concentrated. It is not unlike the hostility between Englishmen and Americans of the same racial stock. It is to be expected that the feeling will always be more or less present between the immigrant and the native born. However it does not extend to the children of the two groups, as they are subject to the same environment and develop identity of speech and psychology. Then, too, there has been an appreciable amount of intermarriage, especially between foreign-born men and native women. Not to be ignored is the fact that congestion in Harlem has forced both groups to be less discriminating in accepting lodgers, thus making for reconciling contacts.

The outstanding contribution of West Indians to American Negro life is the insistent assertion of their manhood in an environment that demands too much servility and unprotesting acquiescence from men of African blood. This unwillingness to conform and be standardized, to accept tamely an inferior status and abdicate their humanity, finds an open expression in the activities of the foreign-born Negro in America.

Their dominant characteristic is that of blazing new paths, breaking the bonds that would fetter the feet of a virile people—a spirit eloquently expressed in the defiant lines of the Jamaican poet, Claude McKay:

> Like men we'll face the murderous, cowardly pack,
> Pressed to the wall, dying, but fighting back.[1]

---

1. These lines come from "If We Must Die," which is included in the creative writing section of this anthology.

Rudolph Fisher

The Caucasian Storms Harlem

I

It might not have been such a jolt had my five years' absence from Harlem been spent otherwise. But the study of medicine includes no courses in cabareting; and, anyway, the Negro cabarets in Washington, where I studied, are all uncompromisingly black. Accordingly I was entirely unprepared for what I found when I returned to Harlem recently.

I remembered one place especially where my own crowd used to hold forth; and, hoping to find some old-timers there still, I sought it out one midnight. The old, familiar plunkety-plunk welcomed me from below as I entered. I descended the same old narrow stairs, came into the same smoke-misty basement, and found myself a chair at one of the ancient white-porcelain, mirror-smooth tables. I drew a deep breath and looked about, seeking familiar faces. "What a lot of 'fays!"[1] I thought, as I noticed the number of white guests. Presently I grew puzzled and began to stare, then I gaped—and gasped. I found myself wondering if this was the right place—if, indeed, this was Harlem at all. I suddenly became aware that, except for the waiters and members of the orchestra, I was the only Negro in the place.

After a while I left it and wandered about in a daze from night-club to night-club. I tried the Nest, Small's, Connie's Inn, the Capitol, Happy's, the Cotton Club. There was no mistake; my discovery was real and was repeatedly confirmed. No wonder my old crowd was not to be found in any of them. The best of Harlem's black cabarets have changed their names and turned white.

Such a discovery renders a moment's recollection irresistible. As irresistible as were the cabarets themselves to me seven or eight years ago. Just out of college in a town where cabarets were something only read about. A year of graduate work ahead. A Sum-

---

1. Short for "ofays," an insulting term for whites.

American Mercury, August 1927.

mer of rest at hand. Cabarets. Cabarets night after night, and one after another. There was no cover-charge then, and a fifteen-cent bottle of Whistle lasted an hour. It was just after the war—the heroes were home—cabarets were the thing.

How the Lybia prospered in those happy days! It was the gathering place of the swellest Harlem set: if you didn't go to the Lybia, why, my dear, you just didn't belong. The people you saw at church in the morning you met at the Lybia at night. What romance in those war-tinged days and nights! Officers from Camp Upton, with pretty maids from Brooklyn! Gay lieutenants, handsome captains—all whirling the lively onestep. Poor non-coms completely ignored; what sensible girl wanted a corporal or even a sergeant? That white, old-fashioned house, standing alone in 138th street, near the corner of Seventh avenue—doomed to be torn down a few months thence—how it shook with the dancing laughter of the dark merry crowds!

But the first place really popular with my friends was a Chinese restaurant in 136th street, which had been known as Hayne's Café and then became the Oriental. It occupied an entire house of three stories, and had carpeted floors and a quiet, superior air. There was excellent food and incredibly good tea and two unusual entertainers: a Cuban girl, who could so vary popular airs that they sounded like real music, and a slender little "brown" with a voice of silver and a way of singing a song that made you forget your food. One could dance in the Oriental if one liked, but one danced to a piano only, and wound one's way between linen-clad tables over velvety, noiseless floors.

Here we gathered: Fritz Pollard, All-American halfback, selling Negro stock to prosperous Negro physicians; Henry Creamer and Turner Layton, who had written "After You've Gone" and a dozen more songs, and were going to write *Strut, Miss Lizzie;* Paul Robeson, All-American end, on the point of tackling law, quite unaware that the stage would intervene; Preacher Harry Bragg, Harvard Jimmie MacLendon and half a dozen others.[2] Here at a little table, just inside the door, Bert Williams had supper every night,[3] and afterward sometimes joined us upstairs and sang songs with us and lampooned the Actors' Equity Association, which had barred him because of his color. Never did white guests come to the Oriental except as guests of Negroes. But the manager soon was stricken with a psychosis of some sort, became a black Jew, grew himself a bushy, square-cut beard, donned a skull-cap and abandoned the Oriental. And so we were robbed of our favorite resort, and thereafter became mere rounders.

II

Such places, those real Negro cabarets that we met in the course of our rounds! There was Edmonds' in Fifth avenue at 130th street. It was a sure-enough honky-tonk, occupying the cellar of a saloon. It was the social center of what was then, and still is, Negro

---

2. Pollard played for Brown University and later became the first black professional football player. Paul Robeson (1898–1976) eventually became a world renowned actor and singer.

3. Bert Williams (1874–1922) was a popular comedian and actor.

Harlem's kitchen. Here a tall brown-skin girl, unmistakably the one guaranteed in the song to make a preacher lay his Bible down, used to sing and dance her own peculiar numbers, vesting them with her own originality. She was known simply as Ethel, and was a genuine drawing-card. She knew her importance, too. Other girls wore themselves ragged trying to rise above the inattentive din of conversation, and soon, literally, yelled themselves hoarse; eventually they lost whatever music there was in their voices and acquired that familiar throaty roughness which is so frequent among blues singers, and which, though admired as characteristically African, is as a matter of fact nothing but a form of chronic laryngitis. Other girls did these things, but not Ethel. She took it easy. She would stride with great leisure and self-assurance to the center of the floor, stand there with a half-contemptuous nonchalance, and wait. All would become silent at once. Then she'd begin her song, genuine blues, which, for all their humorous lines, emanated tragedy and heartbreak:

> Woke up this mawnin'
> The day was dawnin'
> And I was sad and blue, so blue, Lord—
> Didn' have nobody
> To tell my troubles to—

It was Ethel who first made popular the song, "Tryin' to Teach My Good Man Right from Wrong," in the slow, meditative measures in which she complained:

> I'm gettin' sick and tired of my railroad man
> I'm gettin' sick and tired of my railroad man—
> Can't get him when I want him—
> I get him when I can.

It wasn't long before this song-bird escaped her dingy cage. Her name is a vaudeville attraction now, and she uses it all—Ethel Waters. Is there anyone who hasn't heard her sing "Shake That Thing!"?

A second place was Connor's in 135th street near Lenox avenue. It was livelier, less languidly sensuous, and easier to breathe in than Edmonds'. Like the latter, it was in a basement, reached by the typical narrow, headlong stairway. One of the girls there specialized in the Jelly-Roll song, and mad habitués used to fling petitions of greenbacks at her feet—pretty nimble feet they were too—when she sang that she loved 'em but she had to turn 'em down. Over in a corner a group of 'fays would huddle and grin and think they were having a wild time. Slumming. But they were still very few in those days.

And there was the Oriental, which borrowed the name that former Hayne's Café had abandoned. This was beyond Lenox avenue on the south side of 135th street. An upstairs place, it was nevertheless as dingy as any of the cellars, and the music fairly fought its way through the babble and smoke to one's ears, suffering in transit weird and incredible distortion. The prize pet here was a slim, little lad, unbelievably black beneath his high-brown powder, wearing a Mexican bandit costume with a bright-colored head-dress and sash. I see him now, poor kid, in all his glory, shimmying for enraptured women, who marveled at the perfect control of his voluntary abdominal tremors. He used to let the women reach out and put their hands on his sash to palpate those tremors—for a quarter.

Finally, there was the Garden of Joy, an open-air cabaret between 138th and 139th streets in Seventh avenue, occupying a plateau high above the sidewalk—a large, well-laid, smooth wooden floor with tables and chairs and a tinny orchestra, all covered by a propped-up roof, that resembled an enormous lampshade, directing bright light downward and outward. Not far away the Abyssinian Church used to hold its Summer camp-meetings in a great round circus-tent. Night after night there would arise the mingled strains of blues and spirituals, those peculiarly Negro forms of song, the one secular and the other religious, but both born of wretchedness in travail, both with their soarings of exultation and sinkings of despair. I used to wonder if God, hearing them both, found any real distinction.

There were the Lybia, then, and Hayne's, Connor's, the Oriental, Edmonds' and the Garden of Joy, each distinctive, standing for a type, some living up to their names, others living down to them, but all predominantly black. Regularly I made the rounds among these places and saw only incidental white people. I have seen them occasionally in numbers, but such parties were out on a lark. They weren't in their natural habitat and they often weren't any too comfortable.

But what of Barron's, you say? Certainly they were at home there. Yes, I know about Barron's. I have been turned away from Barron's because I was too dark to be welcome. I have been a member of a group that was told, "No more room," when we could see plenty of room. Negroes were never actually wanted in Barron's save to work. Dark skins were always discouraged or barred. In short, the fact about Barron's was this: it simply wasn't a Negro cabaret; it was a cabaret run by Negroes for whites. It wasn't even on the lists of those who lived in Harlem—they'd no more think of going there than of going to the Winter Garden Roof. But these other places were Negro through and through. Negroes supported them, not merely in now-and-then parties, but steadily, night after night.

III

Now, however, the situation is reversed. It is I who go occasionally and white people who go night after night. Time and again, since I've returned to live in Harlem, I've been one of a party of four Negroes who went to this or that Harlem cabaret, and on each occasion we've been the only Negro guests in the place. The managers don't hesitate to say that it is upon these predominant white patrons that they depend for success. These places therefore are no longer mine but theirs. Not that I'm barred, any more than they were seven or eight years ago. Once known, I'm even welcome, just as some of them used to be. But the complexion of the place is theirs, not mine. I? Why, I am actually stared at, I frequently feel uncomfortable and out of place, and when I go out on the floor to dance I am lost in a sea of white faces. As another observer has put it to me since, time was when white people went to Negro cabarets to see how Negroes acted; now Negroes go to these same cabarets to see how white people act. Negro clubs have recently taken to hiring a place outright for a presumably Negro party; and even then a goodly percentage of the invited guests are white.

One hurries to account for this change of complexion as a reaction to the Negro invasion of Broadway not long since. One remembers *Shuffle Along* of four years ago, the first Negro piece in the downtown district for many a moon. One says, "Oh yes, Negroes took their stuff to the whites and won attention and praise, and now the whites are seeking this stuff out on its native soil." Maybe. So I myself thought at first. But one looks for something of oppositeness in a genuine reaction. One would rather expect the reaction to the Negro invasion of Broadway to be apathy. One would expect that the same thing repeated under different names or in imitative fragments would meet with colder and colder reception, and finally with none at all.

A little recollection will show that just what one would expect was what happened. Remember *Shuffle Along*'s successors: *Put and Take, Liza, Strut Miss Lizzie, Runnin' Wild*, and the others? True, none was so good as *Shuffle Along*, but surely they didn't deserve all the roasting they got. *Liza* flared but briefly, during a holiday season. *Put and Take* was a loss, *Strut Miss Lizzie* strutted about two weeks, and the humor of *Runnin' Wild* was derided as Neo-Pleistocene. Here was reaction for you—wholesale withdrawal of favor. One can hardly conclude that such withdrawal culminated in the present swamping of Negro cabarets. People so sick of a thing would hardly go out of their way to find it.

And they *are* sick of it—in quantity at least. Only one Negro entertainment has survived this reaction of apathy in any permanent fashion. This is the series of revues built around the personality of Florence Mills.[4] Without that bright live personality the Broadway district would have been swept clean last season of all-Negro bills. Here is a girl who has triumphed over a hundred obstacles. Month after month she played obscure, unnoticed roles with obscure, unknown dark companies. She was playing such a minor part in *Shuffle Along* when the departure of Gertrude Saunders, the craziest blues-singer on earth, unexpectedly gave her the spotlight. Florence Mills cleaned up. She cleaned up so thoroughly that the same public which grew weary of *Shuffle Along* and sick of its successors still had an eager ear for her. They have yet, and she neither wearies nor disappoints them. An impatient Broadway audience awaits her return from Paris, where she and the inimitable Josephine Baker have been vying with each other as sensations.[5] She is now in London on the way home but London won't release her; the enthusiasm over her exceeds anything in the memory of the oldest reviewers.

Florence Mills, moreover, is admired by her own people too, because, far from going to her head, her success has not made her forgetful. Not long ago, the rumor goes, she made a fabulous amount of money in the Florida real-estate boom, and what do you suppose she plans to do with it? Build herself an Italian Villa somewhere up the Hud-

---

4. Florence Mills (1895–1927) was a popular singer and dancer.

5. Josephine Baker (1906–1975) was a well-known dancer, singer, and civil rights activist who left America in the 1920s and became a star in Paris.

son? Not at all. She plans to build a first-rate Negro theatre in Harlem.

But that's Florence Mills. Others have encountered indifference. In vain has Eddie Hunter, for instance, tried for a first-class Broadway showing, despite the fact that he himself has a new kind of Negro-comedian character to portray—the wise darkey, the "bizthniss man," the "fly" rascal who gets away with murder, a character who amuses by making a goat of others instead of making a goat of himself. They say that some dozen Negro shows have met with similar denials. Yet the same people, presumably, whose spokesmen render these decisions flood Harlem night after night and literally crowd me off the dancing-floor. If this is a reaction, it is a reaction to a reaction, a swinging back of the pendulum from apathy toward interest. Maybe so. The cabarets may present only those special Negro features which have a particular and peculiar appeal, leaving out the high-yaller display that is merely feebly imitative. But a reaction to a reaction—that's differential calculus.

Vivian Schuyler, "The Library Hour," *The Crisis,* February 1928

Elise Johnson McDougald

The Task of Negro Womanhood

Throughout the years of history, woman has been the weather-vane, the indicator, show-ing in which direction the wind of destiny blows. Her status and development have augured now calm and stability, now swift currents of progress. What then is to be said of the Negro woman of today, whose problems are of such import to her race?

A study of her contributions to any one community, throughout America, would illu-minate the pathway being trod by her people. There is, however, an advantage in focus-ing upon the women of Harlem—modern city in the world's metropolis. Here, more than anywhere else, the Negro woman is free from the cruder handicaps of primitive house-hold hardships and the grosser forms of sex and race subjugation. Here, she has con-siderable opportunity to measure her powers in the intellectual and industrial fields of the great city. The questions naturally arise: "What are her difficulties?" and, "How is she solving them?"

To answer these questions, one must have in mind not any one Negro woman, but rather a colorful pageant of individuals, each differently endowed. Like the red and yel-low of the tiger-lily, the skin of one is brilliant against the star-lit darkness of a racial sister. From grace to strength, they vary in infinite degree, with traces of the race's his-tory left in physical and mental outline on each. With a discerning mind, one catches the multiform charm, beauty and character of Negro women, and grasps the fact that their problems cannot be thought of in mass.

Because only a few have caught this vision, even in New York, the general attitude of mind causes the Negro woman serious difficulty. She is conscious that what is left of chivalry is not directed toward her. She realizes that the ideals of beauty, built up in the fine arts, have excluded her almost entirely. Instead, the grotesque Aunt Jemimas of the street-car advertisements proclaim only an ability to serve, without grace or loveli-ness. Nor does the drama catch her finest spirit. She is most often used to provoke the

The New Negro, 1925.

mirthless laugh of ridicule; or to portray feminine viciousness or vulgarity not peculiar to Negroes. This is the shadow over her. To a race naturally sunny comes the twilight of self-doubt and a sense of personal inferiority. It cannot be denied that these are potent and detrimental influences, though not generally recognized because they are in the realm of the mental and spiritual. More apparent are the economic handicaps which follow her recent entrance into industry. It is conceded that she has special difficulties because of the poor working conditions and low wages of her men. It is not surprising that only the most determined women forge ahead to results other than mere survival. To the gifted, the zest of meeting a challenge is a compensating factor which often brings success. The few who do prove their mettle stimulate one to a closer study of how this achievement is won under contemporary conditions.

Better to visualize the Negro woman at her job, our vision of a host of individuals must once more resolve itself into groups on the basis of activity. First, comes a very small leisure group—the wives and daughters of men who are in business, in the professions and a few well-paid personal service occupations. Second, a most active and progressive group, the women in business and the professions. Third, the many women in the trades and industry. Fourth, a group weighty in numbers struggling on in domestic service, with an even less fortunate fringe of casual workers, fluctuating with the economic temper of the times.

The first is a pleasing group to see. It is picked for outward beauty by Negro men with much the same feeling as other Americans of the same economic class. Keeping their women free to preside over the family, these women are affected by the problems of every wife and mother, but touched only faintly by their race's hardships. They do share acutely in the prevailing difficulty of finding competent household help. Negro wives find Negro maids unwilling generally to work in their own neighborhoods, for various reasons. They do not wish to work where there is a possibility of acquaintances coming into contact with them while they serve and they still harbor the misconception that Negroes of any station are unable to pay as much as persons of the other race. It is in these homes of comparative ease that we find the polite activities of social exclusiveness. The luxuries of well-appointed homes, modest motors, tennis, golf and country clubs, trips to Europe and California, make for social standing. The problem confronting the refined Negro family is to know others of the same achievement. The search for kindred spirits gradually grows less difficult; in the past it led to the custom of visiting all the large cities in order to know similar groups of cultured Negro people. In recent years, the more serious minded Negro woman's visit to Europe has been extended from months to years for the purpose of study and travel. The European success which meets this type of ambition is instanced in the conferring of the doctorate in philosophy upon a Negro woman, Dr. Anna J. Cooper,[1] at the last commencement of the Sorbonne, Paris. Similarly, a score of Negro

---

1. Anna Julia Cooper, one of the first African Americans to receive a Ph.D., was committed to education for African Americans and women in particular. She is the author of *A Voice from the South by a Black Woman* (1892).

women are sojourning abroad in various countries for the spiritual relief and cultural stimulation afforded there.

A spirit of stress and struggles characterizes the second two groups. These women of business, profession and trade are the hub of the wheel of progress. Their burden is twofold. Many are wives and mothers whose husbands are insufficiently paid, or who have succumbed to social maladjustment and have abandoned their families. An appalling number are widows. They face the great problem of leaving home each day and at the same time trying to rear children in their spare time—this, too, in neighborhoods where rents are large, standards of dress and recreation high and costly, and social danger on the increase. One cannot resist the temptation to pause for a moment and pay tribute to these Negro mothers. And to call attention to the service she is rendering to the nation, in her struggle against great odds to educate and care for one group of the country's children. If the mothers of the race should ever be honored by state or federal legislation, the artist's imagination will find a more inspiring subject in the modern Negro mother—self-directed but as loyal and tender as the much extolled, yet pitiable black mammy of slavery days.

The great commercial life of New York City is only slightly touched by the Negro woman of our second group. Negro businessmen offer her most of their work, but their number is limited. Outside of this field in Negro offices, custom is once more against her, and competition is keen for all. However, Negro girls are training and some are holding exceptional jobs. One of the professors in a New York college has had a young colored woman as a secretary for the past three or four years. Another holds the head clerical position in an organization where reliable handling of detail and a sense of business ethics are essential. Quietly these women prove their worth, so that when a vacancy exists and there is a call, it is difficult to find even one competent colored secretary who is not employed. As a result of the opportunity in clerical work in the educational system of New York City, a number have qualified for such positions, one having been recently appointed to the office of a high school. In other departments, the civil service in New York City is no longer free from discrimination. The casual personal interview, that tenacious and retrogressive practice introduced into the federal administration during the World War, has spread and often nullifies the Negro woman's success in written tests. The successful young woman cited above was three times "turned down" as undesirable on the basis of the personal interview. In the great mercantile houses, the many young Negro girls who might be well suited to sales positions are barred from all but menial positions. Even so, one Negro woman, beginning as a uniformed maid in the shoe department of one of the largest stores, has pulled herself up to the position of "head of stock." One of the most prosperous monthly magazines of national circulation has for the head of its news service a Negro woman who rose from the position of stenographer. Her duties involve attendance upon staff conferences, executive supervision of her staff of white office workers, broadcasting and journalism of the highest order.

Yet in spite of the claims of justice and proved efficiency, telephone and insurance companies and other corporations which receive considerable patronage from Negroes deny them proportionate employment. Fortunately this is an era of changing customs. There is hope that a less selfish racial attitude will prevail. It is a heartening fact that there is an increasing number of Americans who will lend a hand in the game fight of the worthy.

Throughout the South, where businesses for Negro patronage are under the control of Negroes to a large extent, there are already many opportunities for Negro women. But, because of the nerve strain and spiritual drain of hostile social conditions in that section, Negro women are turning away from opportunities there to find a freer and fuller life in the North.

In the less crowded professional vocations, the outlook is more cheerful. In these fields, the Negro woman is dependent largely upon herself and her own race for work. In the legal, dental and medical professions, successful women practitioners have usually worked their way through college and are "managing" on the small fees that can be received from an under-paid public.

Social conditions in America are hardest upon the Negro because he is lowest in the economic scale. The tendency to force the Negro downward, gives rise to serious social problems and to a consequent demand for trained college women in the profession of social work. The need has been met with a response from young college women, anxious to devote their education and lives toward helping the submerged classes. Much of the social work has been pioneer in nature; the pay has been small, with little possibility of advancement. For, even in work among Negroes, the better paying positions are reserved for whites. The Negro college woman is doing her bit at a sacrifice, along such lines as these: as probation officers, investigators and police women in the correctional departments of the city; as Big Sisters attached to the Children's Court; as field workers and visitors for relief organizations, missions and churches; as secretaries for traveller's aid societies; in the many organizations devoted to preventative and educational medicine; in clinics and hospitals and as boys' and girls' welfare workers in recreation and industry.

In the profession of nursing, there are over three hundred in New York City. In the dark blue linen uniform of Henry Street Visiting Nurse Service, the Negro woman can be seen hurrying earnestly from house to house on her round of free relief to the needy. Again, she is in many other branches of public health nursing, in the public schools, milk stations and diet kitchens. The Negro woman is in the wards of two of the large city hospitals and clinics. After a score of years of service in one such institution, a Negro woman became superintendent of nurses in the war emergency. Deposed after the armistice, though eminently satisfactory, she retained connection with the training school as lecturer, for the inspiration she could be to "her girls." The growing need for the executive nurse is being successfully met, as instanced by the supervisors in day nurseries and private sanitariums, financed and operated in Harlem entirely by Negroes. Throughout the South there is a clear and anxious call to nurses to carry the gospel of hygiene to the rural sections and to minister to the suffering not reached by organizations already in the communities. One social worker, in New York City, though a teacher by profession, is head of an organization whose program is to raise money for the payment of nurses to do the work described above. In other centers, West and South, the professional Negro nurse is supplanting the untrained woman attendant of former years.

In New York City, nearly three hundred women share in the good conditions obtaining there in the teaching profession. They measure up to the high pedagogical requirements of the city and state law, and are increasingly leaders in the community. In a city where the schools are not segregated, she is meeting with success among white as well as colored children in positions ranging from clerk in the elementary school on up through the graded ranks of teachers in the lower grades, of special subjects in the higher grades, in the junior high schools and in the senior high schools. One Negro woman is assistant principal in an elementary school where the other assistant and the principal are white men and the majority of the teachers white. Another Negro woman serves in the capacity of visiting teacher to several schools, calling upon both white and colored families and experiencing no difficulty in making social adjustments. Still another Negro woman is a vocational counsellor under the Board of Education, in a junior high school. She is advising children of both races as to future courses of study to pursue and as to the vocations in which tests prove them to be apt. This position, the result of pioneer work by another Negro woman, is unique in the school system of New York.

With all these forces at work, true sex equality has not been approximated. The ratio of opportunity in the sex, social, economic and political spheres is about that which exists between white men and women. In the large, I would say that the Negro woman is the cultural equal of her man because she is generally kept in school longer. Negro boys, like white boys, are usually put to work to subsidize the family income. The growing economic independence of Negro working women is causing her to rebel against the domineering family attitude of the cruder working-class husband. The masses of Negro men are engaged in menial occupations throughout the working day. Their baffled and suppressed desires to determine their economic life are manifested in overbearing domination at home. Working mothers are unable to instill different ideals in the sons. Conditions change slowly. Nevertheless, education and opportunity are modifying the spirit of the younger Negro men. Trained in modern schools of thought, they begin to show a wholesome attitude of fellowship and freedom for their women. The challenge to young Negro womanhood is to see clearly this trend and grasp the proffered comradeship with sincerity. In this matter of sex equality, Negro women have contributed few outstanding militants, a notable instance being the historic Sojourner Truth. On the whole the Negro woman's feminist efforts are directed chiefly toward the realization of the equality of the races, the sex struggle assuming the subordinate place.

Obsessed with difficulties which might well compel individualism, the Negro woman has engaged in a considerable amount of organized action to meet group needs. She has evolved a federation of her clubs, embracing between eight and ten thousand women in New York state alone. The state federation is a part of the National Association of Colored Women, which, calling together the women from all parts of the country, engages itself in enterprises of general race interest. The national organization of colored women is now firmly established, and under the presidency of Mrs. [Mary McLeod] Bethune is about to strive for conspicuous goals.

In New York City, many associations exist for social betterment, financed and operated by Negro women. One makes child welfare its name and special concern. Others, like the Utility Club, Utopia Neighborhood, Debutantes' League, Semper Fidelis, etc., raise funds for old folks' homes, a shelter for delinquent girls and fresh-air camps for children. The Colored Women's Branch of the Y.W.C.A. and the women's organizations in the many churches as well as the beneficial lodges and associations, care for the needs of their members.

On the other hand, the educational welfare of the coming generation has become the chief concern of the national sororities of Negro college women. The first to be organized in the country, the *Alpha Kappa Alpha,* has a systematized, continuous program of educational and vocational guidance for students of the high schools and colleges. The work of Lambda Chapter, which covers New York City and its suburbs, has been most effective in carrying out the national program. Each year, it gathers together between one and two hundred such students and gives the girls a chance to hear the life stories of Negro women, successful in various fields of endeavor. Recently a trained nurse told how, starting in the same schools as they, she had risen to the executive position in the Harlem Health Information Bureau. A commercial artist showed how real talent had overcome the color line. The graduate physician was a living example of the modern opportunities in the newer fields of medicine open to women. The vocations, as outlets for the creative instinct, became attractive under the persuasion of the musician, the dressmaker and the decorator. A recent graduate outlined her plans for meeting the many difficulties encountered in establishing a dental office and in building up a practice. A journalist spun the fascinating tale of her years of experience. The *Delta Sigma Theta* Sorority (national in scope) works along similar lines. Alpha Beta Chapter of New York City, during the current year, presented a young art student with a scholarship of $1,000 for study abroad. In such ways as these are the progressive and privileged groups of Negro women expressing their community and race consciousness.

We find the Negro woman, figuratively struck in the face daily by contempt from the world about her. Within her soul, she knows little of peace and happiness. But through it all, she is courageously standing erect, developing within herself the moral strength to rise above and conquer false attitudes. She is maintaining her natural beauty and charm and improving her mind and opportunity. She is measuring up to the needs of her family, community and race, and radiating a hope throughout the land.

The wind of the race's destiny stirs more briskly because of her striving.

Marita O. Bonner

On Being Young—a Woman—and Colored

You start out after you have gone from kindergarten to sheepskin covered with sundry Latin phrases.

At least you know what you want life to give you. A career as fixed and as calmly brilliant as the North Star. The one real thing that money buys. Time. Time to do things. A house that can be delectably out of order and as easily put in order as the doll-house of "playing-house" days. And of course, a husband you can look up to without looking down on yourself.

Somehow you feel like a kitten in a sunny catnip field that sees sleek, plump brown field mice and yellow baby chicks sitting coyly, side by side, under each leaf. A desire to dash three or four ways seizes you.

That's Youth.

But you know that things learned need testing—acid testing—to see if they are really, after all, an interwoven part of you. All your life you have heard of the debt you owe "Your People" because you have managed to have the things they have not largely had.

So you find a spot where there are hordes of them—of course below the Line[1]—to be your catnip field while you close your eyes to mice and chickens alike.

If you have never lived among your own, you feel prodigal. Some warm untouched current flows through them—through you—and drags you out into the deep waters of a new sea of human foibles and mannerisms; of a peculiar psychology and prejudices. And one day you find yourself entangled—enmeshed—pinioned in the seaweed of a Black Ghetto.

Not a Ghetto, placid like the Strasse that flows, outwardly unperturbed and calm in a stream of religious belief, but a peculiar group. Cut off, flung together, shoved aside in a bundle because of color with no more in common.

---

1. This is a reference to the Mason-Dixon line, which divided slave states from free states.

The Crisis, December 1925.

Unless color is, after all, the real bond.

Milling around like live fish in a basket. Those at the bottom crushed into a sort of stupid apathy by the weight of those on top. Those on top leaping, leaping; leaping to scale the sides; to get out.

There are two "colored" movies, innumerable parties—and cards. Cards played so intensely that it fascinates and repulses at once.

Movies.

Movies worthy and worthless—but not even a low-caste spoken stage.

Parties, plentiful. Music and dancing and much that is wit and color and gaiety. But they are like the richest chocolate; stuffed costly chocolates that make the taste go stale if you have too many of them. That make plain whole bread taste like ashes.

There are all the earmarks of a group within a group. Cut off all around from ingress or egress to other groups. A sameness of type. The smug self-satisfaction of an inner measurement; a measurement by standards known within a limited group and not those of an unlimited, seeing, world. . . . Like the blind, blind mice. Mice whose eyes have been blinded.

Strange longing seizes hold of you. You wish yourself back where you can lay your dollar down and sit in a dollar seat to hear voices, strings, reeds that have lifted the World out, up, and beyond things that have bodies and walls. Where you can marvel at new marbles and bronzes and flat colors that will make men forget that things exist in a flesh more often than in spirit. Where you can sink your body in a cushioned seat and sink your soul at the same time into a section of life set before you on the boards for a few hours.

You hear that up at New York this is to be seen; that, to be heard.

You decide the next train will take you there.

You decide the next second that that train will not take you, nor the next—nor the next for some time to come.

For you know that—being a woman—you cannot twice a month or twice a year, for that matter, break away to see or hear anything in a city that is supposed to see and hear too much.

That's being a woman. A woman of any color.

You decide that something is wrong with a world that stifles and chokes; that cuts off and stunts; hedging in, pressing down on eyes, ears and throat. Somehow all wrong.

You wonder how it happens here that—say five hundred miles from the Bay State—Anglo-Saxon intelligence is so warped and stunted.

How judgment and discernment are bred out of the race. And what has become of discrimination? Discrimination of the right sort. Discrimination that the best minds have told you weighs shadows and nuances and spiritual differences before it catalogues. The kind they have taught you all your life was best: that looks clearly past generalization and past appearance to dissect, to dig down to the real heart of matters. That casts aside rapid summary conclusions, drawn from primary inference, as Daniel did the spiced meats.

Why can't they then perceive that there is a difference in the glance from a pair of eyes that look, mildly docile, at "white ladies" and those that, impersonally and perceptively—aware of distinctions—see only women who happen to be white?

Why do they see a colored woman only as a gross collection of desires, all uncontrolled, reaching out for their Apollos and the Quasimodos with avid indiscrimination?

Why, unless you talk in staccato squawks—brittle as sea-shells—unless you "champ" gum, unless you cover two yards square when you laugh, unless your taste runs to violent colors—impossible perfumes and more impossible clothes—are you a feminine Caliban craving to pass for Ariel?

An empty imitation of an empty invitation. A mime; a sham; a copy-cat. A hollow re-echo. A froth, a foam. A fleck of the ashes of superficiality?

Everything you touch or taste now is like the flesh of an unripe persimmon. . . . Do you need to be told what that is being . . . ?

Old ideas, old fundamentals seem worm-eaten, out-grown, worthless, bitter, fit for the scrap-heap of Wisdom.

What you had thought tangible and practical has turned out to be a collection of "blue-flower" theories.

If they have not discovered how to use their accumulation of facts, they are useless to you in Their world.

Every part of you becomes bitter.

But—"In Heaven's name, do not grow bitter. Be bigger than they are,"—exhort white friends who have never had to draw breath in a Jim-Crow train. Who have never had petty putrid insults dragged over them—drawing blood—like pebbled sand on your body where the skin is tenderest. On your body where the skin is thinnest and tenderest.

You long to explode and hurt everything white: friendly; unfriendly. But you know that you cannot live with a chip on your shoulder even if you can manage a smile around your eyes—without getting steely and brittle and losing the softness that makes you a woman.

For chips make you bend your body to balance them. And once you bend, you lose your poise, your balance, and the chip gets into you. The real you. You get hard.

. . . And many things in you can ossify . . .

And you know, being a woman, you have to go about it gently and quietly, to find out and discover just what is wrong. Just what can be done.

You see clearly that they have acquired things.

Money; money. Money to build with, money to destroy. Money to swim in. Money to drown in. Money.

An ascendancy of wisdom. An incalculable hoard of wisdom in all fields, in all things collected from all quarters of humanity.

A stupendous mass of things.

Things.

So, too, the Greeks . . . Things.

And the Romans. . . .

And you wonder and wonder why they have not discovered how to handle deftly and skillfully, Wisdom, stored up for them—like the honey for the Gods on Olympus—since time unknown.

You wonder and you wonder until you wander out into Infinity, where if it is to be found anywhere—Truth really exists.

The Greeks had possessions, culture. They were lost because they did not understand.

The Romans owned more than anyone else. Trampled under the heel of Vandals and Civilization, because they would not understand.

Greeks. Did not understand.

Romans. Would not understand.

"They." Will not understand.

So, you find, they have shut Wisdom up and have forgotten to find the key that will let her out. They have trapped, trammeled, lashed her to themselves with thews and thongs and theories. They have ransacked sea and earth and air to bring every treasure to her. But she sulks and will not work for a world with a whitish hue because it has snubbed her twin sister, Understanding.

You see clearly—off there is Infinity—Understanding. Standing alone, waiting for someone to really want her.

But she is so far out there is no way to snatch at her and drag her in.

So—being a woman—you can wait.

You must sit quietly without a chip. Not sodden—and weighted as if your feet were cast in the iron of your soul. Not wasting strength in enervating gestures as if two hundred years of bonds and whips had really tricked you into nervous uncertainty.

But quiet; quiet. Like Buddha—who, brown like I am—sat entirely at ease, entirely sure of himself; motionless and knowing, a thousand years before the white man knew there was so very much difference between feet and hands.

Motionless on the outside. But inside?

Silent.

Still . . . "Perhaps Buddha is a woman."

So you too. Still; quiet; with a smile, ever so slight, at the eyes so that Life will flow into and not by you. And you can gather, as it passes, the essences, the overtones, the tints, the shadows; draw understanding into your self.

And then you can, when Time is ripe, swoop to your feet—at your full height—at a single gesture.

Ready to go where?

Why . . . Wherever God motions.

Alice Dunbar-Nelson

Woman's Most Serious Problem

E. B. Reuter, in his latest book, *The American Race Problem,* makes this comment, "During the past decade there has been a somewhat marked improvement in the economic conditions of the Negroes. This is reflected in the decline of the number of women employed, and in the shift in numbers in different occupations." This statement is followed by a table showing the shift in occupational employment.

From one elevator operator in 1910, the number jumped to 3,073 in 1920. Those engaged in lumber and furniture industries in 1910 were 1,456. In 1920, 4,066. Textile industries jumped from 2,234 to 7,257. On the other hand, chambermaids in 1910 were numbered 14,071, but in 1920 they had declined to 10,443. Untrained nurses from 17,874 to 13,888; cooks from 205,584 to 168,710; laundresses, not in public laundries, from 361,551 to 283,557. On the other hand, cigar and tobacco workers jumped from 10,746 to 21,829, and the teaching profession showed a normal increase from 22,528 to 29,244.

Just what do these figures indicate? That the Negro woman is leaving the industries of home life, cooking, domestic service generally, child nursing, laundry work and going into mills, factories, operation of elevators, clerking, stenography (for in these latter occupations there is an almost 400 percent increase). She is doing a higher grade of work, getting better money, commanding better respect from the community because of her higher economic value, and less menial occupation. Domestic service claims her race no longer as its inalienable right. She is earning a salary, not wages.

This sounds fine. For sixty-three years the Negro woman has been a co-worker with the Negro man. Now that she is more than ever working by his side, she feels a thrill of pride in her new economic status.

But—"the ratio of children to women has declined from census to census for both races. The decline has in general been more rapid for the Negro than for the white elements in the population." In 1850 the number of children under five years of age per 1,000

The Messenger, March 1927.

women from 15 to 44 years of age for Negro women was 741, for white women, 659. In 1920 the Negro birth rate had decreased to 439, the white to 471. While the percentage of children under five years of age had decreased in the case of Negro women from 13.8 in Negro families to 10.9, and in white families from 11.9 to 10.9!

"In spite of the considerable increase in the Negro population and in the increase of the marriage rate, the actual number of Negro children under five years of age was less in 1920 than at any of the previous enumerations." In 1900 the number of Negro children under five years of age was 1,215,655; in 1910, the number was 1,263,288; in 1920 it was 1,143,699!

And this sharp decline in the face of increased knowledge of the care and feeding of infants; the work of the insurance companies in health, Negro Health Week, public health nurses, clinics, dispensaries, and all the active agencies for the conservation and preservation of health.

One startling fact is apparent. Negro women are exercising birth control in order to preserve their new economic independence. Or, because of poverty of the family, they are compelled to limit their offspring.

The same author, Dr. Reuter, tells us that a recent study showed that fifty-five Negro professors at Howard University had come from families averaging 6.5 children, while the professors themselves had an average of 0.7 children. Some were unmarried, but for each family formed, the average number of children was 1.6. "The birth rate of the cultured classes is apparently only one-third of the masses."

The race is here faced with a startling fact. Our birth rate is declining; our infant mortality is increasing; our normal rate of increase must necessarily be slowing up; our educated and intelligent classes are refusing to have children; our women are going into the kind of work that taxes both physical and mental capacities, which of itself, limits fecundity. While white women are beginning to work more away from home, at present, even with the rush of all women into the wage earner's class, in New York City alone, seven times as many colored as white women work away from home.

The inevitable disruption of family life necessitated by the woman being a co-wage earner with the man has discouraged the Negro woman from child-bearing. Juvenile delinquents are recruited largely from the motherless home. That is the home that is without the constant care of the mother or head of the house. For a child to arise in the morning after both parents are gone, get itself an indifferent breakfast, go to school uncared for, lunch on a penny's worth of sweets, and return to a cold and cheerless house or apartment to await the return of a jaded and fatigued mother to get supper, is not conducive to sweetness and light in its behavior. Truancy, street walking, petty thievery and gang rowdyism are the natural results of this lack of family life. The Negro woman is awakening to the fact that the contribution she makes to the economic life of the race is too often made at the expense of the lives of the boys and girls of the race—so she is refusing to bring into the world any more potential delinquents.

This is the bald and ungarnished statement of a startling series of facts. The decline in the birth rate of the Negro. The rise in the economic life of the Negro woman. The sharpest peak of the decline—if a decline can be said to have a peak—is in the birth rate of the more cultured and more nearly leisure classes. The slow increase in the national family life, caused by the women workers not having time to make homes in the strictest sense of homemaking. The sharp rise in juvenile delinquency—in the cities, of course, and among the children of women workers. And worst of all, because more subtle and insinuating in its flattering connotation of economic freedom, handsome salaries and social prestige—the growing use of married women of the child-bearing age as public school teachers, with the consequent temptation to refrain from child-bearing in order not to interfere with the independent life in the school room.

This is the situation. I would not suggest any remedy, make any criticism, raise any question, nor berate the men and women who are responsible for this crisis. For it is a serious crisis. I would only ask the young and intelligent women to give pause.

The new Negro is the topic most dwelt upon these days by the young folks, whom some call, frequently in derisive envy, the "Intelligentsia." In every race, in every nation and in every clime in every period of history there is always an eager-eyed group of youthful patriots who seriously set themselves to right the wrongs done to their race, or nation or sect or sometimes to art or self-expression. No race or nation can advance without them. Thomas Jefferson was an ardent leader of youthful patriots of his day, and Alexander Hamilton would have been dubbed a leader of the intelligentsia were he living now. They do big things, these young people.

Perhaps they may turn their attention, these race-loving slips of girls and slim ardent youths who make hot-eyed speeches about the freedom of the individual and the rights of the Negro, to the fact that at the rate we are going the Negro will become more and more negligible in the life of the nation. For we must remember that while the Negro constituted 19.3 percent of the population in 1790, and 18.9 in 1800, he constitutes only 9.9 percent today, and his percentage of increase has steadily dropped from 37.5 in 1810 to 6.3 in 1920.

No race can rise higher than its women is an aphorism that is so trite that it has ceased to be tiresome from its very monotony. If it might be phrased otherwise to catch the attention of the Negro woman, it would be worth while making the effort. No race can be said to be a growing race, whose birth rate is declining, and whose natural rate of increase is dropping sharply. No race will amount to anything economically, no matter how high the wages it collects nor how many commercial enterprises it supports, whose ownership of homes has not kept proportionate pace with its business holdings. Churches, social agencies, schools and Sunday schools cannot do the work of mothers and heads of families. Their best efforts are as cheering and comforting to the soul of a child in comparison with the welcoming smile of the mother when it comes from school as the machine-like warmth of an incubator is to the chick after the downy comfort of a clucking hen. Incubators are an essential for the mass production of chickens, but the training of human souls needs to begin at home in the old-fashioned family life, augmented later, if necessary, in the expensive schools and settlements of the great cities.

Marion Vera Cuthbert

Problems Facing Negro Young Women

A brown girl sits in the closely packed employment office waiting room. Every piece of her cheap clothing has been put on with care, and the perk of the little green hat is a brave defiance. But despair is in the dark eyes, a little too deeply sunk, and ever so often the set smile must be fastened again upon her lips. No job today. So back to the sister-in-law's again, and taking from the children the little they all have from relief.

———

It is ten o'clock at night. Perhaps by hurrying the tired dark woman bending over the sink of dishes can have them all washed and the kitchen put to rights by ten-thirty. Then the trolley ride home across town. A tub of things to be washed for the children. That will be twelve-thirty. One. Then up again in time to be back on the job at seven. Three dollars and fifty cents a week!

———

A woman stands in the doorway of a shack. Almost up to the very door come the stripped cotton plants. Bare. That is the word for the autumn world without, and the bleak world of her thoughts. The cotton gathered, but no profit to her and hers. Children nearly naked. Almost no food, and what there is [is] part of the burden of debt. This hovel of a home. And the threats of the boss that even this will be taken from them if there is any more talk of "rights." Rights of croppers, indeed!

———

In her smart little bungalow a busy young housewife hurries to get lunch ready before the children storm in from school. It is a good thing that her hands know their tasks so well, for all morning the riveting of the same thought has hammered in her head. What

Opportunity, February 1936.

if he *did* lose his job! Mail carriers' jobs have always been ones to count on. Uncle Sam! Are Negro men to be driven from these, too? What if he *did* lose his job!

———

Because she always ran down the school steps the trim little teacher does so now, but she is really tired this afternoon. Nearly six, and just getting away from the building. Records must be kept, and now with unemployment, undernourished children, and private and public agencies to work with on it all, what a welter of detail, and checking and re-checking. Well, tonight is the bridge party, and she can forget about it all. But can she, and the other young women of her club, they of the good jobs and the good clothes? Is not part of the time at almost every club meeting now taken up with talking about *conditions?*

———

The committee meeting breaks up and the social workers hasten back to offices scattered all over the city. Some important little victories have been won today, and of them none more important than the opening up of the new work to Negro people. The young woman who has made the fight returns to her own office. She closes the door behind her and drops a weary head upon her arms. Exultation slips away and she is just a tired woman knowing that this is gain, yes, but so small, so small. For tomorrow, and all tomorrows, it must be fight, fight, fight.

———

There is no possibility of picturing even so sketchily as is here done the army of Negro women who march with the on-drive of life in our modern world. Sifted with a heavy hand over the whole land is the silt of the dark race. Here it piles up in great masses. There it thins out, and there again the scattering is so scant it is almost lost. But whether it be where her own kind group in thousands and tens of thousands, or where they are few among all the other peoples of our country, the Negro woman stands up under the terrific burden of child bearer, home maker, and toiler. For more than any other group of women in the country is she a toiler outside her home.

Hoeing the fields, stripping the tobacco plants, performing the endless round of household tasks in the homes of others, cleaning shop and office, waiting and serving. And for smaller numbers nursing, making clothing, tending machines, teaching, serving as social workers, working in stores and offices. At these things the Negro woman works.

There is no need to elaborate here upon the fact that the Negro woman suffers from the double discrimination of sex and race. The important thing to make clear is that as she holds her own as a worker the precarious footing of the Negro group is that much more secure; as she is pushed back, because she is so greatly the contributor to the whole group, all lose with her. The loss of work opportunities by Negro women is not compensated for by work gains on the part of Negro men.

There is a subtle deference on the part of Negro men to their women. This is not the remnants of a feudal chivalry, although as much of that as still exists anywhere operates within the westernized dark group; but it is the deference of a comradeship, and a tribute to a great courage. Too many black men owe part or all of what they are to the toil of mothers; too many men today see wives set forth with them daily to earn bread for their children; too many young, unmarried women gallantly carry on for a whole family group. The conditions of life in this country obliterated early any chattel relationship as between women and Negro men, and with women as free as men within the group, there could be the attack by both upon that enslavement coming from without. Considering the terrific oppression of the black people in this country and the little headway made in spite of it, the fact that [that] attack upon the problem of existence was shared by all of the adults of this minority is in large part the answer as to how this bit of headway has been made.

But these are days for Negro women to think again of how they keep the little hold they have on work opportunities, and through these their opportunities for participation in the life and thought of the country. Perhaps "think again" is too pretentious a term to apply to that tenuous process by which dark women have clung to life and fought for expression and expansion. For their way has been that of the vine, clinging to every jut, leafing toward the sun, struggling up and up.

Today, however, demands a more conscious process. The last few years have witnessed the dropping away of much of the tinsel of our boasted wealth, and the sharp outlines of our necessity stand clearly revealed. It is against this stark outline that the Negro woman measures herself and asks herself what must be her way in the immediate years to come.

First of all, the present day has brought a sense of union that could not have been true of the old days, when except for such community contacts as a woman had, she felt herself very much the individual woman struggling alone. But all the modern forms of communication plus the network of organizations of various kinds, combine now to give actuality to the fact that the individual is part of the mass. This realization does not have to be any passion for mass as mass, but it is the knowledge of the hundreds and thousands who, caught in the same situations, struggle in the same fashion, and for the same ends. Nor is it again the bleak cheer of the love of misery for company. It is a plain knowledge of numbers, of the enormity of the situation, of multiple odds that must be faced.

Now from this sense of union can be born a consciousness of what strength can come of union. The Negro woman today is beginning to realize that she is a worker. The few who hold what are called the good jobs know that so slender is their security that the breath of chance, to say nothing of the winds of economic change, can topple almost any of them from this security. Moreover, in compensation there is a limit in range. A few at the very top have salary or income above what has been set as the living wage of the country, but there is a middle point where the job preferred in name or actuality has nothing to distinguish it, as far as compensation is concerned, from the less desired kinds of work.

Here, then, is a truth that gives direction to the course the Negro woman must pursue. She is a worker. She must throw her lot with workers. Nor will an increasingly large number consider this a counsel of hysteria. To labor, to look upon one's self as one who toils and who is justified in asking for adequate rewards for that toil, is not necessarily to run shrill-voiced in the face of the moving currents of life.

But it does mean learning to know something of work and rewards, of the production of goods and their consumption, of the ambitions of wealth, and the self-seeking of nations. And it means also a knowledge that goes deep enough to help one stand firm in that inevitable time when as a group, or as an individual, there must be a demand for the decencies of civilized living for all.

There is a second sense of union that is of great significance at the present time, and that is the unity between women as women, regardless of race and color. This feeling of women for women might spring from something deep in the very biological nature of women. For they who must give birth know the intimacies of pain. Or this feeling may be the result of woman's long battle for her freedom. Or again, sensitivity may be heightened today because woman sees the old terrors of war and the lusts of war threaten all she has made of order in the world.

The Negro woman knows that she can turn to white women, to some of them, for an appreciation of her problems, and that some, they may not be many, but some of them will stand by her in the hour of necessity.

There is scoffing in some quarters that some Negro and white women assert a large measure of trust in each other, for they who scoff believe that here is pretty sentiment and nothing more than that. But there is more. Women as women have more to lose by mankind's periodic indulgences in the major follies. And they know it, that is all. It is this knowledge of what is lost by separateness that may bring the working groups, regardless of race, to a solidarity in our country. Womankind has no perfect knowledge on this point as yet, but there are evidences that they sense the fundamental truth of the strength of union; and there is [a] little evidence that to some degree they are able to act upon it.

Here, then, is a second truth to give direction to the course that Negro women must pursue. They must understand what is involved in the liberal movements among women. For all that is mere sentiment, or shallow thinking in these movements, it is their right, as of any others, to prove the weakness, to expose that which is defective.

It will be no mere friendly acquiescence that will cause Negro women to join with white women in the fight to stop the driving of women back to the kitchen. The Negro woman knows that for years to come, it would seem, she must be a paid worker if her children are to have even the half chance at life that this dual toil of parents makes possible. Nor is it, again, mere friendly gesture that she joins with white women [so] that law may be made real sanctions of the state and operative. Too often have Negro women seen their husbands and sons mobbed by fiends; too often have they seen their daughters despoiled.

It is not likely that in the years of struggle that lie ahead of her the Negro woman will lose her charm of ready sympathy, of understanding born of suffering, of that joy that breaks through when oppression is lifted ever so little. For she has been through much in the years gone by. It is her sensing of the inner character of life, her patience with its varied and often vagrant forms, her belief in its ultimate possibilities for good, that shall remain to her a staff no matter what the road down which she travels. And as such gifts do not come by mere asking, so they do not flourish by mere possession. There is promise that in the days that lie ahead, as in days past, these gifts will be called upon for use, and in the using serve her well.

Alain Locke

The Legacy of the Ancestral Arts

Music and poetry, and to an extent the dance, have been the predominant arts of the American Negro. This is an emphasis quite different from that of the African cultures, where the plastic and craft arts predominate, Africa being one of the great fountain sources of the arts of decoration and design. Except then in his remarkable carry-over of the rhythmic gift, there is little evidence of any direct connection of the American Negro with his ancestral arts. But even with the rude transplanting of slavery, that uprooted the technical elements of his former culture, the American Negro brought over as an emotional inheritance a deep-seated aesthetic endowment. And with a versatility of a very high order, this offshoot of the African spirit blended itself in with entirely different culture elements and blossomed in strange new forms.

There was in this more than a change of art-forms and an exchange of cultural patterns; there was a curious reversal of emotional temper and attitude. The characteristic African art expressions are rigid, controlled, disciplined, abstract, heavily conventionalized; those of the Aframerican,—free, exuberant, emotional, sentimental and human. Only by the misinterpretation of the African spirit, can one claim any emotional kinship between them—for the spirit of African expression, by and large, is disciplined, sophisticated, laconic and fatalistic. The emotional temper of the American Negro is exactly opposite. What we have thought primitive in the American Negro—his naïveté, his sentimentalism, his exuberance and his improvising spontaneity—are then neither characteristically African nor to be explained as an ancestral heritage. They are the result of his peculiar experience in America and the emotional upheaval of its trials and ordeals. True, these are now very characteristic traits, and they have their artistic, and perhaps even their moral compensations; but they represent essentially the working of environmental forces rather than the outcropping of a race psychology; they are really the acquired and not the original artistic temperament.

The New Negro, 1925.

A further proof of this is the fact that the American Negro, even when he confronts the various forms of African art expression with a sense of its ethnic claims upon him, meets them in as alienated and misunderstanding an attitude as the average European Westerner. Christianity and all the other European conventions operate to make this inevitable. So there would be little hope of an influence of African art upon the Western African descendants if there were not at present a growing influence of African art upon European art in general. But led by these tendencies, there is the possibility that the sensitive artistic mind of the American Negro, stimulated by a cultural pride and interest, will receive from African art a profound and galvanizing influence. The legacy is there at least, with prospects of a rich yield. In the first place, there is in the mere knowledge of the skill and unique mastery of the arts of the ancestors the valuable and stimulating realization that the Negro is not a cultural foundling without his own inheritance. Our timid and apologetic imitativeness and overburdening sense of cultural indebtedness have, let us hope, their natural end in such knowledge and realization.

Then possibly from a closer knowledge and proper appreciation of the African arts must come increased effort to develop our artistic talents in the discontinued and lagging channels of sculpture, painting and the decorative arts. If the forefathers could so adroitly master these mediums, why not we? And there may also come to some creative minds among us, hints of a new technique to be taken as the basis of a characteristic expression in the plastic and pictorial arts; incentives to new artistic idioms as well as to a renewed mastery of these older arts. African sculpture has been for contemporary European painting and sculpture just such a mine of fresh *motifs,* just such a lesson in simplicity and originality of expression, and surely, once known and appreciated, this art can scarcely have less influence upon the blood descendants, bound to it by a sense of direct cultural kinship, than upon those who inherit by tradition only, and through the channels of an exotic curiosity and interest.

But what the Negro artist of today has most to gain from the arts of the forefathers is perhaps not cultural inspiration or technical innovations, but the lesson of a classic background, the lesson of discipline, of style, of technical control pushed to the limits of technical mastery. A more highly stylized art does not exist than the African. If after absorbing the new content of American life and experience, and after assimilating new patterns of art, the original artistic endowment can be sufficiently augmented to express itself with equal power in more complex patterns and substance, then the Negro may well become what some have predicted, the artist of American life.

———————

As it is, African art has influenced modern art most considerably. It has been the most influential exotic art of our era, Chinese and Japanese art not excepted. The African art object, a half generation ago the most neglected of ethnological curios, is now universally recognized as a "notable instance of plastic representation," a genuine work of art, masterful over its material in a powerful simplicity of conception, design and effect. This artistic discovery of African art came at a time when there was a marked decadence and sterility in certain forms of European plastic art expression, due to generations of the inbreeding of style and idiom. Out of the exhaustion of imitating Greek classicism and the desperate exploitation in graphic art of all the technical possibilities of color by the Impressionists and Post Impressionists, the problem of form and decorative design became emphasized in one of those reactions which in art occur so repeatedly. And suddenly with this new problem and interest, the African representation of form, previously regarded as ridiculously crude and inadequate, appeared cunningly sophisticated and masterful. Once the strong stylistic conventions that had stood between it and a true aesthetic appreciation were thus broken through, Negro art instantly came into marked recognition. Roger Fry in an essay on Negro Sculpture has the following to say:

> I have to admit that some of these things are great sculpture—greater, I think, than anything we produced in the Middle Ages. Certainly they have the special qualities of sculpture in a higher degree. They have indeed complete plastic freedom, that is to say, these African artists really can see form in three dimensions. Now this is rare in sculpture. . . . So—far from the clinging to two dimensions, as we tend to do, the African artist actually underlines, as it were, the three-dimensionalness of his forms. It is in some such way that he manages to give to his forms their disconcerting vitality, the suggestion that they make of being not mere echoes of actual figures, but of possessing an inner life of their own. . . . Besides the logical comprehension of plastic form which the Negro shows he has also an exquisite taste in the handling of his material.

The most authoritative contemporary Continental criticism quite thoroughly agrees with this verdict and estimate.

Indeed there are many attested influences of African art in French and German modernist art. They are to be found in work of Matisse, Picasso, Derain, Modigliani and Utrillo among the French painters, upon Max Pechstein, Elaine Stern, Franz Marc and others of the German Expressionists, and upon Modigliani, Archipenko, Epstein, Lipschitz, Lembruch, and Zadkine and Faggi among sculptors. In Paris, centering around Paul Guillaume, one of its pioneer exponents, there has grown up an art coterie profoundly influenced by an aesthetic developed largely from the idioms of African art. And what has been true of the African sculptures has been in a lesser degree true of the influence of other African art forms—decorative design, musical rhythms, dance forms, verbal imagery and symbolism. Attracted by the appeal of African plastic art to the study of other modes of African expression, poets like Guillaume Apollinaire and Blaise Cendrars have attempted artistic re-expression of African idioms in poetic symbols and verse forms. So that what is a recognized school of modern French poetry professes the inspiration of African sources—Apollinaire, Reverdy, Salmon, Fargue and others. The bible of this coterie has been Cendrars' *Anthologie Nègre,* now in its sixth edition.

The starting point of an aesthetic interest in African musical idiom seems to have been H. A. Junod's work, *Les Chants et les Contes des Barongas* (1897). From the double source of African folk song and the study of American Negro musical rhythms, many of the leading French modernists have derived inspiration. Bérard, Satie, Poulenc, Auric, and even Honneger, are all in diverse ways and degrees affected, but the most explicit influence has been upon the work of Darius Milhaud, who is an avowed propagandist of the possibilities of Negro musical idiom. The importance of these absorptions of African and Negro material by all of the major forms of contemporary art, some of them independently of any transfer that might be dismissed as a mere contagion of fad or vogue, is striking, and ought to be considered as a quite unanimous verdict of the modern creative mind upon the values, actual and potential, of this yet unexhausted reservoir of art material.

———————

There is a vital connection between this new artistic respect for African idiom and the natural ambition of Negro artists for a racial idiom in their art expression. To a certain extent contemporary art has pronounced in advance upon this objective of the younger Negro artists, musicians and writers. Only the most reactionary conventions of art, then, stand between the Negro artist and the frank experimental development of these fresh idioms. This movement would, we think, be well under way in more avenues of advance at present but for the timid conventionalism which racial disparagement has forced upon the Negro mind in America. Let us take as a comparative instance, the painting of the Negro subject and notice the retarding effect of social prejudice. The Negro is a far more familiar figure in American life than in European, but American art, barring caricature and *genre,* reflects him scarcely at all. An occasional type sketch of Henri, or local color sketch of Winslow Homer represents all of a generation of painters. Whereas in Europe, with the Negro subject rarely accessible, we have as far back as the French romanticists a strong interest in the theme, an interest that in contemporary French, Belgian, German and even English painting has brought forth work of singular novelty and beauty. This work is almost all above the plane of *genre,* and in many cases represents sustained and lifelong study of the painting of the particularly difficult values of the Negro subject. To mention but a few, there is the work of Julius Hüther, Max Slevogt, Max Pechstein, Elaine Stern, von Reuckterschell among German painters; of Dinet, Lucie Cousturier, Bonnard, Georges Rouault, among the French; Klees van Dongen, the Dutch painter; most notably among the Belgians, Auguste Mambour; and among English painters, Neville Lewis, F. C. Gadell, John A. Wells, and Frank Potter. All these artists have looked upon the African scene and the African countenance, and discovered there a beauty that calls for a distinctive idiom both of color and modelling. The Negro physiognomy must be freshly and objectively conceived on its own patterns if it is ever to be seriously and importantly interpreted. Art must discover and reveal the beauty which prejudice and caricature have overlaid. And all vital art discovers beauty and opens our eyes to that which previously we could not see. While American art, including the work of our own Negro artists, has produced nothing above the level of the *genre* study or more penetrating than a Nordicized transcription, European art has gone on experimenting until the technique of the Negro subject has reached the dignity and skill of virtuoso treatment and a distinctive style. No great art will impose alien canons upon its subject matter. The work of Mam-

bour especially suggests this forceful new stylization; he has brought to the Negro subject a modelling of masses that is truly sculptural and particularly suited to the broad
massive features and subtle value shadings of the Negro countenance. After seeing his
masterful handling of mass and light and shade in bold solid planes, one has quite the
conviction that mere line and contour treatment can never be the classical technique for
the portrayal of Negro types.

The work of these European artists should even now be the inspiration and guide-
posts of a younger school of American Negro artists. They have too long been the victims of the academy tradition and shared the conventional blindness of the Caucasian
eye with respect to the racial material at immediate disposal. Thus there have been notably
successful Negro artists, but no development of a school of Negro art. Our Negro American painter of outstanding success is Henry O. Tanner. His career is a case in point. Though
a professed painter of types, he has devoted his art talent mainly to the portrayal of Jewish Biblical types and subjects, and has never maturely touched the portrayal of the Negro
subject. Warrantable enough— for to the individual talent in art one must never dictate—
who can be certain what field the next Negro artist of note will choose to command, or
whether he will not be a landscapist or a master of still life or of purely decorative painting? But from the point of view of our artistic talent in bulk—it is a different matter. We
ought and must have a school of Negro art, a local and a racially representative tradition. And that we have not, explains why the generation of Negro artists succeeding Mr.
Tanner had only the inspiration of his great success to fire their ambitions, but not the
guidance of a distinctive tradition to focus and direct their talents. Consequently they
fumbled and fell short of his international stride and reach. The work of Henri Scott, Edwin
A. Harleson, Laura Wheeler, in painting, and of Meta Warrick Fuller and May Howard Jackson in sculpture, competent as it has been, has nevertheless felt this handicap and has
wavered between abstract expression which was imitative and not highly original, and
racial expression which was only experimental. Lacking group leadership and concentration, they were wandering amateurs in the very field that might have given them concerted mastery.

A younger group of Negro artists is beginning to move in the direction of a racial
school of art. The strengthened tendency toward representative group expression is shared
even by the later work of the artists previously mentioned, as in Meta Warrick Fuller's
Ethiopia Awakening, to mention an outstanding example. But the work of young artists
like Archibald Motley, Otto Farrill, Cecil Gaylord, John Urquhart, Samuel Blount, and especially that of Charles Keene and Aaron Douglas shows the promising beginning of an art
movement instead of just the cropping out of isolated talent. The work of Winold Reiss,
fellow-countryman of Slevogt and von Reuckterschell . . . has been deliberately conceived
and executed as a path-breaking guide and encouragement to this new foray of the younger
Negro artists. In idiom, technical treatment and objective social angle, it is a bold icon-
oclastic break with the current traditions that have grown up about the Negro subject
in American art. It is not meant to dictate a style to the young Negro artist, but to point
the lesson that contemporary European art has already learned—that any vital artistic

expression of the Negro theme and subject in art must break through the stereotypes to a new style, a distinctive fresh technique, and some sort of characteristic idiom.

While we are speaking of the resources of racial art, it is well to take into account that the richest vein of it is not that of portraitistic idiom after all, but its almost limitless wealth of decorative and purely symbolic material. It is for the development of this latter aspect of a racial art that the study and example of African art material is so important. The African spirit, as we said at the outset, is at its best in abstract decorative forms. Design, and to a lesser degree, color, are its original *fortes*. It is this aspect of the folk tradition, this slumbering gift of the folk temperament that most needs reachievement and reexpression. And if African art is capable of producing the ferment in modern art that it has, surely this is not too much to expect of its influence upon the culturally awakened Negro artist of the present generation. So that if even the present vogue of African art should pass, and the bronzes of Benin and the fine sculptures of Gabon and Baoulé, and the superb designs of the Bushongo should again become mere items of exotic curiosity, for the Negro artist they ought still to have the import and influence of classics in whatever art expression is consciously and representatively racial.

Joel A. Rogers

Jazz at Home

Jazz is a marvel of paradox: too fundamentally human, at least as modern humanity goes, to be typically racial, too international to be characteristically national, too much abroad in the world to have a special home. And yet jazz in spite of it all is one part American and three parts American Negro, and was originally the nobody's child of the levee and the city slum. Transplanted exotic—a rather hardy one, we admit—of the mundane world capitals, sport of the sophisticated, it is really at home in its humble native soil wherever the modern unsophisticated Negro feels happy and sings and dances to his mood. It follows that jazz is more at home in Harlem than in Paris, though from the look and sound of certain quarters of Paris one would hardly think so. It is just the epidemic contagiousness of jazz that makes it, like the measles, sweep the block. But somebody had to have it first: that was the Negro.

What after all is this taking new thing, that, condemned in certain quarters, enthusiastically welcomed in others, has nonchalantly gone on until it ranks with the movie and the dollar as a foremost exponent of modern Americanism? Jazz isn't music merely, it is a spirit that can express itself in almost anything. The true spirit of jazz is a joyous revolt from convention, custom, authority, boredom, even sorrow—from everything that would confine the soul of man and hinder its riding free on the air. The Negroes who invented it called their songs the "blues," and they weren't capable of satire or deception. Jazz was their explosive attempt to cast off the blues and be happy, carefree happy, even in the midst of sordidness and sorrow. And that is why it has been such a balm for modern ennui, and has become a safety valve for modern machine-ridden and convention-bound society. It is the revolt of the emotions against repression.

The story is told of the clever group of "Jazz-specialists" who, originating dear knows in what scattered places, had found themselves and the frills of the art in New York and had been drawn to the gay Bohemias of Paris. In a little cabaret of Montmartre they had

The New Negro, 1925.

just "entertained" into the wee small hours fascinated society and royalty; and, of course, had been paid royally for it. Then, the entertainment over and the guests away, the "entertainers" entertained themselves with their very best, which is always impromptu, for the sheer joy of it. That is jazz.

In its elementals, jazz has always existed. It is in the Indian war-dance, the Highland fling, the Irish jig, the Cossack dance, the Spanish fandango, the Brazilian *maxixe,* the dance of the whirling dervish, the hula hula of the South Seas, the *danse du ventre* of the Orient, the *carmagnole* of the French Revolution, the strains of Gypsy music, and the ragtime of the Negro. Jazz proper, however, is something more than all these. It is a release of all the suppressed emotions at once, a blowing off of the lid, as it were. It is hilarity expressing itself through pandemonium, musical fireworks.

The direct predecessor of jazz is ragtime. That both are atavistically African there is little doubt, but to what extent it is difficult to determine. In its barbaric rhythm and exuberance there is something of the bamboula, a wild, abandoned dance of the West African and the Haytian Negro, so stirringly described by the anonymous author of *Untrod-den Fields of Anthropology,* or of the *ganza* ceremony so brilliantly depicted in Maran's *Batouala.* But jazz time is faster and more complex than African music. With its cowbells, auto horns, calliopes, rattles, dinner gongs, kitchen utensils, cymbals, screams, crashes, clankings and monotonous rhythm it bears all the marks of a nerve-strung, strident, mechanized civilization. It is a thing of the jungles—modern man-made jungles.

The earliest jazz-makers were the itinerant piano players who would wander up and down the Mississippi from saloon to saloon, from dive to dive. Seated at the piano with a carefree air that a king might envy, their box-back coats flowing over the stool, their Stetsons pulled well over their eyes, and cigars at an angle of forty-five degrees, they would "whip the ivories" to marvellous chords and hidden racy, joyous meanings, evoking the intense delight of their hearers who would smother them at the close with huzzas and whiskey. Often wholly illiterate, these humble troubadours, knowing nothing of written music or composition, but with minds like cameras, would listen to the rude improvisations of the dock laborers and the railroad gangs and reproduce them, reflecting perfectly the sentiments and the longings of these humble folk. The improvised bands at Negro dances in the South, or the little boys with their harmonicas and jews'-harps, each one putting his own individuality into the air, played also no inconsiderable part in its evolution. "Poverty," says J. A. Jackson of *The Billboard,* "compelled improvised instruments. Bones, tambourines, make-shift string instruments, tin can and hollow wood effects, all now utilized as musical novelties, were among early Negroes the product of necessity. When these were not available 'patting juba' prevailed. Present-day 'Charleston' is but a variation of this. Its early expression was the 'patting' for the buck dance."

The origin of the present jazz craze is interesting. More cities claim its birthplace than claimed Homer dead. New Orleans, San Francisco, Memphis, Chicago, all assert the honor is theirs. Jazz, as it is today, seems to have come into being this way, however: W. C. Handy, a Negro, having digested the airs of the itinerant musicians referred to, evolved the first classic, "Memphis Blues." Then came Jasbo Brown, a reckless musician of a Negro cabaret in Chicago, who played this and other blues, blowing his own extravagant moods and risqué interpretations into them, while hilarious with gin. To give further meanings to his veiled allusions he would make the trombone "talk" by putting a derby hat and later a tin can at its mouth. The delighted patrons would shout, "More, Jasbo. More, Jas, more." And so the name originated.

As to the jazz dance itself: at this time Shelton Brooks, a Negro comedian, invented a new "strut," called "Walkin' the Dog." Jasbo's anarchic airs found in this strut a soul mate. Then as a result of their union came "The Texas Tommy," the highest point of brilliant, acrobatic execution and nifty footwork so far evolved in jazz dancing. The latest of these dances is the "Charleston," which has brought something really new to the dance step. The "Charleston" calls for activity of the whole body. One characteristic is a fantastic fling of the legs from the hip downwards. The dance ends in what is known as the "camel-walk"—in reality a gorilla-like shamble—and finishes with a peculiar hop like that of the Indian war dance. Imagine one suffering from a fit of rhythmic ague and you have the effect precisely.

The cleverest "Charleston" dancers perhaps are urchins of five and six who may be seen any time on the streets of Harlem, keeping time with their hands, and surrounded by admiring crowds. But put it on a well-set stage, danced by a bobbed-hair chorus, and you have an effect that reminds you of the abandon of the Furies. And so Broadway studies Harlem. Not all of the visitors of the twenty or more well-attended cabarets of Harlem are idle pleasure seekers or underworld devotees. Many are serious artists, actors and producers seeking something new, some suggestion to be taken, too often in pallid imitation, to Broadway's lights and stars.

This makes it difficult to say whether jazz is more characteristic of the Negro or of contemporary America. As was shown, it is of Negro origin plus the influence of the American environment. It is Negro-American. Jazz proper, however, is in idiom—rhythmic, musical and pantomimic—thoroughly American Negro; it is his spiritual picture on that lighter comedy side, just as the spirituals are the picture on the tragedy side. The two are poles apart, but the former is by no means to be despised and it is just as characteristically the product of the peculiar and unique experience of the Negro in this country. The African Negro hasn't it, and the Caucasian never could have invented it. Once achieved, it is common property, and jazz has absorbed the national spirit, that tremendous spirit of go, the nervousness, lack of conventionality and boisterous good-nature characteristic of the American, white or black, as compared with the more rigid formal natures of the Englishman or German.

But there still remains something elusive about jazz that few, if any, of the white artists have been able to capture. The Negro is admittedly its best expositor. That elusive something, for lack of a better name, I'll call Negro rhythm. The average Negro, particularly of the lower classes, puts rhythm into whatever he does, whether it be shining shoes or carrying a basket on the head to market as the Jamaican women do. Some years ago while wandering in Cincinnati I happened upon a Negro revival meeting at its height. The majority present were women, a goodly few of whom were white. Under the influence of the "spirit" the sisters would come forward and strut—much of jazz enters where it would be least expected. The Negro women had the perfect jazz abandon, while the white ones moved lamely and woodenly. This same lack of spontaneity is evident to a degree in the cultivated and inhibited Negro.

In its playing technique, jazz is similarly original and spontaneous. The performance of the Negro musicians is much imitated, but seldom equalled. Lieutenant Europe, leader of the famous band of the "Fifteenth New York Regiment," said that the bandmaster of the Garde Républicaine, amazed at his jazz effects, could not believe without demonstration that his band had not used special instruments. Jazz has a virtuoso technique all its own: its best performers, singers and players lift it far above the level of mere "trick" or mechanical effects.

Abbie Mitchell, Ethel Waters, and Florence Mills; the blues singers, Clara, Mamie, and Bessie Smith; Eubie Blake, the pianist; "Buddy" Gilmore, the drummer, and "Bill" Robinson, the pantomimic dancer—to mention merely an illustrative few—are inimitable artists, with an inventive, improvising skill that defies imitation. And those who know their work most intimately trace its uniqueness without exception to the folk-roots of their artistry.

Musically jazz has a great future. It is rapidly being sublimated. In the more famous jazz orchestras like those of Will Marion Cook, Paul Whiteman, Sissle and Blake, Sam Stewart, Fletcher Henderson, Vincent Lopez and the Clef Club units, there are none of the vulgarities and crudities of the lowly origin or the only too prevalent cheap imitations. The pioneer work in the artistic development of jazz was done by Negro artists; it was the lead of the so-called "syncopated orchestras" of Tyers and Will Marion Cook, the former playing for the Castles of dancing fame, and the latter touring as a concertizing orchestra in the great American centers and abroad. Because of the difficulties of financial backing, these expert combinations have had to yield ground to white orchestras of the type of the Paul Whiteman and Vincent Lopez organizations that are now demonstrating the finer possibilities of jazz music. "Jazz," says Serge Koussevitzky, the new conductor of the Boston Symphony, "is an important contribution to modern musical literature. It has an epochal significance—it is not superficial, it is fundamental. Jazz comes from the soil, where all music has its beginning." And Leopold Stokowski says more extendedly of it:

> Jazz has come to stay because it is an expression of the times, of the breathless, energetic, superactive times in which we are living, it is useless to fight against it. Already its new vigor, its new vitality is beginning to manifest itself. . . . America's contribution to the music of the past will have the same revivifying effect as the injection of new, and in the larger sense, vulgar blood into dying aristocracy. Music will then be vulgarized in the best sense of the word, and enter more and more the daily lives of people. . . . The Negro musicians of America are playing a great part in this change. They have an open mind, and unbiased outlook. They are not hampered by conventions or traditions, and with their new ideas, their constant experiment, they are causing new blood to flow in the veins of music. The jazz players make their instruments do entirely new things, things finished musicians are taught to avoid. They are pathfinders into new realms.

And thus it has come about that serious modernist music and musicians, most notably and avowedly in the work of the French modernists Auric, Satie and Darius Milhaud, have become the confessed debtors of American Negro jazz. With the same nonchalance and impudence with which it left the levee and the dive to stride like an upstart conqueror, almost overnight, into the grand salon, jazz now begins its conquest of musical Parnassus.

Whatever the ultimate result of the attempt to raise jazz from the mob-level upon which it originated, its true home is still its original cradle, the none too respectable cabaret. And here we have the seamy side to the story. Here we have some of the charm of Bohemia, but much more of the demoralization of vice. Its rash spirit is in Grey's popular song, "Runnin' Wild":

> Runnin' wild; lost control
> Runnin' wild; mighty bold,
> Feelin' gay and reckless too
> Carefree all the time; never blue
> Always goin' I don't know where
> Always showin' that I don't care
> Don' love nobody, it ain't worth while
> All alone; runnin' wild.

Jazz reached the height of its vogue at a time when minds were reacting from the horrors and strain of war. Humanity welcomed it because in its fresh joyousness men found a temporary forgetfulness, infinitely less harmful than drugs or alcohol. It is partly for some such reasons that it dominates the amusement life of America to-day. No one can sensibly condone its excesses or minimize its social danger if uncontrolled; all culture is built upon inhibitions and control. But it is doubtful whether the "jazz-hounds" of high and low estate would use their time to better advantage. In all probability their tastes would find some equally morbid, mischievous vent. Jazz, it is needless to say, will remain a recreation for the industrious and a dissipater of energy for the frivolous, a tonic for the strong and a poison for the weak.

For the Negro himself, jazz is both more and less dangerous than for the white— less, in that he is nervously more in tune with it; more, in that at his average level of economic development his amusement life is more open to the forces of social vice. The cabaret of better type provides a certain Bohemianism for the Negro intellectual, the artist and the well-to-do. But the average thing is too much the substitute for the saloon, and the wayside inn. The tired longshoreman, the porter, the housemaid and the poor elevator boy in search of recreation, seeking in jazz the tonic for weary nerves and muscles, are only too apt to find the bootlegger, the gambler and the demi-monde who have come there for victims and to escape the eyes of the police.

Yet in spite of its present vices and vulgarizations, its sex informalities, its morally anarchic spirit, jazz has a popular mission to perform. Joy, after all, has a physical basis. Those who laugh and dance and sing are better off even in their vices than those who do not. Moreover, jazz with its mocking disregard for formality is a leveller and makes for democracy. The jazz spirit, being primitive, demands more frankness and sincerity.

Just as it already has done in art and music, so eventually in human relations and social manners, it will no doubt have the effect of putting more reality in life by taking some of the needless artificiality out. . . . Naturalness finds the artificial in conduct ridiculous. "Cervantes smiled Spain's chivalry away," said Byron. And so this new spirit of joy and spontaneity may itself play the rôle of reformer. Where at present it vulgarizes, with more wholesome growth in the future, it may on the contrary truly democratize. At all events, jazz is rejuvenation, a recharging of the batteries of civilization with primitive new vigor. It has come to stay, and they are wise who, instead of protesting against it, try to lift and divert it into nobler channels.

Laura Wheeler, "Woman Playing Harp," cover of *The Crisis*, April 1923

Gwendolyn B. Bennett

The American Negro Paints

From January 6 to 17 an art exhibit was held at the International House on Riverside Drive in New York City. This exhibition was of work in the fine arts by American Negro artists, hung under the auspices of the Harmon Foundation and the Commission on the Church and Race Relations of the Federal Council of Churches. In the catalogue listing the works shown there was this foreword:

> ### Purpose
>
> The Harmon Foundation and the Commission on the Church and Race Relations of the Federal Council of the Churches of Christ in America have placed this exhibition before the public in the hope of accomplishing three things: Creating a wider interest in the work of the Negro artist as a contribution to American culture; stimulating him to aim for the highest standards of achievement, and encouraging the general public in the purchase of his work, with the eventual purpose in view of helping the American Negro to a sounder and more satisfactory economic position in art.

It is in the light of this foreword that I looked at this exhibition. Had it reached all the goals its promulgators set for it, there could be no doubt of its success, and the likes or dislikes of any one individual would be of little account. But let us see whether this exhibition of work by American Negro artists lived up to the sanguine hopes of its fosterers.

Did this particular exhibition create a wider interest in the work of the Negro artist as a contribution to American culture? Had this last phrase been left unsaid I might have bowed my head in cheerful acquiescence. Certainly this hanging of pictures did create quite a widespread interest in the work of the Negro artists, but it is extremely doubtful whether it can be viewed in the light of a contribution to American culture. I wonder if those people who go into ecstatic tantrums over the Negro's contribution to

Southern Workman, January 1928.

American culture realize what such a contribution should entail. Mind you I refer only to the pictorial and sculptural arts. Cultural contributions can be only judged in the light of their artistic permanency. When the pictures here shown are some hundred years old I doubt that they will have any greater value than that of personal record. Regarding them in comparison with the spirituals, which are without question a contribution not only to the culture of America but to the culture of the world, these pictures fall away to nothingness when evaluated as cultural contributions. I doubt if a hundred years from today this showing of pictures by Negro artists will receive more than a passing word of comment from the tongues of even racial historians. It seems to me that they lack the essence of artistic permanency. On the other hand, there can be no cultural contribution unless something distinctive is given, something heightened and developed within the whole form that did not exist before the artist's hand took part in its molding. But where in this exhibition is there any such deftness of hand? Mrs. Laura Wheeler Waring takes the spotlight for having used the existing academic form to its greatest advantage. However, sheer technical facility alone does not make for racial contributions to a culture in the making.

The committee on admissions took a rather roundabout way of realizing their second criterion. Surely the Negro artist needs no greater stimulant to aim higher than to have viewed as a whole the work hung at this exhibit. Many of the pieces were not even of good academic technique. I was surprised to see many pictures in which the actual drawing was out of scale. Here again the work of Mrs. Waring served the committee in good stead. Her work along with that of Palmer C. Hayden, winner of the 1926 Harmon Awards for Distinguished Achievement Among Negroes in Fine Arts, Sargent Johnson, Aaron Douglas, and Hillyard Robinson gave the other competitors an adequate standard of proficiency by which to judge the work that they will send to the committee in the future.

And in accordance with the final aim of the sponsors many of the pictures and pieces of sculpture placed on exhibition were sold. This was indeed a good thing. It is extremely encouraging that most of these purchases were made by Negroes. Too long has the Negro waited for the white man to do his buying for him. However, I must quibble with the point of making a sound economic position for the Negro artist the "eventual purpose" of this exhibit. Seldom have the paths of economic surety and artistic freedom run parallel. It seems that higher aim than economic soundness would be a true expression of real art.

CREATIVE WRITING

Vivian Schuyler, "Lift Every Voice and Sing," cover of *The Crisis,* November 1927

James Weldon Johnson was one of the most influential movers and shakers of the Harlem Renaissance. He was born to James and Helen Louise Dillet Johnson in Jacksonville, Florida, on June 17, 1871. Thanks to his mother's employment as a schoolteacher and his father's position as headwaiter at the prestigious St. James Hotel, Johnson enjoyed a middle-class upbringing. He attended his mother's school, the Stanton School in Jacksonville, until the eighth grade and next attended the preparatory school of Atlanta University, receiving his A.B. from the college division in 1894. After graduation, Johnson became principal

James Weldon Johnson

(1871–1938)

of Stanton School. In 1895–1896 he founded and edited a newspaper, *The Daily American.* In 1897 Johnson became the first African American admitted to the Florida bar. In the summers between 1899 and 1901 Johnson visited his brother, Rosamond, in New York and collaborated in writing light operas, musical comedies, and popular songs. Their 1900 song "Lift Ev'ry Voice and Sing," with Johnson's lyrics and his brother's music, is still considered the "Negro National Anthem."

In 1901 Johnson moved to New York, where he continued to collaborate with his brother and Bob Cole, a vaudeville performer, and pursued literary studies at Columbia University. Despite a successful show business career, Johnson abandoned songwriting to join the diplomatic corps as U.S. consul at Puerto Cabello, Venezuela, in 1906. From 1909 to 1913, he held a similar post at Corinto, Nicaragua. In 1910 Johnson briefly returned to the United States to marry Grace Nail of New York.

Throughout these pre-Renaissance years, Johnson published poems in such journals as *Century Magazine* and *The Independent.* In 1912 he anonymously published his landmark novel, *The Autobiography of an Ex-Coloured Man* (reprinted in 1927 under his own name), one of the most important texts of the Harlem Renaissance. His poetry collection, *God's Trombones: Seven Negro Sermons in Verse,* appeared the same year. These texts, along with his groundbreaking anthology, *The Book of American Negro Poetry* (1922), solidified Johnson's literary reputation as a central figure of the movement.

Johnson left the consular service in 1913 and returned to New York, where he became contributing editor to *The New York Age,* an African American weekly. In 1916 he was asked to become the field secretary for the prestigious civil rights organization, the National Association for the Advancement of Colored People (NAACP), and in 1920 he became the first African American to be elected its executive secretary. Johnson resigned from the NAACP in 1931 to become the Adam K. Spence Professor of Creative Literature at Fisk University. He was killed in an automobile accident in 1938.

Johnson's other major publications include the poetry collections *Fifty Years and Other Poems* (1917) and *Saint Peter Relates an Incident of the Resurrection Day: Selected Poems* (1930); *Black Manhattan* (1930), a history of African Americans in New York; and *Along This Way: The Autobiography of James Weldon Johnson* (1933). He also edited *The Book of American Negro Spirituals* (1925) and *The Second Book of American Negro Spirituals* (1926).

The Creation
(A Negro Sermon)

And God stepped out on space,
And He looked around and said,
"I'm lonely—
I'll make me a world."

And far as the eye of God could see
Darkness covered everything,
Blacker than a hundred midnights
Down in a cypress swamp.

Then God smiled,
And the light broke,
And the darkness rolled up on one side,
And the light stood shining on the other,
And God said, *"That's good!"*

Then God reached out and took the light in His hands,
And God rolled the light around in His hands
Until He made the sun;
And He set that sun a-blazing in the heavens.
And the light that was left from making the sun
God gathered it up in a shining ball
And flung it against the darkness,
Spangling the night with the moon and stars.
Then down between
The darkness and the light
He hurled the world;
And God said, *"That's good!"*

Then God himself stepped down—
And the sun was on His right hand,
And the moon was on His left;
The stars were clustered about His head,
And the earth was under His feet.
And God walked, and where He trod
His footsteps hollowed the valleys out
And bulged the mountains up.

Then He stopped and looked and saw
That the earth was hot and barren.
So God stepped over to the edge of the world
And He spat out the seven seas;
He batted His eyes, and the lightnings flashed;
He clapped His hands, and the thunders rolled;

And the waters above the earth came down,
The cooling waters came down.

Then the green grass sprouted,
And the little red flowers blossomed,
The pine tree pointed his finger to the sky,
And the oak spread out his arms,
The lakes cuddled down in the hollows of the ground,
And the rivers ran down to the sea;
And God smiled again,
And the rainbow appeared,
And curled itself around His shoulder.

Then God raised His arm and He waved His hand
Over the sea and over the land,
And He said, *"Bring forth! Bring forth!"*
And quicker than God could drop His hand,
Fishes and fowls
And beasts and birds
Swam the rivers and the seas,
Roamed the forests and the woods,
And split the air with their wings.
And God said, *"That's good!"*

Then God walked around,
And God looked around
On all that He had made.
He looked at His sun,
And He looked at His moon,
And He looked at His little stars;
He looked on His world
With all its living things,
And God said, *"I'm lonely still."*

Then God sat down
On the side of a hill where He could think;
By a deep, wide river He sat down;
With His head in His hands,
God thought and thought,
Till He thought, *"I'll make me a man!"*

Up from the bed of the river
God scooped the clay;
And by the bank of the river
He kneeled Him down;
And there the great God Almighty
Who lit the sun and fixed it in the sky,
Who flung the stars to the most far corner of the night,
Who rounded the earth in the middle of His hand;

This Great God,
Like a mammy bending over her baby,
Kneeled down in the dust
Toiling over a lump of clay
Till He shaped it in His own image.

Then into it He blew the breath of life,
And man became a living soul.
Amen. Amen.

The Book of American Negro Poetry, 1922.

Mother Night

Eternities before the first-born day,
   Or ere the first sun fledged his wings of flame,
   Calm Night, the everlasting and the same,
   A brooding mother over chaos lay,
And whirling suns shall blaze and then decay,
   Shall run their fiery courses and then claim
   The haven of the darkness whence they came;
   Back to Nirvanic peace shall grope their way.

So when my feeble sun of life burns out,
   And sounded is the hour for my long sleep,
   I shall, full weary of the feverish light,
Welcome the darkness without fear or doubt,
   And heavy-lidded, I shall softly creep
   Into the quiet bosom of the Night.

The Book of American Negro Poetry, 1922.

The White Witch

O brothers mine, take care! Take care!
The great white witch rides out to-night.
Trust not your prowess nor your strength,
Your only safety lies in flight;
For in her glance is a snare,
And in her smile there is a blight.

The great white witch you have not seen?
Then, younger brothers mine, forsooth,

Like nursery children you have looked
For ancient hag and snaggle-tooth;
But no, not so; the witch appears
In all the glowing charms of youth.

Her lips are like carnations, red,
Her face like new-born lilies, fair,
Her eyes like ocean waters, blue,
She moves with subtle grace and air,
And all about her head there floats
The golden glory of her hair.

But though she always thus appears
In form of youth and mood of mirth,
Unnumbered centuries are hers,
The infant planets saw her birth;
The child of throbbing Life is she,
Twin sister to the greedy earth.

And back behind those smiling lips,
And down within those laughing eyes,
And underneath the soft caress
Of hand and voice and purring sighs,
The shadow of the panther lurks,
The spirit of the vampire lies.

For I have seen the great white witch,
And she has led me to her lair,
And I have kissed her red, red lips
And cruel face so white and fair;
Around me she has twined her arms,
And bound me with her yellow hair.

I felt those red lips burn and sear
My body like a living coal;
Obeyed the power of those eyes
As the needle trembles to the pole;
And did not care although I felt
The strength go ebbing from my soul.

Oh! she has seen your strong young limbs,
And heard your laughter loud and gay,
And in your voices she has caught
The echo of a far-off day,
When man was closer to the earth;
And she has marked you for her prey.

She feels the old Antaean strength
In you, the great dynamic beat
Of primal passions, and she sees

In you the last besieged retreat
Of love relentless, lusty, fierce,
Love pain-ecstatic, cruel-sweet.

O, brothers mine, take care! Take care!
The great white witch rides out to-night.
O, younger brothers mine, beware;
Look not upon her beauty bright;
For in her glance there is a snare,
And in her smile there is a blight.

The Book of American Negro Poetry, 1922.

My City

When I come down to sleep death's endless night,
The threshold of the unknown dark to cross,
What to me then will be the keenest loss,
When this bright world blurs on my fading sight?
Will it be that no more I shall see the trees
Or smell the flowers or hear the singing birds
Or watch the flashing streams or patient herds?
No, I am sure it will be none of these.

But, ah! Manhattan's sights and sounds, her smells,
Her crowds, her throbbing force, the thrill that comes
From being of her a part, her subtle spells,
Her shining towers, her avenues, her slums—
O God! the stark, unutterable pity,
To be dead, and never again behold my city!

Caroling Dusk, 1927.

Alice Dunbar-Nelson

(1875–1935)

Born Alice Ruth Moore in New Orleans on July 19, 1875, Dunbar-Nelson was the younger daughter of Patricia Moore, a Louisiana-born freed slave who became a seamstress and Joseph Moore, a seaman. After graduating from Straight College (Dillard University) in 1892, she left New Orleans in 1896 to teach in Brooklyn, New York. Here she helped Viola Earle Matthews establish the White Rose Mission, which became the White Rose Home for Girls in Harlem.

She then married Paul Laurence Dunbar, the most famous African American poet of the day, in March 1898. She joined him in Washington, D.C., where he worked at the Library of Congress, and they became a celebrated artistic couple in the black community, comparing themselves to married nineteenth-century poets Robert and Elizabeth Barrett Browning. Theirs was a stormy marriage; the couple was frequently estranged, and Dunbar-Nelson began living with her mother, divorced sister, and nieces in 1902 in Wilmington, Delaware. From 1902 to 1920 she taught English at Howard High School in Wilmington. When Paul Laurence Dunbar died in 1906 at age thirty-four, she took it upon herself to help preserve his legacy and to use his fame as a springboard for social causes. She accepted speaking engagements throughout the remainder of her life in this capacity.

Beginning in 1904, Dunbar-Nelson pursued her education by enrolling at Cornell University, then Columbia, the Pennsylvania School of Industrial Art, and the University of Pennsylvania. To these activities she added organizational work with the National Association of Colored Women and political activism of all sorts. She also wrote short stories, newspaper columns, poetry, two plays, a diary, and edited scholarly books. Dunbar-Nelson's personal life was equally full. In 1910 she married a fellow teacher at Howard, Arthur Callis, a man twelve years her junior whom she had met at Cornell when he was an undergraduate. The relationship was short-lived and very little is known about the long-concealed marriage. Her third marriage, to Robert Nelson, a journalist with whom she published *The Wilmington Advocate* from 1920 to 1922, lasted from 1916 until her death. Dunbar-Nelson was also involved in passionate relationships with women throughout the 1920s and before, which she recorded in her diary, *Give Us Each Day*.

Dunbar-Nelson's collections of short fiction with New Orleans French and Creole characters, *Violets and Other Tales* (1895) and *The Goodness of St. Rocque and Other Stories* (1899), were published before the Harlem Renaissance. Her primary contribution to the period was her poetry, particularly "Violets" (1917), her signature piece. Her poems were published in the era's major journals and anthologies. She also edited two scholarly anthologies, *Masterpieces of Negro Eloquence* (1914) and *The Dunbar Speaker and Entertainer* (1920). A tireless campaigner for social justice, a feminist, a talented creative writer and scholar, and a hardworking teacher and editor, Alice Dunbar-Nelson left an inspiring legacy of accomplishments. She died of heart disease at age sixty in Philadelphia.

Laura Wheeler, "Spring," cover of *The Crisis*, April 1927

Violets

I had not thought of violets of late,
The wild, shy kind that springs beneath your feet
In wistful April days, when lovers mate
And wander through the fields in raptures sweet.
And thought of violets meant florists' shops,
And bows and pins, and perfumed paper fine;
And garish lights, and mincing little fops
And cabarets and songs, and deadening wine.
So far from sweet real things my thoughts had strayed,
I had forgot wide fields, and clear brown streams;
The perfect loveliness that God has made—
Wild violets shy and heaven-mounting dreams.
And now—unwittingly, you've made me dream
Of violets, and my soul's forgotten gleam.

The Crisis, August 1917.

You! Inez!

Orange gleams athwart a crimson soul
Lambent flames; purple passion lurks
In your dusk eyes.
Red mouth; flower soft,
Your soul leaps up and flashes
Star-like, white, flame-hot.
Curving arms, encircling a world of love.
You! Stirring the depths of passionate desire!

Unpublished, February 1921.

I Sit and Sew

I sit and sew—a useless task it seems,
My hands grown tired, my head weighed down with dreams—
The panoply of war, the martial tread of men,
Grim-faced, stern-eyed, gazing beyond the ken
Of lesser souls, whose eyes have not seen Death
Nor learned to hold their lives but as a breath—
But—I must sit and sew.

I sit and sew—my heart aches with desire—
That pageant terrible, that fiercely pouring fire
On wasted fields, and writhing grotesque things
Once men. My soul in pity flings
Appealing cries, yearning only to go
There in that holocaust of hell, those fields of woe—
But—I must sit and sew.—

The little useless seam, the idle patch;
Why dream I here beneath my homely thatch,
When there they lie in sodden mud and rain,
Pitifully calling me, the quick ones and the slain?
You need me, Christ! It is no roseate seam
That beckons me—this pretty futile seam,
It stifles me—God, must I sit and sew?

Caroling Dusk, 1927.

The Proletariat Speaks

I love beautiful things:
Great trees, bending green winged branches to a velvet lawn,
Fountains sparkling in white marble basins,
Cool fragrance of lilacs and roses and honeysuckle

Or exotic blooms, filling the air with heart-contracting odors;
Spacious rooms, cool and gracious with statues and books,
Carven seats and tapestries, and old masters,
Whose patina shows the wealth of centuries.

And so I work
In a dusty office, whose grimed windows
Look out on an alley of unbelievable squalor,
Where mangy cats, in their degradation, spurn

Swarming bits of meat and bread;
Where odors, vile and breath-taking, rise in fetid waves
Filling my nostrils, scorching my humid, bitter cheeks.

I love beautiful things:
Carven tables laid with lily-hued linen
And fragile china and sparkling iridescent glass;
Pale silver, etched with heraldries,
Where tender bits of regal dainties tempt,
And soft-stepped service anticipates the unspoken wish.

And so I eat
In the food-laden air of a greasy kitchen,
At an oil-clothed table:
Plate piled high with food that turns my head away,
Lest a squeamish stomach reject too soon
The lumpy gobs it never needed.
Or in a smoky cafeteria, balancing a slippery tray
To a table crowded with elbows
Which lately the busboy wiped with a grimy rag.

I love beautiful things:
Soft linen sheets and silken coverlet,
Sweet cool of chamber opened wide to fragrant breeze;
Rose-shaded lamps and golden atomizers,
Spraying Parisian fragrance over my relaxed limbs,
Fresh from a white marble bath, and sweet cool spray.

And so I sleep
In a hot hall-room whose half-opened window,
Unscreened, refuses to budge another inch,
Admits no air, only insects, and hot choking gasps
That make me writhe, nun-like, in sackcloth sheets and lumps of straw
And then I rise
To fight my way to a dubious tub,
Whose tiny, tepid stream threatens to make me late;
And hurrying out, dab my unrefreshed face
With bits of toiletry from the ten cent store.

The Crisis, November 1929.

His Great Career

The travel-scarred motorcar came to a pause in the driveway of the great mountain mansion. "The Squire," as he was lovingly called for miles around, greeted the owner of the car as he rather stiffly set foot on the ground.

"It's good of you to come up here to see us in our mountain fastness," he said warmly.

"Didn't know you lived here until we broke down somewhere in your peaks and crags, and Martin inquired of the nearest civilized house."

The Squire talked cheerfully as he carried the bags of the great criminal lawyer up the broad walk.

"We're having a big house party here," he explained to the group of guests on the veranda. "My wife's birthday, and when we give a party up here, it means a weekend stay, for we have to go so far for our festivities, it would be a pity to go right home."

The great lawyer was introduced to the fluttering and flattered group of maidens and wives, and to the hearty men who hovered on the edges. He bent his great grizzled frame over small eager hands, while his host stood by, enjoying his embarrassment in the pause before he went to his room.

"And so you're married?" asked the lawyer, as they went up the broad stairs.

"Fifteen years. You remember when my health broke eighteen years ago? I found *her* here in a sanitarium, wrecked too, and 'sick of that disease called life.' Between us, we mended our lives, and then she didn't care for the east and all that it means any more than I did—so we stayed, and here we are."

The great lawyer revelled in the scene, a marvelous panorama spreading out from the window.

"Prominent citizen, leader of the community, and the rest?" he asked smilingly.

The Squire was modest. "Well, we've helped build the community, and all that sort of thing. You can't live in a place without being part of it. And you, old Hard-head, you've become one of the most famous lawyers in the country!"

The lawyer waved a deprecating hand. "I'm motoring in out of the way places now to forget it awhile."

The veranda was not in a mood to allow him to forget. Famous celebrities did not drop into their lives often enough for them to be blasé. The lawyer put down the excellent cocktail that his host brought him in lieu of tea, and inquired for the mistress of the house. She had ridden to town for a last bit of foolery for tonight's costume party, explained the Squire.

The almond-eyed widow was subtly intent on opening up a flood of reminiscences. She fluttered slender hands and widened black eyes suggestively. Even the great lawyer's habitual taciturnity relaxed under the enveloping warmth of remembering the night she

Unpublished, ca. 1928–1932.

had sworn to be avenged on the slim, pale woman, who had taken him, her legitimate prey. A wife and a widow since, but the almond eyes still avid for vengeance.

"You must have had some interesting experiences, have you not? Oh, do tell us about some of your early struggles."

The great lawyer expanded under the enveloping perfume of her incense.

"Well," he began, his great voice booming softly in the mountain sunlight, "I shall never forget my first case. I was a briefless barrister, and hungry, or I would not have taken it. Everyone concerned in the affair is dead now, so I can smile at it. My first client was a murderer, a woman. She confessed the truth to me, and expected me to clear her."

"And did you?" chorused an octave of soprano voices.

"Yes. It was the beginning of my career."

A soft intake of breath from the widow, and a flattering flutter from the rest of the veranda left the great lawyer to turn to his host.

But the Squire was oblivious, for coming up the walk was the mistress of the mansion. His soul was in his eyes as he watched her. Her eyes glowed, and her face was windwhipped from riding; she had taken off her hat and her packages dangled from her arm. The lawyer stood in intent stillness. The same lithe form. The same aureole of auburn hair, as yet untinged by gray. The same still, quiet little face with deep pools of eyes. The same questioning droop of the head. She came quickly up the walk and onto the veranda with incredible lightness.

"My dear," said the Squire, his voice a protecting caress, "this is—"

But she extended her hand smilingly to the great lawyer, grasping his with welcoming warmth.

"I did not die, you see," she said in her deep, vibrant voice, "The west gave me health and happiness," and still holding his hand with proprietary grasp, she turned to the group on the veranda.

"Mr. Booth is an old friend of mine, too. You see, I was his very first client, and I flatter myself that I started him on his great career."

Georgia Douglas Johnson

(1877-1966)

Georgia Douglas Camp Johnson was the most prolific woman poet of the Harlem Renaissance and, along with Jessie Fauset, one of its most important female members. She became known as the "lady poet of the Harlem Renaissance," and was the only woman to publish a collection of poetry in her own day. Her poetry was published in every major anthology and journal of the movement, and she published three well-received collections between 1918 and 1928. Johnson's house on S Street in Washington, D.C., affectionately dubbed "Half Way House," became a central gathering place for the most noted African American writers of the 1920s and 1930s. Langston Hughes, Countee Cullen, Angelina Weld Grimké, Zora Neale Hurston, Alain Locke, Marita Bonner, Jessie Fauset, Effie Lee Newsome, Gwendolyn Bennett, and many others found their way to Johnson's home, where she supported them with the creative and intellectual environment they needed. Johnson's friendship was especially important to the careers of Grimké, Hurston, and Newsome. Despite the fact that Johnson rarely made it to Harlem and never to Paris, she was a key artist and organizer of the New Negro movement.

It appears that Johnson falsified her birth date; the recorded date of 1886 in most biographical material is not the date on her birth certificate, September 10, 1877. Her parents were Laura Douglas and George Camp, both of mixed-race descent. They separated when Johnson was a young girl, and Laura Camp resumed her maiden name. Johnson dropped her paternal family name and adopted that of her mother when she married Henry Lincoln Johnson on September 28, 1903. The feminism implicit in this gesture is a hallmark of her verse and life.

Born and raised in Atlanta, Johnson studied at Atlanta University's Normal School, from which she graduated in 1896. She also studied at the Oberlin Conservatory of Music in Ohio, the Cleveland College of Music, and Howard University. She taught music at a high school in Atlanta for ten years, later becoming an assistant principal. When she met and married her attorney husband, Henry Lincoln Johnson, she resigned her position. The couple moved to Washington, D.C. in 1910 with their two sons. "Linc" Johnson was appointed to the prestigious post of recorder of deeds by Republican president Howard Taft in 1912, a position held by a black man since Frederick Douglass's appointment in the nineteenth century. Johnson would remain a lifelong Republican. Johnson's husband died of a stroke in 1925, forcing her to seek employment to support and educate her two sons. Working at government clerical jobs, mostly in the Department of Labor, Johnson sent one son to Bowdoin College and Howard Law School, and the other to Dartmouth and Howard Medical School.

Despite the enormous distraction of full-time employment, it was at this time that Johnson began to play an important role in the Harlem Renaissance. Her Saturday Night gatherings became an important site of contact for Harlem Renaissance writers from 1926 to 1936. Johnson won honorable mention in the 1926 *Opportunity* contest for her play *Blue Blood* and first prize for her play *Plumes* the following year. She was also able to publish a third collection of verse, *An Autumn Love Cycle* (1928), with a foreword by Alain Locke. This joined *The Heart of a Woman and Other Poems* (1918) and *Bronze: A Collection of Verse* (1922), with forewords by William Stanley Braithwaite and W.E.B. Du Bois. (She later self-published one more poetry collection, *Share My World* [1962], with the help of Waring Cuney's brother, who was a printer.) Her numerous poems were published in the leading journals and anthologies of her day, beginning with her first poems in *The Crisis* in 1916. She also wrote a weekly column syndicated in the black press from 1926 to 1932, "Homely Philosophy."

Johnson also wrote many short stories and at least twenty-four plays. Her stories appeared in a variety of magazines but are mainly lost to history because they were published under several male pseudonyms, making proof of authorship difficult. In addition to *Blue Blood* and *Plumes*, which were published in Alain Locke and Montgomery Gregory's *Plays of Negro Life* (1927), Johnson also published two other plays, *Ellen and William Craft* and *Frederick Douglass*. She succeeded in having two of her plays produced on the New York stage in her lifetime. *Plumes* (1927) was performed by the Harlem Experimental Theater, *Blue Blood* (1927) by the Krigwa Players, with playwright May Miller in the lead along with poet Frank Horne. Five others were published posthumously, including *A Sunday Morning in the South* (ca. 1925), the most famous of her eleven anti-lynching dramas.

Johnson never succeeded in getting the fellowships for which she repeatedly applied, which would have released her from the burden of earning a living. Amazingly resilient in the face of repeated rejection by award committees and publishers, she continued to write her entire life, leaving behind an enormous catalogue, which she deposited with Atlanta University. Many of the seventeen books listed in the catalogue, along with countless poems and other writings, were lost when Johnson's home was cleaned out by sanitation workers after her death.

Johnson did, however, receive recognition from her peers. She was given an honorary Ph.D. in literature from Atlanta University the year before she died. Playwright May Miller comforted her in her final days, and Owen Dodson read her poem "I Want to Die While You Love Me" at her funeral.

The Heart of a Woman

The heart of a woman goes forth with the dawn,
As a lone bird, soft winging, so restlessly on,
Afar o'er life's turrets and vales does it roam
In the wake of those echoes the heart calls home.

The heart of a woman falls back with the night,
And enters some alien cage in its plight,
And tries to forget it has dreamed of the stars
While it breaks, breaks, breaks on the sheltering bars.

The Heart of a Woman, 1918.

Motherhood

Don't knock on my door, little child,
I cannot let you in;
You know not what a world this is
Of cruelty and sin.
Wait in the still eternity
Until I come to you.
The world is cruel, cruel, child,
I cannot let you through.

Don't knock at my heart, little one,
I cannot bear the pain
Of turning deaf ears to your call,
Time and time again.
You do not know the monster men
Inhabiting the earth.
Be still, be still, my precious child,
I cannot give you birth.

The Crisis, October 1922.

The Octoroon

One drop of midnight in the dawn of life's pulsating stream
Marks her an alien from her kind, a shade amid its gleam;
Forevermore her step she bends insular, strange, apart—
And none can read the riddle of her wildly warring heart.

The stormy current of her blood beats like a mighty sea
Against the man-wrought iron bars of her captivity.
For refuge, succor, peace and rest, she seeks that humble fold
Whose every breath is kindliness, whose hearts are purest gold.

Bronze, 1922.

Loveless Love

W. C. HANDY
Recorded in 1921.

Love is like a gold brick in a bunco game
Like a banknote with a bogus name
Both have caused many downfalls
Love has done the same.

Love has for its emblem
Cupid with his bow
Loveless love has lots and lots of dough
So carry lots of jack and pick 'em as you go.

Love is like a hydrant, it turns off and on
Like some friendships when your money's gone
Love stands in with the loan sharks
When your heart's in pawn.

If I had some strong wings
Like an aeroplane
Had some broad wings like an aeroplane
I would fly away forever ne'er to come again.

Escape

Shadows, shadows,
Hug me round
So that I shall not be found
By sorrow;
She pursues me
Everywhere,
I can't lose her
Anywhere.

Fold me in your black
Abyss;
She will never look
In this,—
Shadows, shadows,
Hug me round
In your solitude
Profound.

The Crisis, May 1925.

The Black Runner

I'm awake, I'm away!
I have jewels in trust,
They are rights of the soul
That are holy and just;
There are deeds to be done,
There are goals to be won,
I am stripped for the race
In the glare of the sun;
I am throbbing with faith
I can! And I must!
My forehead to God—
My feet in the dust.

Opportunity, September 1925.

Wishes

I'm tired of pacing the petty round of the ring of the thing I know—
I want to stand on the daylight's edge and see where the sunsets go.

I want to sail on a swallow's tail and peep through the sky's blue glass.
I want to see if the dreams in me shall perish or come to pass.

I want to look through the moon's pale crook and gaze on the moon-man's face.
I want to keep all the tears I weep and sail to some unknown place.

The Crisis, April 1927.

Wishes

By GEORGIA DOUGLAS JOHNSON

Illustrated by Laura Wheeler

I'M tired of pacing the petty round of the ring of the thing I know—
I want to stand on the daylight's edge and see where the sunsets go.

I want to sail on a swallow's tail and peep through the sky's blue glass.
I want to see if the dreams in me shall perish or come to pass.

I want to look through the moon's pale crook and gaze on the moon-man's face.
I want to keep all the tears I weep and sail to some unknown place.

Laura Wheeler, "Wishes," *The Crisis,* April 1927

Young Woman's Blues

BESSIE SMITH
Recorded in 1926.

Woke up this mornin' when chickens was crowin' for days
And on the right side of my pilla my man had gone away
By the pilla he left a note reading I'm sorry Jane, you got my goat
No time to marry, no time to settle down
I'm a young woman and ain't done runnin' round
I'm a young woman and ain't done runnin' round.

Some people call me a hobo, some call me a bum
Nobody knows my name, nobody knows what I've done
I'm as good as any woman in your town
I ain't high yeller, I'm a deep killa brown
I ain't gonna marry, ain't gonna settle down
I'm gonna drink good moonshine and run these browns down.

See that long lonesome road
Lord, you know it's gotta end
I'm a good woman and I can get plenty men.

I Want to Die While You Love Me

I want to die while you love me,
   While yet you hold me fair,
While laughter lies upon my lips
   And lights are in my hair.

I want to die while you love me,
   And bear to that still bed
Your kisses turbulent, unspent,
   To warm me when I'm dead.

I want to die while you love me,
   Oh, who would care to live
Till love has nothing more to ask
   And nothing more to give?

I want to die while you love me,
   And never, never see
The glory of this perfect day
   Grow dim or cease to be!

An Autumn Love Cycle, 1928.

Tramp Love

I rode the street car to the end of the line just a little way inside the city limits the north side of Columbus. Then I walked a hundred yards or so and sat down on the grass underneath a tree. It was nice there out of the sun; the ground seemed so cool after hot pavements of the city. Automobiles skimmed almost silently over the highway. A freight engine moved lazily up and down bumping cars around in the yard, across the road, and down in the gully. I could see the engineer in the window mopping his face with a red bandana. The almost colorless smoke went right up straight from the hot stack; little heat waves jiggled before my eyes.

Stretching out on my stomach, I rolled a cigarette. I had turned my back on the highway and the railroad track. A golf course began here, a little way from the road. Men and women moved around in pairs all over the course. The grass was brown and dry, and dust came up in little whirls from their steps. As I watched I envied them just a little. Their nice white clothes, their parked automobiles, their homes and dinners awaiting them. Cool drinks, cool salads. Mothers, fathers, babies, everything that a homeless tramp often longs for, for a moment.

I rolled over on my back and gazed up at the clear, hot sky. Winged seeds drifted by up there in the air. They seemed alive as they moved. I knew they were moving swiftly, for as I looked through the leaves of the tree they passed out of sight like a flash. The air was so dead and still that not a leaf on the tree stirred. I fell to wondering about the air currents that must be moving up above where the seeds floated. I was almost asleep.

Another street car had come out and stopped with a jangling noise at the end of the line. I sat up to watch it. The conductor was already out, changing the trolley around for the return to the city, when a girl stepped down from the car carrying a small black bag. She began walking up the highway. Her hair was very blond. The sun shone from it as she turned her head once to look back at the car. She wore white slacks and seemed quite neat and trim as she tripped swiftly along the highway toward where I was sitting.

I pushed my battered old felt hat back on my head and let the brown paper cigarette dangle unlighted from my lower lip. A car or two passed her before she neared me. I knew by the way she looked up that she was a hitch-hiker. The cars were crowded and didn't stop. When she came opposite where I sat, she looked easily at me. She hesitated only an instant, then the little black bag sailed through the air to light on the ground beside me. She took off her white knitted beret, and with it dangling in her hand, she walked through the shallow ditch toward me.

"Hello," she called out. "It looks cool in the shade there."

She came nearer, fluffing her hair with one hand. It was wispy and curly like white gold.

Challenge, Spring 1937. Published under the name Paul Tremaine.

I lay back on my side and one elbow and watched her as she kicked the bag over with one foot, sat down on it, kicked her slippers off, wiggled her toes and observed them seriously for a moment.

She looked at me. "Have you a cigarette?"

"I have the makin's."

She held out her hand. "Gimme, please."

I picked up the can and papers and handed them to her. She was expert. Her fingers twisted a dandy smoke as rapidly as I could. I scratched a match on my shoe and held it out to her. When she had a light I relighted my own dead butt. She inhaled deeply and then looked around her. She observed everything all around on both sides of us in silence, smoking.

I, too, was silent; just looked at her. She was only a kid. Not more than twenty. Hardly that. Clean and neat, just like she had stepped out of a band-box, so to speak. Her slacks were ordinary white duck. They were men's slacks, worked over. Above them she wore a waist[1] of thin, white silk. I could see the pale green lace brassiere over the tiny breasts. Her throat was delicate and the skin a little red but very smooth. No paint on her face or lips. Just a light coat of powder.

My elbow and shoulder began to ache from lying like that. I dropped down on my back and blew smoke towards the sky.

A motor or two hummed by on the road. The engine over in the yards blew a shrill blast. A bell clanged.

She began to talk. Her voice was soft. It came easily, and not too deep. She had a peculiar, almost Southern accent, or maybe more Western than Southern.

"It's nice to be sitting here in the shade. It's summer—quiet and still. No one cares about us. Automobiles go zipping past. Nothing to bother about. Nothing to worry about. We can sit here as long as we like or leave when we want to. I don't have nothing to—we don't have nothing," she finished suddenly. "Do we?"

I turned my head to look at her. "No, nothing," I agreed. "We just lay down when we're tired and rest. The world is ours. Always there is someone who will give us a ride when we want to go. Some may scowl at us and shake their heads, but always there is one. Yeah, girlie, it's sure nice in the summer. Sure is."

I sat up and began to roll another cigarette.

A couple of men, hitch-hikers, came past on the road. They stopped to wave thumbs, halfheartedly, at a passing car which didn't stop. They looked at us. We looked at them. One of them eyed my tobacco greedily.

"Smoke, fellas," I called.

They scrambled through the grass and eagerly accepted my tobacco and papers. They were dirty and tired out. Long, deeply lined faces. Belts with long flapping tongues pulled tightly around thin waists. The older of the two returned my papers and tobacco with

1. Shirtwaist; a kind of blouse.

a "Thanks, buddy." His eyes lowered as if in shame. I noticed that neither man met the girl's glance.

Her face was a study of pity and sympathy. The men turned swiftly, shambled back to the road, and walked down it out of sight.

We were silent, our thoughts much alike or poles apart. The girl then took a file from her pocket and began to work on her nails. I broke twigs into tiny lengths.

"You're not like the rest of the fellows. I mean like any of the fellows I've met on the road. I mean—I mean—oh, you're different," she finished lamely. Her hand waved uncertainly in a circle. She studied my face, my clothes, my eyes.

"Have you been out a long time, then?" I asked.

Her blue eyes dimmed and again she bent to her manicuring. "Three years. I've been going from place to place three years."

She stopped her manicuring and stretched out beside me on the grass. She nibbled a grass stem as she told me her story.

She was from Nebraska. Her parents were farmers and very poor. That is, there was a big family and they didn't have much money. She had finished high school and gone to the city. No work. She hated to return home and be a burden to them, so she left first one city and then another. Sometimes she worked, sometimes she just traveled, hitchhiking on the highways. She had been in every state, and done all sorts of work, waitress, child's nurse, and everything else. She wanted to work, liked to work, but there were so many girls looking for jobs, and so many reasons for jobs suddenly ending. Most times the reasons were men.

And the men who picked her up on highways. Sure, she had to be nice to them. She had to pay for many a ride. Not with money, but in the only way a poor girl could pay. Especially a nice-looking young girl. She was not bitter about it. It was the only practical way. She had tried to be clean, had tried to find work first, and at first it had seemed tough to find that all the men were alike in one respect. But she held no ill feeling toward the majority of them. It was that or starve or walk. Some of them had been kind, had given her money. She never asked for it. She went to hotels with them or stayed in the car with them. Sometimes they had been rough truck drivers. They had big roomy bunks in those freight trucks. At first it was pretty hard to take, but one learns it doesn't matter. A bath in the morning, and one forgets the bad taste.

She picked up the tobacco and built another smoke. I lighted it for her. After the first puff she talked again.

"But one thing I refuse to do, and that is work at waiting table or something, and then sleep with the boss to hold the job. I'm willing to do one or the other to get by, but both! Nuheugh, not this little gal! I've been waiting table here in Columbus, getting five dollars a week, paying two for a room and three to spend. Not much, but it was enough. The boss has been trying to make me ever since I've been here, three weeks now. Last night he told me plain. I'd either come to his room or get out. I got out. He's the kind of man I hate. The others? Well, I'm just fair game for them."

Her voice went dreamy. "I just keep going and going. Doing the best I can, keeping as close to ways I was taught as I can, and still exist. Lots of soap and water and clean clothes, hoping and dreamin' that a day will come when I can get a break, a good guy, a fairy prince." She broke off, "Oh hell! I'm crazy, I guess."

I lay with my chin on my hands, gazing out across the golf course. In my heart I pitied her, liked her spirit, admired her. She was a square little thing—frank and practical as hell. I had met many girls on the road, but none like her. She had a brain to think with. She lived as best she could.

"Tell me," she questioned. "Why are you so different from the others I've met?"

"I don't know," I answered, "unless it's because I've always been a tramp. Always. I don't care about anything. I'm pretty much like you, I guess, mentally speaking. Of course, I'm a man; that's our only difference. Do you understand?"

"I think I do," she answered. "I see it now. We're alike. I should have known that without asking. But tell me, isn't there anything you long for? Something you're really crazy to have?"

I thought for awhile. "No. There's nothing. And most of the things I do get or have, I care nothing about."

She turned on her side and studied me again. "How about girls? Don't you ever crave that kind of companionship? Most men do."

"There are times when I think about them. There've been times when the idea seemed rather nice, but to really care or crave or long for them or for one, I don't think I ever did."

She put a hand on my arm. "If I stayed here with you all night, I mean. Would it make you happy? Would you like to have me?"

I jerked my head to look into her frank eyes. She was just being kind, wanting to share what she had of happiness with one she thought in need of it.

"I would be happy while you were here," I answered softly, "but tomorrow after you had gone, I would be more unhappy than ever."

She nodded slowly, slapping me once or twice on the back. "Fella," she said, "if things were different I reckon I could learn to love you like I dream of loving someone. You're the kind. But we haven't anything. We don't want anything except security or nothing. Do we?"

I shook my head.

She got to her feet saying, "I better be going. I want to get to another town tonight."

I got up, too, and stretched and sat down again. She combed her hair down smooth and picked up her bag to go. Then she set it down again and reached inside her white blouse. Her brassiere had a pocket in it. She brought out a few folded bills.

"You got any money?" she asked. "I know a guy can't raise money on the road so easy as a girl."

"You're a good little egg, girlie," I replied. "Sure I've got dough. I was in a crap game last night." I showed her a roll of bills.

She tucked hers back into the little pocket and picked up the bag again. She stood looking at me almost tenderly.

"Well, if you ever see me again, sing out, won't you?"

I nodded. She turned and walked out to the road.

A car came. A seaman. I knew from his appearance, for one learns on the road. One glance and a driver is labeled.

He slowed and stopped. She put her bag in the back and got in front beside him. He looked down at her, smiling, then shifted gears. The car started. She turned and looked back. She didn't wave.

I smoked for hours, then I dropped off to sleep. When I awoke it was dark. The skies were clouded. A stiff breeze had come up. Off toward the south a rain storm was blowing up. A train was just whistling out of the yards. I had time to make it, and started to walk over to the yards. A few drops of rain splattered on my hat. I ran then, and just swung up into a car as the skies exploded with tons of water. The whistle sounded eerie and weak as it came drifting back along the train.

Plumes
A Folk Tragedy

Characters

CHARITY BROWN, the mother
EMMERLINE BROWN, the daughter
TILDY, the friend
DOCTOR SCOTT, physician

Scene: A poor cottage in the South.
Time: Contemporary.

Scene: The kitchen of a two-room cottage. A window overlooking the street. A door leading to street, one leading to the back yard and one to the inner room. A stove, a table with a shelf over it, a washtub. A rocking-chair, a cane-bottom chair. Needle, thread, scissors, etc. on table.
    Scene opens with CHARITY BROWN heating a poultice[1] over the stove. A groaning is heard from the inner room.

Charity: Yes, honey, mamma is fixing somethin' to do you good. Yes, my baby, jus' you wait—I'm a-coming. *(knock is heard at door. It is gently pushed open and TILDY comes in cautiously)*

  Tildy: *(whispering)* How is she?

---

1. A poultice is a concoction of ingredients designed to put on a sick person's chest or wound in order to help heal an infection.

Plays of Negro Life, 1927.

Charity: Poorly, poorly. Didn't rest last night none hardly. Move that dress and set in th' rocker. I been trying to snatch a minute to finish it but don't seem like I can. She won't have nothing to wear if she—she—

Tildy: I understands. How near done is it?

Charity: Ain't so much more to do.

Tildy: *(takes up dress from chair; looks at it)* I'll do some on it.

Charity: Thank you, sister Tildy. Whip that torshon[2] on and turn down the hem in the skirt.

Tildy: *(measuring dress against herself)* How deep?

Charity: Let me see, now. *(studies a minute with finger against lip)* I tell you—jus' baste it, 'cause you see—she wears 'em short, but—it might be— *(stops)*

Tildy: *(bowing her head comprehendingly)* Uh-huh, I see exzackly. *(sighs)* You'd want it long—over her feet—then.

Charity: That's it, sister Tildy. *(listening)* She's some easy now! *(stirring poultice)* Jest can't get this poltis' hot enough somehow this morning.

Tildy: Put some red pepper in it. Got any?

Charity: Yes. There ought to be some in one of them boxes on the shelf there. *(Points)*

Tildy: *(goes to shelf, looks about and gets the pepper)* Here, put a-plenty of this in.

Charity: *(groans are heard from the next room)* Good Lord, them pains got her again. She suffers so, when she's 'wake.

Tildy: Poor little thing. How old is she now, sister Charity?

Charity: Turning fourteen this coming July.

Tildy: *(shaking her head dubiously)* I sho' hope she'll be mended by then.

Charity: It don't look much like it, but I trusts so— *(looking worried)* That doctor's mighty late this morning.

Tildy: I expects he'll be 'long in no time. Doctors is mighty onconcerned here lately.

Charity: *(going toward inner room with poultice)* They surely is and I don't have too much confidence in none of 'em. *(You can hear her soothing the child)*

Tildy: *(listening)* Want me to help you put it on, sister Charity?

Charity: *(from inner room)* No, I can fix it. *(coming back from sick room shaking her head rather dejectedly)*

Tildy: How is she, sister Charity?

Charity: Mighty feeble. Gone back to sleep now. My poor little baby. *(bracing herself)* I'm going to put on some coffee now.

Tildy: I'm sho' glad. I feel kinder low-spirited.

Charity: It's me that low-spirited. The doctor said last time he was here he might have

---

2. "Torshon" is a variant of "torsion," which means a twisting of something. Therefore, a torshon here is a decorative twisted piece of material.

to operate—said, she mought have a chance then. But I tell you the truth, I've got no faith a-tall in 'em. They takes all your money for nothing.

Tildy: They sho' do and don't leave a cent for putting you away decent.

Charity: That's jest it. They takes all you got and then you dies jest the same. It ain't like they was sure.

Tildy: No, they ain't sure. That's it exzackly. But they takes your money jest the same, and leaves you flat.

Charity: I been thinking 'bout Zeke these last few days—how he was put away—

Tildy: I wouldn't worry 'bout him now. He's out of his troubles.

Charity: I know. But it worries me when I think about how he was put away . . . that ugly pine coffin, jest one shabby old hack and nothing else to show—to show—what we thought about him.

Tildy: Hush, sister! Don't you worry over him. He's happy now, anyhow.

Charity: I can't help it! Then little Bessie. We all jest scrooged in one hack and took her little coffin in our lap all the way out to the graveyard. *(breaks out crying)*

Tildy: Do hush, sister Charity. You done the best you could. Poor folks got to make the best of it. The Lord understands—

Charity: I know that—but I made up my mind the time Bessie went that the next one of us what died would have a shore nuff funeral, everything grand,—with plumes!—I saved and saved and now—this yah doctor—

Tildy: All they think about is cuttin' and killing and taking your money. I got nothin' to put 'em doing.

Charity: *(goes over to washtub and rubs on clothes)* Me neither. These clothes got to get out somehow, I needs every cent.

Tildy: How much that washing bring you?

Charity: Dollar and a half. It's worth a whole lot more. But what can you do?

Tildy: You can't do nothing—Look there, sister Charity, ain't that coffee boiling?

Charity: *(wipes hands on apron and goes to stove)* Yes, it's boiling good fashioned. Come on, drink some.

Tildy: There ain't nothing I'd rather have than a good strong cup of coffee. *(CHARITY pours TILDY's cup.) (sweetening and stirring hers)* Pour you some. *(CHARITY pours her own cup)* I'd been dead, too, long ago if it hadn't a been for my coffee.

Charity: I love it, but it don't love me—gives me the shortness of breath.

Tildy: *(finishing her cup, taking up sugar with spoon)* Don't hurt me. I could drink a barrel.

Charity: *(drinking more slowly—reaching for coffeepot)* Here, drink another cup.

Tildy: I shore will, that cup done me a lot of good.

Charity: *(looking into her empty cup thoughtfully)* I wish Dinah Morris would drop in now. I'd ask her what these grounds mean.

Tildy: I can read 'em a little myself.

Charity: You can? Well, for the Lord's sake, look here and tell me what this cup says! *(offers cup to TILDY. TILDY wards it off)*

Tildy: You got to turn it 'round in your saucer three times first.

Charity: Yes, that's right, I forgot. *(turns cup 'round, counting)* One, two, three. *(starts to pick it up)*

Tildy: Huhunh. *(meaning no)* Let it set a minute. It might be watery. *(After a minute, while she finishes her own cup)* Now let me see. *(takes cup and examines it very scrutinizingly)*

Charity: What you see?

Tildy: *(hesitatingly)* I ain't seen a cup like this one for many a year. Not since—not since—

Charity: When?

Tildy: Not since jest before ma died. I looked in the cup then and saw things and— I stopped looking . . .

Charity: Tell me what you see, I want to know.

Tildy: I don't like to tell no bad news—

Charity: Go on. I can stan' anything after all I been thru'.

Tildy: Since you're bound to know I'll tell you. *(CHARITY draws nearer)* I sees a big gethering!

Charity: Gethering, you say?

Tildy: Yes, a big gethering. People all crowded together. Then I see 'em going one by one and two by two. Long line stretching out and out and out!

Charity: *(in a whisper)* What you think it is?

Tildy: *(awed like)* Looks like *(hesitates)* a possession![3]

Charity: *(shouting)* You sure!

Tildy: I know it is. *(Just then the toll of a church bell is heard and then the steady and slow tramp, tramp of horses' hoofs. Both women look at each other)*

Tildy: *(in a hushed voice)* That must be Bell Gibson's funeral coming 'way from Mt. Zion. *(gets up and goes to window)* Yes, it sho' is.

Charity: *(looking out of the window also)* Poor Bell suffered many a year; she's out of her pain now.

Tildy: Look, here comes the hearse now!

Charity: My Lord! ain't it grand! Look at them horses—look at their heads—plumes— how they shake 'em! Lawd o' mighty! It's a fine sight, sister Tildy.

Tildy: That must be Jer'miah in that first carriage, bending over like; he shorely is putting her away grand.

Charity: No mistake about it. That's Pickett's best funeral turnout he's got.

---

3. Procession. This may be a deliberate misspelling by the author to indicate the vernacular term for procession, or it may be a typographical error in the original text.

Tildy: I'll bet it cost a lot.

Charity: Fifty dollars, so Matilda Jenkins told me. She had it for Bud. The plumes is what cost.

Tildy: Look at the hacks— *(counts)* I believe to my soul there's eight.

Charity: Got somebody in all of 'em too—and flowers—She shore got a lot of 'em. *(Both women's eyes follow the tail end of the procession, horses' hoofs die away as they turn away from window. The two women look at each other significantly)*

Tildy: *(significantly)* Well!— *(They look at each other without speaking for a minute. CHARITY goes to the washtub)* Want these cups washed up?

Charity: No, don't mind 'em. I'd rather you get that dress done. I got to get these clothes out.

Tildy: *(picking up dress)* Shore, there ain't so much more to do on it now. *(Knock is heard on the door. CHARITY answers knock and admits DR. SCOTT)*

Dr. Scott: Good morning. How's the patient today?

Charity: Not so good, doctor. When she ain't 'sleep she suffers so; but she sleeps mostly.

Dr. Scott: Well, let's see, let's see. Just hand me a pan of warm water and I'll soon find out just what's what.

Charity: All right, doctor. I'll bring it to you right away. *(bustles about fixing water—looking toward dress TILDY is working on)* Poor little Emmerline's been wanting a white dress trimmed with torshon a long time—now she's got it and it looks like—well— *(hesitates)* t'warn't made to wear.

Tildy: Don't take on so, sister Charity—The Lord giveth and the Lord taketh.

Charity: I know—but it's hard—hard— *(goes into inner room with water. You can hear her talking with the doctor after a minute and the doctor expostulating with her—in a minute she appears at the door, being led from the room by the doctor)*

Dr. Scott: No, my dear Mrs. Brown. It will be much better for you to remain outside.

Charity: But, doctor—

Dr. Scott: No. You stay outside and get your mind on something else. You can't possibly be of any service. Now be calm, will you?

Charity: I'll try, doctor.

Tildy: The doctor's right. You can't do no good in there.

Charity: I knows, but I thought I could hold the pan or somethin'. *(lowering her voice)* Says he got to see if her heart is all right or somethin'. I tell you—nowadays—

Tildy: I know.

Charity: *(softly to TILDY)* Hope he won't come out here saying he got to operate. *(goes to washtub)*

Tildy: I hope so, too. Won't it cost a lot?

Charity: That's jest it. It would take all I got saved up.

Tildy: Of course, if he's goin' to get her up—but I don't believe in 'em. I don't believe in 'em.

Charity: He didn't promise tho'—even if he did, he said maybe it wouldn't do no good.

Tildy: I'd think a long time before I'd let him operate on my chile. Taking all yuh money, promising nothing and ten to one killing her to boot.

Charity: This is a hard world.

Tildy: Don't you trus' him. Coffee grounds don't lie!

Charity: I don't trust him. I jest want to do what's right by her. I ought to put these clothes on the line while you're settin' in here, but I jest hate to go outdoors while he's in there.

Tildy: *(getting up)* I'll hang 'em out. You stay here. Where your clothespins at?

Charity: Hanging right there by the back door in the bag. They ought to dry before dark and then I can iron to-night.

Tildy: *(picking up tub)* They ought to blow dry in no time. *(goes toward back door)*

Charity: Then I can shore rub 'em over to-night. Say, sister Tildy, hist 'em up with that long saplin' prop leaning in the fence corner.

Tildy: *(going out)* All right.

Charity: *(standing by the table beating nervously on it with her fingers—listens—and then starts to bustling about the kitchen) (enter DOCTOR from inner room)*

Dr. Scott: Well, Mrs. Brown, I've decided I'll have to operate.

Charity: My Lord! Doctor—don't say that!

Dr. Scott: It's the only chance.

Charity: You mean she'll get well if you do?

Dr. Scott: No, I can't say that—It's just a chance—a last chance. And I'll do just what I said, cut the price of the operation down to fifty dollars. I'm willing to do that for you. *(CHARITY throws up her hands in dismay)*

Charity: Doctor, I was so in hopes you wouldn't operate—-I— I—And yo' say you ain't a bit sure she'll get well—even then?

Dr. Scott: No. I can't be sure. We'll just have to take the chance. But I'm sure you want to do everything—

Charity: Sure, doctor, I do want to—do—everything I can do to—to— Doctor, look at this cup. *(picks up fortune cup and shows the doctor)* My fortune's jes' been told this very morning—look at these grounds—they says— *(softly)* it ain't no use, no use a-tall.

Dr. Scott: Why, my good woman, don't you believe in such senseless things! That cup of grounds can't show you anything. Wash them out and forget it.

Charity: I can't forget it. I feel like it ain't no use; I'd just be spendin' the money that I needs—for nothing—nothing.

Dr. Scott: But you won't though—You'll have a clear conscience. You'd know that you did everything you could.

Charity: I know that, doctor. But there's things you don't know 'bout—there's other things I got to think about. If she goes—if she must go . . . I had plans—I been getting ready—now—Oh, doctor, I jest can't see how I can have this operation— you say you can't promise—nothing?

Dr. Scott: I didn't think you'd hesitate about it—I imagined your love for your child—

Charity: *(breaking in)* I do love my child. My God, I do love my child. You don't understand . . . but . . . but—can't I have a little time to think about it, doctor? It means so much—to her—and—me!

Dr. Scott: I tell you. I'll go on over to the office. I'd have to get my— *(hesitates)* my things, anyhow. And as soon as you make up your mind, get one of the neighbors to run over and tell me. I'll come right back. But don't waste any time now, Mrs. Brown, every minute counts.

Charity: Thank you, doctor, thank you. I'll shore send you word as soon as I can. I'm so upset and worried I'm half crazy.

Dr. Scott: I know you are . . . but don't take too long to make up your mind. . . . It ought to be done to-day. Remember—it may save her. *(exits)*

Charity: *(goes to door of sick room—looks inside for a few minutes, then starts walking up and down the little kitchen, first holding a hand up to her head and then wringing them. Enter TILDY from yard with tub under her arm)*

Tildy: Well, they're all out, sister Charity— *(stops)* Why, what's the matter?

Charity: The doctor wants to operate.

Tildy: *(softly)* Where [is] he—gone?

Charity: Yes—he's gone, but he's coming back—if I send for him.

Tildy: You going to? *(puts down tub and picks up white dress and begins sewing)*

Charity: I dunno—I got to think.

Tildy: I can't see what's the use myself. He can't save her with no operation— Coffee grounds don't lie.

Charity: It would take all the money I got for the operation and then what about puttin' her away? He can't save her—don't even promise ter. I know he can't— I feel it . . . I feel it . . .

Tildy: It's in the air . . . *(Both women sit tense in the silence. TILDY has commenced sewing again. Just then a strange, strangling noise comes from the inner room)*

Tildy: What's that?

Charity: *(running toward and into inner room)* Oh, my God! *(from inside)* Sister Tildy—Come here—No,— Some water, quick. *(TILDY with dress in hand starts toward inner room. Stops at door, sighs and then goes hurriedly back for the water pitcher. CHARITY is heard moaning softly in the next room, then she appears at doorway and leans against jamb of door)* Rip the hem out, sister Tildy.

Curtain

Angelina Weld Grimké

(1880–1958)

Angelina Weld Grimké was born in Boston on February 27, 1880, the only child of an emancipated slave and Harvard Law School graduate, Archibald Henry Grimké, and a white woman, Sarah Stanley. Archibald was the son of Henry Grimké, himself the son of a South Carolina slaveholder, and Nancy Weston, a slave on the Grimké plantation. Henry's sisters were the famous abolitionists Sarah Moore Grimké and Angelina Grimké Weld, after the latter of whom Angelina was named. When her parents separated in 1883, Grimké lived with her mother for another year and then returned to her father, a U.S. consul and attorney. Grimké was educated at elite schools where she was frequently the only African American student; she attended the Fairmount School in Hyde Park, the Carleton Academy in Minnesota, the Cushing Academy in Massachusetts, and the Boston Normal School of Gymnastics. After her graduation from Normal School in 1902, she taught high school in Washington, D.C., first at the Armstrong Manual Training School and then, in 1916, at the Dunbar High School, where she stayed until her retirement in 1926.

Despite the absence of her mother (who died when Grimké was eighteen) during most of her life, Grimké's creative writing frequently centered on motherhood and contained loving mother figures. Grimké herself, however, vowed early on, when she was only twenty-three, not to marry or have children. This decision appears to have resulted from an unhappy love affair, perhaps with a woman, that ended with Grimké in despair. It is known that she formed a close romantic attachment to African American actress and playwright Mary Burrill in the mid-1890s when they were schoolmates, but it is not clear that Burrill was the person with whom she was involved. Grimké's biographer, Gloria Hull, relates that her unpublished poetry contains many explicitly lesbian allusions and that she was probably a lesbian herself but without an intimate relationship beyond girlhood.

Grimké's fame rests on a slender, though distinguished, selection of poems written in the 1920s and published in *Opportunity* and every major anthology of her day, except *The Book of American Negro Poetry* (1922). Countee Cullen's *Caroling Dusk* (1927) included more of Grimké's poems than of any other female poet in the collection. Her poetry is lyrical, imagistic, poignant, and frequently woman-centered; Grimké is known for her meditations on nature and her love poetry to women. She is also known for her anti-lynching play, *Rachel* (1916), which was credited by Alain Locke as the first successful drama written by an African American interpreted by African American actors. *Rachel* was produced in Washington, D.C., by the NAACP and a year later in Harlem and Cambridge. It was self-financed for publication by Cornhill Publishers in 1920 and reprinted in 1969. Grimké wrote a second anti-lynching play, *Mara*, that was neither produced nor published. Grimké's fiction also centered on lynching. "Goldie," published in *The Atlantic Monthly* in 1920, was based on an actual lynching of a married couple that occurred in Georgia in 1918. This lynching also became the subject of Anne Spencer's 1923 poem "White Things," included in this volume. These writings grew out of Grimké's political activism, which began in 1899 when she was only nineteen and continued through her support of the Dyer Anti-Lynching Bill of 1922.

Grimké was an accomplished writer who excelled in three genres, especially poetry, but most of her work remains unpublished. She tried to publish a novella, *Jettisoned,* which was praised by *Opportunity* editor Charles S. Johnson when he read it in 1925, but she could find no takers. She also assembled a collection of poems at this time entitled *Dusk Dreams,* but it too failed to materialize. Although encouraged and befriended by Georgia Douglas Johnson, who also lived in Washington, D.C., Grimké could not sustain her writing career beyond the twenties. After a railway accident in 1911 that severely injured her back, she struggled with her health. She finally retired in 1926, largely as a result of poor health, and nursed her father through a long illness of his own. After his death in 1930, she moved permanently to New York City. There she lived quietly and in relative financial comfort until her death.

El Beso

Twilight—and you
Quiet—the stars;
Snare of the shine of your teeth,
Your provocative laughter,
The gloom of your hair;
Lure of you, eye and lip;
Yearning, yearning,
Languor, surrender;
Your mouth,
And madness, madness,
Tremulous, breathless, flaming,
The space of a sigh;
Then awakening—remembrance,
Pain, regret—your sobbing;
And again, quiet—the stars,
Twilight—and you.

Negro Poets and Their Poems, 1923. The title means *The Kiss* in Spanish.

The Black Finger

I have just seen a most beautiful thing:
    Slim and still,
  Against a gold, gold sky,
  A straight, black cypress
      Sensitive
      Exquisite
    A black finger
  Pointing upwards.
Why, beautiful still finger, are you black?
And why are you pointing upwards?

Opportunity, November 1923.

The Want of You

A hint of gold where the moon will be;
Through the flocking clouds just a star or two;
Leaf sounds, soft and wet and hushed;
And oh! the crying want of you.

Negro Poets and Their Poems, 1923.

Dusk

Twin stars through my purpling pane,
  The shriveling husk
Of a yellowing moon on the wane—
  And the dusk.

Opportunity, April 1924.

A Mona Lisa

1

I should like to creep
Through the long brown grasses
    That are your lashes;
I should like to poise
    On the very brink
Of the leaf-brown pools
    That are your shadowed eyes;
I should like to cleave
    Without sound,
Their glimmering waters,
    Their unrippled waters;
I should like to sink down
    And down
        And down . . .
            And deeply drown.

2

Would I be more than a bubble breaking?
    Or an ever-widening circle
    Ceasing at the marge?
Would my white bones
    Be the only white bones
Wavering back and forth, back and forth
    In their depths?

Caroling Dusk, 1927.

Tenebris

There is a tree by day,
That, at night,
Has a shadow,
A hand huge and black,
With fingers long and black.
  All through the dark,
Against the white man's house,
  In the little wind,
The black hand plucks and plucks
  At the bricks.
The bricks are the color of blood and very small.
  Is it a black hand,
  Or is it a shadow?

Caroling Dusk, 1927.

Goldie

He had never thought of the night, before, as so sharply black and white; but then, he had never walked before, three long miles, after midnight, over a country road. A short distance only, after leaving the railroad station, the road plunged into the woods and stayed there most of the way. Even in the day, he remembered, although he had not traveled over it for five years, it had not been the easiest to journey over. Now, in the almost palpable darkness, the going was hard, indeed; and he was compelled to proceed, it almost seemed to him, one careful step after another careful step.

Singular fancies may come to one, at such times: and, as he plodded forward, one came, quite unceremoniously, quite unsolicited, to him and fastened its tentacles upon him. Perhaps it was born of the darkness and the utter windlessness with the resulting great stillness; perhaps—but who knows from what fancies spring? At any rate, it seemed to him, the woods, on either side of him, were really not woods at all but an ocean that had flowed down in a great rolling black wave of flood to the very lips of the road itself and paused there as though suddenly arrested and held poised in some strange and sinister spell. Of course, all of this came, he told himself over and over, from having such a cursed imagination; but whether he would or not, the fancy persisted and the growing feeling with it, that he, Victor Forrest, went in actual danger, for at any second the spell might snap and with that snapping, this boundless, deep upon

The Atlantic Monthly, November–December 1920.

deep of horrible, waiting sea, would move, rush, hurl itself heavily and swiftly together from the two sides, thus engulfing, grinding, crushing, blotting out all in its path, not excluding what he now knew to be that most insignificant of insignificant pigmies, Victor Forrest.

But there were bright spots, here and there in the going—he found himself calling them white islands of safety. These occurred where the woods receded at some little distance from the road.

"It's as though," he thought aloud, "they drew back here in order to get a good deep breath before plunging forward again. Well, all I hope is, the spell holds O.K. beyond."

He always paused, a moment or so, on one of these islands to drive out expulsively the dank, black oppressiveness of the air he had been breathing and to fill his lungs anew with God's night air, that here, at least, was sweet and untroubled. Here, too, his eyes were free again and he could see the dimmed white blur of road for a space each way; and, above, the stars, millions upon millions of them, each one hardly brilliant, stabbing its way whitely through the black heavens. And if the island were large enough there was a glimpse, scarcely more, of a very pallid, slightly crumpled moon sliding furtively down the west. —Yes, sharply black and sharply white, that was it, but mostly it was black.

And as he went, his mind busy enough with many thoughts, many memories, subconsciously always the aforementioned fancy persisted, clung to him; and he was never entirely able to throw off the feeling of his very probable and imminent danger in the midst of this arrested wood-ocean.

—Of course, he thought, it was downright foolishness, his expecting Goldie, or rather Cy, to meet him. He hadn't written or telegraphed.—Instinct he guessed, must have warned him that wouldn't be safe; but, confound it all! This was the devil of a road.—Gosh! What a lot of noise a man's feet could make—couldn't they?—All alone like this.—Well, Goldie and Cy would feel a lot worse over the whole business than he did.—After all it was only once in a lifetime, wasn't it?—Hoofing it was good for him, anyway.—No doubt about his having grown soft.—He'd be as lame as the dickens tomorrow.—Well, Goldie would enjoy that—liked nothing better than fussing over a fellow.—If (But he very resolutely turned away from that if.)

—In one way, it didn't seem like five years and yet, in another, it seemed longer— since he'd been over this road last. It had been the sunshiniest and the saddest May morning he ever remembered.—He'd been going in the opposite direction, then; and that little sister of his, Goldie, had been sitting very straight beside him, the two lines held rigidly in her two little gold paws and her little gold face stiff with repressed emotion. He felt a twinge, yet, as he remembered her face and the way the great tears would well up and run over down her cheeks at intervals.—Proud little thing!—She had disdained even to notice them and treated them as a matter with which she had no concern.—No, she hadn't wanted him to go.—Good, little Goldie!—Well, she never knew, how close, how very close he had been to putting his hand out and telling her to turn back—he'd changed his mind and wasn't going after all.—

He drew a sharp breath.—He hadn't put out his hand.

—And at the station, her face there below him, as he looked down at her through the open window of the train.—The unwavering way her eyes had held his—and the look in them, he hadn't understood then, or didn't now, for that matter.

"Don't," he had said. "Don't, Goldie!"

"I must. Vic, I must.—I don't know.—Don't you understand I may never see you again?"

"Rot!" he had said. "Am I not going to send for you?"

—And then she had tried to smile and that had been worse than her eyes.

"You think so, now, Vic—but will you?"

"Of course."

"Vic!"

"Yes."

"Remember, whatever it is—it's all right. *It's all right.*—I mean it.—See! I couldn't smile—could I?—if I didn't?"

And then, when it had seemed as if he couldn't stand any more—he had leaned over, even to pick up his bag to get off, give it all up—the train had started and it was too late. The last he had seen of her, she had been standing there, very straight, her arms at her sides and her little gold paws little tight fists.—And her eyes!—And her twisted smile!—God! That was about enough of that.—He was going to her, now, wasn't he?

—Had he been wrong to go?—Had he?—Somehow, now, it seemed that way.—And yet, at the time, he had felt he was right.—He still did for that matter.—His chance, that's what it had meant.—Oughtn't he to have had it?—Certainly a colored man couldn't do the things that counted in the South.—To live here, just to *live* here, he had to swallow his self-respect.—Well, he had tried, honestly, too, for Goldie's sake, to swallow his.—The trouble was he couldn't keep it swallowed—it nauseated him.—The thing for him to have done, he saw that now, was to have risked everything and taken Goldie with him.—He shouldn't have waited, as he had from year to year, to send for her.—It would have meant hard sledding, but they could have managed somehow.—Of course, it wouldn't have been the home she had had with her Uncle Ray and her Aunt Millie, still.—Well, there wasn't any use in crying over spilt milk. One thing was certain, never mind how much you might wish to, you couldn't recall the past.—

—Two years ago—(gosh!) but time flew!—when her letter had come telling him she had married Cy Harper.—Queer thing, this life!—Darned queer thing!—Why, he had been in the very midst of debating whether or not he could afford to send for her—had almost decided he could.—Well, sisters, even the very best of them, it turned out, weren't above marrying and going off and leaving you high and dry—just like this.—Oh! of course, Cy was a good enough fellow, clean, steady going, true, and all the rest of it—no one could deny that—still, confound it all! how could Goldie prefer a fathead like Cy to him.—Hm!—peeved yet, it seemed!—Well, he'd acknowledge it—he was peeved all right.

Involuntarily he began to slow up.

—Good! Since he was acknowledging things—why not get along and acknowledge the rest.—Might just as well have this out with himself here and now.— Peeved first, then, what?

He came to an abrupt stop in the midst of the black silence of the arrested wood-ocean.

—There was one thing, it appeared, a dark road could do for you—it could make it possible for you to see yourself quite plainly—almost too plainly.—Peeved first, then what?—No blinking now, the truth.—He'd evaded himself very cleverly—hadn't he?—up until tonight?—No use any more.—Well, what was he waiting for?—Out with it. —Peeved first; go ahead, now.—Louder!—*Relief!*—Honest, at last.—Relief! Think of it, he had felt relief when he had learned he wasn't to be bothered, after all, with little, loyal, big-hearted Goldie.—*Bothered!*—And he had prided himself upon being rather a decent, upright, respectable fellow.—Why, if he had heard this about anybody else, he wouldn't have been able to find language strong enough to describe him—a rotter, that's what he was, and a cad.

"And Goldie would have sacrificed herself for you any time, and gladly, and you know it."

To his surprise he found himself speaking aloud.

—Why once, when the kid had been only eight years old and he had been taken with a cramp while in swimming, she had jumped in too!—Goldie, who couldn't swim a single stroke!—Her screams had done it and they were saved. He could see his mother's face yet, quizzical, a little puzzled, a little worried.

"But what on earth, Goldie, possessed you to jump in too?" she had asked. "Didn't you *know* you couldn't save him?"

"Yes, I knew it."

"Then, why?"

"I don't know. It just seemed that if Vic had to drown, why, I had to drown with him.—Just couldn't live *afterwards,* Momsey. If I lived *then* and he drowned."

"Goldie! Goldie!—If Vic fell out of a tree, would you have to fall out too?"

"Proberbly." Goldie had never been able to master "probably," but it fascinated her.

"Well, for Heaven's sake. Vic, do be careful of yourself hereafter. You see how it is," his mother had said.

And Goldie had answered—how serious, how quaint, how true her little face had been.—

"Yes, that's how it is, isn't it?" Another trick of hers, ending so often what she had to say with a question.—And he hadn't wished to be bothered with her!—

He groaned and started again.

—Well, he'd try to even up things a little, now.—He'd show her (there was a lump in his throat) if he could.—

For the first time Victor Forrest began to understand the possibilities of tragedy that may lie in those three little words, "If I can."

—Perhaps Goldie had understood and married Cy so that he needn't bother any more about having to have her with him. He hoped, as he had never hoped for anything before, that this hadn't been her reason. She was quite equal to marrying, he knew, for such a motive—and so game, too, you'd never dream it was a sacrifice she was making. He'd rather believe, even, that it had been just to get the little home all her own.—When Goldie was only a little thing and you asked her what she wanted most in all the world when she grew up, she had always answered:

"Why, a little home—all my own—a cunning one—and young things in it and about it. "

And if you asked her to explain, she had said:

"Don't you *know*?—not *really*?"

And, then, if you had suggested children, she had answered:

"Of course, all my own; and kittens and puppies and little fluffy chickens and ducks and little birds in my trees, who will make little nests and little songs there because they will know that the trees near the little home all my own are the very nicest ever and ever."—

—Once, she must have been around fifteen, then—how well he remembered that once—he had said:

"Look here, Goldie, isn't this an awful lot you're asking God to put over for you?"

Only teasing, he had been—but Goldie's face!

"Oh! Vic, am I?—Do you *really* think that?"

And then, before he could reply, in little, eager, humble rushes:

"I hadn't thought of it—*that* way—before.—Maybe you're right.—If—if—I gave up something, perhaps—the ducks—or the chickens—or the—birds—or the kittens—or the puppies?"

Then very slowly:

"Or—the—children?—Oh!—But I couldn't!—Not any of them.—Don't you think, perhaps—just perhaps, Vic—if—if—I'm—good—always—from now on—that—that—maybe—maybe—sometime, Vic, sometime—I—I—might?—Oh! Don't you?"—

He shut his mouth hard.

—Well, she had had the little home all her own. Cy had made a little clearing, she had written, just beyond the great live oak. Did he remember it? And did he remember, too, how much Cy loved the trees?—

—No, he hadn't forgotten that live oak—not the way he had played in it—and carved his initials all over it; and he hadn't forgotten Cy and the trees, either. —Silly way, Cy had had, even after he grew up, of mooning among them.

"Talk to me—they do—sometimes.—Tell me big, quiet things, nice things."

—Gosh! After *his* experience, *this* night among them. *Love* 'em!—Hm!—Damned, waiting, greedy things!—Cy could have them and welcome.—

—It had been last year Goldie had written about the clearing with the little home all her own in the very "prezact" middle of it.—They had had to wait a whole year after they were married before they could move in—not finished or something—he'd forgotten the reason.—How had the rest of that letter gone? —Goldie's letters were easy to remember—had, somehow, a sort of burrlike quality about them. He had it, now, something like this:

She wished she could tell him how cunning the little home all her own was, but there was really no cunning word cunning enough to describe it. —Why even the very trees came right down to the very edges of the clearing on all four sides just to look at it. — If he could only *see* how proudly they stood there and nodded their entire approval one to the other!—

Four rooms the little home, all her own, had—Four! —And a little porch in the front and a "littler" one in the back, and a hall that had really the most absurd way of trying to get out both the front and rear doors at the same time. Would he believe it, they had to keep both the doors shut tight in order to hold that ridiculous hall in. Had he ever, in all his life, heard of such a thing? And just off of this little hall, at the right of the front door, was their bedroom, and back of this, at the end of this same very silly hall, was their dining room, and opposite, across the hall again—she hoped he saw how this hall simply refused to be ignored—again—opposite was the kitchen.—He was, then, to step back into the hall once more, but *this* time he was to pretend very hard not to see it. There was no telling, its vanity was so great, if you paid too much attention to it, what it might do. Why, the unbearable little thing might rise up, break down the front and back doors and escape; and then where'd they be, she'd like to know, without any little hall at all? —He was to step, then, quite nonchalantly—if he knew what that was—back into the hall and come forward, but this time he was to look at the room at the left of the front door; and *there,* if he pleased, he would see something really to repay him for his trouble, for here he would behold her sitting room and parlor both in one. And if he couldn't believe how perfectly adorable this little room could be and was, why she was right there to tell him all about it. —Every single bit of the little home all her own was built just as she had wished and furnished just as she had hoped. And, well, to sum it all up, it wasn't safe, if you had any kind of heart trouble at all, to stand in the road in front of the little home all her own, because it had such a way of calling you that before you knew it, you were running to it and running fast. She could vouch for the absolute truth of this statement.

And she had a puppy, yellow all over, all but his little heart—she dared him even to suggest such a thing!—with a funny wrinkled forehead and a most impudent grin. And he insisted upon eating up all the uneatable things they possessed, including Cy's best straw hat and her own Sunday-go-to-meeting slippers. And she had a kitten, a grey one; and the busiest things he did were to eat and sleep. Sometimes he condescended to play with his tail and to keep the puppy in his place. He had a way of looking at you out of blue, very young, very innocent eyes that you knew perfectly well were not a bit young nor yet a bit innocent. And she had the darlingest, downiest little chickens and ducks and a canary bird, which Emma Elizabeth lent her sometimes when she went away to work, and the canary had been made of two golden songs. And outside of the little home all her own—in the closest trees—the birds were, lots of them, and they had nested there. —If, of a morning, he could only hear them singing! —As if they knew—and did it on purpose—just as she had wished. —How happy it had all sounded—and yet—and yet—once or twice—he had had the feeling that something wasn't quite right.

—He hoped it didn't mean she wasn't caring for Cy. —He would rather believe it was because there hadn't been children. —The latter could be remedied—from little hints he had been gathering lately, he rather thought it was already being remedied; but if she didn't *care* for Cy, there wasn't much to be done about that. —Well, he was going to her, at last. —She couldn't fool him—couldn't Goldie; and if that fathead, Cy, couldn't take care of her, now. Just let somebody start something. —

—That break ahead there, in the darkness, ought to be just about where the settlement was. —No one need ever tell *him* again it was only three miles from the station— he guessed he knew better. —More like ten or twenty. —The settlement, all right. —Thought he hadn't been mistaken. —So far, then, so good.

The road, here, became the main street of the little colored settlement. Three or four smaller ones cut it at right angles and then ran off into the darkness. The houses, for the most part, sat back, not very far apart; and, as the shamed moon had entirely disappeared, all he could make out of them was their silent, black little masses. His quick eyes and his ears were busy. No sound broke the stillness. He drew a deep breath of relief. As nearly as he could make out, everything was as it should be.

He did not pause until he was about midway of the settlement. Here he set his bag down, sat on it and looked at the illuminated hands of his watch. It was half past two. In the woods he had found it almost cold, but in this spot the air was warm and close. He pulled out his handkerchief, took off his hat, mopped his face, head and neck, finally the sweatband of his hat.

—Queer!—But he wouldn't have believed that the mere sight of all this, after five years, could make him feel this way. There was something to this home idea, after all. —Didn't feel, hardly, as though he had ever been away.—

Suddenly he wondered if old man Tom Jackson had fixed that gate of his yet. Curiosity got the better of him. He arose, went over and looked. Sure enough the gate swung outward on a broken hinge. Forrest grinned.

"Don't believe over much here in change, do they? —That gate was that way ever since I can remember.—Bet every window is shut tight too. Turrible, the night air always used to be. —Wonder if my people will ever get over these things."

He came back and sat down again. He was facing a house that his eyes had returned to more than any other.

"Looks just the same.—Wonder who lives there now. —Suppose someone does. — Looks like it.—Mother sure had courage—more than I would have had—to give up a good job in the North, teaching school, to come down here and marry a poor doctor in a colored settlement. I give it to her. —Game!—Goldie's just like her—she'd have done it too."

—How long had it been since his father had died? —Nine—ten—why, it was ten years and eight since his mother—. They'd both been born there—he and Goldie. —What was that story his mother had used to tell about him when he had first been brought in to see her? —He had been six at the time.

"Mother," he had asked, "is her gold?"

"What, son?"

"I say, is her gold?"

"Oh! I see," his mother had said and smiled, he was sure, that very nice understanding smile of hers. "Why, she *is* gold, isn't she?"

"Yes, all of her. What's her name?"

"She hasn't any yet, son."

"She ain't got no name? —Too bad! —I give her one. Her name's Goldie, 'cause."

"All right, son, Goldie it shall be." And Goldie it had always been.

—No, you couldn't call Goldie pretty exactly. —Something about her, though, mighty attractive. —Different looking! —That was it. —Like herself. —She had never lost that beautiful even gold color of hers. —Even her hair was "goldeny" and her long eyelashes. Nice eyes Goldie had, big and brown with flecks of gold in them—set in a little wistful, pointed face. —

He came to his feet suddenly and picked up his bag. He moved swiftly now, but not so swiftly as not to notice things still as he went.

"Why, hello!" he exclaimed and paused a second or so before going on again. "What's happened to Uncle Ray's house?—Something's not the same. —Seems larger, somehow. —Wonder what it is?—Maybe a porch. —So they do change here a little. —That there ought to be Aunt Phoebe's house. —But she must be dead—though I don't remember Goldie's saying so. —Why, she'd be way over ninety. —Used to be afraid of the dark or something and never slept without a dim light. —Gosh! If there isn't the light—just the same as ever. —And way over ninety. —Whew! —Wonder how it feels to be that old.—Bet I wouldn't like it.—Gee! What's that?"

Victor Forrest stopped short and listened. The sound was muffled but continuous, it seemed to come from the closed, faintly lighted pane of Aunt Phoebe's room. It was a sound, it struck him, remarkably like the keening he had heard in an Irish play. It died out slowly and, though he waited, it did not begin again.

"Probably dreaming or something and woke herself up," and he started on once more.

He soon left the settlement behind and, continuing along the same road, found himself (he hoped for the last time) in the midst of the arrested wood-ocean.

But the sound of that keening, although he had explained it quite satisfactorily to himself, had left him disturbed. Thoughts, conjectures, fears that he had refused, until now, quite resolutely to entertain no longer would be denied. They were rooted in Goldie's last two letters, the cause of his hurried trip South.

"Of course, there's no *real* danger. —I'm foolish, even, to entertain such a thought. —Women get like that sometimes—nervous and overwrought. —And if it is with her as I suspect and hope—why the whole matter's explained. —Why it had really sounded *frightened!* —And parts of it were—hm! —almost incoherent. —The whole thing's too ridiculous, however, to believe. —Well, when she sees me we'll have a good big laugh over it all. —Just the same, I'm glad I came. —Rather funny—somehow—thinking of Goldie—with a kid—in her arms. —Nice, though."

—Lafe Coleman! —Lafe Coleman! —He seemed to remember dimly a stringy, long white man with stringy colorless hair quite disagreeably unclean; eyes a pale grey and fishlike. —He associated a sort of toothless grin with that face. —No, that wasn't it, either. —Ah!

That was it! —He had it clearly, now. —The grin was all right but it displayed the dark and rotting remains of tooth stumps.—

He made a grimace of strong disgust and loathing.

—And—this—this—*thing* had been annoying Goldie, had been in fact, for years. — She hadn't told anybody, it seems, because she had been able to take care of herself. —But since she had married and been living away from the settlement—it had been easier for him, and much more difficult for her. He wasn't to worry, though, for the man was stupid and so far she'd always been able to outwit [him]— What she feared was Cy. It was true Cy was amiability itself—but—well—she had seen him angry once. —Ought she to tell him? —She didn't believe Cy would kill the creature—not outright—but it would be pretty close to it. —The feeling between the races was running higher than it used to. —There had been a very terrible lynching in the next county only last year. —She hadn't spoken of it before—for there didn't seem any use going into it. —As he had never mentioned it, she supposed it had never gotten into the papers. Nothing, of course, had been done about it, nothing ever was. Everybody knew who was in the mob. —Even he would be surprised at some of the names. —The brother of the lynched man, quite naturally, had tried to bring some of the leaders to justice; and he, too, had paid with his life. Then the mob, not satisfied, had threatened, terrorized, cowed all the colored people in the locality. —He was to remember that when you were under the heel it wasn't the most difficult of matters to be terrorized and cowed. There was absolutely no law, as he knew, to protect a colored man. —That was one of the reasons she had hesitated to tell Cy, for not only Cy and she might be made to pay for what Cy might do, but the little settlement as well. Now, keeping all this in mind, ought she to tell Cy?

And the letter had ended:

"I'm a little nervous, Vic, and frightened and not quite sure of my judgment. Whatever you advise me to do, I am sure will be right."

—On the very heels of this had come the "special" mailed by Goldie in another town. —She hadn't dared, it seemed, to post it in Hopewood. —It had contained just twelve words, but they had brought him South on the next train.

"Cy knows," it had said, "and O! Vic, if you love me, come, come, come!"

Way down inside of him, in the very depths, a dull, cold rage began to glow, but he banked it down again, carefully, very carefully, as he had been able to do, so far, each time before that the thoughts of Lafe Coleman and little Goldie's helplessness had threatened anew to stir it.

—That there ought to be the great live oak—and beyond should be the clearing, in the very "prezact" middle of which should be the little home all Goldie's own. —

For some inexplicable reason his feet suddenly began to show a strange reluctance to go forward.

"Damned silly ass!" he said to himself. "There wasn't a thing wrong with the settlement. That ought to be a good enough sign for anybody with a grain of sense."

And then, quite suddenly, he remembered the keening.

He did not turn back to pause, still his feet showed no tendency to hasten. Of necessity, however, it was only a matter of time before he reached the live oak. He came to a halt beside it, ears and every sense keenly on the alert. Save for the stabbing, white stars above the clearing, there was nothing else in all the world, it seemed, but himself and the heavy black silence.

Once more he advanced but, this time, by an act of sheer will. He paused, set his jaw and faced the clearing. In the very center was a small dark mass; it must be the little home. The breath he had drawn in sharply, while turning, he emitted in a deep sigh. His knees felt strangely weak. —What he had expected to see exactly, he hardly knew. He was almost afraid of the reaction going on inside of him. The relief, the blessed relief at merely finding it there, the little house all her own!

It made him feel suddenly very young and joyous and the world, bad as it was, a pretty decent old place after all. Danger! —Of course, there was no danger. —How could he have been so absurd? —Just wait until he had teased Goldie aplenty about this. He started to laugh aloud but caught himself in time. —No use awaking them. —He'd steal up and sit on the porch—there'd probably be a chair there or something—and wait until dawn. —They shouldn't be allowed to sleep one single second after that. —And then he'd bang on their window, and call out quite casually:

"O, Goldie Harper, this is a nice way—isn't it? —to treat a fellow; not even to leave the latch string out for him?"

He could hear Goldie's little squeal now.

And then he'd say to Cy:

"Hello, you big fathead, you! —What do you mean, anyhow, by making a perfectly good brother-in-law hoof it the whole way here, like this?"

He had reached the steps by this time and he began softly to mount them. It was very dark on the little porch and he wished he dared to light a match, but he mustn't risk anything that might spoil the little surprise he was planning. He transferred his bag from his right to his left hand, the better to feel his way. With his fingers outstretched in front of him he took a cautious step forward and stumbled over something.

"Clumsy chump!" he exclaimed below his breath. "That will about finish your little surprise I am thinking." He stood stockstill for several seconds, but there was no sound.

"Some sleepers," he commented.

He leaned over to find out what it was he had stumbled against and discovered that it was a broken chair lying on its side. Slowly he came to a standing posture. He was not as happy for some reason. He stood there, very quiet, for several moments. Then his hand stretched out before he started forward again. This time, after only a couple of steps, his hand came in contact with the housefront. He was feeling his way along, cautiously still, when all of a sudden his fingers encountered nothing but air. Surprised, he paused. He thought, at first, he had come to the end of the porch. He put out a carefully exploring foot only to find firm boards beneath. A second time he experimented, with the same result. And then, as suddenly, he felt the housefront once more beneath his fingers. Gradually it came to him where he must be. He was standing before the door and it was open, wide open!

He could not have moved if he had wished. He made no sound and none broke the blackness all about.

It was sometime afterwards when he put his bag down upon the porch, took a box of matches out of his pocket, lit one and held it up. His hand was trembling, but he managed, before it burned his fingers and he blew it out automatically, to see four things— two open doors to right and left, a lamp in a bracket just beyond the door at the left and a dirty mudtrodden floor.

The minutes went by and then it seemed to him, somebody else called out:

"Goldie! Cy!" This was followed by silence only.

Again the voice tried, a little louder this time:

"Goldie! Cy!" —There was no response.

_____

This other person, who seemed, somehow, to have entered into his body, moved forward, struck another match, lit the lamp and took it down out of the bracket. Nothing seemed to make very much difference to this stranger. He moved his body stiffly; his eyes felt large and dry. He passed through the open door at the left and what he saw there did not surprise him in the least. In some dim way, only he knew that it affected him.

There was not, in this room, one single whole piece of furniture. Chairs, tables, a sofa, a whatnot, all had been smashed, broken, torn apart; the stuffing of the upholstery, completely ripped out; and the entirety thrown, scattered, here, there and everywhere. The piano lay on one side, its other staved in. —Something, it reminded him of—something to do with a grin—the black notes like the rotting stumps of teeth. Oh, yes! Lafe Coleman! —That was it. The thought aroused no particular emotion in him. Only, again he knew it affected him in some far off way.

Every picture on the walls had been wrenched down and the moulding with it, the pictures themselves defaced and torn, and the glass splintered and crushed under foot. Knickknacks, vases, a china clock, all lay smashed and broken. Even the rug upon the floor had not escaped, but had been ripped up, torn into shreds and fouled by many dirty feet. The frail white curtains and window shades had gone down too in this human whirlwind; not a pane of glass was whole. The white woodwork and the white walls were soiled and smeared. Over and over the splay-fingered imprint of one dirty hand repeated itself on the walls. A wanton boot had kicked through the plastering in places.

This someone else went out of the door, down the hall, into the little kitchen and dining room. In each room he found precisely the same conditions prevailing.

There was one left, he remembered, so he turned back into the hall, went along it to the open door and entered in. —What was the matter, here, with the air? —He raised the lamp higher above his head. He saw the same confusion as elsewhere. A brass bed was overturned and all things else shattered and topsy-turvy. There was something dark at the foot of the bed. He moved nearer, and understood why the air was not pleasant. The dark object was a little dead dog, a yellow one, with a wrinkled forehead. His teeth were bared in a snarl. A kick in the belly had done for him. He leaned over; the little leg was quite stiff. Less dimly this time, he knew that this affected him.

He straightened up. When he had entered the room there had been something he had noticed for him to do. But what was it? This stranger's memory was not all that it should be. —Oh, yes! He knew, now. The bed. He was to right the bed. With some difficulty he cleared a space for the lamp and set it down carefully. He raised the bed. Nothing but the mattress and the rumpled and twisted bed clothing. He didn't know exactly just what this person was expecting to find.

He was sitting on the steps, the extinguished lamp at his side. It was dawn. Everything was veiled over with grey. As the day came on, a breeze followed softly after, and with the breeze there came to him there on the steps a creaking, two creakings! —Somewhere there to the right they were, among the trees. The grey world became a shining green one. Why were the birds singing like that, he wondered. —It didn't take the day long to get here—did it?—once it started. A second time his eyes went to the woods at the right. He was able to see now. Nothing there, as far as he could make out. His eyes dropped from the trees to the ground and he beheld what looked to him like a trampled path. It began there at the trees; it approached the house; it passed over a circular bed of little pansies. It ended at the steps. Again his eyes traversed the path, but this time from the steps to the trees.

Quite automatically he arose and followed the path. Quite automatically he drew the branches aside and saw what he saw. Underneath those two terribly mutilated swinging bodies, lay a tiny unborn child, its head crushed in by a deliberate heel.

Something went very wrong in his head. He dropped the branches, turned and sat down. A spider, in the sunshine, was reweaving the web someone had just destroyed while passing through the grass. He sat slouched far forward, watching the spider for hours. He wished the birds wouldn't sing so. —Somebody had said something once about them. He wished, too, he could remember who it was.

About midday, the children of the colored settlement, playing in the road, looked up and saw a man approaching. There was something about him that frightened them, the little ones in particular, for they ran screaming to their mothers. The larger ones drew back as unobtrusively as possible into their own yards. The man came on with a high head and an unhurried gait. His should have been a young face, but it was not. Out of its set sternness looked his eyes, and they were very terrible eyes indeed. Mothers with children, hanging to them from behind and peering around, came to their doors. The man was passing through the settlement now. A woman, startled, recognized him and called the news out shrilly to her man eating his dinner within. He came out, went down to the road rather reluctantly. The news spread. Other men from other houses followed the first man's example. They stood about him, quite a crowd of them. The stranger, of necessity, came to a pause. There were no greetings on either side. He eyed them over, this crowd, coolly, appraisingly, contemptuously. They eyed him, in turn, but surreptitiously. They were plainly very uncomfortable. Wiping their hands on aprons, women joined the crowd. A larger child or two dared the outskirts. No one would meet his eye.

Suddenly a man was speaking. His voice came sharply, jerkily. He was telling a story. Another took it up and another.

One added a detail here; one a detail there. Heated arguments arose over insignificant particulars; angry words were passed. Then came too noisy explanations, excuses, speeches in extenuation of their own actions, pleas, attempted exoneration of themselves. The strange man said never a word. He listened to each and to all. His contemptuous eyes made each writhe in turn. They had finished. There was nothing more that they could see to be said. They waited, eyes on the ground, for him to speak.

But what he said was:

"Where is Uncle Ray?"

Uncle Ray, it seemed, was away—had been for two weeks. His Aunt Millie with him. No one had written to him, for his address was not known.

The strange man made no comment.

"Where is Lafe Coleman?" he asked.

No one there knew where he was to be found—no one. They regretted the fact, they were sorry, but they couldn't say. They spoke with lowered eyes, shifting their bodies uneasily from foot to foot.

Watching their faces he saw their eyes suddenly lift, as if with one accord, and focus upon something behind him and to his right. He turned his head. In the brilliant sunshine, a very old, very bent form leaning heavily on a cane was coming down the path from the house in whose window he had seen the dimmed light. It was Aunt Phoebe.

He left the crowd abruptly and went to meet her. When she was quite sure he was coming she paused where she was, bent over double, her two hands, one over the other, on the knob of her cane, and waited for him. No words, either, between these two. He looked down at her and she bent back her head, tremulous from age, and looked up at him.

The wrinkles were many and deep-bitten in Aunt Phoebe's dark skin. A border of white wool fringed the bright bandana tied tightly around her head. There were grey hairs in her chin; two blue rings encircled the irises of her dim eyes. But all her ugliness could not hide the big heart of her, kind yet, and brave, after ninety years on earth.

And as he stood gazing down at her, quite suddenly he remembered what Goldie had once said about those circled eyes.

"Kings and Queens may have *their* crowns and welcome. What's there to *them?* — But the kind Aunt Phoebe wears—that's different. She earned hers, Vic, earned them through many years and long of sorrow, and heartbreak and bitter, bitter tears. She bears with her the unforgetting heart. —And though they could take husband and children and sell them South, though she lost them in the body—never a word of them, since—she keeps them always in her heart. —I know, Vic, I know—and God who is good and God who is just touched her eyes, both of them and gave her blue crowns, beautiful ones, a crown for each. Don't you see *she is of God's Elect?*"

For a long time Victor Forrest stood looking down into those crowned eyes. No one disturbed these two in the sun-drenched little yard. They, in the road, drew closer together and watched silently.

And then he spoke:

"You are to tell me, Aunt Phoebe—aren't you? —where I am to find Lafe Coleman?"

Aunt Phoebe did not hesitate a second. "Yes," she said, and told him.

The crowd in the road moved uneasily, but no one spoke.

And then Victor Forrest did a thing he had never done before: he leaned over swiftly and kissed the wrinkled parchment cheek of Aunt Phoebe.

"Goldie loved you," he said and straightened up, turned on his heel without another word and went down the path to the road. Those there made no attempt to speak. They drew closer together and made way for him. He looked neither to the right nor to the left. He passed them without a glance. He went with a steady, purposeful gait and a high head. All watched him for they knew they were never to see him alive again. The woods swallowed Victor Forrest. A low keening was to be heard. Aunt Phoebe had turned and was going more feebly, more slowly than ever toward her house.

Those that know whereof they speak say that when Lafe Coleman was found he was not a pleasant object to see. There was no bullet in him—nothing like that. It was the marks upon his neck and the horror of his blackened face.

And Victor Forrest died, as the other two had died, upon another tree.

There is a country road upon either side of which grow trees even to its very edges. Each tree has been chosen and transplanted here for a reason and the reason is that at some time each has borne upon its boughs a creaking victim. Hundreds of these trees there are, thousands of them. They form a forest—"Creaking Forest" it is called. And over this road many pass, very, very many. And they go jauntily, joyously here—even at night. They do not go as Victor Forrest went, they do not sense the things that Victor Forrest sensed. If their souls were not deaf, there would be many things for them to hear in Creaking Forest. At night the trees become an ocean dark and sinister, for it is made up of all the evil in all the hearts of all the mobs that have done to death their creaking victims. It is an ocean arrested at the very edges of the road by a strange spell. But this spell may snap at any second and with that snapping this sea of evil will move, rush, hurl itself heavily and swiftly together from the two sides of the road, engulfing, grinding, crushing, blotting out all in its way.

THE CRISIS

JUNE 1927　　　　　　　　　　15¢ A COPY

Vivian Schuyler, "Drawing from Life," cover of *The Crisis,* June 1927

Rachel

In Raoma, was there a voice heard, lamentation, and weeping, and great mourning. Rachel weeping for her children, and would not be comforted, because they are not.

—Matthew 2:18

Cast of Characters

MRS. LOVING, mother
RACHEL LOVING, her daughter
TOM LOVING, her son
JOHN STRONG, Tom's friend
JIMMY, the neighbor's small boy
MRS. LANE, a black woman
ETHEL, her daughter
EDITH, LOUISE, NANCY, MARY, MARTHA, JENNY, children

ACT ONE

The scene is a room scrupulously neat and clean and plainly furnished. The walls are painted green, the woodwork, white. In the rear at the left (left and right are from the spectator's point of view) an open doorway leads into a hall. Its bare, green wall and white baseboard are all that can be seen of it. It leads into the other rooms of the flat. In the center of the rear wall of the room is a window. It is shut. The white sash curtains are pushed to right and left as far as they will go. The green shade is rolled up to the top. Through the window can be seen the red bricks of a house wall, and the tops of a couple of trees moving now and then in the wind. Within the window, and just below the sill, is a shelf upon which are a few potted plants. Between the window and the door is a bookcase full of books and above it, hanging on the wall, a simply framed, inexpensive copy of Millet's The Reaper.[1] *There is a run extending from the right center to just below the right upper entrance. It is the vestibule of the flat. Its open doorway faces the left wall. In the right wall near the front is another window. Here the sash curtains are drawn together and the green shade is partly lowered. The window is up from the bottom. Through it street noises can be heard. In front of this window is an open, threaded sewing-machine. Some frail, white fabric is lying upon it. There is a chair in front of the machine and at the machine's left a small table covered with a green cloth. In the rear of the left wall and directly opposite to the entrance to the flat is the doorway leading into the kitchenette; dishes on shelves can be seen behind glass doors.*

In the center of the left wall is a fireplace with a grate in it for coals; over this is a wooden mantel painted white. In the center is a small clock. A pair of vases, green and white in coloring, one at each end, complete the ornaments. Over the mantel is a narrow mirror; and over this, hanging on the wall, Burne-Jones' Golden Stairs,[2] *simply framed. Against the front end*

---

1. Jean-François Millet, a nineteenth-century French landscape painter. *The Reaper* (1866–1868) portrays a (white) male peasant working in a field.

2. Sir Edward Burne-Jones, a late-nineteenth-century British painter. *The Golden Stairs* (1880) portrays angels (white women) dressed in white classical gowns descending a staircase.

Produced in 1916; published in 1920.

of the left wall is an upright piano with a stool in front of it. On top is music neatly piled. Hanging over the piano is Raphael's Sistine Madonna.[3] *In the center of the floor is a green rug, and in the center of this, a rectangular dining-room table, the long side facing front. It is covered with a green tablecloth. Three dining-room chairs are at the table, one at either end and one at the rear facing front. Above the table is a chandelier with four gas jets enclosed by glass globes. At the right front center is a rather shabby armchair upholstered in green.*

Before the sewing-machine, MRS. LOVING is seated. She looks worried. She is sewing swiftly and deftly by hand upon a waist in her lap.[4] It is a white, beautiful thing and she sews upon it delicately. It is about half-past four in the afternoon; and the light is failing. Mrs. Loving pauses in her sewing, rises and lets the window-shade near her go up to the top. She pushes the sash-curtains to either side, the corner of a red brick house wall being thus brought into view. She shivers slightly, then pushes the window down at the bottom and lowers it a trifle from the top. The street noises become less distinct. She takes off her thimble, rubs her hands gently, puts the thimble on again, and looks at the clock on the mantel. She then reseats herself, with her chair as close to the window as possible and begins to sew. Presently a key is heard, and the door opens and shifts noisily. RACHEL comes in from the vestibule. In her left arm she carries four or five books strapped together, under her right, a roll of music. Her hat is twisted over her left ear and her hair is falling in tendrils about her face. She brings into the room with her the spirit of abounding life, health, joy, youth. MRS. LOVING pauses, needle in hand, as soon as she hears the turning key and the banging door. There is a smile on her face. For a second, mother and daughter smile at each other. Then RACHEL throws her books upon the dining-room table, places the music there also, but with care, and rushing to her mother, gives her a bear hug and a kiss.

Rachel: Ma dear! Dear old Ma dear!

Mrs. Loving: Look out for the needle, Rachel! The waist! Oh, Rachel!

Rachel: (on her knees and shaking her finger directly under her mother's nose) You old, old fraud! You know you adore being hugged. I've a good mind . . .

Mrs. Loving: Now, Rachel, please! Besides, I know your tricks. You think you can make me forget you are late. What time is it?

Rachel: (looking at the clock and expressing surprise) Jiminy Xmas! (whistles) Why, it's five o'clock!

Mrs. Loving: (severely) Well!

Rachel: (plaintively) Now, Ma dear, you're going to be horrid and cross.

Mrs. Loving: (laughing) Really, Rachel, that expression is not particularly affecting, when your hat is over your ear, and you look, with your hair over your eyes, exactly like some one's pet poodle. I wonder if you are ever going to grow up and be ladylike.

Rachel: Oh! Ma dear, I hope not, not for the longest time, two long, long years at least. I just want to be silly and irresponsible, and have you to love and torment, and, of course, Tom, too.

3. Raphael, an Italian Renaissance painter. The *Sistine Madonna* (1513) is one of his most famous works.
4. Shirtwaist; a kind of blouse, normally white.

Mrs. Loving: (*smiling down at RACHEL*) You'll not make me forget, young lady. Why are you late, Rachel?

Rachel: Well, Ma dear, I'm your pet poodle, and my hat is over my ear, and I'm late, for the loveliest reason.

Mrs. Loving: Don't be silly, Rachel.

Rachel: That may sound silly, but it isn't. And please don't "Rachel" me so much. It was honestly one whole hour ago when I opened the front door down stairs. I know it was, because I heard the postman telling some one it was four o'clock. Well, I climbed the first flight, and was just starting up the second, when a little shrill voice said, "Lo!" I raised my eyes, and there, half-way up the stairs, sitting in the middle of a step, was just the dearest, cutest, darlingest little brown baby boy you ever saw. "Lo! yourself," I said. "What are you doing, and who are you anyway?" "I'm Jimmy; and I'm widing to New York on the choo-choo tars." As he looked entirely too young to be going such a distance by himself, I asked him if I might go too. For a minute or two he considered the question and me very seriously, and then he said, "Es," and made room for me on the step beside him. We've been everywhere: New York, Chicago, Boston, London, Paris and Oshkosh. I wish you could have heard him say that last place. I suggested going there just to hear him. Now, Ma dear, is it any wonder I am late? See all the places we have been in just one "teeny, weeny" hour? We would have been traveling yet, but his horrid, little mother came out and called him in. They're in the flat below, the new people. But before he went, Ma dear, he said the "cunningest" thing. He said, "Will you turn out an' p'ay wif me aden in two minutes?" I nearly hugged him to death, and it's a wonder my hat is on my head at all. Hats are such unimportant nuisances anyway!

Mrs. Loving: Unimportant nuisances! What ridiculous language you do use, Rachel! Well, I'm no prophet, but I see very distinctly what is going to happen. This little brown baby will be living here night and day. You're not happy unless some child is trailing along in your rear.

Rachel: (*mischievously*) Now, Ma dear, who's a hypocrite? What? I suppose you don't like children! I can tell you one thing, though, it won't be my fault if he isn't here night and day. Oh, I wish he were all mine, every bit of him! Ma dear, do you suppose that "the woman" he calls mother would let him come up here until it is time for him to go to bed? I'm going down there this minute. (*rises impetuously*)

Mrs. Loving: Rachel, for Heaven's sake! No! I am entirely too busy and tired today without being bothered with a child romping around in here.

Rachel: (*reluctantly and a trifle petulantly*) Very well, then. (*For several moments she watches her mother, who has begun to sew again. The displeasure vanishes from her face*) Ma dear!

Mrs. Loving: Well.

Rachel: Is there anything wrong today?

Mrs. Loving: I'm just tired, chickabiddy, that's all.

Rachel: *(moves over to the table. Mechanically takes off her hat and coat and carries them out into the entryway of the flat. She returns and goes to the looking glass over the fireplace and tucks in the tendrils of her hair in rather a preoccupied manner. The electric doorbell rings. She returns to the speaking tube in the vestibule. Her voice is heard answering)* Yes!—Yes! —No, I'm not Mrs. Loving. She's here, yes!— What? Oh! come right up! *(appearing in the doorway)* Ma dear, it's some man, who is coming for Mrs. Strong's waist.

Mrs. Loving: *(pausing and looking at RACHEL)* It is probably her son. She said she would send for it this afternoon. *(RACHEL disappears. A door is heard opening and closing. There is the sound of a man's voice. RACHEL ushers in MR. JOHN STRONG)*

Strong: *(bowing pleasantly to MRS. LOVING)* Mrs. Loving? *(MRS. LOVING bows, puts down her sewing, rises and goes toward STRONG)* My name is Strong. My mother asked me to come by and get her waist this afternoon. She hoped it would be finished.

Mrs. Loving: Yes, Mr. Strong, it is all ready. If you'll sit down a minute, I'll wrap it up for you. *(She goes into hallway leading to other rooms in flat)*

Rachel: *(manifestly ill at ease at being left alone with a stranger; attempting, however, to be the polite hostess)* Do sit down, Mr. Strong. *(They both sit)*

Rachel: *(nervously after a pause)* It's a very pleasant day, isn't it, Mr. Strong?

Strong: Yes, very. *(He leans back composedly, his hat on his knee, the faintest expression of amusement in his eyes)*

Rachel: *(after a pause)* It's quite a climb up to our flat, don't you think?

Strong: Why, no! It didn't strike me so. I'm not old enough yet to mind stairs.

Rachel: *(nervously)* Oh! I didn't mean that you are old! Anyone can see you are quite young, that is, of course, not too young, but,— *(STRONG laughs quietly)* There! I don't blame you for laughing. I'm always clumsy just like that.

Mrs. Loving: *(calling from the other room)* Rachel, bring me a needle and the sixty cotton, please.

Rachel: All right, Ma dear! *(rummages for the cotton in the machine drawer, and upsets several spools upon the floor. To STRONG)* You see! I can't even get a spool of cotton without spilling things all over the floor. *(STRONG smiles, RACHEL picks up the spools and finally gets the cotton and needle)* Excuse me! *(goes out door leading to other rooms. STRONG, left to himself, looks around casually. The* Golden Stairs *interests him and the* Sistine Madonna*)*

Rachel: *(reenters, evidently continuing her function of hostess)* We were talking about the climb to our flat, weren't we? You see, when you're poor, you have to live in a top flat. There is always a compensation, though; we have bully— I mean nice air, better light, a lovely view, and nobody "thud-thudding" up and down over our heads night and day. The people below have our "thud-thudding," and it must be something *awful*, especially when Tom and I play "Ivanhoe" and have a tournament up here. We're entirely too old, but we still play. Ma dear rather dreads the climb up three flights, so Tom and I do all the errands. We don't mind climbing the stairs, particularly when we go up two or three at a time,—that is—Tom still does. I can't; Ma dear stopped me. *(sighs)* I've got to grow up it seems.

Strong: *(evidently amused)* It is rather hard being a girl, isn't it?

Rachel: Oh, no! It's not hard at all. That's the trouble; they won't let me be a girl. I'd love to be.

Mrs. Loving: *(reentering with parcel. She smiles)* My chatterbox, I see, is entertaining you, Mr. Strong. I'm sorry to have kept you waiting, but I forgot, I found, to sew the ruching in the neck. I hope everything is satisfactory. If it isn't, I'll be glad to make any changes.

Strong: *(who has risen upon her entrance)* Thank you, Mrs. Loving, I'm sure everything is all right.

(He takes the package and bows to her and RACHEL. He moves towards the vestibule, MRS. LOVING following him. She passes through the doorway first. Before leaving, Strong turns for a second and looks back quietly at RACHEL. He goes out too. RACHEL returns to the mirror, looks at her face for a second, and then begins to touch and pat her hair lightly and delicately here and there. MRS. LOVING returns)

Rachel: *(still at the glass)* He *was* rather nice, wasn't he Ma dear?—for a man? *(laughs)* I guess my reason's a vain one,—he let me do all the talking. *(pauses)* Strong? Strong? Ma dear, is his mother the little woman with the sad, black eyes?

Mrs. Loving: *(resuming her sewing; sitting before the machine)* Yes. I was rather curious, I confess, to see this son of hers. The whole time I'm fitting her she talks of nothing else. She worships him. *(pauses)* It's rather a sad case, I believe. She is a widow. Her husband was a doctor and left her a little money. She came up from the South to educate this boy. Both of them worked hard and the boy got through college. Three months he hunted for work that a college man might expect to get. You see he had the tremendous handicap of being colored. As the two of them had to live, one day, without her knowing it, he hired himself out as a waiter. He has been one now for two years. He is evidently goodness itself to his mother.

Rachel: *(slowly and thoughtfully)* Just because he is *colored!* *(pauses)* We sing a song at school, I believe, about "The land of the free and the home of the brave." What an amusing nation it is.

Mrs. Loving: *(watching RACHEL anxiously)* Come, Rachel, you haven't time for "amusing nations." Remember, you haven't practised any this afternoon. And put your books away; don't leave them on the table. You didn't practise any this morning either, did you?

Rachel: No, Ma dear,—didn't wake up in time. *(goes to the table and in an abstracted manner puts books on the bookcase; returns to the table; picks up the roll of sheet music she has brought home with her; brightens; impulsively)* Ma dear, just listen to this lullaby. It's the sweetest thing. I was so "daffy" over it, one of the girls at school lent it to me. *(She rushes to the piano with the music and plays the accompaniment through softly and then sings, still softly and with great expression, Jessie Gaynor's "Slumber Boat")*[5] . . . Listen, Ma dear, right here. Isn't it lovely? *(plays and sings very softly and slowly)* . . . *(pauses, in hushed tones)* Ma dear, it's so beautiful—it—hurts.

Mrs. Loving: *(quietly)* Yes, dear, it is pretty.

Rachel: *(for several minutes watches her mother's profile from the piano stool. Her expression is rather wistful)* Ma dear!

Mrs. Loving: Yes, Rachel.

Rachel: What's the matter?

Mrs. Loving: *(without turning)* Matter! What do you mean?

Rachel: I don't know. I just *feel* something is not quite right with you.

Mrs. Loving: I'm only tired—that's all.

Rachel: Perhaps. But— *(watches her mother a moment or two longer; shakes her head; turns back to the piano. She is thoughtful; looks at her hands in her lap)* Ma dear, wouldn't it be nice if we could keep all the babies in the world—always little babies? Then they'd be always little, and cunning, and lovable; and they could never grow up, then, and—and—be bad. I'm so sorry for mothers whose little babies—grow up—and—and—are bad.

Mrs. Loving: *(startled; controlling herself, looks at RACHEL anxiously, perplexedly. RACHEL's eyes are still on her hands. Attempting a light tone)* Come, Rachel, what experience have you had with mothers whose babies have grown up to be bad? You—you talk like an old, old woman.

Rachel: *(without raising her eyes, quietly)* I know I'm not old; but, just the same I know that is true. *(softly)* And I'm so sorry for the mothers.

Mrs. Loving: *(with a forced laugh)* Well, Miss Methuselah, how do you happen to know all this? Mothers whose babies grow up to be bad don't, as a rule, parade their faults before the world.

Rachel: That's just it—that's *how* you know. They don't talk at all.

Mrs. Loving: *(involuntarily)* Oh! *(ceases to sew; looks at RACHEL sharply; she is plainly worried. There is a long silence. Presently RACHEL raises her eyes to Raphael's Madonna over the piano. Her expression becomes rapt; then, very softly, her eyes still on the picture, she plays and sings Nevin's "Mighty Lak a Rose")*[6] . . .

Rachel: *(with head still raised, after she has finished, she closes her eyes. Half to herself and slowly)* I think the loveliest thing of all the lovely things in this world is just *(almost in a whisper)* being a mother!

Mrs. Loving: *(turns and laughs)* Well, of all the startling children, Rachel! I am getting to feel, when you're around, as though I'm shut up with dynamite. What next? *(RACHEL rises, goes slowly to her mother, and kneels down beside her. She does not touch her mother)* Why so serious, chickabiddy?

5. "Slumber Boat" was a popular song of the period.
6. Ethelbert Nevin, a white turn-of-the-century songwriter known for his sentimental lyrics.

Rachel: (slowly and quietly) It is not kind to laugh at sacred things. When you laughed, it was as though you laughed—at God!

Mrs. Loving: (startled) Rachel!

Rachel: (still quietly) It's true. It was the best in me that said that—it was God! *(pauses)* And, Ma dear, if I believed that I should grow up and not be a mother, I'd pray to die now. I've thought about it a lot, Ma dear, and once I dreamed, and a voice said to me—oh! it was so real— "Rachel, you are to be a mother to little children." Wasn't that beautiful? Ever since I have known how Mary felt at the "Annunciation." *(almost in a whisper) God spoke to me through some one, and I believe.* And it has explained so much to me. I know now why I just can't resist any child. I have to love it—it calls me—it—draws me. I want to take care of it, wash it, dress it, live for it. I want the feel of its little warm body against me, its breath on my neck, its hands against my face. *(pauses thoughtfully for a few moments)* Ma dear, here's something I don't understand: I love the little black and brown babies best of all. There is something about them that—that—clutches at my heart. Why—why— should they be—oh!—pathetic? I don't understand. It's dim. More than the other babies, I feel that I must protect them. They're in danger, but from what? I don't know. I've tried so hard to understand, but I can't. *(her face radiant and beautiful)* Ma dear, I think their white teeth and the clear whites of their big black eyes and their dimples everywhere—are—are— *(breaks off)* And, Ma dear, because I love them best, I pray God every night to give me, when I grow up, little black and brown babies—to protect—and guard. *(wistfully)* Now, Ma dear, don't you see why you must never laugh at me again? Dear, dear, Ma dear? *(buries her head in her mother's lap and sobs)*

Mrs. Loving: (for a few seconds, sits as though dazed, and then instinctively begins to caress the head in her lap. To herself) And I suppose my experience is every mother's. Sooner or later—of a sudden she finds her own child a stranger to her. *(to RACHEL, very tenderly)* Poor little girl! Poor little chickabiddy!

Rachel: (raising her head) Why do you say, "Poor little girl," like that? I don't understand. Why, Ma dear, I never saw tears in your eyes before. Is it—is it— because you know the things I do not understand? Oh! it *is* that.

Mrs. Loving: (simply) Yes, Rachel, and I cannot save you.

Rachel: Ma dear, you frighten me. Save me from *what*?

Mrs. Loving: Just life, my little chickabiddy! . . .

[(MRS. LOVING sends RACHEL to the store. Tom enters shortly after she leaves.)]

Tom: 'Lo, Ma! Where's Sis,—out? The door's off the latch. *(kisses his mother and hangs hat in entryway)*

Mrs. Loving: (greeting him with the same beautiful smile with which she greeted RACHEL) Rachel just went after the rolls and pie. She'll be back in a few minutes. You're late, Tommy.

Tom: No, Ma—you forget—it's pay day. *(with decided shyness and awkwardness he hands her his wages)* Here, Ma!

Mrs. Loving: *(proudly counting it)* But, Tommy, this is every bit of it. You'll need some.

Tom: Not yet! *(constrainedly)* I only wish—. Say, Ma, I hate to see you work so hard. *(fiercely)* Some day—some day—. *(breaks off)*

Mrs. Loving: Son, I'm as proud as though you had given me a million dollars.

Tom: *(emphatically)* I may some day,—you'll see. *(abruptly changing the subject)* Gee! Ma, I'm hungry. What's for dinner? Smells good.

Mrs. Loving: Lamb and dumplings and rice.

Tom: Gee! I'm glad I'm living—and a pie too?

Mrs. Loving: Apple pie, Tommy.

Tom: Say, Ma, don't wake me up. And shall "muzzer's" own little boy set the table?

Mrs. Loving: Thank you, Son.

Tom: *(folds the green cloth, hangs it over the back of the arm-chair, gets white tablecloth from kitchenette and sets the table. The whole time he is whistling blithely a popular air. He lights one of the gas jets over the table)* Ma!

Mrs. Loving: Yes, Son.

Tom: I made "squad" today,—I'm quarter-back. Five other fellows tried to make it. We'll all have to buy new hats, now.

Mrs. Loving: *(with surprise)* Buy new hats! Why?

Tom: *(makes a ridiculous gesture to show that his head and hers are both swelling)* Honest, Ma, I had to carry my hat in my hand tonight,—couldn't even get it to perch aloft.

Mrs. Loving: *(smiling)* Well, I for one, Son, am not going to say anything to make you more conceited.

Tom: You don't *have* to say anything. Why, Ma, ever since I told you, you can almost look down your own back your head is so high. What? *(MRS. LOVING laughs. The outer door of the flat opens and shuts. RACHEL's voice is heard)*

Rachel: *(without)* My! that was a "dreful" climb, wasn't it? Ma, I've got something here for you. *(appears in the doorway carrying packages and leading a little boy by the hand. The little fellow is shy but smiling)* Hello, Tommy! Here, take these things for me. This is Jimmy. Isn't he a dear? Come, Jimmy. *(TOM carries the packages into the kitchenette. RACHEL leads JIMMY to MRS. LOVING)* Ma dear, this is my brown baby. I'm going to take him right down stairs again. His mother is as sweet as can be, and let me bring him up just to see you. Jimmy, this is Ma dear. *(MRS. LOVING turns expectantly to see the child. Standing before her, he raises his face to hers with an engaging smile. Suddenly, without word or warning, her body stiffens; her hands grip her sewing convulsively; her eyes stare. She makes no sound)*

Rachel: *(frightened)* Ma dear! What is the matter? Tom! Quick! *(TOM reenters and goes to them)*

Mrs. Loving: *(controlling herself with an effort and breathing hard)* Nothing, dears, nothing. I must be—I am—nervous tonight. *(with a forced smile)* How-do-you-do,

Jimmy? Now, Rachel—perhaps—don't you think—you had better take him back to his mother? Goodnight, Jimmy! *(eyes the child in a fascinated way the whole time he is in the room. RACHEL, very much perturbed, takes the child out)* Tom, open that window, please! There! That's better! *(still breathing deeply)* What a fool I am!

Tom: *(patting his mother awkwardly on the back)* You're all pegged out, that's the trouble—working entirely too hard. Can't you stop for the night and go to bed right after supper?

Mrs. Loving: I'll see, Tommy dear. Now I must look after the supper.

Tom: Huh! Well, I guess not. How old do you think Rachel and I are anyway? I see; you think we'll break some of this be-au-tiful Hav-i-land china, we bought at the "Five and Ten Cent Store." *(to RACHEL, who has just reentered wearing a puzzled and worried expression. She is without hat and coat)* Say, Rachel, do you think you're old enough?

Rachel: Old enough for what, Tommy?

Tom: To dish up the supper for Ma.

Rachel: *(with attempted sprightliness)* Ma dear thinks nothing can go on in this little flat unless she does it. Let's show her a thing or two. *(They bring in the dinner. MRS. LOVING with trembling hands tries to sew. TOM and RACHEL watch her covertly. Presently she gets up)*

Mrs. Loving: I'll be back in a minute, children. *(goes out the door that leads to the other rooms of the flat. TOM and RACHEL look at each other)*

Rachel: *(in a low voice, keeping her eyes on the door)* Why do you suppose she acted so strangely about Jimmy?

Tom: Don't know—nervous, I guess, —worn out. I wish— *(breaks off)*

Rachel: *(slowly)* It may be that; but she hasn't been herself this afternoon. I wonder—Look out! Here she comes!

Tom: *(in a whisper)* Liven her up. *(RACHEL nods, MRS. LOVING reenters. Both rush to her and lead her to her place at the right end of the table. She smiles and tries to appear cheerful. They sit down, TOM opposite MRS. LOVING and RACHEL at the side facing front. MRS. LOVING asks grace. Her voice trembles. She helps the children bountifully, herself sparingly. Every once in a while she stops eating and stares blankly into her plate; then, remembering where she is suddenly, looks around with a start and goes on eating. TOM and RACHEL appear not to notice her)*

Tom: Ma's "some" cook, isn't she?

Rachel: Is she! Delmonico's isn't in it.[7]

Tom: *(presently)* Say, Rachel, do you remember that Reynolds boy in the fourth year?

Rachel: Yes. You mean the one who is flat-nosed, freckled, and who squints and sneers?

---

7. Delmonico's was a famous New York restaurant, known for its fine cuisine. It was closed to African American patrons.

Tom: *(looking at RACHEL admiringly)* The same.

Rachel: *(vehemently)* I hate him!

Mrs. Loving: Rachel, you do use such violent language. Why hate him?

Rachel: I do—that's all.

Tom: Ma, if you saw him just once, you'd understand. No one likes him. But, then, what can you expect? His father's in "quod" doing time for something, I don't know just what. One of the fellows says he has a real decent mother, though. She never mentions him in any way, shape or form, he says. Hard on her, isn't it? Bet I'd keep my head shut too; —you'd never get a yap out of me. *(RACHEL looks up quickly at her mother; MRS. LOVING stiffens perceptibly, but keeps her eyes on her plate. RACHEL catches TOM's eye; silently draws his attention to their mother; and shakes her head warningly at him)*

Tom: *(continuing hastily and clumsily)* Well, anyway, he called me "Nigger" today. If his face isn't black, his eye is.

Rachel: Good! Oh! Why did you let the other one go?

Tom: *(grinning)* I knew he said things behind my back; but today he was hopping mad, because I made quarter-back. He didn't!

Rachel: Oh, Tommy! How lovely! Ma dear, did you hear that? *(chants)* Our Tommy's on the team! Our Tommy's on the team!

Tom: *(trying not to appear pleased)* Ma dear, what did I say about er—er "capital" enlargements?

Mrs. Loving: *(smiling)* You're right, Son.

Tom: I hope you got that "capital," Rachel. How's that for Latin knowledge? Eh?

Rachel: I don't think much of your knowledge, Tommy dear; but *(continuing to chant)* Our Tommy's on the team! Our Tommy's on the team! Our— *(breaks off)* I've a good mind to kiss you.

Tom: *(threateningly)* Don't you dare.

Rachel: *(rising and going toward him)* I will! I will! I will!

Tom: *(rising, too, and dodging her)* No, you don't, young lady. *(A tremendous tussle and scuffle ensues)*

Mrs. Loving: *(laughing)* For Heaven's sake! children, do stop playing and eat your supper. *(They nod brightly at each other behind her back and return smiling to the table)*

Rachel: *(sticking out her tongue at Tom)* I will!

Tom: *(mimicking her)* You won't!

Mrs. Loving: Children! *(They eat for a time in silence)*

Rachel: Ma dear, have you noticed Mary Shaw doesn't come here much these days?

Mrs. Loving: Why, that's so, she doesn't. Have you two quarreled?

Rachel: No, Ma dear. *(uncomfortably)* I—think I know the reason—but I don't like to say, unless I'm certain.

Tom: Well, I know. I've seen her lately with those two girls who have just come from the South. Twice she bowed stiffly, and the last time made believe she didn't see me.

Rachel: Then you think—? Oh! I was afraid it was that.

Tom: *(bitterly)* Yes—we're "niggers"—that's why.

Mrs. Loving: *(slowly and sadly)* Rachel, that's one of the things I can't save you from. I worried considerably about Mary, at first—you do take your friendships so seriously. I knew exactly how it would end. *(pauses)* And then I saw that if Mary Shaw didn't teach you the lesson—someone else would. They don't want you, dearies, when you and they grow up. You may have everything in your favor—but they don't *dare* to like you.

Rachel: I know all that is generally true—but I had hoped that Mary— *(breaks off)*

Tom: Well, I guess we can still go on living even if people don't speak to us. I'll never bow to *her* again—that's certain.

Mrs. Loving: But, Son, that wouldn't be polite, if she bowed to you first.

Tom: Can't help it. I guess I can be blind, too.

Mrs. Loving: *(wearily)* Well—perhaps you are right—I don't know. It's the way I feel about it too—but—but I wish my son always to be a *gentleman.*

Tom: If being a *gentleman* means not being a *man*—I don't wish to be one.

Rachel: Oh! well, perhaps we're wrong about Mary—I hope we are. *(sighs)* Anyway, let's forget it. Tommy guess what I've got. *(rises, goes out into entryway swiftly, and returns holding up a small bag)* Ma dear treated. Guess!

Tom: Ma, you're a thoroughbred. Well, let's see—it's—a dozen dill pickles?

Rachel: Oh! stop fooling.

Tom: I'm not. Tripe?

Rachel: Silly!

Tom: Hog's jowl?

Rachel: Ugh! Give it up—quarter-back.

Tom: Pig's feet?

Rachel: *(in pretended disgust)* Oh! Ma dear—send him from the table. It's CANDY!

Tom: Candy? Funny, I never thought of that! And I was just about to say some nice, delicious chitlings. Candy! Well! Well! *(RACHEL disdainfully carries the candy to her mother, returns to her own seat with the bag and helps herself. She ignores TOM)*

Tom: *(in an aggrieved voice)* You see, Ma, how she treats me. *(in affected tones)* I have a good mind, young lady, to punish you, er—er corporeally speaking. Tut! Tut! I have a mind to master thee—I mean—you. Methinks that if I should advance upon you, apply, perchance, two or three digits to your glossy locks and extract—aha!—say, a strand—you would no more defy me. *(He starts to rise)*

Mrs. Loving: *(quickly and sharply)* Rachel! Give Tom the candy and stop playing. *(RACHEL obeys. They eat in silence. The old depression returns. When the candy is all gone, RACHEL pushes her chair back, and is just about to rise, when her mother, who is very evidently nerving herself for something, stops her)* Just a moment, Rachel. *(pauses, continuing slowly and very seriously)* Tom and Rachel! I have been trying to make up my mind for some time whether a certain thing is my duty or not. Today—I have decided it is. You are old enough, now, —and I see you ought to be told. Do you know what day this is? *(both TOM and RACHEL have been watching their mother intently)* It's the sixteenth of October. Does that mean anything to either of you?

Tom and
Rachel: *(wonderingly)* No.

Mrs. Loving: *(looking at both of them thoughtfully, half to herself)* No—I don't know why it should. *(slowly)* Ten years ago—today—your father and your half-brother died.

Tom: I do remember, now, that you told us it was in October.

Rachel: *(with a sigh)* That explains—today.

Mrs. Loving: Yes, Rachel. *(pauses)* Do you know—how they—died?

Tom and
Rachel: Why, no.

Mrs. Loving: Did it ever strike you as strange—that they—died—the same day?

Tom: Well, yes.

Rachel: We often wondered, Tom and I; but—but somehow we never quite dared to ask you. You—you—always refused to talk about them, you know, Ma dear.

Mrs. Loving: Did you think—that—perhaps—the reason—I—I—wouldn't talk about them—was—because, because—I was ashamed—of them? *(TOM and RACHEL look uncomfortable)*

Rachel: Well, Ma dear—we—we—did wonder.

Mrs. Loving: *(questioningly)* And you thought?

Rachel: *(haltingly)* W-e-l-l—

Mrs. Loving: *(sharply)* Yes?

Tom: Oh! come, now, Rachel, you know we haven't bothered about it at all. Why should we? We've been happy.

Mrs. Loving: But when you have thought—you've been ashamed? *(intensely)* Have you?

Tom: Now, Ma, aren't you making a lot out of nothing?

Mrs. Loving: *(slowly)* No. *(half to herself)* You evade—both—of you. You have been ashamed. And I never dreamed until today you *could* take it this way. How blind— how almost criminally blind, I have been.

Rachel: *(tremulously)* Oh! Ma dear, don't! *(TOM and RACHEL watch their mother anxiously and uncomfortably. MRS. LOVING is very evidently nerving herself for something)*

Mrs. Loving: *(very slowly, with restrained emotion)* Tom—and Rachel!

Tom: Ma!

Rachel: Ma dear! *(a tense, breathless pause)*

Mrs. Loving: (bracing herself) They—they—were lynched!!

Tom and
Rachel: (in a whisper) Lynched!

Mrs. Loving: (slowly, laboring under strong but restrained emotion) Yes—by Christian people—
in a Christian land. We found out afterwards they were all church members
in good standing—the best people. *(a silence)* Your father was a man among
men. He was a fanatic. He was a Saint!

Tom: (breathing with difficulty) Ma—can you—will you—tell us—about it?

Mrs. Loving: I believe it to be my duty. *(a silence)* When I married your father I was a widow.
My little George was seven years old. From the very beginning he worshipped
your father. He followed him around—just like a little dog. All children were
like that with him. I myself have never seen anybody like him. "Big" seems
to fit him better than any other word. He was big-bodied—big-souled. His
loves were big and his hates. You can imagine, then, how the wrongs of the
Negro—ate into his soul. *(pauses)* He was utterly fearless. *(a silence)* He edited
and owned, for several years, a small Negro paper. In it he said a great many
daring things. I used to plead with him to be more careful. I was always
afraid for him. For a long time, nothing happened—he was too important
to the community. And then—one night—ten years ago—a mob made up
of the respectable people in the town lynched an innocent black man—and
what was worse—they knew him to be innocent. A white man was guilty.
I never saw your father so wrought up over anything: he couldn't eat; he
couldn't sleep; he brooded night and day over it. And then—realizing
fully the great risk he was running, although I begged him not to—and all
his friends also—he deliberately and calmly went to work and published
a most terrific denunciation of that mob. The old prophets in the Bible were
not more terrible than he. A day or two later, he received an anonymous
letter, very evidently from an educated man, calling upon him to retract
his words in the next issue. If he refused his life was threatened. The next
week's issue contained an arraignment as frightful, if not more so, than the
previous one. Each word was white-hot, searing. That night, some dozen
masked men came to our house.

Rachel: (moaning) Oh, Ma dear! Ma dear!

Mrs. Loving: (too absorbed to hear) We were not asleep—your father and I. They broke
down the front door and made their way to our bedroom. Your father
kissed me—and took up his revolver. It was always loaded. They broke
down the door. *(a silence. She continues slowly and quietly)* I tried to shut
my eyes—I could not. Four masked men fell—they did not move any
more—after a little. *(pauses)* Your father was finally overpowered and
dragged out. In the hall—my little seventeen-year-old George tried to res-
cue him. Your father begged him not to interfere. He paid no attention.
It ended in their dragging them both out. *(pauses)* My little George—
was—a man! *(controls herself with an effort)* He never made an outcry. His

last words to me were: "Ma, I am glad to go with Father." I could only nod to him. *(pauses)* While they were dragging them down the steps, I crept into the room where you were. You were both asleep. Rachel, I remember, was smiling. I knelt down by you—and covered my ears with my hands—and waited. I could not pray—I couldn't for a long time—afterwards. *(a silence)* It was very still when I finally uncovered my ears. The only sounds were the faint rustle of leaves and the "tap-tapping of the twig of a tree" against the window. I hear it still—sometimes in my dreams. *It was the tree—where they were. (a silence)* While I had knelt there waiting—I had made up my mind what to do. I dressed myself and then I woke you both up and dressed you. *(pauses)* We set forth. It was a black, still night. Alternately dragging you along and carrying you—I walked five miles to the house of some friends. They took us in, and we remained there until I had seen my dead laid comfortably at rest. They lent me money to come North—I couldn't bring you up—in the South. *(a silence)* Always remember this: There never lived anywhere—or at any time—any two whiter or more beautiful souls. God gave me one for a husband and one for a son and I am proud. *(brokenly)* You—must—be proud—too. *(a long silence. MRS. LOVING bows her head in her hands. TOM controls himself with an effort. RACHEL creeps softly to her mother; kneels beside her and lifts the hem of her dress to her lips. She does not dare touch her. She adores her with her eyes)*

Mrs. Loving: *(presently raising her head and glancing at the clock)* Tom, it's time, now, for you to go to work. Rachel and I will finish up here.

Tom: *(still laboring under great emotion, goes out into the entryway and comes back and stands in the doorway with his cap. He twirls it around and around nervously)* I want you to know, Ma, before I go—how—how proud I am. Why, I didn't believe two people could be like that and live. And then to find out that one—was your own father—and one—your own brother. —It's wonderful! I'm—not much yet, Ma, but—I've—I've just got to be something now. *(breaks off. His face becomes distorted with passion and hatred)* When I think—when I think—of those devils with white skins—living somewhere today—living and happy—I—see red! I—I—goodbye! *(rushes out, the door bangs)*

Mrs. Loving: *(half to herself)* I was afraid of just that. I wonder—if I did the wise thing—after all.

Rachel: *(with a gesture infinitely tender, puts her arm around her mother)* Yes, Ma dear, you did. And, hereafter, Tom and I share and share alike with you. To think, Ma dear, of ten years of this—all alone. It's wicked! *(a short silence)*

Mrs. Loving: And, Rachel, about that dear, little boy, Jimmy.

Rachel: Now, Ma dear, tell me tomorrow. You've stood enough for one day.

Mrs. Loving: No, it's better over and done with—all at once. If I had seen that dear child suddenly any other day than this—I might have borne it better. When he lifted his little face to me—and smiled—for a moment—I thought it was the end—of all things. Rachel, he is the image of my boy—my George!

Rachel: Ma dear!

Mrs. Loving: And, Rachel—it will hurt to see him again.

Rachel: I understand, Ma dear. *(a silence; suddenly)* Ma dear, I am beginning to see—to understand—so much. *(slowly and thoughtfully)* Ten years ago, all things being equal, Jimmy might have been—George? Isn't that so?

Mrs. Loving: Why—yes, if I understand you.

Rachel: I guess that doesn't sound very clear. It's only getting clear to me, little by little. Do you mind my thinking out loud to you?

Mrs. Loving: No, chickabiddy.

Rachel: If Jimmy went South now—and grew up—he might be—a George?

Mrs. Loving: Yes.

Rachel: Then, the South is full of tens, hundreds, thousands of little boys, who, one day may be—and some of them with certainty—Georges?

Mrs. Loving: Yes, Rachel.

Rachel: And the little babies, the dear, little, helpless babies, being born today—now—and those who will be, tomorrow, and all the tomorrows to come—have *that* sooner or later to look forward to? They will laugh and play and sing and be happy and grow up, perhaps, and be ambitious—just for *that*?

Mrs. Loving: Yes, Rachel.

Rachel: Then, everywhere, everywhere, throughout the South, there are hundreds of dark mothers who live in fear, terrible, suffocating fear, whose rest by night is broken, and whose joy by day in their babies on their hearts is three parts—pain. Oh, I know this is true—for this is the way I should feel, if I were little Jimmy's mother. How horrible! Why—it would be more merciful—to strangle the little things at birth. And so this nation—this white Christian nation—has deliberately set its curse upon the most beautiful—the most holy thing in life—motherhood! Why—it—makes—you doubt—God!

Mrs. Loving: Oh, hush! Little girl, hush!

Rachel: *(suddenly with a great cry)* Why, Ma dear, *you know.* You were a *mother, George's mother.* So, this is what it means. Oh, Ma dear! Ma dear! *(faints in her mother's arms)*

ACT TWO

Time: October sixteenth, four years later; seven o'clock in the morning.

Scene: The same room. There have been very evident improvements made. The room is not so bare; it is cosier. On the shelf, before each window, are potted geraniums. At the windows are green denim drapery curtains covering fresh white dotted Swiss inner curtains. At each doorway are green denim portieres. On the wall between the kitchenette and the entrance to the other rooms of the flat, a new picture is hanging, Millet's The Man With the Hoe. *Hanging against the side of the run that faces front is Watts's* Hope.[8] *There is another easy-chair at the left front.*

8. Jean-François Millet's *The Man with the Hoe* (1848, a.k.a. *The Winnower*) depicts a (white) peasant working in a field. George Frederic Watts was a nineteenth-century British painter and sculptor. *Hope* (1886) is one of his best-known paintings and depicts a white woman, blindfolded, playing a lyre on which only one string remains. Clad in a pale blue robe and seated on the top of the earth, she bends down to listen to the sound she can still make.

The table in the center is covered with a white tablecloth. A small asparagus fern is in the middle of this. When the curtain rises there is the clatter of dishes in the kitchenette. Presently RACHEL enters with dishes and silver in her hands. She is clad in a bungalow apron. She is noticeably all of four years older. She frowns as she sets the table. There is a set expression about the mouth. A child's voice is heard from the rooms within.

Jimmy: *(still unseen)* Ma Rachel!

Rachel: *(pauses and smiles)* What is it, Jimmy boy?

Jimmy: *(appearing in rear doorway, half-dressed, breathless, and tremendously excited over something. Rushes toward RACHEL)* Three guesses! Three guesses! Ma Rachel!

Rachel: *(her whole face softening)* Well, let's see—maybe there is a circus in town.

Jimmy: No siree! *(in a sing-song)* You're not right! You're not right!

Rachel: Well, maybe Ma Loving's going to take you somewhere.

Jimmy: No! *(vigorously shaking his head)* It's—

Rachel: *(interrupting quickly)* You said I could have three guesses, honey. I've only had two.

Jimmy: I thought you had three. How many are three!

Rachel: *(counting on her fingers)* One! Two! Three! I've only had one! two!—See? Perhaps Uncle Tom is going to give you some candy.

Jimmy: *(dancing up and down)* No! No! No! *(catches his breath)* I leaned over the bathtub, way over, and got hold of the chain with the button on the end, and dropped it into the little round place in the bottom. And then I runned lots of water in the tub and climbed over and fell in splash! Just like a big stone; *(loudly)* and took a bath all by myself alone.

Rachel: *(laughing and hugging him)* All by yourself, honey? You ran the water, too, boy, not "runned" it. What I want to know is, where was Ma Loving all this time?

Jimmy: I stole in "creepy-creep" and looked at Ma Loving and she was awful fast asleep. *(proudly)* Ma Rachel, I'm a "nawful" big boy now, aren't I? I are almost a man, aren't I?

Rachel: Oh! Boy, I'm getting tired of correcting you—"I am almost a man, am I not?" Jimmy, boy, what will Ma Rachel do, if you grow up? Why, I won't have a little boy any more! Honey, you mustn't grow up, do you hear? You mustn't.

Jimmy: Oh, yes, I must; and you'll have me just the same, Ma Rachel. I'm going to be a policeman and make lots of money for you and Ma Loving and Uncle Tom, and I'm going to buy you some trains and fire-engines, and little, cunning ponies, and some rabbits, and some great 'normous banks full of money—lots of it. And then, we are going to live in a great, big castle and eat lots of ice cream, all the time, and drink lots and lots of nice pink lemonade.

Rachel: What a generous Jimmy boy! *(hugs him)* Before I give you "morning kiss," I must see how clean my boy is. *(inspects teeth, ears and neck)* Jimmy, you're sweet and clean enough to eat. *(kisses him; he tries to strangle her with hugs)* Now the hands. Oh! Jimmy, look at those nails! Oh! Jimmy! *(JIMMY wriggles and tries to get his hands away)* Honey, get my file off of my bureau and go to Ma Loving; she must be awake by this time. Why, honey, what's the matter with your feet?

Jimmy: I don't know. I thought they looked kind of queer, myself. What's the matter with them?

Rachel: *(laughing)* You have your shoes on the wrong feet.

Jimmy: *(bursts out laughing)* Isn't that most 'normously funny? I'm a case, aren't I— *(pauses thoughtfully)* I mean—am I not, Ma Rachel?

Rachel: Yes, honey, a great big case of molasses. Come, you must hurry now, and get dressed. You don't want to be late for school, you know.

Jimmy: Ma Rachel! *(shyly)* I—I have been making something for you all the morning—ever since I waked up. It's awful nice. It's—stoop down, Ma Rachel, please—a great, big— *(puts both arms about her neck and gives her a noisy kiss. RACHEL kisses him in return, then pushes his head back. For a long moment they look at each other; and, then, laughing joyously, he makes believe he is a horse, and goes prancing out of the room. RACHEL, with a softer, gentler expression, continues setting the table. Presently, MRS. LOVING, bent and worn-looking, appears in the doorway in the rear. She limps a trifle)*

Mrs. Loving: Good morning, dearie. How's my little girl, this morning? *(looks around the room)* Why, where's Tom? I was certain I heard him running the water in the tub, sometime ago. *(limps into the room)*

Rachel: *(laughing)* Tom isn't up yet. Have you seen Jimmy?

Mrs. Loving: Jimmy? No. I didn't know he was awake, even.

Rachel: *(going to her mother and kissing her)* Well! What do you think of that! I sent the young gentleman to you, a few minutes ago, for help with his nails. He is very much grown up this morning, so I suppose that explains why he didn't come to you. Yesterday, all day, you know, he was a puppy. No one knows what he will be by tomorrow. All of this, Ma dear, is preliminary to telling you that Jimmy boy has stolen a march on you, this morning.

Mrs. Loving: Stolen a march! How?

Rachel: It appears that he took his bath—all by himself and, as a result, he is so conceited, peacocks aren't in it with him.

Mrs. Loving: I heard the water running and thought, of course, it was Tom. Why, the little rascal! I must go and see how he has left things. I was just about to wake him up.

Rachel: Rheumatism's not much better this morning, Ma dear. *(confronting her mother)* Tell me the truth, now, did you or did you not try that liniment I bought you yesterday?

Mrs. Loving: *(guiltily)* Well, Rachel, you see—it was this way, I was—I was so tired, last night, —I—I really forgot it.

Rachel: I thought as much. Shame on you!

Mrs. Loving: As soon as I walk around a bit it will be all right. It always is. It's bad, when I first get up—that's all. I'll be spry enough in a few minutes. *(limps to the door; pauses)* Rachel, I don't know why the thought should strike me, but how very strangely things turn out. If any one had told me four years ago that Jimmy would be living with us, I should have laughed at him. Then it hurt to see him; now it would hurt not to. *(softly)* Rachel, sometimes—I wonder—if, perhaps, God—hasn't relented a little—and given me back my boy,—my George.

Rachel: The whole thing was strange, wasn't it?

Mrs. Loving: Yes, God's ways are strange and often very beautiful; perhaps all would be beautiful—if we only understood.

Rachel: God's ways are certainly very mysterious. Why, of all the people in this apartment-house, should Jimmy's father and mother be the only two to take the smallpox, and the only two to die. It's queer!

Mrs. Loving: It doesn't seem like two years ago, does it?

Rachel: Two years, Ma dear! Why it's three the third of January.

Mrs. Loving: Are you sure, Rachel?

Rachel: *(gently)* I don't believe I could ever forget that, Ma dear.

Mrs. Loving: No, I suppose not. That is one of the differences between youth and old age—youth attaches tremendous importance to dates,—old age does not.

Rachel: *(quickly)* Ma dear, don't talk like that. You're not old.

Mrs. Loving: Oh! yes, I am, dearie. It's sixty long years since I was born; and I am much older than that, much older.

Rachel: Please, Ma dear, please!

Mrs. Loving: *(smiling)* Very well, dearie, I won't say it any more. *(a pause)* By the way,—how—does Tom strike you, these days?

Rachel: *(avoiding her mother's eye)* The same old, bantering, cheerful Tom. Why?

Mrs. Loving: I know he's all that, dearie, but it isn't possible for him to be really cheerful. *(pauses; goes on wistfully)* When you are little, we mothers can kiss away all the trouble, but when you grow up—and go out—into the world—and get hurt—we are helpless. There is nothing we can do.

Rachel: Don't worry about Tom, Ma dear, he's game. He doesn't show the white feather.[9]

Mrs. Loving: Did you see him, when he came in, last night?

Rachel: Yes.

Mrs. Loving: Had he had—any luck?

Rachel: No. *(firmly)* Ma dear, we may as well face it—it's hopeless, I'm afraid.

9. A white feather is a traditional sign of cowardice.

Mrs. Loving: I'm afraid—you are right. *(shakes her head sadly)* Well, I'll go and see how Jimmy has left things and wake up Tom, if he isn't awake yet. It's the waking up in the mornings that's hard. *(goes limping out rear door. RACHEL frowns as she continues going back and forth between the kitchenette and the table. Presently TOM appears in the door at the rear. He watches RACHEL several moments before he speaks or enters. RACHEL looks grim enough)*

Tom: *(entering and smiling)* Good-morning, "Merry Sunshine"! Have you, perhaps, been taking a—er—prolonged draught of that very delightful beverage— vinegar? *(RACHEL, with a knife in her hand, looks up unsmiling. In pretended fright)* I take it all back, I'm sure. May I request, humbly, that before I press my chaste, morning salute upon your forbidding lips, that you—that you—that you—er—in some way rid yourself of that—er—knife? *(bows as RACHEL puts it down)* I thank you. *(He comes to her and tips her head back; gently)* What's the matter with my little Sis?

Rachel: *(her face softening)* Tommy dear, don't mind me. I'm getting wicked, I guess. At present I feel just like—like curdled milk. Once upon a time, I used to have quite a nice disposition, didn't I, Tommy?

Tom: *(smiling)* Did you, indeed! I'm not going to flatter you. Well, brace yourself, old lady. Ready, One! Two! Three! Go! *(kisses her, then puts his hands on either side of her face, and raising it, looks down into it)* You're a pretty, decent little sister, Sis, that's what T. Loving thinks about it; and he knows a thing or two. *(abruptly looking around)* Has the paper come yet?

Rachel: I haven't looked; it must have, though, by this time. *(TOM, hands in his pockets, goes into the vestibule. He whistles. The outer door opens and closes, and presently he saunters back, newspaper in hand. He lounges carelessly in the arm-chair and looks at RACHEL)* . . .

Mrs. Loving: *(solemnly and slowly breaking the silence)* Rachel, do you know what day this is?

Rachel: *(looking at her plate; slowly)* Yes, Ma dear.

Mrs. Loving: Tom.

Tom: *(grimly and slowly)* Yes, Ma.

(a silence)

Mrs. Loving: *(impressively)* We must never—as long—as we live—forget this day.

Rachel: No, Ma dear.

Tom: No, Ma.

(another silence)

Tom: *(slowly; as though thinking aloud)* I hear people talk about God's justice—and I wonder. There are you, Ma. There isn't a sacrifice—that you haven't made. You're still working your fingers to the bone—sewing just so all of us may keep on living. Rachel is a graduate in Domestic Science; she was high in her class; most of the girls below her in rank have positions in the schools. I'm an electrical engineer—and I've tried steadily for several months—to practice my profession. It seems our educations aren't of much use to us: we aren't allowed to make good—because our skins are dark. *(pauses)* And, in the South today, there are white men— *(controls himself)* They have everything; they're well-dressed, well-fed, well-housed; they're prosperous in business; they're important politically; they're pillars in the church. I know all this is true—I've inquired. Their children (our ages, some of them) are growing up around them; and they are having a square deal handed out to them—college, position, wealth, and best of all, freedom, without galling restrictions, to work out their own salvations. With ability, they may become—anything; and all this will be true of their children's children after them. *(a pause)* Look at us—and look at them. We are destined to failure— they, to success. Their children shall grow up in hope; ours, in despair. Our hands are clean;—theirs are red with blood—red with the blood of a noble man—and a boy. They're nothing but low, cowardly, bestial murderers. The scum of the earth shall succeed.—God's justice, I suppose.

Mrs. Loving: *(rising and going to TOM; brokenly)* Tom, promise me—one thing.

Tom: *(rises gently)* What is it, Ma?

Mrs. Loving: That—you'll try—not to lose faith—in God. I've been where you are now and it's black. Tom, we don't understand God's ways. My Son, I know, now—He is beautiful. Tom, won't you try to believe, again?

Tom: *(slowly, but not convincingly)* I'll try, Ma.

Mrs. Loving: *(sighs)* Each one, I suppose, has to work out his own salvation. *(after a pause)* Rachel, if you'll get Jimmy ready, I'll take him to school. I've got to go downtown shopping for a customer this morning. *(RACHEL rises and goes out the rear doorway; MRS. LOVING, limping very slightly now, follows. She turns and looks back yearningly at TOM, who has seated himself again, and is staring unseeingly at his plate. She goes out. TOM sits without moving until he hears MRS. LOVING's voice within and RACHEL's faintly; then he gets the paper, sits in the arm-chair and pretends to read)*

Mrs. Loving: *(from within)* A yard, you say, Rachel? You're sure that will be enough? Oh! you've measured it. Anything else?—What?—Oh! all right. I'll be back by one o'clock, anyway. Good-bye. *(enters with JIMMY. Both are dressed for the street. TOM looks up brightly at JIMMY)*

Tom: Hello! Big Fellow, where are you taking *my* mother, I'd like to know? This is a pretty kettle of fish.

Jimmy: *(laughing)* Aren't you funny, Uncle Tom! Why, I'm not taking her anywhere. She's taking me. *(importantly)* I'm going to school.

Tom: Big Fellow, come here. *(JIMMY comes with a rush)* Now, where's that penny I gave you? No, I don't want to see it. All right. Did Ma Loving give you another? *(vigorous noddings of the head from JIMMY)* I wish you to promise me solemnly—Now, listen! Here, don't wriggle so! not to buy—Listen! too many pints of ice-cream with my penny. Understand?

Jimmy: *(very seriously)* Yes, Uncle Tom, cross my "tummy"! I promise.

Tom: Well, then, you may go. I guess that will be all for the present. *(JIMMY loiters around looking up wistfully into his face)* Well?

Jimmy: Haven't you—aren't you—isn't you—forgetting something?

Tom: *(grabbing at his pockets)* Bless my stars! What now?

Jimmy: If you could kind of lean over this way. *(TOM leans forward)* No, not that way. *(TOM leans toward the side away from JIMMY)* No, this way, this way! *(laughs and pummels him with his little fists)* This way!

Tom: *(leaning toward JIMMY)* Well, why didn't you say so, at first?

Jimmy: *(puts his arms around TOM's neck and kisses him)* Good-bye, dear old Uncle Tom. *(Tom catches him and hugs him hard)* I likes to be hugged like that—I can taste—sau-sa-ges.

Tom: You 'barrass me, son. Here, Ma, take your boy. Now remember all I told you, Jimmy.

Jimmy: I 'members.

Mrs. Loving: God bless you, Tom, Good luck.

Jimmy: *(to TOM)* God bless you, Uncle Tom. Good luck!

Tom: *(much affected, but with restraint, rising)* Thank you—Good-bye. *(MRS. LOVING and JIMMY go out through the vestibule. TOM lights a cigarette and tries to read the paper. He soon sinks into a brown study. Presently RACHEL enters, humming. TOM relights his cigarette; and RACHEL proceeds to clear the table. In the midst of this, the bell rings three distinct times)*

Rachel and
Tom: John!

Tom: I wonder what's up—It's rather early for him.—I'll go. *(rises leisurely and goes out into the vestibule. The outer door opens and shuts. Men's voices are heard. TOM and JOHN STRONG enter. During the ensuing conversation RACHEL finishes clearing the table, takes the fern off, puts on the green tablecloth, places a doily carefully in the center, and replaces the fern. She apparently pays no attention to the conversation between her brother and STRONG. After she has finished, she goes to the kitchenette. The rattle of dishes can be heard now and then)*

Rachel: *(brightly)* Well, stranger, how does it happen you're out so early in the morning?

Strong: I hadn't seen any of you for a week, and I thought I'd come by, on my way to work, and find out how things are going. There is no need of asking how you are, Rachel. And the mother and the boy?

Rachel: Ma dear's rheumatism still holds on.—Jimmy's fine.

Strong: I'm sorry to hear that your mother is not well. There isn't a remedy going that my mother doesn't know about. I'll get her advice and let you know. *(turning to TOM)* Well, Tom, how goes it? *(STRONG and TOM sit)*

Tom: *(smiling grimly)* There's plenty of "go," but no "git there."

(There is a pause)

Strong: I was hoping for better news.

Tom: If I remember rightly, not so many years ago, you tried—and failed. Then, a colored man had hardly a ghost of a show;—now he hasn't even the ghost of a ghost.

Strong: That's true enough. *(a pause)* What are you going to do?

Tom: *(slowly)* I'll do this little "going act" of mine the rest of the week; *(pauses)* and then, I'll do anything I can get to do. If necessary, I suppose, I can be a "White-wing." [10]

Strong: Tom, I came— *(breaks off; continuing slowly)* Six years ago, I found I was up against a stone wall—your experience, you see, to the letter. I couldn't let my mother starve, so I became a waiter. *(pauses)* I studied waiting; I made a science of it, an art. In a comparatively short time, I'm a head-waiter and I'm up against another stone wall. I've reached my limit. I'm thirty-two now, and I'll die a head-waiter. *(a pause)* College friends, so-called, and acquaintances used to come into the restaurant. One or two at first—attempted to commiserate with me. They didn't do it again. I waited upon them—I did my best. Many of them tipped me. *(pauses and smiles grimly)* I can remember my first tip, still. They come in yet; many of them are already powers, not only in this city, but in the country. Some of them make a personal request that I wait upon them. I am an artist, now, in my proper sphere. They tip me well, extremely well—the larger the tip, the more pleased they are with me. Because of me, in their own eyes, they're philanthropists. Amusing, isn't it? I can stand their attitude now. My philosophy—learned hard, is to make the best of everything you can, and go on. At best, life isn't so very long. You're wondering why I'm telling you all this. I wish you to see things exactly as they are. There are many disadvantages and some advantages in being a waiter. My mother can live comfortably; I am able, even, to see that she gets some of the luxuries. Tom, it's this way—I can always get you a job as a waiter; I'll teach you the art. If you care to begin the end of the week—all right. And remember this, as long as I keep my job— this offer holds good.

Tom: I—I— *(breaks off)* Thank you. *(a pause; then smiling wryly)* I guess it's safe enough to say, you'll see me at the end of the week. John, you're— *(breaking off again. A silence interrupted presently by the sound of much vigorous rapping on the outer door of the flat. RACHEL appears and crosses over toward the vestibule)*

Rachel: Hear the racket! My kiddies gently begging for admittance. It's about twenty minutes of nine, isn't it? *(TOM nods)* I thought so. *(goes into the entry-way; presently reappears with a group of six little girls ranging in age from five to about nine. All are fighting to be close to her; and all are talking at once. There is one exception: the smallest tot is self-possessed and self-sufficient. She carries a red geranium in her hand and gives it her full attention)*

Little Mary: It's my turn to get "morning kiss" first this morning, Miss Rachel. You kissed Louise first yesterday. You said you'd kiss us "alphebetically." *(ending in a shriek)* You promised! *(RACHEL kisses MARY, who subsides)*

10. " White-wing" is a slang term for "waiter." The reference is to a white napkin draped over the arm.

Little Nancy: *(imperiously)* Now, me. *(RACHEL kisses her, and then amid shrieks, recriminations, pulling of hair, jostling, etc., she kisses the rest. The small tot is still oblivious to everything that is going on)*

Rachel: *(laughing)* You children will pull me limb from limb; and then I'll be all dead; and you'll be sorry—see, if you aren't. *(They fall back immediately. TOM and JOHN watch in amused silence. RACHEL loses all self-consciousness, and seems to bloom in the children's midst)* Edith! come here this minute, and let me tie your hair-ribbon again. Nancy, I'm ashamed of you, I saw you trying to pull it off. *(NANCY looks abashed but mischievous)* Louise, you look as sweet as sweet, this morning; and Jenny, where did you get the pretty, pretty dress?

Little Jenny: *(snuffling, but proud)* My mother made it. *(pauses with more snuffles)* My mother says I have a very bad cold. *(there is a brief silence interrupted by the small tot with the geranium)*

Little Martha: *(in a sweet, little voice)* I—have—a—pitty—'ittle flower.

Rachel: Honey, it's beautiful. Don't you want "morning kiss" too?

Little Martha: Yes, I do.

Rachel: Come, honey. *(RACHEL kisses her)* Are you going to give the pretty flower to Jenny's teacher? *(vigorous shakings of the head in denial)* Is it for—mother? *(more shakings of the head)* Is it for—let's see—Daddy? *(more shakings of the head)* I give up. To whom are you going to give the pretty flower, honey?

Little Martha: *(shyly)* "Oo."

Rachel: You, darling!

Little Martha: Muzzer and I picked it—for "oo." Here 'tis. *(puts her finger in her mouth, and gives it shyly)*

Rachel: Well, I'm going to pay you with three big kisses. One! Two! Three!

Little Martha: I can count, One! Two! Free! Tan't I? I am going to school soon; and I wants to put the flower in your hair.

Rachel: *(kneels)* All right, baby. *(LITTLE MARTHA fumbles and RACHEL helps her)*

Little Martha: *(dreamily)* Miss Rachel, the 'ittle flower loves you. It told me so. It said it wanted to lie in your hair. It is going to tell you a pitty 'ittle secret. You listen awful hard—and you'll hear. I wish I were a fairy and had a little wand, I'd turn everything into flowers. Wouldn't that be nice, Miss Rachel?

Rachel: Lovely, honey!

Little Jenny: *(snuffling loudly)* If I were a fairy and had a wand, I'd turn you, Miss Rachel, into a queen—and then I'd always be near you and see that you were happy.

Rachel: Honey, how beautiful!

Little Louise: I'd make my mother happy—if I were a fairy. She cries all the time. My father can't get anything to do.

Little Nancy: If I were a fairy, I'd turn a boy in my school into a spider. I hate him.

Rachel: Honey, why?

Little Nancy: I'll tell you sometime—I hate him.

Little Edith: Where's Jimmy, Miss Rachel?

Rachel: He went long ago; and chickies, you'll have to clear out, all of you, now, or you'll be late. Shoo! Shoo! *(She drives them out prettily before her. They laugh merrily. They all go into the vestibule)*

Tom: *(slowly)* Does it ever strike you—how pathetic and tragic a thing—a little colored child is?

Strong: Yes.

Tom: Today, we colored men and women, everywhere—are up against it. Every year, we are having a harder time of it. In the South, they make it as impossible as they can for us to get an education. We're hemmed in on all sides. Our one safeguard—the ballot—in most states is taken away already, or is being taken away. Economically, in a few lines, we have a slight show—but at what a cost! In the North, they make a pretense of liberality: they give us the ballot and a good education, and then—snuff us out. Each year, the problem just to live, gets more difficult to solve. How about these children—if we're fools enough to have any? *(RACHEL reenters. Her face is drawn and pale. She returns to the kitchenette)*

Strong: *(slowly, with emphasis)* That part—is damnable! *(a silence)*

Tom: *(suddenly looking at the clock)* It's later than I thought. I'll have to be pulling out of here now, if you don't mind. *(raising his voice)* Rachel! *(RACHEL, still drawn and pale, appears in the doorway of the kitchenette. She is without her apron)* I've got to go now, Sis. I leave John in your hands.

Strong: I've got to go, myself, in a few minutes.

Tom: Nonsense, man! Sit still. I'll begin to think, in a minute, you're afraid of the ladies.

Strong: I am.

Tom: What! And not ashamed to acknowledge it?

Strong: No.

Tom: You're lots wiser than I dreamed. So long! *(gets hat out in the entry-way and returns; smiles wryly)* "Morituri [Te] Salutamus." [11] *(They nod at him—RACHEL wistfully. He goes out. There is the sound of an opening and closing door. RACHEL sits down. A rather uncomfortable silence, on the part of RACHEL, ensues. STRONG is imperturbable)*

Rachel: *(nervously)* John!

Strong: Well?

Rachel: I—I listened.

Strong: Listened! To what?

Rachel: To you and Tom.

---

11. Latin; "Being about to die, we salute you." Gladiators' greeting in the arena.

Strong: Well,—what of it?

Rachel: I didn't think it was quite fair not to tell you. It—it seemed, well, like eavesdropping.

Strong: Don't worry about it. Nonsense!

Rachel: I'm glad—I want to thank you for what you did for Tom. He needs you, and will need you. You'll help him?

Strong: *(thoughtfully)* Rachel, each one has his own little battles. I'll do what I can. After all, an outsider doesn't help much.

Rachel: But friendship—just friendship—helps.

Strong: Yes. *(a silence)* Rachel, do you hear anything encouraging from the schools? Any hope for you yet?

Rachel: No, nor ever will be. I know that now. There's no more chance for me than there is for Tom,—or than there was for you—or for any of us with dark skins. It's lucky for me that I love to keep house, and cook, and sew. I'll never get anything else. Ma dear's sewing, the little work Tom has been able to get, and the little sewing I sometimes get to do—keep us from the poorhouse. We live. According to your philosophy, I suppose, make the best of it—it might be worse.

Strong: *(quietly)* You don't want to get morbid over these things, you know.

Rachel: *(scornfully)* That's it. If you see things as they are, you're either pessimistic or morbid.

Strong: In the long run, do you believe, that attitude of mind—will be—beneficial to you? I'm ten years older than you. I tried your way. I know. Mine is the only sane one. *(goes over to her slowly; deliberately puts his hands on her hair, and tips her head back. He looks down into her face quietly without saying anything)*

Rachel: *(nervous and startled)* Why, John, don't! *(He pays no attention, but continues to look down into her face)*

Strong: *(half to himself)* Perhaps—if you had—a little more fun in your life, your point of view would be—more normal. I'll arrange it so I can take you to some theatre, one night, this week.

Rachel: *(irritably)* You talk as though I were a—a jelly-fish. You'll take me, how do you know *I'll* go?

Strong: You will.

Rachel: *(sarcastically)* Indeed! *(STRONG makes no reply)* I wonder if you know how—how—maddening you are. Why, you talk as though my will counts for nothing. It's as if you're trying to master me. I think a domineering man is detestable.

Strong: *(softly)* If he's, perhaps, *the* man?

Rachel: *(hurriedly, as though she had not heard)* Besides, some of these theatres put you off by yourself as though you had leprosy. I'm not going.

Strong: *(smiling at her)* You know I wouldn't ask you to go, under those circumstances. *(a silence)* Well, I must be going now. *(He takes her hand, and looks at it reverently. RACHEL at first resists; but he refuses to let go. When she finds it useless, she ceases to resist. He turns his head and smiles down into her face)* Rachel, I am coming back to see you, this evening.

Rachel: I'm sure *we'll* all be very glad to see you.

Strong: *(looking at her calmly)* I said—you. *(Very deliberately, he turns her hand palm upwards, leans over and kisses it; then he puts it back into her lap. He touches her cheek lightly)* Good-bye—little Rachel. *(turns in the vestibule door and looks back, smiling)* Until tonight. *(He goes out. RACHEL sits for some time without moving. She is lost in a beautiful day-dream. Presently she sighs happily, and after looking furtively around the room lifts the palm JOHN has kissed to her lips. She laughs shyly and jumping up, begins to hum. She opens the window at the rear of the room and then commences to thread the sewing-machine. She hums happily the whole time. A light rapping is heard at the outer door. RACHEL listens. It stops, and begins again. There is something insistent, and yet hopeless in the sound. RACHEL looking puzzled, goes out into the vestibule. . . . The door closes. RACHEL, and a black woman, poorly dressed, and a little ugly, black child come in. There is the stoniness of despair in the woman's face. The child is thin, nervous, suspicious, frightened)*

Mrs. Lane: *(in a sharp, but toneless voice)* May I sit down? I'm tired.

Rachel: *(puzzled, but gracious; draws up a chair for her)* Why, certainly.

Mrs. Lane: No, you don't know me—never even heard of me—nor I of you. I was looking at the vacant flat on this floor—and saw your name—on your door,— "Loving!" It's a strange name to come across—in this world.—I thought, perhaps, you might give me some information. *(The child hides behind her mother and looks around at RACHEL in a frightened way)*

Rachel: *(smiling at the woman and child in a kindly manner)* I'll be glad to tell you anything I am able, Mrs.—

Mrs. Lane: Lane. What I want to know is, how do they treat the colored children in the school I noticed around the corner? *(The child clutches at her mother's dress)*

Rachel: *(perplexed)* Very well—I'm sure.

Mrs. Lane: *(bluntly)* What reason have you for being sure?

Rachel: Why, the little boy I've adopted goes there; and he's very happy. All the children in this apartment-house go there too; and I know they're happy.

Mrs. Lane: Do you know how many colored children there are in the school?

Rachel: Why, I should guess around thirty.

Mrs. Lane: I see. *(pauses)* What color is this little adopted boy of yours?

Rachel: *(gently)* Why—he's brown.

Mrs. Lane: Any black children there?

Rachel: *(nervously)* Why—yes.

Mrs. Lane: Do you mind if I send Ethel over by the piano to sit?

Rachel: N—no, certainly not. *(places a chair by the piano and goes to the little girl, holding out her hand. She smiles beautifully. The child gets farther behind her mother)*

Mrs. Lane: She won't go to you—she's afraid of everybody now but her father and me. Come, Ethel. *(MRS. LANE takes the little girl by the hand and leads her to the chair. In a gentler voice)* Sit down, Ethel. *(ETHEL obeys. When her mother starts back again toward RACHEL, she holds out her hands pitifully. She makes no sound)* I'm not going to leave you, Ethel. I'll be right over here. You can see me. *(The look of agony on the child's face, as her mother leaves her, makes RACHEL shudder)* Do you mind if we sit over here by the sewing-machine? Thank you. *(They move their chairs)*

Rachel: *(looking at the little, pitiful figure watching its mother almost unblinkingly)* Does Ethel like apples, Mrs. Lane?

Mrs. Lane: Yes.

Rachel: Do you mind if I give her one?

Mrs. Lane: No. Thank you very much.

Rachel: *(goes into the kitchenette and returns with a fringed napkin, a plate, and a big, red apple, cut into quarters. She goes to the little girl, who cowers away from her; very gently)* Here, dear little girl, is a beautiful apple for you. *(The gentle tones have no appeal for the trembling child before her)*

Mrs. Lane: *(coming forward)* I'm sorry, but I'm afraid she won't take it from you. Ethel, the kind lady has given you an apple. Thank her nicely. Here! I'll spread the napkin for you, and put the plate in your lap. Thank the lady like a good little girl.

Ethel: *(very low)* Thank you. *(They return to their seats. ETHEL with difficulty holds the plate in her lap. During the rest of the interview between RACHEL and her mother, she divides her attention between the apple on the plate and her mother's face. She makes no attempt to eat the apple, but holds the plate in her lap with a care that is painful to watch. Often, too, she looks over her shoulder fearfully. The conversation between RACHEL and her mother is carried on in low tones)*

Mrs. Lane: I've got to move—it's *Ethel.*

Rachel: What is the matter with that child? It's—it's heartbreaking to see her.

Mrs. Lane: I understand how you feel,—I don't feel anything, myself, any more. *(a pause)* My husband and I are poor, and we're ugly and we're black. Ethel looks like her father more than she does like me. We live on 55th Street—near the railroad. It's a poor neighborhood, but the rent's cheap. My husband is a porter in a store; and, to help out, I'm a caretaker. *(pauses)* I don't know why I'm telling you all this. We had a nice little home—and the three of us were happy. Now we've got to move.

Rachel: Move! Why?

Mrs. Lane: It's Ethel. I put her in school this September. She stayed two weeks. *(pointing to ETHEL)* That's the result.

Rachel: *(in horror)* You mean—that just two weeks—in school—did that?

Mrs. Lane: Yes. Ethel never had a sick day in her life—before. *(a brief pause)* I took her to the doctor at the end of the two weeks. He says she's a nervous wreck.

Rachel: But what could they have done to her?

Mrs. Lane: *(laughs grimly and mirthlessly)* I'll tell you what they did the first day. Ethel is naturally sensitive and backward. She's not assertive. The teacher saw that, and, after I had left, told her to sit in a seat in the rear of the class. She was alone there—in a corner. The children, immediately feeling there was something wrong with Ethel because of the teacher's attitude, turned and stared at her. When the teacher's back was turned they whispered about her, pointed their fingers at her and tittered. The teacher divided the class into two parts, divisions, I believe, they are called. She forgot all about Ethel, of course, until the last minute, and then, looking back, said sharply: "That little girl there may join this division," meaning the group of pupils standing around her. Ethel naturally moved slowly. The teacher called her sulky and told her to lose a part of her recess. When Ethel came up—the children drew away from her in every direction. She was left standing alone. The teacher then proceeded to give a lesson about kindness to animals. Funny, isn't it, *kindness to animals*? The children forgot Ethel in the excitement of talking about their pets. Presently, the teacher turned to Ethel and said disagreeably—"Have you a pet?" Ethel said, "Yes," very low. "Come, speak up, you sulky child, what is it?" Ethel said: "A blind puppy." They all laughed, the teacher and all. Strange, isn't it, but Ethel loves that puppy. She spoke up: "It's mean to laugh at a little blind puppy. I'm glad he's blind." This remark brought forth more laughter. "Why are you glad?" the teacher asked curiously. Ethel refused to say. *(pauses)* When I asked her why, do you know what she told me? "If he saw me, he might not love me any more." *(a pause)* Did I tell you that Ethel is only seven years old?

Rachel: *(drawing her breath sharply)* Oh! I didn't believe any one could be as cruel as that—to a little child.

Mrs. Lane: It isn't very pleasant, is it? When the teacher found out that Ethel wouldn't answer, she said severely: "Take your seat!" At recess, all the children went out. Ethel could hear them playing and laughing and shrieking. Even the teacher went too. She was made to sit there all alone—in that big room—because God made her ugly—and black. *(pauses)* When the recess was half over the teacher came back. "You may go now," she said coldly. Ethel didn't stir. "Did you hear me!" "Yes'm." "Why don't you obey," "I don't want to go out, please." "You don't, don't you, you stubborn child! Go immediately!" Ethel went. She stood by the school steps. No one spoke to her. The children near her moved away in every direction. They stopped playing, many of them, and watched her. They stared as only children can stare. Some began whispering about her. Presently one child came up and ran her hand roughly over Ethel's face. She looked at her hand and Ethel's face and ran screaming back to the others, "It won't come off! See!" Other children followed the first child's example. Then one boy spoke up loudly: "I know what she is, she's a nigger!" Many took up the cry. God or the devil interfered—the bell rang. The children filed in. One boy boldly called her "Nigger!" before the teacher. She said, "That isn't nice," —but she smiled at the boy. Things went on about the same for the rest of the day. At the end of school, Ethel put on her hat and coat—the teacher made her hang them at a distance from the other pupils' wraps, and started for home. Quite a crowd escorted her. They called her "Nigger!" all the way. I *made* Ethel go the next day. I complained to the authorities. They treated me lightly. I was determined not to let them force my child out of school. At the end of two weeks— I had to take her out.

Rachel: (*brokenly*) Why, —I never—in all my life—heard anything—so—pitiful.

Mrs. Lane: Did you ever go to school here?

Rachel: Yes. I was made to feel my color—but I never had an experience like that.

Mrs. Lane: How many years ago were you in the graded schools?

Rachel: Oh—around ten.

Mrs. Lane: (*laughs grimly*) Ten years! Every year things are getting worse. Last year wasn't as bad as this. (*pauses*) So they treat the children all right in this school?

Rachel: Yes! Yes! I know that.

Mrs. Lane: I can't afford to take this flat here, but I'll take it. I'm going to have Ethel educated. Although, when you think of it,—it's all rather useless—this education! What are our children going to do with it, when they get it? We strive and save and sacrifice to educate them—and the whole time—down underneath, we know—they'll have no chance.

Rachel: (*sadly*) Yes, that's true, all right. God seems to have forgotten us.

Mrs. Lane: God! It's all a lie about God. I know.—This fall I sent Ethel to a white Sunday-school near us. She received the same treatment there she did in the day school. Her being there nearly broke up the school. At the end, the superintendent called her to him and asked her if she didn't know of some nice colored Sunday-school. He told her she must feel out of place and uncomfortable there. That's your Church of God!

Rachel: Oh! how unspeakably brutal. (*controls herself with an effort; after a pause*) Have you any other children?

Mrs. Lane: (*dryly*) Hardly! If I had another—I'd kill it. It's kinder. (*rising presently*) Well, I must go, now. Thank you, for your information—and for listening. (*suddenly*) You aren't married, are you?

Rachel: No.

Mrs. Lane: Don't marry—that's my advice. Come, Ethel. (*ETHEL gets up and puts down the things in her lap, carefully upon her chair. She goes in a hurried, timid way to her mother and clutches her hand*) Say good-bye to the lady.

Ethel: (*faintly*) Good-bye.

Rachel: (*kneeling by the little girl—a beautiful smile on her face*) Dear little girl, won't you let me kiss you good-bye? I love little girls. (*The child hides behind her mother; continuing brokenly*) Oh!—no child—ever did—that to me—before!

Mrs. Lane: *(in a gentler voice)* Perhaps, when we move in here, the first of the month, things may be better. Thank you, again. Good morning! You don't belie your name. *(All three go into the vestibule. The outside door opens and closes. RACHEL, as though dazed and stricken, returns. She sits in a chair, leans forward, and clasping her hands loosely between her knees, stares at the chair with the apple on it where ETHEL LANE has sat. She does not move for some time. Then she gets up and goes to the window in the rear center and sits there. She breathes in the air deeply and then goes to the sewing-machine and begins to sew on something she is making. Presently her feet slow down on the pedals; she stops; and begins brooding again. After a short pause, she gets up and begins to pace up and down slowly, mechanically, her head bent forward. The sharp ringing of the electric bell breaks in upon this. RACHEL starts and goes slowly into the vestibule. She is heard speaking dully through the tube)*

Rachel: Yes!—All right! Bring it up! *(Presently she returns with a long flower box. She opens it listlessly at the table. Within are six beautiful crimson rosebuds with long stems. RACHEL looks at the name on the card. She sinks down slowly on her knees and leans her head against the table. She sighs wearily)* Oh! John! John!—What are we to do?—I'm—I'm afraid! Everywhere—it is the same thing. My mother! My little brother! Little, black, crushed Ethel! *(in a whisper)* Oh! God! You who I have been taught to believe are so good, so beautiful, how could—You permit—these—things? *(pauses, raises her head and sees the rosebuds. Her face softens and grows beautiful; very sweetly)* Dear little rosebuds—you—make me think—of sleeping, curled up, happy babies. Dear beautiful, little rosebuds! *(pauses; goes on thoughtfully to the rosebuds)* When—I look—at you—I believe— God is beautiful. He who can make a little exquisite thing like this, and this, can't be cruel. Oh! He can't mean me to give up—love—and the hope of little children. *(There is the sound of a small hand knocking at the outer door. RACHEL smiles)* My Jimmy! It must be twelve o'clock. *(rises)* I didn't dream it was so late. *(starts for the vestibule)* Oh! the world can't be so bad. I don't believe it. I won't. I must forget that little girl. My little Jimmy is happy—and today John sent me beautiful rosebuds. Oh, there are lovely things, yet. *(goes into the vestibule. A child's eager cry is heard, and RACHEL, carrying Jimmy in her arms, comes in. He has both arms about her neck and is hugging her. With him in her arms, she sits down in the armchair at the right front)*

Rachel: Well, honey, how was school today?

Jimmy: *(sobering a trifle)* All right, Ma Rachel. *(suddenly sees the roses)* Oh! look at the pretty flowers. Why, Ma Rachel, you forgot to put them in water. They'll die.

Rachel: Well, so they will. Hop down this minute, and I'll put them in right away. *(gathers up box and flowers and goes into the kitchenette. JIMMY climbs back into the chair. He looks thoughtful and serious. RACHEL comes back with the buds in a tall, glass vase. She puts the fern on top of the piano, and places the vase in the center of the table)* There, honey, that's better, isn't it? Aren't they lovely?

Jimmy: Yes, that's lots better. Now they won't die, will they? Rosebuds are just like little "chilyun," aren't they, Ma Rachel? If you are good to them, they'll grow up into lovely roses, won't they? And if you hurt them, they'll die. Ma Rachel, do you think all peoples are kind to little rosebuds?

Rachel: (watching JIMMY shortly) Why, of course. Who could hurt little children? Who would have the heart to do such a thing?

Jimmy: If you hurt them, it would be lots kinder, wouldn't it, to kill them all at once, and not a little bit and a little bit?

Rachel: (sharply) Why, honey boy, why are you talking like this?

Jimmy: Ma Rachel, what is a "Nigger?"

(RACHEL recoils as though she had been struck).

Rachel: Honey boy, why—why do you ask that?

Jimmy: Some big boys called me that when I came out of school just now. They said: "Look at the little nigger!" And they laughed. One of them runned, no ranned, after me and threw stones; and they all kept calling "Nigger! Nigger! Nigger!" One stone struck me hard in the back, and it hurt awful bad; but I didn't cry, Ma Rachel. I wouldn't let them make me cry. The stone hurts me there, Ma Rachel; but what they called me hurts and hurts here. What is a "Nigger," Ma Rachel?

Rachel: (controlling herself with a tremendous effort. At last she sweeps down upon him and hugs and kisses him) Why, honey boy, those boys didn't mean anything. Silly, little, honey boy! They're rough, that's all. How *could* they mean anything?

Jimmy: You're only saying that, Ma Rachel, so I won't be hurt. I know. It wouldn't ache here like it does—if they didn't mean something.

Rachel: (abruptly) Where's Mary, honey?

Jimmy: She's in her flat. She came in just after I did.

Rachel: Well, honey, I'm going to give you two big cookies and two to take to Mary; and you may stay in there and play with her, till I get your lunch ready. Won't that be jolly?

Jimmy: (brightening a little) Why, you never give me but one at a time. You'll give me two?—One? Two?

Rachel: (gets the cookies and brings them to him. JIMMY climbs down from the chair) Shoo! now, little honey boy. See how many laughs you can make for me, before I come after you. Hear? Have a good time, now.

(JIMMY starts for the door quickly; but he begins to slow down. His face gets long and serious again. RACHEL watches him)

Rachel: (jumping at him) Shoo! Shoo! Get out of here quickly, little chicken. (She follows him out. The outer door opens and shuts. Presently she returns. She looks old and worn and grey; calmly pauses) First, it's little, black Ethel and then it's Jimmy. Tomorrow, it will be some other little child. The blight—sooner or later—strikes all. My little Jimmy, only seven years old, poisoned! (Through the open window comes the laughter of little children at play. RACHEL, shuddering, covers her ears) And once I said, centuries ago, it must have been: "How can life be so terrible, when there are little children in the world?" Terrible!

Terrible! *(in a whisper, slowly)* That's the reason it is so terrible. *(The laughter reaches her again; this time she listens)* And suddenly, some day, from out of the black, the blight shall descend, and shall still forever—the laughter on those little lips, and in those little hearts. *(pauses thoughtfully)* And the loveliest thing—almost, that ever happened to me, that beautiful voice, in my dream, those beautiful words: "Rachel, you are to be the mother to little children." *(pauses, then slowly and with dawning surprise)* Why, God, you were making a mock of me; you were laughing at me. I didn't believe God could laugh at our sufferings, but He can. We are accursed, accursed! We have nothing, absolutely nothing. *(STRONG's rosebuds attract her attention. She goes over to them, puts her hand out as if to touch them, and then shakes her head; very sweetly)* No, little rosebuds, I may not touch you. Dear, little, baby rosebuds,— I am accursed. *(Gradually her whole form stiffens, she breathes deeply; at last slowly)* You God! You terrible, laughing God! Listen! I swear and may my soul be damned to all eternity, if I do break this oath—I swear—that no child of mine shall ever lie upon my breast, for I will not have it rise up, in the terrible days that are to be—and call me cursed. *(a pause, very wistfully; questioningly)* Never to know the loveliest thing in all the world—the feel of a little head, the touch of little hands, the beautiful utter dependence—of a little child? *(with sudden frenzy)* You can laugh, Oh God! Well, so can I. *(bursts into terrible, racking laughter)* But I can be kinder than You. *(Fiercely she snatches the rosebuds from the vase, grasps them roughly, tears each head from the stem, and grinds it under her feet. The vase goes over with a crash; the water drips unheeded over the tablecloth and floor)* If I kill, You Mighty God, I kill at once—I do not torture. *(falls face downward on the floor. The laughter of the children shrills loudly through the window)*

ACT THREE

Time: Seven o'clock in the evening, one week later.

[Scene]: The same room. There is a coal fire in the grate. The curtains are drawn. A lighted oil lamp with a dark green porcelain shade is in the center of the table. MRS. LOVING and TOM are sitting by the table, MRS. LOVING sewing, TOM reading. There is the sound of much laughter and the shrill screaming of a child from the bedroom. Presently JIMMY, clad in a flannelet sleeping suit, covering all of him but his head and hands, chases a pillow, which has come flying through the doorway at the rear. He struggles with it, finally gets it in his arms, and rushes as fast as he can through the doorway again. RACHEL jumps at him with a cry. He drops the pillow and shrieks. There is a tussle for possession of it, and they disappear. The noise grows louder and merrier. TOM puts down his paper and grins. He looks at his mother.

Tom: Well, who's the giddy one in this family now?

Mrs. Loving: *(shaking her head in troubled manner)* I don't like it. It worries me. Rachel— *(breaks off)*

Tom: Have you found out, yet— . . .

[TOM and MRS. LOVING discuss RACHEL's recent withdrawal and gloomy mood.]

Mrs. Loving: (*slowly, as though thinking aloud*) I try to make out what could have happened; but it's no use—I can't. Those four days, she lay in bed hardly moving, scarcely speaking. Only her eyes seemed alive. I never saw such a wide, tragic look in my life. It was as though her soul had been mortally wounded. But how? how? What could have happened?

Tom: (*quietly*) I don't know. She generally tells me everything; but she avoids me now. If we are alone in a room—she gets out. I don't know what it means.

[(*RACHEL enters and TOM leaves the room*)]

Rachel: My kiddies! They're late, this evening. (*goes out into the vestibule. A door opens and shuts. There is the shrill, excited sound of childish voices. RACHEL comes in surrounded by the children, all trying to say something to her at once. RACHEL puts her finger on her lips and points toward the doorway in the rear. They all quiet down. She sits on the floor in the front of the stage, and the children all cluster around her. Their conversation takes place in a half-whisper. As they enter they nod brightly at MRS. LOVING, who smiles in return*) Why so late, kiddies? It's long past "sleepy-time."

Little Nancy: We've been playing "Hide and Seek," and having the mostest fun. We promised, all of us, that if we could play until half-past seven tonight we wouldn't make any fuss about going to bed at seven o'clock the rest of the week. It's awful hard to go. I *hate* to go to bed!

Little Mary,
Louise,
and Edith: So do I! So do I! So do I!

Little Martha: I don't. I love bed. My bed, after my muzzer tucks me all in, is like a nice warm bag. I just stick my nose out. When I lifts my head up I can see the light from the dining room come in the door. I can hear my muzzer and fazzer talking nice and low; and then, before I know it, I'm fast asleep, and I dream pretty things, and in about a minute it's morning again. I love my little bed, and I love to dream.

Little Mary: (*aggressively*) Well, I guess I love to dream too. I wish I could dream, though, without going to bed.

Little Nancy: When I grow up, I'm never doing to bed at night! (*darkly*) You'll see.

Little Louise: "Grown-ups" just love to poke their heads out of windows and cry, "Child'run, it's time for bed now; and you'd better hurry, too, I can tell you." They "sure" are queer, for sometimes when I wake up, it must be about twelve o'clock, I can hear my big sister giggling and talking to some silly man. If it's good for me to go to bed early—I should think—

Rachel: (*interrupting suddenly*) Why, where is my little Jenny? Excuse me, Louise dear.

Little Martha: Her cold is awful bad. She coughs like this (*giving a distressing imitation*) and snuffles all the time. She can't talk out loud, and she can't go to sleep. Muzzer says she's fev'rish—I thinks that's what she says. Jenny says she knows she could go to sleep, if you would come and sit with her a little while.

Rachel: I certainly will. I'll go when you do, honey.

Little Martha: (*softly stroking RACHEL's arm*) You're the very nicest "grown-up," (*loyally*) exept my muzzer, of course, I ever knew. You knows all about little chil'run and you can be one, although you're all grown up. I think you would make a lovely muzzer. (*to the rest of the children*) Don't you?

All: (*in excited whispers*) Yes, I do.

Rachel: (*winces, then says gently*) Come, kiddies, you must go now, or your mothers will blame me for keeping you. (*rises, as do the rest. LITTLE MARTHA puts her hand into RACHEL's*) Ma dear, I'm going down to sit a little while with Jenny. I'll be back before you go, though. Come, kiddies, say good-night to my mother.

All: (*gravely*) Good-night! Sweet dreams! God keep you all the night.

Mrs. Loving: Good-night dears! Sweet dreams, all!

(*Exeunt RACHEL and the children. MRS. LOVING continues to sew. The bell presently rings three distinct times. In a few moments, MRS. LOVING gets up and goes out into the vestibule. A door opens and closes. MRS. LOVING and JOHN STRONG come in. He is a trifle pale but his imperturbable self. MRS. LOVING, somewhat nervous, takes her seat and resumes her sewing. She motions STRONG to a chair. He returns to the vestibule, leaves his hat, returns, and sits down*)

Strong: Well, how is everything?

Mrs. Loving: Oh! about the same, I guess. Tom's out. John, we'll never forget you—and your kindness.

Strong: That was nothing. And Rachel?

Mrs. Loving: She'll be back presently. She went to sit with a sick child for a little while.

Strong: And how is she?

Mrs. Loving: She's not herself yet, but I think she is better. . . .

Strong: (*slowly*) It is rather strange. (*a long silence during which the outer door opens and shuts. RACHEL is heard singing. She stops abruptly. In a second or two she appears in the door. There is an air of suppressed excitement about her*)

Rachel: Hello! John. (*STRONG rises, nods at her, and brings forward for her the big armchair near the fire*) I thought that was your hat in the hall. It's brand new, I know—but it looks—"Johnlike." How are you? Ma! Jenny went to sleep like a little lamb. I don't like her breathing, though. (*looks from one to the other flippantly*) Who's dead? (*nods her thanks to STRONG for the chair and sits down*)

Mrs. Loving: Dead, Rachel?

Rachel: Yes. The atmosphere here is so funereal,—it's positively "crapey."

Strong: I don't know why it should be—I was just asking how you are.

Rachel: Heavens! Does the mere inquiry into my health precipitate such an atmosphere? Your two faces were as long, as long— (*breaks off*) Kind sir, let me assure you, I am in the very best of health. And how are you, John?

Strong: Oh! I'm always well. (*sits down*)

Mrs. Loving: Rachel, I'll have to get ready to go now. John, don't hurry. I'll be back shortly, probably in three-quarters of an hour—maybe less.

Rachel: And maybe more, if I remember Mrs. Jordan. However, Ma dear, I'll do the best I can—while you are away. I'll try to be a credit to your training. *(MRS. LOVING smiles and goes out the rear doorway)* Now, let's see—in the books of etiquette, I believe, the properly reared young lady always asks the young gentleman caller—you're young enough, aren't you, to be classed still as a "young gentleman caller?" *(no answer)* Well, anyway, she always asks the young gentleman caller, sweetly, something about the weather. *(primly)* This has been an exceedingly beautiful day, hasn't it, Mr. Strong? *(no answer from STRONG, who, with his head resting against the back of the chair, and his knees crossed is watching her in an amused, quizzical manner)* Well, really, every properly brought up young gentleman, I'm sure, ought to know, that it's exceedingly rude not to answer a civil question.

Strong: *(lazily)* Tell me what to answer, Rachel.

Rachel: Say, "Yes, very"; and look interested and pleased when you say it.

Strong: *(with a half-smile)* Yes, very.

Rachel: Well, I certainly wouldn't characterize that as a particularly animated remark. Besides, when you look at me through half-closed lids like that— and kind of smile—what are you thinking? *(no answer)* John Strong, are you deaf or—just plain stupid?

Strong: Plain stupid, I guess.

Rachel: *(in wheedling tones)* What were you thinking, John?

Strong: *(slowly)* I was thinking— *(breaks off)*

Rachel: *(irritably)* Well?

Strong: I've changed my mind.

Rachel: You're not going to tell me?

Strong: No.

(MRS. LOVING, dressed for the street, comes in)

Mrs. Loving: Goodbye, children. Rachel, don't quarrel so much with John. Let me see if I have my key. *(feels in her bag)* Yes, I have it. I'll be back shortly. Good-bye. *(STRONG and RACHEL rise. He bows)*

Rachel: Good-bye, Ma dear. Hurry back as soon as you can, won't you? *(exit MRS. LOVING through the vestibule. STRONG leans back again in his chair, and watches RACHEL through half-closed eyes. RACHEL sits in her chair nervously)*

Strong: Do you mind if I smoke?

Rachel: You know I don't.

Strong: I am trying to behave like—Reginald—"the properly reared young gentleman caller." *(lights a cigar; goes over to the fire, and throws his match away. RACHEL goes into the kitchenette, and brings him a saucer for his ashes. She places it on the table near him)* Thank you. *(They both sit again, STRONG very evidently enjoying his cigar and RACHEL)* Now this is what I call cosy.

Rachel: Cosy! Why?

Strong: A nice warm room—shut in—curtains drawn—a cheerful fire crackling at my back—a lamp, not an electric or gas one, but one of your plain, old-fashioned kerosene ones—

Rachel: (*interrupting*) Ma dear would like to catch you, I am sure, talking about *her* lamp like that. "Old-fashioned! plain!"—You have nerve.

Strong: (*continuing as though he had not been interrupted*) A comfortable chair—a good cigar—and not very far away, a little lady, who is looking charming, so near, that if I reached over, I could touch her. You there—and I here.—It's living.

Rachel: Well! of all things! A compliment—and from *you*! How did it slip out, pray? (*no answer*) I suppose that you realize that a conversation between two persons is absolutely impossible, if one has to do her share all alone. Soon my ingenuity for introducing interesting subjects will be exhausted; and then will follow what, I believe, the story books call, "an uncomfortable silence."

Strong: (*slowly*) Silence—between friends—isn't such a bad thing.

Rachel: Thanks awfully. (*leans back; cups her cheek in her hand, and makes no pretense at further conversation. The old look of introspection returns to her eyes. She does not move*)

Strong: (*quietly*) Rachel! (*RACHEL starts perceptibly*) You must remember I'm here. I don't like looking into your soul—when you forget you're not alone.

Rachel: I hadn't forgotten.

Strong: Wouldn't it be easier for you, little girl, if you could tell—someone?

Rachel: No. (*a silence*)

Strong: Rachel,—you're fond of flowers, aren't you?

Rachel: Yes.

Strong: Rosebuds—red rosebuds—particularly?

Rachel: (*nervously*) Yes.

Strong: Did you—dislike—the giver?

Rachel: (*more nervously; bracing herself*) No, of course not.

Strong: Rachel,—why—why—did you—kill the roses—then?

Rachel: (*twisting her hands*) Oh, John! I'm so sorry, Ma dear told you that. She didn't know you sent them.

Strong: So I gathered. (*pauses and then leans forward; quietly*) Rachel, little girl, why—did you kill them?

Rachel: (*breathing quickly*) Don't you believe—it—a—a—kindness—sometimes—to kill?

Strong: (*after a pause*) You—considered—it—a—kindness—to kill them?

Rachel: Yes. (*another pause*)

Strong: Do you mean—just—the roses?

Rachel: (*breathing more quickly*) John!—Oh! must I say?

Strong: Yes, little Rachel.

Rachel: *(in a whisper)* No. *(there is a long pause. RACHEL leans back limply, and closes her eyes. Presently STRONG rises, and moves his chair very close to hers. She does not stir. He puts his cigar on the saucer)* . . .

[*JOHN proposes marriage to her and describes an apartment he has picked out for them*]

(Suddenly there comes to their ears the sound of a child's weeping. It is monotonous, hopeless, terribly afraid. RACHEL recoils) Oh! John!—Listen!—It's my boy, again.—I—John—I'll be back in a little while. *(goes swiftly to the door in the rear, pauses and looks back. The weeping continues. Her eyes are tragic. Slowly she kisses her hand to him and disappears. JOHN stands where she has left him, looking down. The weeping stops. Presently RACHEL appears in the doorway. She is haggard and grey. She does not enter the room. She speaks as one dead might speak tonelessly, slowly)*

Rachel: Do you wish to know why Jimmy is crying?

Strong: Yes.

Rachel: I am twenty-two—and I'm old; you're thirty-two—and you're old; Tom's twenty-three—and he is old. Ma dear's sixty—and she said once she is much older than that. She is. We are all blighted; we are all accursed—all of us—everywhere, we whose skins are dark—our lives blasted by the white man's prejudice. *(pauses)* And my little Jimmy—seven years old, that's all—is blighted too. In a year or two, at best, he will be made old by suffering. *(pauses)* One week ago, today, some white boys, older and larger than my little Jimmy, as he was leaving the school—called him "Nigger"! They chased him through the streets calling him, "Nigger! Nigger! Nigger!" One boy threw stones at him. There is still a bruise on his little back where one struck him. That will get well; but they bruised his soul—and that—will never—get well. He asked me what "Nigger" meant. I made light of the whole thing, laughed it off. He went to his little playmates, and very naturally asked them. The oldest of them is nine!—and they knew, poor little things—and they told him. *(pauses)* For the last couple of nights he has been dreaming—about these boys. And he always awakes—in the dark—afraid—afraid—of the now—and the future—I have seen that look of deadly fear—in the eyes—of other little children. I know what it is myself.—I was twelve—when some big boys chased me and called me names.—I never left the house afterwards—without being afraid. I was afraid, in the streets—in the school—in the church, everywhere, always, afraid of being hurt. And I—was not—afraid in vain. *(The weeping begins again)* He's only a baby and he's blighted. *(to JIMMY)* Honey, I'm right here. I'm coming in just a minute. Don't cry. *(to STRONG)* If it nearly kills me to hear my Jimmy's crying, do you think I could stand it, when my own child, flesh of my flesh, blood of my blood—learned the same reason for weeping? Do you? *(pauses)* Ever since I fell here—a week ago—I am afraid—to go—to sleep, for every time I do—my children come—and beg me—weeping—not to—bring them here—to suffer. Tonight, they came—when I was awake. *(pauses)* I have promised them again, now—by Jimmy's bed. *(in a whisper)* I have damned—my soul to all eternity—if I do. *(to JIMMY)* Honey, don't! I'm coming. *(to STRONG)* And John, dear John—

you see—it can never be—all the beautiful, beautiful things—you have told me about. *(wistfully)* No—they—can never be—now. *(STRONG comes toward her)* No, —John dear,—you—must not—touch me—any more. *(pauses)* Dear, this—is—"Good-bye."

Strong: *(quietly)* It's not fair—to you, Rachel, to take you—at your word—tonight. You're sick; you've brooded so long, so continuously, —you've lost—your perspective. Don't answer, yet. Think it over for another week and I'll come back.

Rachel: *(wearily)* No,—I can't think—any more.

Strong: You realize—fully—you're sending me [away]—for always?

Rachel: Yes.

Strong: And you care?

Rachel: Yes.

Strong: It's settled, then for all time—"Good-bye!"

Rachel: *(after a pause)* Yes.

Strong: *(stands looking at her steadily a long time, and then moves to the door and turns, facing her; with infinite tenderness)* Good-bye, dear little Rachel—God bless you.

Rachel: Good-bye, John! *(STRONG goes out. A door opens and shuts. There is finality in the sound. The weeping continues. Suddenly; with a great cry)* John! John! *(runs out into the vestibule. She presently returns. She is calm again. Slowly)* No! No! John. Not for us. *(a pause; with infinite yearning)* Oh! John,—if it only—if it only— (breaks off, controls herself. Slowly again; thoughtfully)* No—No sunshine— no laughter—always—darkness. That is it. Even our little flat— *(in a whisper)* John's and mine—the little flat—that calls, calls us—through darkness. It shall wait—and wait—in vain—in darkness. Oh, John! *(pauses)* And my little children! my little children! *(the weeping ceases; pauses)* I shall never— see—you—now. Your little, brown, beautiful bodies—I shall never see.— Your dimples—everywhere—your laughter—your tears—the beautiful, lovely feel of you here. *(puts her hands against her heart)* Never—never—to be. *(a pause, fiercely)* But you are somewhere—and wherever you are, you are mine! You are mine! All of you! Every bit of you! Even God can't take you away. *(a pause; very sweetly; pathetically)* Little children! My little children!—No more need you come to me—weeping—weeping. You may be happy now—you are safe. Little weeping, voices, hush! hush! *(the weeping begins again. To JIMMY, her whole soul in her voice)* Jimmy! My little Jimmy! Honey! I'm coming.—Ma Rachel loves you so. *(sobs and goes blindly, unsteadily to the rear doorway; she leans her head there one second against the door; and then stumbles through and disappears. The light in the lamp flickers and goes out. . . . It is black. The terrible, heartbreaking weeping continues)*

Curtain

Anne Spencer

(1882–1975)

The only child of Joel Cephus and Sarah Louise Scales Bannister, Annie Bethel Scales (the name she assumed in school) was born on February 6, 1882 on a Virginia plantation, where her mother was the daughter of a former slave woman and a white member of the slave-owning aristocracy. Anne's father was also of mixed descent, African American and Seminole. She spent her early childhood in Martinsville, Virginia, where her father owned a saloon, until her mother fled the marriage and took her to North Carolina, then to Bramwell, West Virginia, in 1887. There her mother served as cook for a mining camp and placed Anne in the middle-class home of an African American barber to protect her from the camp's rough atmosphere. Bramwell was virtually an all-white town, and although Anne lived in the segregated section reserved for blacks, she was able to cross the color barrier through her friendship with a white girl, a relationship the town accepted. She received no formal schooling until the age of eleven because her mother did not want her to attend the school for blacks, at which the miners' children were also educated. In 1893, Anne was enrolled in the Virginia Seminary, a boarding school for African Americans in Lynchburg, Virginia. She graduated at the head of her class in 1899.

While in school, Anne met Edward Spencer, another student, and in 1901 they married and settled in Lynchburg for the rest of their lives. They had three children. The first black postal worker in Lynchburg, Edward took the unusual step of hiring housekeepers to take over the domestic chores so that Anne could write and tend her beloved garden. In the early 1920s, Anne's mother came to live with the Spencers and took responsibility for the household work. Anne became a librarian at Dunbar High School in 1924, remaining in the position for twenty years.

Although Spencer published only thirty poems in her lifetime, she became one of the most respected poets of the Harlem Renaissance, and her work was frequently anthologized. Her poetry appeared in *Opportunity, The Crisis, Survey Graphic, Palms*, and all the major anthologies of her day: James Weldon Johnson's *The Book of American Negro Poetry* (1922), Robert Kerlin's *Negro Poets and Their Poems* (1923), Alain Locke's *The New Negro* (1925), Charles S. Johnson's *Ebony and Topaz* (1927), and Countée Cullen's *Caroling Dusk* (1927). Known for her nature poetry and feminist themes, Spencer was one of the few women poets to be included in anthologies of the Harlem Renaissance after it was over, so highly regarded was her verse. She did not start publishing until she was thirty-eight, when James Weldon Johnson read her poetry during a visit to the Spencer home when he was in Lynchburg organizing a branch of the NAACP. He became her mentor from 1920, when the first poem was published, until his death in 1938. Johnson was one of several prominent intellectuals and artists who visited the Spencers at 1313 Pierce Street over several decades, including Langston Hughes, Georgia Douglas Johnson, W.E.B. Du Bois, Claude McKay, and Paul Robeson. Anne Spencer fought as a political activist against racism in Lynchburg while continuing to write poetry and prose in the cottage her husband built for her as a study. Most of it is unpublished. Her final piece of writing was a long poem about John Brown, which she did not finish. After her husband's death in 1964, Anne Spencer became reclusive, although she continued to write until her own death at the age of ninety-three.

White Things

Most things are colorful things—the sky, earth, and sea.
    Black men are most men; but the white are free!
White things are rare things; so rare, so rare
They stole from out a silvered world—somewhere.
Finding earth-plains fair plains, save greenly grassed,
They strewed white feathers of cowardice, as they passed;
    The golden stars with lances fine,
    The hills all red and darkened pine,
They blanched with their wand of power;
And turned the blood in a ruby rose
To a poor white poppy-flower.

They pyred a race of black, black men,
And burned them to ashes white; then,
Laughing, a young one claimed a skull,
For the skull of a black is white, not dull,
    But a glistening awful thing
    Made, it seems, for this ghoul to swing
In the face of God with all his might,
And swear by the hell that sired him:
    "Man-maker, make white!"

The Crisis, March 1923.

Lady, Lady

Lady, Lady, I saw your face,
Dark as night withholding a star . . .
The chisel fell, or it might have been
You had borne so long the yoke of men.
Lady, Lady, I saw your hands,
Twisted, awry, like crumpled roots,
Bleached poor white in a sudsy tub,
Wrinkled and drawn from your rub-a-dub.
Lady, Lady, I saw your heart,
And altared there in its darksome place
Were the tongues of flames the ancients knew,
Where the good God sits to spangle through.

Survey Graphic, March 1925.

Letter to My Sister

It is dangerous for a woman to defy the gods;
To taunt them with the tongue's thin tip,
Or strut in the weakness of mere humanity,
Or draw a line daring them to cross;
The gods own the searing lightning,
The drowning waters, tormenting fears
And anger of red sins.

Oh, but worse still if you mince timidly—
Dodge this way or that, or kneel or pray,
Be kind, or sweat agony drops
Or lay your quick body over your feeble young;
If you have beauty or none, if celibate
Or vowed—the gods are juggernaut,
Passing over . . . over . . .

This you may do:
Lock your heart, then, quietly,
And lest they peer within,
Light no lamp when dark comes down
Raise no shade for sun;
Breathless must your breath come through
If you'd die and dare deny
The gods their god-like fun.

Ebony and Topaz, 1927. This poem is also known under the title "Sybil Warns Her Sister."

Grapes: Still-Life

Snugly you rest, sweet globes,
Aged essence of the sun;
Copper of the platter
Like that you lie upon.

Is so well your heritage
You need feel no change
From the ringlet of your stem
To this bright rim's flange;

You, green-white Niagara,
Cool dull Nordic of your kind,—
Does your thick meat flinch
From these . . . touch and press your rind?

Caco, there, so close to you,
Is the beauty of the vine;
Stamen red and pistil black
Thru the curving line;

Concord, the too peaceful one,
Purpling at your side,
All the colors of his flask
Holding high in pride . . .

This, too, is your heritage,
You who force the plight;
Blood and bone you turn to them
For their root is white.

The Crisis, April 1929.

Black Man o' Mine

Black man o' mine,
If the world were your lover,
It could not give you what I give to you,
Or the ocean would yield and you could discover
Its ages of treasure to hold and to view;
Could it fill half the measure of my heart's portion . . .
Just for you living, just for you giving all this devotion,
Black man o' mine.

Black man o' mine,
As I hush and caress you, close to my heart,
All your loving is just your needing what's true;
Then with your passing dark comes my darkest part,
For living without your loving is only rue.
Black man o' mine, if the world were your lover,
It could not give what I give to you.

Unpublished.

Jessie Redmon Fauset

(1882–1961)

Jessie Fauset was one of the most important figures of the Harlem Renaissance: a brilliant woman who excelled at literary production and scholarly study. She is best known for her central role as literary editor of *The Crisis* from 1919 to 1926; she discovered and helped promote Langston Hughes, Countee Cullen, Claude McKay, and other major writers of the period. So important was Fauset that she became known as the midwife of the Harlem Renaissance. In addition to her prowess as an editor, however, Fauset was herself a major writer in the movement she helped create. She was one of its most prolific novelists, producing four novels: *There Is Confusion* (1924), *Plum Bun* (1928), *The Chinaberry Tree* (1931), and *Comedy, American Style* (1933). Fauset also wrote numerous short stories and essays and published many poems in *The Crisis;* the latter were also widely anthologized in important collections such as Countee Cullen's *Caroling Dusk* (1927), Robert Kerlin's *Negro Poets and Their Poems* (1923), and Charles S. Johnson's *Ebony and Topaz* (1927). Along with her friends Angelina Weld Grimké and Georgia Douglas Johnson, Jessie Fauset was the best-known African American woman poet of her day, and together they mentored other women writers in their homes, which they opened as literary salons.

Born in a suburb of Philadelphia to an African Methodist Episcopal minister, the Rev. Redmon Fauset, and his wife Anna Seamon, Fauset was the seventh child in her family. Her mother died when Fauset was a child, and her father remarried. Educated at prestigious schools, she was the only black person in her classes in high school and college. She was denied admission to Bryn Mawr because of her race and was the only African American student at Cornell University, from which she graduated Phi Beta Kappa in 1905, the first black woman to join that society and to graduate from Cornell. Denied teaching employment in Philadelphia, again because of racism, Fauset taught French and Latin at Dunbar High School in Washington, D.C., from 1906 until 1918, when she enrolled in an M.A. program in French at the University of Pennsylvania.

She moved to New York and joined *The Crisis* staff in 1919 under the editorship of W.E.B. Du Bois. Along with her editing duties there, Fauset was the first literary editor (and later managing editor) of *The Brownies' Book*, a children's monthly begun by Du Bois. She was one of the few Harlem Renaissance women who traveled to Europe. She attended the Second Pan African Congress in 1921 and later studied at the Sorbonne, where she polished her French; the language frequently appears in her writing. When she quit *The Crisis* after a dispute with Du Bois in 1926, Fauset resumed teaching at De Witt Clinton High School in New York. In 1929, when she was forty-five, she married Herbert Harris, an insurance broker. The couple moved to Montclair, New Jersey, in 1939, though she continued to teach in New York until 1944. After Harris's death in 1958, she lived with her stepbrother in Philadelphia until her death. Jessie Fauset's contributions to the Harlem Renaisssance cannot be overstated, although her creative writing is only now beginning to garner the critical respect it deserves.

Laura Wheeler, "The Veil of Spring," cover of *The Crisis,* April 1924

Oriflamme

I can remember when I was a little, young girl, how my old mammy would sit out of doors in the evenings and look up at the stars and groan, and I would say, "Mammy, what makes you groan so?" And she would say, "I am groaning to think of my poor children; they do not know where I be and I don't know where they be. I look up at the stars and they look up at the stars!"
— Sojourner Truth

I think I see her sitting, bowed and black,
    Stricken and seared with slavery's mortal scars,
Reft of her children, lonely, anguished, yet
    Still looking at the stars.

Symbolic mother, we thy myriad sons,
    Pounding our stubborn hearts on Freedom's bars,
Clutching our birthright, fight with faces set,
    Still visioning the stars!

The Crisis, January 1920.

Here's April!

I

This town that yesterday was dark and mean,
    And dank and raw with Winter's freezing air,
Is Light itself today, and verdant Sheen
    Gold-tinted, and besprent with perfume rare;
Translated over night to a parterre
    That makes me dream of Araby and Spain,
And all the healing places of the Earth,
    Where one lays by his woe, his bitter pain,—
        For peace and mirth.

II

Old Winter that stayed by us black and drear,
    And laid his blighting seal on everything,
Is vanished.—Is it true he once was here?
    Mark how the ash-trees bud, and children sing,
And birds set up a faint, shy jargoning;
    And healing balm pours out from bole and leaf.
For Spring—sweet April's here in tree and grass!
    Oh foolish heart to fret so with your grief!
        This too shall pass!

The Crisis, April 1924.

Words! Words!

How did it happen that we quarreled?
We two who loved each other so!
Only the moment before we were one,
Using the language that lovers know.
And then of a sudden, a word, a phrase,
That struck at the heart like a poignard's blow.
And you went berserk, and I saw red,
And love lay between us, bleeding and dead!
Dead! When we'd loved each other so!

How *could* it happen that we quarreled!
Think of the things we used to say!
"What does it matter, dear, what you do?
Love such as ours has to last for aye!"
—"Try me! I long to endure your test!"
—"Love, we shall always love, come what may!"
What are the words the apostle saith?
"In the power of the tongue are Life and Death!"
Think of the things we used to say!

Palms, October 1926.

Touché

Dear, when we sit in that high, placid room,
"Loving" and "doving" as all lovers do,
Laughing and leaning so close in the gloom,—

What is the change that creeps sharp over you?
Just as you raise your fine hand to my hair,
Bringing that glance of mixed wonder and rue?

"Black hair," you murmur, "so lustrous and rare,
Beautiful too, like a raven's smooth wing;
Surely no gold locks were ever more fair."

Why do you say every night that same thing?
Turning your mind to some old constant theme,
Half meditating and half murmuring?

Tell me, that girl of your young manhood's dream,
Her you loved first in that dim long ago—
Had *she* blue eyes? Did *her* hair goldly gleam?

Does *she* come back to you softly and slow,
Stepping wraith-wise from the depths of the past?
Quickened and fired by the warmth of our glow?

There, I've divined it! My wit holds you fast.
Nay, no excuses; 'tis little I care.
I knew a lad in my own girlhood's past,—
Blue eyes he had and such waving gold hair!

Caroling Dusk, 1927.

La Vie C'Est la Vie

On summer afternoons I sit
Quiescent by you in the park,
And idly watch the sunbeams gild
And tint the ash-trees' bark.

Or else I watch the squirrels frisk
And chaffer in the grassy lane;
And all the while I mark your voice
Breaking with love and pain.

I know a woman who would give
Her chance of heaven to take my place;
To see the love-light in your eyes,
The love-glow on your face!

And there's a man whose lightest word
Can set my chilly blood afire;
Fulfilment of his least behest
Defines my life's desire.

But he will none of me. Nor I
Of you. Nor you of her. 'Tis said
The world is full of jests like these.—
I wish that I were dead.

Caroling Dusk, 1927.

Mary Elizabeth

Mary Elizabeth was late that morning. As a direct result, Roger left for work without telling me goodbye, and I spent most of the day fighting the headache which always comes if I cry.

For I cannot get a breakfast. I can manage a dinner, one just puts the roast in the oven and takes it out again. And I really excel in getting lunch. There is a good delicatessen near us, and with dainty service and flowers. I get along very nicely. But breakfast! In the first place, it's a meal I neither like nor need. And I never, if I live a thousand years, shall learn to like coffee. I suppose that is why I cannot make it.

"Roger," I faltered, when the awful truth burst upon me and I began to realize that Mary Elizabeth wasn't coming. "Roger, couldn't you get breakfast downtown this morning? You know last time you weren't so satisfied with my coffee."

Roger was hostile. I think he had just cut himself shaving. Anyway, he was horrid.

"No, I can't get my breakfast downtown!" He actually snapped at me. "Really, Sally, I don't believe there's another woman in the world who would send her husband out on a morning like this on an empty stomach. I don't see how you can be so unfeeling."

Well, it wasn't "a morning like this," for it was just the beginning of November. And I had only proposed his doing what I knew he would have to do eventually.

I didn't say anything more, but started on that breakfast. I don't know why I thought I had to have hot cakes! The breakfast really was awful! The cakes were tough and gummy and got cold one second, exactly, after I took them off the stove. And the coffee boiled, or stewed, or scorched, or did whatever the particular thing is that coffee shouldn't do. Roger sawed at one cake, took one mouthful of the dreadful brew, and pushed away his cup.

"It seems to me you might learn to make a decent cup of coffee," he said icily. Then he picked up his hat and flung out of the house.

I think it is stupid of me, too, not to learn how to make coffee. But really, I'm no worse than Roger is about lots of things. Take "Five Hundred." Roger knows I love cards, and with the Cheltons right around the corner from us and as fond of it as I am, we could spend many a pleasant evening. But Roger will not learn. Only the night before, after I had gone through a whole hand with him, with hearts as trumps, I dealt the cards around again to imaginary opponents and we started playing. Clubs were trumps, and spades led. Roger, having no spades, played triumphantly a Jack of Hearts and proceeded to take the trick.

"But Roger," I protested, "you threw off."

"Well," he said, deeply injured, "didn't you say hearts were trumps when you were playing before?"

And when I tried to explain, he threw down the cards and wanted to know what difference it made; he'd rather play casino, anyway! I didn't go out and slam the door.

The Crisis, December 1919.

But I couldn't help from crying this particular morning. I not only value Roger's good opinion, but I hate to be considered stupid.

Mary Elizabeth came in about eleven o'clock. She is a small, wizened woman, very dark, somewhat wrinkled, and a model of self-possession. I wish I could make you see her, or that I could reproduce her accent, not that it is especially colored,—Roger's and mine are much more so—but her pronunciation, her way of drawing out her vowels, is so distinctively Mary Elizabethan!

I was ashamed of my red eyes and tried to cover up my embarrassment with sternness.

"Mary Elizabeth," said I, "you are late!" just as though she didn't know it.

"Yas'm, Mis' Pierson," she said, composedly, taking off her coat. She didn't remove her hat,—she never does until she has been in the house some two or three hours. I can't imagine why. It is a small, black, dusty affair, trimmed with black ribbon, some dingy white roses and a sheaf of wheat. I give Mary Elizabeth a dress and hat now and then, but, although I recognize the dress from time to time, I never see any change in the hat. I don't know what she does with my ex-millinery.

"Yas'm," she said again, and looked comprehensively at the untouched breakfast dishes and the awful viands, which were still where Roger had left them.

"Looks as though you'd had to git breakfast yourself," she observed brightly. And went out in the kitchen and ate all those cakes and drank that unspeakable coffee. Really she did, and she didn't warm them up either.

I watched her miserably, unable to decide whether Roger was too finicky or Mary Elizabeth a natural born diplomat.

"Mr. Gales led me an awful chase last night," she explained. "When I got home yestiddy evenin', my cousin whut keeps house for me tole me Mr. Gales went out in the mornin' en hadn't come back."

"Mr. Gales," let me explain, is Mary Elizabeth's second husband, an octogenarian, and the most original person, I am convinced, in existence.

"Yas'm," she went on, eating a final cold hot cake, "en I went to look fer 'im, en had the whole perlice station out all night huntin' 'im. Look like they wusn't never goin' to find 'im. But I ses, 'Jes' let me look fer enough en long enough en I'll find 'im,' I ses, en I did. Way out Georgy Avenue, with the hat on ole Mis' give 'im. Sent it to 'im all the way fum Chicago. He's had it fifteen years, high silk beaver. I knowed he wusn't goin' too fer with that hat on.

"I went up to 'im, settin' by a fence all muddy, holdin' his hat on with both hands. En I ses, 'Look here, man, you come erlong home with me, en let me put you to bed.' En he come jest as meek! No-o-me! I knowed he wusn't goin' fer with ole Mis' hat on."

"Who was old 'Mis,' Mary Elizabeth?" I asked her.

"Lady I used to work fer in Noo York," she informed me. "Me en Rosy, the cook, lived with her fer years. Ole Mis' was turrible fond of me, though her en Rosy used to querrel all the time. Jes' seemed like they couldn't git erlong. 'Member once Rosy run after her one Sunday with a knife, en I kep 'em apart. Reckon Rosy musta bin right put out with ole Mis' that day. By en by, her en Rosy move to Chicaga, en when I married Mr. Gales, she sent 'im that hat. That old white woman shore did like me. It's so late, reckon I'd better put off sweepin' tel termorrer, ma'am."

I acquiesced, following her about from room to room. This was partly to get away from my own doleful thoughts. Roger really had hurt my feelings, but just as much to hear her talk. At first I used not to believe all she said, but after I investigated once and found her truthful in one amazing statement, I capitulated.

She had been telling me some remarkable tale of her first husband and I was listening with the stupefied attention to which she always reduces me. Remember she was speaking of her first husband.

"En I ses to him, I ses, 'Mr. Gale, —'"

"Wait a moment, Mary Elizabeth," I interrupted, meanly delighted to have caught her for once. "You mean your first husband, don't you?"

"Yas'm," she replied. "En I ses to 'im, 'Mr. Gale,' I ses—'"

"But Mary Elizabeth," I persisted, "that's your second husband, isn't it,—Mr. Gale?"

She gave me her long drawn "No-o-me! My first husband was Mr. Gale and my second husband is Mr. *Gales.* He spells his name with a Z, I reckon. I ain't never see it writ. Ez I wus sayin' I ses to Mr. Gale—"

And it was true! Since then I have never doubted Mary Elizabeth.

She was loquacious that afternoon. She told me about her sister, "where's got a home in the country and where's got eight children." I used to read Lucy Pratt's stories about little Ephraim or Ezekiel, I forget his name, who always said "where's" instead of "who's," but I never believed it really till I heard Mary Elizabeth use it. For some reason or other she never mentions her sister without mentioning the home too. "My sister where's got a home in the country" is her unvarying phrase.

"Mary Elizabeth," I asked her once, "does your sister live in the country, or does she simply own a house there?"

"Yas'm," she told me.

She is fond of her sister. "If Mr. Gales wus to die," she told me complacently, "I'd go to live with her."

"If he should die," I asked her idly, "would you marry again?"

"Oh, no-o-me!" She was emphatic. "Though I don't know why I shouldn't, I'd come by it hones'. My father wus married four times."

That shocked me out of my headache. "Four times, Mary Elizabeth, and you had all those stepmothers!" My mind refused to take it in.

"Oh, no-o-me! I always lived with mamma. She was his first wife."

I hadn't thought of people in the state in which I had instinctively placed Mary Elizabeth's father and mother as indulging in divorce, but as Roger says slangily, "I wouldn't know."

Mary Elizabeth took off the dingy hat. "You see, papa and mamma—" the ineffable pathos of hearing this woman of sixty-four, with a husband of eighty, use the old childish terms!

"Papa and mamma wus slaves, you know, Mis' Pierson, and so of course they wusn't exackly married. White folks wouldn't let 'em. But they wus awf'ly in love with each other. Heard mamma tell erbout it lots of times, and how papa wus the han'somest man! Reckon she wus long erbout sixteen or seventeen then. So they jumped over a broom-stick,[1] en they wus jes as happy! But not long after I come erlong, they sold papa down South, and mamma never see him no mo' fer years and years. Thought he was dead. So she married again."

"And he came back to her, Mary Elizabeth?" I was overwhelmed with the woefulness of it.

"Yas'm. After twenty-six years. Me and my sister where's got a home in the country— she's really my half-sister, see Mis' Pierson,—her en mamma en my step-father en me wus all down in Bumpus, Virginia, workin' fer some white folks, and we used to live in a little cabin, had a front stoop to it. En one day an ole cullud man come by, had a lot o' whiskers. I'd saw him lots of times there in Bumpus, lookin' and peerin' into every cullud woman's face. En jes' then my sister she call out 'Come here, you Ma'y Elizabeth,' en that old man stopped, en he looked at me en he looked at me, en he ses to me, 'Chile, is yo name Ma'y Elizabeth?'

"You know, Mis' Pierson, I thought he wus jes' bein' fresh, en I ain't paid no 'tention to 'im. I ain't sed nuthin' ontel he spoke to me three or four times, en then I ses to 'im, 'Go 'way fum here, man, you ain't got no call to be fresh with me. I'm a decent woman. You'd oughta be ashamed of yorself, an ole man like you!'"

Mary Elizabeth stopped and looked hard at the back of her poor wrinkled hands.

"En he says to me, 'Daughter,' he ses jes' like that, 'daughter,' he ses, 'hones' I ain't bein' fresh. Is yo' name shore enough Ma'y Elizabeth?'

"En I tole him, 'Yas'r.'

"'Chile,' he ses, 'whar is yo' daddy?'

"'Ain't got no daddy,' I tole him pert-like. 'They done tuk 'im away fum me twenty-six years ago, I wusn't but a mite of a baby. Sol' 'im down the river. My mother often talks about it.' And oh, Mis' Pierson, you shoulda see the glory come into his face!

"'Yore mother!' he ses, kinda out of breath, 'yore mother! Ma'y Elizabeth, whar is your mother?'

"'Back thar on the stoop,' I tole 'im. 'Why, did you know my daddy?'

"But he didn't pay no 'tention to me, jes' turned and walked up the stoop whar mamma wus settin'! She wus feelin' sorta porely that day. En you oughta see me steppin' erlong after 'im.

"He walked right up to her and giv' her one look. 'Oh, Maggie,' he shout out, 'oh, Maggie! Ain't you know me? Maggie, ain't you know me?'

"Mamma look at 'im and riz up outa her cheer. 'Who're you?' she ses kinda trimbly, 'callin' me Maggie thata way? Who're you?'

---

1. Jumping over a broomstick was part of the marriage ceremony for slaves. The bride and groom would jump over a broomstick held parallel to the ground as a sign that they were married.

"He went up real close to her, then, 'Maggie,' he ses jes' like that, kinda sad 'n tender, 'Maggie!' and hel' out his arms.

"She walked right into them. 'Oh!' she ses, 'it's Cassius! It's Cassius! It's my husban' come back to me! It's Cassius!' They wus like two mad people.

"My sister Minnie and me, we jes' stood and gawped at 'em. There they wus, holding on to each other like two pitiful childrun, en he tuk her hands and kissed 'em.

"'Maggie,' he ses, 'you'll come away with me, won't you? You gonna take me back, Maggie? We'll go away, you en Ma'y Elizabeth en me. Won't we Maggie?'

"Reckon my mother clean forgot about my step-father. 'Yes, Cassius,' she ses, 'we'll go away.' And then she sees Minnie, en it all comes back to her. 'Oh, Cassius,' she ses 'I cain't go with you, I'm married again, en this time fer real. This here gal's mine and three boys, too, another chile comin' in November!'"

"But she went with him, Mary Elizabeth," I pleaded. "Surely she went with him after all those years. He really was her husband."

I don't know whether Mary Elizabeth meant to be sarcastic or not. "Oh, no-o-me, mamma couldn't a done that. She wus a good woman. Her ole master, whut done sol' my father down river, brung her up too religious fer that, en anyways, papa was married again, too. Had his fourth wife there in Bumpus with 'im."

The unspeakable tragedy of it!

I left her and went up to my room, and hunted out my dark blue serge dress which I had meant to wear again that winter. But I had to give Mary Elizabeth something, so I took the dress down to her.

She was delighted with it. I could tell she was, because she used her rare and untranslatable expletive.

"Haytian!" she said. "My sister where's got a home in the country, got a dress look somethin' like this but it ain't as good. No-o-me. She got hers to wear at a friend's weddin',—gal she wus riz up with. Thet gal married well, too, lemme tell you; her husband's a Sunday School sup'rintender."

I told her she needn't wait for Mr. Pierson, I would put dinner on the table. So off she went in the gathering dusk, trudging bravely back to her Mr. Gales and his high silk hat.

I watched her from the window till she was out of sight. It had been such a long time since I had thought of slavery. I was born in Pennsylvania, and neither my parents nor grandparents had been slaves; otherwise I might have had the same tale to tell as Mary Elizabeth, or worse yet, Roger and I might have lived in those black days and loved and lost each other and futilely, damnably, met again like Cassius and Maggie.

Whereas it was now, and I had Roger and Roger had me.

How I loved him as I sat there in the hazy dark. I thought of his dear, bronze perfection, his habit of swearing softly in excitement, his blessed stupidity. Just the same I didn't meet him at the door as usual, but pretended to be busy. He came rushing to me with *The Saturday Evening Post,* which is more to me than rubies. I thanked him warmly, but aloofly, if you can get that combination.

We ate dinner almost in silence for my part. But he praised everything,—the cooking, the table, my appearance.

After dinner we went up to the little sitting-room. He hoped I wasn't tired,—couldn't he fix the pillows for me? So!

I opened the magazine and the first thing I saw was a picture of a woman gazing in stony despair at the figure of a man disappearing around the bend of the road. It was too much. Suppose that were Roger and I! I'm afraid I sniffled. He was at my side in a moment.

"Dear loveliest! Don't cry. It was all my fault. You aren't any worse about coffee than I am about cards! And anyway, I needn't have slammed the door! Forgive me, Sally. I always told you I was hard to get along with. I've had a horrible day,—don't stay cross with me, dearest."

I held him to me and sobbed outright on his shoulder. "It isn't you, Roger," I told him, "I'm crying about Mary Elizabeth."

I regret to say he let me go then, so great was his dismay. Roger will never be half the diplomat that Mary Elizabeth is.

"Holy smokes!" he groaned. "She isn't going to leave us for good, is she?"

So then I told him about Maggie and Cassius. "And oh, Roger," I ended futilely, "to think that they had to separate after all those years, when he had come back, old and with whiskers!" I didn't mean to be so banal, but I was crying too hard to be coherent.

Roger had got up and was walking the floor, but he stopped then aghast.

"Whiskers!" he moaned. "My hat! Isn't that just like a woman?" He had to clear his throat once or twice before he could go on, and I think he wiped his eyes.

"Wasn't it the—" I really can't say what Roger said here, —"wasn't it the darndest hard luck that when he did find her again, she should be married? She might have waited."

I stared at him astounded. "But, Roger," I reminded him, "he had married three other times, he didn't wait."

"Oh—!" said Roger, unquotable, "married three fiddlesticks! He only did that to try to forget her."

Then he came over and knelt beside me again. "Darling, I do think it is a sensible thing for a poor woman to learn how to cook, but I don't care as long as you love me and we are together. Dear loveliest, if I had been Cassius," he caught my hands so tight he hurt them,—"and I had married fifty times and had come back and found you married to someone else, I'd have killed you, killed you."

Well, he wasn't logical, but he was certainly convincing.

So thus, and not otherwise, Mary Elizabeth healed the breach.

Effie Lee Newsome

(a k a Mary Effie Lee)

(1885-1979)

Born Mary Effie Lee on January 19, 1885, in Philadelphia, Effie Lee Newsome was one of two daughters born to Benjamin Franklin and Mary Elizabeth Ashe Lee. Her sister, Consuelo, was also a poet, and both were illustrators for children's magazines. Their childhood was spent in Texas and then Ohio, where their father was a bishop. Newsome attended Wilberforce University (1901–1904), Oberlin College (1904–1905), the Philadelphia Academy of Fine Arts (1907–1908), and the University of Pennsylvania (1911–1914). She married the Rev. Henry Nesby Newsome in 1920 and moved with him to Birmingham, Alabama. She later returned to Wilberforce, Ohio, where she worked as a librarian in an elementary school. Newsome is best known for her children's literature. She edited "The Little Page" in *The Crisis,* contributing both poems and drawings. She also edited children's columns for *Opportunity* and published several children's stories. She also wrote articles, poems, and reviews for adults. Over one hundred of her poems appeared in *The Crisis* from 1917 to 1934, and she published one volume of poetry, *Gladiola Gardens,* in 1940.

The Bronze Legacy (To a Brown Boy)

'Tis a noble gift to be brown, all brown,
   Like the strongest things that make up this earth,
Like the mountains grave and grand,
   Even like the trunks of trees—
   Even oaks, to be like these!
God builds His strength in bronze.

To be brown like thrush and lark!
   Like the subtle wren so dark!
Nay, the king of beasts wears brown;
   Eagles are of this same hue.
I thank God, then, I am brown.
      Brown has mighty things to do.

The Crisis, October 1922.

Exodus

Rank fennel and broom
Grow wanly beside
The cottage and room
We once occupied,
But sold for the snows!

The dahoon berry weeps in blood,
I know,
Watched by the crow—
I've seen both grow
In those weird wastes of Dixie!

The Crisis, January 1925.

The Bird in the Cage

I am not better than my brother over the way,
But he has a bird in a cage and I have not.
It beats its little fretted green wings
Against the wires of its prison all day long.
Backward and forward it leaps,
While summer air is tender and the shadows of leaves
Rock on the ground,
And the earth is cool and heated in spots,
And the air from rich herbage rises teeming,
And gold of suns spills all around,

And birds within the maples
And birds upon the oaks fly and sing and flutter.
And there is that little green prisoner,
Tossing its body forward and up,
Backward and forth mechanically!
I listen for its hungry little song,
Which comes unsatisfying,
Like drops of dew dispelled by drought.
O, rosebud doomed to ripen in a bud vase!
O, bird of song within that binding cage!
Nay, I am not better than my brother over the way,
Only he has a bird in a cage and I have not.

The Crisis, February 1927.

The Quilt

I have the greatest fun at night,
When casement windows are all bright.
I make believe each one's a square
Of some great quilt up in the air.

The blocks of gold have black between,
Wherever only night is seen.
It surely makes a mammoth quilt—-
With bits of dark and checks of gilt—
—To cover up the tired day
In such a cozy sort of way.

Caroling Dusk, 1927.

John F. Matheus

(1887–1983)

John Frederick Matheus was born September 10, 1887, in Keyser, West Virginia, one of Mary Susan Brown and John William Matheus's four sons. His mother was a housewife, his father a bank messenger and a part-time tannery worker. While Matheus was still quite young, the family moved to Steubenville, Ohio. Matheus was educated at Western Reserve University in Cleveland, where he studied classics and graduated cum laude with an A.B. degree in 1910. While an undergraduate, he married Martha Miller Roberts, a singer who introduced him to black theater. In 1921 he received an A.M. degree from Columbia University. After visiting Cuba in 1924, he studied at the Sorbonne; he also attended the University of Chicago in 1927. Matheus taught Latin and modern foreign languages at Florida A & M College in Tallahassee from 1910 to 1922, then took a position as a professor of romance languages at West Virginia State College, where, for the next thirty years, he taught French.

Matheus traveled extensively, and in 1930 he spent some time in Liberia, serving as secretary to Dr. Charles S. Johnson, founding editor of *Opportunity* and the American member of the League of Nations commission to investigate slavery in Liberia. After traveling to Haiti in 1927 to research his opera, *Ouanga!*, he spent a year there from 1945 to 1946 as director for the teaching of English in the national schools. After his retirement in 1953, Matheus remained academically active and taught at a number of institutions, including Dillard University in New Orleans, Morris Brown College in Atlanta, Texas Southern University in Houston, Hampton Institute in Hampton, Virginia, and Kentucky State University. He also served as treasurer of the College Language Association until 1975.

By the mid 1920s, Matheus had garnered critical acclaim as a creative writer. His most famous short story, "Fog," won first prize in the 1925 *Opportunity* contest. The story was also included in Edward J. O'Brien's *Best Short Stories of 1925*. The next year, he won first prize in *The Crisis* contest for his story "Swamp Moccasin." It was also in 1926 that he was awarded first prize in the *Opportunity* contest for his popular play, *'Cruiter*. Matheus published as many as fifty short stories, several articles, and wrote at least four other plays, *Tambour, Ti Yette, Black Damp, Guitar*, and one opera, *Ouanga!* His plays were included in Alain Locke and Montgomery Gregory's *Plays of Negro Life* (1927) and Willis Richardson's *Plays and Pageants from the Life of the Negro* (1930). His numerous short stories were published in *Opportunity* and *Carolina Magazine* as well as in such anthologies as *The New Negro* (1925), *Ebony and Topaz* (1927), and *The Negro Caravan* (1941). In 1974 Matheus privately printed *A Collection of Short Stories*, edited by Leonard A. Slade, Jr. Matheus spent the last years of his life in Tallahassee, Florida, and died at age ninety-five.

Requiem

She wears, my beloved, a rose upon her head.
Walk softly angels, lest your gentle tread
Awake her to the turmoil and the strife,
The dissonance and hates called life.

She sleeps, my beloved, a rose upon her head.
Who says she will not hear, that she is dead?
The rose will fade and lose its lovely hue,
But not, my beloved, will fading wither you.

Caroling Dusk, 1927.

In Haiti Is Riot of Color—

In Haiti is riot of color:
The sea with its salt, salt tang,
The land, the sky and the palm trees,
Dancing a wild *meringue.*

The mountains are royal purple,
The flamboyant flowering red,
The houses, the walks and the garments
Are white, like shrouds for the dead.

The moon is more than of silver,
The sun has dazzlinger glow;
The mangoes peep over bananas,
Painting a marvelous show.

The oranges are matching the cane stalks,
The coffee plantations are glad,
The hills are happy in splendor,
Only the people are sad.

The Crisis, November 1929.

Fog

The stir of life echoed. On the bridge between Ohio and West Virginia was the rumble of heavy trucks, the purr of high power engines in Cadillacs and Paiges, the rattle of Fords. A string of loaded freight cars pounded along on the C. & P. tracks, making a thunderous, if tedious way to Mingo. A steamboat's hoarse whistle boomed forth between the swish, swish, chug, chug of a mammoth stern paddle wheel with the asthmatic poppings of the pistons. The raucous shouts of smutty-speaking street boys, the noises of a steam laundry, the clank and clatter of a pottery, the godless voices of women from Water Street houses of ill fame, all these blended in a sort of modern babel, common to all the towers of destruction erected by modern civilization.

These sounds were stirring when the clock sounded six on top of the Court House, that citadel of Law and Order, with the statue of Justice looming out of an alcove above the imposing stone entrance, blindfolded and in her right hand the scales of Judgment. Even so early in the evening the centers from which issued these inharmonious notes were scarcely visible. This sinister cloak of late November twilight Ohio Valley fog had stealthily spread from somewhere beneath the sombre river bed, down from somewhere in the lowering West Virginia hills. This fog extended its tentacles over city and river, gradually obliterating traces of familiar landscapes. At five-thirty the old Panhandle bridge, supported by massive sandstone pillars, stalwart, as when erected fifty years before to serve a generation now passed behind the portals of life, this *old* bridge had become a spectral outline against the sky as the toll keepers of the *new* bridge looked northward up the Ohio River.

Now at six o'clock the fog no longer distorted; it blotted out, annihilated. One by one the street lights came on, giving an uncertain glare in spots, enabling peeved citizens to tread their way homeward without recognizing their neighbor ten feet ahead, whether he might be Jew or Gentile, Negro or Pole, Slav, Croatian, Italian or one hundred per cent American.

An impatient crowd of tired workers peered vainly through the gloom to see if the headlights of the interurban car were visible through the thickening haze. The car was due at Sixth and Market at six-ten and was scheduled to leave at six-fifteen for many little towns on the West Virginia side.

At the same time as these uneasy toilers were waiting, on the opposite side of the river the car had stopped to permit some passengers to descend and disappear in the fog. The motorman, flagged and jaded by the monotony of many stoppings and startings, waited mechanically for the conductor's bell to signal, "Go ahead."

The fog was thicker, more impenetrable. It smothered the headlight. Inside the car in the smoker, that part of the seats nearest the motorman's box, partitioned from the rest, the lights were struggling bravely against a fog of tobacco smoke, almost as opaque as the dull grey blanket of mist outside.

Opportunity, May 1925.

A group of red, rough men, sprawled along the two opposite bench-formed seats, parallel to the sides of the car, were talking to one another in the thin, flat colorless English of their mountain state, embellished with the homely idioms of the coal mine, the oil field, the gas well.

"When does this here meetin' start, Bill?"

"That air notice read half after seven."

"What's time now?"

"Damned 'f I know. Hey, Lee, what time's that pocket clock of yourn's got?"

"Two past six."

There was the sound of a match scratching against the sole of a rough shoe.

"Gimme a light, Lafe."

In attempting to reach for the burning match before its flame was extinguished, the man stepped forward and stumbled over a cheap suitcase of imitation leather. A vile looking stogie fell in the aisle.

"God! Your feet're bigger'n Bill's."

The crowd laughed uproariously. The butt of this joke grinned and showed a set of dirty nicotine stained teeth. He recovered his balance in time to save the flaring match. He was a tremendous man, slightly stooped, with taffy colored, straggling hair and little pig eyes.

Between initial puffs he drawled: "Now you're barkin' up the wrong tree. I only wear elevens."

"Git off'n me, Lee Cromarty," growled Bill. "You hadn't ought to be rumlin' of *my* feathers the wrong way—and you a-plannin' to ride the goat."[1]

Lafe, a consumptive-appearing, undersized, bovine-eyed individual, spat out the remark: "Naow, there! You had better be kereful. Men have been nailed to the cross for less than that."

"Ha! Ha!—ho! ho! ho!"

There was a joke to arouse the temper of the crowd.

A baby began to cry lustily in the rear and more commodious end of the car reserved for nonsmokers. His infantine wailing smote in sharp contrast upon the ears of the hilarious joshers, filling the silence that followed the subsidence of the laughter.

"Taci, bimba. Non aver paura!"[2]

Nobody understood the musical words of the patient, Madonna-eyed Italian mother, not even the baby, for it continued its yelling. She opened her gay colored shirt waist and pressed the child to her bosom. He was quieted.

"She can't speak United States, but I bet her Tony Spaghetti votes the same as you an' me. The young 'un 'll have more to say about the future of these United States than your children an' mine unless we carry forward the word such as we are going to accomplish tonight."

---

1. "Riding the goat" was an expression referring to the joining of a lodge. Sometimes new initiates did ride a goat as part of the initiation ceremony.

2. Italian for "Hush, baby. Don't be afraid."

"Yeh, you're damned right," answered the scowling companion of the lynx-eyed citizen in khaki clothes, who had thus commented upon the foreign woman's offspring.

"They breed like cats. They'll outnumber us, unless—"

A smell of garlic stifled his speech. Nick and Mike Axaminter, late for the night shift at the LaBelle, bent over the irate American deluging him with the odor of garlic and voluble, guttural explosions of a Slovak tongue.

"What t' hell! Git them buckets out o' my face, you hunkies, you!"[3]

Confused and apologetic the two men moved forward.

"Isn't this an awful fog, Barney," piped a gay, girlish voice.

"I'll tell the world it is," replied her red-haired companion, flinging a half smoked cigarette away in the darkness as he assisted the girl to the platform.

They made their way to a vacant seat in the end of the car opposite the smoker, pausing for a moment respectfully to make the sign of the cross before two Sisters of Charity, whose flowing black robes and ebon headdress contrasted strikingly with the pale whiteness of their faces. The nuns raised their eyes, slightly smiled and continued their orisons on dark decades of rosaries with pendant crosses of ivory.

"Let's sit here," whispered the girl. "I don't want to be by those niggers."

In a few seconds they were settled. There were cooings of sweet words, limpid-eyed soul glances. They forgot all others. The car was theirs alone.

"Say, boy, ain't this some fog. Yuh can't see the old berg."

"'Sthat so. I hadn't noticed."

Two Negro youths thus exchanged words. They were well dressed and sporty.

"Well, it don't matter, as long as it don't interfere with the dance."

"I hope Daisy will be there. She's some stunnin' high brown an' I don't mean maybe."

"O boy!"

Thereupon one began to hum "Daddy, O Daddy" and the other whistled softly the popular air from *Shuffle Along* entitled "Old Fashioned Love."[4]

"Oi, oi! Ven, I say, vill dis car shtart. Ve must mek dot train fur Pittsburgh."

"Ach, Ish ka bibble.[5] They can't do a thing without us, Laban."

They settled down in their seats to finish the discussions in Yiddish, emphasizing the conversation with shrugs of the shoulder and throaty interjections.

In a seat apart to themselves, for two seats in front and behind were unoccupied, sat an old Negro man and a Negro woman, evidently his wife. Crowded between them was a girl of fourteen or fifteen.

"This heah is suah cu'us weather,"[6] complained the old man.

---

3. Derogatory slang for Hungarians.

4. *Shuffle Along* (1921) was the first African American musical on Broadway. It was written by Aubrey Lyles and Flournoy Miller, with music and lyrics by Noble Sissle and Eubie Blake. It starred Florence Mills, with Josephine Baker in the chorus line. It is credited by some as starting the Harlem Renaissance.

5. A Yiddish expression.

6. "This here is sure curious weather."

"We all nevah had no sich fog in Oklahoma."

The girl's hair was bobbed and had been straightened by "Poro" treatment, giving her an Egyptian cast of features.

"Gran' pappy," said the girl, "yo' cain't see ovah yander."

"Ain't it de troot, chile."

"Ne' min', sugah," assured the old woman. "Ah done paid dat 'ployment man an' he sayed yo' bound tuh lak de place. Dis here lady what's hirin yo' is no po' trash an' she wants a lively gal lak yo' tuh ten' huh baby."

Now these series of conversations did not transpire in chronological order. They were uttered more or less simultaneously during the interval that the little conductor stood on tiptoe in an effort to keep one hand on the signal rope, craning his neck in a vain and dissatisfied endeavor to pierce the miasma of the fog. The motorman chafed in his box, thinking of the drudging lot of the laboring man. . . .

The garrulous group in the smoker were smouldering cauldrons of discontent. In truth their dissatisfaction ran the gamut of hate. It was stretching out to join hands with an unknown and clandestine host to plot, preserve, defend their dwarfed and twisted ideals.

The two foreign intruders in the smoker squirmed under the merciless, half articulate antipathy. They asked nothing but a job to make some money. In exchange for that magic English word job, they endured the terror that walked by day, the boss. They grinned stupidly at profanity, dirt, disease, disaster. Yet they were helping to make America.

Three groups in the car on this foggy evening were united under the sacred mantle of a common religion. Within its folds they sensed vaguely a something of happiness. The Italian mother radiated the joy of her child. Perhaps in honor of her and in reverence the two nuns with downcast eyes, trying so hard to forget the world, were counting off the rosary of the blessed Virgin—"Ave, Maria," "Hail, Mary, full of grace, the Lord is with thee; blessed art thou among women."

The youth and his girl in their tiny circle of mutual attraction and affection could not as in Edwin Markham's poem widen the circle to include all or even to embrace that small circumscribed area of humanity within the car.[7]

And the Negroes? Surely there was no hate in their minds. The gay youths were rather indifferent. The trio from the South, journeying far for a greater freedom of self expression philosophically accepted the inevitable "slings and arrows of outrageous fortune."

The Jews were certainly enveloped in a racial consciousness, unerringly fixed on control and domination of money, America's most potent factor in respectability.

The purplish haze of fog contracted. Its damp presence slipped into the car and every passenger shivered and peered forth to see. Their eyes were as the eyes of the blind!

----

7. (Charles) Edwin Markham (1852–1940) was a well-known American poet. The reference is to his poem "Outwitted" (1902): "He drew a circle that shut me out— / Heretic, rebel, a thing to flout. / But Love and I had the wit to win: / We drew a circle that took him in!"

At last the signal bell rang out staccato. The car suddenly lurched forward, shaking from side to side the passengers in their seats. The wheels scraped and began to turn. Almost at once a more chilling wetness filtered in from the river. In the invisibility of the fog it seemed that one was traveling through space, in an aeroplane perhaps, going nobody knew where.

The murmur of voices buzzed in the smoker, interrupted by the boisterous outbursts of laughter. A red glare tinted the fog for a second and disappeared. LaBelle was "shooting" the furnaces.[8] Then a denser darkness and the fog.

The car lurched, scintillating sparks flashed from the trolley wire, a terrific crash—silence. The lights went out. Before anybody could think or scream, there came a falling sensation, such as one experiences when dropped unexpectedly in an elevator or when diving through the scenic railways of the city amusement parks, or more exactly when one has a nightmare and dreams of falling, falling, falling.

"The bridge has given way. God! The muddy water! The fog! Darkness. Death."

These thoughts flashed spontaneously in the consciousness of the rough ignorant fellows, choking in the fumes of their strong tobacco, came to the garlic-scented "hunkies," to the Italian Madonna, to the Sisters of Charity, to the lover boy and his lover girl, to the Negro youths, to the Jews thinking in Yiddish idioms, to the old Negro man and his wife and the Egyptian-faced girl, with the straightened African hair, even to the bored motorman and the weary conductor.

To drown, to strangle, to suffocate, to die! In the dread silence the words screamed like exploding shells within the beating temples of terror-stricken passengers and crew.

Then protest, wild, mad, tumultuous, frantic protest. Life at bay and bellowing furiously against its ancient arch-enemy and antithesis—Death. An oath, screams,—dull, paralyzing, vomit-stirring nausea. Holy, unexpressed intimacies, deeply rooted prejudices were roughly shaken from their smug moorings. The Known to be changed for an Unknown, the ever expected, yet unexpected, Death. No! No! Not that.

Lee Cromarty saw things in that darkness. A plain, one-story frame house, a slattern woman on the porch, an overgrown, large hipped girl with his face. Then the woman's whining, scolding voice and the girl's bashful confidences. What was dimming that picture? What cataract was blurring his vision? Was it fog?

To Lafe, leader of the crowd, crouched in his seat, his fingers clawing the air for a grasping place, came a vision of a hill-side grave,—his wife's—and he saw again how she looked in her coffin—then the fog.

"I'll not report at the mine," thought Bill. "Wonder what old Bunner will say to that." The mine foreman's grizzled face dangled for a second before him and was swallowed in the fog.

Hoarse, gasping exhalations. Men, old men, young men, sobbing. "Pietà! Madre mia! —Mercy, Virgin Mary! My child!"

8. Feeding the furnaces.

No thoughts of fear or pain on the threshold of death, that shadow from whence all children flow, but all the Mother Love focused to save the child.

"*Memorare*, remember, O most gracious Virgin Mary, that never was it known that any one who fled to thy protection, implored thy help and sought thy intercession was left unaided."

The fingers sped over the beads of the rosary. But looming up, unerasable, shuttled the kaleidoscope of youth, love, betrayal, renunciation, the vows. *Miserere, Jesu!*

> Life is ever lord of Death
> And Love can never lose its own.

The girl was hysterical, weeping, screaming, laughing. Did the poet dream an idle dream, a false mirage? Death is master. Death is stealing Love away. How could a silly girl believe or know the calm of poesie?

The boy crumbled. His swagger and bravado melted. The passionate call of sex became a blur. He was not himself, yet he was looking at himself, a confusion in space, in night, in fog. And who was she hanging limp upon his arm?

That dance? The jazz dance? Ah, the dance! The dance of Life was ending. The orchestra was playing a dirge and Death was leading the Grand March. Fog! Impenetrable fog!

All the unheeded, forgotten warnings of ranting preachers, all the prayers of simple black mothers, the Mercy-Seat, the Revival, too late. Terror could give no articulate expression to these muffled feelings. They came to the surface of a blunted consciousness, incoherent.

Was there a God in Israel? Laban remembered Russia and the pogrom. The old Negro couple remembered another horror. They had been through the riots in Tulsa. There they had lost their son and his wife, the Egyptian-faced girl's father and mother. They had heard the whine of bullets, the hiss of flame, the howling of human wolves, killing in the most excruciating manner. The water was silent. The water was merciful.

The old woman began to sing in a high quavering minor key:

> Lawdy, won't yo' ketch mah groan,
> Oh Lawdy, Lawdy, won't yo' ketch my groan.

The old man cried out: "Judgment! Judgment!"

The Egyptian-faced girl wept. She was sore afraid, sore afraid. And the fog was round about them.

Time is a relative term. . . . What happened inside the heads of these men and women seemed to them to have consumed hours instead of seconds. The conductor mechanically grabbed the trolley rope, the motorman threw on the brakes.

The reaction came. Fear may become inarticulate and paralyzed. Then again it may become belligerent and self-protective, striking blindly in the maze. Darkness did not destroy completely the sense of direction.

"The door! the exit!"

A mad rush to get out, not to be trapped without a chance, like rats in a trap.

"Out of my way! Damn you—out of my way!"

Somebody yelled: "Sit still!"

Somebody hissed: "Brutes! Beasts!"

Another concussion, accompanied by the grinding of steel. The car stopped, lurched backward, swayed, and again stood still. Excited shouts reechoed from the ends of the bridge. Automobile horns tooted. An age seemed to pass, but the great smash did not come. There was still time—maybe. The car was emptied.

"Run for the Ohio end!" someone screamed.

The fog shut off every man from his neighbor. The sound of scurrying feet reverberated, of the Italian woman and her baby, of the boy carrying his girl, of the Negro youths, of the old man and his wife, half dragging the Egyptian-faced girl, of the Sisters of Charity, of the miners. Flitting like wraiths in Homer's Hades, seeking life.

In five minutes all were safe on Ohio soil. The bridge still stood. A street light gave a ghastly glare through the fog. The whore houses on Water Street brooded evilly in the shadows. Dogs barked, the Egyptian-faced girl had fainted. The old Negro woman panted, "Mah Jesus! Mah Jesus!"

The occupants of the deserted car looked at one another. The icy touch of the Grave began to thaw. There was a generous intermingling. Everybody talked at once, inquiring, congratulating.

"Look after the girl," shouted Lee Cromarty. "Help the old woman, boys."

Bells began to ring. People came running. The ambulance arrived. The colored girl had recovered. Then everybody shouted again. Profane miners, used to catastrophe, were strangely moved. The white boy and girl held hands.

"Sing us a song, old woman," drawled Lafe.

"He's heard mah groan. He done heard it," burst forth the old woman in a song flood of triumph.

> Yes, he conquered Death and Hell,
> An' He never said a mumblin' word,
> Not a word, not a word.

"How you feelin', Mike," said Bill to the garlic eater.

"Me fine. Me fine."

The news of the event spread like wildfire. The street was now crowded. The police arrived. A bridge official appeared, announcing the probable cause of the accident, a slipping of certain supports. The girders fortunately had held. A terrible tragedy had been prevented.

"I'm a wash-foot Baptist an' I don't believe in Popery," said Lafe, "but, fellers, let's ask them ladies in them air mournin' robes to say a prayer of thanksgiving for the bunch."

The Sisters of Charity did say a prayer, not an audible petition for the ears of men, but a whispered prayer for the ears of God, the Benediction of Thanksgiving, uttered by the Catholic Church through many years, in many tongues and places.

"De profundis," added the silently moving lips of the white-faced nuns. "Out of the depths have we cried unto Thee, O Lord. And Thou hast heard our cries."

The motorman was no longer dissatisfied. The conductor's strength had been renewed like the eagle's.

"Boys," drawled Lafe, "I'll be damned if I'm goin' to that meetin' tonight."

"Nor me," affirmed Lee Cromarty.

"Nor me," repeated all the others.

The fog still crept from under the bed of the river and down from the lowering hills of West Virginia—dense, tenacious, stealthy, chilling, but from about the hearts and minds of some rough, unlettered men another fog had begun to lift.

Aaron Douglas, "'Cruiter," *Plays of Negro Life,* 1927

'Cruiter

Characters

GRANNY, aged seventy-seven, a typical Negro "Mammy"
SONNY, her grandson, aged twenty-three
SISSY, his wife, aged twenty
A WHITE MAN, a recruiting agent for a Northern munitions factory

    Scene: A farm cottage in lower Georgia.
    Time: Just after the entry of the United States into the World War.

Early morning and Spring, 1918, in lower Georgia. The rising of the curtain reveals the large room of a Negro cabin. The walls are the reverse of the outside weatherboarding. A kerosene lamp is on a shelf. At the end of the room looking toward the audience is a door leading to a bedroom, where the starchy whiteness of a well-made bed is visible. In front of the spectators, at the rear of the room, is a window without glass, half-closed by a heavy wooden shutter. Four feet from the window is a door, wide open, leading to a garden. Rows of collards are seen, an old hoe, and in the background a path to the big road.

    On the right is a wide, old-fashioned fireplace, where a big pine log makes a smoldering blaze. GRANNY, her head swathed in a blue bandana, is bending over the fire, stirring the contents of a huge iron kettle. In the center of the room is a rough table. A hunk of salt pork is on the table and a rusty knife. Under the window is another table supporting a fifteen quart galvanized iron bucket. A gourd dipper is hanging on the wall between the window and the door. Under the gourd a tin washpan is suspended. Below the basin is a box in which oranges have been crated. A backless chair is under the center table. A mongrel dog is curled under it.

SCENE I

    Granny: (with her profile to the audience, stirring the kettle and singing)
           Nobody knows de trouble Ah've seen,
           Nobody knows but Jesus;
           Nobody knows de trouble Ah've seen—
    (stopping abruptly) —Ah mus' put some mo' watah to dese plague-taked grits. *(walks to the water bucket, takes down the gourd dipper and fills it with water. Returning to the kettle she slowly pours in the water, stirring as she pours and singing)* "Nobody knows de trouble Ah've seen"—dah now! *(hobbles to the open door and looks across the big road toward the east)* 'Pears like Sonny and Sissy ought to be hyar. It is *(squinting at the sun)* it's mighty nigh onto six o'clock. *(A rooster crows lustily beyond the door. She claps her hands and stamps her feet)* —Skat! Skat, sir. Yo' honery rascal—bringin' me company so early in the mornin'. Ah ain't wantin' to see nobody wid all Ah got tuh do. *(A mocking bird sings.)* Jes' listen tuh dat bird. Hallelujah! Praise de Lam'. *(sings)*
           Oh, when de world's on fiah,
           Ah wants God's bosom
           Fo' mah piller.

Opportunity, 1926.

(goes to the table in the center of the room and begins to slice the bacon) "Fo' mah piller." *(voice is heard outside)*

Sonny: Whoa, mule, whoa, Ah say.

Granny: *(putting the bacon in a large iron spider)[1]* Ah knowed dey'd be a-gwine fum de field. *(sound of two pairs of shoes is heard; the heavy tread of Sonny, the lighter tread of Sissy)*

Sonny: *(wearing brogans and overalls)* Mo'in', Granny. Dat bacon sho' smells good.

Sissy: *(enters, wearing a blue calico wrapper)* How yo' feelin', Granny?

Granny: Ah ain't feelin' so peart dis mo'in'. Mus' be needin' some spring tonic.

Sonny: *(taking down the washpan and dipping water from the bucket into the pan)* Well, us done planted a haf'n acre co'n. *(washing his face vigorously)* Ah don't know whut Ah'm goin' to do 'bout de cotton dis yeah, ef Ah don't go tuh wah.[2]

Sissy: *(dropping down in the doorsill)* Phew! Mah back is sho' breakin'—stoopin' an' stoopin', drappin' dat co'n.

Granny: Well, yo' know yo' po' pappy allus use tuh put in de cotton tuh pay Mistah Bob fo' he's rations fum de Commissary.

Sonny: But dere warn't nary a pesky ole weevil[3] then neither. 'Sides Mistah Bob done tol' me de guv'ment wanted somethin' t'eat. Say dat de Germans ah goin' to sta've us out an' we mus' plant co'n an' 'taters an' sich. He lows, too, Ah got tuh gi' 'em all us maks dis yeah, 'scusin' ouh keep, tuh he'p him fo' not sendin' me to camp.[4]

Granny: How come? He ain't no sheriff.

Sonny: Don't kere, he somethin' t'other wif dis here Draftin' Bo'd. Yo know dey done sent off Aunt Ca'line's crazy Jim?

Granny: Mah Jesus! Mah Jesus! Yo'se all Ah's lef', Sonny. Gi' it tuh him. Yo' sho'll git kilt ef yo' has to go off fightin'; like yo' gran'pappy bruder, Samuel, was kilt, when he jined de Yankee Army.

Sonny: But 'tain't his'n an' Ah jest as leef die a fightin' dan stay heah an' tek his sass an 'uptiness an' gi' him all Ah mak, lak Ah was on de chain gang.

Sissy: *(coming in from the doorsill and throwing out the dirty water in the basin)* Sonny, Sonny, don't yo' know dese hyar whi' foks?

Sonny: *(wiping his hands on his overalls)* Don't Ah know 'em? Co'se Ah knows 'em. When Ah was in town Sat'day didn't Ah see Mistah Bob 'sputin' wif ol' Judge Wiley? Didn't Ah heah him say dis wah was raisin' hell wid his business, takin' all de niggahs fum de plantations?

---

1. A spider is a frying pan with feet.

2. "War."

3. A boll weevil is an insect that destroys cotton.

4. "He says, too, I've got to give them all [the money] we make this year, aside from our room and board, to help him for not sending me to [boot] camp."

Granny: Ah knowed dis here disturbance was comin', 'cause Ah seed a light in de sky eb'ry night dis week.

Sissy: *(washing her hands and wiping them on her dress)* Where's dey takin' 'em to, Sonny? Do yo' think dey goin' to take yo'?

Sonny: How does Ah know? Whatevah whi' fo'ks wants o' we-all, we-all jes' nacherly got tuh do, Ah spose, but Ah ain't ter gwine tuh give Mistah Bob all my wuk an' Sissy's fo' tuh keep me out a wah. Ah ain't skeered.

Granny: Boy, yo' don't know whut yo' talkin' 'bout. Ah done seed one wah.[5] Men kilt, heads shot off—all de whi' fo'ks in dey big houses, de wimmins, cryin' dey eyes out an' ol' Gen'ral Sherman shootin' an' sottin' on fiah evahthing waht 'ud bu'n. *(mechanically takes the spider off the fire, then the kettle of grits, dishing up both on a large, heavy crockery platter)*

Sissy: *(looking at GRANNY with tenderness. She and SONNY exchange glances, showing appreciation of her)* Heah, Granny, lemme he'p yo' fix breakfas'.

Granny: Go 'way chile. Yo' got a heap to do he'pin' Sonny all day in de field.

Sissy: Oh, that ain't nothin'. *(pulling out the backless chair, then bringing up the orange box and turning it lengthwise so that she and SONNY can sit upon it)*

Sonny: *(patting Sissy's hand)* Po' chile, Ah ain't gwine to have yo' wukin' dis er-way. 'Tain't right.

Sissy: Hush, chile, Granny's askin' de blessin'.

Granny: *(bowing her head)* Bress dis food we'se 'bout tuh receive fo' Christ's sake. Amen. *(She serves their plates generously of the bacon and grits and some gravy made with the bacon)*

Sonny: *(eating with his knife)* Er, ah, Granny—

Granny: Sonny, de co'n meal's 'bout gone. Dere's enough fo' co'npone to-day.

Sonny: *(laying down his knife)* Sissy, don't lemme fergit to take some co'n meal when Ah goes tuh town to-morrow, Sat'day, ef us is heah.

Sissy: Ef us is heah? Whut yo' mean, Sonny?

Granny: He mean ef de Lawd's willin'. How come, chile, yo' don't tek Him into yo' plannin'?

Sonny: *(absent-mindedly)* No, Granny, Ah means jes' whut Ah say, ef all o' us is heah.

Sissy and
Granny: *(looking at SONNY in amazement)* Wha' we gwine tuh be?

Sonny: *(hangin' his head)* Ah don't know how to tell yo' 'bout it. Ah been a-thinkin' an' a-plannin' an' skeered to let on.

Sissy: *(impatiently)* Whut's yo' talkin' bout?

Sonny: *(doggedly)* Ah'm talkin' 'bout leavin' heah.

Granny: How we goin' tuh leave? Wha' to? Hit teks heaps o' money to git away.

5. She's alluding to the Civil War.

Sonny: Yo' don't have tuh have no money, no nuthin'. Jes' git away.

Sissy: *(incredulous)* How?

Granny: What's ailin' yo' boy?

Sonny: When Ah was in town las' Sat'day a whi' man done tol' me he was lookin' fo' wukers.

Granny: Whut whi' man?

Sonny: He said he was a 'cruiter. Lots a fo'ks ah talkin' 'bout him. Yo' all out heah in de country, yo' don't know nothin' 'bout whut's goin' on. Ah'm tellin' yo'. He sez tuh me ez Ah was standin' in de Gen'ral Sto', kin' o' whisperin' lak: "Do yo' wan' tuh mek some money?"

Granny: Be keerful o' dese heady fo'ks. Dey ain't out fuh no good.

Sonny: But, Granny, he talked hones'.

Granny: Ah know dey ain't no mo' wuk roun' heah dan whut we all is doin'.

Sonny: But dis ain' 'round heah.

Sissy: Wha' is ut, Sonny?

Sonny: Up No'th.

Sissy: *(lighting up)* Up No'th!

Granny: *(with scorn)* UP NO'TH!

Sonny: *(bubbling with enthusiasm)* Yes. Up No'th—wha' we kin be treated lak fo'ks. He told me he would tek us all, tek us an' put us on de train at River Station below town, 'cause a deputy sheriff done 'rested[6] a pa'cel o' niggahs, whut was tryin' tuh follow some other 'cruiter.

Sissy: Wha' he now? When could he come?

Sonny: He say he wus comin' tuh see 'bout ut Friday, today. *(with hesitation)* Dat's why Ah had to tell yo' all.

Granny: Up No'th? Sonny, dey tell me it's too col' up No'th.

Sonny: No, Granny, de 'cruiter say us kin live ez wa'm ez down heah—houses all het by steam. An' Sissy won't have to wuk in no fields neither, ner yo'.

Granny: But Ah done been down heah seventy-seven yeahs.

Sonny: *(triumphantly)* But, Granny, Ah won't have tuh leave yo' tuh fight de wa' 'gin dem Germans.

Granny: Who say so?

Sonny: De 'cruiter.

Granny: How he know?

Sonny: Oh—Ah jes' knows he knows. He sounds lak it when he talks.

Sissy: Sonny, why wouldn't yo' have to go tuh wa'?

---

6. "Arrested."

Sonny: He say somethin' Ah don't quite git de meanin' ob, but Ah 'membahs dis. He say Ah could wuk in some kin' o' a—a 'nition factory,[7] wha' dey meks guns an' things, tuh fight de Germans. Dat's why Ah wouldn't have to go.

Granny: *(looking off into space and tapping her foot slowly)* But yo' can't believe dese whi' fo'ks. Dey're sich liars.

Sonny: But he's tellin' de troof.

Sissy: Ah hope he's tellin' de troof.

Sonny: *(emphatically)* He *is*. He's talkin' sense.

Granny: Eat yo' breakfus', chillun. Hit's gittin' col'. 'Spec yo'll nebbah heah any mo' fum dat 'cruiter. *(They begin to eat. GRANNY gets up to get some hot grits, carrying the pot around and replenishing each plate)*

Sonny: *(his mouth full)* We wuk—wuk—wuk. Whut does us git fo' ut? Ouah victuals an' keep. De mules git dat. We ain't no bettern de mules down heah.

Granny: Yo' ain't seen no slavery days, Sonny.

Sonny: Why, slavery days ah right heah now.

Granny: Dey can't sell yo'.

Sonny: But dey kin buy us. Ole Mistah Bob thinks he's done bought us. Dey put bloodhounds on some po' niggah who was tryin' tuh leave ol' man Popperil's plantation. Whut's dat but slavery?

Sissy: But, Sonny, Lincum[8] done sot us free. Didn't he, Granny?

Granny: 'Course he did. Sonny know dat.

Sonny: He ain't sot me free. *(An automobile horn is heard at a distance)*

Sonny: *(jumping from the orange crate and speaking joyfully)* Dere now. Whut did Ah say? Ah bet dat's him, de 'cruiter.

Granny: Comin' on Friday. No day to mek new business on Friday. Bad luck's bound to follow yo'.

Sissy: 'Pears lak tuh me bad luck's been follering us. *(The horn sounds near. They all go to the door to look)* There 'tis, comin' down de road lickity-split.

Sonny: Sho' nuf! Sissy, da hit is, an' hit sho' looks lak de 'cruiter's cah.

Granny: Looks say nuthin'.

Sonny: See. He's stoppin' right by ouah place.

Sissy: Sho' is. *(A brisk voice is heard)* Hey there!— *(steps sound. The WHITE MAN is seen coming down the path. He stops in front of the open door, hat on and wearing gloves. He talks rapidly and with finality)*

---

7. "Munitions factory."

8. "Abraham Lincoln."

The White Man: This woman your wife?

Sonny: Yas, this is her, Mr. 'Cruiter,[9] an' hyah is mah Granny. *(GRANNY nods her head coldly)*

The White Man: Well, everything is ready. I came through the country early this morning to avoid other cars on the road. If you say the word I will be back here after you about eleven o'clock to-night. Don't miss this opportunity, folks.

Granny: Yo' don't know whut yo're axin', Mistah 'Cruiter.

The White Man: Why, Missus, I am giving this boy a chance to get out, to be a man, like anybody else, make plenty money and have time to enjoy it. *(turning to SISSY)* What do you say? Don't you want to live like a lady and wear fine clothes?

Sissy: *(grinning bashfully)* Yas, sir.

Sonny: 'Course, Mr. 'Cruiter, Ah sho' wants tuh go.

The White Man: You know there are many jumping at the chance.

Granny: Honey, yo' can't tell him now. Whut yo' gwine tuh do wif yo' things?

Sonny: Us ain't got nothin' nohow, Granny.

The White Man: *(looking at his watch)* Well, I must hurry. Tell you what I'll do. I have to come down the road tonight anyway as far as the adjoining plantation.

Sissy: *(turning to GRANNY)* Mistah Popperil's place.

The White Man: I'll blow the horn three times. If you want to come I'll take you. Don't miss this chance of your lifetime. Good wages, transportation to Detroit straight, a good job waiting for you and freedom. *(He leaves hastily)*

Granny: *(sinks down on the steps)* Huh! *(SISSY looks at SONNY expectantly. SONNY stands undecided, scratching his head. The automobile is heard leaving in the distance, down the big road)*

Granny: *(singing)*
Nobody knows de trouble Ah've seen,
Nobody knows but Jesus.
(SISSY and SONNY stand looking on the ground.) 'Twon't be right fo' tuh run dat er-way—widout tellin' nobody. 'Tain't Christian, Sonny.

Sonny: Ah ain't stud'in' 'bout Christian.

Granny: Yo' talk lak a po' sinnah, boy.

Sissy: Well, Granny, let us try it. Come on.

Granny: Ef we leave dis place dis a-way, we dasn't come back, even ef yo' didn't lak it.

---

9. This is not his name. Recruiters like this character came South around this time to encourage black workers to move North and take jobs in the labor-short industries they represented, such as railroads, slaughterhouses, wartime factories, and so on. Often these recruiters paid moving expenses for the worker and his family. So many African Americans responded to such overtures that Southern sheriffs forcibly restrained them from leaving at times, such as is described in this play.

Sonny: Ah wish Ah knowed whut tuh do.

Granny: Yo' ain't got no faith, son. Yo' ought tuh trust God, lak us did way back dar in slavery days. An' He heard ouah prayahs.

Sissy: Sonny prays, Granny.

Sonny: But Ah neveh gits no answer.

Sissy: Mebbe dis is an answer.

Sonny: (*looking at the heavens*) De sun's risin'. Even ef we go we got tuh keep on wukin' today, 'cause ol' Mistah Bob's liable to come heah any time.

Granny: Sonny, Sissy, Ah can't leave dis place. Why, bress me, my mammy's died heah, ol' Missus is buried heah, yo' gran'daddy crossed ovah Jordan in dis ve'y house, yo' own po' mammy, atter yo' worthless pappy was kilt in de cotton mill, died heah too. Ah'm too puny to leave heah now, too far gone mahself.

Sonny: Granny, ain't Ah allus wuked and he'p to tek kere o' yo' evah sence Ah been big enough to hoe a row?

Granny: Yo' has been a mighty dutiful chile, Sonny. Ah ain't sayin' nuttin' 'gin yo' honey. Ah ain't wantin' tuh stan' in yo' light. But Ah can't he'p ut. Ah can't beah tuh leave heah, wha all mah fo'ks ah a-layin' an' go 'way 'mongst heathen people.

Sissy: But, Granny, you'd be happy wif us, won't yo'?

Granny: Yas, chile, Ah'd be happy all right, but Ah'm lak Ephraim Ah reckon, wedded to mah idols.[10] (*forcing the words*) Yo'-all go 'long an' lemme stay heah.

Sonny: (*fiercely*) But, Granny, yo' know how Mistah Bob's gwine tuh tek it, when he fin's us done gone. Ah nevah'd feel safe leavin' yo' behin'.

Granny: Dat's a'right. Ain't Ah wuked fo' he's pappy?

Sonny: He ain't keerin' fo' 'at. He's liable to th'ow yo' out wif nuttin'.

Granny: Ain't dis mah cabin? (*looks around tenderly*) Ain't Ah lived heah fo' fifty yeahs?

Sonny: But it's on Mistah Bob's lan'.

Granny: Yo' kin sen' me some money an' excusin' de asthma an' de misery in mah head Ah kin keep a youngah 'oman dan me pantin', when it come tuh wuk.

Sissy: Granny, yo' *mus'* come wid us.

Sonny: Ah can't think o' leavin' yo' behin'.

Granny: (*getting up from the steps and walking wearily into the kitchen*) Don't pester me now. Mebbe—mebbe—Ah knowed trouble was comin', seein' dem lights in de elements.

Sissy: (*whispers to SONNY*) She say "Mebbe."

Sonny: (*whispering*) Ah wished Ah knowed what to do.

10. She is referring to a biblical figure.

Granny: *(looking up and seeing them whispering)* Go long, chillun, yo' needn't be keepin' secrets fum yo' ol' Granny. Mebbe yo're right; mebbe Ah'm right. Dis is a cu'ios worl' anyhow. But dat whi' man ain't come back yit. Dey ain't tekin' niggahs on steam cahs fo' nuttin'. Whi' fo'ks *is* whi' fo'ks.

Sonny: Well, Granny, we'll see.

Granny: Ah'll fix yo'-all's dinner an' bring it down yander to de bottom tree.

Sonny: *(to SISSY)* Come on, Sissy, us'll put in one day more anyhow. *(They leave. As the sound of their footsteps ceases the rooster is heard to crow again)*

Granny: *(going to the door)* Plague tek yo' honery self.[11] *(picks up a spoon and throws in direction of the sound)* Cl'ar out a heah—crowin' up company. Ah don't need no 'cruiters. *(She becomes silent and then sings)*
> Down in de Valley—couldn't heah mah Jesus,
> Couldn't heah nobody pray, O Lord! —

SCENE II

Same Place: Ten forty-five that night. The faint glow of the kerosene lamp accentuates the desolate shadows. GRANNY is sitting on the backless chair, her hands folded. Sissy is packing clothes in an old dress suitcase. A big bag with a string tied around it rests beside GRANNY. SONNY, dressed in overalls and a gray coat, walks back and forth as he talks.

Granny: He ain't comin'.

Sonny: 'Tain't time yit. *(looking at his dollar watch)* It's only a quarter tuh 'leven.

Granny: He ain't comin', Ah say.

Sonny: Don't put a bad mouf on us, Granny.

Sissy: *(to SONNY)* Come heah, he'p me shet dis thing. *(SONNY helps her close the stuffed suitcase)*

Granny: Bad mouf, chile, Ah's been sittin' heah prayin' fo' yo'-all. We ain't nuttin', but wif de ol' Marster we ah pow'ful strong.

Sissy: *(holding her head)* Mah head's turnin' 'round all in a whirl.

Sonny: Ah yo' ready, Granny?

Granny: Reckon so.

Sissy: Do yo' think he's comin'?

Sonny: Sho'.

Granny: *(shaking her head)* Can't keep fum thinkin' 'bout yo' mammy, how she wouldn't wan' yo' tuh leab heah dis a-way.

Sonny: Ah believe she'd wan' us tuh go.

Sissy: Whut yo' all talkin' 'bout sich fo'? Yo' mak me skeert.

Granny: 'Tain't no use bein' skeert. Yo' got tuh face de ol' Marster some o' dese times.

---

11. "May the plague take your ornery self [kill you]."

Sissy: Oh, Ah ain't skeert o' no ol' Marster, but yo' mek me think o' ghos'es.

Sonny: Ah'm skeert o' de clutches o' ol' Mistah Bob. He don't mean us no good. Ah jes' know ef mammy an' pappy could speak dey'd shoo us on.

Granny: How yo' know so much?

Sonny: Ain't Ah done seed de way he looked at niggahs—wicked lak he could swallow 'em whole?

Granny: (sighs) —Lordy! Lordy!

Sissy: Whut time is it, Sonny?

Sonny: (looking at his watch) —Ten tuh 'leven.

Granny: (singing) —O Lordy, Lordy, won't yo' ketch mah groan.

Sonny: Us ain't goin' tuh no funeral, Granny. Ah feels lak it's a picnic—a 'Mancipation Celebration picnic.

Sissy: Ah'm rarin' tuh go, too, 'specially sence yo' tol' me 'bout de schools up yander. Ouah chillun kin go tuh whi' fo'ks school.

Granny: Whi' fo'ks ain't goin' treat niggahs wif book learnin' any bettern we-all.

Sonny: We kin treat each othah bettah den. Ah kin treat mahself bettah. An' so kin mah chillun.

Granny: Yo' young niggahs ah sho' uppity, but Ah hope yo' ain't got no wool ovah yo' eyes. We mought a sont ouah chickens tuh Sis Ca'line.

Sissy: She mought a tol' somebody, too, an' dere we'd be.

Granny: Yo' got dat box fixed for Berry?

Sonny: He's already in ut. He ain't used tuh bein' shut up lak dat, de lazy varmint.

Granny: (walks to the door and looks out) The stars ah shinin'. (comes back and gets a drink from the bucket)

Sissy: (excitedly) SAKES ALIVE! Ah see de lights a-comin', 'mobile lights.

Sonny: (running to the door) She is. We goin' fum heah.

Granny: (moodily silent. The glare from the headlights of the automobile lights up the room, shining in through the open door. GRANNY looks in wonder at the light) Ah, chillun, de Lawd is wif us. (sings) Shine on me. Let de light fum de lighthouse, shine on me.

(The chug of the engine is heard and the grinding of the brakes, as the car pulls up. The horn blows three times. THE WHITE MAN runs down the walk)

The White Man: Are you ready? We have no time to lose.

Sonny: We's waitin'. (gathers up bag, suitcase and hat and starts towards the door)

Sissy: Don't forgit Berry.

The White Man: Who's Berry?

Sissy: De dog.

The White Man: What do you mean? We can't take dogs on this trip.

Granny: Whut's de mattah wif yo', man? Think we're goin' tuh leave Berry?

The White Man: See here. It is impossible to take any dog. He'll make too much noise and besides I can't be bothered looking out for him.

Sonny: Well, Berry 'll have tuh stay heah, dat's all.

Granny: Den Ah stays too.

Sonny: Whut yo' say?

Granny: *(stubbornly)* Ah ain't goin' tuh leave Berry.

The White Man: Ah, come on—cut the argument. We got to make that train.

Sissy: *(worried)* He kin fend fo' hisself.

Granny: Go on yo' chillun, go on. Ah don't wan' tuh go nohow. Ah jes' been a-pretendin' tuh git yo' started. Ah kin git along. Ain't Ah got along wif whi' fo'ks fo' seventy yeahs an' mo'?

Sonny: *(angrily)* Whut yo' wan' tuh act dis a-way fo'?

The White Man: Well, come on or stay, people. Time's passing.

Sonny: Ah'm goin', Granny. Don't yo' see Ah can't stay heah? Ef Ah stay Ah'm goin' tuh git kilt fo' sassin' dese whi' fo'ks; ef Ah go tuh wa', Ah hastuh leave yo' jes' de same an' mebbe git kilt. Ef Ah go No'th and die, Ah'll be a dead free man. *(He puts down bundles and embraces GRANNY)* Mah po' ol' Granny. Ah'm goin' tuh send yo' plenty a money an' Ah'll be back, come Christmas, mebbe to tek yo' atter we gits settled.

Granny: *(frightened)* Don't, don't come back, not heah. Promise me dat, chile. Yo' know Mistah Bob. He git yo'.

Sonny: No, he won't. Ah'll show him.

The White Man: *(impatiently)* We must be going.

Sissy: Fo' God, Granny, come on.

Granny: *(firmly)* Ah done said mah say.

Sonny: Den, good-bye, Granny. *(gives her money)* Ah send yo' plenty mo' fust pay day an' Ah'm goin' tuh have a pay day ebery week.

Sissy: *(kissing GRANNY)* Good-bye.

Granny: *(her arms around them both)* Mah po' chillun. Mah po' chillun. *(They tear themselves from her embrace. THE WHITE MAN leads the way to the car. SONNY takes up the suitcase, but leaves the bag. Sissy follows. The sound of the three pairs of footsteps dies away)*

Sonny and Sissy: *(calling from the car)* Granny?

Granny: *(standing in the doorway)* CHILLUN.

Sissy: Pray fo' us, Granny. *(The car is heard lurching ahead. The light disappears. The sounds die away. GRANNY stands for a minute in the deep silence, looking in the direction of the vanished car. A whining is heard. She looks out in the darkness)*

Granny: Bress mah soul! Berry! *(She pulls in a crated box, containing the cur. She gets a poker and pries the box open. The dog is wild with appreciation)* Come heah, Berry. *(pulls up the backless chair by the table and sits down, patting the dog)* Berry, you'se all Ah got lef' now. *(rests her elbow on the table, shuts her eyes)* Lordy, Ah'm so tiahed, so tiahed. *(She sits up suddenly, listening attentively)* Who dat knockin' at mah do'? *(She gets up slowly and looks out. Nothing. Shuts the door and bolts it. Sits down again and buries her face in her hands. Again she raises up and listens)* Who dat, knockin' agin? *(Once more she gets up more painfully, unbolts and opens the door. Nothing. Closing it, she totters feebly to the chair)* Berry, Ah'm tuckered out. *(croons)* "Somebody knockin' at mah do'!" *(stops. Listens)* Come in. *(falls back in chair, her head rests on the table, her arms limp. She mumbles)* Come in, 'Cruiter. Reckon Ah'm all ready.

Curtain

Fenton Johnson

(1888–1958)

Fenton Johnson is generally considered a forerunner of the Harlem Renaissance writers, but his work was also included in its major texts, including Countee Cullen's *Caroling Dusk* (1927). Johnson was born in Chicago on May 7, 1888, one of the two sons of Jessie Taylor and Elijah Johnson. His father, a railroad porter, was one of the wealthiest African Americans in Chicago. Johnson attended Englewood and Wendell Phillips High School. He then attended Northwestern University, the University of Chicago, and Columbia University School of Journalism, evidently graduating from none of them. From 1910 to 1911 Johnson worked as an English instructor at Louisville State University (now Simmons University), a private black Baptist school in Louisville, Kentucky. After his marriage to Cecilia Rhone, Johnson lived primarily in Chicago and New York. His employment included work for the Eastern Press Association as a special writer and as acting dramatic editor for *The New York News*.

Johnson was a playwright, editor, essayist, and short story writer, but he is primarily known as a poet. He published three books of poetry: *A Little Dreaming* (1913), *Visions of the Dark* (1915), and *Songs of the Soil* (1916). Johnson also published a short story collection, *Tales of Darkest Highest Good* (1920) and an essay collection, *For the Highest Good* (1920). He was only nineteen when his plays began to be produced at the Old Pekin Theatre in Chicago. He continued to write plays through 1925, when his *The Cabaret Girl* was performed at the Shadow Theatre in Chicago. Unfortunately, Johnson's plays are not extant. Johnson also founded two magazines, *The Champion Magazine* (1916–1917) and *The Favorite Magazine* (1917–1920). He became a recluse in the 1930s and died in 1958.

The Banjo Player

There is music in me, the music of a peasant people.
I wander through the levee, picking my banjo and singing my songs of the cabin and
    the field. At the Last Chance Saloon I am as welcome as the violets of March; there
    is always food and drink for me there, and the dimes of those who love honest
    music. Behind the railroad tracks the little children clap their hands and love me
    as they love Kris Kringle.
But I fear that I am a failure. Last night a woman called me a troubadour.
    What is a troubadour?

The Book of American Negro Poetry, 1922.

Aaron Douglas, "The Broken Banjo," *Plays of Negro Life,* 1927

The Scarlet Woman

Once I was good like the Virgin Mary and the Minister's wife.
My father worked for Mr. Pullman[1] and white people's tips; but he died two days after
      his insurance expired.
I had nothing, so I had to go to work.
All the stock I had was a white girl's education and a face that enchanted the men of
      both races.
Starvation danced with me.
So when Big Lizzie, who kept a house for white men, came to me with tales of fortune
      that I could reap from the sale of my virtue I bowed my head to Vice.
Now I can drink more gin than any man for miles around.
Gin is better than all the water in Lethe.

1. G. M. Pullman was the inventor of Pullman sleeping cars. African Americans worked as porters on
these cars.

The Book of American Negro Poetry, 1922.

Tired

I am tired of work; I am tired of building up somebody else's civilization.
Let us take a rest, M'Lissy Jane.
I will go down to the Last Chance Saloon, drink a gallon or two of gin, shoot a game or
      two of dice and sleep the rest of the night on one of Mike's barrels.
You will let the old shanty go to rot, the white people's clothes turn to dust, and the
      Calvary Baptist Church sink to the bottomless pit.
You will spend your days forgetting you married me and your nights hunting the
      warm gin Mike serves the ladies in the rear of the Last Chance Saloon.
Throw the children into the river; civilization has given us too many. It is better to die
      than to grow up and find that you are colored.
Pluck the stars out of the heavens. The stars mark our destiny. The stars marked my
      destiny.
I am tired of civilization.

The Book of American Negro Poetry, 1922.

It was a poem by Claude McKay, "If We Must Die" (1919), that many people credit with providing the militant spirit so identified with the Harlem Renaissance. His novel *Home to Harlem* (1928) is the text most closely aligned with the movement's proletarian radicalism. Unlike most of the Harlem Renaissance figures, however, McKay was not born in the United States, and he spent most of the Renaissance years outside its borders.

Claude McKay
(1889–1948)

Born September 15, 1889, in Jamaica, British West Indies, McKay spent the first twenty-three years of his life in the West Indies, the same area from which Marcus Garvey came. McKay was the youngest of eleven children born to Ann Elisabeth Edwards Kennedy and Thomas Francis McKay. The McKays resided in Sunny Ville in Clarendon Parish and prospered as peasant farmers. McKay considered agriculture for a career, but at the age of seventeen he was sponsored by the government to become an apprentice wheelwright and cabinetmaker in Brown's Town. In 1910, after his mother's death, he moved to Kingston to serve as a police constable, but within a year he proved unsuited for the position because of his sympathy for the people who were arrested.

He returned to Clarendon Parish, where his mentor Walter Jekyll, an English folklore collector, encouraged him to write Jamaican dialect poetry. In 1912 Jekyll helped McKay publish two volumes, *Songs of Jamaica* and *Constab Ballads*. For these books, McKay became the first black person to be honored with the medal of the Jamaican Institute of Arts and Sciences. Deciding to use the substantial award money to finance his education at Tuskegee Institute in Alabama, McKay came to the United States in 1912. However, after only two months he left Alabama because of his frustration with the racism there. He then studied agriculture at Kansas State College for two years before resuming his writing career in New York. On July 30, 1914, he married another Jamaican, Eulalie Imelda Edwards, but she soon returned to her homeland where she gave birth to their daughter, Ruth. McKay never met his daughter, and he never married again.

In 1917 McKay published his first poems in America, using the pseudonym Eli Edwards and dropping dialect in favor of standard English. His work appeared regularly in *Pearson's Magazine* and *The Liberator*. He worked during World War I as a stevedore, porter, houseman, and dining car waiter on the Pennsylvania Railroad; these experiences were important sources of his poetry and his working-class leftist politics. It was at this time that he became friends with the celebrated literati and political radicals of Greenwich Village and Harlem.

In 1919 McKay traveled to London for a year, where he worked for Sylvia Pankhurst at *Worker's Dreadnought*, a Communist weekly, and became an active socialist. He returned to the United States in 1920, working for several publications, including *The Liberator*, which he edited with Michael Gold, and Marcus Garvey's *Negro World*. However, after a political disagreement in 1922, he parted company with Garvey. This same year he published his most important poetry collection, *Harlem Shadows*. With this collection, McKay became the most famous poet in the African American community of New York and beyond, but he remained estranged from the United States and left the same year. For twelve years he traveled extensively, living in the Soviet Union, France, Spain, and Morocco. While abroad, McKay published several novels: *Home to Harlem* (1928), *Banjo: A Story without a Plot* (1929), and *Banana Bottom* (1933) as well as a short story collection, *Gingertown and Other Stories* (1932). However, with the exception of *Home to Harlem,* which was the first bestseller by a Harlem Renaissance writer and the source of heated debate about the role of art within the movement, his fiction was not well received by critics, though royalties allowed McKay to become a full-time writer. He returned to the United States in 1934.

In 1937 McKay finished his autobiography, *A Long Way from Home,* and in 1940 he published his last book, the essay collection *Harlem: Negro Metropolis.* However, neither book sold well, and McKay had to supplement his writing income by employment with the Federal Writers' Project. In 1940, only eight years before his death, McKay became a U.S. citizen. With his writing career and health in decline, McKay became more involved in Friendship House, a Catholic-sponsored community center in Harlem. This, his friendship with Catholic writer Ellen Tarry, and his move to Chicago in 1944 at the invitation of Bishop Bernard Sheil led to his eventual conversion to Catholicism. Until his death in 1948 from heart failure, McKay taught at the Catholic Youth Organization in Chicago and compiled *The Selected Poems of Claude McKay,* published posthumously in 1953. Though he died in Chicago, McKay was buried in Queens after a final service in Harlem.

The Harlem Dancer

Applauding youths laughed with young prostitutes
And watched her perfect, half-clothed body sway;
Her voice was like the sound of blended flutes
Blown by black players upon a picnic day.
She sang and danced on gracefully and calm,
The light gauze hanging loose about her form;
To me she seemed a proudly-swaying palm
Grown lovelier for passing through a storm.
Upon her swarthy neck black shiny curls
Luxuriant fell; and tossing coins in praise,
The wine-flushed, bold-eyed boys, and even the girls,
Devoured her shape with eager, passionate gaze;
But looking at her falsely-smiling face,
I knew her self was not in that strange place.

The Seven Arts, 1917. Published under the name Eli Edwards.

If We Must Die

If we must die, let it not be like hogs
Hunted and penned in an inglorious spot,
While round us bark the mad and hungry dogs,
Making their mock at our accursèd lot.
If we must die, O let us nobly die,
So that our precious blood may not be shed
In vain; then even the monsters we defy
Shall be constrained to honor us though dead!
O kinsmen! we must meet the common foe!
Though far outnumbered let us show us brave,
And for their thousand blows deal one death-blow!
What though before us lies the open grave?
Like men we'll face the murderous, cowardly pack,
Pressed to the wall, dying, but fighting back!

The Liberator, July 1919.

Africa

The sun sought thy dim bed and brought forth light,
The sciences were sucklings at thy breast;
When all the world was young in pregnant night
Thy slaves toiled at thy monumental best.
Thou ancient treasure-land, thou modern prize,
New peoples marvel at thy pyramids!
The years roll on, thy sphinx of riddle eyes
Watches the mad world with immobile lids.
The Hebrews humbled them at Pharaoh's name.
Cradle of Power! Yet all things were in vain!
Honor and Glory, Arrogance and Fame!
They went. The darkness swallowed thee again.
Thou art the harlot, now thy time is done,
Of all the mighty nations of the sun.

The Liberator, August 1921.

Laura Wheeler, "The Strength of Africa," cover of *The Crisis,* September 1924

America

Although she feeds me bread of bitterness,
And sinks into my throat her tiger's tooth,
Stealing my breath of life, I will confess
I love this cultured hell that tests my youth!
Her vigor flows like tides into my blood,
Giving me strength erect against her hate.
Her bigness sweeps my being like a flood.
Yet as a rebel fronts a king in state,
I stand within her walls with not a shred
Of terror, malice, not a word of jeer.
Darkly I gaze into the days ahead,
And see her might and granite wonders there,
Beneath the touch of Time's unerring hand,
Like priceless treasures sinking in the sand.

The Liberator, December 1921.

Baptism

Into the furnace let me go alone;
Stay you without in terror of the heat.
I will go naked in—for thus 'tis sweet—
Into the weird depths of the hottest zone.
I will not quiver in the frailest bone,
You will not note a flicker of defeat;
My heart shall tremble not its fate to meet,
Nor mouth give utterance to any moan.
The yawning oven spits forth fiery spears;
Red aspish tongues shout wordlessly my name.
Desire destroys, consumes my mortal fears,
Transforming me into a shape of flame.
I will come out, back to your world of tears,
A stronger soul within a finer frame.

Harlem Shadows, 1922.

Harlem Shadows

I hear the halting footsteps of a lass
  In Negro Harlem when the night lets fall
Its veil. I see the shapes of girls who pass
  To bend and barter at desire's call.
Ah, little dark girls who in slippered feet
Go prowling through the night from street to street!

Through the long night until the silver break
  Of day the little gray feet know no rest;
Through the lone night until the last snow-flake
  Has dropped from heaven upon the earth's white breast,
The dusky, half-clad girls of tired feet
Are trudging, thinly shod, from street to street.

Ah, stern harsh world, that in the wretched way
  Of poverty, dishonor and disgrace,
Has pushed the timid little feet of clay,
  The sacred brown feet of my fallen race!
Ah, heart of me, the weary, weary feet
In Harlem wandering from street to street.

Harlem Shadows, 1922.

To O.E.A.

Your voice is the color of a robin's breast,
  And there's a sweet sob in it like rain—still rain in the night.
Among the leaves of the trumpet-tree, close to his nest,
  The pea-dove sings, and each note thrills me with strange delight
Like the words, wet with music, that well from your trembling throat.
  I'm afraid of your eyes, they're so bold,
  Searching me through, reading my thoughts, shining like gold.
But sometimes they are gentle and soft like the dew on the lips of the eucharist
Before the sun comes warm with his lover's kiss,
  You are sea-foam, pure with the star's loveliness,
Not mortal, a flower, a fairy, too fair for the beauty-shorn earth,
All wonderful things, all beautiful things, gave of their wealth to your birth:
  O I love you so much, not recking[1] of passion, that I feel it is wrong,
  But men will love you, flower, fairy, non-mortal spirit burdened with flesh,
Forever, life-long.

1. Taking heed.

The Book of American Negro Poetry, 1922.

Like a Strong Tree

Like a strong tree that in the virgin earth
Sends far its roots through rock and loam and clay,
And proudly thrives in rain or time of dearth,
When the dry waves scare rainy sprites away;
Like a strong tree that reaches down, deep, deep,
For sunken water, fluid underground,
Where the great-ringed unsightly blind worms creep,
And queer things of the nether world abound:

So would I live in rich imperial growth,
Touching the surface and the depth of things,
Instinctively responsive unto both,
Tasting the sweets of being and the stings,
Sensing the subtle spell of changing forms,
Like a strong tree against a thousand storms.

Survey Graphic, March 1925.

The Tropics in New York

Bananas ripe and green, and ginger root,
    Cocoa in pods and alligator pears,
And tangerines and mangoes and grape fruit,
    Fit for the highest prize at parish fairs.

Set in the window, bringing memories
    Of fruit-trees laden by low-singing rills,
And dewy dawns, and mystical blue skies
    In benediction over nun-like hills.

My eyes grew dim, and I could no more gaze;
    A wave of longing through my body swept,
And, hungry for the old familiar ways,
    I turned aside and bowed my head and wept.

The New Negro, 1925.

Mamie's Blues

JELLY ROLL MORTON

Date unknown.

De Two-Nineteen done took mah baby away
Two-Nineteen took mah baby away
Two-Seventeen bring her back some day

Stood on the corner with her feets soakin' wet
Stood on the corner with her feets soakin' wet
Beggin' each an' every man that she met

If you can't give me a dollar, give me a lousy dime
Can't give a dollar, give me a lousy dime
I wanna feed that hongry man of mine

Mattie and Her Sweetman

In the neighborhood of 135th Street and Lenox Avenue a parlor social was taking place in the flat of a grass widow called Rosie.

Rosie had sent out invitations to a number of chambermaids, bellhops, waiters, long-shoremen, and railroad men whom she knew personally. She asked them to bring their friends and to tell their friends to bring their friends.

The price of admission was twenty-five cents. Soda pop and hard drinks were sold at prices a little more than what was paid in the saloon. At ten o'clock Rosie's place began filling up with guests. It was that type of apartment called [a] railroad flat. The guests put their wraps in Rosie's bedroom and danced in the dining-room and parlor.

Rosie kept the soda pop and beer cold in the ice-box in the kitchen. Whisky, wine, and gin were locked up in a cabinet whose key was secured by a red ribbon suspended from her waist.

The parlor social was good company. There was a fascinating melange of color: choco-late, cocoa, chestnut, ginger, yellow, and cream. The people for whom these parlor maids and chambermaids worked would have gazed wonder-eyed at them now. Aprons and caps set aside, the maids were radiant in soft shimmering chiffon, crêpe de Chine and satin stuff. How do they do it? those people would have commented, wearing the things they do on their wages?

Gingertown, 1932.

In that merry crowd was one strange person—a black woman in her fifties. She wore a white dress, long white gloves, black stockings and black shoes, and a deep-fringed purple shawl. She was of average height and very thin. Her neck was extraordinary; it was such a long, excessively skinny neck, a pathetic neck. Her face was much finer than her neck, thin also, but marked by a quiet, dark determination.

She danced with a codfish-complexioned strutter wearing a dress suit. He was tall with a trim ready-to-wear appearance and his hair was plastered down, glistening with brilliantine. His mouth wore a perpetual sneer. The woman danced badly. Her partner was a good dancer and tried to make her look as awkward as he could. The music stopped and they found seats near the piano.

"What youse gwina drink, Jay?" she asked.

"Gin," he said, casually.

"Rosie!" the woman called.

Rosie bustled over, a marvel of duck-chested amiability. Rosie's complexion was a flat café-au-lait, giving the impression of a bad mixture, coffee over-parched, or burned with skimmed milk, and the generous amount of powder she used did not make the effect any pleasanter.

"Whaz you two agwine to hev, Mattie?" She knew, of course, that Jay was Mattie's sweet-man and Mattie did the paying.

"One gin and one beer," said Mattie.

"Gwine to treat the pianist to something?" Rosie knew how to tease her guests into making her parlor socials things worth giving.

"You throw me a good ball and whisky, sistah" said the pianist, a slight-built, sharp-featured black, whose eyes were intense, the whites appearing inflamed. . . .

Hands waved at Rosie from a group seated at a small table wedged against the mantel-piece, and an impatient young man called:

"Seven whiskies, Rosie, and four bottles a ginger ale jest as cold as you c'n makem."

"Right away, right away, mah chilluns." Rosie started a quick-time duck step to the cabinet.

Two girls pushed their way through a jam of men blocking the way between the din-ing-room and the parlor. The smaller was a satin-skinned chocolate; the other, attractive in a red frock, was cocoa.

The cocoa girl saw Jay with Mattie and cried: "Hello, Jay! Howse you?"

"Hello, you Marita!" said Jay.

"Having a good time?"

"Kinder," he sneered.

Marita was the waitress at Aunt Hattie's pigs'-feet-and-chittlings joint. Jay went there to eat sometimes. Marita rather liked him, put more food than ordinary in his dish, and chatted with him. She would have liked to keep company with Jay, but he made her realize that he had no desire to go with a girl in the regular way. He never felt that sort of feeling that would urge a fellow on to rent a room for two and live, a good ele-vator boy, in the Black Belt. For it was easier going with the Matties and grass widows of Harlem. Marita couldn't imagine herself down to the level of Jay's women. Not yet—when she was young and strong and pretty. But she rather admired his casual way of getting along and felt a romantic fascination for the sneer that sharp living had marked him by.

The pianist turned his inflamed eyes to the ceiling and banged the piano. Jay left Mattie alone to jazz with Marita.

"What a scary way she's dressed up!" said Marita as they wiggled past Mattie.

Jay grinned. Marita went liltingly with his movement. He disliked toting a middle-aged black hen round the room. Not that he minded being Mattie's sweetman. He was very proud of his new job. For three months before he met her he had been dogged by hard luck. The bottom had been eaten out of his nigger-brown pants. A flashy silk shirt, the gift of his last lady, had given way around the neck and at the cuffs. For thirteen weeks it had not seen the washtub, and when it did it went all to pieces. The toes of his ultra-pointed shoes were turned pathetically heavenward and the pavement had gnawed through his rubber heels down to the base of the leather.

Meeting Mattie at a parlor social in the Belt's Fifth Avenue had materially changed Jay's condition. He had been taken to 125th Street and fitted to a good pair of shoes. Mattie chose also a decent shirt for him. But it was not silk. He hadn't achieved a new suit yet. The choice was between that and an overcoat. Mattie's resources could not cover both at once. One would have to wait until she could put by enough out of their daily living to get it. And so she decided that a heavy, warm overcoat was more necessary, for it was mid-January and in his ruined summer suit Jay had been freezing along the streets of Harlem.

It was not quite a month since Mattie and Jay had come together, and docile as she seemed, she was well worn in experience and carried a smoldering fire in her ugly black body. Years ago she had had a baby for a white man in South Carolina. But being one black woman who did not feel proud having a yellow pickaninny at any price, she had got rid of the thing, strangling it at birth and, quitting relatives and prayer-meeting sisters, made her way up North.

Marita's girl pal discovered friends and went to drink with them. Marita followed, and Jay danced after her and got in with the gang. They were making rapid time with Old Crow whisky. They sent Rosie over to the pianist with a double drink of whisky to spur him on.

"Play that theah 'Baby Blues,'" she said. "Them good spenders ovah theah done buys you this drink and ask foh it."

The pianist tossed off his whisky, turned his eyes to the ceiling, and banged, "Baby blues, Baby blues."

Mattie stood up and went over to Jay. "Le's dance," she said. She loved dancing as a pastime, but it wasn't in her blood, and so she was a bad dancer.

"Not now," Jay said, angrily. "Ahm chinning with the gang."

He was putting away a lot of the boys' good liquor and it was working on him in a bad way for Mattie. Disappointed, she looked round for Rosie. Rosie was bustling about in the kitchen getting new glasses. Mattie gulped down two stiff drinks of gin and returned to her seat by the piano. . . .

Baby Blues! Baby Blues!

"Le's do this heah sweet strut, gal." And before Jay, Marita was on her feet and poised for movement. Her pal was jigging with one of the chocolate boys. The space was filled thick and warm with dancers just shuffling round and round. Hot cheeks yellow, chestnut, chocolate, each perspiring against each.

"Is that theah thing you' lady now?" Marita asked.

"She ain't a bad ole mammy as she looks," said Jay. "She's good giving. Fixed me up all right."

"Did she buy you this heah dress suit? Youse the only one here all dressed up so swell."

Jay grinned for the compliment.

"No. I hired this off a ole Greenbaum. The other was so bad. But she got me these heah shoes and a swell overcoat. And she's gwina get me a nifty suit."

"But youse kinder rough on her, though. You ain't treating her right, is you?"

Young and pretty, Marita disapproved of Mattie, old and ugly, having Jay, but she also resented with feminine feeling Jay's nastiness to the older woman.

"I ain't soft and sissified with no womens," said Jay. "Them's all cats, always mewing or clawing. The harder a man is with them the better."

"Think so?" Marita said. Her resentment rose to anger and she wanted to stop wriggling, but Jay's casual manner (which said, I don't care whether you dance or quit) held her tethered to him.

Mattie, sitting alone, had swallowed her sixth glass of gin. Rosie, feeling sympathetic, went and gossiped with her for a while.

"Ain't dancing, honey?"

"No, but I guess I'll take the next one."

"Don't you sit heah and get too lonely drinking all by you'se'f and that yaller strutter a yourn having such a wicked time."

"I don't mind him fooling with his own crowd when we goes to a pahty, 'causen Ise pass their age."

Finished "Baby Blues."

Jay went back to the waiters' table. One of his poolroom pals came in and joined the group, greeting Jay with enthusiasm and praising his rig-out.

In the poolroom where Jay loafed and played, he had become the hero of the place since his new affair. Colored boys who washed water-closets and cleaned spittoons for a living, with no hope of ever doing better, envied the way Jay could always get on to some woman to do everything for him. They wished they had Jay's magic. Jay might have his bad days getting by sometimes, but his luck never deserted him. He toted a charm.

The pianist turned his face to the ceiling and began a plaintive "Blues." He cast down his eyes for a moment and said to Mattie, "Ain't you gwina dance, sistah?"

Mattie essayed a smile. "Guess I will."

She crossed over to Jay and asked, "Wanta dance this with me?"

Jay glared at her, "Wha's scratching you? I don't wanta dance. Ahm having a good time heah."

The sneer deepened under the influence of the mixed drinks working on his temper. Mattie lingered near the table, but nobody asked her to sit down. Turning to go, she said to Jay hesitatingly, "Well—any time you feels like dancing with me Ise ready."

"Oh, foh Gawd's sake," he exclaimed, "gimme a chance! Shake a leg, black woman."

Everybody within hearing turned to look at Mattie, some with suppressed giggling, others with pity. Marita and her pal were ashamed and could not look at Mattie. For there is no greater insult among Aframericans than calling a black person black. That is never done. In Aframerican literature, perhaps, but never in social life. A black person may be called "nigger" as a joke in Aframerica, but never "black," which is considered a term of reproach in the mouths of colored people quite as contemptuous as "nigger" in the mouths of whites. And so Aframericans have invented pretty names such as low-brown, seal-skin brown, chocolate, and even prune as substitutes for black.

Oh, Blues, Blues, brown-skin Blues: the piano wailed.

"That was a mean one," said Marita.

"Oh, mean hell. I guess the ole mug likes when you handle her rough. Don't she, Jay?" said his pal.

"Ain't nobody wanting their bad points thrown up to them as nasty as that," declared Marita.

Her pal agreed. The girls imagined themselves growing old some day and ridden by a special passion like Mattie.

And Mattie by the piano, thinking that everybody was laughing at her, called for another gin. She wanted not to care. She knew she did not belong to a fast parlor-social set where everybody was young or acting young. Rosie with her hostess's tricks looked like a vampire beside her. But although she was ugly and unadjustable, she loved amusement and was always ready to pay for it.

Mattie worked hard doing half-time and piece-work, washing and ironing and mending for white people. Her work was finely done and her patrons recommended her to their friends. She earned twenty to thirty and forty dollars a week.

Living for Mattie was harder than working. Having an irresistible penchant for the yellow daddy-boys of the Black Belt, she had realized, when she was much younger, that because she was ugly she would have to pay for them.

She occupied a large rear room on the second floor of a private house, situated in the cheapest section of the Belt. The price was moderate and she was allowed the use of the kitchen and the spacious back yard for laundry work.

Mattie's coming and going quietly through the block was remarked by the good and churchy neighbors of the African Methodist, the Colored Methodist, and the Abyssinian and Cyrenian churches. And they marveled at her, a steady, reliable worker, refusing to be persuaded into membership in a church. . . .

Mattie brooded. Nevah befoh I been slapped like that by an insult so public. Slam in the face: Black woman! Black woman! Didn't I know I was that and old and no beauty?

Oh, mamma, sweet papa. Blues, Blues, seal-skin, brown-skin Blues. The pianist was gone on a wailing Blues.

Mattie got up to go home. She looked round for Jay. He had hurt her, but her pride had fallen, humbled and broken, under desire. Jay was not in the room. Mattie found him in the kitchen with his poolroom pal and a boozy gang over a bottle of gin.

"I'm gwine along home, Jay," she said. "Youse coming?"

Jay was getting drunk. "Why you nosing and smelling after a fellah like that foh?" he demanded.

"Don't get mad, Jay. I ain't bothering you. If you wanta stay—"

"Oh, beat it outa here, you no-'count black bitch."

Mattie slunk off to Rosie's bedroom and put on her coat. She saw Jay's overcoat and felt it and after a slight hesitation slipped it on over hers. Outside it was snowing. She dove her hands into the deep pockets and said: "A man's clothes is that much more solid and protecting than a woman's is." She went home, southward, along Lenox Avenue.

The gang finished the gin. Jay suggested to the waiters they should all go and hunt up a speak-easy.[1] Marita and her pal said they were going home.

"No, you come on along with us," said Jay.

"Not me. I gotta work tomorrow," said Marita.

"Me too. That don't make no difference," said the darkest waiter. The others joined him asking the two girls to change their minds; but the girls went home.

The fellows stood up, arguing just what they should do next, when Rosie elbowed through them and waved a bottle of gin in their faces.

"Le's have another round," said the mulatto waiter.

"You'd bettah," said Rosie. "Wha's this heah talk about you all going when is jest the time to start in on some real fun."

The boys sat down again, each waiter paying a round of drinks. The waiters had been paying all along. Jay and his friend had not paid for anything. The darkest waiter was soft. He began sifting a pack of cards, crying: "Coon-can! Coon-can! Le's play coon-can!"

"Ahm feeling high, ahm feeling cocky," said Jay.

The bottle of gin was finished and they were now ready to leave, but Jay could not find his overcoat.

"Ain't nobody could take it 'cep'n the one that done buys it." Rosie grinned maliciously.

Jay was mad and blew Mattie to hell with curses. Just a hussy trick to get me home to bed. Ain't got no shame nor pride, that woman. But I'll punish her some more.

Outside the snow had turned to sleet and a high wind was driving through the shivering naked trees.

"It'll be some sweet skating on the sidewalk tomorrow," said one of the waiters.

"And bitter cold, too," said Jay. And the thought of his overcoat gave him a comfortable, warm, and luxurious feeling.

---

1. A speakeasy was a nightclub that served alcohol during the Prohibition era. Because its liquor sales were illegal, patrons gave a password at the door to get in.

The boys had decided to visit a certain speak-easy. They walked along Fifth Avenue, and Jay stopped before an apartment house.

"It's here, fellahs," he said.

"All right," said the chocolate boy. "Le's go on in and look the fair browns ovah."

Jay, with his hands in his pockets and his dress suit slightly damp, gleaming in the far-flung flare of the arc-light, was the picture of perfect aplomb.

"But, buddies, I ain't got no money on me," he announced.

"And I ain't got none, neither," said Jay's pal.

The waiters exchanged eye-flecks with one another.

"Well," said the mulatto waiter, "after Rosie she done ate up so much I ain't none so flush to treat anybody else again 'cep'n' mahself. What about you fellahs?"

His workmates took his cue and said they had just enough each for himself.

"Tell you what, then; we'll call this show off until some other night," said the mulatto.

The waiters said good night to Jay and his pal. They were unanimous about not treating them in the speak-easy. If Jay hadn't any money to pay in the speak-easy, let him go home to Mattie. They had seen and felt so much as servitors, that they had not wasted any pity on Mattie. There were women whose special problems made them stand for that kind of hoggishness. But, neither had they any servile praise for Jay's attitude.

The waiters saw Jay and his pal out of sight, then entered the apartment house and rang the bell of the speak-easy. They worked. Creatures of service, waiters—that moment serving up a rarebit, this moment a cocktail, next a high-ball; bellhops in livery with ridiculous buttons before and behind, leaping up like rabbits at the touch of a knob. And they were fool spenders having that curious psychology of some servants who never feel like such good living as when they are making a big splurge imitation of their employers. . . .

"Come on, buddies," said the mulatto. "We may be suckers all right in Rosie's joint, but we won't be suckers in a cat dog bite mah laig hear the player piano crying fair chile baby oh boy house."

Jay said good-by to his pal and hurried homewards, head bent against the sleety wind, his hands in his trousers pockets, and thinking aloud: Well I was setting for an all-night laying-off, but I guess I'll have to warm up the ole black hen tonight, after all.

————————

But Mattie, too, had been thinking hard in the meanwhile.

I don't know what love is, but I know what's a man!

The cabaret song was singing in her head. She remembered when she first left Dixie and "went No'th" to Philadelphia, how she had liked a yellow man and he had laughed in her ugly face and called her "black giraffe." She had forgotten the incident, it was so long ago, but Jay made her remember it now. She had hated that man deeply and wanted to do him real hurt. And now she felt the same kind of hatred for Jay.

She lay in bed without sleeping, waiting for Jay, but not in the mood he anticipated. Dawn was creeping along the walls when the bell rang. Mattie raked up a window and craned out her giraffe neck. She had on a white nightcap and looked like a scarifying ghost.

"Who's it?"

"It's me—Jay."

"Wait a minute."

Mattie opened the closet where she kept her soiled linen and took out the little bandanna bundle that she had made of Jay's rags of a suit, his old greasy cap, his old shoes, and the remains of his silk shirt.

"Theah's you' stuff. Take a walk."

The bundle fell against Jay, nearly knocking him over. Mattie raked down the window. The sleet blew in Jay's face and the wind sang round his rump. He turned up his collar and walked shivering toward Lenox Avenue.

Willis
Richardson
(1889–1977)

During his thirty-year career, Willis Richardson wrote forty-eight plays in a variety of formats, including children's fairy tales, histories, and domestic plays. He was the premier playwright of the Harlem Renaissance and has the distinction of being the first African American to have a nonmusical produced on Broadway, *The Chip Woman's Fortune* (1923) performed by the Ethiopian Art Players, opening first at Harlem's Lafayette Theatre and then at the Frazee Theatre, where it shared the playbill with Oscar Wilde's *Salome*.

Richardson was born on November 5, 1889, in Wilmington, North Carolina, to Willis Wilder and Agnes Ann Harper Richardson. After the Wilmington race riots of 1898, the family moved to Washington, D.C. Richardson attended the M Street School, later known as Dunbar High School, and his teachers included Angelina Weld Grimké and Mary Burrill, two of the earliest African American playwrights. Burrill, who was writing and staging her own plays, encouraged Richardson to pursue his interest in drama. He graduated in 1910 and was awarded a scholarship to Howard University, but his family still could not afford the expense. Thus Richardson was forced to put his love of drama on hold while he earned a living as a clerk in the U.S. Bureau of Engraving and Printing.

In 1914 he married Mary Ellen Jones; the couple had three children between 1916 and 1920. But seeing a production of Grimké's *Rachel* (1916), which premiered in Washington, D.C., inspired him to return to his studies, and from 1916 to 1918 Richardson took correspondence courses in poetry, drama, and the novel. Then he began to write his own plays. Between December 1920 and October 1921, four of his early one-act children's dramas were published under Jessie Fauset's editorship of *The Brownies' Book*, a monthly magazine founded by W.E.B. Du Bois for African American children. Richardson's first adult one-act play, *The Deacon's Awakening,* was published by *The Crisis* in 1920 and produced on stage the following year. Throughout the 1920s Richardson wrote prize-winning plays that were staged by the Howard Players in Washington, D.C., the Gilpin Players at Karamu House in Cleveland, and the Krigwa Players in New York. His *Plays and Pageants from the Life of the Negro* (1930) was the first collection of plays for black youth. In 1935 he coedited, with May Miller, *Negro History in Thirteen Plays.*

Despite his prolific output and fame during the Harlem Renaissance, with the exception of a performance of his one-act play, *Miss or Mrs.,* nothing was heard from Richardson during the 1940s. He continued to work at the Bureau of Engraving and Printing until retiring in 1954. In 1956 he published his last collection of plays, *The King's Dilemma and Other Plays for Children;* however, it did not include any new work. Although he was honored in his hometown of Wilmington by the establishment of the Willis Richardson Players in 1974, he died in 1977 in relative obscurity. Richardson's important role in African American theater, however, is increasingly being recognized today.

The Chip Woman's Fortune

Cast

AUNT NANCY, the chip woman
JIM, her son
LIZA, a friend
SILAS, her husband
EMMA, a girl of eighteen, Liza's daughter

ACT ONE

The scene is the very plain dining room of a poor colored family. The floor is without covering and the walls are without pictures. At the center of the floor is a rectangular table with a couple of chairs near it. In the rear wall is a fireplace in which a low fire is burning, and at the left of this sits LIZA in a rocker. She is wrapped from shoulders to ankles in blankets, for she is just up from a spell of sickness. At the right of the fireplace is a window. A door at the right leads through to other rooms and to the back yard. Another door at the left leads to the front of the house. Against the left side near the door stands a Victrola. There is a deep silence as LIZA sits gazing into the fire. She looks up at the clock on the mantel, then looks toward the right and calls.

    Liza: (calling) Emma! Emma!

(Presently AUNT NANCY appears at the right. Every one of us has seen her kind—those old women who go about the streets picking up chips of wood and lumps of coal, or searching in trash cans for whatever they can find. Such is AUNT NANCY. She is old and her back is bent on account of constant stooping. She is wearing a bonnet which partly hides her black, wrinkled face, and is wearing a shawl over her shoulders)

Aunt Nancy: You callin' Emma, Miss Liza?

    Liza: Yes'm, Aunt Nancy. You seen her?

Aunt Nancy: No'm, Ah ain't seen her.

    Liza: Wonder where she is? Ah want her to go to the store for me.

Aunt Nancy: Ah don't know where she is. Ah ain't seen her for the last two hours, but I reckon she'll drop in in a minute or two. How you feelin' now?

    Liza: Ah'm feelin' pretty good. The medicine you give me last night must be doin' me good.

Aunt Nancy: Ah don't reckon you need no more medicine today.

    Liza: Ah reckon not. How you feelin'? Seems like Ah ought to be askin' you that instead of you askin' me.

Aunt Nancy: Ah'm feelin' right sharp for a old woman. To tell you the truth, Ah ain't felt better since the day Ah got married. Ah'm 'spectin' somethin'.

Produced in 1923; published in 1927.

Liza: You 'spectin' somethin'?

Aunt Nancy: Yes'm.

Liza: What you 'spectin'?

Aunt Nancy: Ah can't tell you that, Miss Liza; but maybe you'll find out before the day's gone.

Liza: Is it anythin' good?

Aunt Nancy: Didn' Ah tell you Ah ain't felt better since the day I got married?

Liza: Ah'm glad somethin' good's happenin' to somebody. Ain't nothin' good happenin' to me.

Aunt Nancy: You gettin' better, ain't you?

Liza: Yes'm. Ah'm gettin' better.

Aunt Nancy: That sure is good; and besides, you're young yet; lot o' good things can happen to you before you die.

Liza: Ah hope so.

Aunt Nancy: *(going close to her)* Lemme look in your eyes. *(after looking into her eyes)* Your eyes is startin' to shine. You'll be gettin' all right pretty soon. *(She whispers something in LIZA's ear)*

Liza: *(blushing)* Oh, no'm. Aunt Nancy!

Aunt Nancy: *(laughing)* That's all right, you wait. Ah likes to see a woman's eyes shinin'. It shows she's got some life in her. Ah don't like to see no woman with dead eyes, 'specially a young woman. Ah likes to see 'em pert.

Liza: You ain't by yourself. Everybody likes to see a young woman pert.

Aunt Nancy: Ah was goin' in the woods to dig up some roots, but Ah reckon Ah'll wait 'til tomorrow.

Liza: Tomorrow'll be all right. You don't have to go today.

Aunt Nancy: Ah'll go now and set out on the back steps and think. Ah like to set in the sun and think.

Liza: Think about what?

Aunt Nancy: Ah got somethin' to think about.

Liza: What?

Aunt Nancy: Ah can't tell you everythin'. It ain't good to tell everythin' you think about, you know. 'Spose everybody told all their thoughts?

Liza: That wouldn't never do.

Aunt Nancy: 'Deed it wouldn't never do. Everythin' ud be upside down with other people knowin' what you was thinkin' about. *(She starts out right)*

Liza: If you see Emma out there send her in to me.

Aunt Nancy: All right, Ah will. *(She looks through the right door)* Here comes Emma now.

(EMMA enters. She is a pretty brown girl of eighteen)

Emma: You want me, Ma?

   Liza: Yes, Ah want you. Where you been?

Emma: Upstairs.

   Liza: Upstairs doin' what?

Emma: Combin' ma hair.

   Liza: Combin' your hair this time o' day? You combed your hair once this mornin'. What you comb it again for?

Emma: Ah wanted it combed.

   Liza: You wasn't always so fond o' combin' your hair. What's comin' off?

Emma: Nothin'.

   Liza: *(looking at her more closely)* Come here, gal. *(EMMA moves nearer to her)* Ah believe before God you been puttin' powder on your face. Is you been puttin' powder on your face? *(EMMA looks away without answering)* Where'd you get that powder from?

Emma: Ah bought it.

   Liza: Bought it with what? *(as EMMA is silent)* Don't you hear me talkin' to you? Bought it with what?

Emma: Bought it with some change Pa gave me.

   Liza: Well, wipe it off! Wipe it right off and don't put no more on! Leave it up there and Ah'll use it when Ah get on ma feet. You too young to be powderin'.

Aunt Nancy: *(who still stands near)* Let the gal alone, Liza. You was young like that once and she ain't goin' to be that young but once.

   Liza: She don't have to paint herself up like a billboard just because she's young. *(to EMMA)* Get the basket, Ah want you to go to the store for me.

(EMMA goes out right)

Aunt Nancy: Ah'll be out on the back steps if you want me.

   Liza: All right'm. Ah hope Ah won't need you.

(AUNT NANCY goes out right and LIZA sits rocking until EMMA returns. She speaks just as EMMA comes in)

   Liza: There's somethin' mighty funny goin' on round here. You primpin' and Aunt Nancy thinkin'. Ah reckon we goin' to have a thunder storm.

Emma: Ain't nothin' funny goin' on.

   Liza: What you doin' plasterin' your face up and combin' your hair if somethin' funny ain't goin' on? You know you ain't never combed your hair twice the same day in your life if it wasn't Sunday.

Emma: *(anxious to change the subject)* What did you say to get from the store?

   Liza: Get some potatoes and chops and some cakes. Some o' the little ones your Pa likes so much.

Emma: Is that all?

Liza: Yes, that's all. Look a here, tell me this. Did Aunt Nancy take you in the woods and show you how to dig them roots yesterday?

Emma: Yes'm, she showed me, but Ah don't remember much.

Liza: Why don't you? You ain't got your mind on no boy, is you?

Emma: No'm. She says she's goin' to show me all over again so Ah'll know how to find 'em for you when she's gone.

Liza: Aunt Nancy ain't goin' nowhere.

Emma: Ah hope she won't, but if she does Ah'll be sorry. She's so good to me. Ah love her a lot.

Liza: 'Deed she is good. Everybody loves her and they can't help it. Ain't no way in the world to help lovin' somebody that's good to you.

Emma: And Aunt Nancy sure has been good to us.

Liza: Nobody knows that like Ah do.

Emma: *(starting out)* Ah'm goin' now.

Liza: Wait a minute. Start the Victrola off before you go, and go out the back way, it's nearer.

Emma: *(adjusting the needle)* When we goin' to get some new records, Ma?

Liza: New records? You better wait 'til the Victrola gets paid for. You got a plenty o' records.

Emma: But they're all old.

Liza: That's all right, you can keep on usin' 'em. You ought to be glad to get bread to eat and let new records alone.

(EMMA starts the machine and goes out right)

Liza: Don't stay long.

Emma: *(outside the door)* No'm, Ah'll be right back.

(LIZA is listening to the Victrola when SILAS, her husband, enters from the left. He is a man about forty and is wearing the uniform of a store porter. As he enters LIZA looks up at him in surprise)

Liza: Why, Silas, what you doin' home?

Silas: *(throwing his cap down and moving to the table)* They sent me home.

Liza: Not discharged?

Silas: *(not in the best of spirits)* No, Ah ain't discharged, but it's almost as bad; Ah'm furloughed a couple o' days without pay.

Liza: Furloughed for what?

Silas: *(motioning toward the Victrola)* On account o' that old Victrola. Seems like it's bringin' us more trouble than it's worth.

Liza: What's the Victrola got to do with your job?

Silas: It's just like everything else. When a man's got trouble o' one kind seems like everything goes wrong.

Liza: That ain't tellin' me nothin'.

Silas: Well, you know we ain't paid nothin' on that Victrola since the first payment, don't you?

Liza: Yes, Ah know that. But you been promisin'.

Silas: That's the trouble. Ah been doin' a lot o' promisin' and no payin'.

Liza: *(impatiently)* Well, what else? You just as well tell me all of it at once. Ah don't feel like askin' a million questions.

Silas: The man said he was goin' to send here and get the thing if we didn't pay this month, didn't he?

Liza: Yes.

Silas: Well, you know we ain't been able to pay, so he's goin' to send after it.

Liza: Goin' to take it away?

Silas: Yes.

Liza: So, that's why you got furloughed, is it? 'Cause they goin' to take the Victrola away.

Silas: No, that ain't it exactly.

Liza: Ah see you ain't told me. What is it exactly?

Silas: The manager o' that music place is a friend o' ma boss; and this mornin' while Ah was sweepin' off the front pavement he passed by me goin' in the store. When he seen me he stopped and looked at me hard, then he went in. Ah thought trouble was comin' when Ah seen him look at me so hard. After he came out the boss called me in and told me they was goin' to send after that Victrola; and then he says, "Go home and stay a few days and maybe you'll learn how to pay your debts." So here Ah am.

Liza: Ah'll be mighty sorry to lose that Victrola; but if it can't be helped, it can't be helped.

Silas: No, it can't be helped, but that ain't the worst of it. If Ah don't pay and they take it back, when Ah go back the boss'll always have his eyes on me, and Ah bet it won't be long before Ah'll be losin' ma job.

Liza: What you goin' to do?

Silas: Ah'll do anything to save ma job.

Liza: Ah know you'd like to pay and keep the Victrola; but Ah don't see where you goin' to get the fifty dollars from.

Silas: Ah know one thing.

Liza: What?

Silas: Aunt Nancy's got to start payin' for her room and board.

Liza: *(surprised)* Aunt Nancy!

Silas: Yes. We can't keep her around here as high as everything is.

Liza: *(earnestly)* But look what she done for me. She brought me from flat o' ma back. Ah had one foot in the grave before she come here. And look at me now. Ah'm almost on ma feet.

Silas: Ah can't help it. Ah know she done a whole lot for us, but Ah can't keep things goin' if she don't pay—

Liza: She helps along. She picks up chips and pieces o' coal on the street. That keeps you from havin' to buy 'em.

Silas: Everythin' you sayin' is true, but she's either got to give us some money for stayin' here or she's got to go.

Liza: *(greatly concerned)* If she goes who's goin' to nurse me? Who's goin' in the woods to get the roots to make ma medicine?

Silas: If that old woman didn't have money, Ah wouldn't say nothin'.

Liza: *(not understanding)* If she didn't have what?

Silas: If she didn't have money; but Ah know she's got money.

Liza: *(angrily)* Where in the devil would Aunt Nancy get any money from?

Silas: Ain't no use to get mad about it. Ah know what Ah'm sayin'.

Liza: How do you know she's got money?

Silas: Ah know because Ah been watchin' her the last week or so.

Liza: You been watchin' her, is you? Well, what did you find out?

Silas: Ah found out that people passin' in the street give her money every day.

Liza: You ain't talkin' about a cent or two anybody might give a poor old woman, is you?

Silas: No, every day Ah see people givin' her dimes and nickels and quarters. And it ain't no longer than yesterday that Ah seen two rich lookin' men givin' her greenbacks.

Liza: Ah ain't never seen her with no money.

Silas: Ah know you ain't. She hides it.

Liza: Hides it where?

Silas: In the back yard. I know the very place.

Liza: Did you see her hide it there?

Silas: No, Ah didn't see her hide it there, but every time I go out there by that spot she comes right behind me.

Liza: Ah hope you ain't mean enough to try to take her money. Ah mean if she's got any.

Silas: No, Ah ain't been tryin' to take it. Ah just wanted to see what she had there. Ah tried it time and time again, and every time I went close to that spot she come right up.

Liza: Why didn't you wait 'til she went away?

Silas: I done that twice; but every time Ah went out there she come right back just like somethin' drawed her back. Once Ah went out there with a spade and up she comes and stands right on the spot. Ah told her Ah wanted to dig a hole for a post and she said, "Please don't dig it right here, Mr. Silas; Ah got somethin' planted here." You know if somebody has anything planted, they wouldn't go and stand right on the spot.

Liza: (*after a moment's thought*) Well, whether she's got money or not, Ah don't think you ought to put her out after what she's done for us.

Silas: That's the only way I know we can get by.

Liza: That won't make it the right thing to do. A lot o' people get by by doin' the wrong thing. Ah know Emma won't like it.

Silas: It's got to happen just the same if she don't hand out some money. Where's Emma?

Liza: She went after somethin' for dinner.

Silas: When she comes in, tell her what Ah said. 'Course the old woman might get open-hearted and let us have fifty dollars or so; then we won't have no trouble at all and Ah can go back to work tomorrow.

Liza: Maybe she'll let us have that much if she's got it, but Ah don't believe she's got that much.

Silas: (*determined*) Somethin's got to be done. (*as he starts out*) Ah reckon Ah better change these clothes so they'll be clean when Ah do go back.

(*He goes out, leaving LIZA gazing into the fire. Presently EMMA returns with the basket on her arm*)

Liza: Ah got a lot o' sad news for you, Emma.

Emma: (*a little frightened at her mother's tone, rests the basket on the table and gazes at her*) What's the matter? Anythin' bad happened?

Liza: They goin' to take the Victrola away.

Emma: The Victrola! Who's goin' to take it away?

Liza: The men from the store's comin' 'cause we ain't been makin' no payments.

Emma: Does Pa know about it?

Liza: Yes, he's the one told me.

Emma: He been here?

Liza: He's here now. They sent him home from work because we ain't been makin' no payments.

Emma: (*fearfully*) He ain't been discharged, is he?

Liza: He ain't been discharged, but he's furloughed and that's just as bad.

Emma: You mean they goin' to let him go back?

Liza: Yes, they'd let him go back today if he could make a good payment on that Victrola; but he reckons he'll have to stay out two or three days as it is.

Emma: Ah'm mighty sorry they put him off, and Ah'm mighty sorry we can't keep that Victrola. Hearin' that thing was about the only pleasure Ah had.

Liza: That ain't the worst yet.

Emma: What, somethin' more? What else is it?

Liza: Your Pa says if Aunt Nancy don't pay some money for stayin' here she's got to go.

Emma: Where's Aunt Nancy goin' to get any money from?

Liza: He says he's been seein' people give her money almost every day, and she's got it buried in the back yard.

Emma: If she's got any money at all, it's just a few cents; but Ah don't believe she's got none.

Silas: (*entering just in time to hear what EMMA says. He is now wearing overalls*) Yes, she is got money, too; and she'll either have to pay some or get out.

Emma: (*turning on him*) Ah don't see nothin' fair in that. She picks up chips, she brings home wood and coal, and she nurses Ma. What more do you want?

Silas: (*sitting at the right of the table*) If she'll give me a few dollars or let me borrow a few dollars, maybe Ah can go back to ma job tomorrow.

Emma: If you put her out, Ah believe Ma'll go right back to bed 'cause there won't be nobody that'll know what to do for her. So Ah don't see nothin' you'll gain by puttin' her out.

Silas: If she'll let us have the money—

Emma: If she's got any money it's just a little she's savin' for her son.

Silas: (*surprised*) Her son! Ah didn't know she had no son.

Emma: Yes, seh, she's got a son.

Silas: Where's he? Ah ain't heard nothin' about him.

Emma: He's been in the pen[1] a long time, but Ah reckon he's out now.

Silas: In the pen?

Emma: Yes, seh.

Silas: (*still puzzled*) And she's savin' money for him?

Emma: Ah reckon that's what she's savin' it for if she's got any.

Silas: (*in disgust*) Well, for God's sake! Savin' money for a jailbird!

Emma: She says she wants him to have a few cents to keep him 'til he can get a job.

Silas: Did she tell you all this?

Emma: Yes, seh. Ah wrote a letter for her the other day.

Silas: (*turning to LIZA*) Did you know anything about this, Liza?

Liza: No, this is the first time Ah've heard a word about it.

Silas: Why didn't you say somethin' about it?

1. "Pen" is a slang word for prison.

Emma: You always told me to tend to ma own business. Ah didn't want to be tellin' her business around.

Silas: It's all right to tend to your business, but it ain't all right to keep secrets from your parents when it concerns 'em. You say her son's out now.

Emma: He was to be out yesterday. She's lookin' for him to come here today.

Silas: What was he sent up for?

Emma: Ah don't know, seh; somethin' about a woman, Ah believe.

Silas: And he means to come here, does he?

Emma: Yes, seh.

Silas: You hear that, Liza?

Liza: Yes, and Ah ain't particular about havin' no jailbird comin' here neither.

Silas: Ah reckon Ah just as well talk to her now as any other time. Was she out there when you come in, Emma?

Emma: Yes, seh, she was sittin' out on the back steps; but she got up when Ah came in and started off.

Silas: Well, go tell her to come in here a minute.

Emma: *(as she goes out)* Ah'll have to catch her 'cause Ah reckon she's gone.

Silas: Just go out there and stand by that middle clothes prop and she'll come right in sight. Ah've already tried it a lot o' times myself.

(EMMA goes out)

Silas: Liza, Ah want you to understand Ah'm not actin' this way 'cause Ah mean to be hardhearted. Ah've just got to get out o' this trouble.

Liza: *(discouraged)* Ah'm sorry everything turned out like this, 'cause I reckon Ah'll have to go back to bed if she goes.

Silas: *(concerned)* Don't say that. The Lord couldn't be that hard on us.

Liza: Ah hope you're right; goodness knows Ah do.

Silas: If Ah can get her to do us this favor before the men come after that Victrola, everything'll be all right. *(There is a pause while they ponder over their situation)* And even if she will agree to help us, Ah'm tired o' this kind o' life. Ah'm sick o' livin' from hand to mouth.

Liza: Ah reckon we ought to be thankful to be livin' any kind o' way with all the trouble we had. Some people get along better'n we do, but a whole lot o' others don't get along as good. Ah only got one consolation besides believin' in the Lord.

Silas: What's that?

Liza: That things ain't always been like this, and they might not always be like this.

Silas: Ah hope not. *(after he listens)* Here they come.

Liza: Now don't be hard on her, Silas. You know she's been mighty good to us.

Silas: Ah ain't goin' to be hard on her. Ah'm goin' to be as fair as Ah can.

(EMMA enters followed by AUNT NANCY)

Aunt Nancy: (moving to the table and speaking to SILAS) You want to see me, seh?

Silas: (kindly) Yes'm, Aunt Nancy, Ah want to talk to you. Get a chair so she can sit down, Emma.

(AUNT NANCY looks around for a chair, EMMA brings her one and she sits above the table)

Silas: The first thing Ah want to do, Aunt Nancy, is to thank you for all the good things you done for us. And then Ah want to tell you that we're in trouble.

Aunt Nancy: You all in trouble, Mister Silas?

Silas: Yes'm. The men'll be here today after the Victrola, and Ah'm put off from work a few days 'cause Ah didn't pay for it.

Aunt Nancy: Ah'm mighty sorry for that.

Silas: And you know you been stayin' here with us for six months or more and we ain't been chargin' you a thing.

Aunt Nancy: No, and Ah wouldn't a been able to pay you nothin' no how.

Silas: Now Ah'm askin' if you'll pay us for stayin' or let us borrow a few dollars from you?

Aunt Nancy: (with a long face) 'Deed the Lord knows Ah can't pay you nothin', Mister Silas. Ah ain't got nothin for myself.

Silas: But we know you got money hid out there in the back yard.

Aunt Nancy: Ah got a little money out there, but that ain't for me; that's for ma child.

Silas: (feigning surprise) You didn't tell us you had no child.

Aunt Nancy: Ah reckon you'd call him a man, but Ah call him ma child. He's grown.

Silas: Where is he?

Aunt Nancy: Ah reckon he's on his way here now.

Silas: (still pretending ignorance) Ah don't see what a old woman like you wants to be savin' money for a grown man for. He ought to be workin' and takin' care o' you. Ain't he workin'?

Aunt Nancy: He's been locked up.

Silas: In jail?

Aunt Nancy: In the pen.

Silas: That's so much the worse. You oughtn't to be savin' money to give to a jail-bird.

Aunt Nancy: (offended) He ain't no jailbird, Mister Silas; don't call him that. He's ma son.

Silas: He ought to be shamed of hisself for not workin' and takin' care o' you.

Aunt Nancy: That used to be the way when Ah was comin' up. When children used to get grown they used to take care o' the old folks, but now it's different. The old folks has to take care o' the children.

Silas: Ah wouldn't never look out for no grown man.

Aunt Nancy: Ah reckon you wouldn'. Fathers wasn't never like mothers and never will be.

Silas: And 'specially if he went to the pen.

Aunt Nancy: Goin' to the pen ain't nothin'. Some o' the best men in the world's been to the pen. It ain't the goin' to the pen that counts, it's what you go there for. Once it used to be a big disgrace to be locked up; but the people in them days forgot that the Lord was locked up. No, seh, it ain't the bein' locked up, it's what you locked up for. If the Lord had a got locked up for stealin' somethin' or killin' somebody do you think people would be praisin' him like they do?

Silas: I know they wouldn't; but what did your son get locked up for?

Aunt Nancy: He got locked up about a woman, but he done what any other man might a done. He was goin' with a woman what he thought was clean, but she was crooked. He run up on her one night when another man was handlin' her kind o' rough and beat the man up—he beat the man up bad. Then he found out the woman was crooked and he lost his head and beat her up too. That's the worse part of it.

Silas: *(doubtfully)* And they sent him to the pen for that? Just for that?

Aunt Nancy: Yes, seh. The man he beat up was one o' these big fellows what went to church every Sunday, and looked so clean and nice in his biled[2] shirts and white collars and fine clothes all through the week days, but in the night he trailed in the gutter. He used his pull and put up a job on Jim that sent him to the pen.

Silas: Ah don't mean to hurt your feelin's, Aunt Nancy, but your boy can't be much if he beat a woman up.

Liza: 'Deed he can't.

Aunt Nancy: *(hanging her head)* That's the worse part of it. Ah didn't mind him beatin' the man, but Ah never did care much for a man that ud hit a woman—no man but ma own son. *(looking him in the eyes)* And you know a mother can't help that.

Silas: Ah always did think some mothers was too kindhearted.

Aunt Nancy: No, they ain't. Mothers ain't half as kindhearted as God is. If God was hard as some people is, everybody in this world would be farin' mighty bad. You know there ain't no man perfect, and no woman neither.

Silas: I reckon you might be right about that, but the main reason I sent for you was to ask you if you wouldn't let us have a little money. If you can't do it we'll be in a hole sure enough.

Aunt Nancy: Ah wish Ah could. Ah'd be willin' to do anything in the world for you, but he comes first, you know.

Silas: Do you reckon he'll let us have it?

2. "Boiled;" clean.

Aunt Nancy: Ah don't know; he's mighty kindhearted. He's takin' a mighty long time to come here too.

(At this time, there is a loud knocking on the outside door)

Aunt Nancy: (starting to rise) Ah reckon that's him now.

> *Liza:* Don't get up, Aunt Nancy; Emma'll let him in.

(EMMA goes out)

> *Silas: (to AUNT NANCY)* Why don't you take your bonnet off? You don't want to look like you ain't home.

Aunt Nancy: Never mind. Ah'll keep it on. We won't be here long, Ah reckon.

> *Emma: (returning)* It's the men after the Victrola.

(SILAS hastens out left)

Aunt Nancy: (sighing) Oh, Lord. Ah thought that was Jim. Ah wonder why he don't come?

> *Liza:* Don't worry, Aunt Nancy, it ain't late.

> *Emma:* Ah reckon he might be lookin' for the place.

Aunt Nancy: But you put this number in the letter, didn' you?

> *Emma:* Yes'm, Ah put it in.

> *Silas: (returning)* Ah don't know why Ah done it, but Ah told 'em to wait a few minutes.

(He sits again)

Aunt Nancy: Ah don't know. Jim might come in a few minutes.

(There is another knock on the door)

> *Silas: (rising)* Ah wonder what they want now?

(He goes out again)

Aunt Nancy: That might be Jim.

> *Liza:* Ah hope it is.

(SILAS returns followed by JIM. When AUNT NANCY sees him she flies toward him. JIM opens his arms and draws her to him)

Aunt Nancy: (holding him off and looking at him) It is you, sure enough? Jim, is it you?

> *Jim: (smiling)* Yes'm, it's me.

Aunt Nancy: Come over here.

(She draws him over to the table and we have an opportunity to get a good view of him. He is about thirty, standing over six feet in height and large in proportion. He is wearing a blue shirt with collar attached and a blue suit)

Aunt Nancy: These is the people Ah been stayin' with all the winter, Jim. *(She names each one in her way of introduction)* This is Mr. Silas.

Jim: (*smiling as they shake hands*) Glad to meet you, Mr. Silas.

Aunt Nancy: This is Miss Liza.

Jim: (*bowing to LIZA*) Glad to meet you, Miss Liza.

Aunt Nancy: And this is Emma. (*JIM and EMMA bow and smile at each other*) These people been mighty good to me, Jim.

Jim: (*speaking to all of them*) Ah'm glad to hear that and Ah thank you all for it.

Liza: We ain't been half as good to her as she's been to us.

Emma: Indeed we ain't.

Aunt Nancy: Ah ain't done nothin' that no good woman wouldn't a done. Jim knows me.

Jim: Ah know her well, too.

Aunt Nancy: (*to JIM*) What made you take so long to get here?

Jim: Well, Ah hung around a little while—

Aunt Nancy: Now, Jim, you ain't got no business hangin' 'round when Ah'm waitin' for you.

Jim: And even when Ah got here Ah wasn't sure this was the right place 'cause Ah seen two men hangin' 'round on the outside and they looked kinder like bootleggers.

Silas: Them's the men that come to take the Victrola away.

Jim: (*turning to AUNT NANCY*) You say these people been good to you, Ma?

Aunt Nancy: Yes, they been mighty good to me.

Jim: (*reaching into his pocket*) Ah got fifteen dollars. You can have that if it'll do you any good. (*He gives it to SILAS*)

Silas: (*taking the money*) Thanks for that. Maybe some o' these days—

(*The two men who have been waiting outside enter*)

First Man: Ah'm sorry, but we can't wait all day; we got to get back to the store.

Jim: (*to SILAS*) How much do you owe on it?

Silas: Fifty dollars.

Jim: Fifteen dollars won't do much good then, will it?

Silas: Well, it'll help. Ah been tryin' to borrow it from your Ma.

Second Man: (*roughly*) Come on, Dan, let's take it; they ain't got nothin'.

Silas: (*as they take hold of the Victrola*) Wait a minute!

Jim: (*turning to his mother*) You got any money, Ma?

Aunt Nancy: Ah got a little Ah been savin' for you.

Jim: How much?

Aunt Nancy: (*who is not very good at figures*) Ah don't know, but Ah reckon it's enough. Ah'll get it. (*She goes out right*)

Second Man: (*impatiently*) Come on, Dan; this is all a bluff.

(They move the Victrola toward the door)

> Jim: *(getting in the doorway)* There ain't nobody or nothin' goin' out o' here 'til she comes back!

(JIM is such a large man and so nearly fills the doorway that the two men stop and reconsider their plan. They decide to wait)

> Jim: Ah don't mean no harm to nobody and Ah wouldn't hurt a hair in nobody's head; but when Ah say wait, Ah mean wait.

> First Man: But you see, mister, we been waitin' a long time already.

> Jim: Well, you won't have to wait much longer. She'll be back in a minute.

(AUNT NANCY returns with a rather dirty box which she puts on the table and opens. All gaze into it)

> Aunt Nancy: *(pouring the contents of the box on the table)* This is yours. Jim. Ah been savin' it for you ever since you went away.

> Jim: *(staring at the money)* All this for me?

> Aunt Nancy: Yes, and you can do anything you want to do with it.

> Jim: *(pushing half of the money to SILAS)* Here, take this; maybe it'll be enough.

(Judging from the expression on AUNT NANCY's face JIM is giving away too much)

> Silas: *(drawing the money to him)* 'Deed it will be enough. *(After counting the money he hands part of it to one of the men)* Here's your fifty dollars.

(The first man takes the money and with the aid of the second man pushes the Victrola back to its place. Having done this they start out)

> Jim: *(to SILAS)* You better get a receipt for that.

> Silas: *(to the men)* Hey, wait a minute. *(The men stop)* Gimme a receipt for that money. *(The first man writes him a receipt and then they go out)* That's better. *(after indicating the money left on the table)* Ah reckon you better take the rest of it back, Jim.

> Jim: No, you keep it. You all been good to Ma, and ain't nothin' Ah got too good for you.

> Liza: She done a whole lot more for us than we could ever do for her.

> Aunt Nancy: Ah'd a give you that money before, Mr. Silas, but Ah was savin' it for Jim, and Ah just didn't have the heart to give it away.

> Silas: That's all right, Auntie; Ah 'preciated it just as much as if you had give it to me when Ah first ask you.

> Aunt Nancy: *(taking up her basket)* Well, Jim, Ah reckon we better be goin'.

> Liza: *(quickly in surprise)* Goin'! Where you goin'?

> Aunt Nancy: Goin' to get a place to stay.

> Jim: Then Ah'm goin' to look for a job.

Liza: But Ah' thought you was goin' to stay here with us.

Aunt Nancy: You ain't got no room for both of us, chile.

Silas: (*shifting the chairs around*) Yes'm, we is. We'll make room.

Jim: No, seh, Ah don't want you to cramp yourself on ma account. It won't take us long to find another place.

Liza: But how'll Ah get along, Aunt Nancy, with you gone?

Aunt Nancy: Ah won't be far away. Ah'll come in and look after you every day.

Liza: Ah'm mighty sorry you goin'; and Ah want to thank you for what you done for us.

Aunt Nancy: (*as she and JIM stand near the door*) Maybe we'll ask you all to do us a favor sometime.

Silas: And we'll be mighty glad to do it.

Aunt Nancy: Well, good day 'til tomorrow.

Silas, Liza,
and Emma: Good day.

Jim: Good day to all of you.

Silas, Liza,
and Emma: Good day.

(*AUNT NANCY and JIM go out*)

Emma: Ah'm sorry she's gone.

Liza: You must be mighty sorry he's gone too by the way you looked at him.

Silas: 'Deed she must be. She looked at him like her life depended on it.

Liza: To tell the truth, Ah'm mighty sorry she's gone too. She's sure goin' to be a loss to me.

Silas: But she says she's goin' to come around every day to look after you.

Liza: Yes, but that ain't like stayin' here.

Silas: Well, there ain't nothin' Ah can do.

Emma: Ah reckon you're mighty glad you didn't put her out.

Silas: Ah am, Ah'm mighty glad.

Liza: She got us out o' trouble, all right.

Emma: Indeed she did.

Silas: Ah got to go and get ma work clothes on and go and see about ma job.

Liza: She saved your job too, Ah'm thinkin'.

Silas: You bet your life she did.

Curtain

Aaron Douglas, "The Flight of the Natives," *Plays of Negro Life,* 1927

The Flight of the Natives

Characters

MOSE, a slave
PET, his wife
JUDE, an informer
TOM, a slave
SALLIE, his wife
LUKE, another slave—a mulatto, evidently an illegitimate son
MONK, a slave lasher
JOHN, the white slave owner

> *Scene:* A South Carolina slave cabin.
> *Time:* 1860. A spring afternoon, towards sunset.

We see the interior of a crude candlelighted hut. There is no floor save the bare ground and no ceiling save the rough boards, shingles and rafters of the roof itself. At the right is a door which leads outside and above this against the same wall are bunks such as are used by steerage passengers. In the rear wall are two windows below which are two rough benches. On the left side against the wall are bunks similar to those on the right. At the center of the rear wall exactly between the two windows hangs an old quilt on a cord. The cord leads forward and fastens to one of the rafters so that when the quilt is pulled forward on it the hut is temporarily divided into two compartments, the one on the right for men and the other for women. It is the early part of the night and on each windowsill is a lighted candle. The quilt is drawn partly forward on the cord. JUDE, a small, narrow shouldered man of thirty-five, is seated on the end of the men's bench with his elbows on his knees and his head in his hands; TOM, another man, is lying in a bunk; while LUKE is standing by the wall with the quilt pulled slightly aside at the rear end so that he can look through the window. PET, MOSE's wife, is sitting on her bench sewing, and SALLIE, TOM's wife, is lying in a bunk.

Sallie: *(looking at LUKE)* What you watchin', Luke?

Luke: Ah'm watchin' the river and wishin' y'awl wuz menfolks so's we could all make way from heah, same's Slim.

Sallie: Ah hope to God Slim gets away, but Ah ain't thinkin' there's much chance.

Pet: There ought to be much chance. He's gone.

Sallie: Ah know he's gone, but dere's Marse an' his hound dogs right on his heels.

Pet: Slim went fo' daybreak—and lessen de Lawd's ag'in him, I reckon Marse John nevah ketch up wid him.

Sallie: He mought have a chance, but ain't no man can outrun dogs and horses.

Pet: Who knows they went the right way? Slim left in de dark and nobody ain't seen him go.

Sallie: (knowingly) Yes, somebody did see him go. Ah seen him go. Ah know which a-way he went and Ah know somebody else that knows which a-way he went.

Pet: Who den?

Sallie: Somebody done told Marse John the way he went. Ah seen him. (At this JUDE raises his head and listens)

Pet: (interested) Who told on Slim?

Sallie: It wasn't nobody but Jude. Jude, that they lets come tuh the big house. Jude, that they lets eat the scraps off'n the table in the big house.

Jude: (going quickly to the front end of the curtain) You talkin' about me, Sallie?

Sallie: You the only one what's named Jude around here, ain't you? Ah reckon your mammy named you Jude 'cause she knowed you'd be a 'trayer.[1]

Jude: You stan' there an' tell me Ah told Marse John de way Slim went?

Sallie: Yes, I say you tole him!

Jude: Ah didn't!

Sallie: You did! Ah heered you! An' Ah seen you with ma own eyes!

Jude: It ain't true!

Tom: (who has risen in his bunk) 'Tis true! If Sallie says it's de truf, it's de truf!

Jude: (more humbly) Ah didn't tell him, Tom! Ah swear to de Lawd Ah didn't!

Tom: Ain't no use o' swearin' to a lie! You tole it and if Mose finds out you tattled on Slim he's goin' to beat the life out o' you!

Luke: (who has been staring at JUDE ever since SALLIE accused him) He'll half kill you, niggah, and he ought to!

Jude: Mose ain't goin' to tech me! Marse John done said if Mose put his hands on me he'll sell him down the river.

Pet: (indignantly) So you been talkin' about Mose too, is you? You keep your mouth off Mose!

Jude: Ah ain't goin' to say nothin' about him if he don't do nothin' to me.

Sallie: If Slim gets away and dey don't catch him Ah won't say nothin'; but sho's you bawn if Slim gets caught Ah'm goin' to tell Mose on you!

Tom: Slim an' Mose wuz bosom friends and Mose was moughty glad when Slim got away. Now, if Slim gets caught 'count o' you, Mose'll half kill yuh.

Pet: Don't you-all say nothin' to Mose, neither one of yuh. Ah don't want Mose to put his hands on Jude, 'cause they might sell Mose down the river sho 'nough, and if they done that Ah'd die. Ah 'clare to the Lawd, Ah'd die.

Luke: We mought not tell Mose and Mose mought not do nothin' to you; but Ah mought mahself. You can't tattle on none of us and get away with it.

Sallie: You can't beat him up half as much as Mose can, Luke; and Mose is the one Ah'm goin' to tell if Slim gets caught.

1. "Betrayer."

Pet: I done tole you, Sallie; don't you do it!

Sallie: You reckon we'd let that big-house Judas 'tray Slim, and do nothin' to him?

Pet: But Mose is ma husband! He ain't yo' husband, an' Ah don't want ma husband sold away from me, does I?

Jude: You-all don't like me! Ah know you don't; you just want to get me in trouble!

Sallie: You get yourself in trouble! If you had 'a' kept your tongue still in yo' mouth this never would 'a' happened. They never would 'a' found out the way Slim went!

Jude: Ah doan' care what you-all likes, but the one that lays his hands on me'll be sold down the river. Marse done said so.

Luke: Ah'd like to know what good that'll do you after you get busted to pieces.

Jude: It might not do me much good, you white-man's trash, but it'll do one of you-all a lot o' harm. *(LUKE sneers at him to hide his discomfort)*

Sallie: All Ah hope is they don't catch Slim.

Pet: Ah hope they don't neither.

Tom: *(to JUDE)* All Ah've got to say,—ef you cares fo' yo' hide, you bettah pray dey don't ketch Slim. *(Just then MOSE, a large, broad-shouldered man of thirty, enters. PET at once goes to him. JUDE slinks back to his seat)*

Tom: *(after MOSE closes the door)* What's [the] news, Mose?

Mose: Marse is back and back swearin'. Slim must 'a' made it.

Pet: Ah hope the Lord he's sho nuff gone lak de chillen ub Isreel.

Mose: Lawd a-mussy, Ah hopes so. *(He goes on PET's side and sits on the bench with her)*

Tom: Haven't heerd de hound dogs yet. Whah's dey at?

Mose: Ain't back yit. Dey's on de udder side wid Bark's men.

Pet: *(hopefully)* Slim ought to be miles and miles away from hyah by now, oughtn't he, Mose?

Mose: Yes, he ought to be out o' reach, way out o' reach. I reckon he's ketchin' his breath by now. Ah reckon there ain't nothin' in the whole world that's better'n bein' free.

Pet: Ah reckon not. Just like heaven.

Luke: *(going towards the door)* Must be a moughty fine thing to be out wha you kin stretch yo' ahms and laigs and breathe the air deep, and you know you ain't no mo' slave. Ah'm goin' out here and see how they're talkin'. *(He goes out)*

Mose: Ah'd give ten years o' ma life if Ah could live ten years a free man.

Tom: Ah'm a common dog if Ah wouldn't give the rest o' ma life for five years free.

Mose: Sometimes Ah reckon Ah'd jus' like to break loose and make a dash for it. If it wasn't for Pet Ah'd 'a' done it long ago.

Pet: Ah'd be willin' to go with you, Mose. Ah'd be willin' to go with you to the end o' time.

Mose: Ah know you would, but the chances is too big. You couldn't never swim the river in no kind o' time, and then you mought get shot.

Pet: When you talk like that Ah feel like Ah'm a millstone 'round yo' neck.

Mose: You mustn't think that. If it hadn't 'a' been for you Ah'd 'a' been dead long ago. Ah take a lot o' things every day Ah wouldn't take if it don't be fo' you.

Sallie: Mose, what you reckon ud happen if Slim got caught?

Mose: It ud be a mighty bad thing, Sallie. There ain't no tellin' what they wouldn't do to him.

Tom: You think he's got a good chance, sho' nuff?

Mose: Bes' he's evah had. He's done gone over twelve hours and he's a powerful good swimmer and knows the woods like a fox. Ah'm thinkin' it won't be long before Slim'll be real free and out o' danger and brushin' elbows with men.

Tom: Brushin' elbows with men—how Ah'd love dat. *(Here LUKE enters hurriedly and speaks with great excitement)*

Luke: Mose! Mose! For God's sake!

Mose: *(leaping up)* What?

Luke: They done got Slim!

Mose: Got Slim! How you know?

Luke: That's what dey's sayin' out there! *(JUDE starts hastily towards the door but LUKE blocks him)*

Luke: No, you don't! You don't go nowhere, you dirty rat!

Mose: What' the matter 'tween you-all?

Sallie: He's the one that tole on Slim! He's done tole Marse John de way Slim went!

Mose: You-all mean to say he done that!

Sallie: Yes, he done it! Ah seen him! Ah heard him!

Mose: *(catching JUDE by the collar of his shirt)* You tole on Slim, did you?

Jude: *(frightened)* Ah didn't tattle on him! Ah didn't!

Mose: I reckon you did! Ah can see it in your lyin' eyes! Slim was ma friend and you done tole on him and now he's caught! Ah'll break your neck! *(As he draws back his fist to strike JUDE, PET runs to him)*

Pet: *(excitedly)* Don't hit him, Mose! Don't do it! He'll get you sent down the river! What'll become o' me if they sell you down the river? For God's sake, Mose, don't hit him! *(MONK, a short, ugly negro, enters with a whip in his hand)*

Monk: Marse John wants Jude.

Pet: Let him go, Mose! Let him go! Oh, it's the best to let him go! *(MOSE finally relinquishes JUDE, who hurries out where there is a great commotion)*

Mose: *(sitting on the bench hopelessly)* They got him! They got Slim and Jude's the cause of it! Jude better look out for me when dis done blowed over!

Pet: Don't you put your big hands on Jude, Mose; he's moughty dangerous!

Sallie: Somebody ought to put de cat-er-nine-tails on him, dat's waht.

Pet: (*to SALLIE*) You doan' want Mose sold down the river, does you? Well den, take it quiet.

Sallie: The master wouldn't never sell Mose. He's too good a worker 'round here.

Pet: You don't know. Marse does mos' anything when he's in [a] temper.

Mose: (*as the commotion outside continues*) Lemme see what's goin' on out here. (*He goes to the door and opens it just a little*) The dogs! They're tyin' him to a tree and Monk's goin' to lash him!

Pet: Sho bad 'nuff, lashes on your bare back, but it's better'n bein' sold down the river.

Mose: No real man'd let hisself be tied to a tree and beat till the blood runs out o' him! (*suddenly becomes infuriated*) Let me out o' heah! (*LUKE and TOM hold him back. Then comes the sound of SLIM being lashed. The lashing is mingled with SLIM's moans; each time he is struck every person in the room shudders. Finally when the lashing is over there is a sigh of relief from everyone*)

Sallie: Lord, Ah'm glad it's over. Slim must be almost dead.

Mose: (*with determination*) And Jude'll be almost dead when Ah get ma hands on him!

Pet: Don't you lay your hands on Jude, Mose! They'll do you the same way they just done Slim!

Mose: Ain't no man goin' to whip me! (*Just then the door is thrown open suddenly and JOHN, the slave owner, enters with the whip in his hand. He is followed by MONK and JUDE*)

John: (*to all save MOSE and PET*) You-all get out o' here! (*to MOSE after they have gone*) Mose, Ah hear you been sympathizin' with Slim! And Ah hear you laid your hands on Jude for tellin' me the way Slim went!

Mose: Slim was ma friend.

John: (*scornfully*) Friend! What you doin' havin' a friend? You belong to me and Slim belongs to me and Jude belongs to me! All of you supposed to look out for what's mine and you ain't supposed to be glad when Ah lose it! You been a good worker, but for what you done tonight you goin' to be lashed just like Slim was!

Mose: (*in a determined tone*) Ah ain't never been lashed! Ain't no man goin' to lash me!

John: They ain't, ain't they? (*with a motion towards the door*) Come on out o' here!

Mose: (*not moving*) Ain't nobody goin' to lash me!

John: (*handing the whip to MONK*) If you won't come out you'll be lashed right here! Lash him, Monk! Give him the same you just gave Slim!

Monk: (*afraid of the task*) Ma arm's almost dead from lashin' Slim, Master John.

John: (*handing the whip to JUDE*) You lash him, Jude! You the one to lash him anyhow! He laid his hands on you! After you get through with him maybe he won't be so anxious to lay his hands on you next time!

Jude: (*whiningly*) Don't make me do it, Master John; Ah'm scared of him! He'd kill me soon as he got me by mahself.

John: (*raging*) All of you scared of him? Give me that whip, Ah'll lash him! (*Taking the whip he starts towards MOSE, but at the same time MOSE starts towards him and he stops. He knows that a man as big and strong as MOSE is dangerous to strike under any circum-stances)*

John: You threaten me!

Mose: Ain't no man ever whipped me! Ah always done ma work and took a lot o' things Ah didn't want to take, but ain't no man goin' to whip me!

John: Ah'll do worse'n whip you! Slim's just been whipped and he's goin' to be sold down the river in the mornin'! You won't be whipped, but you'll be sold down the river in the mornin' along with Slim! And Pet'll stay here on the plantation! *(MOSE shows no emotion save a slight shudder, but PET flies past him and falls on her knees before JOHN)*

Pet: Massa John! Massa John! For God's sake don't sell Mose away from me! He's good! He don't mean nobody no harm! Please don't sell him away from me!

John: Mose'll be sold down the river in the mornin' and you'll stay here! *(With this he goes out followed by MONK and JUDE)*

Mose: *(lifting PET from the ground)* That's all right, Pet; don't worry. De Lawd'll git us out o' dis somehow.

Pet: *(fearfully)* But goin' down the river! Don't you know what dat'll mean? They'll kill you! They'll beat you to death!

Mose: *(taking her over to the bench)* Ah ain't goin' down no river.

Pet: What you goin' to do? They'll make you go! They'll tie you and take you!

Mose: Ah might start out from here, but Ah ain't goin' down no river.

Pet: What you goin' to do?

Mose: After dey gets started good, Ah'm goin' to jump in the river and swim for it.

Pet: But they'll shoot you! They'll shoot you like a dog!

Mose: Ah'll take the chance. If they shoot me Ah'll be gone to Glory, but if they miss me Ah'll be gone north for freedom. Freedom is wuth it, ain't it?

Pet: Ah reckon it is; but what'll 'come o' me? What'll 'come o' me without you?

Mose: Ah hear they're talkin' about war in the north—talkin' about war and whisperin' about freedom. If the war comes and the freedom comes Ah'm comin' back and get you, Pet. And if freedom don't come Ah'm comin' back and get you anyhow. Ah'll have a taste o' freedom then and Ah'll take you somehow or 'nuther.

Pet: *(hopefully)* Will you, Mose? Will you come back after me?

Mose: Ah promise Ah will, Pet; Ah promise to God Ah will.

Pet: *(putting her arm around his neck)* Ah'll wait for you, then; Ah'll wait for you till Ah die. *(LUKE enters, followed by TOM and SALLIE)*

Luke: *(after TOM closes the door)* What did they do, Mose? What did they say?

Mose: They didn't do nothin' to me.

Pet: *(almost in tears)* But Marse John said he was goin' to sell Mose and Slim down the river in the mornin'.

Sallie: *(hardly able to believe it)* Sell Mose down the river?

Pet: (angrily to SALLIE) Yes, they goin' to sell him! Goin' to sell 'em both! Ah told you not to make Mose lay his hands on Jude!

Tom: Is that what they goin' to sell Mose for?

Mose: No, it's cause Ah wouldn't stand up and let 'em whip me. Wouldn't Ah be a big ninny to stand up and let any man whip me? Ain't no man livin' goin' to whip me!

Luke: But they'll do worse 'n whip you down the river, Mose.

Mose: Ah ain't goin' down no river!

Tom: What you goin' to do?

Mose: Goin' to make a break for it!

Luke: (shaking his head doubtfully) I dunno, Mose, as yuh could make it, but Gawd help yuh. (in a sudden mood) The Lawd help us all, fo' we needs deliverance.

Pet: Amen!—But what we gwine to do wid'out Mose?

Luke: We-all better go 'long wif Mose whichever way he's gwine; an' it don't much matteh. 'Sposin' we all made a breakaway! (They stand aghast) Yassuh, I mean it—ain't crazy, neither. (They huddle round about him) Ah got a plan, I has. (He ponders and then whispers)

Tom: These women can't swim no river.

Luke: An' ain't goin' to—We's takin' the boat.

Mose: What! What yer sayin'?

Luke: I keep a' tellin' yuh, the boat.

Mose: D'yuh think we ought make it that a-way?

Tom: We mought make it like a' that!

Mose: (shaking his head and changing his tone at once) No, we cain't make it nowhere like that. Fust thing, Jude'll be watchin' like a hawk tonight, an' we jes' cain't make it together.

Tom: (pressing his point) Jes' wait a minute, Mose! Le's listen to Luke,—what he says 'bout it.

Pet: Ah'm willin' to try anything, ef it's being wif' Mose. Ah reckon Ah can swim de river—

Sallie: (impatiently) Let the men talk, Pet; let the men talk!

Luke: Jude's got to go ter the woodhouse shortly, ain't he? Well, he ain't comin' out to tell no tales on nobody. Mose kin sneak in behind him and fix him fo' sure. (turning to MOSE) An' be sho' an' lock de woodhouse door, Mose—de keys is allus in Jude's back pocket. You heah dat, Mose? Now that's ou'ah onliest chance!

Mose: (elated) Sho is—an Ah'm perticlar glad to go.

Tom: (detaining him) No, Mose, you'd ruin it. Time Jude set his eyes on you he'd holler murder and everybody on the plantation ud be comin' round here. Let Luke do it.

Luke: Ain't likin' to go, mahself—but Mose sho' would spile it. (after a minute) Ah'm a-goin'. An'— (hesitates) Ah got a plan too. Dat's all right 'bout Mose bein' the stronges' man on the place, but— *(pointing to his forehead with his index finger)* folks, yo' jes' got ter use this sometimes.

Mose: *(grumpily)* Aw, go on den, an' hurry up.

Tom: *(after cracking the door stealthily and peeping out)* Da' Jude now. Mought 'a' been list'nin'. No. Ah reckon he goin' to the woodhouse now. *(pause)* He be! *(LUKE goes out stealthily but with precision)*

Tom: What we gwine do now?

Mose: *(rising to a sense of power)* Dat talkin', Luke! Ah got an ideah mahself! Got it clear as a whistle!

Tom: What?

Mose: Luke an' me'll go steal out and hide fus', an' then you go tell Marse John we done run away—an' dat Sallie knows de way we went.

Sallie: *(surprised)* Me?

Mose: Yes, can you lie?

Sallie: Lie? Ah can do worse'n lie for a chance to get free!

Mose: When Marse John comes to you to tell him the way we went you put him off an' tell him wrong—yah hear?

Sallie: Ah won't never tell him!

Mose: Yuh got to tell him sumthin'. Tell him we took a boat and said we was goin' up the river and cross at Moseby's Landin' and goin' north from there.

Sallie: But you ain't goin' that a-way?

Mose: No, we all goin' together and we goin' a different way.

Tom: Which-a-way.

Mose: When they take the dogs and the rowboats and go up the river lookin' for us on the other side, we'll take the flatboat and go south— *(proudly)* Now,—that Luke think he know so much!

Tom: Go south!

Mose: Yes, we'll go down the river a mile or two and get out on this side and walk all around the plantation, then beat it north like the devil! That'll keep the dogs off our trail! We'll have the river between them and us.

Tom: By daybreak we ought to be a long ways off, oughtn't we?

Mose: A long ways off.

Tom: Ah wonder how Luke's makin' out.

Sallie: Ah hope to the Lord he makes out all right. *(TOM cracks the door and peeps out)*

Pet: If we can get away and get free it'll be just like goin' to heaven.

Tom: *(suddenly)* Here he comes! Here comes Luke!

Sallie: Is he runnin'?

Tom: No, and he don't want to be runnin'. Somebody mought notice him, moughtn't they?

Pet: What about Slim?

Mose: Po' Slim. We'll have tuh look after Slim! But he cain't travel none. *(LUKE enters and closes the door quickly)*

Luke: Ah got him! Got him good, gagged and tied! An' I found Slim in de woodhouse.

Mose: Sho' nuff! Po' Slim—we cain't hardly make it,—but Ah don't see how he can. *(pulling himself together quickly)* Now, you got to do your part, Sallie. Come on, Luke, we'll go hide! Ah'll tell you mo' 'bout it while we'se hidin'! Tom, you go and tell 'em we got away! *(MOSE and LUKE hurry out)*

Tom: *(earnestly)* Sallie, if you ever lied in your life, lie this time!

Sallie: Ah'll lie, all right. I 'clar I will.

Tom: All right, Ah'm goin'. *(He hurries out)*

Sallie: Everything generally happens to a woman, Pet; but this is goin' to be somethin' that ain't never happened to us before in our life.

Pet: Ah know it ain't. They can say sickness is hard and bearin' children is hard; but ain't nothin' in the whole world as hard as livin' in slavery.

Sallie: 'Deed it ain't. If Ah can only lie right and make the master believe what Ah'm sayin' Ah reckon Ah'll be doin' ma part.

Pet: You will be doin' your part. Ah wish there was somethin' Ah could do.

Sallie: You can do somethin'. Get in the bunk and make believe you're 'sleep and Ah'll do the same thing; cause the master'll be here in a minute ravin' like a thunderstorm.

Pet: *(getting into the bunk)* If things work out all right it won't be long before we'll be able to stop sayin' "Marsa," sho' 'nuff.

Sallie: *(getting into another bunk)* I 'clar Ah'll be glad of it. *(They hear the noise of running feet)* Shet up. Here they come, Ah can hear 'em comin'! *(Presently the door is thrown open suddenly and JOHN enters, followed by TOM)*

John: *(to those outside)* You-all wait out there! Shut that door, Tom! *(looking around)* Where's Sallie?

Tom: In the bunk, Ah reckon.

John: *(sharply)* Sallie!

Sallie: *(raising up)* Seh?

John: Come here! *(SALLIE gets out of the bunk and goes to him)* Where's Mose and Luke?

Sallie: *(in trembling tones)* Ah don't know, seh.

John: *(angrily)* Yes, you do know! Stop lyin'! You do know! Tom just told me you did!

Sallie: Ah don't know where they went, Marse John; 'deed Ah don't.

John: *(turning to TOM)* Tom, didn't you just tell me she knowed where they went?

Tom: Yes, seh.

John: *(turning to SALLIE again)* Do you want to be sold down the river in the mornin'?

Sallie: (*pleading*) No, seh; for God's sake, Marse John, don't sell me down the river! Ah don't want to be sold down no river!

John: Which a-way did they go?

Sallie: Ah promised 'em not to tell.

John: Either you tell me the way they went or you'll be goin' down the river yo'self in the mornin'!

Sallie: They said— (*She hesitates*)

John: (*impatiently*) They said what? Hurry up!

Sallie: They said they was goin' to take a boat and go up the river and cross at Moseby's Landin', and goin' north from there.

John: If Ah gets ma hands on 'em they'll wish they wuz north, I'll tell ye! (*He hurries out*)

Sallie: (*to TOM*) Where's Mose? Where's Luke?

Tom: (*going to the window*) Wait a minute, can't yah! Give 'em time to get out on the river! Mose and Luke's close by watchin' 'em, ain't dey?

Sallie: Is they goin'?

Tom: Yes, dey's goin' down to the boats now.

Sallie: All of 'em?

Tom: Yes, and takin' the dogs and guns. You-all better get some things together. But what we goin' tuh do 'bout po' Slim? (*The two women hustle about getting together the things they want to carry*)

Tom: (*from the window*) Now, they're off! Mose and Luke ought to be runnin' in pretty soon!

Sallie: Tom, is you glad?

Tom: Glad! You wait till Ah get away from here, Ah'll show you how glad Ah am!

Sallie: Pet, is you glad? Ah ain't heard you say a word in Ah don't know when!

Pet: Glad! Sallie, Ah'm jes' too scared ter talk! (*She cowers as MOSE enters*)

Mose: You folkses ready?

Tom: Yes, Mose. Wha's Luke?

Mose: I knows wha' Slim is but I done los' Luke. He's a kind a' ondependable niggah, any-how.

Pet: Now, Mose, don't you talk 'gainst Luke. He fixed Jude, didn't he?

Mose: Yas, Ah reckon so—but what's he doin' stayin' so long out dere? We got t' be get-tin' away. Doubt's we get fuh anyway.

(*After several minutes of silent tension in the cabin, the door opens and a lank figure dressed in planter's costume, with a broad-brim hat well down over his eyes, enters. They all cower, but SALLIE shrieks. The man springs forward and stops her mouth with his palm, and discloses himself. It is LUKE*)

Sallie: Oh, Gawd, I thought you was Massa John or someone! What you doin'—

Luke: (*interrupting as they stand out in amazement*) Now folks, 'membah! You-alls my nig-gahs when we get away from heah. You understan'? (*They gradually come out of their stupefaction as the idea dawns on them*) An' you-all's— (*They begin to chorus "Yassuhs" in the intervals of his speech*) you-all's jes' been purchus', understand that?

All: (*except MOSE, who turns skeptically*) Yassuh, Yassuh!

Luke: An' we-all had to turn off de road after Slim, 'cause he run away—an' yo' helpin' me back with him. (*grandiosely and making an effort to talk correctly*) You-all understand that?

Sallie: Yassuh! An', please yo', what shill we call yuh?

Luke: Marse John, of co'se! Ain't dese yeah Marse John's? (*pointing to the clothes*) I done took Jude's keys. (*drawing himself up proudly*) Ah told yo' I had plans. Does Ah look de part? (*They all draw close to scrutinize him. MOSE surveys him suspiciously and spreads LUKE's tie to hide his lack of a shirt*)

Sallie: Lawd a' mussy, you sho' does look like quality! —I hopes we makes it.

Mose: Well, we'se got to try anyhow. (*to the women*) Don't you stan' there lookin' crazy like, come on! Come on, Ah tell yuh, ef you-all wants to be free. Ah'm not 'pendin' so much on Luke's foolin's, Ah'm goin' ta run. Ah am.

(*LUKE with a commanding gesture marshals them all out of the door and closes it*)

Curtain

Anita Scott Coleman

(1890–1960)

The daughter of a Cuban father who purchased his wife as a slave, Anita Scott Coleman was raised in New Mexico and became a teacher. She later married, had four children, and lived in Los Angeles, where she established a children's boarding home. Coleman published numerous short stories and poems from 1920 to 1939, some of them prize-winning, in *The Messenger*, *Opportunity*, *The Crisis*, and *Half-Century* and is one of the few African American women of her era to publish poetry collections: *Reason for Singing* (1948) and *The Singing Bells* (1961).

Wash Day

The rain has hung her washing out
The earth is cool and dry;
Dirty faces are descried in silver pools
Of water as men go by.

Opportunity, April 1927.

Definition

Night is a velvet cloak
Wrapped 'round a gay Lothario;
Day is a flash-light
In the hand of a prude.

Opportunity, November 1927.

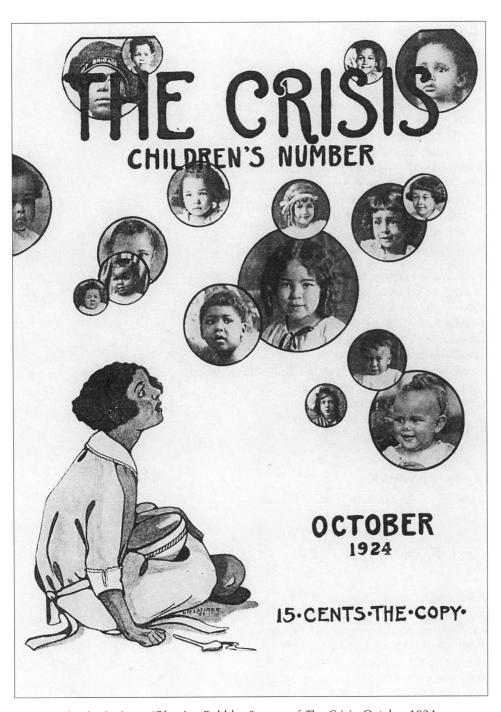

Louise Latimer, "Blowing Bubbles," cover of *The Crisis,* October 1924

Black Baby

The baby I hold in my arms is a black baby.
   Today I set him in the sun and
   Sunbeams danced on his head.
The baby I hold in my arms is a black baby.
   I toil, and I cannot always cuddle him.
   I place him on the ground at my feet.
   He presses the warm earth with his hands,
   He lifts the sand and laughs to see
   It flow through his chubby fingers.
   I watch to discern which are his hands,
   Which is the sand. . . .
Lo . . . the rich loam is black like his hands.

The baby I hold in my arms is a black baby.
   Today the coal-man brought me coal.
   Sixteen dollars a ton is the price I pay for coal.—
   Costly fuel . . . though they say:—
   Men must sweat and toil to dig it from the ground.
   Costly fuel . . . 'Tis said:—
If it is buried deep enough and lies hidden long enough
'Twill be no longer coal but diamonds. . . .
My black baby looks at me.
His eyes are like coals,
They shine like diamonds.

Opportunity, February 1929.

Black Faces

I love black faces. . . .
They are full of smould'ring fire.
And Negro eyes, white—with white desire,
And Negro lips so soft and thick,
Like rich velvet within
Fine jewelry cases.
I love black faces. . . .

Opportunity, October 1929.

Negro Laughter

Negro laughter . . .
  is not the laughter of those others
Who force their distrait mirth
  through thin pale lips.

Negro laughter . . .
  is a stem of joyousness, a hardy tendril
Thrusting through the moraines
  of long distress.

The Crisis, March 1930.

Two Old Women A-Shopping Go!
A Story of Man, Marriage and Poverty

Without a doubt, Nell had Horace on her mind. There was no forgetting the way he had pleaded with her, the night before. She had fallen to sleep thinking of him, not as on other nights when imagery made vivid by love, brought his dear presence near in her last wakeful moments to drift pleasantly through her dreams. No, not that way, but an unhappy picture of him, nervous and moody, penetrated her sleep and leaped to aliveness with her first wakefulness.

She remembered every word he had said, unfair, cruel words; now they formed crookedly and apart like bits of a jig-saw puzzle as she dressed. His arguments repeated themselves:

"Each day, we are growing older—"

Nell leaned nearer the mirror, and scanned her piquant face. Could it be that she really was aging and losing her charm, as surely as yesterday's flowers that drooped beside her in their squat, brown jar. A tiny line brought Nell's brows, silky, high-arched brows like the sweep of bird wings, together. She brushed her hair with brisk strokes, while thinking dejectedly:

"You will be old and gray."

Sudden panic seized her; she would not look for gray strands; no, not yet. She was not old, and she would not allow Horace to hurry her, frighten her into marrying him.

She put on her hat, a little round crocheted affair that she had made herself. She put on her coat and drew on her gloves, picked up her bag, and went out, an altogether lovely colored girl.

The Crisis, May 1933.

Nell thought how many mornings had she gone out, thus. Five years and every morning except Sundays, she had taken this same way: three steps down the cobble-stoned walk to the green latticed gate; half a block to the corner, turn North; four blocks to the car-line; a wait five or more minutes for the car; an hour's ride to work.

Last night, Horace had said, pleadingly. . .

"You'll be worn out, all fagged-to-death and, I—I—don't want the girl I marry worked to death before I get her."

Nell tried to brush her troublesome thoughts aside and quickened her steps, then as quickly found herself agreeing with Horace. She was tired, so tired. Unconsciously, the line that drew her lovely brows together, deepened.

She heard voices, and looking up, she saw two old women come trundling towards her.

One was a very black and very stout old lady buttoned to the throat in a long black coat that fitted tightly about the waist and bulged loosely about the hips. She carried a basket on her arm.

One was a very stout and white old lady with near-white-folk's hair straggling from beneath a brown bonnet. She was buttoned into a red knitted sweater. She wore a heavy worsted skirt, and over that, a white, starched apron that tied around her waist. She carried a black shopping-bag in her hand.

Thought Nell: two old ladies out to do their shopping. Making a lark of it, too, she decided as their high cackling old voices came to her. Said one:

"No suh, they'll never come through what we done come through."

The other old woman tuned in quaveringly:

"Lord, chile, they couldn't begin to do 't."

"Not wantin' 'im 'cause he ain't rich," chimed the first.

"Ain't none of us that, neither," vouchsafed the other.

"The ideas and the whimsies of these 'ere young 'uns do beat me." They broke into high cackling laughter. The black old woman changed the basket to her other arm. The old white woman shortened the strings of her bag.

Then they were abreast of Nell. They smiled broadly upon her. The old mulatto[1] nodded her head until the brown feather atop her brown bonnet danced like a live thing. The black old woman called out: "Howdy!"

"None of 'em will ever stand what we done stood," floated to Nell, like the refrain of a song, as she waited for the car.

Somehow the passing of those two old women changed Nell's day. For the first time, she noticed that the morning was very bright, the sky was blue and tiny knobs of green were putting out on a tree near by.

"They were so cheery, the dears!" she said of the two old women, and sought to dismiss them. She wanted to think of her own perplexities, but the old ladies insisted upon

---

1. A mulatto is someone who is part African and part European ancestry. This character is described as "white," but she is here identified as mulatto. She is likely a person of mixed race who can pass for white.

rising up before her . . . Their cackling words: "None of 'em will ever stand what we done stood," caused Nell to toss her head defiantly. How could they know, those two . . . Old issues that they were! Why, she herself had had her share of trouble, and she was but one of a legion of "young 'uns" as they termed them.

Had she not toiled every day except Sundays for five years, denying herself everything save sheer necessities for a chance to enjoy at some future time the heritage of every human creature, love and home and children? Undoubtedly, she had saved a little, her dowry, she called it, but its amount was written in her brain and on her heart. Tolling off their joint income, dollar by dollar, penny by penny, she and Horace together, was a part of their Sunday's routine.

Sundays, Nell often said, were Horace-days. Horace had Sundays off also, and they spent their one free day together. For the most part they spent the day planning, making schemes to make their dreams come true. While she had merely worked, Horace had slaved; he had scraped together a sum that matched her own savings and there was a little place up-state where he wished to make their home.

He wanted to marry at once, now that the little place was paid for, but then, Nell countered, when during the long years since they had known they belonged to each other, had he not wanted to do so?

As though some of the glow from the steady flame of his adoration reached out to her, Nell felt her cheeks grow hot.

Suddenly, she knew that it was hard on Horace, harder than upon herself. Black men really had tougher sledding than black women, she thought, tenderly. She loved him so, she communed in her heart. That's why she wanted things; demanded them, those things that later, would insure their peace and contentment in their nest of a home. That's why . . . She checked herself, smiling whimsically at finding herself beginning to use all the arguments that she was wont to use upon Horace over and over to convince him that they must work on and wait a little longer.

Then for no reason at all, two old figures lumbered through her consciousness, glimmeringly like moving shadows on a wall.

One very black and stout old lady, one very stout and white old lady said: "No suh, they'll never come through what we done come through."

"Lord, chile, they couldn't begin to do 't."

Nell tossed back her head and laughed. . . . The darling funny old dears!

Aroused from her day-dreams, her slender brown fingers played for a time on the keys of her typewriter, but thoughts of Horace would not down. As the moments sped, her thoughts became laden with foreboding: she decided to call him. It was against the rules, but just this once.

—Employees must not use telephone during working-hours, except emergencies.—

A placard advised her as she dialed. It was [an] emergency, she concluded grimly. Never before had such warning intuition driven her. Never before had a desire to call to Horace through space tormented her as it did now; never before had longing, intense as pain, made her want to stretch out her arms and encircle him, close to her heart . . .

"Horace Canning has quit the company," an ironic voice informed her over the wire.

"Horace—quit—his—job?" Nell gasped the words foolishly and was restored to sanity only by the sound of the faint click striking into her ear.

She alighted from the car four blocks from home. She had not found Horace, though she had verified the information received by telephone. Horace had given up his job, though that no longer mattered; she had lost hers too. She had given it up to look for Horace.

She could not avoid seeing the knot of people gathered on the corner. A cursory glance revealed it to be several boys in their teens and younger mingling with the usual motley street-crowd that is attracted willy-nilly to anything that happens. Intent with her own concern she was hastening on when some horrid cataclysm rushed out to meet her, paralyzing her until sight and sound and feeling swirled and clashed into one agonizing tempest of emotion that sent her running, screaming headlong into the crowd. Horace was in the midst of it, a disheveled funny-looking Horace, but her Horace!

Magically, they made way for her to pass . . . Save for a few taunts—a prolonged "Boo," "Sic 'em, Sic 'em," "Atta Girl," "Geese"—nothing was done to hinder her. Presently she was beside Horace, placing trembling hands upon his shoulder. At her touch, he turned, looked at her a moment, unknowingly, and announced thickly: —

"I need-sh my girl, hic, but she-sh won't-sh have me!"

Nell's grasp on his shoulder tightened; she shook him furiously . . . "Horace, oh Horace, how could you? How could you?"

The crowd dwindled away. As for that, Nell had forgotten that there ever was a crowd. She looked for a taxi. Horace lurched heavily against her, and asked in ludicrous bewilderment:

"Is-sh you, hic, Nellie by-sh any chanc-sh?"

"Tut, tut . . ." said someone close beside her, with a voice whose high old cackle dropped through Nell's dismay like a ray of sunlight into a dark crevice.

"He be your'n, honey, your man?" queried the voice. Nell knew it belonged to the old black woman of the morning.

"Take 'im, chile don't you dast to leave 'im, when he needs yo'," chimed in another quavering old voice.

"Just you take 'im home. A cup of right hot coffee'll fix 'im or a speck of tomatoes will be better."

Without more ado, they were walking together. The trundling gait of the two old women matching nicely with Horace's unsteady steps.

"'Tis a trouble men folks be," offered one.

"But a sweet trouble 'tis," proffered the other.

"Trouble ain't never harmed nary one of us. What's more, us wimens can make men folks what us choose to."

"'Deed so! Us 'tis what makes 'em or breaks 'ems."

Then they performed a tempered replica of their high cackling laughter of the morning. Soon afterwards, they left her, turning off down their street.

The next day, while Nell sat waiting proudly high-headed looking straight ahead, she was not certain that these two old ladies had really joined her. Yet without effort, she could vision the black old woman in her queer black coat and the old white woman in her brown bonnet and red-knitted sweater. Oddly enough, their high cackling old voices still rang in her ears:

"Trouble ain't never harmed nary one of us," made a tune like a Spiritual . . .

"The ideas and the whimsies of these 'ere young 'uns do beat me," was an epitome of the wisdom of old age.

"No suh, they'll never come through what we done come through."

"Lord, chile, they couldn't begin to do 't," was like a skit of Negro comedy and Nell tossed back her head and laughed.

The intangibleness of those two old women enthralled her. Life, too, was like that, Nell mused, made up of intangible veils that became real only as you lifted them one by one, always, to find others and yet others, on and on. Love was one of the veils, so gossamer and fine, so fragile and easily broken. Love was one of life's veils that could never be brushed aside to grasp another. If you dared, once having it, to let it go, it was lost forever. You had to take it when you came to it, but once you caught and held it, it became for all time, a magic carpet.

Horace was coming towards her; tickets were in his hand. The porter was calling their train. Above all the ensuing bustle of departure, she caught the sound of a high, old cackle:

"'Deed so! . . . 'tis us what makes 'em or breaks 'em."

All Aboard!

At last, Horace and she were settled in their seats, on their way to the little place up-state, still short thousands of dollars of what they intended having. But she was glad, oh so glad.

"Happy?" asked Horace suddenly, his arm going around her.

"Happy!" breathed Nell with a great content.

Zora Neale Hurston

(1891–1960)

Zora Neale Hurston contributed to the Harlem Renaissance as a playwright, short story writer, novelist, essayist, anthropologist, musicologist, and folklorist. She is one of the movement's most celebrated artists and, along with Langston Hughes, arguably its most innovative and accomplished writer.

She was born the sixth of eight children on January 15, 1891, in Notasulga, Alabama, but raised in Eatonville, Florida, an all-black town. Her parents, John Hurston and Lula (Lucy) Potts, were both natives of Notasulga, but moved to Eatonville in search of better opportunities. John Hurston found a position preaching and soon became pastor of the Zion Hope Baptist Church in Sanford, Florida, and later served as the mayor of Eatonville from 1912 to 1916. Her mother's death in 1904, when Zora was thirteen, ended what had been a fairly happy childhood. In less than a year, John Hurston married a woman half his age and only six years older than Zora. After a fight with her stepmother, Hurston was removed from the home and spent time in boarding school and with relatives. She eventually traveled to Baltimore, where she lived with her sister Sarah, attended Morgan Academy, and worked a variety of jobs. In 1918 she earned her high school diploma from Morgan Academy and then moved to Washington, D.C., where she studied intermittently at Howard University from 1918 to 1924.

While at Howard, Hurston met Alain Locke, a professor of philosophy. He, recognizing her talent, encouraged her to submit her story "Drenched in Light" to *Opportunity*. It was published in the December 1924 issue, and her career was launched. The following year Hurston traveled to New York City and established herself among the Harlem set. Her story "Spunk," awarded second prize at the first *Opportunity* awards dinner in May, appeared in the June 1925 issue and was later included in Locke's prestigious *The New Negro* (1925). The success of this story brought her to the attention of well-known novelist Fannie Hurst, who hired her as a secretary, and philanthropist Annie Nathan Meyer, who arranged for Hurston to become the first African American sudent at Barnard College. Wallace Thurman selected her story "Sweat" and her play *Color Struck* for the groundbreaking single issue of *Fire!!* (November 1926).

After her graduation from Barnard, Hurston did graduate work with Franz Boas, a renowned anthropologist at Columbia University. Under his tutelage, Hurston earned a grant to collect black folklore in rural Louisiana, Florida, and the Bahamas. (While on this trip, in May 1927, she married Herbert Sheen, whom she had met while they were students at Howard, but they divorced four months later when Sheen returned to medical school.) Besides the training she received from Boas, Hurston also benefited from the financial patronage of Charlotte Osgood Mason, who funded Hurston's travels through the South from December 1927 to September 1932. This support, critical to Hurston's success, had been arranged by Locke, who introduced the two. In 1936, Hurston received a Guggenheim Fellowship to conduct additional fieldwork in Haiti and Jamaica. Hurston's anthropological research provided the material for two collections,

Mules and Men (1935) and *Tell My Horse* (1938), several articles, including her ground-breaking essay "Characteristics of Negro Expression" (1935), and novels, including her first, *Jonah's Gourd Vine* (1934) and her finest, *Their Eyes Were Watching God* (1937).

Hurston's later life was fraught with professional and personal disappointment. Her attempts to establish an academic career at Bethune-Cookman College in Florida and at Fisk University in Tennessee failed. In 1938 she found employment with the Federal Writers' Project. The following year she married Albert Price, a man half her age (he was twenty-three; she was forty-eight), but they were divorced within a year. When her stint with the Federal Writers' Project ended in 1939, Hurston found work, briefly, as a drama instructor at the North Carolina College for Negroes at Durham. (She was able to obtain this position because of her experience working on musical productions throughout the 1930s. She had collaborated on the play *Mule Bone* with Langston Hughes, but the play was not staged during Hurston's lifetime, due in part to a quarrel with Hughes.) Hurston then moved to California, where she was supported by a wealthy white woman while she wrote her autobiography. She returned to Florida in 1942 and taught creative writing at Florida Normal College.

By 1951 Hurston was struggling to support herself as a substitute teacher, librarian, and domestic worker while trying to continue writing. Her last novel was published in 1948, but her publisher rejected subsequent submissions. Hurston's publishing difficulties followed a false accusation of child molestation. In September 1948, she was charged with committing an "immoral act" with a ten-year-old boy—despite being out of the country at the time of the alleged incident. But Hurston's reputation never recovered from the charge, and she published little in the remaining years of her life. She was eventually forced to enter a welfare home in St. Lucie, Florida, and there she died in 1960. She was buried in an unmarked grave at an African American cemetery in Fort Pierce.

Alice Walker revived interest in Hurston during the 1970s and put up a gravestone in this cemetery to commemorate her achievements. This led to a resurgence of interest in Hurston, whose work is regularly taught on college campuses. Her other publications include *Moses, Man of the Mountain* (1941), *Dust Tracks on a Road* (1942), and *Seraph on the Sewanee* (1948) as well as two plays and dozens of short stories and articles.

Wild Women Don't Have the Blues

IDA COX

Recorded in 1924.

I've got a disposition and a way of my own,
When my man starts to kicking I let him find a new home,
I get full of good liquor, walk the street all night,
Go home and put my man out if he don't act right.
Wild women don't worry,
Wild women don't have the blues.

You never get nothing by being an angel child,
You'd better change your ways an' get real wild.
I wanta' tell you something, I wouldn't tell you no lie,
Wild women are the only kind that ever get by.
Wild women don't worry,
Wild women don't have the blues.

Passion

When I look back
On days already lived
I am content.

For I have laughed
With the dew of morn,
The calm of night;
With the dawn of youth
And spring's bright days.

Mid-summer's bloom
And autumn's ripening glory
My youth rejoiced.

And when winter bleak
Spread melancholy 'round
I still smiled on.
And I have loved
With quivering arms that
Clung, and throbbing breast—
With all the white-hot blood
Of mating's flaming urge.

My cool, white soul
Has oft fared forth
In Astral ways,
For none may lag
When star dust hides the earth.

The wings of dreams
Have swept me up
To touch my feet on cloud
And wander where none
But souls dare climb.

Negro World, 1922.

Spunk

A giant of a brown skinned man sauntered up the one street of the Village and out into the palmetto thickets with a small pretty woman clinging lovingly to his arm.

"Looka theah, folkses!" cried Elijah Mosley, slapping his leg gleefully. "Theah they go, big as life an' brassy as tacks."

All the loungers in the store tried to walk to the door with an air of nonchalance but with small success.

"Now pee-eople!" Walter Thomas gasped. "Will you look at 'em!"

"But that's one thing Ah likes about Spunk Banks—he ain't skeered of nothin' on God's green foot-stool—*nothin'!* He rides that log down at saw-mill jus' like he struts round wid another man's wife—jus' don't give a kitty. When Tes' Miller got cut to giblets on that circle-saw, Spunk steps right up and starts ridin'. The rest of us was skeered to go near it."

A round-shouldered figure in overalls much too large, came nervously in the door and the talking ceased. The men looked at each other and winked.

"Gimme some soda-water. Sass'prilla Ah reckon," the newcomer ordered, and stood far down the counter near the open pickled pig-feet tub to drink it.

Elijah nudged Walter and turned with mock gravity to the newcomer.

"Say Joe, how's everything up yo' way? How's yo' wife?"

Joe started and all but dropped the bottle he held in his hands. He swallowed several times painfully and his lips trembled.

"Aw 'Lige, you oughtn't to do nothin' like that," Walter grumbled. Elijah ignored him.

"She jus' passed heah a few minutes ago goin' thata way," with a wave of his hand in the direction of the woods.

Opportunity, June 1925.

Now Joe knew his wife had passed that way. He knew that the men lounging in the general store had seen her, moreover, he knew that the men knew *he* knew. He stood there silent for a long moment staring blankly, with his Adam's apple twitching nervously up and down his throat. One could actually *see* the pain he was suffering, his eyes, his face, his hands and even the dejected slump of his shoulders. He set the bottle down upon the counter. He didn't bang it, just eased it out of his hand silently and fiddled with his suspender buckle.

"Well, Ah'm goin' after her today. Ah'm goin' an' fetch her back. Spunk's done gone too fur."

He reached deep down into his trouser pocket and drew out a hollow ground razor, large and shiny, and passed his moistened thumb back and forth over the edge.

"Talkin' like a man, Joe. Course that's *yo'* fambly affairs, but Ah like to see grit in anybody."

Joe Kanty laid down a nickel and stumbled out into the street.

Dusk crept in from the woods. Ike Clarke lit the swinging oil lamp that was almost immediately surrounded by candle-flies. The men laughed boisterously behind Joe's back as they watched him shamble woodward.

"You oughtn't to said whut you did to him, 'Lige,—look how it worked him up," Walter chided.

"And Ah hope it did work him up. 'Tain't even decent for a man to take and take like he do."

"Spunk will sho' kill him."

"Aw, Ah doan't know. You never kin tell. He might turn him up an' spank him fur gettin' in the way, but Spunk wouldn't shoot no unarmed man. Dat razor he carried outa heah ain't gonna run Spunk down an' cut him, an' Joe ain't got the nerve to go up to Spunk with it knowing he totes that Army 45. He makes that break outa heah to bluff us. He's gonna hide that razor behind the first likely palmetto root an' sneak back home to bed. Don't tell me nothin' 'bout that rabbit-foot colored man. Didn't he meet Spunk an' Lena face to face one day las' week an' mumble sumthin' to Spunk 'bout lettin' his wife alone?"

"What did Spunk say?" Walter broke in—"Ah like him fine but 'tain't right the way he carries on wid Lena Kanty, jus' cause Joe's timid 'bout fightin.'"

"You wrong theah, Walter. 'Tain't cause Joe's timid at all, it's cause Spunk wants Lena. If Joe was a passel of wile cats Spunk would tackle the job just the same. He'd go after *anything* he wanted the same way. As Ah wuz sayin' a minute ago, he tole Joe right to his face that Lena was his. 'Call her,' he says to Joe. 'Call her and see if she'll come. A woman knows her boss an' she answers when he calls.' 'Lena, ain't I yo' husband?' Joe sorter whines out. Lena looked at him real disgusted but she don't answer and she don't move outa her tracks. Then Spunk reaches out an' takes hold of her arm an' says: 'Lena, youse mine. From now on Ah works for you an' fights for you an' Ah never wants you to look to nobody for a crumb of bread, a stitch of close or a shingle to go over yo' head, but *me* long as Ah live. Ah'll git the lumber foh owah house tomorrow. Go home an' git yo' things together!' 'Thass mah house,' Lena speaks up. 'Papa gimme that.' 'Well,' says

Spunk, 'doan give up whut's yours, but when youse inside don't forgit youse mine, an' let no other man git outa his place wid you!' Lena looked up at him with her eyes so full of love that they wuz runnin' over an' Spunk seen it an' Joe seen it too, and his lips started to tremblin' and his Adam's apple was galloping up and down his neck like a race horse. Ah bet he's wore out half a dozen Adam's apples since Spunk's been on the job with Lena. That's all he'll do. He'll be back heah after while swallowin' an' workin' his lips like he wants to say somethin' an' can't."

"But didn't he do *nothin'* to stop 'em?"

"Nope, not a frazzlin' thing—jus' stood there. Spunk took Lena's arm and walked off jus' like nothin' ain't happened and he stood there gazin' after them till they was outa sight. Now you know a woman don't want no man like that. I'm jus' waitin' to see whut he's goin' to say when he gits back."

II

But Joe Kanty never came back, never. The men in the store heard the sharp report of a pistol somewhere distant in the palmetto thicket and soon Spunk came walking leisurely, with his big black Stetson set at the same rakish angle and Lena clinging to his arm, came walking right into the general store. Lena wept in a frightened manner.

"Well," Spunk announced calmly, "Joe come out there wid a meatax an' made me kill him."

He sent Lena home and led the men back to Joe—Joe crumpled and limp with his right hand still clutching his razor.

"See mah back? Mah close cut clear through. He sneaked up an' tried to kill me from the back, but Ah got him, an' got him good, first shot," Spunk said.

The men glared at Elijah, accusingly.

"Take him up an' plant him in 'Stoney lonesome,'" Spunk said in a careless voice. "Ah didn't wanna shoot him but he made me do it. He's a dirty coward, jumpin' on a man from behind."

Spunk turned on his heel and sauntered away to where he knew his love wept in fear for him and no man stopped him. At the general store later on, they all talked of locking him up until the sheriff should come from Orlando, but no one did anything but talk.

A clear case of self-defense, the trial was a short one, and Spunk walked out of the court house to freedom again. He could work again, ride the dangerous log-carriage that fed the singing, snarling, biting, circle-saw; he could stroll the soft dark lanes with his guitar. He was free to roam the woods again; he was free to return to Lena. He did all of these things.

III

"Whut you reckon, Walt?" Elijah asked one night later. "Spunk's gittin' ready to marry Lena!"

"Naw! Why Joe ain't had time to git cold yit. Nohow Ah didn't figger Spunk was the marryin' kind."

"Well, he is," rejoined Elijah. "He done moved most of Lena's things—and her along wid 'em—over to the Bradley house. He's buying it. Jus' like Ah told yo' all right in heah the night Joe wuz kilt. Spunk's crazy 'bout Lena. He don't want folks to keep on talkin' 'bout her—thass reason he's rushin' so. Funny thing 'bout that bob-cat, wan't it?"

"Whut bob-cat, 'Lige? Ah ain't heered 'bout none."

"Ain't cher? Well, night befo' las' was the fust night Spunk an' Lena moved together an' jus' as they was goin' to bed, a big black bob-cat, black all over, you hear me, *black,* walked round and round that house and howled like forty, an' when Spunk got his gun an' went to the winder to shoot it, he says it stood right still an' looked him in the eye, an' howled right at him. The thing got Spunk so nervoused up he couldn't shoot. But Spunk says twan't no bob-cat nohow. He says it was Joe done sneaked back from Hell!"

"Humph!" sniffed Walter, "he oughter be nervous after what he done. Ah reckon Joe come back to dare him to marry Lena, or to come out an' fight. Ah bet he'll be back time and agin, too. Know what Ah think? Joe wuz a braver man than Spunk."

There was a general shout of derision from the group.

"Thass a fact," went on Walter. "Lookit whut he done; took a razor an' went out to fight a man he knowed toted a gun an' wuz a crack shot, too; 'nother thing Joe wuz skeered of Spunk, skeered plumb stiff! But he went jes' the same. It took him a long time to get his nerve up. 'Tain't nothin' for Spunk to fight when he ain't skeered of nothin'. Now, Joe's done come back to have it out wid the man that's got all he ever had. Y'all know Joe ain't never had nothin' nor wanted nothin' besides Lena. It musta been a h'ant[1] cause ain' nobody never seen no black bob-cat."

"'Nother thing," cut in one of the men, "Spunk wuz cussin' a blue streak today 'cause he 'lowed dat saw wuz wobblin'—almos' got 'im once. The machinist come, looked it over an' said it wuz alright. Spunk musta been leanin' t'wards it some. Den he claimed somebody pushed 'im but 'twant nobody close to 'im. Ah wuz glad when knockin' off time come. I'm skeered of dat man when he gits hot. He'd beat you full of button holes as quick as he'd look atcher."

IV

The men gathered the next evening in a different mood, no laughter. No badinage this time.

"Look 'Lige, you goin' to set up wid Spunk?"[2]

"Naw, Ah reckon not, Walter. Tell yuh the truth, Ah'm a lil bit skittish. Spunk died too wicket—died cussin' he did. You know he thought he wuz done outa life."

"Good Lawd, who'd he think done it?"

"Joe."

---

1. Ghost.

2. That is, "sit up" with his corpse through the night, a rural tradition.

"Joe Kanty? How come?"

"Walter, Ah b'leeve Ah will walk up thata way an' set. Lena would like it Ah reckon."

"But whut did he say, 'Lige?"

Elijah did not answer until they had left the lighted store and were strolling down the dark street.

"Ah wuz loadin' a wagon wid scantlin' right near the saw when Spunk fell on the carriage but 'fore Ah could git to him the saw got him in the body—awful sight. Me an' Skint Miller got him off but it was too late. Anybody could see that. The fust thing he said wuz: 'He pushed me, 'Lige—the dirty hound pushed me in the back!'—He was spittin' blood at ev'ry breath. We laid him on the sawdust pile with his face to the East so's he could die easy. He helt mah han' till the last, Walter, and said: 'It was Joe, 'Lige—the dirty sneak shoved me . . . he didn't dare come to mah face . . . but Ah'll git the son-of-a-wood louse soon's Ah get there an' make hell too hot for him. . . . Ah felt him shove me . . . !' Thass how he died.

"If spirits kin fight, there's a powerful tussle goin' on somewhere ovah Jordan 'cause Ah b'leeve Joe's ready for Spunk an' ain't skeered anymore—yas, Ah b'leeve Joe pushed 'im mahself."

They had arrived at the house. Lena's lamentations were deep and loud. She had filled the room with magnolia blossoms that gave off a heavy sweet odor. The keepers of the wake tipped about whispering in frightened tones. Everyone in the Village was there, even old Jeff Kanty, Joe's father, who a few hours before would have been afraid to come [within] ten feet of him, stood leering triumphantly down upon the fallen giant as if his fingers had been the teeth of steel that laid him low.

The cooling board consisted of three sixteen-inch boards on saw horses, a dingy sheet was his shroud.

The women ate heartily of the funeral baked meats and wondered who would be Lena's next. The men whispered coarse conjectures between guzzles of whiskey.

Sweat

It was eleven o'clock of a Spring night in Florida. It was Sunday. Any other night, Delia Jones would have been in bed for two hours by this time. But she was a washwoman, and Monday morning meant a great deal to her. So she collected the soiled clothes on Saturday when she returned the clean things. Sunday night after church, she sorted them and put the white things to soak. It saved her almost a half day's start. A great hamper in the bedroom held the clothes that she brought home. It was so much neater than a number of bundles lying around.

She squatted in the kitchen floor beside the great pile of clothes, sorting them into

Fire!!, November 1926.

small heaps according to color, and humming a song in a mournful key, but wondering through it all where Sykes, her husband, had gone with her horse and buckboard.

Just then something long, round, limp and black fell upon her shoulders and slithered to the floor beside her. A great terror took hold of her. It softened her knees and dried her mouth so that it was a full minute before she could cry out or move. Then she saw that it was the big bull whip her husband liked to carry when he drove.

She lifted her eyes to the door and saw him standing there bent over with laughter at her fright. She screamed at him.

"Sykes, what you throw dat whip on me like dat? You know it would skeer me—looks just like a snake, an' you knows how skeered Ah is of snakes."

"Course Ah knowed it! That's how come Ah done it." He slapped his leg with his hand and almost rolled on the ground in his mirth. "If you such a big fool dat you got to have a fit over a earth worm or a string, Ah don't keer how bad Ah skeer you."

"You aint got no business doing it. Gawd knows it's a sin. Some day Ah'm gointer drop dead from some of yo' foolishness. 'Nother thing, where you been wid mah rig? Ah feeds dat pony. He aint fuh you to be drivin' wid no bull whip."

"You sho is one aggravatin' nigger woman!" he declared and stepped into the room. She resumed her work and did not answer him at once. "Ah done tole you time and again to keep them white folks' clothes outa dis house."

He picked up the whip and glared down at her. Delia went on with her work. She went out into the yard and returned with a galvanized tub and set it on the washbench. She saw that Sykes had kicked all of the clothes together again, and now stood in her way truculently, his whole manner hoping, *praying,* for an argument. But she walked calmly around him and commenced to re-sort the things.

"Next time, Ah'm gointer kick'em outdoors," he threatened as he struck a match along the leg of his corduroy breeches.

Delia never looked up from her work, and her thin, stooped shoulders sagged further.

"Ah aint for no fuss t'night Sykes. Ah just come from taking sacrament at the church house."

He snorted scornfully. "Yeah, you just come from de church house on a Sunday night, but heah you is gone to work on them clothes. You aint nothing but a hypocrite. One of them amen-corner Christians—sing, whoop, and shout, then come home and wash white folks' clothes on the Sabbath."

He stepped roughly upon the whitest pile of things, kicking them helterskelter as he crossed the room. His wife gave a little scream of dismay and quickly gathered them together again.

"Sykes, you quit grindin' dirt into these clothes! How can Ah git through by Sat'day if Ah don't start on Sunday?"

"Ah don't keer if you never git through. Anyhow, Ah done promised Gawd and a couple of other men, Ah aint gointer have it in mah house. Don't gimme no lip neither, else Ah'll throw 'em out and put mah fist up side yo' head to boot."

Delia's habitual meekness seemed to slip from her shoulders like a blown scarf. She was on her feet; her poor little body, her bare knuckly hands bravely defying the strapping hulk before her.

"Looka heah, Sykes, you done gone too fur. Ah been married to you fur fifteen years, and Ah been takin' in washin' fur fifteen years. Sweat, sweat, sweat! Work and sweat, cry and sweat, pray and sweat!"

"What's that got to do with me?" he asked brutally.

"What's it got to do with you, Sykes? Mah tub of suds is filled yo' belly with vittles more times than yo' hands is filled it. Mah sweat is done paid for this house and Ah reckon Ah kin keep on sweatin' in it."

She seized the iron skillet from the stove and struck a defensive pose, which act surprised him greatly, coming from her. It cowed him and he did not strike her as he usually did.

"Naw you won't," she panted, "that ole snaggle-toothed black woman you runnin' with aint comin' heah to pile up on *mah* sweat and blood. You aint paid for nothin' on this place, and Ah'm gointer stay right heah till Ah'm toted out foot foremost."

"Well, you better quit gittin' me riled up, else they'll be totin' you out sooner than you expect. Ah'm so tired of you Ah don't know whut to do. Gawd! how Ah hates skinny wimmen!"

A little awed by this new Delia, he sidled out of the door and slammed the back gate after him. He did not say where he had gone, but she knew too well. She knew very well that he would not return until nearly daybreak also. Her work over, she went on to bed but not to sleep at once. Things had come to a pretty pass!

She lay awake, gazing upon the debris that cluttered their matrimonial trail. Not an image left standing along the way. Anything like flowers had long ago been drowned in the salty stream that had been pressed from her heart. Her tears, her sweat, her blood. She had brought love to the union and he had brought a longing after the flesh. Two months after the wedding, he had given her the first brutal beating. She had the memory of his numerous trips to Orlando with all of his wages when he had returned to her penniless, even before the first year had passed. She was young and soft then, but now she thought of her knotty, muscled limbs, her harsh knuckly hands, and drew herself up into an unhappy little ball in the middle of the big feather bed. Too late now to hope for love, even if it were not Bertha it would be someone else. This case differed from the others only in that she was bolder than the others. Too late for everything except her little home. She had built it for her old days, and planted one by one the trees and flowers there. It was lovely to her, lovely.

Somehow, before sleep came, she found herself saying aloud: "Oh well, whatever goes over the Devil's back, is got to come under his belly. Sometime or ruther, Sykes, like everybody else, is gointer reap his sowing." After that she was able to build a spiritual earthworks against her husband. His shells could no longer reach her. *Amen.* She went to sleep and slept until he announced his presence in bed by kicking her feet and rudely snatching the cover away.

"Gimme some kivah heah, an' git yo' damn foots over on yo' own side! Ah oughter mash you in yo' mouf fuh drawing dat skillet on me."

Delia went clear to the rail without answering him. A triumphant indifference to all that he was or did.

———

The week was as full of work for Delia as all other weeks, and Saturday found her behind her little pony, collecting and delivering clothes.

It was a hot, hot day near the end of July. The village men on Joe Clarke's porch even chewed cane listlessly. They did not hurl the cane-knots as usual. They let them dribble over the edge of the porch. Even conversation had collapsed under the heat.

"Heah come Delia Jones," Jim Merchant said, as the shaggy pony came round the bend of the road toward them. The rusty buckboard was heaped with baskets of crisp, clean laundry.

"Yep," Joe Lindsay agreed. "Hot or col', rain or shine, jes ez reg'lar ez de weeks roll roun' Delia carries 'em an' fetches 'em on Sat'day."

"She better if she wanter eat," said Moss. "Sykes Jones aint wuth de shot an' powder hit would tek tuh kill 'em. Not to *huh* he aint."

"He sho' aint," Walter Thomas chimed in. "It's too bad, too, cause she wuz a right pritty lil trick when he got huh. Ah'd uh mah'ied huh mahseff if he hadnter beat me to it."

Delia nodded briefly at the men as she drove past.

"Too much knockin' will ruin *any* 'oman. He done beat huh 'nough tuh kill three women, let 'lone change they looks," said Elijah Mosely. "How Sykes kin stommuck dat big black greasy Mogul he's layin' roun' wid, gits me. Ah swear dat eight-rock[1] couldn't kiss a sardine can Ah done thowed out de back do' 'way las' yeah."

"Aw, she's fat, thass how come. He's allus been crazy 'bout fat women," put in Merchant. "He'd a' been tied up wid one long time ago if he could a' found one tuh have him. Did Ah tell yuh 'bout him come sidlin' roun' *mah* wife—bringin' her a basket uh pee-cans outa his yard fuh a present? Yessir, mah wife! She tol' him tuh take 'em right straight back home, cause Delia works so hard ovah dat washtub she reckon everything on de place taste lak sweat an' soapsuds. Ah jus' wisht Ah'd a' caught 'im 'roun' dere! Ah'd a' made his hips ketch on fiah down dat shell road."

"Ah know he done it, too. Ah sees 'im grinnin' at every 'oman dat passes," Walter Thomas said. "But even so, he useter eat some mighty big hunks uh humble pie tuh git dat lil' 'oman he got. She wuz ez pritty ez a speckled pup! Dat wuz fifteen yeahs ago. He useter be so skeered uh losin' huh, she could make him do some parts of a husband's duty. Dey never wuz de same in de mind."

"There oughter be a law about him," said Lindsay. "He aint fit tuh carry guts tuh a bear."

Clarke spoke for the first time. "Taint no law on earth dat kin make a man be decent if it aint in 'im. There's plenty men dat takes a wife lak dey do a joint uh sugar-cane. It's

———

1. Eight-rock is a slang reference for someone with dark skin color.

round, juicy an' sweet when dey gits it. But dey squeeze an' grind, squeeze an' grind an' wring tell dey wring every drop uh pleasure dat's in 'em out. When dey's satisfied dat dey is wrung dry, dey treats 'em jes lak dey do a cane-chew. Dey thows 'em away. Dey knows whut dey is doin' while dey is at it, an' hates theirselves fuh it but they keeps on hangin' after huh tell she's empty. Den dey hates huh fuh bein' a cane-chew an' in de way."

"We oughter take Sykes an' dat stray 'oman uh his'n down in Lake Howell swamp an' lay on de rawhide till they cain't say 'Lawd a' mussy.' He allus wuz uh ovahbearin' nig-gah, but since dat white 'oman from up north done teached 'im how to run a automo-bile, he done got too biggety to live—an' we oughter kill 'im," Ole Man Anderson advised.

A grunt of approval went around the porch. But the heat was melting their civic virtue and Elijah Mosely began to bait Joe Clarke.

"Come on, Joe, git a melon outa dere an' slice it up for yo' customers. We'se all suf-ferin' wid de heat. De bear's done got *me!*"

"Thass right, Joe, a watermelon is jes' whut Ah needs tuh cure de eppizudicks,"[2] Walter Thomas joined forces with Mosely. "Come on dere, Joe. We all is steady customers an' you aint set us up in a long time. Ah chooses dat long, bowlegged Floridy favorite."

"A god, an' be dough.[3] You all gimme twenty cents and slice away," Clarke retorted. "Ah needs a col' slice m'self. Heah, everybody chip in. Ah'll lend y'll mah meat knife."

The money was quickly subscribed and the huge melon brought forth. At that moment, Sykes and Bertha arrived. A determined silence fell on the porch and the melon was put away again.

Merchant snapped down the blade of his jackknife and moved toward the store door.

"Come on in, Joe, an' gimme a slab uh sow belly an' uh pound uh coffee—almost fuh-got 'twas Sat'day. Got to git on home." Most of the men left also.

Just then Delia drove past on her way home, as Sykes was ordering magnificently for Bertha. It pleased him for Delia to see.

"Git whutsoever yo' heart desires, Honey. Wait a minute, Joe. Give huh two bottles uh strawberry soda-water, uh quart uh parched ground-peas, an' a block uh chewin' gum."

With all this they left the store, with Sykes reminding Bertha that this was his town and she could have it if she wanted it.

The men returned soon after they left, and held their watermelon feast.

"Where did Sykes Jones git dat 'oman from nohow?" Lindsay asked.

"Ovah Apopka. Guess dey musta been cleanin' out de town when she lef'. She don't look lak a thing but a hunk uh liver wid hair on it."

"Well, she sho' kin squall," Dave Carter contributed. "When she gits ready tuh laff, she jes' opens huh mouf an' latches it back tuh de las' notch. No ole grandpa alligator down in Lake Bell ain't got nothin' on huh."

Bertha had been in town three months now. Sykes was still paying her room rent at Della Lewis'—the only house in town that would have taken her in. Sykes took her

---

2. An epidemic of some sort; slang for not feeling well.

3. "Oh god, and be damned."

frequently to Winter Park to "stomps."[4] He still assured her that he was the swellest man in the state.

"Sho' you kin have dat lil' ole house soon's Ah kin git dat 'oman outa dere. Everything b'longs tuh me an' you sho' kin have it. Ah sho' 'bominates uh skinny 'oman. Lawdy, you sho' is got one portly shape on you! You kin git *anything* you wants. Dis is *mah* town an' you sho' kin have it."

Delia's work-worn knees crawled over the earth in Gethsemane and up the rocks of Calvary many, many times during these months. She avoided the villagers and meeting places in her efforts to be blind and deaf. But Bertha nullified this to a degree, by coming to Delia's house to call Sykes out to her at the gate.

Delia and Sykes fought all the time now with no peaceful interludes. They slept and ate in silence. Two or three times Delia had attempted a timid friendliness, but she was repulsed each time. It was plain that the breaches must remain agape.

The sun had burned July to August. The heat streamed down like a million hot arrows, smiting all things living upon the earth. Grass withered, leaves browned, snakes went blind in shedding and men and dogs went mad. Dog days!

Delia came home one day and found Sykes there before her. She wondered, but started to go on into the house without speaking, even though he was standing in the kitchen door and she must either stoop under his arm or ask him to move. He made no room for her. She noticed a soap box beside the steps, but paid no particular attention to it, knowing that he must have brought it here. As she was stooping to pass under his outstretched arm, he suddenly pushed her backward, laughingly.

"Look in de box dere Delia, Ah done brung yuh somethin'!"

She nearly fell upon the box in her stumbling, and when she saw what it held, she all but fainted outright.

"Sykes! Sykes, mah Gawd! You take dat rattlesnake 'way from heah! You *gottuh*. Oh, Jesus, have mussy!"

"Ah aint gut tuh do nuthin' uh de kin'—fact is Ah aint got tuh do nothin' but die. Taint no use uh you puttin' on airs makin' out lak you skeered uh dat snake—he's gointer stay right heah tell he die. He wouldn't bite me cause Ah knows how tuh handle 'im. Nohow he wouldn't risk breakin' out his fangs 'gin *yo'* skinny laigs."

"Naw, now Sykes, don't keep dat thing 'roun' heah tuh skeer me tuh death. You knows Ah'm even feared uh earth worms. Thass de biggest snake Ah evah did see. Kill 'im Sykes, please."

"Doan ast me tuh do nothin' fuh yuh. Goin' 'round tryin' tuh be so damn asterperious.[5] Naw, Ah aint gonna kill it. Ah tink uh damn sight mo' uh him dan you! Dat's a nice snake an' anybody doan lak 'im kin jes' hit de grit."[6]

---

4. Slang for dancing.
5. "Imperious"; slang for bossy.
6. "Hit the road"; get out.

The village soon heard that Sykes had the snake, and came to see and ask questions.

"How de hen-fire did you ketch dat six-foot rattler, Sykes?" Thomas asked.

"He's full uh frogs so he caint hardly move, thass how Ah eased up on 'm. But Ah'm a snake charmer an' knows how tuh handle 'em. Shux, dat aint nothin'. Ah could ketch one eve'y day if Ah so wanted tuh."

"Whut he needs is a heavy hick'ry club leaned real heavy on his head. Dat's de bes 'way tuh charm a rattlesnake."

"Naw, Walt, y'll jes' don't understand dese diamon' backs lak Ah do," said Sykes in a superior tone of voice.

The village agreed with Walter, but the snake stayed on. His box remained by the kitchen door with its screen wire covering. Two or three days later it had digested its meal of frogs and literally came to life. It rattled at every movement in the kitchen or the yard. One day as Delia came down the kitchen steps she saw his chalky-white fangs curved like scimitars hung in the wire meshes. This time she did not run away with averted eyes as usual. She stood for a long time in the doorway in a red fury that grew bloodier for every second that she regarded the creature that was her torment.

That night she broached the subject as soon as Sykes sat down to the table.

"Sykes, Ah wants you tuh take dat snake 'way fum heah. You done starved me an' Ah put up widcher, you done beat me an Ah took dat, but you done kilt all mah insides bringin' dat varmint heah."

Sykes poured out a saucer full of coffee and drank it deliberately before he answered her.

"A whole lot Ah keer 'bout how you feels inside uh out. Dat snake aint goin' no damn wheah till Ah gits ready fuh 'im tuh go. So fur as beatin' is concerned, yuh aint took near all dat you gointer take ef yuh stay 'roun' *me*."

Delia pushed back her plate and got up from the table. "Ah hates you, Sykes," she said calmly. "Ah hates you tuh de same degree dat Ah useter love yuh. Ah done took an' took till mah belly is full up tuh mah neck. Dat's de reason Ah got mah letter fum de church an' moved mah membership tuh Woodbridge—so Ah don't haftuh take no sacrament wid yuh. Ah don't wantuh see yuh 'roun' me atall. Lay 'roun' wid dat 'oman all yuh wants tuh, but gwan 'way fum me an' mah house. Ah hates yuh lak uh suck-egg dog."

Sykes almost let the huge wad of corn bread and collard greens he was chewing fall out of his mouth in amazement. He had a hard time whipping himself up to the proper fury to try to answer Delia.

"Well, Ah'm glad you does hate me. Ah'm sho' tiahed uh you hangin' ontuh me. Ah don't want yuh. Look at yuh stringey ole neck! Yo' rawbony laigs an' arms is enough tuh cut uh man tuh death. You looks jes' lak de devvul's doll-baby tuh *me*. You cain't hate me no worse dan Ah hates you. Ah been hatin' *you* fuh years."

"Yo' ole black hide don't look lak nothin' tuh me, but uh passle uh wrinkled up rubber, wid yo' big ole yeahs flappin' on each side lak uh paih uh buzzard wings. Don't think Ah'm gointer be run 'way fum mah house neither. Ah'm goin' tuh de white folks bout *you*, mah young man, de very nex' time you lay yo' han's on me. Mah cup is done run ovah."

Delia said this with no signs of fear and Sykes departed from the house, threatening her, but made not the slightest move to carry out any of them.

That night he did not return at all, and the next day being Sunday, Delia was glad that she did not have to quarrel before she hitched up her pony and drove the four miles to Woodbridge.

She stayed to the night service—"love feast"—which was very warm and full of spirit. In the emotional winds her domestic trials were borne far and wide so that she sang as she drove homeward,

> Jurden water, black an' col'
> Chills de body, not de soul
> An' Ah wantah cross Jurden in uh calm time.

She came from the barn to the kitchen door and stopped.

"Whut's de mattah, ol' satan, you aint kickin' up yo' racket?" She addressed the snake's box. Complete silence. She went on into the house with a new hope in its birth struggles. Perhaps her threat to go to the white folks had frightened Sykes! Perhaps he was sorry! Fifteen years of misery and suppression had brought Delia to the place where she would hope *anything* that looked towards a way over or through her wall of inhibitions.

She felt in the match safe behind the stove at once for a match. There was only one there.

"Dat niggah wouldn't fetch nothin' heah tuh save his rotten neck, but he kin run thew whut Ah brings quick enough. Now he done toted off nigh on tuh haff uh box uh matches. He done had dat 'oman heah in mah house, too."

Nobody but a woman could tell how she knew this even before she struck the match. But she did and it put her into a new fury.

Presently she brought in the tubs to put the white things to soak. This time she decided she need not bring the hamper out of the bedroom; she would go in there and do the sorting. She picked up the pot-bellied lamp and went in. The room was small and the hamper stood hard by the foot of the white iron bed. She could sit and reach through the bedposts—resting as she worked.

"Ah wantah cross Jurden in uh calm time." She was singing again. The mood of the "love feast" had returned. She threw back the lid of the basket almost gaily. Then, moved by both horror and terror, she leapt back, toward the door. *There lay the snake in the basket!* He moved sluggishly at first, but even as she turned round and round, jumped up and down in an insanity of fear, he began to stir vigorously. She saw him pouring his awful beauty from the basket upon the bed, then she seized the lamp and ran as fast as she could to the kitchen. The wind from the open door blew out the light and the darkness added to her terror. She sped to the darkness of the yard, slamming the door after her before she thought to set down the lamp. She did not feel safe even on the ground, so she climbed up in the hay barn.

There for an hour or more she lay sprawled upon the hay a gibbering wreck.

Finally she grew quiet, and after that, coherent thought. With this, stalked through her a cold, bloody rage. Hours of this. A period of introspection, a space of retrospection, then a mixture of both. Out of this an awful calm.

"Well, Ah done de bes' Ah could. If things aint right, Gawd knows taint mah fault."

She went to sleep—a twitchy sleep—and woke up to a faint gray sky. There was a loud hollow sound below. She peered out. Sykes was at the wood-pile, demolishing a wire-covered box.

He hurried to the kitchen door, but hung outside there some minutes before he entered, and stood some minutes more inside before he closed it after him.

The gray in the sky was spreading. Delia descended without fear now, and crouched beneath the low bedroom window. The drawn shade shut out the dawn, shut in the night. But the thin walls held back no sound.

"Dat ol' scratch is woke up now!" She mused at the tremendous whirr inside, which every woodsman knows, is one of the sound illusions. The rattler is a ventriloquist. His whirr sounds to the right, to the left, straight ahead, behind, close under foot—everywhere but where it is. Woe to him who guesses wrong unless he is prepared to hold up his end of the argument! Sometimes he strikes without rattling at all.

Inside, Sykes heard nothing until he knocked a pot lid off the stove while trying to reach the match safe in the dark. He had emptied his pockets at Bertha's.

The snake seemed to wake up under the stove and Sykes made a quick leap into the bedroom. In spite of the gin he had had, his head was clearing now.

"Mah Gawd!" he chattered, "ef Ah could on'y strack uh light!"

The rattling ceased for a moment as he stood paralyzed. He waited. It seemed that the snake waited also.

"Oh, fuh de light! Ah thought he'd be too sick"—Sykes was muttering to himself when the whirr began again, closer, right underfoot this time. Long before this, Sykes' ability to think had been flattened down to primitive instinct and he leaped—onto the bed.

Outside Delia heard a cry that might have come from a maddened chimpanzee, a stricken gorilla. All the terror, all the horror, all the rage that man possibly could express, without a recognizable human sound.

A tremendous stir inside there, another series of animal screams, the intermittent whirr of the reptile. The shade torn violently down from the window, letting in the red dawn, a huge brown hand seizing the window stick, great dull blows upon the wooden floor punctuating the gibberish of sound long after the rattle of the snake had abruptly subsided. All this Delia could see and hear from her place beneath the window, and it made her ill. She crept over to the four-o'clocks[7] and stretched herself on the cool earth to recover.

She lay there, "Delia, Delia!" she could hear Sykes calling in a most despairing tone as one who expected no answer. The sun crept on up, and he called. Delia could not move—her legs were gone flabby. She never moved, he called, and the sun kept rising.

"Mah Gawd!" She heard him moan, "Mah Gawd fum Heben!" She heard him stumbling

---

7. A kind of flower.

about and got up from her flower-bed. The sun was growing warm. As she approached the door she heard him call out hopefully, "Delia, is dat you Ah heah?"

She saw him on his hands and knees as soon as she reached the door. He crept an inch or two toward her—all that he was able, and she saw his horribly swollen neck and his one open eye shining with hope. A surge of pity too strong to support bore her away from the eye that must, could not, fail to see the tubs. He would see the lamp. Orlando with its doctors was too far. She could scarcely reach the chinaberry tree, where she waited in the growing heat while inside she knew the cold river was creeping up and up to extinguish that eye which must know by now that she knew.

Color Struck

> *Time:* Twenty years ago and present
> *Place:* A Southern City

Persons

JOHN, a light brown-skinned man
EMMALINE, a black woman
WESLEY, a boy who plays an accordion
EMMALINE'S DAUGHTER, a very white girl
EFFIE, a mulatto girl
A RAILWAY CONDUCTOR
A DOCTOR
Several who play mouth organs, guitars, banjos
Dancers, passengers, etc.

SCENE I

Setting: Early night. The inside of a "Jim Crow" railway coach. The car is parallel to the footlights. The seats on the down stage side of the coach are omitted. There are the luggage racks above the seats. The windows are all open. There are exits in each end of the car—right and left.

Action: Before the curtain goes up there is the sound of a locomotive whistle and a stopping engine, loud laughter, many people speaking at once, good-natured shrieks, strumming of stringed instruments, etc. The ascending curtain discovers a happy lot of Negroes boarding the train dressed in the gaudy, tawdry best of 1900. They are mostly in couples—each couple bearing a covered-over market basket which the men hastily deposit in the racks as they scramble for seats. There is a little friendly pushing and shoving. One pair just miss a seat three times, much to the enjoyment of the crowd. Many "plug" silk hats are in evidence, also sunflowers in button holes. The women are showily dressed in the manner of the time, and quite conscious of their finery. A few seats remain unoccupied.

Enter EFFIE (left) above, with a basket.

Fire!!, November 1926.

One of the Men: (standing, lifting his "plug" in a grand manner) Howdy do, Miss Effie, You'se lookin' jes lak a rose. (EFFIE blushes and is confused. She looks up and down for a seat) Fack is, if you wuzn't walkin' long, ah'd think you wuz a rose— (He looks timidly behind her and the others laugh) Looka here, where's Sam at?

Effie: (tossing her head haughtily) I don't know an' I don't keer.

The Man: (visibly relieved) Then lemme scorch you to a seat.[1] (He takes her basket and leads her to a seat center of the car, puts the basket in the rack and seats himself beside her with his hat at a rakish angle)

Man: (sliding his arm along the back of the seat) How come Sam ain't heah—y'all on a bust?[2]

Effie: (angrily) A man dat don't buy me nothin tuh put in *mah* basket, ain't goin' wid me tuh no cake walk.[3] (The hand on the seat touches her shoulder and she thrusts it away) Take yo' arms from 'round me, Dinky! Gwan hug yo' Ada!

Man: (in mock indignation) Do you think I'd look at Ada when Ah got a chance tuh be wid you? Ah always wuz sweet on you, but you let ole Mullet-head Sam cut me out.

Another Man: (with head out of the window) Just look at de darkies coming! (with head inside coach) Hey, Dinky! Heah come Ada wid a great big basket.

(DINKY jumps up from beside EFFIE and rushes to exit right. In a moment they re-enter and take a seat near entrance. Everyone in coach laughs. DINKY's girl turns and calls back to EFFIE)

Girl: Where's Sam, Effie?

Effie: Lawd knows, Ada.

Girl: Lawd a mussy! Who you gointer walk de cake wid?

Effie: Nobody, Ah reckon. John and Emma gointer win it nohow. They's the bestest cake walkers in dis state.

Ada: You'se better than Emma any day in de week. Cose Sam cain't walk lak John. (She stands up and scans the coach) Looka heah, ain't John an' Emma going? They ain't on heah! (The locomotive bell begins to ring)

Effie: Mah Gawd, s'pose dey got left!

Man: (with head out of window) Heah they come, nip and tuck—whoo-ee! They'se gonna make it! (He waves excitedly) Come on Jawn! (Everybody crowds the windows, encouraging them by gesture and calls. As the whistle blows twice, and the train begins to move, they enter panting and laughing at left. The only seat left is the one directly in front of EFFIE)

1. "Then let me escort you to a seat."
2. "Are you quarreling, not speaking to one another?"
3. The cake walk was a popular dance contest in the early twentieth century that involved couples walking in a pattern to music, usually ragtime waltzes. The winner of the contest was awarded a cake.

Dinky: *(standing)* Don't y'all skeer us no mo' lak dat! There couldn't be no cake walk thout y'all. Dem shad-mouf St. Augustine coons[4] would win dat cake and we would have tuh kill 'em all bodaciously.

John: It was Emmaline nearly made us get left. She says I wuz smiling at Effie on the street car and she had to get off and wait for another one.

Emma: *(removing the hatpins from her hat, turns furiously upon him)* You wuz grinning at her and she wuz grinning back jes lak a ole chessy cat![5]

John: *(positively)* I wuzn't.

Emma: *(about to place her hat in rack)* You wuz. I seen you looking jes lak a possum.

John: I wuzn't. I never gits a chance tuh smile at nobody—you won't let me.

Emma: Jes the same every time you sees a yaller face,[6] you *takes* a chance. *(They sit down in peeved silence for a minute)*

Dinky: Ada, les we all sample de basket. I bet you got huckleberry pie.

Ada: No I aint, I got peach an' tater pies, but we aint gonna tetch a thing tell we gits tuh de hall.

Dinky: *(mock alarm)* Naw, don't do dat! It's all right tuh save the fried chicken, but pies is *always* et, on trains.

Ada: Aw shet up! *(He struggles with her for a kiss. She slaps him but finally yields)*

John: *(looking behind him)* Hellow, Effie, where's Sam?

Effie: Deed, I don't know.

John: Y'all on a bust?

Emma: None ah yo' bizness, you got enough tuh mind yo' own self. Turn 'round!

(She puts up a pouting mouth and he snatches a kiss. She laughs just as he kisses her again and there is a resounding smack which causes the crowd to laugh. And cries of "Oh you kid!" "Salty dog!")

(Enter conductor left calling tickets cheerfully and laughing at the general merriment)

Conductor: I hope somebody from Jacksonville wins this cake.

John: You live in the "Big Jack?"[7]

Conductor: Sure do. And I wanta taste a piece of that cake on the way back tonight.

John: Jes rest easy—them Augustiners aint gonna smell it. *(turns to Emma)* Is they, baby?

Emma: Not if Ah kin help it.

---

4. "Shad-mouf" means shut-mouth, which refers to a quiet person. Coon is a derogatory word for a black person. The derogatory reference is probably used because they are competing against the favored couple.

5. "Cheshire cat."

6. "Yellow" is a slang term for light-skinned blacks.

7. Jacksonville.

Somebody with a guitar sings: "Ho babe, mah honey taint no lie"

(The conductor takes up tickets, passes on and exits right)

> Wesley: Look heah, you cake-walkers—y'all oughter git up and limber up yo' joints. I heard them folks over to St. Augustine been oiling up wid goose-grease, and over to Ocala they ban rubbing down in snake oil.

> A Woman's
> Voice: You better shut up, Wesley, you just joined de church last month. Somebody's going to tell the pastor on you.

> Wesley: Tell it, tell it, take it up and smell it. Come on out you John and Emma and Effie, and limber up.

> John: Naw, we don't wanta do our walking steps—nobody won't wanta see them when we step out at the hall. But we kin do something else just to warm ourselves up.

(WESLEY begins to play "Goo Goo Eyes" on his accordion, the other instruments come in one by one and JOHN and EMMA step into the aisle and "parade" up and down the aisle— EMMA holding up her skirt, showing the lace on her petticoats. They two-step back to their seat amid much applause)

> Wesley: Come on out, Effie! Sam aint heah so you got to hold up his side too. Step on out. *(There is a murmur of applause as she steps into the aisle. Wesley strikes up "I'm gointer live anyhow till I die." It is played quite spiritedly as Effie swings into the pas-me-la)*[8]

> Wesley: *(in ecstasy)* Hot stuff I reckon! Hot stuff I reckon! *(The musicians are stamping. Great enthusiasm. Some clap time with hands and feet. She hurls herself into a modified Hoochy Koochy, and finishes up with an ecstatic yell)*

(There is a babble of talk and laughter and exultation)

> John: *(applauding loudly)* If dat Effie can't step nobody can.

> Emma: Course you'd say so cause it's her. Everything she do is pretty to you.

> John: *(caressing her)* Now don't say that, Honey. Dancing is dancing no matter who is doing it. But nobody can hold a candle to you in nothing.

(Some men are heard tuning up—getting pitch to sing. Four of them crowd together in one seat and begin the chorus of "Daisies Won't Tell." JOHN and EMMA grow quite affectionate)

> John: *(kisses her)* Emma, what makes you always picking a fuss with me over some yaller girl. What makes you so jealous, nohow? I don't do nothing.

(She clings to him, but he turns slightly away. The train whistle blows, there is a slackening of speed. Passengers begin to take down baskets from their racks)

> Emma: John! John, don't you want me to love you, honey?

> John: *(turns and kisses her slowly)* Yes, I want you to love me, you know I do. But I don't like to be accused o' ever light colored girl in the world. It hurts my feeling. I don't want to be jealous like you are.

8. A kind of dance step.

(Enter at right CONDUCTOR, crying "St. Augustine, St. Augustine." He exits left. The crowd has congregated at the two exits, pushing good-naturedly and joking. All except JOHN and EMMA. They are still seated with their arms about each other)

> Emma: *(sadly)* Then you don't want my love, John, cause I can't help mahself from being jealous. I loves you so hard, John, and jealous love is the only kind I got.

(JOHN kisses her very feelingly)

> Emma: Just for myself alone is the only way I knows how to love.

(They are standing in the aisle with their arms about each other as the curtain falls)

SCENE II

Setting: A weather-board hall. A large room with the joists bare. The place has been divided by a curtain of sheets stretched and a rope across from left to right. From behind the curtain there are occasional sounds of laughter, a note or two on a stringed instrument or accordion. General stir. That is the dance hall. The front is the ante-room where the refreshments are being served. A "plank" seat runs all around the hall, along the walls. The lights are kerosene lamps with reflectors. They are fixed to the wall. The lunch-baskets are under the seat. There is a table on either side upstage with a woman behind each. At one, ice cream is sold, at the other, roasted peanuts and large red-and-white sticks of peppermint candy.

People come in by twos and three, laughing, joking, horse-plays, gaudily flowered dresses, small waists, bulging hips and busts, hats worn far back on the head, etc. People from Ocala greet others from Palatka, Jacksonville, St. Augustine, etc. Some find seats in the ante-room, others pass on into the main hall. Enter the Jacksonville delegation, laughing, pushing proudly.

> Dinky: Here we is, folks—here we *is*. Gointer take dat cake on back tuh Jacksonville where it belongs.

> Man: Gwan! Whut wid you mullet-head Jacksonville coons know whut to do wid a cake. It's gointer stay right here in Augustine where de *good* cake walkers grow.

> Dinky: Taint no "Walkers" never walked till John and Emmaline prance out—you mighty come a tootin'.

(Great laughing and joshing as more people come in. John and Emma are encouraged, urged on to win)

> Emma: Let's we git a seat, John, and set down.

> John: Sho will—nice one right over there. *(They push over to wall seat, place basket underneath, and sit. Newcomers shake hands with them and urge them on to win)*

(Enter JOE CLARKE and a small group. He is a rotund, expansive man with a liberal watch chain and charm)

> Dinky: *(slapping Clarke on the back)* If you don't go 'way from here! Lawdy, if it aint Joe.

Clarke: *(jovially)* Ah thought you had done forgot us people in Eatonville since you been living up here in Jacksonville.

Dinky: Course Ah aint. *(turning)* Looka heah folks! Joe Clarke oughta be made chairman uh dis meetin'—Ah mean Past Great-Grand Master of Ceremonies, him being the onliest mayor of de onliest colored town in de state.

General Chorus: Yeah, let him be—thass fine *(etc.)*

Dinky: *(setting his hat at a new angle and throwing out his chest)* And *Ah'll* scorch him to de platform. Ahem!

(Sprinkling of laughter as JOE CLARKE is escorted into next room by DINKY)

(The musicians are arriving one by one during this time. A guitar, accordion, mouth organ, banjo, etc. Soon there is a rapping for order heard inside and the voice of JOE CLARKE)

Clarke: Git yo' partners one an' all for de gran' march! Git yo' partners, gent-mens!

A Man: *(drawing basket from under bench)* Let's we all eat first. *(JOHN and EMMA go buy ice cream. They coquettishly eat from each other's spoons. Old Man LIZZIMORE crosses to EFFIE and removes his hat and bows with a great flourish)*

Lizzimore: Sam ain't here t'night, is he, Effie.

Effie: *(embarrassed)* Naw suh, he aint.

Lizz: Well, you like chicken? *(extends arm to her)* Take a wing! *(He struts her up to the table amid the laughter of the house. He wears no collar)*

John: *(squeezes EMMA's hand)* You certainly is a ever loving mamma—when you aint mad.

Emma: *(smiles sheepishly)* You oughtn't to make me mad then.

John: Ah don't make you! You makes yo'self mad, den blame it on me. Ah keep on tellin' you Ah don't love nobody but you. Ah knows heaps uh half-white girls Ah could git ef Ah wanted to. But *(he squeezes her hand again)* Ah jus' wants you! You know what they say! De darker de berry, de sweeter de taste!

Emma: *(pretending to pout)* Oh, you tries to run over me an' keep it under de cover, but Ah won't let yuh. *(both laugh)* Les' we eat our basket!

John: Alright. *(He pulls the basket out and she removes the table cloth. They set the basket on their knees and begin to eat fried chicken)*

Male Voice: Les' everybody eat—motion's done carried. *(Everybody begins to open baskets. All have fried chicken. Very good humor prevails. Delicacies are swapped from one basket to the other. JOHN and EMMA offer the man next to them some supper. He takes a chicken leg. EFFIE crosses to JOHN and EMMA with two pieces of pie on a plate)*

Effie: Y'll have a piece uh mah blueberry pie—it's mighty nice! *(She proffers it with a timid smile to EMMA who "freezes" up instantly)*

Emma: Naw! We don't want no pie. We got cocoanut layer-cake.

John: Ah—Ah think Ah'd choose a piece uh pie, Effie. *(he takes it)* Will you set down an' have a snack wid us? *(He slides over to make room)*

Effie: *(nervously)* Ah, naw, Ah got to run on back to mah basket, but Ah thought maybe y'll mout' want tuh taste mah pie. *(She turns to go)*

John: Thank you, Effie. It's mighty good, too. *(He eats it. EFFIE crosses to her seat. EMMA glares at her for a minute, then turns disgustedly away from the basket, JOHN catches her shoulder and faces her around)*

John: *(pleadingly)* Honey, be nice. Don't act lak dat!

Emma: *(jerking free)* Naw, you done ruint mah appetite now, carryin' on wid dat punkin-colored ole gal.

John: Whut kin Ah do? If you had a acted polite Ah wouldn't a had nothin' to say.

Emma: Naw, youse jus' hog-wile ovah er cause she's half-white! No matter whut Ah say, you keep carryin' on wid her. Act polite? Naw Ah aint gonna be deceitful an' bust mah gizzard fuh nobody! Let her keep her dirty ole pie ovah there where she is!

John: *(looking around to see if they are overheard)* Sh-sh! Honey, you mustn't talk so loud.

Emma: *(louder)* Ah-Ah ain't gonna bite mah tongue! If she don't like it she can lump it. Mah back is broad— *(JOHN tries to cover her mouth with his hand)* She calls herself a big cigar, but I kin smoke her!

(The people are laughing and talking for the most part and pay no attention. EFFIE is laughing and talking to those around her and does not hear the tirade. The eating is over and everyone is going behind the curtain. John and Emma put away their basket like the others, and sit glum. Voice of Master-of-Ceremonies can be heard from beyond curtain announcing the pas-me-la contest. The contestants, mostly girls, take the floor. There is no music except the clapping of hands and the shouts of "Parse-me-lah" in time with the hand-clapping. At the end Master announces winner. Shadows seen on curtain)

Master: Mathilda Clarke is [the] winner—if she will step forward she will receive a beautiful wool fascinator.[9] *(The girl goes up and receives it with great hand-clapping and good humor.)* And now since the roosters is crowin' foah midnight, an' most of us got to git up an' go to work tomorrow, The Great Cake Walk will begin. Ah wants de floor cleared, cause de representatives of de several cities will be announced an' we wants 'em to take de floor as their names is called. Den we wants 'em to go a gran' promenade roun' de hall. An' they will then commence to walk fuh de biggest cake ever baked in dis state. Ten dozen eggs—ten pounds of flour—ten pounds of butter and so on and so forth. Now then— *(he strikes a pose)* for St. Augustine—Miss Lucy Taylor, Mr. Ned Coles.

(They step out amid applause and stand before stage)

9. A fascinator is a scarf.

For Daytona—Miss Janie Bradley, Enoch Nixon.

(same business)

For Ocala—Miss Docia Boger, Mr. Oscar Clarke.

(same business)

For Palatka—Miss Maggie Lemmons, Mr. Senator Lewis.

(same business)

And for Jacksonville the most popular "walkers" in de state—Miss Emmaline Beazely, Mr. John Turner.

(tremendous applause. JOHN rises and offers his arm grandiloquently to EMMA)

Emma: *(pleadingly, and clutching his coat)* John, let's we all don't go in there with all them. Let's we all go on home.

John: *(amazed)* Why, Emma?

Emma: Cause, cause all them girls is going to pulling and hauling on you, and—

John: *(impatiently)* Shucks! Come on. Don't you hear the people clapping for us and calling our names? Come on! *(He tries to pull her up—she tries to drag him back)* Come on, Emma! Taint no sense in your acting like this. The band is playing for us. Hear 'em? *(He moves feet in a dance step)*

Emma: Naw, John, Ah'm skeered. I loves you—I—. *(He tries to break away from her. She is holding on fiercely)*

John: I got to go! I been practising almost a year—I—we done come all the way down here. I can walk the cake, Emma—we got to—I got to go in! *(He looks into her face and sees her tremendous fear)* What you skeered about?

Emma: *(hopefully)* You won't go in—You'll come on go home with me all by ourselves. Come on John. I can't, I just can't go in there and see all them girls—Effie hanging after you—.

John: I got to go in— *(he removes her hand from his coat)* —whether you come with me or not.

Emma: Oh—them yaller wenches! How I hate 'em! They gets everything they wants—.

Voice Inside: We are waiting for the couple from Jacksonville—Jacksonville! Where is the couple from—.

(Wesley parts the curtain and looks out)

Wesley: Here they is, out here spooning![10] You all can't even hear your names called. Come on John and Emma.

John: Coming. *(He dashes inside. Wesley stands looking at Emma in surprise)*

Wesley: What's the matter, Emma? You and John spatting again? *(He goes back inside)*

10. Flirting, carrying on like lovers.

Emma: *(calmly bitter)* He went and left me. If we is spatting we done had our last one. *(She stands and clenches her fists)* Ah, mah God! He's in there with her— Oh, them half whites, they gets everything, they gets everything every-body else wants! The men, the jobs—everything! The whole world is got a sign on it. Wanted: Light colored. Us blacks was made for cobble stones. *(She muffles a cry and sinks limp upon the seat)*

Voice Inside: Miss Effie Jones will walk for Jacksonville with Mr. John Turner in place of Miss Emmaline Beazely.

SCENE III

Setting: Dance Hall

EMMA springs to her feet and flings the curtains wide open. She stands staring at the gay scene for a moment defiantly, then creeps over to a seat along the wall and shrinks into the Span-ish moss, motionless.

Dance hall decorated with palmetto leaves and Spanish moss—a flag or two. Orchestra con-sists of guitar, mandolin, banjo, accordion, church organ and drum.

Master: *(on platform)* Couples take yo' places! Wen de music starts, gentlemen parade yo' ladies once round de hall, den de walk begins. *(The music begins. Four men come out from behind the platform bearing a huge chocolate cake. The couples are "prancing" in their tracks. The men lead off the procession with the cake—the contestants make a grand slam around the hall)*

Master: Couples to de floor! Stan' back, ladies an' gentlemen—give 'em plenty room.

(Music changes to "Way Down in Georgia." Orchestra sings. Effie takes the arm that John offers her and they parade to the other end of the hall. She takes her place. JOHN goes back upstage to the platform, takes off his silk hat in a graceful sweep as he bows deeply to EFFIE. She lifts her skirts and curtsies to the floor. Both smile broadly. They advance toward each other, meet midway, then, arm in arm, begin to "strut." JOHN falters as he faces her, but recovers promptly and is perfection in his style. [Seven to nine minutes to curtain] Fervor of spectators grows until all are taking part in some way—either hand-clapping or singing the words. At curtain they have reached a frenzy)

Quick Curtain

(It stays down a few seconds to indicate ending of contest and goes up again on JOHN and EFFIE, being declared winners by judges)

Master: *(on platform, with JOHN and EFFIE on the floor before him)* By unanimous decision de cake goes to de couple from Jacksonville! *(great enthusiasm. The cake is set down in the center of the floor and the winning couple parade around it arm in arm. JOHN and EFFIE circle the cake happily and triumphantly. The other contestants and then the entire assembly fall in behind and circle the cake, singing and clapping. The festivities continue. The Jacksonville quartet step upon the platform and sing a verse and chorus of "Daisies Won't Tell." Cries of "Hurrah for Jacksonville! Glory for the big town," "Hurrah for Big Jack")*

A Man: (seeing Emma) You're from Jacksonville, aint you? *(He whirls her around and around)* Aint you happy? Whoopee! *(He releases her and she drops upon a seat. She buries her face in the moss)*

(Quartet begins on chorus again. People are departing, laughing, humming, with quartet cheering. JOHN, the cake, and EFFIE being borne away in triumph)

SCENE IV

Time: present. The interior of a one-room shack in an alley. There is a small window in the rear wall upstage left. There is an enlarged crayon drawing of a man and woman—man sitting cross-legged, woman standing with her hand on his shoulder. A center table, red cover, a low, cheap rocker, two straight chairs, a small kitchen stove at left with a wood-box beside it, a water-bucket on a stand close by. A hand towel and a wash basin. A shelf of dishes above this. There is an ordinary oil lamp on the center table but it is not lighted when the curtain goes up. Some light enters through the window and falls on the woman seated in the low rocker. The door is center right. A cheap bed is against the upstage wall. Someone is on the bed but is lying so that the back is toward the audience.

Action: As the curtain rises, the woman is seen rocking to and fro in the low rocker. A dead silence except for the sound of the rocker and an occasional groan from the bed. Once a faint voice says "water" and the woman in the rocker arises and carries the tin dipper to the bed.

Woman: No mo' right away—Doctor says not too much. *(returns dipper to pail. Pause)* You got right much fever—I better go git the doctor agin.

(There comes a knocking at the door and she stands still for a moment, listening. It comes again and she goes to door but does not open it)

Woman: Who's that?

Voice Outside: Does Emma Beazely live here?

Emma: Yeah— *(pause)* —who is it?

Voice: It's me—John Turner.

Emma: (puts hand eagerly on the fastening) John? Did you say John Turner?

Voice: Yes, Emma, it's me.

(The door is opened and the man steps inside)

Emma: John! Your hand. *(she feels for it and touches it)* John, flesh and blood.

John: (laughing awkwardly) It's me alright, old girl. Just as bright as a basket of chips. Make a light quick so I can see how you look. I'm crazy to see you. Twenty years is a long time wait, Emma.

Emma: (nervously) Oh, let's we all just sit in the dark awhile. *(apologetically)* I wasn't expecting nobody and my house aint picked up. Sit down. *(She draws up the chair. She sits in rocker)*

John: Just to think! Emma! Me and Emma sitting down side by each. Know how I found you?

Emma: (*dully*) Naw. How?

John: (*brightly*) Soon's I got in town I hunted up Wesley and he told me how to find you. That's who I come to see, you!

Emma: Where you been all these years, up North somewheres? Nobody round here could find out where you got to.

John: Yes, up North. Philadelphia.

Emma: Married yet?

John: Oh yes, seventeen years ago. But my wife is dead now and so I came as soon as it was decent to find you. I wants to marry *you*. I couldn't die happy if I didn't. Couldn't get over you—couldn't forget. Forget me, Emma?

Emma: Naw, John. How could I?

John: (*leans over impulsively to catch her hand*) Oh, Emma, I love you so much. Strike a light honey so I can see you—see if you changed much. You was such a handsome girl!

Emma: We don't exactly need no light, do we, John, tuh jus' set an' talk?

John: Yes, we do, Honey. Gwan, make a light. Ah wanna see you.

(*There is a silence*)

Emma: Bet you' wife wuz some high-yaller dickty-doo.[11]

John: Naw she wasn't neither. She was jus' as much like you as Ah could get her. Make a light an' Ah'll show you her pictcher. Shucks, Ah gotta look at mah old sweetheart. (*He strikes a match and holds it up between their faces and they look intently at each other over it until it burns out.*) You aint changed none atall, Emma, jus' as pretty as a speckled pup yet.

Emma: (*lighter*) Go long, John! (*short pause*) 'Member how you useter bring me magnolias?

John: Do I? Gee, you was sweet! 'Member how Ah useter pull mah necktie loose so you could tie it back for me? Emma, Ah cain't see to mah soul how we lived all this time, way from one another. 'Member how you useter make out mah ears had done run down and you useter screw 'em up agin for me? (*They laugh*)

Emma: Yeah, Ah useter think you wuz gointer be mah husban' then—but you let dat ole—.

John: Ah aint gonna let you alibi on me lak dat. Light dat lamp! You cain't look me in de eye and say no such. (*He strikes another match and lights the lamp*) Course, Ah don't wanta look too bossy, but Ah b'lieve you got to marry me tuh git rid of me. That is, if you aint married.

Emma: Naw, Ah aint. (*She turns the lamp down*)

___

11. Dickty is slang for high class, stuck up.

John: (*looking about the room*) Not so good, Emma. But wait till you see dat little place in Philly! Got a little "Rolls-Rough,"[12] too—gointer teach you to drive it, too.

Emma: Ah been havin' a hard time, John, an' Ah lost you—oh, aint nothin' been right for me! Ah aint never been happy. (*JOHN takes both of her hands in his*)

John: You gointer be happy now, Emma. Cause Ah'm gointer make you. Gee whiz! Ah aint but forty-two and you aint forty yet—we got plenty time. (*There is a groan from the bed*) Gee, what's that?

Emma: (*ill at ease*) Thass mah chile. She's sick. Reckon Ah bettah see 'bout her.

John: You got a chile? Gee, that great! Ah always wanted one, but didn't have no luck. Now we kin start off with a family. Girl or boy?

Emma: (*slowly*) A girl. Comin' tuh see me agin soon, John?

John: Comin' agin? Ah aint gone yet! We aint talked, you aint kissed me an' nothin', and you aint showed me our girl. (*another groan, more prolonged*) She must be pretty sick—let's see. (*He turns in his chair and EMMA rushes over to the bed and covers the girl securely, tucking her long hair under the covers, too—before he arises. He goes over to the bed and looks down into her face. She is mulatto.[13] Turns to EMMA teasingly*) Talkin' 'bout me liking high-yallers—*yo* husband musta been pretty near white.

Emma: (*slowly*) Ah never wuz married, John.

John: It's alright, Emma. (*kisses her warmly*) Everything is going to be O.K. (*turning back to the bed*) Our child looks pretty sick, but she's pretty. (*feels her forehead and cheek*) Think she oughter have a doctor.

Emma: Ah done had one. Course Ah cain't git no specialist an' nothin' lak dat. (*She looks about the room and his gaze follows hers*) Ah aint got a whole lot lak you. Nobody don't git rich in no white-folks' kitchen, nor in de wash-tub. You know Ah aint no school-teacher an' nothin' lak dat. (*JOHN puts his arm about her*)

John: It's all right, Emma. But our daughter is bad off—run out an' git a doctor—she needs one. Ah'd go if Ah knowed where to find one—you kin git one the quickest—hurry, Emma.

Emma: (*looks from JOHN to her daughter and back again*) She'll be all right, Ah reckon, for a while. John, you love me—you really want me sho' nuff?

John: Sure Ah do—think Ah'd come all de way down here for nothin'? Ah wants to marry agin.

Emma: Soon, John?

John: Real soon.

---

12. Rolls-Royce, a luxury car.
13. A mulatto is someone who is part African and part white.

Emma: Ah wuz jus' thinkin', mah folks is away now on a little trip—be home day after tomorrow—we could git married tomorrow.

John: All right. Now run on after the doctor—we must look after our girl. Gee, she's got a full suit of hair! Glad you didn't let her chop it off. *(looks away from bed and sees EMMA standing still)*

John: Emma, run on after the doctor, honey. *(She goes to the bed and again tucks the long braids of hair in, which are again pouring over the side of the bed by the feverish tossing of the girl)* What's our daughter's name?

Emma: Lou Lillian. *(She returns to the rocker uneasily and sits rocking jerkily. He returns to his seat and turns up the light)*

John: Gee, we're going to be happy—we gointer make up for all them twenty years. *(another groan)* Emma, git up an' gwan git dat doctor. You done forgot Ah'm de boss uh dis family now—gwan, while Ah'm here to watch her whilst you're gone. Ah got to git back to mah stoppin'-place after a while.

Emma: You go git one, John.

John: Whilst Ah'm blunderin' round tryin' to find one, she'll be gettin' worse. She sounds pretty bad *(takes out his wallet and hands her a bill)* —get a taxi if necessary. Hurry!

Emma: *(does not take the money, but tucks her arms and hair in again, and gives the girl a drink)* Reckon Ah better go git a doctor. Don't want nothin' to happen to *her.* After you left, Ah useter have such a hurtin' in heah *(touches bosom)* till she come an' eased it some.

John: Here, take some money and get a good doctor. There must be some good colored ones around here now.

Emma: *(scornfully)* I wouldn't let one of 'em tend my cat if I had one! But let's we don't start a fuss.

(JOHN caresses her again. When he raises his head he notices the picture on the wall and crosses over to it with her—his arm still about her)

John: Why, that's you and me!

Emma: Yes, I never could part with that. You coming tomorrow morning, John, and we're gointer get married, aint we? Then we can talk over everything.

John: Sure, but I aint gone yet. I don't see how come we can't make all our arrangements now. *(groans from bed and feeble movement)* Good lord, Emma, go get that doctor!

(EMMA stares at the girl and the bed and seizes a hat from nail on the wall. She prepares to go but looks from JOHN to bed and back again. She fumbles about the table and lowers the lamp. Goes to door and opens it. John offers the wallet. She refuses it)

Emma: Doctor right around the corner. Guess I'll leave the door open so she can get some air. She won't need nothing while I'm gone, John.

(She crosses and tucks the girl in securely and rushes out, looking backward and pushing the door wide open as she exits. JOHN sits in the chair beside the table. Looks about him—shakes

his head. The girl on the bed groans, "Water," "so hot." JOHN looks about him excitedly. Gives her a drink. Feels her forehead. Takes a clean handkerchief from his pocket and wets it and places it upon her forehead. She raises her hand to the cool object. Enter EMMA running. When she sees John at the bed she is full of fury. She rushes over and jerks his shoulder around. They face each other)

> Emma: I knowed it! *(She strikes him)* A half white skin. *(She rushes at him again. JOHN staggers back and catches her hands)*

> John: Emma!

> Emma: *(struggles to free her hands)* Let me go so I can kill you. Come sneaking in here like a pole cat!

> John: *(slowly, after a long pause)* So this is the woman I've been wearing over my heart like a rose for twenty years! She so despises her own skin that she can't believe any one else could love it!

(EMMA writhes to free herself)

> John: Twenty years! Twenty years of adoration, of hunger, of worship! *(On the verge of tears he crosses to door and exits quietly, closing the door after him)*

(EMMA remains standing, looking dully about as if she is half asleep. There comes a knocking at the door. She rushes to open it. It is the doctor. White. She does not step aside so that he can enter)

> Doctor: Well, shall I come in?

> Emma: *(stepping aside and laughing a little)* That's right, doctor, come in.

(DOCTOR crosses to bed with professional air. Looks at the girl, feels the pulse and draws up the sheet over the face. He turns to her)

> Doctor: Why didn't you come sooner? I told you to let me know of the least change in her condition.

> Emma: *(flatly)* I did come—I sent for the doctor.

> Doctor: Yes, but you waited. An hour more or less is mighty important sometimes. Why didn't you come?

> Emma: *(passes hand over face)* Couldn't see.

> Doctor: *(looks at her curiously, then sympathetically takes out a small box of pills, and hands them to her)* Here, you're worn out. Take one of these every hour and try to get some sleep. *(He departs)*

(She puts the pill-box on the table, takes up the low rocking chair and places it by the head of the bed. She seats herself and rocks monotonously and stares out of the door. A dry sob now and then. The wind from the open door blows out the lamp and she is seen by the little light from the window rocking in an even, monotonous gait, and sobbing)

Curtain

Nella Larsen

(1891–1964)

Nella Larsen was born Nellie Walker in Chicago on April 13, 1891, to a Danish mother, Mary Hanson, and a "colored" West Indian father, Peter Walker. Her father purportedly died when she was two and her mother married a Dane, by whom she had another daughter, Anna, in 1893. However, Larsen's biographer, Thadious Davis, speculates that Walker in fact did not die, but passed as white in 1893 when their second daughter was born fair enough to pass for white. She contends that Walker became Peter Larson (later Larsen), even though mother, father, and child were all listed as white on Anna's birth certificate. There are no extant records of a marriage between Walker and Hanson, although the couple did apply for a marriage license in 1890, nor is there a death certificate for Peter Walker. Larson and Hanson were married on February 7, 1894. Whatever Nella Larsen's actual patrimony, it must have troubled her to be a "colored" child in a family identifying as "white."

She and Anna attended a Chicago elementary school, where their classmates were mainly of Scandinavian and German ancestry. She then attended the integrated Wendell Phillips High School. From 1907 to 1908, after her family moved to Nashville, she went to Fisk University as a high school student but was uncomfortable in that predominantly black environment. She claimed to have audited classes at the University of Copenhagen from 1910 to 1912; however, Davis contends no records can be found to show that she studied there or indeed ever lived in Denmark. In 1912 Larsen studied at the Lincoln Hospital Training School for Nurses in New York. She completed the program in 1915 and accepted a position as assistant superintendent of nurses at the John A. Andrew Hospital and Nurse Training School at Tuskegee Institute in Alabama. Very unhappy there, she returned to New York in 1916 and worked for Lincoln Hospital until 1918. She then joined the New York Department of Health. In 1921 Larsen resigned to attend the New York Public Library Training School, becoming in 1923 a children's librarian at the 135th Street branch in Harlem, a vital center of literary activity during the Harlem Renaissance.

On May 3, 1919, Larsen married Dr. Elmer S. Imes, a research physicist with a Ph.D. from the University of Michigan. As Imes was a member of a prominent New York society family, the marriage provided Larsen with a high social standing in the Harlem community. In October 1925, Larsen took a year off from her job for health reasons. During this period she wrote her first novel, *Quicksand* (1928), one of the finest novels of the period. She published two stories in *Young's Magazine* in 1926 under the pseudonym Allen Semi: "The Wrong Man" and "Freedom." *Quicksand*, published two years later, was widely acclaimed by reviewers. Her next novel, *Passing* (1929), secured her reputation as an emerging artist of great potential. In 1930 Larsen became the first black woman and only the third black person to be awarded a Guggenheim Fellowship for creative writing, and she embarked on a two-year trip to Europe financed by the award to do research for a third novel, *Fall Fever*. This honor was overshadowed by an accusation of plagiarism regarding her story "Sanctuary" (1930), published in *Forum* magazine. Despite evidence vindicating her, Larsen never seemed to recover from the accusation. Although she completed the novel funded by the Guggenheim Fellowship, it was never published and she did not complete the next two novels she began, *The Wingless Hour* and *Adrian and Evodne*, which she was coauthoring. None of these manuscripts is extant.

She also had trouble in her personal life, suffering a painful divorce from Imes in 1933 after his public affair with a white woman. After her divorce, she moved from Harlem to Greenwich Village and ceased to write; she was supported by her alimony until Imes's death in 1941. Aptly named the "mystery woman of the Harlem Renaissance," Larsen pretended to emigrate to South America in 1937 and withdrew from the friends and acquaintances she had made during the 1920s and 1930s. Larsen lived as a recluse under the name Nella Imes and earned her living after 1941 as a nurse on the night shift at Gouverneur Hospital on the Lower East Side, where she lived and died in a one-room apartment.

Sanctuary

I

On the Southern coast, between Merton and Shawboro, there is a strip of desolation some half a mile wide and nearly ten miles long between the sea and old fields of ruined plantations. Skirting the edge of this narrow jungle is a partly grown-over road which still shows traces of furrows made by the wheels of wagons that have long since rotted away or been cut into firewood. This road is little used, now that the state has built its new highway a bit to the west and wagons are less numerous than automobiles.

In the forsaken road a man was walking swiftly. But in spite of his hurry, at every step he set down his feet with infinite care, for the night was windless and the heavy silence intensified each sound; even the breaking of a twig could be plainly heard. And the man had need of caution as well as haste.

Before a lonely cottage that shrank timidly back from the road the man hesitated a moment, then struck out across the patch of green in front of it. Stepping behind a clump of bushes close to the house, he looked in through the lighted window at Annie Poole, standing at her kitchen table mixing the supper biscuits.

He was a big, black man with pale brown eyes in which there was an odd mixture of fear and amazement. The light showed streaks of gray soil on his heavy, sweating face and great hands, and on his torn clothes. In his woolly hair clung bits of dried leaves and dead grass.

He made a gesture as if to tap on the window, but turned away to the door instead. Without knocking he opened it and went in.

The Forum, January 1930.

II

The woman's brown gaze was immediately on him, though she did not move. She said, "You ain't in no hurry, is you, Jim Hammer?" It wasn't, however, entirely a question.

"Ah's in trubble, Mis' Poole," the man explained, his voice shaking, his fingers twitching.

"Wat you done done now?"

"Shot a man, Mis' Poole."

"Trufe?" The woman seemed calm. But the word was spat out.

"Yas'm. Shot 'im." In the man's tone was something of wonder, as if he himself could not quite believe that he had really done this thing which he affirmed.

"Daid?"

"Dunno, Mis' Poole. Dunno."

"White man o' niggah?"

"Cain't say, Mis' Poole. White man, Ah reckons."

Annie Poole looked at him with cold contempt. She was a tiny, withered woman— fifty perhaps—with a wrinkled face the color of old copper, framed by a crinkly mass of white hair. But about her small figure was some quality of hardness that belied her appearance of frailty. At last she spoke, boring her sharp little eyes into those of the anxious creature before her.

"An' w'at am you lookin' foh me to do 'bout et?"

"Jes' lemme stop till dey's gone by. Hide me till dey passes. Reckon dey ain't fur off now." His begging voice changed to a frightened whimper. "Foh de Lawd's sake, Mis' Poole, lemme stop."

And why, the woman inquired caustically, should she run the dangerous risk of hiding him?

"Obadiah, he'd lemme stop ef he was home," the man whined.

Annie Poole sighed. "Yas," she admitted, slowly, reluctantly, "Ah spec' he would. Obadiah, he's too good to youall no 'count trash." Her slight shoulders lifted in a hopeless shrug. "Yas, Ah reckon he'd do et. Emspecial' seein' how he allus set such a heap o' store by you. Cain't see w'at foh, mahse'f. Ah shuah don' see nuffin' in you but a heap o' dirt."

But a look of irony, of cunning, of complicity passed over her face. She went on, "Still, 'siderin' all an' all, how Obadiah's right fon' o' you, an' how white folks is white folks, Ah'm a-gwine hide you dis one time."

Crossing the kitchen, she opened a door leading into a small bedroom, saying "Git yo'se'f in dat dere feather baid an' Ah'm a-gwine put de clo's on de top. Don' reckon dey'll fin' you ef dey does look foh you in mah house. An Ah don' spec' dey'll go foh to do dat. Not lessen you been keerless an' let 'em smell you out gittin' hyah." She turned on him a withering look. "But you allus been triflin'. Cain't do nuffin' propah. An' Ah'm a-tellin' you ef dey warn't white folks an' you a po' niggah, Ah shuah wouldn't be lettin' you mess up mah feather baid dis ebenin', 'cose Ah jes' plain don' want you hyah. Ah done kep' mahse'f outen trubble all mah life. So's Obadiah."

"Ah's powahful 'bliged to you, Mis' Poole. You shuah am one good oman. De Lawd'll mos' suttinly—"

Annie Poole cut him off. "Dis ain't no time foh all dat kin' o' fiddle-de-roll. Ah does mah duty as Ah sees et 'thout no thanks from you. Ef de Lawd had gib you a white face 'stead o' dat dere black one, Ah shuah would turn you out. Now hush yo' mouf an' git you'se'f in. An' don' git movin' and scrunchin' undah dose covahs and git yo'se'f kotched in mah house."

Without further comment the man did as he was told. After he had laid his soiled body and grimy garments between her snowy sheets, Annie Poole carefully rearranged the covering and placed piles of freshly laundered linen on top. Then she gave a pat here and there, eyed the result, and finding it satisfactory, went back to her cooking.

III

Jim Hammer settled down to the racking business of waiting until the approaching danger should have passed him by. Soon savory odors seeped in to him and he realized that he was hungry. He wished that Annie Poole would bring him something to eat. Just one biscuit. But she wouldn't, he knew. Not she. She was a hard one, Obadiah's mother.

By and by he fell into a sleep from which he was dragged back by the rumbling sound of wheels in the road outside. For a second fear clutched so tightly at him that he almost leaped from the suffocating shelter of the bed in order to make some active attempt to escape the horror that his capture meant. There was a spasm at his heart, a pain so sharp, so slashing that he had to suppress an impulse to cry out. He felt himself falling. Down, down, down . . . Everything grew dim and very distant in his memory . . . Vanished . . . Came rushing back.

Outside there was silence. He strained his ears. Nothing. No footsteps. No voices. They had gone on then. Gone without even stopping to ask Annie Poole if she had seen him pass that way. A sigh of relief slipped from him. His thick lips curled in an ugly, cunning smile. It had been smart of him to think of coming to Obadiah's mother's to hide. She was an old demon, but he was safe in her house.

He lay a short while longer listening intently, and, hearing nothing, started to get up. But immediately he stopped, his yellow eyes glowing like pale flames. He had heard the unmistakable sound of men coming toward the house. Swiftly he slid back into the heavy hot stuffiness of the bed and lay listening fearfully.

The terrifying sounds drew nearer. Slowly. Heavily. Just for a moment he thought they were not coming in—they took so long. But there was a light knock and the noise of a door being opened. His whole body went taut. His feet felt frozen, his hands clammy, his tongue like a weighted, dying thing. His pounding heart made it hard for his straining ears to hear what they were saying out there.

"Ebenin', Mistah Lowndes." Annie Poole's voice sounded as it always did, sharp and dry.

There was no answer. Or had he missed it? With slow care he shifted his position, bringing his head nearer the edge of the bed. Still he heard nothing. What were they waiting for? Why didn't they ask about him?

Annie Poole, it seemed, was of the same mind. "Ah don' reckon youall done traipsed way out hyah jes' foh yo' healf," she hinted.

"There's bad news for you, Annie, I'm 'fraid." The sheriff's voice was low and queer.

Jim Hammer visualized him standing out there—a tall, stooped man, his white tobacco-stained mustache drooping limply at the ends, his nose hooked and sharp, his eyes blue and cold. Bill Lowndes was a hard one too. And white.

"W'atall bad news, Mistah Lowndes?" The woman put the question quietly, directly.

"Obadiah—" the sheriff began—hesitated—began again. "Obadiah—ah—er—he's outside, Annie. I'm 'fraid—"

"Shucks! You done missed. Obadiah, he ain't done nuffin', Mistah Lowndes. Obadiah!" she called stridently, "Obadiah! git hyah an' splain yose'f."

But Obadiah didn't answer, didn't come in. Other men came in. Came in with steps that dragged and halted. No one spoke. Not even Annie Poole. Something was laid carefully upon the floor.

"Obadiah, chile," his mother said softly, "Obadiah, chile." Then, with sudden alarm, "He ain't daid, is he? Mistah Lowndes! Obadiah, he ain't daid?"

Jim Hammer didn't catch the answer to that pleading question. A new fear was stealing over him.

"There was a to-do, Annie," Bill Lowndes explained gently, "at the garage back o' the factory. Fellow tryin' to steal tires. Obadiah heerd a noise an' run out with two or three others. Scared the rascal all right. Fired off his gun an' run. We allow et to be Jim Hammer. Picked up his cap back there. Never was no 'count. Thievin' an' sly. But we'll git 'im, Annie. We'll git 'im."

The man huddled in the feather bed prayed silently. "Oh, Lawd! Ah didn't go to do et. Not Obadiah, Lawd. You knows dat. You knows et." And into his frenzied brain came the thought that it would be better for him to get up and go out to them before Annie Poole gave him away. For he was lost now. With all his great strength he tried to get himself out of the bed. But he couldn't.

"Oh Lawd!" he moaned, "Oh Lawd!" His thoughts were bitter and they ran through his mind like panic. He knew that it had come to pass as it said somewhere in the Bible about the wicked. The Lord had stretched out his hand and smitten him. He was paralyzed. He couldn't move hand or foot. He moaned again. It was all there was left for him to do. For in the terror of this new calamity that had come upon him he had forgotten the waiting danger which was so near out there in the kitchen.

His hunters, however, didn't hear him. Bill Lowndes was saying, "We been a-lookin' for Jim out along the old road. Figured he'd make tracks for Shawboro. You ain't noticed anybody pass this evenin', Annie?"

The reply came promptly, unwaveringly. "No, Ah ain't seen nobody pass. Not yet."

IV

Jim Hammer caught his breath.

"Well," the sheriff concluded, "we'll be gittin' along. Obadiah was a mighty fine boy. Ef they was all like him—. I'm sorry, Annie. Anything I c'n do, let me know."

"Thank you, Mistah Lowndes."

With the sound of the door closing on the departing men, power to move came back to the man in the bedroom. He pushed his dirt-caked feet out from the covers and rose up, but crouched down again. He wasn't cold now, but hot all over and burning. Almost he wished that Bill Lowndes and his men had taken him with them.

Annie Poole had come into the room.

It seemed a long time before Obadiah's mother spoke. When she did there were no tears, no reproaches; but there was a raging fury in her voice as she lashed out, "Git outen mah feather baid, Jim Hammer, an' outen mah house, an' don' nevah stop thankin' yo' Jesus he done gib you dat black face."

Eulalie Spence
(1894–1981)

Eulalie Spence was born on June 11, 1894, in Nevis, British West Indies. When she was eight years old, Spence's family emigrated to Harlem, later moving to Brooklyn. She attended Wadleigh High School in New York City and the New York Training School for Teachers. She graduated from New York University in 1937 with a B.A., and in 1939 she received her M.A. in speech from Teachers College, Columbia University. Unlike most of her female contemporaries who were playwrights, Spence lived in New York City rather than Washington, D.C., and worked until her retirement at Eastern District High School in Brooklyn, where she began teaching speech in 1914 and served as the dramatic society coach.

After writing a number of skits, Spence met W.E.B. Du Bois around 1926 and became involved in the black theater movement. She is arguably the period's most prolific and accomplished black woman playwright. Her work is notable for its avoidance of propaganda and for its focus on the humor of everyday life for black people in Harlem, rather than its painful side; thus, the majority of her plays were comedies. Spence won second prize in the Krigwa Players contest sponsored by *The Crisis* in October 1926 for her comedy *Foreign Mail*. Her comedy *Fool's Errand* was produced by the Krigwa Players, Little Negro Theater of Harlem, and won second prize at the National Little Theatre Tournament in 1927.

Spence's contribution to the Harlem Renaissance, in large part, grew out of her determination to direct and produce plays. In 1929 she directed the Dunbar Garden Players in productions of Eugene O'Neill's *Before Breakfast* and her own *Joint Owners of Spain*. Some of Spence's other one-act plays include *Hot Stuff* (1927), *Her* (1927), *The Hunch* (1927), *The Starter* (1927), *Episode* (1928), *Help Wanted* (1929), and *Undertow* (1927). Her three-act comedy, *The Whipping* (1933), based on a Ray Flanagan novel, was optioned by Paramount Productions but was never produced; this was her last play.

Aaron Douglas, poster of the Krigwa Players, Little Negro Theatre of Harlem, New York City, *The Crisis,* May 1926

Undertow

Persons in the Play

DAN, the man
HATTIE, the man's wife
CHARLEY, their son
CLEM, the other woman
MRS. WILKES, a lodger

Scene: Harlem. The dining room in HATTIE's private house. It is a cheerful room, never sunny, but well furnished and spotless from shining floor to snowy linen. The supper dishes have been cleared away, but the table is still set for one who did not appear. Double doors opening upon the hall are at center back. At right there is a door leading to the kitchen. At the left there are two windows facing the street.

Time: About 8 o'clock one winter's night.

At Rise HATTIE is sitting at the head of the table frowning heavily at the place of the one who did not appear. She drums impatiently with her fingers for a few seconds then pushing her chair back with more violence than grace, rises. HATTIE's dark face is hard and cold. She has a disconcerting smile—a little contempt and a great deal of distrust. Her body is short and spreads freely in every direction. Her dark dress is covered by an apron which makes her look somewhat clumsy. CHARLEY, dressed in an overcoat and hat of the latest mode, bursts noisily into the room. He is a slender fellow, about the same complexion of his mother, but possessing none of her strength of character. His good-looking face is weak, with a suggestion of stubbornness about it. His manner is arrogant and somewhat insolent.

Charley: Ah'm off, Ma.

  Hattie: So Ah see.

Charley: (his glance falls on the table) Say, Ma—Gee whiz! Ain't Dad bin home fer supper yet?

  Hattie: (shortly) No.

Charley: (with a low whistle) Dat's funny, he ain't never stayed out befo' has he?

  Hattie: Not sence Ah married him—'cept—

Charley: (curiously) 'Cept whut, Ma?

  Hattie: 'Cept wunce 'fo yuh was born.

Charley: (with an uproarious laugh) An' the old man ain't tried it sence! Reckon yuh fixed him, didn't yuh, Ma! *(He sits down beside the table and laughs once more)*

  Hattie: (sharply) Ah ain't trained yuh half's as well's Ah's trained yo' Dad. *(She resumes her seat)* Ah shoulda made yuh stay in school fer one thing.

Charley: Yuh had mo' sense Ma! If yuh'd a bossed me lak yuh's bossed Dad, Ah'd runned away long 'fo now.

The Crisis, December 1927.

Hattie: Thar ain't no danger uh Dan runnin' off. He ain't got de nerve. Sides, no-buddy'd want him.

Charley: Now doan' fool yuhself, Ma! An easy simp lak Dad'd be snapped up soon 'nuff ef he ever got it intuh his head dat he could do sech a thing.

Hattie: Dan's a fool, but he knows which side his bread's buttered on.

Charley: (*giving his thigh a loud slap*) Holy smoke!

Hattie: (*irritably*) Whut's eatin' yuh?

Charley: Nuthin'.

Hattie: (*impatiently*) Never mind lyin'! Whut's on yuh mind?

Charley: Oh, nuthin'! Ah jes' thought er sumpth'n dat's all. Say, Ma—

Hattie: Well?

Charley: Ah gotta have five bucks ter-night,—Need 'em bad.

Hattie: It doan do no harm tuh need 'em. Thar's a plenty things Ah's wanted dat Ah ain't never got.

Charley: (*roughly*) Where the devil do yuh think Ah kin git it, ef Ah doan ask yuh?

Hattie: Yuh might wuk 'cassionally. Dan ain't bin home a day dese twenty-five years.

Charley: (*with a sneer*) An' yuh's jes' done callin' him a fool, ain't yuh? The guys in mah crowd doan do no work see? We lives by our brains.

Hattie: Not by exercisin' 'em, Lawd knows!

Charley: How come yuh think we hits de Number ev'y week?[1] Brain work!

Hattie: Ef yuh hits so often whut yuh allus comin' ter me 'bout money fer?

Charley: Ef dat ain't lak a woman! It takes money ter make money!

Hattie: Charley, yuh's gotta cut out dis gamblin'. Ah ain't goin' give yuh no mo' money.

Charley: (*insolently*) Yuh think Ah'm Dad, doan' yuh? Well, Ah ain't! Ah wish ter Gawd Ah knew whut yuh's got over on him. No free man would er stood yuh nag-gin' all dese years.

Hattie: (*coldly*) Dem whut can't stan' fer in mah ways knows whut dey kin do.

Charley: Wouldn't 'sprise me none ef Dad has walked off—

Hattie: (*quickly*) Whut makes yuh think so?

Charley: Reckon yu'd like tuh know, wouldn't yuh?

Hattie: 'Tain't likely whut yuh could say's wurth five dollars tuh hear.

Charley: Whut Ah seen wouldn't ah bin wuth nuthin' las' week, but sence Dad ain't showed up fer supper, it's wuth a damn sight mo'. Yuh'd never guess whut Ah seen him doin' one night las' week up on Lenox Avenue.

Hattie: Well, yuh might's well say it. Yuh kin have dat five, but lemme tell yuh dat yuh'll be de loser, later, if yuh's lied tuh me.

1. Bets on the correct number in a game of gambling.

Charley: Whut Ah's gotta lie fer? *(He stretches his hand across the table, palm upturned)* Hand it over, Ma. *(HATTIE takes a bill from her stocking and puts it on the table, beside her. She places her closed fist upon the money. CHARLEY frowns and draws his hand back)*

Hattie: Ah ain't never refused tuh pay fer whut Ah gits.

Charley: Oh, all right. Here goes. Me an' Nat Walker was strollin' up Lenox Avenue one night las' week 'bout half past six. Right ahead uh me Ah seen Dad. He was walkin' 'long, slow ez usual wid his head bent, not seein' nobuddy. All uv a sudden, a woman comin' down de Avenue, went up tuh him an' stops him. He looked up kinda dazed like an' stared at her lak he'd seen a ghost. She jes' shook him by de arm an' laughed. By dat time, we come along side an' Ah got a good look at her. She warn't young an' she warn't old. But she looked—well—Ah jes' doan know how she did look—all laughin' an' happy an' tears in her eyes. Ah didn't look at her much fer starin' at Dad. He looked—all shaken up—an' scared like—Not scared like neither fer Ah seen him smile at her, after a minute. He ain't never smiled lak that befo'—not's Ah kin remember. Nat said—"Reckin yuh Dad met an ole gal 'er his"—But Ah only laughed—Struck me kinda funny—that! Dad's meetin' an ole flame uh his—Ah meant tuh ask Dad 'bout her but it went clean outa mah head. *(He reaches once more for the money. This time he takes it easily, enough. HATTIE has forgotten it)*

Hattie: *(after a pause)* Was she tall?

Charley: Kinda. Plenty taller'n you. *(He rises and takes his hat from the table)*

Hattie: *(after a pause)* Light?

Charley: So-so—lighter'n you. *(He moves toward the door)*

Hattie: Pretty?

Charley: Mebbe. She warn't no chicken[2]—but she was good tuh look at. 'Tain't no use mopin', Ma. Dad ain't de fus' husban' tuh take dinner wid his girl friend. Funny, though his never doin' it befo'. Well, s'long!

(He goes out and the door slams noisily. HATTIE rouses up at that and starts clearing the table. She has just left the room with the last handful of dishes when the hall door is opened quietly and DAN enters. He is a dark man of medium height, slender of build. He looks a little stooped. There is a beaten look about his face—a tired, patient look. He takes off his overcoat and stands there hesitating. HATTIE re-enters, frowns darkly but does not speak. She places a scarf upon the table and a little silver-plated basket from the sideboard)

Dan: *(dropping his coat and hat upon a chair)* Sorry, Ah'm late, Hattie. *(She does not answer)* Ah ain't had no supper. Reckon Ah'll get it an' eat in de kitchen.

Hattie: *(icily)* Reckon yuh'll hang dat coat an' hat in de hall whar dey belongs.

Dan: *(apologetically)* Sure. Dunno how Ah come tuh ferget. *(He goes out with his clothes and returns almost immediately. He looks timidly at HATTIE, then passes on toward the kitchen door)*

---

2. Spring chicken; that is, she wasn't young.

Hattie: *(fiercely)* Keep outa dat kitchen!

Dan: But Ah'm hungry, Hattie. Ah ain't had nuthin' tuh eat.

Hattie: Whar yuh bin, dat yur ain't had nuthin' tuh eat? *(DAN doesn't answer)* Yuh kain't say, kin yuh?

Dan: Ah went tuh see a friend uh mine.

Hattie: Half past six ain't callin' hours! *(DAN looks unhappily at the floor)* Less'n yuh's asked ter dine!

Dan: It was important! Ah had tuh go.

Hattie: Had tuh go whar? Yuh ain't said whar yuh's bin. *(DAN does not answer)* An' yuh ain't got no intention uh saying, has yuh? *(DAN does not answer. He moves once more toward the kitchen)*

Hattie: *(in a shrill voice)* Yuh keep outa thar! Keep outa mah kitchen! Ah kep yuh supper till eight o'clock. Yuh didn' come, and Ah's throwed it out!

Dan: Ah'll fix sumpth'n else. Ah doan want much.

Hattie: Yuh ain't goin' messin' in mah kitchen! Yuh's hidin' sumpth'n, Dan Peters, and Ah's gwine fine it out 'fo long. Yuh ain't gonna trow no dust in mah eyes no second time—not ef Ah knows it!

Dan: All right, Ah doan' want no fuss, Hattie. Ah'll go out an' git sumpth'n.

Hattie: Yuh kin fix de furnace 'fo yuh go. Ah's got 'nuff tuh do runnin' a lodgin' house, 'thout fixin' fires day an' night.

Dan: Charley was home. Yuh coulda asked Charley tuh do it.

Hattie: Charley doan' never fix no furnace. It's yo' job when yuh's home an' Ah ain't got no reason tuh wish it on Charley.

Dan: Ah'll fix it when Ah gits back. Ah'm hungry now an' Ah's gwine tuh git sumpth'n tuh eat.

(He goes out. HATTIE listens for the click of the iron gate, then hurries to the window and peers after him. The door is opened softly and a little brown woman sidles in. Her eyes rove constantly, always seeking—seeking. HATTIE turns around and glares fiercely at her)

Hattie: What yuh want?

Mrs Wilkes: *(startled slightly at the grimness of the other's voice)* Ah declare, Mis' Peters, yuh sho' does look put out! Anything de matter?

Hattie: *(shortly)* Did yuh come down here tuh tell me dat?

Mrs. Wilkes: *(with an uneasy laugh)* Co'se not, Mis' Peters! . . . It's pretty cold upstairs. Ah s'pose de fire's goin' ez usual?

Hattie: Yes.

Mrs. Wilkes: It's gettin' colder, Ah reckon. *(HATTIE does not answer)* It's warmer down here. As Ah always tells Mr. Wilkes, gimme a parlor floor an' basement any time. Ef thar's any heat goin' yuh's sure tuh git it—Co'se, Ah ain't complainin', Mis' Peters—

Hattie: H'm!

Mrs. Wilkes: See Mr. Peters got home pretty late tuh-night, didn' he? *(HATTIE answers only with a venomous glance)* Thar's a man with reg'lar habits. Ah often tells Mr. Wilkes dat I wish tuh goodness he was a home lovin' man lak Mr. Peters. . . Well, reckon Ah'll be gwine up again seein' ez yuh's got comp'ny.

Hattie: *(with a puzzled frown)* Comp'ny?

Mrs. Wilkes: Thar's a lady tuh see yuh. She's upstairs settin' in de parlor.

Hattie: Who let her in?

Mrs. Wilkes: Mr. Wilkes did. He seen her on de stoop. She was jes' gwine tuh ring de bell when Mr. Wilkes come up wid his key. She ask tuh see Mis' Peters an' he tole her tuh set in de parlor. Ef thar's ever a stupid man it sure is mah husban'. 'Stead uh goin' down an tellin' yuh, 'er hollerin' tuh yuh, 'er sendin' her on down, he comes upstairs an' tells me ter go down an' tell yuh. He'd oughta sent her down de basement do' fust place.

Hattie: Send her down, will yuh? Some fine day, Ah 'spec we'll be cleaned out, ef yuh all's gwine let strangers in de house that 'a-way.

Mrs. Wilkes: *(with a little cough)* Thought yuh might want tuh see her in de parlor. Ah reckon she ain't no thief, not judgin' from her looks.

Hattie: H'h! Whut she look lak?

Mrs. Wilkes: She's tall—but not too tall.

Hattie: *(forcing her stiffening lips to move)* Light?

Mrs. Wilkes: Lighter'n yuh an' me—

Hattie: *(with a supreme effort)* Pretty?

Mrs. Wilkes: Well, yuh knows her all right! She ain't never bin here befo' ez Ah knows— but yuh knows her frum de way yuh's 'scribed her. Well, 'slong! Ah'll send her down. *(She opens the hall door)* B'r! *(She shivers)* Dis hall cert'nly is cold!

(The door closes after her. For a moment HATTIE looks bewildered. But only for a moment. With a sudden harsh laugh she rips the apron from about her waist and pushes it quickly into the side-board drawer. She goes up to the mirror over the mantle, but one look at herself is all that she can bear. As she turns sharply away the door opens and CLEM enters. In one glance HATTIE's burning eyes take in the tall, well-dressed figure. The graying hair, the youthful face. If CLEM's glance is less piercing, it is nevertheless just as comprehensive)

Clem: *(softly)* It's bin a long time, Hattie. *(HATTIE opens her lips to speak, but she doesn't. She sits, rather heavily, and continues to stare at CLEM)* Ah doan' wonder yuh's sprised Hattie. *(She hesitates and then drawing up a chair facing HATTIE, she too sits.)* Ah know yuh's waitin' tuh hear whut brought me. . . . It's a long story, Hattie. *(At that, HATTIE moves impatiently)*

Hattie: Yuh kin start—at de end—

Clem: At de end?

Hattie: At de end. Whut yuh come fer? Yuh's come ter git sumpth'n—Is it—Dan?

Clem: *(leaning back in her chair with a sigh)* De same ole Hattie! De years ain't changed yuh, none.

Hattie: *(with a bitter laugh)* An' de years ain't changed *you,* none.

Clem: Yes. Ah reckon they has, Hattie, Ah's suffered a-plenty.

Hattie: *(with a curl of her lip)* An' yuh think dat yuh's de only one?

Clem: Oh no! Ah kin see yuh's not bin over happy, Hattie, an' Ah knows dat Dan ain't bin happy.

Hattie: Whut reason yuh got ter bring up all dis talk 'bout suff'rin'? Yuh bin seein' Dan agin, ain't yuh?

Clem: Yes. Ah met him jes' by accident one night las' week.

Hattie: An' yuh's bin seein' him sence?

Clem: Yes, ev'y night. Ah's bein' gwine down town ter meet him 'roun six o'clock an' Ah's ride home wid him in de "L."[3]

Hattie: An' tuh-night yuh had him out tuh dinner. *(HATTIE's voice has a deadly calm)*

Clem: No. Tuh-night Ah couldn' go tuh meet him. Ah was called away on business. Ah ain't seen him tuh-night.

Hattie: Did he know yuh was comin' here?

Clem: No.

Hattie: Why'nt yuh tell him, yuh was comin'.

Clem: He wouldn' 'er let me come.

Hattie: Well, say whut yuh's come fer, an' go. It ain't easy settin' here an' listenin' tuh yuh talkin' 'bout Dan.

Clem: *(abruptly)* Yuh's almost driv' him crazy. An' yuh said yuh loved him. *(HATTIE's fingers clench slowly)*

Hattie: Whar'd yuh go to? Whar you bin all dese years?

Clem: South—Virginia, whar I come frum.

Hattie: H'm!

Clem: Ef Ah'd knowed yuh was gwine tuh be unkind tuh him, Ah'd never let him go! Dan ain't knowed a day's happiness since Ah went away.

Hattie: He—he tole yuh dat?

Clem: Yes! Ah kin fergive yuh fer takin' him 'way frum me—an' de way yuh done it—but it ain't easy fergivin' yuh fer makin' him suffer.

Hattie: An' dat's whut yuh's come here tuh tell me?

Clem: *(passionately)* Dan's dyin' here, right under yo' eyes, an' yo' doan see it. He's dyin' fer kindness—he's dyin' frum hard wuk. He's dyin' frum de want uv love. Ah could allus read him lak a book. He won't talk 'gainst yuh, Hattie, but Ah kin see it all in de way he looks—in de way he looks at me. *(CLEM dabs at her eyes with her handkerchief)*

Hattie: Go on. *(She marvels at her own quietness)*

3. The elevated subway line.

Clem: (accusingly) He's shabby—all uv him—hat an' shoes an' coat. Ef he had one suit fer ev'y five dat yuh son has, he'd be pretty well dressed.

Hattie: (slowly) Yuh fergit, Charley is Dan's son ez well ez mine.

Clem: An' yuh's set him 'gainst his dad. He sides with yuh ev'y time, doan' he?

Hattie: (with a faint sneer) Did yuh read dat too, in de way Dan—looked—at yuh?

Clem: Ef yuh had a brought Charley up diff'rent yuh mighta held on tuh Dan. 'Stead uh dat, yuh's brought him up tuh look down on him.

Hattie: (She is breathing heavily, her voice comes thick and choked) Is yuh tru?[4] *(rises)*

Clem: Yuh doan' need Dan an yo' son doan' need him. Well, sence yuh ain't got no use fer him, Ah's gwine take him frum yuh, Hattie. Now yuh knows why Ah's come. *(She rises also and looks down at HATTIE, much to the latter's disadvantage)*

Hattie: (forcing the words out, as though each one pains her) Funny—how—thoughtful yuh's got sence Ah's las' seen yuh. Yuh come inta mah house twenty years ago as a frien'—an' yuh took Dan when Ah hadn't bin married ter him a year. Yuh didn' give no 'nouncement den 'bout whut yuh was gwine ter do. Yuh jes' took him—an' me expectin' tuh be de mother uv his chile. Gawd! *(A deep shudder runs through her body)* But now—dat yuh's got mo' stylish—mo' lady-like in yuh ways yuh come tuh tell me ve'y politely, dat yuh's gwine tuh take him agin. Is it mah blessin' yuh's waitin' fer? Yuh doan' need no permission.

Clem: Yuh, yuh doan' un'erstan'—Yuh never did un'erstan' Hattie.

Hattie: Mebbe not. Some things is hard tuh un'erstan'.

Clem: Co'se Dan an' me could go off tergether, 'thout yuh permission. Yuh knows dat well 'nuff. It's bein' done ev'y day. But we doan' want ter go lak dat.

Hattie: Yuh mean Dan doan' want ter go that 'a-way!

Clem: Yuh's wrong, Hattie. Dan ain't thinkin' 'er nuthin' 'er nobuddy but me. He's fer quittin' an' never sayin' a word tuh yuh but jes' goin' off, me an' him together. But Ah ain't gwine tuh go lak dat. Dis time it's gotta be diff'rent.

Hattie: Diff'rent—how?

Clem: Hattie, Ah wants yuh tuh free Dan. Yuh owes it tuh him. He ain't never bin free sence he's knowed yuh. Will yuh free him?

Hattie: Free him—how?

Clem: Give him a devo'ce.

Hattie: A devo'ce—tuh marry you?

Clem: (pleadingly) Yes. 'Taint lak yuh loved him Hattie. Ef yuh loved him Ah couldn' ask yuh. But yuh only holds onta him tru spite—Yuh hates him, mebbe—Yuh treats him lak yuh does.

Hattie: Yuh knows Ah kain't keep him ef he wants tuh go. Reckon Ah knows it, too. Well, ef he wants tuh go he kin go.

Clem: (with an exclamation of relief) Thank Gawd! Ah didn' think yuh'd do it, Hattie.

4. "Are you through," finished?

Hattie: Yuh coulda spared yuhself de trubble comin' here—an' jes' gone off. It woulda bin more lak yuh.

Clem: But—but—how? Yuh'd have ter know 'bout de devo'ce, Hattie.

Hattie: Devo'ce? Ah ain't said nuthin' 'bout gettin' no devo'ce!

Clem: But—but—yuh—Ah thought—Whut yuh mean, Hattie?

Hattie: Yuh didn' need no devo'ce de fust time, did yuh?

Clem: (biting her lips to keep back the tears) Dat—dat was diff'rent.

Hattie: Ah doan' see it.

Clem: Well, it was. It's gotta be a devo'ce dis time.

Hattie: Ah see Dan's morals has improved some sence you went away.

Clem: It ain't Dan whut's holdin' out fer devo'ce—It's—it's me.

Hattie: (HATTIE's laugh has a bitter edge) Den it's yo' morals dat's bin improvin'—Well, dey could stan' improvin' a-plenty. (The fierce edge returns suddenly to her voice) Yuh's wastin' yo' time an' mine an' Dan's! 'Bout lettin' him go—He coulda gone all dese years—Ah warn't holdin' him back! He'd gone too, ef he'd knowed whar to find yuh. Ah knowed ef he ever found yuh, he'd leave me. Well, he didn' find yuh tell now. But long's Ah's got breaf tuh breathe, Ah ain't gwine say "Yes!" 'bout no devo'ce. Ef he kin git one 'thout me, let him git it! Yuh hear me? Now ef yuh's tru, yuh better get outa here. Ah ain't 'sponsible fer whut Ah says frum now on!

Clem: Hattie, 'fore Gawd, yuh's hard!

Hattie: Ah was soft 'nuff, when yuh fust stepped on me. Ef Ah's hard now, 'tis yo' fault!

Clem: Hattie—Ah ain't tole yuh de real reason why Ah wants dat devo'ce— (a note of despair has crept into her voice)

Hattie: No? Well, Ah ain't in'trested none.

Clem: Still Ah wants yuh tuh hear! It's sumpthin' dat Ah ain't tole Dan. (The door is opened quietly and DAN enters. He starts—looks fearfully from CLEM to HATTIE and then back again to CLEM) Come in, Dan. Ah hope yuh doan' mind ma comin' tuh see Hattie. Ah jes' had tuh come.

Dan: (swallowing painfully) It won' do no good. (HATTIE is gazing at him curiously)

Clem: Mebbe not, but Ah had tuh come.

Dan: Ah'm sorry, Hattie. We—we— (He turns away as if ashamed)

Clem: Hattie knows ev'ything Dan. Ah's tole her. (DAN turns toward her)

Dan: Clem, whut was yuh sayin' when Ah come on in? Ah heard yuh—

Clem: (embarrassed) Ah didn' want tuh tell yuh—lak dis—

Dan: (gently) We kain't go back now, Clem. Sence we's in de middle we's gotta git tru, somehow.

Clem: (turning from him to HATTIE) Ah didn' mean tuh beg, 'less'n Ah had tuh—

Hattie: (coldly) Yuh doan' have tuh—

Clem: Ef 'twas only me—but it ain't. It's fer mah Lucy, —Dan's chile *(There is a terrible silence)* Dan's chile—Ah didn' tell yuh, Hattie, an' Ah didn' tell Dan. Whut woulda bin de use? She's a woman now an' good—an' pretty. She thinks her dad died when she was a baby an' she thinks—she thinks—Ah'm a good woman. She's proud uh me. *(As if unconscious of HATTIE's presence, DAN grips CLEM's hands. They look at each other)*

Hattie: *(as if to herself. She seems to be trying to get it all quite clear)* She thinks yuh's a good woman! An' dat's why yuh expects me tuh give Dan a devo'ce.

Clem: *(eagerly)* Yes, Yes! Yuh see, doan' yuh?

Hattie: Yes, Ah see. Gawd, ef dat ain't funny! She thinks yuh's a good woman. *(She laughs loudly,—hysterically)* Oh, my Gawd!

Dan: *(sharply)* Hattie!

Hattie: *(ignoring him)* Tell me mo'—'bout dis—dis new relation, uh Dan's.

Clem: Ah's wuked hard tuh git her de chances Ah didn' have. She's bin tuh school—she's got an eddication. An' now she's goin' tuh git married tuh a fine feller whut'll be able tuh take care uv her. Now yuh see dat Ah kain't jes' go off wid Dan. It's got tuh be proper—a devo'ce an' all. Yuh see, doan' yuh, Hattie?

Hattie: *(nodding)* Mother an' daughter—double weddin'.

Clem: *(anxiously)* An yuh'll do it, Hattie? Gawd'll bless yuh, Hattie.

Hattie: *(derisively)* How come *you's* passin' on blessin's? Yuh knows a lot, doan' yuh 'bout blessin's? Wonder ef yuh knows ez much 'bout curses?

Clem: Now, Hattie—

Hattie: *(darkly)* Yuh doan' know nuthin' much 'bout curses, does yuh? Well, yuh's cursed, Clem Jackson! Cursed! Yuh's allus bin cursed sence de day yuh cast yuh eyes on Dan!

Dan: *(harshly)* Hattie, yuh ain't got no call tuh go on lak dat.

Hattie: *(who does not seem to hear him)* Dan was cursed when he set eyes on yuh. An' Ah was cursed when Ah took yuh fer a frien'.

Clem: *(hurriedly)* Ah'm goin', Hattie! Ah see yuh ain't gwine give in.

Hattie: Whut's yuh hurry? Yuh better hear whut Ah's gwine tuh say . . . Curses. Yes, we's all bin cursed, Clem. Mah Charley's cursed an' yo' Lucy—too bad.

Clem: *(angrily)* Doan' yuh call mah Lucy's name 'long uv yours.

Hattie: *(with a sneer)* Too bad. Wonder how she'll feel when she hears whut a good woman yuh is?

Clem: *(shrinking as if from a blow)* Whut? Yuh—yuh wouldn'—yuh wouldn'—

Hattie: Wouldn'— wouldn'— *(She laughs again—crazily)* Sure, Ah'll fine her! Ef it takes de rest uh mah life, Ah'll fine her. It's too good—tuh keep. How she'll stare when she knows her ma was a prostitute an' her dad—

Dan: *(hoarsely)* Damn yuh, Hattie! Doan' yuh say no mo'.

Hattie: Ah'll tell her all—all—leavin' out nuthin'.

Clem: *(pleading as if for life)* Yuh couldn', Hattie! Yuh couldn'! Hattie—Hattie—

Hattie: How she play me false—when Ah trusted her—an' how she lie tuh me—How she ruin' mah life—an' come on back tuh take de leavin's once more—

Dan: Doan' yuh say no mo, Hattie!

Hattie: Yuh'd shut mah mouf wouldn' yuh? How? How—

Dan: Let's go, Clem. Let's go—

Hattie: (*shrilly*) G'wan. Is Ah keepin' yuh? Take yuh street walker back whar she come frum. Yuh kin give Lucy mah regahds. Tell her dat a frien's gwine call on her— real soon—an' ole frien' uv her ma's.

Dan: (*with a cry of rage, grips Hattie by the shoulder and shakes her*) Yoh'll shut yo' mouf, Hattie. Promise, 'er 'fo' Gawd-A-Mighty.

Hattie: (*scornfully*) How yuh's thinkin' 'er shuttin' mah mouf, Dan Peters?

Dan: Yuh'll keep 'way frum Lucy. Yuh'll promise not tuh say nuthin' 'bout Clem. (*DAN shakes her again roughly*)

Hattie: (*her speech broken with little gasping cries*) Never! An' yuh kain't make me! Ah'll tell her 'bout dis good woman! Dis thief! Dis dirty minded whore! (*Without a word, DAN grips her by the throat and forces her back—back against the table. Her arms claw awkwardly and then drop to her sides. CLEM utters a low cry and springs upon DAN, tearing wildly at his fingers*)

Clem: Dan! Leggo! Leggo, fer Gawd's sake! Dan! (*With a violent movement of disgust he thrusts HATTIE from him. She falls heavily from the chair, her head striking the marble base of the mantle—an ugly sound. She lies very still. DAN looks at her stupidly. CLEM throws her arms about his neck, sobbing hysterically*) Dan! Dan! Yuh come near killin' her!

Dan: (*breathing heavily*) Ah'd a done it too, ef yuh hadn't bin thar.

Clem: (*stooping over HATTIE*) She hit her head an awful crack!

Dan: Hattie's head's harder'n mos'. Come on, Clem. We kain't stay here, now. She'll be comin' to, 'fo long! An raisin' de roof.

Clem: (*who is still peering at HATTIE*) Dan, thar's blood comin' out de corner uv her mouf.

Dan: She'll be waggin' it again 'fo yuh knows it.

Clem: (*going up to DAN and putting her hand on his shoulder*) Dan, Ah wish yuh hadn't done it! 'Twon' do no good!

Dan: Ah couldn' stan' it no longer. Ah clean los' mah head when she call yuh—whut she did.

Clem: Yes, Ah know. Poor Danny boy! Ah doan' see how yuh's stood it all dese years.

Dan: (*putting his arms about her*) Ah was allus thinkin' uv yuh, Clem. Yuh shouldn' 'a lef' me behin'. Yuh'd oughta tole me whar tuh fine yuh. Yuh shoulda tole me 'bout Lucy.

Clem: Yes, Ah see dat now. But yuh b'longed tuh Hattie 'n Ah thought—

Dan: Ah never b'longed tuh Hattie. (*He kisses her*) Let's go, Clem. (*She draws away from him*) Why, whut's wrong?

Clem: Ah's gotta think uh Lucy.

Dan: Lucy?

Clem: Yes, Lucy. She's yo' chile Dan, an' she doan' know—'bout us.

Dan: An' me—Whut 'bout me, an' you—Clem—Clem—

Clem: Ah you musn'. Then thar's Hattie. Yuh's gotta think uv Hattie— *(They both turn and look at the figure huddled there on the floor)* Dan, we'd better try'n bring her to. Get some water, Dan.

Dan: Ah won't touch her!

Clem: It ain't human leavin' her lak dat. Help me lif' her, Dan. She'll catch her death uh cold on dat flo'! *(Very unwillingly DAN assists. Together he and CLEM get HATTIE into a chair. Her head lolls persistently to one side. CLEM rubs her hands)* Lak ice! Why, Dan, her fingers all stiff! An'—an' Dan! Feel her pulse! Dan!

(She draws back terrified. HATTIE's body, unsupported, sags awkwardly against the table. DAN quickly seizes her hands, feeling her pulse. He tilts her head backward, looks into her face—feels her heart, then straightens up—his face distorted, his eyes blank)

Clem: *(in a whisper)* Dan—she ain't—dead?

Dan: Dead. *(He looks down at his hands in horror)*

Clem: *(wildly)* Dan! Whut'll we do! Whut'll we do!

Dan: Yuh'll go back tuh Lucy. She needs yuh.

Clem: You needs me mo', Dan!

Dan: Yuh kain't help none! Ah doan' stan' no chance—reckon Ah owes it tuh Lucy tuh send yuh back tuh her. Ah ain't never had de chance tuh do nuthin' fer her—but dis.

Clem: Ah kain't go, Dan! Doan' mek me. *(Her body is wracked with sobs)*

Dan: *(taking her in his arms and kissing her)* We's gotta think 'bout Lucy—We's brung each other bad luck, Clem. Hattie was right.

Clem: But Ah loved yuh Dan, an' yuh loved me.

Dan: Ah ain't never loved nobuddy else.

Clem: Whut'll dey do tuh yuh Dan? Dey won't kill yuh? *(She clings tightly to him)* Will dey, Dan?

Dan: Co'se not, Honey! Reckon Ah'll git twenty—er fifteen years—mebbe ten— *(He buttons her coat and draws her firmly toward the door)*

Clem: Ten years! *(She wrings her hands with a low moaning cry)*

Dan: Ah'll spend 'em all dreamin' 'bout yuh, Clem, an'—an' Lucy! Yuh musn' grieve, Honey. Go, now, fer Gawd's sake! Ah hears sombuddy comin' down! *(He pushes her out, forcibly. And then the door is shut. The outer door slams. DAN listens for the click of the gate. Finally he turns and looks down at HATTIE)* Ah'm sorry, Hattie! 'Fore Gawd, Ah didn' mean tuh do it!

Curtain

While Jean Toomer's reputation rests on only one work, *Cane* (1923), he was a significant contributor to the Harlem Renaissance. Toomer was born December 26, 1894, in Washington, D.C., to Nathan and Nina Pinchback Toomer. Toomer claimed a mixed ancestry that included French, Dutch, Welsh, African American, German, Jewish, and Native American. Less than a year after Toomer's birth, his father abandoned the family and his mother moved back home with her parents. Her father was the well-known P.B.S. Pinchback, a mixed-race man who identified as African American and a former Reconstruction lieutenant governor and acting governor of Louisiana. After the Republicans lost power, Pinchback's family was light enough that they were able to move to a white neighborhood in Washington, D.C. In 1906 Nina Toomer remarried and moved with her son and new husband to New Rochelle, New York. When she died three years later, Toomer, then fourteen, returned to live with his maternal grandparents. They had resettled in a black neighborhood, and here Toomer grappled on a personal level for the first time with the issue of race. He attended M Street High School, later known as Dunbar High School. After he graduated in 1914, Toomer attended the University of Wisconsin but only stayed a semester. He attended four other colleges between 1914 and 1917, including New York University and City College of New York, but he never received a degree. He supported himself and financed his education with odd jobs selling cars, teaching physical education, and working in a shipyard.

Jean Toomer

(1894–1967)

In 1921 he accepted a temporary position as superintendent of a black industrial school in Sparta, Georgia. This four-month experience was a dramatic turning point in his life. Much of the material for *Cane* was a result of this time spent in rural Georgia. *Cane* was published in 1923, and although the book did not initially sell well, it was a critical success, garnering praise from all quarters and propelling Toomer into the vanguard of the Harlem Renaissance. Its significance and impact on American letters has been far-reaching, as it is arguably the most highly regarded prose work of the Renaissance. During the 1920s Toomer's poems and sketches were published in *Broom, The Crisis, The Dial, The Prairie Schooner, Nomad, Opportunity, Little Review*, and other magazines. His play, *Balo* (1924), was included in *Plays of Negro Life* (1927), edited by Alain Locke and Montgomery Gregory.

Soon after the publication of *Cane*, however, Toomer sought to leave racial tensions behind him and dropped out of the movement with which he would remain so closely associated. He became interested in the work of George I. Gurdjieff, an Armenian spiritualist, and in the summer of 1924, Toomer made his first visit to Gurdjieff's Institute for the Harmonious Development of Man, located in France. His interest in Gurdjieff's philosophy led Toomer to proselytize for Unitism in Harlem, and he temporarily attracted Nella Larsen, Wallace Thurman, and Aaron Douglas into the movement. Much of Toomer's later work reflects the influence of Gurdjieff's philosophy, and nothing he wrote after *Balo*, with the exception of "Blue Meridian"

(1936), pertains to African American subjects. That long poem depicts the fusion of black, white, and red people into the blue man.

In 1932 Toomer married one of his white students, Margery Latimer, but she died the next year during childbirth. He married another white woman, Marjorie Content, in 1934. The couple relocated to Bucks County, Pennsylvania, and Toomer turned from Unitism to the Quaker Society of Friends, becoming a Quaker in 1940. By the time Toomer died in 1967, he had completely disavowed his black ancestry and in fact claimed that he had no race.

"Blue Meridian" was his last major publication, although he did publish two books after his conversion to Quakerism: *An Interpretation of Friends Worship* (1947) and *The Flavor of Man* (1949). Darwin Turner's *The Wayward and the Seeking* (1980) includes the best of Toomer's previously unpublished fiction and poetry.

Song of the Son

Pour O pour that parting soul in song,
O pour it in the sawdust glow of night,
Into the velvet pine-smoke air to-night,
And let the valley carry it along.
And let the valley carry it along.

O land and soil, red soil and sweet-gum tree,
So scant of grass, so profligate of pines,
Now just before an epoch's sun declines
Thy son, in time, I have returned to thee,
Thy son, I have in time returned to thee.

In time, for though the sun is setting on
A song-lit race of slaves, it has not set;
Though late, O soil, it is not too late yet
To catch thy plaintive soul, leaving, soon gone,
Leaving, to catch thy plaintive soul soon gone.

O Negro slaves, dark purple ripened plums,
Squeezed, and bursting in the pine-wood air,
Passing, before they stripped the old tree bare
One plum was saved for me, one seed becomes

An everlasting song, a singing tree,
Caroling softly souls of slavery,
What they were, and what they are to me,
Caroling softly souls of slavery.

The Crisis, June 1922.

Georgia Dusk

The sky, lazily disdaining to pursue
　The setting sun, too indolent to hold
　A lengthened tournament for flashing gold,
Passively darkens for night's barbeque,

A feast of moon and men and barking hounds,
　An orgy for some genius of the South
　With blood-hot eyes and cane-lipped scented mouth,
Surprised in making folk-songs from soul sounds.

The sawmill blows its whistle, buzz-saws stop,
　And silence breaks the bud of knoll and hill,
　Soft settling pollen where plowed lands fulfill
Their early promise of a bumper crop.

Smoke from the pyramidal sawdust pile
　Curls up, blue ghosts of trees, tarrying low
　Where only chips and stumps are left to show
The solid proof of former domicile.

Meanwhile, the men, with vestiges of pomp,
　Race memories of king and caravan,
　High-priests, an ostrich, and a juju-man,
Go singing through the footpaths of the swamp.

Their voices rise . . . the pine trees are guitars,
　Strumming, pine-needles fall like sheets of rain . . .
　Their voices rise . . . the chorus of the cane
Is caroling a vesper to the stars . . .

O singers, resinous and soft your songs
　Above the sacred whisper of the pines,
　Give virgin lips to cornfield concubines,
Bring dreams of Christ to dusky cane-lipped throngs.

The Liberator, September 1922.

Portrait in Georgia

Hair—braided chestnut,
　coiled like a lyncher's rope,
Eyes—fagots,
Lips—old scars, or the first red blisters,
Breath—the last sweet scent of cane,
And her slim body, white as the ash
　of black flesh after flame.

Cane, 1923.

James Lesesne Wells, Untitled, *Plays and Pageants from the Life of the Negro,* 1930

Blood-Burning Moon

1

Up from the skeleton stone walls, up from the rotting floor boards and the solid hand-hewn beams of oak of the pre-war cotton factory, dusk came. Up from the dusk the full moon came. Glowing like a fired pine-knot, it illumined the great door and soft showered the Negro shanties aligned along the single street of factory town. The full moon in the great door was an omen. Negro women improvised songs against its spell.

Louisa sang as she came over the crest of the hill from the white folks' kitchen. Her skin was the color of oak leaves on young trees in fall. Her breasts, firm and up-pointed like ripe acorns. And her singing had the low murmur of winds in fig trees. Bob Stone, younger son of the people she worked for, loved her. By the way the world reckons things, he had won her. By measure of that warm glow which came into her mind at thought of him, he had won her. Tom Burwell, whom the whole town called Big Boy, also loved her. But working in the fields all day, and far away from her, gave him no chance to show it. Though often enough of evenings he had tried to. Somehow, he never got along. Strong as he was with hands upon the ax or plow, he found it difficult to hold her. Or so he thought. But the fact was that he held her to factory town more firmly than he thought for. His black balanced, and pulled against, the white of Stone, when she thought of them. And her mind was vaguely upon them as she came over the crest of the hill, coming from the white folks' kitchen. As she sang softly at the evil face of the full moon.

A strange stir was in her. Indolently, she tried to fix upon Bob or Tom as the cause of it. To meet Bob in the canebrake, as she was going to do an hour or so later, was nothing new. And Tom's proposal which she felt on its way to her could be indefinitely put off. Separately, there was no unusual significance to either one. But for some reason, they jumbled when her eyes gazed vacantly at the rising moon. And from the jumble came the stir that was strangely within her. Her lips trembled. The slow rhythm of her song grew agitant and restless. Rusty black and tan spotted hounds, lying in the dark corners of porches or prowling around back yards, put their noses in the air and caught its tremor. They began plaintively to yelp and howl. Chickens woke up and cackled. Intermittently, all over the countryside dogs barked and roosters crowed as if heralding a weird dawn or some ungodly awakening. The women sang lustily. Their songs were cotton-wads to stop their ears. Louisa came down into factory town and sank wearily upon the step before her home. The moon was rising towards a thick cloud-bank which soon would hide it.

> Red nigger moon. Sinner!
> Blood-burning moon. Sinner!
> Come out that fact'ry door.

Cane, 1923.

2

Up from the deep dusk of a cleared spot on the edge of the forest a mellow glow arose and spread fan-wise into the low-hanging heavens. And all around the air was heavy with the scent of boiling cane. A large pile of cane-stalks lay like ribboned shadows upon the ground. A mule, harnessed to a pole, trudged lazily round and round the pivot of the grinder. Beneath a swaying oil lamp, a Negro alternately whipped out at the mule, and fed cane-stalks to the grinder. A fat boy waddled pails of fresh ground juice between the grinder and the boiling stove. Steam came from the copper boiling pan. The scent of cane came from the copper pan and drenched the forest and the hill that sloped to factory town, beneath its fragrance. It drenched the men in a circle seated around the stove. Some of them chewed at the white pulp of stalks, but there was no need for them to, if all they wanted was to taste the cane. One tasted it in factory town. And from factory town one could see the soft haze thrown by the glowing stove upon the low-hanging heavens.

Old David Georgia stirred the thickening syrup with a long ladle, and ever so often drew it off. Old David Georgia tended his stove and told tales about the white folks, about moonshining and cotton picking, and about sweet nigger gals, to the men who sat there about his stove to listen to him. Tom Burwell chewed cane-stalk and laughed with the others till some one mentioned Louisa. Till some one said something about Louisa and Bob Stone, about the silk stockings she must have gotten from him. Blood ran up Tom's neck hotter than the glow that flooded from the stove. He sprang up. Glared at the men and said, "She's my gal." Will Manning laughed. Tom strode over to him. Yanked him up and knocked him to the ground. Several of Manning's friends got up to fight for him. Tom whipped out a long knife and would have cut them to shreds if they hadn't ducked into the woods. Tom had had enough. He nodded to Old David Georgia and swung down the path to factory town. Just then, the dogs started barking and the roosters began to crow. Tom felt funny. Away from the fight, away from the stove, chill got to him. He shivered. He shuddered when he saw the full moon rising towards the cloud-bank. He who didn't give a godam for the fears of old women. He forced his mind to fasten on Louisa. Bob Stone. Better not be. He turned into the street and saw Louisa sitting before her home. He went towards her, ambling, touched the brim of a marvelously shaped, spotted, felt hat, said he wanted to say something to her, and then found that he didn't know what he had to say, or if he did, that he couldn't say it. He shoved his big fists in his overalls, grinned, and started to move off.

"Youall want me, Tom?"

"Thats sho what us wants, sho, Louisa."

"Well, here I am—"

"An here I is, but that aint ahelpin none, all th same."

"You wanted to say something? . . ."

"I did that, sho. But words is like th spots on dice: no matter how y fumbles em, there's times when they jes wont come. I dunno why. Seems like th love I feels fo yo done stole m tongue. I got it now. Whee! Louisa, honey, I oughtnt tell y, I feel I oughtnt cause yo is young an goes t church an I has had other gals, but Louisa I sho do love y. Lil gal, Ise watched y from them first days when youall sat right here befo yo door befo th well an sang sometimes in a way that like t broke m heart. Ise carried y with me into th fields, day after day, an after that, an I sho can plow when yo is there, an I can pick cotton. Yassur! Come near beatin Barlo yesterday. I sho did. Yassur! An next year if ole Stone'll trust me, I'll have a farm. My own. My bales will buy yo what y gets from white folks now. Silk stockings an purple dresses—course I dont believe what some folks been whisperin as t how y gets them things now. White folks always did do for niggers what they likes. An they jes cant help alikin yo, Louisa. Bob Stone likes y. Course he does. But not th way folks is awhisperin. Does he, hon?"

"I dont know what you mean, Tom."

"Course y dont. Ise already cut two niggers. Had t hon, t tell em so. Niggers always tryin t make somethin out a nothin. An then besides, white folks aint up t them tricks so much nowadays. Godam better not be. Leastawise not with yo. Cause I wouldnt stand f it. Nassur."

"What would you do, Tom?"

"Cut him jes like I cut a nigger."

"No, Tom—"

"I said I would an there aint no mo to it. But that aint th talk f now. Sing, honey Louisa, an while I'm listenin t y I'll be makin love."

Tom took her hand in his. Against the tough thickness of his own, hers felt soft and small. His huge body slipped down to the step beside her. The full moon sank upward into the deep purple of the cloud-bank. An old woman brought a lighted lamp and hung it on the common well whose bulky shadow squatted in the middle of the road, opposite Tom and Louisa. The old woman lifted the well-lid, took hold the chain, and began drawing up the heavy bucket. As she did so, she sang. Figures shifted, restlesslike, between lamp and window in the front rooms of the shanties. Shadows of the figures fought each other on the gray dust of the road. Figures raised the windows and joined the old woman in song. Louisa and Tom, the whole street, singing:

> Red nigger moon. Sinner!
> Blood-burning moon. Sinner!
> Come out that fact'ry door.

3

Bob Stone sauntered from his veranda out into the gloom of fir trees and magnolias. The clear white of his skin paled, and the flush of his cheeks turned purple. As if to balance this outer change, his mind became consciously a white man's. He passed the house with its huge open hearth which, in the days of slavery, was the plantation cookery. He saw Louisa bent over that hearth. He went in as a master should and took her. Direct, honest, bold. None of this sneaking that he had to go through now. The contrast was repulsive to him. His family had lost ground. Hell no, his family still owned the niggers, practically. Damned if they did, or he wouldn't have to duck around so. What would they think if they knew? His mother? His sister? He shouldn't mention them, shouldn't think of them in this connection. There in the dusk he blushed at doing so. Fellows about town were all right, but how about his friends up North? He could see them incredible, repulsed. They didn't know. The thought first made him laugh. Then, with their eyes still upon him, he began to feel embarrassed. He felt the need of explaining things to them. Explain hell. They wouldn't understand, and moreover, who ever heard of a Southerner getting on his knees to any Yankee, or anyone. No sir. He was going to see Louisa tonight, and love her. She was lovely—in her way. Nigger way. What way was that?

Damned if he knew. Must know. He'd known her long enough to know. Was there something about niggers that you couldn't know? Listening to them at church didn't tell you anything. Looking at them didn't tell you anything. Talking to them didn't tell you anything—unless it was gossip, unless they wanted to talk. Of course, about farming, and licker, and craps—but those weren't nigger. Nigger was something more. How much more? Something to be afraid of, more? Hell no. Who ever heard of being afraid of a nigger? Tom Burwell. Cartwell had told him that Tom went with Louisa after she reached home. No sir. No nigger had ever been with his girl. He'd like to see one try. Some position for him to be in. Him, Bob Stone, of the old Stone family, in a scrap with a nigger over a nigger girl. In the good old days . . . Ha! Those were the days. His family had lost ground. Not so much, though. Enough for him to have to cut through old Lemon's canefield by way of the woods, that he might meet her. She was worth it. Beautiful nigger gal. Why nigger? Why not, just gal? No, it was because she was nigger that he went to her. Sweet . . . The scent of boiling cane came to him. Then he saw the rich glow of the stove. He heard the voices of the men circled around it. He was about to skirt the clearing when he heard his own name mentioned. He stopped. Quivering. Leaning against a tree, he listened.

"Bad nigger. Yassur, he sho is one bad nigger when he gets started."

"Tom Burwell's been on th gang three times fo cuttin men."

"What y think he's agwine t do t Bob Stone?"

"Dunno yet. He aint found out. When he does—Baby!"

"Aint no tellin."

"Young Stone aint no quitter an I ken tell y that. Blood of th old uns in his veins."

"Thats right. He'll scrap, sho."

"Be gettin too hot f niggers round this away."

"Shut up, nigger. Y don't know what y talkin bout."

Bob Stone's ears burned as though he had been holding them over the stove. Sizzling heat welled up within him. His feet felt as if they rested on red-hot coals. They stung him to quick movement. He circled the fringe of the glowing. Not a twig cracked beneath his feet. He reached the path that led to factory town. Plunged furiously down it. Halfway along, a blindness within him veered him aside. He crashed into the bordering canebrake. Cane leaves cut his face and lips. He tasted blood. He threw himself down and dug his fingers in the ground. The earth was cool. Cane-roots took the fever from his hands. After a long while, or so it seemed to him, the thought came to him that it must be time to see Louisa. He got to his feet and walked calmly to their meeting place. No Louisa. Tom Burwell had her. Veins in his forehead bulged and distended. Saliva moistened the dried blood on his lips. He bit down on his lips. He tasted blood. Not his own blood; Tom Burwell's blood. Bob drove through the cane and out again upon the road. A hound swung down the path before him towards factory town. Bob couldn't see it. The dog loped aside to let him pass. Bob's blind rushing made him stumble over it. He fell with a thud that dazed him. The hound yelped. Answering yelps came from all over the countryside.

Chickens cackled. Roosters crowed, heralding the bloodshot eyes of southern awakening. Singers in the town were silenced. They shut their windows down. Palpitant between the rooster crows, a chill hush settled upon the huddled forms of Tom and Louisa. A figure rushed from the shadow and stood before them. Tom popped to his feet.

"Whats y want?"

"I'm Bob Stone."

"Yassur—an I'm Tom Burwell. Whats y want?"

Bob lunged at him. Tom side-stepped, caught him by the shoulder, and flung him to the ground. Straddled him.

"Let me up."

"Yassur—but watch yo doins, Bob Stone."

A few dark figures, drawn by the sound of scuffle, stood about them. Bob sprang to his feet.

"Fight like a man, Tom Burwell, an I'll lick y."

Again he lunged. Tom side-stepped and flung him to the ground. Straddled him.

"Get off me, you godam nigger you."

"Yo sho has started somethin now. Get up."

Tom yanked him up and began hammering at him. Each blow sounded as if it smashed into a precious, irreplaceable soft something. Beneath them, Bob staggered back. He reached in his pocket and whipped out a knife.

"Thats my game, sho."

Blue flash, a steel blade slashed across Bob Stone's throat. He had a sweetish sick feeling. Blood began to flow. Then he felt a sharp twitch of pain. He let his knife drop. He slapped one hand against his neck. He pressed the other on top of his head as if to hold it down. He groaned. He turned, and staggered towards the crest of the hill in the direction of white town. Negroes who had seen the fight slunk into their homes and blew the lamps out. Louisa, dazed, hysterical, refused to go indoors. She slipped, crumbled, her body loosely propped against the woodwork of the well. Tom Burwell leaned against it. He seemed rooted there.

Bob reached Broad Street. White men rushed up to him. He collapsed in their arms.

"Tom Burwell. . . ."

White men like ants upon a forage rushed about. Except for the taut hum of their moving, all was silent. Shotguns, revolvers, rope, kerosene, torches. Two high-powered cars with glaring searchlights. They came together. The taut hum rose to a low roar. Then nothing could be heard but the flop of their feet in the thick dust of the road. The moving body of their silence preceded them over the crest of the hill into factory town. It flattened the Negroes beneath it. It rolled to the wall of the factory, where it stopped. Tom knew that they were coming. He couldn't move. And then he saw the searchlights of the two cars glaring down on him. A quick shock went through him. He stiffened. He started to run. A yell went up from the mob. Tom wheeled about and faced them. They poured down on him. They swarmed. A large man with dead-white face and flabby cheeks came to him and almost jabbed a gun-barrel through his guts.

"Hands behind y, nigger."

Tom's wrists were bound. The big man shoved him to the well. Burn him over it, and when the woodwork caved in, his body would drop to the bottom. Two deaths for a godam nigger. Louisa was driven back. The mob pushed in. Its pressure, its momentum was too great. Drag him to the factory. Wood and stakes already there. Tom moved in the direction indicated. But they had to drag him. They reached the great door. Too many to get in there. The mob divided and flowed around the walls to either side. The big man shoved him through the door. The mob pressed in from the sides. Taut humming. No words. A stake was sunk into the ground. Rotting floor boards piled around it. Kerosene poured on the rotting floor boards. Tom bound to the stake. His breast was bare. Nails' scratches let little lines of blood trickle down and mat into the hair. His face, his eyes were set and stony. Except for irregular breathing, one would have thought him already dead. Torches were flung onto the pile. A great flare muffled in black smoke shot upward. The mob yelled. The mob was silent. Now Tom could be seen within the flames. Only his head, erect, lean, like a blackened stone. Stench of burning flesh soaked the air. Tom's eyes popped. His head settled downward. The mob yelled. Its yell echoed against the skeleton stone walls and sounded like a hundred yells. Like a hundred mobs yelling. Its yell thudded against the thick front wall and fell back. Ghost of a yell slipped through the flames and out the great door of the factory. It fluttered like a dying thing down the single street of factory town. Louisa, upon the step before her home, did not hear it, but her eyes opened slowly. They saw the full moon glowing in the great door. The full moon, an evil thing, an omen, soft showering the homes of folks she knew. Where were they, these people? She'd sing, and perhaps they'd come out and join her. Perhaps Tom Burwell would come. At any rate, the full moon in the great door was an omen which she must sing to:

> Red nigger moon. Sinner!
> Blood-burning moon. Sinner!
> Come out that fact'ry door.

Joseph Seamon Cotter, Jr.

(1895–1919)

Joseph Cotter, Jr., was the son of a prolific writer, Joseph Cotter, Sr., who furnished him with an extensive library in the Louisville, Kentucky, home where he was born. After graduating from Louisville Central High School, he entered Fisk University in Nashville, Tennessee, but his school days were brought to a halt in his second year when he contracted tuberculosis (a disease that claimed the lives of many African Americans at the time) and had to return to Louisville. There he edited and wrote for *The Louisville Leader* and produced poetry. He died when he was only twenty-three.

Cotter is best known for his volume of verse, *The Band of Gideon*, published in 1918. It includes both traditional and the experimental free-verse poems for which he is lauded. Cotter is also known for his poems and one-act play, *On the Fields of France*, about black soldiers in World War I, inspired by his friend Abram Simpson, the youngest African American army captain of that conflict. His final notable works, the sonnet series *Out of the Shadows* and *Poems*, were published posthumously by the *A.M.E. Zion Quarterly Review* in 1920 and 1921.

And What Shall You Say?

Brother, come!
And let us go unto our God.
And when we stand before Him
I shall say—
"Lord, I do not hate,
I am hated.
I scourge no one,
I am scourged.
I covet no lands,
My lands are coveted.
I mock no peoples,
My people are mocked."
And, brother, what shall you say?

The Band of Gideon, 1918.

Is It Because I Am Black?

Why do men smile when I speak,
And call my speech
The whimperings of a babe
That cries but knows not what it wants?
Is it because I am black?

Why do men sneer when I arise
And stand in their councils,
And look them eye to eye,
And speak their tongue?
Is it because I am black?

The Band of Gideon, 1918.

Sonnet to Negro Soldiers

They shall go down unto Life's Borderland,
    Walk unafraid within that Living Hell,
    Nor heed the driving rain of shot and shell
That 'round them falls; but with uplifted hand,
Be one with mighty hosts, an armed band
    Against man's wrong to man—for such full well
    They know. And from their trembling lips shall swell
A song of hope the world can understand.
All this to them shall be a glorious sign,
    A glimmer of that resurrection morn,
When age-long Faith, crowned with a grace benign,
    Shall rise and from their brows cast down the thorn
Of prejudice. E'en though through blood it be,
There breaks this day their dawn of Liberty.

The Band of Gideon, 1918.

Rain Music

On the dusty earth-drum
  Beats the falling rain;
Now a whispered murmur,
  Now a louder strain.

Slender, silvery drumsticks,
  On an ancient drum,
Beat the mellow music
  Bidding life to come.

Chords of earth awakened,
  Notes of greening spring,
Rise and fall triumphant
  Over every thing.

Slender, silvery drumsticks
  Beat the long tattoo—
God, the Great Musician,
  Calling life anew.

A.M.E. Zion Quarterly Review, 1921.

On the Fields of France

Cast

A WHITE AMERICAN OFFICER
A COLORED AMERICAN OFFICER

Time: Present
Place: Battlefield of Northern France

Curtain rises on WHITE AMERICAN OFFICER and COLORED AMERICAN OFFICER, both mortally wounded.

White Officer: (rises on elbow and sees someone across the field. Speaks slowly as if in pain) I say there, my good fellow, have you a drop of water to spare? The Boches[1] have about done for me, I fear.

Colored Officer: (turns over) Who calls?

White Officer: (sees that he is a fellow officer) It is I, a fellow-officer, my friend. A shell has gone through my body and the fever has parched my lips. Have you a drop to spare?

Colored Officer: (speaks in catches) I am—about done for—myself. They've got me—through the lung. I've enough water—to moisten our—lips about as long—as either of—us will be here.

(They drag themselves across toward each other. They get close enough to touch hands. COLORED OFFICER hands his canteen to WHITE OFFICER, who moistens his lips and hands it back)

White Officer: That is much better, my friend. I have been lying here for several hours, it seems, waiting for someone. We went over the Boches' trenches in a bombing squad and they got me coming back.

Colored Officer: I was range-finding—and the snipers—got me. I have been dragging— myself towards our trenches—for an hour or so. I got this—far and decided to—stop and close my eyes—and wait for the—end here. It won't be—far off anywhere.

(WHITE OFFICER's strength begins to fail and he slips back. COLORED OFFICER takes his hand and he raises himself up with an effort and speaks)

White Officer: I thought I was gone then. My strength is going fast. Hold my hand. It won't feel so lonesome dying way over here in France.

Colored Officer: (takes his hand) I feel much better—myself. After all—it isn't so hard—to die when—you are dying—for Liberty.

---

1. French slang for Germans.

The Crisis, June 1920.

White Officer: Do you feel that way too? I've often wondered how your people felt. We've treated you so badly mean over home and I've wondered if you could feel that way. I've been as guilty as the rest, maybe more so than some. But that was yesterday.—What is that I see? *(rises with unbelievable strength and points toward the heavens)* Do you see it? It is a white-haired figure clad in the Old Continentals, standing there within the gates of heaven. And he is beckoning for me. It is Washington.

Colored Officer: *(speaks excitedly and rapidly)* I see him, I see him. And who is that beside him with his swarthy chest bare and torn? It is Attucks—Crispus Attucks,[2] and he beckons to me. *(He gasps for breath, fatigued with his rapid talk)*

White Officer: They stand hand in hand. And there is Lee.[3] He beckons to me. Those serried hosts behind him,—they're Forrest and his men.[4] They call me to join them.

Colored Officer: *(speaks slowly now, gasping for breath all the while)* And there is—Carney[5] with the Old Flag—still in the air. And back of—him, those swarthy—hosts, they're Shaw[6]—and his black—heroes. And they—beckon to me.

White Officer: *(slips back on elbow)* They stand hand in hand over there and we die hand in hand over here on the fields of France. Why couldn't we have lived like this at home? They beckon to us, to you and to me. It is one country she will some day be, in truth as well as in spirit—the country of Washington and Attucks, *(speaks slowly and painfully)* of Lee and Carney. The country of the whites and the country of the blacks. *Our* country!

White Officer and Colored Officer: *(together)* America! *(They fall back hand in hand as their life blood ebbs away.)*

Curtain

2. Crispus Attucks was the first African American to die in the American revolutionary struggle.

3. Robert E. Lee, head of the Confederate Army in the Civil War.

4. Nathan Bedford Forrest was a Confederate cavalry officer.

5. Carney was a Union soldier.

6. Robert Gould Shaw was an African American Bostonian who led an all-black battalion, the 54th Massachusetts Volunteer Regiment, in a battle against Confederate forces.

Rudolph Fisher

(1897–1934)

Harlem physician and roentgenologist, author, and musical arranger, Rudolph Fisher was a true Renaissance man. Born on May 9, 1897, to Reverend John Wesley Fisher and Glendora Williamson Fisher, in Washington, D.C., one of three children, he was raised in New York and Providence, Rhode Island, where he graduated in 1915 with honors from Classical High School. Fisher attended Brown University as a James Manning and Francis Wayland Scholar, majoring in English and biology. In 1917 he represented Brown in a public speaking contest at Harvard and won first prize. He graduated in 1919 and the following year completed his M.A. at Brown. He then studied at the Howard University Medical School from 1920 to 1924. He graduated in 1924 with highest honors and began an internship at Washington's Freedman's Hospital. This same year he married Jane Ryder, a teacher; the couple had one son. After completing his internship, he moved to New York to become a fellow of the National Research Council at Columbia University's College of Physicians and Surgeons. He specialized in roentgenology (the diagnostic and therapeutic uses of x-rays) at Columbia before going into private practice in Harlem in 1927, and later opened an x-ray laboratory. From 1929 to 1932, he served as superintendent of the International Hospital in Harlem. Concomitantly he was associated with the X-ray Division of the New York Department of Health from 1930 to 1934, and from 1931 to 1934 he was first lieutenant in the medical division of the 369th Infantry.

Despite his successful medical career, Fisher found time to pursue his love of literature. In fact, his first published story, "The City of Refuge," was written while he was in medical school. It first appeared in the February 1925 issue of *Atlantic Monthly* and brought him instant fame within the Harlem literary scene. "The South Lingers On" appeared in the special issue of *Survey Graphic* (1925), edited by Alain Locke, and was reprinted in Locke's *The New Negro* (1925) as "Vestiges, Harlem Sketches." His influential essay "The Caucasian Storms Harlem" was published in *American Mercury* in 1927. He continued to publish stories in such well-known journals as *Atlantic Monthly*, *McClure's*, *Opportunity*, *The Crisis*, *Redbook*, and *Story Magazine*. "Miss Cynthie" (1933), published in *Story*, is one of his most admired works and appeared in Edward O'Brien's *The Best Short Stories for 1934*. Many of his stories address the recent southern migrant's encounter with Harlem.

While best known for his fiction, Fisher is also the author of two novels. *The Walls of Jericho* (1928) was hailed by critics and considered the "clean" view of Harlem when contrasted (favorably) with Claude McKay's *Home to Harlem* (1928) and Carl Van Vechten's *Nigger Heaven* (1926). Fisher's second novel, *The Conjure-Man Dies: A Mystery Tale of Dark Harlem* (1932) is considered the first African American detective novel. Fisher was working on a dramatization of *The Conjure-Man Dies* when he died from intestinal cancer at the age of thirty-seven. His novelette, *John Archer's Nose*, was published posthumously in 1935, while *The Conjure-Man Dies* was produced in 1936 at the Lafayette Theater in Harlem. Despite his influential writings, so well received in his own time, Fisher fell into obscurity among literary critics until Sterling Brown, a professor at Howard University, revived interest in him in 1959.

Aaron Douglas, "Rebirth," *The New Negro,* 1925

The City of Refuge

Confronted suddenly by daylight, King Solomon Gillis stood dazed and blinking. The railroad station, the long, white-walled corridor, the impassible slot-machine, the terrifying subway train—he felt as if he had been caught up in the jaws of a steam-shovel, jammed together with other helpless lumps of dirt, swept blindly along for a time, and at last abruptly dumped.

There had been strange and terrible sounds: "New York! Penn Terminal—all change!" "Pohter, hyer, pohter, suh?" Shuffle of a thousand soles, clatter of a thousand heels, innumerable echoes. Cracking rifleshots—no, snapping turnstiles. "Put a nickel in!" "Harlem? Sure. This side—next train." Distant thunder, nearing. The screeching onslaught of the fiery hosts of hell, headlong, breath-taking. Car doors rattling, sliding, banging open. "Say, wha' d'ye think this is, a baggage car?" Heat, oppression, suffocation—eternity—"Hundred'n turdy-fif' next!" More turnstiles. Jonah emerging from the whale.

Clean air, blue sky, bright sunlight.

Gillis set down his tan cardboard extension-case and wiped his black, shining brow. Then slowly, spreadingly, he grinned at what he saw: Negroes at every turn; up and down Lenox Avenue, up and down One Hundred and Thirty-Fifth Street; big, lanky Negroes, short, squat Negroes; black ones, brown ones, yellow ones; men standing idle on the curb, women, bundle-laden trudging reluctantly homeward, children rattle-trapping about the sidewalks; here and there a white face drifting along, but Negroes predominantly, overwhelmingly everywhere. There was assuredly no doubt of his whereabouts. This was Negro Harlem.

Back in North Carolina Gillis had shot a white man and, with the aid of prayer and an automobile, probably escaped a lynching. Carefully avoiding the railroads, he had reached Washington in safety. For his car a Southwest bootlegger had given him a hundred dollars and directions to Harlem; and so he had come to Harlem.

Ever since a traveling preacher had first told him of the place, King Solomon Gillis had longed to come to Harlem. The Uggams were always talking about it; one of their boys had gone to France in the draft and, returning, had never got any nearer home than Harlem. And there were occasional "colored" newspapers from New York: newspapers that mentioned Negroes without comment, but always spoke of a white person as "So-and-so, white." That was the point. In Harlem, black was white. You had rights that could not be denied you; you had privileges, protected by law. And you had money. Everybody in Harlem had money. It was a land of plenty. Why, had not Mouse Uggam sent back as much as fifty dollars at a time to his people in Waxhaw?

The shooting, therefore, simply catalyzed whatever sluggish mental reaction had been already directing King Solomon's fortunes toward Harlem. The land of plenty was more than that now: it was also the city of refuge.

Atlantic Monthly, February 1925.

Casting about for direction, the tall newcomer's glance caught inevitably on the most conspicuous thing in sight, a magnificent figure in blue that stood in the middle of the crossing and blew a whistle and waved great white-gloved hands. The Southern Negro's eyes opened wide; his mouth opened wider. If the inside of New York had mystified him, the outside was amazing him. For there stood a handsome, brass-buttoned giant directing the heaviest traffic Gillis had ever seen; halting unnumbered tons of automobiles and trucks and wagons and pushcarts and street-cars; holding them at bay with one hand while he swept similar tons peremptorily on with the other; ruling the wide crossing with supreme self-assurance; and he, too, was a Negro!

Yet most of the vehicles that leaped or crouched at his bidding carried white passengers. One of these overdrove bounds a few feet and Gillis heard the officer's shrill whistle and gruff reproof, saw the driver's face turn red and his car draw back like a threatened pup. It was beyond belief—impossible. Black might be white, but it couldn't be that white!

"Done died an' woke up in Heaven," thought King Solomon, watching, fascinated; and after a while, as if the wonder of it were too great to believe simply by seeing, "Cullud policemans!" he said, half aloud; then repeated over and over, with greater and greater conviction, "Even got cullud policemans—even got cullud—"

"Where y'want to go, big boy?"

Gillis turned. A little, sharp-faced yellow man was addressing him. "Saw you was a stranger. Thought maybe I could help y'out."

King Solomon located and gratefully extended a slip of paper. "Wha' dis hyeh at, please, suh?"

The other studied it a moment, pushing back his hat and scratching his head. The hat was a tall-crowned, unindented brown felt; the head was brown patent-leather, its glistening brush-back flawless save for a suspicious crimpiness near the clean-grazed edges.

"See that second corner? Turn to the left when you get there. Number forty-five's about halfway [down] the block."

"Thank y', suh."

"You from—Massachusetts?"

"No, suh, Nawth Ca'lina."

"Is 'at so? You look like a Northerner. Be with us long?"

"Till I die," grinned the flattered King Solomon.

"Stoppin' there?"

"Reckon I is. Man in Washin'ton 'lowed I'd find lodgin' at dis address."

"Good enough. If y' don't, maybe I can fix y' up. Harlem's pretty crowded. This is me." He proffered a card.

"Thank y', suh," said Gillis, and put the card in his pocket.

The little yellow man watched him plod flat-footedly on down the street, long awkward legs never quite straightened, shouldered extension-case bending him sidewise, wonder upon wonder halting or turning him about. Presently, as he proceeded, a pair of bright-green stockings caught and held his attention. Tony, the storekeeper, was crossing the sidewalk with a bushel basket of apples. There was a collision; the apples rolled; Tony exploded; King Solomon apologized. The little yellow man laughed shortly, took out a notebook, and put down the address he had seen on King Solomon's slip of paper.

"Guess you're the shine[1] I been waitin' for," he surmised.

As Gillis, approaching his destination, stopped to rest, a haunting notion grew into an insistent idea. "Dat li'l yaller nigger was a sho' 'nuff gen'man to show me de road. Seem lak I knowed him befo'—" he pondered. That receding brow, that sharp-ridged, spreading nose, that tight upper lip over the two big front teeth, that chinless jaw—He fumbled hurriedly for the card he had not looked at and eagerly made out the name.

"Mouse Uggam, sho' 'nuff! Well, dog-gone!"

II

Uggam sought out Tom Edwards, once a Pullman porter, now prosperous proprietor of a cabaret, and told him: —

"Chief, I got him: a baby jess in from the land o' cotton and so dumb he thinks ante bellum's an old woman."

"Where d'you find him?"

"Where you find all the jay birds when they first hit Harlem—at the subway entrance. This one come up the stairs, batted his eyes once or twice, an' froze to the spot—with his mouth open. Sure sign he's from 'way down behind the sun an' ripe f' the pluckin'."

Edwards grinned a gold-studded, fat-jowled grin. "Gave him the usual line, I suppose?"

"Didn't miss. An' he fell like a ton o'bricks. 'Course I've got him spotted, but damn 'f I know jess how to switch 'em on to him."

"Get him a job around a store somewhere. Make out you're befriendin' him. Get his confidence."

"Sounds good. Ought to be easy. He's from my state. Maybe I know him or some of his people."

"Make out you do, anyhow. Then tell him some fairy tales that'll switch your trade to him. The cops'll follow the trade. We could even let Froggy[2] flop into some dumb white cop's hands and 'confess' where he got it. See?"

"Chief, you got a head, no lie."

"Don't lose no time. And remember, hereafter, it's better to sacrifice a little than to get squealed on. Never refuse a customer. Give him a little credit. Humor him along till you can get rid of him safe. You don't know what that guy that died may have said; you don't know who's on to you now. And if they get you—I don't know you."

"They won't get me," said Uggam.

King Solomon Gillis sat meditating in a room half the size of his hen coop back home, with a single window opening into an airshaft.

1. Vulgar slang for African American or black.
2. Derogatory slang for a Frenchman. Here, it is the nickname of a black character.

An airshaft: cabbage and chitterlings cooking; liver and onions sizzling, sputtering; three player-pianos out-plunking each other; a man and woman calling each other vile things; a sick, neglected baby wailing; a phonograph broadcasting blues; dishes clacking; a girl crying heartbrokenly; waste noises, waste odors of a score of families, seeing issue through a common channel; pollution from bottom to top—a sewer of sounds and smells.

Contemplating this, King Solomon grinned and breathed, "Doggone!" A little later, still gazing into the sewer, he grinned again. "Green stockin's," he said; "loud green!" The sewer gradually grew darker. A window lighted up opposite, revealing a woman in camisole and petticoat, arranging her hair. King Solomon, staring vacantly, shook his head and grinned yet again. "Even got culled policemans!" he mumbled softly.

III

Uggam leaned out of the room's one window and spat maliciously into the dinginess of the airshaft. "Damn glad you got him," he commented, as Gillis finished his story. "They's a thousand shines in Harlem would change places with you in a minute jess f' the honor of killin' a cracker."[3]

"But, I didn't go to do it. 'Twas a accident."

"That's the only part to keep secret."

"Know whut dey done? Dey killed five o' Mose Joplin's hawses 'fo he lef'. Put groun' glass in de feed-trough. Sam Cheevers come up on three of 'em one night pizenin' his well. Bleesom beat Crinshaw out o' sixty acres o' lan' an' a year's crops. Dass jess how 't is. Soon's a nigger make a li'l sump'n he better git to leavin'. An' 'fo long ev'ybody's goin' be lef'!"

"Hope to hell they don't all come here."

The doorbell of the apartment rang. A crescendo of footfalls in the hallway culminated in a sharp rap on Gillis's door. Gillis jumped. Nobody but a policeman would rap like that. Maybe the landlady had been listening and had called in the law. It came again, loud, quick, angry. King Solomon prayed that the policeman would be a Negro.

Uggam stepped over and opened the door. King Solomon's apprehensive eyes saw framed therein, instead of a gigantic officer, calling for him, a little blot of a creature, quite black against even the darkness of the hallway, except for a dirty, wide-striped silk shirt, collarless, with the sleeves rolled up.

"Ah hahve bill fo' Mr. Gillis." A high, strongly accented Jamaican voice, with its characteristic singsong intonation, interrupted King Solomon's sigh of relief.

"Bill? Bill fo' me? What kin' o' bill?"

"Wan bushel appels. T'ree seventy-fife."

"Apples? I ain' bought no apples." He took the paper and read aloud, laboriously, "Antonio Gabrielli to K. S. Gillis, Doctor—"

3. A derogatory term for a white person.

"Mr. Gabrielli say, you not pays him, he send policeman."

"What I had to do wid 'is apples?"

"You bumps into him yesterday, no? Scatter appels everywhere—on de sidewalk, in de gutter. Kids pick up an' run away. Others all spoil. So you pays."

Gillis appealed to Uggam. "How 'bout it, Mouse?"

"He's a damn liar. Tony picked up most of 'em; I seen him. Lemme look at that bill—Tony never wrote this thing. This baby's jess playin' you for a sucker."

"Ain' had no apples, ain' payin' fo' none," announced King Solomon, thus prompted. "Didn't have to come to Harlem to git cheated. Plenty o' dat right wha' I come fum."

But the West Indian warmly insisted. "You cahn't do daht, mon. Whaht you t'ink, 'ey? Dis mon loose 'is appels an' 'is money too?"

"What diff'ence it make to you, nigger?"

"Who you call nigger, mon? Ah hahve you understahn'—"

"Oh, well, white folks, den. What all you got t' do wid dis hyeh, anyhow?"

"Mr. Gabrielli send me to collect bill!"

"How I know dat?"

"Do Ah not bring bill? You t'ink Ah steal t'ree dollar, 'ey?"

"Three dollars an' sebenty-fi' cent," corrected Gillis. "'Nuther thing: wha' you ever see me befo'? How you know dis is me?"

"Ah see you, sure. Ah help Mr. Gabrielli in de store. When you knocks down de baskette appels, Ah see. Ah follow you. Ah know you comes in dis house."

"Oh, you does? An' how come you know my name an' flat an' room so good? How come dat?"

"Ah fin' out. Sometime Ah brings up here vegetables from de store."

"Humph! Mus' be workin' on shares."

"You pays, 'ey? You pays me or de policeman?"

"Wait a minute," broke in Uggam, who had been thoughtfully contemplating the bill. "Now listen, big shorty. You haul hips on back to Tony. We got your menu all right"—he waved the bill—"but we don't eat your kind o' cookin', see?"

The West Indian flared. "Whaht it is to you, 'ey? You can not mind your own business? Ah hahve not spik to you!"

"No, brother. But this is my friend, an' I'll be john-browned if there's a monkey-chaser in Harlem can gyp him if I know it, see?[4] Bes' thing f' you to do is catch air, toot sweet."[5]

Sensing frustration, the little islander demanded the bill back. Uggam figured he could use the bill himself, maybe. The West Indian hotly persisted; he even menaced. Uggam pocketed the paper and invited him to take it. Wisely enough, the caller preferred to catch air.

---

4. John Brown was a white martyr in the abolition of slavery movement. Monkey-chaser is vulgar slang for a West Indian.

5. From the French *toute de suite;* right now.

When he had gone, King Solomon sought words of thanks.

"Bottle it," said Uggam. "The point is this: I figger you got a job."

"Job? No I ain't! Wh'at?"

"When you show Tony this bill, he'll hit the roof and fire that monk."

"Wha ef he do?"

"Then you up 'n ask f' the job. He'll be too grateful to refuse. I know Tony some, an' I'll be there to put in a good word. See?"

King Solomon considered this. "Sho' needs a job, but ain' after stealin' none."

"Stealin'? 'Twouldn't be stealin'. Stealin' 's what that damn monkey-chaser tried to do from you. This would be doin' Tony a favor an' gettin' y'self out o' the barrel. What's the hold-back?"

"What make you keep callin' him monkey-chaser?"

"West Indian. That's another thing. Any time y'can knife a monk, do it. They's too damn many of 'em here. They're an achin' pain."

"Jess de way white folks feels 'bout niggers."

"Damn that. How' bout it? Y' want the job?"

"Hm—well—I'd ruther be a policeman."

"Policeman?" Uggam gasped.

"M-hm. Dass all I wants to be, a policeman, so I kin police all de white folks right plumb in jail!"

Uggam said seriously, "Well, y' might work up to that. But it takes time. An' y've got to eat while y're waitin'." He paused to let this penetrate. "Now, how 'bout this job at Tony's in the meantime? I should think y'd jump at it."

King Solomon was persuaded.

"Hm—well—reckon I does," he said slowly.

"Now y're tootin'!" Uggam's two big front teeth popped out in a grin of genuine pleasure. "Come on. Let's go."

IV

Spitting blood and crying with rage, the West Indian scrambled to his feet. For a moment he stood in front of the store gesticulating furiously and jabbering shrill threats and unintelligible curses. Then abruptly he stopped and took himself off.

King Solomon Gillis, mildly puzzled, watched him from Tony's doorway. "I jess give him a li'l shove," he said to himself, "an' he roll' clean 'cross de sidewalk." And a little later, disgustedly, "Monkey-chaser!" he grunted, and went back to his sweeping.

"Well, big boy, how y' comin' on?"

Gillis dropped his broom. "Hay-o, Mouse. Wha' you been las' two-three days?"

"Oh, around. Gettin' on all right here? Had any trouble?"

"Deed I ain't—'ceptin' jess now I had to throw 'at li'l jigger out."

"Who? The monk?"

"M-hm. He sho' Lawd doan like me in his job. Look like he think I stole it from him, stiddy him tryin' to steal from me. Had to push him down sho' 'nuff 'fo I could git rid of 'im. Den he run off talkin' Wes' Indi'man an' shakin' his fis' at me."

"Ferget it." Uggam glanced about. "Where's Tony?"

"Boss man? He be back direckly."

"Listen—like to make two or three bucks a day extra?"

"Huh?"

"Two or three dollars a day more'n what you're gettin' already?"

"Ain' I near 'nuff in jail now?"

"Listen." King Solomon listened. Uggam hadn't been in France for nothing.[6] Fact was, in France he'd learned about some valuable French medicine. He'd brought some back with him,—little white pills,—and while in Harlem had found a certain druggist who knew what they were and could supply all he could use. Now there were any number of people who would buy and pay well for as much of this French medicine as Uggam could get. It was good for what ailed them, and they didn't know how to get it except through him. But he had no store in which to set up an agency and hence no single place where his customers could go to get what they wanted. If he had, he could sell three or four times as much as he did.

King Solomon was in a position to help him now, same as he had helped King Solomon. He would leave a dozen packages of the medicine—just small envelopes that could all be carried in a coat pocket—with King Solomon every day. Then, he could simply send his customers to King Solomon at Tony's store. They'd make some trifling purchase, slip him a certain coupon which Uggam had given them, and King Solomon would wrap the little envelope of medicine with their purchase. Mustn't let Tony catch on, because he might object, and then the whole scheme would go gaflooey. Of course it wouldn't really be hurting Tony any. Wouldn't it increase the number of his customers?

Finally, at the end of each day, Uggam would meet King Solomon some place and give him a quarter for each coupon he held. There'd be at least ten or twelve a day—two and a half or three dollars plumb extra! Eighteen or twenty dollars a week!

"Dog-gone!" breathed Gillis.

"Does Tony ever leave you heer alone?"

"M-hm. Jess started dis mawnin'. Doan nobody much come round 'tween ten an' twelve, so he done took to doin' his buyin' right 'long 'bout dat time. Nobody hyeh but me fo' 'n hour or so."

"Good. I'll try to get my folks to come 'round here mostly while Tony's out, see?"

"I doan miss."

"Sure y' get the idea, now?" Uggam carefully explained it all again. By the time he had finished, King Solomon was wallowing in gratitude.

"Mouse, you sho' is been a friend to me. Why, 'f 't had n' been fo' you—"

"Bottle it," said Uggam. "I'll be round to your room tonight with enough stuff for tomorrer, see? Be sure'n be there."

---

6. A reference to Uggam's experience in France during World War I.

"Won't be no wha' else."

"An' remember, this is all jess between you 'n me."

"Nobody else but," vowed King Solomon.

Uggam grinned to himself as he went on his way. "Dumb Oscar! Wonder how much can we make before the cops nab him? French medicine—Hmph!"

V

Tony Gabrielli, an oblate Neapolitan of enormous equator, waddled heavily out of his store and settled himself over a soap box.

Usually Tony enjoyed sitting out front thus in the evening, when his helper had gone home and his trade was slackest. He liked to watch the little Gabriellis playing over the sidewalk with the little Levys and Johnsons; the trios and quartettes of brightly dressed, dark-skinned girls merrily out for a stroll; the slovenly gaited, darker men, who eyed them up and down and commented to each other with an unsuppressed "Hot damn!" or "Oh, no, now!"

But tonight Tony was troubled. Something was different since the arrival of King Solomon Gillis. The new man had seemed to prove himself honest and trustworthy, it was true. Tony had tested him, as he always tested a new man, by apparently leaving him alone in charge for two or three mornings. Tony's store was a modification of the front rooms of his flat and was in direct communication with it by way of a glass-windowed door in the rear. Tony always managed to get back into his flat via the sidestreet entrance and watch the new man through this unobtrusive glass-windowed door. If anything excited his suspicion, like unwarranted interest in the cash register, he walked unexpectedly out of this door to surprise the offender in the act. Thereafter he would have no more such trouble. But he had not succeeded in seeing King Solomon steal even an apple.

What he had observed, however, was that the number of customers that came into the store during the morning's slack hour had pronouncedly increased in the last few days. Before, there had been three or four. Now there were twelve or fifteen. The mysterious thing about it was that their purchases totaled little more than those of the original three or four.

Yesterday and today Tony had elected to be in the store at the time when, on the other days, he had been out. But Gillis had not been overcharging or short-changing; for when Tony waited on the customers himself—strange faces all—he found that they bought something like a yeast cake or a five-cent loaf of bread. It was puzzling. Why should strangers leave their own neighborhoods and repeatedly come to him for a yeast cake or a loaf of bread? They were not new neighbors. New neighbors would have bought more variously and extensively and at different times of day. Living near by, they would have come in, the men often in shirtsleeves and slippers, the women in kimonos, with boudoir caps covering their lumpy heads. They would have sent in strange children for things like yeast cakes and loaves of bread. And why did not some of them come in at night when the new helper was off duty?

As for accosting Gillis on suspicion, Tony was too wise for that.

Patronage had a queer way of shifting itself in Harlem. You lost your temper and let slip a single "*nègre*."[7] A week later you sold your business.

Spread over his soap box, with his pudgy hands clasped on his preposterous paunch, Tony sat and wondered. Two men came up, conspicuous for no other reason than that they were white. They displayed extreme nervousness, looking about as if afraid of being seen; and when one of them spoke to Tony it was in a husky, toneless, blowing voice, like the sound of a dirty phonograph record.

"Are you Antonio Gabrielli?"

"Yes, sure." Strange behavior for such lusty-looking fellows. He who had spoken unsmilingly winked first one eye then the other, and indicated by a gesture of his head that they should enter the store. His companion looked cautiously up and down the Avenue, while Tony, wondering what ailed them, rolled to his feet and puffingly led the way.

Inside, the spokesman snuffled, gave his shoulders a queer little hunch, and asked, "Can you fix us up, buddy?" The other glanced restlessly about the place as if he were constantly hearing unaccountable noises.

Tony thought he understood clearly now. "Booze, 'ey?" he smiled. "Sorry—I no got."

"Booze? Hell, no!" The voice dwindled to a throaty whisper. "Dope. Coke, milk, dice—anything.[8] Name your price. Got to have it."

"Dope?" Tony was entirely at a loss. "What's a dis, dope?"

"Aw, lay off, brother. We're in on this. Here." He handed Tony a piece of paper. "Froggy gave us a coupon. Come on. You can't go wrong."

"I no got," insisted the perplexed Tony; nor could he be budged on that point.

Quite suddenly the manner of both men changed. "All right," said the first angrily, in a voice as robust as his body. "All right, you're clever. You no got. Well, you will get. You'll get twenty years!"

"Twenty year? Whadda you talk?"

"Wait a minute, Mac," said the second caller. "Maybe the wop's[9] on the level. Look here, Tony, we're officers, see? Policemen." He produced a badge. "A couple of weeks ago a guy was brought in dying for the want of a shot, see? Dope—he needed some dope—like this—in his arm. See? Well we tried to make him tell us where he'd been getting it, but he was too weak. He croaked next day. Evidently he hadn't had money enough to buy any more.

"Well, this morning a little nigger that goes by the name of Froggy was brought into the precinct pretty well doped up. When he finally came to, he swore he got the stuff here at your store. Of course, we've just been trying to trick you into giving yourself away, but you don't bite. Now what's your game? Know anything about this?"

---

7. French for Negro or black. Here it's an insult.
8. Dope is slang for drugs, especially heroin. Coke is cocaine; milk, heroin; dice, hashish.
9. Wop is derogatory slang for an Italian.

Tony understood. "I dunno," he said slowly; and then his own problem, whose contemplation his callers had interrupted, occurred to him. "Sure!" he exclaimed. "Wait. Maybe so I know somet'ing."

"All right. Spill it."

"I got a new man, work-a for me." And he told them what he had noted since King Solomon Gillis came.

"Sounds interesting. Where is this guy?"

"Here in da store—all day."

"Be here tomorrow?"

"Sure. All day."

"All right. We'll drop in tomorrow and give him the eye. Maybe he's our man."

"Sure. Come ten o'clock. I show you," promised Tony.

VI

Even the oldest and rattiest cabarets in Harlem have sense of shame enough to hide themselves under the ground—for instance, Edwards's. To get into Edwards's you casually enter a dimly lighted corner saloon, apparently—only apparently—a subdued memory of brighter days. What was once the family entrance is now a side entrance for ladies. Supporting yourself against close walls, you crouchingly descend a narrow, twisted staircase until, with a final turn, you find yourself in a glaring, long, low basement. In a moment your eyes become accustomed to the haze of tobacco smoke. You see men and women seated at wire-legged, white-topped tables, which are covered with half-empty bottles and glasses; you trace the slow-jazz accompaniment you heard as you came down the stairs to a pianist, a cornetist, and a drummer on a little platform at the far end of the room. There is a cleared space from the foot of the stairs, where you are standing, to the platform where this orchestra is mounted, and in it a tall brown girl is swaying from side to side and rhythmically proclaiming that she has the world in a jug and the stopper in her hand. Behind a counter at your left sits a fat, bald, tea-colored Negro, and you wonder if this is Edwards—Edwards, who stands in with the police, with the political bosses, with the importers of wines and worse. A white-vested waiter hustles you to a seat and takes your order. The song's tempo changes to a quicker; the drum and the cornet rip out a fanfare, almost drowning the piano; the girl catches up her dress and begins to dance. . . .

Gillis's wondering eyes had been roaming about. They stopped.

"Look, Mouse!" he whispered. "Look a-yonder!"

"Look at what?"

"Dog-gone if it ain' de self-same gal!"

"Wha' d'ye mean, self-same girl?"

"Over yonder, wi' de green stockin's. Dass de gal made me knock over dem apples fust day I come to town. 'Member? Been wishin' I could see her ev'y sence."

"What for?" Uggam wondered.

King Solomon grew confidential. "Ain but two things in dis world, Mouse, I really wants. One is to be a policeman. Been wantin' dat ev'ry sence I seen dat cullud traffic-cop dat day. Other is to git myse'f a gal lak dat one over yonder!"

"You'll do it," laughed Uggam, "if you live long enough."

"Who dat wid her?"

"How'n hell do I know?"

"He cullud?"

"Don't look like it. Why? What of it?"

"Hm—nuthin—"

"How many coupons y' got tonight?"

"Ten." King Solomon handed them over.

"Y'ought to've slipt 'em to me under the table, but it's all right now, long as we got this table to ourselves. Here's y' medicine for tomorrer."

"Wha'?"

"Reach under the table."

Gillis secured and pocketed the medicine.

"An' here's two-fifty for a good day's work." Uggam passed the money over. Perhaps he grew careless; certainly the passing this time was above the table, in plain sight.

"Thanks, Mouse."

Two white men had been watching Gillis and Uggam from a table near by. In the tumult of merriment that rewarded the entertainer's most recent and daring effort, one of these men, with a word to the other, came over and took the vacant chair beside Gillis.

"Is your name Gillis?"

"Tain' nuthin' else."

Uggam's eyes narrowed.

The white man showed King Solomon a police officer's badge.

"You're wanted for dope-peddling. Will you come along, without trouble?"

"Fo' what?"

"Violation of the narcotic law—dope-selling."

"Who—me?"

"Come on, now, lay off that stuff. I saw what happened just now myself." He addressed Uggam. "Do you know this fellow?"

"Nope. Never saw him before tonight."

"Didn't I just see him sell you something?"

"Guess you did. We happened to be sittin' here at the same table and got to talkin'. After a while I says I can't seem to sleep nights, so he offers me sump'n he says'll make me sleep, all right. I don't know what it is, but he says he uses it himself an' I offers to pay him what it cost him. That's how I come to take it. Guess he's got more in his pocket there now."

The detective reached deftly into the coat pocket of the dumbfounded King Solomon and withdrew a packet of envelopes. He tore off a corner of one, emptied a half-dozen tiny white tablets into his palm, and sneered triumphantly. "You'll make a good witness," he told Uggam.

The entertainer was issuing an ultimatum to all sweet mammas who dared to monkey around her loving man. Her audience was absorbed and delighted, with the exception of one couple—the girl with the green stockings and her escort. They sat directly in the line of vision of King Solomon's wide eyes, which, in the calamity that had descended upon him, for the moment saw nothing.

"Are you coming without trouble?"

Mouse Uggam, his friend. Harlem. Land of plenty. City of refuge—city of refuge. If you live long enough—

Consciousness of what was happening between the pair across the room suddenly broke through Gillis's daze like flame through smoke. The man was trying to kiss the girl and she was resisting. Gillis jumped up. The detective, taking the act for an attempt at escape, jumped with him and was quick enough to intercept him. The second officer came at once to his fellow's aid, blowing his whistle several times as he came.

People overturned chairs getting out of the way, but nobody ran for the door. It was an old crowd. A fight was a treat; and the tall Negro could fight.

"Judas Priest!"

"Did you see that?"

"Damn!"

White—both white. Five of Mose Joplin's horses. Poisoning a well. A year's crops. Green stockings—white—white—

"That's the time, papa!"

"Do it, big boy!"

"Good night!"

Uggam watched tensely, with one eye on the door. The second cop had blown for help.

Downing one of the detectives a third time and turning to grapple again with the other, Gillis found himself face to face with a uniformed black policeman.

He stopped as if stunned. For a moment he simply stared. Into his mind swept his own words like a forgotten song, suddenly recalled: —

"Cullud policemans!"

The officer stood ready, awaiting his rush.

"Even—got—cullud—policemans—"

Very slowly King Solomon's arms relaxed; very slowly he stood erect; and the grin that came over his features had something exultant about it.

Miss Cynthie

For the first time in her life somebody had called her "madam." She had been standing, bewildered but unafraid, while innumerable Red Caps appropriated piece after piece of the baggage arrayed on the platform.[1] Neither her brief seventy years' journey through life nor her long two days' travel northward had dimmed the live brightness of her eyes, which, for all their bewilderment, had accurately selected her own treasures out of the row of luggage and guarded them vigilantly. "These yours, madam?"

The biggest Red Cap of all was smiling at her. He looked for all the world like Doc Crinshaw's oldest son back home. Her little brown face relaxed; she smiled back at him.

"They got to be. You all done took all the others."

He laughed aloud. Then—"Carry 'em in for you?"

She contemplated his bulk. "Reckon you can manage it—puny little feller like you?"

Thereupon they were friends. Still grinning broadly, he surrounded himself with her impedimenta, the enormous brown extension-case on one shoulder, the big straw suit-case in the opposite hand, the carpet-bag under one arm. She herself held fast to the umbrella. "Always like to have sump'm in my hand when I walk. Can't never tell when you'll run across a snake."

"There aren't any snakes in the city."

"There's snakes everywhere, chile."

They began the tedious hike up the interminable platform. She was small and quick. Her carriage was surprisingly erect, her gait astonishingly spry. She said:

"You liked to took my breath back yonder, boy, callin' me 'madam.' Back home everybody call me 'Miss Cynthie.' Even their chillun. Black folks, white folks too. 'Miss Cynthie.' Well, when you come up with that 'madam' o' yourn, I say to myself, 'Now, I wonder who that chile's a-grinnin' at? 'Madam' stands for mist'ess o' the house, and I sho' ain' mist'ess o' nothin' in this hyeh New York.'"

"Well, you see, we call everybody 'madam.'"

"Everybody?—Hm." The bright eyes twinkled. "Seem like that'd worry me some—if I was a man."

He acknowledged his slip and observed, "I see this isn't your first trip to New York."

"First trip any place, son. First time I been over fifty mile from Waxhaw. Only travelin' I've done is in my head. Ain' seen many places, but I's seen a passel o' people. Reckon places is pretty much alike after people been in 'em awhile."

"Yes, ma'am. I guess that's right."

"You ain' no reg'lar bag-toter, is you?"

"Ma'am?"

---

1. Red Caps were porters. At this time railroad porters were mainly African Americans. It was an occupation segregated by race.

Story, 1933.

"You talk too good."

"Well, I only do this in vacation-time. I'm still in school."

"You is. What you aimin' to be?"

"I'm studying medicine."

"You is?" She beamed. "Aimin' to be a doctor, huh? Thank the Lord for that. That's what I always wanted my David to be. My grandchile hyeh in New York. He's to meet me hyeh now."

"I bet you'll have a great time."

"Mussn't bet, chile. That's sinful. I tole him 'for' he left home, I say, 'Son, you the only one o' the chillun what's got a chance to amount to sump'm. Don't th'ow it away. Be a preacher or a doctor. Work yo' way up and don' stop short. If the Lord don' see fit for you to doctor the soul, then doctor the body. If you don' get to be a reg'lar doctor, be a tooth-doctor. If you jes' can't make that, be a foot-doctor. And if you don' get that fur, be a undertaker. That's the least you must be. That ain' so bad. Keep you acquainted with the house of the Lord. Always mind the house o' the Lord—whatever you do, do like a church-steeple: aim high and go straight.'"

"Did he get to be a doctor?"

"Don' b'lieve he did. Too late startin', I reckon. But he's done succeeded at sump'm. Mus' be at least a undertaker, 'cause he started sendin' the homefolks money, and he come home las' year dressed like Judge Pettiford's boy what went off to school in Virginia. Wouldn't tell none of us 'zackly what he was doin', but he said he wouldn' never be happy till I come and see for myself. So hyeh I is." Something softened her voice. "His mammy died befo' he knowed her. But he was always sech a good chile—" The something was apprehension. "Hope he *is* a undertaker."

They were mounting a flight of steep stairs leading to an exit gate, about which clustered a few people still hoping to catch sight of arriving friends. Among these a tall young brown-skinned man in a light grey suit suddenly waved his panama[2] and yelled, "Hey, Miss Cynthie!"

Miss Cynthie stopped, looked up, and waved back with a delighted umbrella. The Red Cap's eyes lifted too. His lower jaw sagged.

"Is that your grandson?"

"It sho' is," she said and distanced him for the rest of the climb. The grandson, with an abandonment that superbly ignored onlookers, folded the little woman in an exultant, smothering embrace. As soon as she could, she pushed him off with breathless mock impatience.

"Go 'way, you fool, you. Aimin' to squeeze my soul out my body befo' I can get a look at this place?" She shook herself into the semblance of composure. "Well. You don't look hungry, anyhow."

"Ho-ho! Miss Cynthie in New York! Can y' imagine this? Come on. I'm parked on Eighth Avenue."

---

2. A panama hat is a broad-brimmed, usually white, hat.

The Red Cap delivered the outlandish luggage into a robin's egg blue open Packard with scarlet wheels, accepted the grandson's dollar and smile, and stood watching the car roar away up Eighth Avenue.

Another Red Cap came up. "Got a break, hey, boy?"

"Dave Tappen himself—can you beat that?"

"The old lady hasn't seen the station yet—starin' at him."

"That's not the half of it, bozo. That's Dave Tappen's grandmother. And what do you s'pose she hopes?"

"What?"

"She hopes that Dave has turned out to be a successful undertaker!"

"Undertaker? Undertaker!"

They stared at each other a gaping moment, then doubled up with laughter.

"Look—through there—that's the Chrysler Building. Oh, helleluhah! I meant to bring you up Broadway—"

"David—"

"Ma'am?"

"This hyeh wagon yourn?"

"Nobody else's. Sweet buggy, ain't it?"

"David—you ain't turned out to be one of them moonshiners,[3] is you?"

"Moonshiners—? Moon—Ho! No indeed, Miss Cynthie. I got a better racket 'n that."

"Better which?"

"Game. Business. Pick-up."[4]

"Tell me, David. What is yo' racket?"

"Can't spill it yet, Miss Cynthie. Rather show you. Tomorrow night you'll know the worst. Can you make out till tomorrow night?"

"David, you know I always wanted you to be a doctor, even if 'twasn' nothin' but a foot-doctor. The very leas' I wanted you to be was a undertaker."

"Undertaker! Oh, Miss Cynthie!—with my sunny disposition?"

"Then you ain' even a undertaker?"

"Listen, Miss Cynthie. Just forget 'bout what I am for awhile. Must till tomorrow night. I want you to see for yourself. Tellin' you will spoil it. Now stop askin', you hear? —because I'm not answerin'—I'm surprisin' you. And don't expect anybody you meet to tell you. It'll mess up the whole works. Understand? Now give the big city a break. There's the elevated train going up Columbus Avenue. Ain't that hot stuff?"

Miss Cynthie looked. "Humph!" she said. "Tain' half high as that trestle two mile from Waxhaw."

She thoroughly enjoyed the ride up Central Park West. The stagger lights, the extent of the park, the high, close, kingly buildings, remarkable because their stoves cooled them in summer as well as heated them in winter, all drew nods of mild interest. But what gave

---

3. Moonshine is slang for illegal alcohol made at home.
4. Gambling.

her special delight was not these: it was that David's car so effortlessly sped past the headlong drove of vehicles racing northward.

They stopped for a red light; when they started again their machine leaped forward with a triumphant eagerness that drew from her an unsuppressed "Hot you, David! That's it!"

He grinned appreciatively. "Why, you're a regular New Yorker already."

"New York nothin'! I done the same thing fifty years ago—befo' I knowed they was a New York."

"What!"

"'Deed so. Didn' I use to tell you 'bout my young mare, Betty? Chile, I'd hitch Betty up to yo' grandpa's buggy and pass anything on the road. Betty never knowed what another horse's dust smelt like. No 'ndeedy. Shuh, boy, this ain' nothin' new to me. Why that broke-down Fo'd yo uncle Jake's got ain' nothin'—nothin' but a sorry mess. Done got so slow I jes' won' ride in it—I declare I'd rather walk. But this hyeh thing, now, this is right nice." She settled back in complete, complacent comfort, and they sped on, swift and silent.

Suddenly she sat erect with abrupt discovery.

"David—well—bless my soul!"

"What's the matter, Miss Cynthie?"

Then he saw what had caught her attention. They were traveling up Seventh Avenue now, and something was miraculously different. Not the road; that was as broad as ever, wide, white gleaming in the sun. Not the houses; they were lofty still, lordly, disdainful, supercilious. Not the cars; they continued to race impatiently onward, innumerable, precipitate, tumultuous. Something else, something at once obvious and subtle, insistent, pervasive, compelling.

"David—this mus' be Harlem!"

"Good Lord, Miss Cynthie—!"

"Don' use the name of the Lord in vain, David."

"But I mean—gee!—you're no fun at all. You get everything before a guy can tell you."

"You got plenty to tell me, David. But don' nobody need to tell me this. Look a yonder."

Not just a change of complexion. A completely dissimilar atmosphere. Sidewalks teeming with leisurely strollers at once strangely dark and bright. Boys in white trousers, berets, and green shirts, with slickened black heads and proud swagger. Bareheaded girls in crisp organdie dresses, purple, canary, gay scarlet. And laughter, abandoned strong Negro laughter, some falling full on the ear, some not heard at all, yet sensed—the warm life-breath of the tireless carnival to which Harlem's heart quickens in summer.

"This is it," admitted David. "Get a good eyeful. Here's One Hundred and Twenty-fifth Street—regular little Broadway. And here's the Alhambra, and up ahead we'll pass the Lafayette."

"What's them?"

"Theatres."

"Theatres? Theatres. Humph! Look, David—is that a colored folks' church?" They were passing a fine gray-tone edifice.

"That? Oh. Sure it is. So's this one on this side."

"No! Well, ain' that fine? Splendid big church like that for colored folks."

Taking his cue from this, her first tribute to the city, he said, "You ain't seen nothing yet. Wait a minute."

They swung left through a side street and turned right on a boulevard. "What do you think o' that?" And he pointed to the quarter-million-dollar St. Mark's.

"That a colored church, too?"

"'Tain' no white one. And they built it themselves, you know. Nobody's hand-me-down gift."

She heaved a great happy sigh. "Oh, yes, it was a gift, David. It was a gift from on high." Then, "Look a hyeh—which a one you belong to?"

"Me? Why, I don't belong to any—that is, none o' these. Mine's over in another section. Y'see, mine's Baptist. These are all Methodist. See?"

"M-m. Uh-huh. I see."

They circled a square and slipped into a quiet narrow street overlooking a park, stopping before the tallest of the apartment-houses in the single commanding row.

Alighting, Miss Cynthie gave this imposing structure one sideways, upward glance, and said, "Y'all live like bees in a hive, don't y'? —I boun' the women does all the work, too." A moment later, "So this is a elevator? Feel like I'm glory-bound, sho' nuff."

Along a tiled corridor and into David's apartment. Rooms leading into rooms. Luxurious couches, easy-chairs, a brown-walnut grand piano, gay-shaded floor lamps, panelled walls, deep rugs, treacherous glass-wood floors—and a smiling golden-skinned girl in a gingham housedress, approaching with outstretched hands.

"This is Ruth, Miss Cynthie."

"Miss Cynthie!" said Ruth.

They clasped hands. "Been wantin' to see David's girl ever since he first wrote us 'bout her."

"Come—here's your room this way. Here's the bath. Get out of your things and get comfy. You must be worn out with the trip."

"Worn out? Worn out? Shuh. How you gon' get worn out on a train? Now if 'twas a horse, maybe, or Jake's no-count Fo'd—but a train—didn' but one thing bother me on that train."

"What?"

"When the man made them beds down, I jes' couldn' manage to undress same as at home. Why, s'posin' sump'm bus' the train open—where'd you be? Naked as a jay-bird in dew-berry time."

David took in her things and left her to get comfortable. He returned, and Ruth, despite his reassuring embrace, whispered:

"Dave, you can't fool old folks—why don't you go ahead and tell her about yourself? Think of the shock she's going to get at her age."

David shook his head. "She'll get over the shock if she's there looking on. If we just told her, she'd never understand. We've got to railroad her into it. Then she'll be happy."

"She's nice. But she's got the same ideas as all old folks—"

"Yea—but with her you can change 'em. Specially if everything is really all right. I know her. She's for church and all, but she believes in good times too, if they're right. Why, when I was a kid—" He broke off. "Listen!"

Miss Cynthie's voice came quite distinctly to them, singing a jaunty little rhyme:

> Oh I danced with the gal with the hole in her stockin,'
> And her toe kep' a-kickin' and her heel kep' a-knockin'—

> "Come up, Jesse, and get a drink o' gin,
> 'Cause you near to the heaven as you'll ever get ag'in."

"She taught me that when I wasn't knee-high to a cricket," David said.

Miss Cynthie still sang softly and merrily:

> Then I danced with the gal with the dimple in her cheek,
> And if she'd 'a' kep' a-smilin', I'd 'a' danced for a week—

"God forgive me," prayed Miss Cynthie as she discovered David's purpose the following night. She let him and Ruth lead her, like an early Christian martyr, into the Lafayette Theatre. The blinding glare of the lobby produced a merciful self-anaesthesia, and she entered the sudden dimness of the interior as involuntarily as in a dream. . . .

Attendants outdid each other for Mr. Dave Tappen. She heard him tell them, "Fix us up till we go on," and found herself sitting between Ruth and David in the front row of a lower box. A miraculous device of the devil, a motion-picture that talked, was just ending. At her feet the orchestra was assembling. The motion-picture faded out amid a scattered round of applause. Lights blazed and the orchestra burst into an ungodly rumpus.

She looked out over the seated multitude, scanning row upon row of illumined faces, black faces, white faces, yellow, tan, brown; bald heads, bobbed heads, kinky and straight heads; and upon every countenance, expectancy—scowling expectancy in this case, smiling in that, complacent here, amused there, commentative elsewhere, but everywhere suspense, abeyance, anticipation.

Half a dozen people were ushered down the nearer aisle to reserved seats in the second row. Some of them caught sight of David and Ruth and waved to them. The chairs immediately behind them in the box were being shifted. "Hello, Tap!" Miss Cynthie saw David turn, rise, and shake hands with two men. One of them was large, bald and pink, emanating good cheer; the other short, thin, sallow with thick black hair and a sour mien. Ruth also acknowledged their greeting. "This is my grandmother," David said proudly. "Miss Cynthie, meet my managers, Lou and Lee Goldman." "Pleased to meet you," managed Miss Cynthie. "Great lad, this boy of yours," said Lou Goldman. "Great little partner he's got, too," added Lee. They also settled back expectantly.

"Here we go!"

The curtain rose to reveal a cotton-field at dawn. Pickers in blue denim overalls, bandanas, and wide-brimmed straws, or in gingham aprons and sun-bonnets, were singing as they worked. Their voices, from clearest soprano to richest bass, blended in low concordances, first simply humming a series of harmonies, until, gradually, came words, like figures forming in mist. As the sound grew, the mist cleared, the words came round and full, and the sun rose bringing light as if in answer to the song. The chorus swelled, the radiance grew, the two, as if emanating from a single source, fused their crescendos, till at last they achieved a joint transcendence of tonal and visual brightness.

"Swell opener," said Lee Goldman.

"Ripe," agreed Lou.

David and Ruth arose. "Stay here and enjoy the show, Miss Cynthie. You'll see us again in a minute."

"Go to it, kids," said Lou Goldman.

"Yea—burn 'em up," said Lee.

Miss Cynthie hardly noted that she had been left, so absorbed was she in the spectacle. To her, the theatre had always been the antithesis of the church. As the one was the refuge of righteousness, so the other was the stronghold of transgression. But this first scene awakened memories, captured and held her attention by offering a blend of truth and novelty. Having thus baited her interest, the show now proceeded to play it like the trout through swift-flowing waters of wickedness. Resist as it might, her mind was caught and drawn into the impious subsequences.

The very music that had just rounded out so majestically now distorted itself into ragtime. The singers came forward and turned to dancers; boys, a crazy, swaying background, threw up their arms and kicked out their legs in a rhythmic jamboree; girls, an agile, brazen foreground, caught their skirts up to their hips and displayed their copper calves, knees, thighs, in shameless, incredible steps. Miss Cynthie turned dismayed eyes upon the audience, to discover that mob of sinners devouring it all with fond satisfaction. Then the dancers separated and with final abandon flung themselves off the stage in both directions.

Lee Goldman commented through the applause, "They work easy, them babies."

"Yea," said Lou. "Savin' the hot stuff for later."

Two black-faced cotton-pickers appropriated the scene, indulging in dialogue that their hearers found uproarious.

"Ah'm tired."

"Ah'm hongry."

"Dis job jes' wears me out."

"Starves me to death."

"Ah'm so tired—you know what Ah'd like to do?"

"What?"

"Ah'd like to go to sleep and dream I was sleepin'."

"What good dat do?"

"Den I could wake up and still be 'sleep."

"Well y'know what Ah'd like to do?"

"No. What?"

"Ah'd like to swaller me a hog and a hen."

"What good dat do?"

"Den Ah'd always be full o' ham and eggs."

"Ham? Shuh. Don't you know a hog has to be smoked 'fo' he's a ham?"

"Well, if I swaller him, he'll have a smoke all around him, won' he?" Presently Miss Cynthie was smiling like everyone else, but her smile soon fled. For the comics departed, and the dancing girls returned, this time in scant travesties of their earlier voluminous costumes—tiny sun-bonnets perched jauntily on one side of their glistening bobs, bandanas reduced to scarlet neck-ribbons, waists mere brassieres, skirts mere gingham sashes.

And now Miss Cynthie's whole body stiffened with a new and surpassing shock; her bright eyes first widened with unbelief, then slowly grew dull with misery. In the midst of a sudden great volley of applause her grandson had broken through that bevy of agile wantons and begun to sing.

He too was dressed as a cotton-picker, but a Beau Brummel[5] among cotton-pickers; his hat bore a pleated green band, his bandana was silk, his overalls blue satin, his shoes black patent leather. His eyes flashed, his teeth gleamed, his body swayed, his arms waved, his words came fast and clear. As he sang, his companions danced a concerted tap, uniformly wild, ecstatic. When he stopped singing, he himself began to dance, and without sacrificing crispness of execution, seemed to absorb into himself every measure of the energy which the girls, now merely standing off and swaying, had relinquished.

"Look at that boy go," said Lee Goldman.

"He ain't started yet," said Lou.

But surrounding comment, Dave's virtuosity, the eager enthusiasm of the audience were all alike lost on Miss Cynthie. She sat with stricken eyes watching this boy whom she'd raised from a babe, taught right from wrong, brought up in the church, and endowed with her prayers, this child whom she had dreamed of seeing a preacher, a regular doctor, a tooth-doctor, a foot-doctor, at the very least an undertaker—sat watching him disport himself for the benefit of a sin-sick, flesh-hungry mob of lost souls, not one of whom knew or cared to know the loving kindness of God; sat watching a David she'd never foreseen, turned tool of the devil, disciple of lust, unholy prince among sinners.

For a long time she sat there watching with wretched eyes, saw portrayed on the stage David's arrival in Harlem, his escape from 'old friends' who tried to dupe him; saw him working as a trap-drummer in a night-club, where he fell in love with Ruth, a dancer; not the gentle Ruth Miss Cynthie knew, but a wild and shameless young savage who danced like seven devils—in only a girdle and breast-plates; saw the two of them join in a song-and-dance act that eventually made them Broadway headliners, an act presented *in toto* as the pre-finale of this show. And not any of the melodies, not any of the sketches, not all the comic philosophy of the tired-and-hungry duo, gave her figure a moment's relaxation or brightened the dull defeat in her staring eyes. She sat apart, alone in the box, the symbol, the epitome of supreme failure. Let the rest of the theatre be riotous,

5. Beau Brummel was an eighteenth-century figure of great style.

clamoring for more and more of Dave Tappen, "Tap," the greatest tapster of all time, idol of uptown and downtown New York. For her, they were lauding simply an exhibition of sin which centered about her David.

"This'll run a year on Broadway," said Lee Goldman.

"Then we'll take it to Paris."

Encores and curtains with Ruth, and at last David came out on the stage alone. The clamor dwindled. And now he did something quite unfamiliar to even the most consistent of his followers. Softly, delicately, he began to tap a routine designed to fit a particular song. When he had established the rhythm, he began to sing the song:

> Oh I danced with the gal with the hole in her stockin,'
> And her toe kep' a-kickin' and her heel kep' a-knockin'—
>
> "Come up, Jesse, and get a drink o' gin,
> 'Cause you near to the heaven as you'll ever get ag'in."

As he danced and sang this song, frequently smiling across at Miss Cynthie, a visible change transformed her. She leaned forward incredulously, listened intently, then settled back in limp wonder. Her bewildered eyes turned on the crowd, on those serried rows of shriftless sinners.[6] And she found in their faces now an overwhelmingly curious thing: a grin, a universal grin, a gleeful and sinless grin such as not the nakedest chorus in the performance had produced. In a few seconds, with her own song, David had dwarfed into unimportance, wiped off their faces, swept out of their minds every trace of what had seemed to be sin; had reduced it all to mere trivial detail and revealed these revelers as a crowd of children, enjoying the guileless antics of another child. And Miss Cynthie whispered, "Bless my soul! They didn' mean nothin'. . . They jes' didn' see no harm in it—"

> Then I danced with the gal with the dimple in her cheek,
> And if she'd 'a' kep' a-smilin', I'd 'a' danced for a week—
> "Come up, Jesse—"

The crowd laughed, clapped their hands, whistled. Someone threw David a bright yellow flower. "From Broadway!"

He caught the flower. A hush fell. He said:

"I'm really happy tonight, folks. Y'see this flower? Means success, don't it? Well, listen. The one who is really responsible for my success is here tonight with me. Now what do you think o' that?"

The hush deepened.

"Y'know folks, I'm sump'm like Adam—I never had no mother. But I've got a grandmother. Down home everybody calls her Miss Cynthie. And everybody loves her. Take that song I just did for you. Miss Cynthie taught me that when I wasn't knee-high to a cricket. But that wasn't all she taught me. Far back as I can remember, she always used

---

6. Unrepentant sinners.

to say one thing: Son, do like a church steeple—aim high and go straight. And for doin' it—" he grinned, contemplating the flower— "I get this."

He strode across to the edge of the stage that touched Miss Cynthie's box. He held up the flower.

"So y'see folks, this isn't mine. It's really Miss Cynthie's." He leaned over to hand it to her. Miss Cynthie's last trace of doubt was swept away. She drew a deep breath of revelation; her bewilderment vanished, her redoubtable composure returned, her eyes lighted up; and no one but David, still holding the flower toward her, heard her sharply whispered reprimand:

"Keep it, you fool. Where's yo' manners—givin' 'way what somebody give you?"

David grinned:

"Take it, tyro. What you tryin' to do—crab my act?"

Thereupon, Miss Cynthie, smiling at him with bright, meaningful eyes, leaned over without rising from her chair, jerked a tiny twig off the stem of the flower, then sat decisively back, resolutely folding her arms with only a leaf in her hand.

"This'll do for me," she said.

The finale didn't matter. People filed out of the theatre. Miss Cynthie sat awaiting her children, her foot absently patting time to the orchestra's jazz recessional. Perhaps she was thinking, "God moves in a mysterious way," but her lips were unquestionably forming the words:

—danced with the gal—hole in her stockin'—
—toe kep' a-kickin'—heel kep' a-knockin'.

Eric Walrond

(1898–1966)

Eric Walrond was born in Georgetown, British Guyana, to a Barbadian mother and a Guyanese father. His first eight years were spent in Guyana, but after his father left in 1906, Walrond and his mother moved to Barbados to live with relatives. Walrond attended St. Stephen's Boys School in Black Rock until 1910, when his mother took him to the Panama Canal Zone in hopes of finding his father. However, the reunion was not successful and by 1913, Walrond was attending school in Colón, where he became fluent in Spanish. He used his training as a secretary and stenographer to gain employment with the Health Department of the Canal Commission at Cristobal. He also worked as a reporter for the Panama *Star-Herald* before emigrating to New York in 1918 at the age of twenty. It was these experiences that furnished the material for Walrond's single book and the basis of his literary fame, the modernist collection of stories, *Tropic Death* (1926). It is often compared in stature to Jean Toomer's *Cane* (1923).

Walrond attended City College of New York for three years and took creative writing courses at Columbia University for a year, but never received a degree. While taking classes, he supported himself with clerical positions, working as a stenographer in the British Recruiting Mission and as secretary to the superintendent of Broad Street Hospital. In 1921 Walrond became an owner and editor of *The Brooklyn and Long Island Informer*. He remained with the paper until 1923, when he became involved with Marcus Garvey's Universal Negro Improvement Association (UNIA) and was made an associate editor of *Negro World*. While working for the paper, Walrond also wrote articles for such periodicals as *Current History*, *The Messenger*, and *The Independent*. Before long he became dissatisfied with Garvey's organization, left the UNIA, and was recruited by Charles S. Johnson to work for *Opportunity* as an associate editor from 1925 to 1927. Throughout the early twenties, he published short stories in such journals as *Opportunity*, *Smart Set*, and *The New Republic*.

His short story "The Voodoo's Revenge" won third prize in the 1925 *Opportunity* short story contest and demonstrates the impressionistic style that distinguishes his collection, *Tropic Death*. The book did not sell well, but it was highly regarded by reviewers, and in 1928 he became one of the first three blacks to win a Guggenheim Fellowship in creative writing (the others were Countee Cullen and Nella Larsen). He had been given a contract by publishers Boni and Liveright to write a history of the French role in the Panama Canal. The fellowship enabled Walrond to travel extensively throughout the Caribbean and France. In Paris he shared a studio with Countee Cullen in the summer of 1929 and became involved with the African American expatriate community. After a brief visit to Brooklyn to see his mother in 1931, Walrond settled in a small village near Avignon and published a long article on the Panama Canal in the Spanish magazine *Ahora* (1934). He never returned to the United States nor published again, aside from a few pieces in French magazines.

Very little is known about Eric Walrond's personal life. He never married, and whatever close relationships he had are unknown. After living for a long time in rural France, Walrond settled in London, where he spent his last days still working on his book about the Panama Canal. He died in 1966.

The Voodoo's Revenge

At the edge of Faulke's River a fleet of cayukas lay at anchor. It was a murky slice of water front. Half Latin, it was a rendezvous for those French creoles who had left the service of the Americans to go into business for themselves as liquor dealers, fishermen, coal burners, black artists, etc. On the side of it facing the muddy rivulet with its coral islets and turtle shoals, were the usual cafes, dance halls and fish markets. Behind these stretched a line of "Silver" quarters—cabins of the black Antillian canal diggers.

One ran across in this part of the Silver City Negroes who spoke *patois*[1]—blacks and brunettes from St. Lucia and Trinidad and Martinique. Fronting their quarters a road meandered, dusty on sunny days and a lake of mud and slush on rainy ones, up to Monkey Hill.

Along Faulke's River folk gathered each morning to buy up the offerings of the fishermen and the pearl divers who had come in the night before. In the group of traders one saw pretty Negresses from the isles of the Caribbean who wore flame-colored skirts and East Indian earrings and heavy silver bangles reaching up to their elbows. Some, those of "higher caste," wore in their bosoms cameos and pearls and Birds of Paradise feathers to ornament their already gorgeous head dress. In those days short skirts were foreign to women of the tropics—and one saw long beautiful silk dresses, a faint echo of Louis Quinze, trailing behind the dusky grande dames as they went from stall to stall and with bamboo baskets bought dolphins and pigeon peas and guinea birds. For hours, as the tropical sun beat down upon them, these lovely angels of Ethiopia would shop and dye their lips with the wine of luscious pomegranates and talk lightly of the things on sale. With them it was a Spring rite. They made a holiday out of it. And far into the morning cayukas full of coral and oranges and yam-pies would come swinging up out of the dark tremulous bowls of the lagoon beyond, to empty themselves upon the wharf while the *patois* men would stand by and fill their pipes, chin, and oft-times steal away in soft bits of voodoo melody.

1. A dialect of French and other languages.

Opportunity, July 1925.

Zoomie maca le
Maca le la
Le a le a le

Zoomie tell me
Pape say kiss
'Am a' ready

Tell me mama say wahlo . . .

Zerry wuz a mambe
Zerry.
Wahlo, wahlo, wahlo.
Zamba le a le a le a
Zoke! Zoke! Zoke!

A queer lot these men. Huge, gigantic, black as night, each grew a mustache or a grizzly beard. In them one saw a transplantation of the ancient culture of Europe. In the old Maiden Islands one saw big hairy black ship chandlers and fishing boat men who walked with the grace and majesty of university professors. And in these silent old witch-worshipping seamen on Faulke's River, unlike the voluble Maches and Spaniards who infested the crumbling wharves along Limon Bay, was a lingering strain of those heroic men who set out at the beginning of the Nineteenth Century to conquer in the name of France the tropic isles of the Caribbean.

Night in the tropics is an erotic affair. As it flung its mantle over the shining form of the lake the fishermen along it would sit on the bottoms of upturned cayukas and for hours dream of far off weird things. Dreaming; dreaming; dreaming. That is all they seemed to do. For it was difficult to penetrate the mind of a *patois* man. He spoke little. He preferred solitude. He preferred to smoke his cow-dung pipe for days in silence. But he never slept. The fire in his lustreless eyes never went out.

One of these *patois* men was a robust son of the soil who still went by the name of Nestor Villaine. Certainly it had been a comparatively easy thing for him to get in, jabber a few mouthfuls of broken French, and live as an *obeah* man.[2] Up in the hills he lived the life of a hermit, ate *bobo* fish and iguanas and corn cakes and grew up as hardy and as hairy-chested as the oaks and mahogany he tore down to burn his coal. Away from the society of men and the endearments of women Nestor grew to be a stern son of the jungle. Hard, cold, relentless, he hated the sight of human beings.

Villaine plotted revenge!

II

Caught in the maelstrom of local politics Editor Villaine of the *Aspinwall Voice* drew a breath of righteous indignation as he was jostled into the *alcaldia*. Alongside him was

2. An obeah man or woman was a sacred person versed in the art of voodoo.

a crouching bit of humanity—a short, brown-skinned stranger whose immaculate duck, white and tan shoes, jippi-jappa hat, branded him an enemy; in all probability in the pay of the reactionary Ex-Governor Tejada. One of his arms was in a sling; a bit of plaster adorned his left temple. His nose was cut. Dark spots, of ink, soiled the caballero's otherwise white suit.

As if they were made by sharply pointed finger nails, gashes and bruises covered his copper-coloured face. His eyes threatened to close up. His lips hung unbeautifully. Not only an arm was in a sling, but tied about his head was a red neckerchief. Unlike his fistic antagonist he had on workmen's clothes. Ink stained his jacket. Dust and dirt disfigured his already ink-stained trousers. Indubitably Nestor was not at his best.

In walked the *alcalde.* He was a tall, finely built man. Former Deputy Salzedo was one of the handsomest men in the Republic. Friend and foe admitted that. It had an added significance, especially when one is brilliant and fearless and something of a radical. That was what he was. He was the hope of the Liberal Party. He had been swept into office, a few weeks previous, on the crest of a mighty wave of rebellion. In the coastal provinces he was hailed as a Messiah, a man to lead the people out of the chaos brought on by the Tejadistas.

"Orden!"

The *tinterillos* came to a verbal halt. The *alcaldia* was full of them. They sat in the best wicker chairs. They buzzed around it like a nest of hungry bees. Out at the door Pablo, the black porter, who belonged pathologically to the leper asylum as Palo Seco, kept order with an *agente's* baton. Leaning up against the newly papered wall was the dean of the *tinterillos,* the celebrated Dr. Cecilio Rhodes, a West Indian Negro. As the *alcalde* entered, and malleted for order, Rhodes, dragging the toothpick out of his mouth, yelled to his colleagues engulfed in the soft wicker chairs to "Rise, in respect to His Excellency, El Senor Alcalde!"

The *tinterillos* rose with one accord out of respect to His Excellency El Senor Alcalde.

Alcalde Salzedo gazed at the prisoners, Editor Villaine and the truculent *extranjero* with the white and tan shoes.

"Well, what is the trouble with you two?"

The *agente* testified. At high noon, as the labor train had emptied its freight and had started on its way back to the round house, he had been standing in front of the kiosk at the corner of Sixth and Bolivar Streets when a shrill cry attracted his attention. Seizing his baton he raced in the direction whence it had come. In the middle of the block, in the offices of the *Aspinwall Voice,* he found the prisoners wrestling and throwing rolling pins at each other. After a terrific struggle in which he lost a button off his coat and a bit of skin off the third finger of his left hand, he had succeeded in arresting the scoundrels and there they were. . . .

"Now, what have you got to say for yourself!" asked His Excellency as the *agente* retired.

Villaine bristled. Ah, to hear his master's voice! To be able to look into his mentor's dusky eyes and tell him the story of his love and fidelity to him! To relate, by a striking tale of primordial lust, just how far he was willing to go for the Liberal Party! To do that! For years, as a fly-by-night pamphleteer, he had longed for an opportunity to show these native leaders, like Salzedo, just how loyal a "Chumbo"—that is, a black from the English colonies—could be. For Nestor was a native of Anguilla who had come to the isthmus as a "contract laborer" to dig the canal. But he didn't want to do that; he had ideas, big, earth-quaking ideas. So when the *Magdalena,* the ship on which he had arrived, docked, he managed, as the laborers disembarked, to slip out of the line and secrete himself behind a bale of merchandise in front of the wharf. When the car in which the men were sardined began to pull out, he had raced across the railroad tracks and had joined the carnival of folk which swept leisurely up Front Street. Dusk found him safely ensconced in a Chinese lice-ridden rooming house on Bottle Alley.

But that was six years before.

"Nothing to say?" the *alcalde* inquired impatiently. He was annoyed at the glow in Villaine's dreamy black eyes.

"Ah," he breathed, "I was—was—this brute came in my office and without provocation at all began to abuse the Liberal Party, began to swear at Alcalde Salzedo—vilely—criminally! And when he did that I got red in the eyes, and I—well, I went after him, that's all!"

"And you?" inquired the *alcalde,* turning to the other.

"Nada!"

"All right then, sixty days, both of you!"

"Madre de Dios!" Villaine staggered under the weight of the sentence. Sixty days—sixty days—

Naively, very naively, he went up to the desk, put his black ink-stained hands on it, and faced his gaoler.

"Surely," he smiled eagerly, "surely, you do not mean me?"

"Yes, you too. Both of you. Next."

The *tinterillos* began beseiging the *alcalde* with their preposterous requests. Pablo with his baton hopped in and escorted the prisoners to the cuartel, which was nearby.

Villaine was in a psychic stupor. It took a long time for it to sink into him. He couldn't understand it. It was a nightmare, a hideous dream. His head ached.

On a cold, wet slab he sat in the cuartel, staring at the crumbling ceiling. Why, he had been fighting Salzedo's battles! He fought for him! He was—get away you rat! Yes, come to think of it he had been Salzedo's champion right along. *The Aspinwall Voice* was willingly and freely his. It boosted him. It came to be known as the Liberal Party's keenest weapon of satire.

Still . . . ah, the fleas in this place! Still Salzedo, on his magisterial throne, had sentenced him to sixty days in jail as if he were a common felon. His body was sore. It was full of cuts and bruises. Cuts and bruises that he had suffered while fighting his jailer's battles.

Revolution surged through him. And at night when the prisoners conspired to break through the walls of that terrible inquisition Nestor Villaine, the "Chumbo" *herido*, would be plotting, plotting.

At Porto Bello, where he broke rocks, he was gruff and brooding. His fellow prisoners avoided him. The *guardias* chucked the food at him and had as little dealings with him as possible. Plainly Villaine had something on his mind.

III

One of the show places of the river front was a cafe with a brothel in the rear. Here the *patois* men drank goblets of anisette and vermouth and met their women. It was the prototype of Sablo's Baron Bolivar Street. But this nameless rendezvous also served a deadly purpose. It was here that the black artists met "their" cooks and servant girls who worked for the white Americans—folk of the "Golden City"—and gave them for a pittance tips on secret poisoning through vegetable alkaloids, etc. And here it was one dark still night Nestor agreed to meet a young St. Lucian by the name of Sambola.

As the clock struck twelve the boy flung aside the dingy curtain and stepped into the room. Except for Nestor, alone at a table with a glass of green liquor, it was deserted. Squeezing through a network of demijohns the boy came and sat at Nestor's table. Silently the man pushed the bottle over to him and pretending to take a puff at his pipe threw out a haze of smoke to hide the flames that had leapt into his eyes. Sambola poured out a drink and dashed it down his throat. Nestor lowered his eyes in assurance.

Yes, this boy was just the one for it. He came from a family that wallowed in *obeah*. His brother, who was a time-keeper on the Zone, which was a big job for a grammar-school boy to hold, had kept his job there all three years by virtue of it. His other brother, the one all of whose front teeth were capped with gold, steered clear of dagger-gemmed combs and senorita's vials simply because his old witch-stricken mother sat of nights and burned *obeah* for the dusky ladies with whom he consorted in *El Barrio Rojo*.

"Now, look a here," he dashed the pipe away, "I don't wan' no bunglin', *oui*?"

"Non," Sambola dared not blink, so potent was the power Nestor exerted over him.

"You must hide it safely in yo' pocket till the men begin fo' get sleepy—till it is late. Lissen out fo' de polise wissle fo' one o'clock. Pape is likely fo' go a bit early, you say? But that don't matter. Be sure you get it in his, though . . ."

Far into the night the older man talked to the boy. He talked to him with the petulance and the nervous gestures of an Oriental. But the thing was Nestor's life balm. For ten long years he had been cherishing it. And there it was—within his grasp!

"Here, take this, and don't lose it, *oui*?"

"Non!"

He took the green vial and tucked it safely in his bosom. Nestor gleamed at him fiendishly. Drink after drink he made the boy swallow. Thru the curtain of the night came the sound of fish splashing in the molten river. From atop the undulating *cordilleras* in the distance a lion howled.

About four o'clock in the morning Sambola slipped out.

Later in the day, as the dusky folk flocked to the waterfront to gobble up the oysters and cayukas of venison, among the things offered for sale was the big yellow cayuka of the trader Villaine.

IV

"Sambola, don't forget the Chess Club meets tonight. And I want you to run over to Calavaggio's and get some of that Jamaica rum he's got."

Mr. Newbold, the manager of the West Indian Telegraph Company, was a social climber. A mulatto, he was something of a mogul. In a small place like Aspinwall, it was easy to know and talk with the mayor and the governor and the agents of the steamship lines that plied to the city. Born in the Cayman Islands he had been to Liverpool, Calais, Bremen. He was a cosmopolitan. In Aspinwall, where life is more precarious than it is elsewhere, white men found time to cultivate one another. On the native side Mr. Newbold was well liked. Alcalde Munoz and Governor Salzedo were great friends of his. And at the governor's reception he was one of the principal guests. Moreover, his wife, a dark brown woman from one of the islands, passed as a shawl-swept *senora*. And his idea of a chess club had originated with Mr. Newbold. A few men in the Republic played it and he was bent on popularizing the game. It was too good to limit to a straggling few.

In Sambola, the West Indian office boy, he had a faithful and obedient servant. Sambola was a good boy. Unlike the others Mr. Newbold had had he never smoked or whistled or stayed out late at nights or read "Old Sleuth," "Dick Turpin" or "Dead-Wood Dick."[3] He hadn't any imagination. That, Mr. Newbold felt, was good for him. He would sit, out there in the front office, and watch Mr. Newbold's collie lying on the hot sun-drenched pavement growl and snap viciously at the flies on his nose.

"You know, Sambola," said Mr. Newbold as the boy returned, "I want you to put on a white apron—like a regular waiter. I was thinking of that the other day. Serving drinks to such a distinguished assemblage in your working clothes looks a bit out of place, don't you think?" So that night Sambola had on a white apron to serve the liqueurs.

The chess club met upstairs in Padros' Bar, facing Slifer's Park. On Friday nights the park band did not play. In consequence the park was deserted—shrouded in darkness. It was a good night for chess.

Sambola got there first. He opened the door, turned on the gas, and arranged the table. The place was in ship shape for Mr. Newbold always saw to it that Sambola clean and tidy it up the day after each game. In one corner was an ice box. Opening it Sambola examined the array of liqueurs, and again closed it. A moment later Mr. Newbold arrived.

"Well, Sambola, how's tricks? Are all the bottles there?" He went to the icebox, poked a nose in, and took out a bottle of champagne. He took down a glass.

"Don't drink, eh Sambola?" he asked as he filled the glass and put it to his lips.

---

3. These are all titles of dime novels from America, small cheap paperbacks with formulaic stories.

"No, sir."

"Not even champagne?"

"No, sir."

"That's a good boy."

A few minutes later Herr Pape, the agent of the Hamburg American Line, blond, grey-eyed, a pipe in his mouth, entered. Following him Sir Winfield Baxter, the agent of the Royal Mail Steam Packet Company, a flippant, youngish old man, a perpetual twinkle in his cat grey eyes; Vincent Childers, the British Vice-Consul, hoarse, hump-backed, anaemic, and dribbling at a brown paper cigarette. Lastly came the Governor and Mayor Munoz.

The years of triumph had heightened the charms of the populist idol. Salzedo wore the usual duck, the same long French shoes with the narrow instep and pointed toes, the same gold and brown peacock charm at his watch, the same fascinating light in his eyes.

"Well, gentlemen," said Mr. Newbold, "this is our club's first anniversary. Let's drink to its health."

After which, the game began. Herr Pape and Mr. Newbold, Governor Salzedo and Sir Winfield, Alcalde Munoz and Vice-Consul Childers.

Thus it was for hours. Between times the men were served sherry and ice, whiskey and soda, coca-cola. Silently Sambola served the drinks, got a check signed, and stole softly back to his stool out on the porch to watch the shadows of the barques and brigantines and big ocean liners tied to their piers. Below, in the dusky shadows, he saw, too, brown boys and girls spooning.[4] And Sambola grew reminiscent. For down in the Silver City he also had a girl, a yellow beauty from one of the isles, A'Minta who went with him to the *parque* on Sunday evenings . . .

Hours he sprawled on the balcony, the vial clutched to his bosom . . . Ah, Pape was going. He always left early.

"Good luck, gentlemen, I've got to run along. Big day before me tomorrow."

Another hour slipped by. The policeman downstairs blew a long owlish wail. Once, twice, thrice. Twelve o'clock. Somewhere on the roof Sambola heard the unmistakable snarl of a lust-bound boar cat. He dimly glimpsed a yacht in the bay.

One more drink he served. Ensued a long sleeping spell . . . a sleep in which he dreamt of a shark tugging at his gizzard and of being washed up on the ebony shores of Faulke's River.

"Sambola!"

Sir Winfield wanted his glass refilled. He hadn't had anything for an age. The others also wanted theirs refilled. Alert, on the job, a wonderful host, Mr. Newbold also saw it.

"Here, Sambola, fill up the glasses. Why, governor, yours is quite empty."

"Oh, let me see, I'll take vermouth."

---

4. Spooning is an old-fashioned term for lovemaking, that is, hugging and kissing.

Unemotional as a clam, Sambola went to the ice box and began pouring out the liqueurs. As if he had forgotten something he turned to make sure. No, no one was looking at him. They were deeply engrossed in the game. The boy took the vial out of his bosom and uncorked it. Odorless. Colorless. He put three tiny drops in the governor's anisette. It scarcely created a ripple.

V

The next day the Republic was thrown into a paroxysm of grief over the strange death of Governor Manual Salzedo. The physicians said it was due to heart failure. Others privately attributed it to a vendetta in *El Barrio Rojo.* Donna Teresa demanded an autopsy. But it did not reveal anything. The newspapers, in dealing with it, threw a cloak of still further mystery over it. They hinted at assault by the ousted Tejadistas. *El Dario* went so far as to dig up or fabricate a parallel in the Republic's bloody history.

But no one ever got to the bottom of it. Not even the enterprising reporters of the fictional press—not one of them ever thought of linking the governor's death with the finding a few days later of a Negro's shark bitten body fished up out of the black lagoon on Faulke's River.

Soon, like everything else, it died down. And if you asked any of the old residents about it they'd say, "Ah, that is one of the legends of this legendary country. Like the failure of the French."

Yet, Sambola, as meek as before, continued to serve liqueurs on Friday evenings to the members of Mr. Newbold's Chess Club. Only sometimes a strange, smoky gleam would creep into his eyes. On nights when he'd go to that brothel on the banks of the river by the Silver City there were those who couldn't help compare it with the cat-like light they had often seen in the eyes of the old grouchy trader, Nestor Villaine. As a matter of fact, folk oftimes, for no reason they could explain, referred to Sambola as Nestor Villaine.

May Miller

(1899–1995)

Born in Washington, D.C., on January 26, 1899, and raised in the Howard University community, May Miller was the daughter of Annie May Butler and sociologist Kelly Miller, a professor at Howard during the Harlem Renaissance. Miller attended Paul Laurence Dunbar High School where she was taught by notable dramatist and poet Angelina Weld Grimké. In 1916 she enrolled in Howard University where she studied drama and participated in the Howard University Dramatic Club, organized by Montgomery Gregory and Alain Locke. Upon graduating from Howard in 1920, Miller did graduate work in drama and poetry at American and Columbia Universities. She taught English and speech at the Frederick Douglass High School in Baltimore, Maryland, for twenty years. She also supervised the Baltimore Junior High School English Program and participated in the Negro Little Theatre Movement. After her marriage to John Sullivan, an accountant with the U.S. Postal Service, Miller returned to Washington, D.C., and focused on her literary career with the help of close friend Georgia Douglas Johnson, whose weekly Saturday evening gatherings helped acquaint her with leading figures of the movement, most notably Zora Neale Hurston. She was later appointed to the D.C. Commission on the Arts and Humanities and chaired a project to publish poetry by children.

Although Miller is best known today for her poetry and served as poet-in-residence at several universities including the University of Wisconsin, Southern University, and Wellesley College, her poetry was published mainly after 1943; during the Harlem Renaissance, she was better known as a dramatist. She won third prize in the 1925 *Opportunity* contest for the play *Bog Guide*. The next year she received honorable mention for *The Cuss'd Thing*. She also coedited with Willis Richardson *Negro History in Thirteen Plays* (1935). Her most popular play is *Riding the Goat* (1930), but other plays include *Scratches* (1929), *Graven Images* (1929), *Stragglers in the Dust* (1930), *Nails and Thorns* (1933), *Harriet Tubman* (1935), and *Sojourner Truth* (1935). Miller stopped writing plays in 1943 when she retired from teaching and thereafter focused on poetry. She published seven books of poetry including *Into the Clearing* (1959), *Dust of Uncertain Journey* (1975), and *The Ransomed West* (1983).

James Lesesne Wells, Untitled, *Plays and Pageants from the Life of the Negro,* 1930

Riding the Goat

Persons of the Play

WILLIAM CARTER, a young physician
RUTH CHAPMAN
ANT HETTY, Ruth's grandmother
CHRISTOPHER COLUMBUS JONES, the lodge inspector

Scene: The sitting-room of ANT HETTY's home. The action takes place in South Baltimore in a community of draymen.

Time: Six o'clock of a June evening in the early part of the twentieth century.

Scene: The stuffy sitting room of ANT HETTY's home. In the side right wall down stage, a door leading outside. When the door is open, a white stoop and a few white steps can be seen. In the middle of the left wall is a door leading into the kitchen. The room is furnished with the usual three-piece parlor set upholstered in red plush. Diagonally across the corner, an easel supports a portrait of a heavy-set man. Stretched from the table in the middle of the room to the back of a chair is an ironing board before which ANT HETTY stands ironing. She is a stout dark woman of about sixty. Her gingham house dress is open at the throat and a pair of well worn bedroom slippers are more off her feet than on. When the curtain rises, she pauses in her ironing of a stiffly starched white dress. She turns the iron upon the board and wetting her finger tests the heat. She sighs, shakes her head, dries her face on the end of her apron, and then taking the iron goes into the kitchen humming. She returns with another iron and continues her work singing "Such a Meetin's Goin' Be Here To-Night." When she is half through the second chorus, a knock is heard at the outer door. ANT HETTY calls without stopping her work.

Ant Hetty: Who's there?

Carter: It's I, Carter.

Ant Hetty: Why don't cha come on in then?

(CARTER enters with a physician's bag in his hand and a bundle under his arm. He is a slender brown fellow of medium height, neatly dressed in a dark suit. As he enters he takes off his straw hat and mops his brow with a pocket handkerchief)

Carter: Good evening. How're you this time, Ant Hetty?

(He sits on the sofa and ANT HETTY adjusts the ironing board so that she may see him as she talks)

Ant Hetty: Well, son, I guess I can't complain none. Is it hot 'nough fo' you?

Carter: Too hot with all the work I've had to do.

Ant Hetty: You jest wait, honey, 'til I finishes ironin' this dress an' I'll make you some cool mint water.

Carter: Thanks.

Plays and Pageants from the Life of the Negro, 1930.

Ant Hetty: An' the worse is there ain't no change in sight. That wasn't no wet moon that riz las' night. It was there a-shinin' over them roof tops as clear as a whistle—nary a rain ring 'bout it.

Carter: You can't tell; maybe we'll catch a stray shower.

Ant Hetty: No, I don't b'lieve it. Them stray showers might fool the moon, but they nevah fools Ant Hetty. Sho as it's gonna rain, my feet and limbs begins to trouble me; an' ain't I been standin' on my feet most nigh all day widout ache nor pain? Anyhow who'd want a shower today—the day of the perade?

Carter: I would.

Ant Hetty: (*turning around abruptly*) Huh!

Carter: Nothing.

Ant Hetty: (*She takes the dress off the board and drapes it carefully over the back of a chair. She talks to the dress as she smooths its folds*) Now you'se already spick and span fo' that perade tonight; ain't cha? (*Looking up, she remembers CARTER. She takes the ironing board under her left arm and carries the iron in her right hand. She starts toward the kitchen*) Wait a minute, son, an' your Ant Hetty'll fix you up. (*She goes into the kitchen*)

(*CARTER stares at the white dress with a frown. He opens the bundle that he brought with him and shakes out his uniform. Holding it at arm's length, he views it with disgust*)

Carter: Damn that lodge and all its parades! (*He throws the costume on the floor as ANT HETTY enters carrying a glass of her concoction. He hastily, almost guiltily, replaces the costume on the sofa*)

Ant Hetty: Now drink that, honey, 'cause you mus' be tir'd chasin' roun' all day in this heat 'tending niggers. Since you been gran' mastah[1] looks lak folks tryin' to outdo one 'nother callin' you.

Carter: And before I joined the lodge, the same people wouldn't even consider me. (*He takes the proffered glass*) Thanks.

Ant Hetty: (*Sitting in the rocker and watching CARTER as he drinks*) What was you doin' down in Haw Street so lon' befo' perade time?

Carter: I had a call down the street and I dropped in thinking maybe Ruth would be home early today.

Ant Hetty: Yes, Ruth'll be alon' in a little while now. But Lawd, who's sick in our street now?

Carter: Mrs. Riles called me to see Mr. Ike.

Ant Hetty: I 'clare ev'ry time that nigger gets tir'd of workin' he gits 'nother spell of rheumatics.[2]

---

1. Grand Master, head of a lodge or club. Such lodges were popular among both black and white people during this era. They were characterized by a high degree of ritual and ceremony and were often segregated by gender.

2. Rheumatic pains.

Carter: Ant Hetty!

Ant Hetty: It's the truf. Lon' time ago I tol' Mary Riles that there wasn't nothin' the mattah wid Ike but laziness, an' she knows it.

Carter: But he is sick.

Ant Hetty: 'Course he's sick. He's made hisself sick a-thinkin' so. Ain't he been arguin' wid hisself fo' twenty years 'til now even him is convinced he's dyin'?

Carter: But it's not so easy to convince a doctor.

Ant Hetty: Yes 'tis. Don't I remember ten years ago Mary Riles come runnin' in here. Me an' Mistah Chapman was settin' at the dinner table. She was a-weepin' an' sobbin' out that the doctor said Ike couldn't live 'nother week. I says to her then, "Mary Riles, you dry them tears. Ike'll bury the three of us." There was my Sam a-settin' there as strong as 'n ox; ain't he gone now an' Ike's a-livin' on? Too bad though he can't march in that perade to-day.

Carter: It's too hot for parades.

Ant Hetty: That you, the gran' mastah, a-talkin' 'bout it's too hot fo' perades?

Carter: The heat's enough without having to wear that heavy regalia.

Ant Hetty: But it's only round the block that you has to go. Jest think of all the folks from Fremont to Green Street that'll be standin' on the corners to see the candidates in review!

Carter: (bitterly) How interesting for me!

Ant Hetty: Yes, you know Sara Blake's boy, James, jest turned eighteen an' that reformed scape-goat of a husban' of Rachel Lee's is both 'mong the candidates.

Carter: Plague the candidates and their parade! I'm getting tired of all this useless thumping over cobblestones. Work all day, and parade all night. I can be just as good a doctor to them outside the lodge as in it.

Ant Hetty: Sh! son, be careful there. Of course, you'se talkin' to your Ant Hetty, but there's them that wouldn't understan'. The gran' 'xalted ruler of the United Order of Moabites can't afford to talk thata way.

Carter: No, I guess not. All in the line of duty.

Ant Hetty: Now ain't that jest lak a man atalkin' 'bout duty an' there's fifty others wantin' your place. A woman ought to have it; she'd know a good thing.

Carter: Any woman who'd want it is welcome to the trouble.

Ant Hetty: Oh, there's plenty. I ustah hear my poor dead Sam talk 'bout a woman who hid in a closet at her husban's lodge meeting an' heard an' saw all the 'nitiation.[3] Nobody knew that she was there; but jes' as they was 'bout to leave, she sneezed an' they opens the closet an' there she was.

Carter: (laughing) What did they do to her?

Ant Hetty: They give her her choice—she could jine the lodge or die.

---

3. "Initiation rites."

    Carter: Which did she take?

Ant Hetty: She went aridin' the goat,[4] of course.

    Carter: *(rising and taking his bag)* It must have been funny. I wish I could have seen that performance. *(He starts to roll the uniform to make a bundle)* Ant Hetty, I guess I had better not wait for Ruth. I have a call to make on Fremont Avenue and I'll be back this way later.

Ant Hetty: All right; but why you gotta tote that uniform up an' down the street to get it all messed up?

    Carter: *(quickly dropping the uniform)* Thanks. I hated to have to bring it with me, but I feared that I could not get uptown again. *(laughing as he pauses in the doorway)* And, Ant Hetty, be sure to take good care of the grand regalia of the grand exalted ruler of the United Order of Moabites. *(He goes out)*

Ant Hetty: *(following CARTER to the door)* I wonder why he was laffin', the young upstart! *(ANT HETTY goes to the sofa and smooths the rumpled uniform. She straightens the chairs, carefully arranges the much fondled white dress over her arm and starts toward the kitchen. RUTH enters. She is a tall, well developed brown girl of about eighteen. Her smoothly brushed hair and the pretty checked gingham she wears bespeak personal care)*

    Ruth: Hello, grandma!

Ant Hetty: *(pausing at the kitchen door)* How'd you make out this time, child?

    Ruth: Very well. I rode down though; I was too tired to walk.

Ant Hetty: Did you meet Doctor Carter?

    Ruth: *(a little excited)* No. Was he here?

Ant Hetty: Jes' lef' the minute befo' you come in. He lef' that uniform an' I guess he'll be back.

    Ruth: *(talking rapidly as if to change the subject)* Grandma, you should have looked in the sewing room today. You know the Framinghams on Charles Street, don't you?

Ant Hetty: *(coming back into the room to listen)* Now listen, who you'se askin'! 'Course I do; ain't them the folks Mary Riles works fo'?

    Ruth: Well, the Framingham girl marries next week.

Ant Hetty: You don't say so!

    Ruth: Yes, and we finished her wedding clothes today—every stitch by hand. I'm so tired now that I can't see anything but ruffles, tucks, and laces. I think I'll lie down a little. *(She starts toward the door)*

Ant Hetty: *(shocked)* You ain't got no time to sleep an' eat an' see the perade too.

    Ruth: It's too hot for parades.

Ant Hetty: *(looking at RUTH closely)* I've heard that 'nough fo' one day. You young ones gits me. You'se too pert fo' your years. There's Doctor Carter now agettin' too

---

4. "Riding the goat" is part of the ceremony for this lodge.

high an' mighty fo' perades, says he's tir'd of useless marchin'. Did you evah hear the lak of it?

Ruth: I don't blame him.

Ant Hetty: Huh!

Ruth: No, mam, I don't see any sense in all that parading either.

Ant Hetty: O Lawd! an' did I evah think I'd live to hear Sam Chapman's granddaughter talk lak that!

Ruth: But, grandma, what sense is there in it?

Ant Hetty: What would your grandpap's funeral 've been without his lodges?

Ruth: I don't know; I hardly remember it.

Ant Hetty: The peradin' of his brothers wid their swords ashinin' an' their plumes awavin' was a gran' sight.

Ruth: Yes, mam.

Ant Hetty: But the brightest spot in the whole affair was when they lit them candles 'round the coffin an' the gran' mastah stood at the head ahittin' Sam wid his sword yellin' "Rise, Brother Chapman, an' jine the order of departed Moabites." They beat on him so lon' an' I was alookin' so close I thought I seen Sam move under them dim lights.

Ruth: Yes, mam, I am sure that was a grand funeral.

Ant Hetty: 'Course there was them as called him a habitual jiner,[5] but I didn't mind. They was only jealous of that turnout, cause Sam was a member of three lodges an' nary a one failed to show up on his big day.

Ruth: But I can't see that it made any difference to him then.

Ant Hetty: I didn't 'speck you to see. But, child, you'd better hurry an' learn that you gotta see lak some other folks sees if you wanta git alon'! Take Doctor Carter now. He needn't 'spect to get too uppish fo' the lodge an' still come down hopin' to 'tend these folks.

Ruth: But, grandma, they need him so.

Ant Hetty: 'Course they does but they won't have him.

Ruth: What will they do then?

Ant Hetty: Jes' what they done befo' he come. That good ol' white doctor is still livin' an' I guess he's got a few mo' of them pills.

Ruth: Yes, and just a few more of us will die.

Ant Hetty: Well, what diff'rence do that make? Ain't people been dyin' since there was folks?

Ruth: It's all right if it can't be helped, but Doctor Carter can cure them and he wants to.

---

5. "Joiner"; Sam is described as a habitual joiner because of his membership in three lodges.

Ant Hetty: If he's so set on helpin' his folks why don't he act lak it? Instid he laffs at our peradin'—I know.

Ruth: Grandma, why are you so anxious about the parade?

Ant Hetty: Ain't your Ant Sara's Jim marchin' wid the candidates? It seems lak ev'ryone's got somebody an' me widout a frazzlin' soul in the line.

Ruth: I don't understand why you would worry.

Ant Hetty: It was so different when your grandpap was livin'; I had somethin' to watch fo' then. Since he died I been out of it. Then recently I been thinkin', "Here's Ruthie growd up wid a nice doctor an' he gran' mastah." I could hold my haid higher 'n the res'. Now he's 'bout to spoil it all, an' you aidin' an' abettin' him in it.

Ruth: It's not exactly that, grandma.

Ant Hetty: You know, sometimes I wishes you had liked Chris.

Ruth: Please, grandma, don't start that again.

Ant Hetty: 'Course I thinks Doctor's all right in some ways, but them educated chaps always manages to think a little diff'rent. I guess that's where the trouble comes wid you—them sisters at that convent kinda educated you 'way from me.

Ruth: Grandma, I'm not away from you in any way, but I just can't marry Chris. *(Her voice breaks)*

Ant Hetty: There now, honey, I didn't mean fo' you to git all riz up 'bout it. You'se tired. Set down a minute an' res' while I fixes you a bite to eat.

(ANT HETTY goes to the kitchen. A knock is heard at the outer door. RUTH walks wearily over and opens the door. JONES enters. He is a very dark, stockily built fellow of about twenty-three. He wears the uniform of the order, the long-tail, double-breasted coat with bright brass buttons. The badges of the order decorate his breast. His helmet-like hat is decorated with a finely curled white ostrich feather. As he enters, he grins broadly)

Ruth: Hello, Chris! Coming in?

Jones: I guess mebbe I kin fin' time to tell some of my good friends hello; but 'course this is the busy day an' I ain't got much time—me bein' made the gran' inspector fo' the lodge.

Ruth: *(with an effort)* Isn't that lovely!

Ant Hetty: *(entering from kitchen)* Christopher Columbus Jones, they ain't gone an' made you lodge inspector, has they?

Jones: *(proudly drawing himself up)* Yes, mam, that's jest what they done.

Ant Hetty: You know I always tol' your ma when she give you that gran' an' mighty name that you was gonna be a great man some day. If your ma had only lived to see this day!

Jones: *(complacently)* Yes, 'tis too bad she can't see me, ain't it? What's the mattah, Ruth, you ain't sayin' nothin'?

Ruth: Your uniform does look nice.

Ant Hetty: It sho does but you wouldn't go doublin' it up an throwin' it all roun', would you? (*She looks significantly at CARTER's rumpled suit but JONES is busy surveying himself in the mirror which hangs on the back wall*)

Jones: No, Ant Hetty, 'course not. When my pa give me this suit, it was such a decent suit that I jest keeps it decent.

Ant Hetty: Your pappy bein' the richest drayman[6] down this way, I bet he could give you many a suit.

Jones: Yes, he is rich; but I does take good care of this suit. 'Course I'm not talkin' 'bout nobody, but there is them that is high in the order what don't look haf so good.

Ruth: Many of them haven't got the time you have, Chris, because most of them are working since they have no rich fathers.

Jones: Yes, that's too bad, but they oughta fin' time.

Ant Hetty: We that stands an' watches you pass knows who's keerful an' who ain't. (*sniffing toward the kitchen*) That my baby's dinner burnin'? (*She goes into the kitchen*)

Jones: I thinks mebbe the lodge oughta stan' an' watch itself in perade sometime, then it might reward them as deserves it.

Ruth: Who is unrewarded now, Chris?

Jones: Nobody perticular. 'Course lodge inspector is a mighty good job, but I don't see why I couldn't be gran' mastah same as some nigger from the outside. I'm jest as fittin' as that doctor chap.

Ruth: Then you aren't satisfied?

Jones: I'm proud all right of this job, but I'd be prouder of that one. Mebbe if I was gran' mastah you'd like me a little better.

Ruth: Chris, I do like you. Haven't we been friends since we were kids?

Jones: You remember how we ustah race scrubbin' the front stoop. You always made yourn whiter'n mine an' got through sooner.

Ruth: You never did like to work.

Jones: Is that the reason you ain't lovin' me?

Ruth: No, I can't say it's that.

Jones: You'se right, 'taint that. You ustah be my gal 'til you went up on Vine Street to that there place wid the high wall 'roun' it. Since then, you ain't been yourself—wantin' something new all the time.

Ruth: No, Chris, I haven't been the same.

Jones: Turned me down wid all them ol' things, huh.

Ruth: I told you I am still your friend.

Jones: Frien'! I don't want you fo' no frien' when that doctor fella's got you fo' a sweetheart. But don't think I'm givin' you up so easy. Remember how I ustah fight

---

6. Someone who drives a dray or wagon, usually a brewer's dray.

all the gang in Haw Street fo' you? I'm grown a little but I ain't changed much. *(He starts toward the door. RUTH starts after him)*

Ruth: Chris, come back a minute.

Jones: What'cha want?

Ruth: What did you mean by that?

Jones: Nothin'.

Ruth: Oh, yes, you did, too.

Jones: Well, do you think I'm gonna let any fella step in an' take the job that oughta be mine an' my gal to boot an' not raise my hand to stop it?

Ruth: What are you going to do?

Jones: Don't think doctors can't make no mistakes an' just remember Christopher Columbus Jones is watchin' him. *(He goes out the front door. RUTH stands in the doorway looking down the street. ANT HETTY enters from the kitchen)*

Ant Hetty: I 'clare wid all these hinderances nobody kin get a bite. Come now, Ruthie, 'cause I know you're most nigh starved to death.

Ruth: *(standing in the doorway)* No'm, I'm not so hungry now.

Ant Hetty: Chris take your appetite?

Ruth: No'm.

Ant Hetty: But you does lak him a little, don't you, honey?

Ruth: Yes, mam, of course, I do.

Ant Hetty: That's right. Jest remember you'll please your granny. Chris is a right nice boy even if he won't work; but Lawd, he don't have to wid his pappy stablin' five horses an' buggies an' everythin'.

Ruth: Chris is all right.

Ant Hetty: Much better 'n some uppish niggers I knows wid new fangled ideas. Now Doctor Carter—

Ruth: *(turning back into the room)* Sh! here he comes.

Ant Hetty: Talk 'bout the devil!

Carter: *(standing in the open door)* Here I am, back again, Ant Hetty. Hello, Ruth!

Ruth: Hello, Doctor!

Ant Hetty: Anybody out yit?

Carter: A few folks dressed in white are sitting on their stoops.

Ant Hetty: I know'd it. I was atellin' Sara this mornin' as how them folks 'ud have on every-thin' but the kitchen stove. *(She goes toward the kitchen door)* Ruthie, don't for-git your dinner. I'm gonna dress.

Ruth: No'm.

Carter: What's the matter, Ruth? You haven't much to say today.

Ruth: Nothing.

Carter: I know better than that.

Ruth: It's nothing much, Doctor Carter—

Carter: How many more times shall I tell you to drop the "Doctor"?

Ruth: I remember, but you're so different from the rest of the men I know.

Carter: Tell me about that later. Right now I want to know what is troubling you. *(He pushes his uniform in the corner of the sofa and sits down)*

Ruth: *(sitting in a chair near the sofa)* Are you—going to give up the lodge?

Carter: Why do you ask?

Ruth: Grandma said you were talking doubtful about it.

Carter: Oh, Ruth, I am sick of all that foolishness. From the day I put on that little white apron and rode a bony gray mare around the block, I've been hating it, and I'm just about through with all of it.

Ruth: They don't think of it as foolishness.

Carter: They've got to be taught.

Ruth: But not in that way.

Carter: Why?

Ruth: Because I know them better than you do. If you leave their lodge now, they won't have you attend them; even grandma wouldn't and she's no member.

Carter: Well, if that's the way they feel, let them cut me. I guess I can manage to get along.

Ruth: But they will suffer for it.

Carter: Which will be their own fault. They ought to suffer.

Ruth: But aren't they your people?

Carter: Of course they are, but not even for my people am I going to don that regalia again. *(He grabs the uniform, looks at it a minute in disgust and drops it in a heap on the floor)*

Ruth: Don't say that! There are too many waiting for you to take just that attitude.

Carter: Maybe, but let's forget them. *(He goes over to RUTH's chair and takes her hand to help her rise)* Come here, I want to say something to you.

Ruth: *(standing beside him and nervously measuring heights with her hand)* In these new shoes, I'm as tall as you are—not quite so big, though.

Carter: Bigger in some ways. I guess that's why I care so much.

Ruth: Do you mean that?

Carter: Surely. Why?

Ruth: Wouldn't you do almost anything for a person you liked that way?

Carter: You know I would.

Ruth: *(slipping her hand on his coat, coaxingly)* Well, march today—just today, please.

Carter: *(looking away)* That's another matter.

Ruth: Then you didn't mean what you said?

Carter: Certainly I did. I'll always mean that part.

Ruth: But you won't march?

Carter: Ruth, I am tired. I've been working all day in this heat and heaven knows when I will collect some of those bills.

Ruth: And if you don't stay in the lodge, they may never pay you.

Carter: Consider it then my contribution to charity.

Ruth: You have definitely decided?

Carter: Yes, and I wish you wouldn't say anything more about it.

Ruth: I can't help feeling that you're unwise.

Carter: Since you are so crazy about parading, it's really a pity you can't march yourself.

Ruth: William!

Carter: Excuse me, Ruth. I'd better be going. I'm talking all kinds of ways. Good-by, Ruth. *(He takes his bag from the table and goes toward the door hurriedly)*

Ruth: Good-by! *(starting after him)* William! *(ANT HETTY appears in the kitchen doorway with her white dress on. She is struggling with the many hooks and eyes. RUTH turns abruptly away from the door)*

Ant Hetty: Fix this, Ruthie. *(RUTH goes to her grandmother and fastens the hooks)* Doctor Carter gone?

Ruth: *(slyly kicking CARTER's uniform under the sofa)* Yes, mam.

Ant Hetty: It's gittin' late, an' me not dressed yit. I leaned out the window upstairs an' heard them callin' the line together. Them folks'll be havin' a monkey an' parrot time,[7] an' I'll be missin' it. Have you ate yit?

Ruth: No'm.

Ant Hetty: *(going back to the kitchen)* Well, hurry.

Ruth: Yes, mam. *(She hears a bugle call, goes to the door and looks out. She comes back into the room, views herself in the mirror a minute. Hastily she goes to the sofa, reaches under it and pulls out the suit. Without taking off her dress she dons the costume which is like JONES' except for a bright golden plume on the hat and a large black mask. She views herself in the mirror and goes out as ANT HETTY calls from the kitchen)*

Ant Hetty: Ruthie, Ruthie, how many mo' times has I got to call you? *(entering the room fully dressed)* I 'clare that gal's gone on. *(she rushes to the door and meets CARTER entering)* Ain't you gone yit?

Carter: I had. Where's Ruth?

Ant Hetty: She always sets on the Riles' stoop; the steps is higher an' you can see better. I guess she's there. Why?

7. This means a good time, a party.

Carter: Nothing particularly. I just wanted to tell her something. *(He looks for his uniform on the sofa)*

Ant Hetty: Why don't you hurry an' git in line? You'se late already.

Carter: I want my uniform; I thought I left it here.

Ant Hetty: You taken it wid you when you left befo', didn't you?

Carter: No, I left it right here. *(He looks nervously under the couch. The strains of "Maryland, My Maryland" are heard)* Oh, well, it's too late now. I could never fall in in time.

Ant Hetty: *(harshly)* You didn't mean to go in the first place.

Carter: Yes, I did.

Ant Hetty: But you said as how it was too warm fo' perades.

Carter: I did, but I have changed my mind about that and a number of other things.

Ant Hetty: You sho'lly had me upset 'cause I was athinkin' you was giving up the lodge an' everythin'. I'm sartinly glad to fin' you'se still got good sense. *(The strains of the music are heard again. ANT HETTY opens the street door wide and sits in the doorway. CARTER looks from the window)* I won't make the corner now. I guess I kin see jest as well from the stoop mebbe. You'd better set here wid me.

Carter: No, I don't think it wise to be seen. I'm here and not here.

Ant Hetty: You'll have to tell them that you was called on a mattah of life an' death.

Carter: All right, Ant Hetty, I guess I shall have to depend on you to help me tell it. *(The strains of music grow louder and there is silence for a minute as both ANT HETTY and CARTER watch intently)*

Ant Hetty: Doctor, ain't they gran'? In the twilight, they looks jest lak 'n army acomin' on. Look undah that lamppost 'cross the street. See Linda Dodd?

Carter: Who?

Ant Hetty: Her wid the new silk parasol an' no rain in sight.

Carter: Uh-huh!

Ant Hetty: Watch her bowin' an' scrapin' to ev'rybody jest ahopin' somebody'll ask fo' Lew.

Carter: Which one do you call Lew? *(The music is very near)*

Ant Hetty: That's Lew—the fella what's leadin' the ban'. I 'clare I don' know when that nigger prances mos'—when he's leadin' that ban' in perades or shoutin' in church on Sundays. *(They continue to look intently)*

Ant Hetty: Doctor, look! Who's leading them candidates?

Carter: Only my assistant could ride for me, and that isn't he, for he's very fat. *(pressing closer to the window)* That's my outfit, too—mask and all!

Ant Hetty: If I didn't see you asettin' right there, I'd vow it was you. Even got that sway of yourn. *(The strains of music become fainter)*

Carter: Of all odd things! How did any one get my uniform? I would have sworn that I left it right here. I wonder if I could have taken the bundle out and lost it in my hurry; but who in creation had nerve enough to wear it?

Ant Hetty: Some low-down rascal wid the nerve of Judas.

     Carter: (*starting toward the table and reaching for his hat*) I'm going to find out.

Ant Hetty: Wait a minute. They're disbandin' at the corner. Well, will you look at Sara Blake! She's gone to cryin' on her James' neck. An' there's Rachel Lee jest makin' a fool of herself over that no-count man. (*In disgust she comes into the room but goes to the window*) I 'clare Chris jest keeps tryin' to talk to that scape-goat in your outfit. The rascal's sho in a hurry an' he's haided this way.

     Carter: (*grasping his hat*) Well, I'll meet him.

Ant Hetty: (*Suddenly turning away from the window, she grasps CARTER's arm, and almost drags him into the kitchen*) Now we'll fin' out somethin' 'bout this rascal. (*As ANT HETTY closes the kitchen door, RUTH dashes in and locks the outer door. She is panting breathlessly, but without pausing tears off the mask and helmet and undresses rapidly. A knock is heard at the outer door. She rolls the regalia together and opening the kitchen door tosses it in without looking. She opens the door for JONES who enters sword in hand*)

     Jones: (*breathlessly*) Where's gran' mastah?

     Ruth: (*nervously*) Grand master! What made you think that he was here?

     Jones: You ain't foolin' Christopher Columbus Jones. I seen the one what marched in that perade come in here aracin' an' I believes you was the one.

     Ruth: I—the grand master!

     Jones: What'cha call yourself adoin'? Tryin' to save him—huh. You ain't bided your time right 'cause all us knowed how that doctor fella's been gittin' tir'd of us an' we's been watchin' him. When I goes back an' tells them what you done fo' him he better make hisself scarce in this neighborhood.

     Ruth: But, Chris, what can you tell them?

     Jones: Tell 'em that I knows the doctor got you to march fo' him in our line.

     Ruth: You would tell them that!

     Jones: Ruth, you oughta be 'shamed of yourself agoin' back on your own folks fo' some outside nigger. (*The kitchen door opens and CARTER, dressed in the uniform, hat in hand, stands in the doorway almost overshadowing ANT HETTY who is behind him. RUTH and JONES stare at him stupidly*)

     Carter: Good evening, inspector. Didn't our parade move along smoothly?

     Jones: (*with an effort*) Yes, sah, yes, sah, it sho did.

     Carter: Ant Hetty said she enjoyed it a great deal. What did your friends think of it?

     Jones: I ain't seen my friends, but I guess I got time to speak to 'em an' ax how the new inspector done. Well, folks, I guess I'll be movin' 'lon'.

     Ruth: Don't forget to tell them how grand I thought you looked.

     Jones: All right. Bye, folks.

Ant Hetty: Good-by, Chris. (*she follows JONES to the door and closes it after him*) Ruthie, how'd you evah do it?

     Ruth: (*sitting on the couch and sighing with relief*) I don't know.

Ant Hetty: Well, you sartinly saved the doctor's skin 'cause there's mo' lak Chris jest waitin' to give him the devil up Sixth Street.

Carter: But, Ruth, how did you carry it through?

Ruth: I couldn't have if you hadn't put on the suit and come in at just the right moment.

Carter: I confess that I was a little alarmed when I came back and couldn't find that suit.

Ruth: Then you did change your mind? *(She goes toward CARTER and starts to embrace him)* Oh, Doctor—William!

Ant Hetty: There, now, ain't you got no respect fo' my presence. *(chuckling)* Go on, Doctor, when a gal does that much fo' a man, he oughta hug her. *(She starts toward the door)*

Ruth: Where're you going, grandma?

Ant Hetty: Jest keep your shirt on, Miss, I'm goin'. I got to talk to Mary Riles 'bout the perade. *(calling from the doorway)* Lawd, child, I knows you mus' be faint wid hunger. You go right out in that kitchen an' eat 'cause nobody's fixin' to lose you. *(She goes out the front door)*

Ruth: Yes, mam. *(sinking on sofa exhausted)* I'm so glad that's over.

Carter: *(standing before her)* Ruth, I don't know what to say.

Ruth: Please don't let's talk about it at all. I tremble every time I think of what I did.

Carter: *(stooping and placing his helmet on her head)* Very well, grand master, just as you command. *(As the curtain falls he kneels before RUTH in mock salute)*

Curtain

Marita O. Bonner

(1899-1971)

A singer as well as a prolific and versatile writer, Marita Odette Bonner was born in Brookline, Massachusetts, on June 16, 1899, to Joseph Bonner and Mary Anne Noel, who had three other children. She attended Brookline High School. In 1918 she entered Radcliffe College, where she studied music and English and German literature, becoming fluent in German. After graduating from Radcliffe in 1922 and teaching for two years in a small Virginia town, Bonner moved to Washington, D.C., to teach at Armstrong High School. There she became involved with Georgia Douglas Johnson's weekly gatherings of African American artists, an important group for mentoring new writers, and wrote plays after joining the Krigwa Players at Howard University. Like many women of the Harlem Renaissance era, Bonner never lived in Harlem.

In 1925 Bonner won first prize in *The Crisis* essay contest for "On Being Young—a Woman—and Colored," one of the best known prose pieces of the Harlem Renaissance (see the essay section). She published numerous pieces of short fiction, essays, plays, and reviews in the leading journals of her day between 1922 and 1942. She published three plays of note: *The Pot Maker* (1927), *The Purple Flower* (1928), and *Exit, an Illusion* (1929). *The Pot Maker* (published in *Opportunity*) and *The Purple Flower* (which won first prize for best play in the 1927 *Crisis* contest), were well regarded, but none of her dramas was produced.

After marrying an accountant and Brown University graduate, William Occomy, in 1930, Bonner moved to Chicago. Here she wrote several short stories about the black and immigrant communities there that were later collected and published as *Frye Street and Environs* (1987). She stopped publishing in 1941, devoting her energies to her husband and three children, teaching high school, and the Church of Christ Scientist.

One Boy's Story

I'm glad they got me shut up in here. Gee, I'm glad! I used to be afraid to walk in the dark and to stay by myself.

That was when I was ten years old. Now I am eleven.

My mother and I used to live up in the hills right outside of Somerset. Somerset, you know, is way up State and there aren't many people there. Just a few rich people in big houses and that's all.

Our house had a nice big yard behind it, beside it and in front of it. I used to play it was my fortress and that the hills beside us were full of Indians. Some days I'd go on scouting parties up and down the hills and fight.

The Crisis, November 1927.

That was in the summer and fall. In the winter and when the spring was rainy, I used to stay in the house and read.

I love to read. I love to lie on the floor and put my elbows down and read and read myself right out of Somerset and America—out of the world, if I want to.

There was just my mother and I. No brothers—no sisters—no father. My mother was awful pretty. She had a roundish plump, brown face and was all plump and round herself. She had black hair all curled up on the end like a nice autumn leaf.

She used to stay in the house all the time and sew a lot for different ladies who came up from the big houses in Somerset. She used to sew and I would pull the bastings out for her. I did not mind it much. I liked to look at the dresses and talk about the people who were to wear them.

Most people, you see, wear the same kind of dress all the time. Mrs. Ragland always wore stiff silk that sounded like icicles on the window. Her husband kept the tea and coffee store in Somerset and everybody said he was a coming man.

I used to wonder where he was coming to.

Mrs. Gregg always had the kind of silk that you had to work carefully for it would ravel into threads. She kept the boarding house down on Forsythe Street. I used to like to go to that house. When you looked at it on the outside and saw all the windows and borders running up against it you thought you were going in a palace. But when you got inside you saw all the little holes in the carpet and the mended spots in the curtains and the faded streaks in the places where the draperies were folded.

The pale soft silk that always made me feel like burying my face in it belonged to Mrs. Swyburne. She was rich—awful rich. Her husband used to be some kind of doctor and he found out something that nobody else had found out, so people used to give him plenty of money just to let him tell them about it. They called him a specialist.

He was a great big man. Nice and tall and he looked like he must have lived on milk and beef-juice and oranges and tomato juice and all the stuff Ma makes me eat to grow. His teeth were white and strong so I guess he chewed his crusts too.

Anyhow, he was big but his wife was all skinny and pale. Even her eyes were almost skinny and pale. They were sad like and she never talked much. My mother used to say that those who did not have any children did not have to talk much anyhow.

She said that to Mrs. Swyburne one time. Mrs. Swyburne had been sitting quiet like she used to, looking at me. She always looked at me anyhow, but that day she looked harder than ever.

Every time I raised up my head and breathed the bastings out of my face, I would see her looking at me.

I always hated to have her look at me. Her eyes were so sad they made me feel as if she wanted something I had.

Not that I had anything to give her because she had all the money and cars and everything and I only had my mother and Cato, my dog, and some toys and books.

But she always looked that way at me and that day she kept looking so long that pretty soon I sat up and looked at her hard.

She sort of smiled then and said, "Do you know, Donald. I was wishing I had a little boy just like you to pull out bastings for me, too."

"You couldn't have one just like me," I said right off quick. Then I quit talking because Ma commenced to frown even though she did not look up at me.

I quit because I was going to say, "Cause I'm colored and you aren't," when Ma frowned.

Mrs. Swyburne still sort of smiled; then she turned her lips away from her teeth the way I do when Ma gives me senna and manna tea.

"No," she said, "I couldn't have a little boy like you, I guess."

Ma spoke right up, "I guess you do not want one like him! You have to talk to him so much."

I knew she meant I talked so much and acted so bad sometimes.

Mrs. Swyburne looked at Ma then. She looked at her hair and face and right down to her feet. Pretty soon she said: "You cannot mind that surely. You seem to have all the things I haven't anyway." Her lips were still held in that lifted, twisted way.

Ma turned around to the machine then and turned the wheel and caught the thread and it broke and the scissors fell and stuck up in the floor. I heard her say "Jesus," to herself like she was praying.

I didn't say anything. I ripped out the bastings. Ma stitched. Mrs. Swyburne sat there. I sort of peeped up at her and I saw a big fat tear sliding down her cheek.

I kind of wiggled over near her and laid my hand on her arm. Then Ma yelled: "Donald, go and get a pound of rice! Go now, I said."

I got scared. She had not said it before and she had a lot of rice in a jar in the closet. But I didn't dare say so. I went out.

I couldn't help but think of Mrs. Swyburne. She ought not to cry so easy. She might not have had a little boy and Ma might have—but she should have been happy. She had a great big house on the swellest street in Somerset and a car all her own and some one to drive it for her. Ma only had me and our house which wasn't so swell, but it was all right.

Then Mrs. Swyburne had her husband and he had such a nice voice. You didn't mind leaning on his knee and talking to him as soon as you saw him. He had eyes that looked so smiling and happy and when you touched his hands they were soft and gentle as Ma's even if they were bigger.

I knew him real well. He and I were friends. He used to come to our house a lot of time and bring me books and talk to Ma while I read.

He knew us real well. He called Ma Louise and me Don. Sometimes he'd stay and eat supper with us and then sit down and talk. I never could see why he'd come way out there to talk to us when he had a whole lot of rich friends down in Somerset and a wife that looked like the only doll I ever had.

A lady gave me that doll once and I thought she was really pretty—all pale and blonde and rosy. I thought she was real pretty at first but by and by she seemed so dumb. She never did anything but look pink and pale and rosy and pretty. She never went out and ran with me like Cato did. So I just took a rock and gave her a rap up beside her head and threw her in the bushes.

Maybe Mrs. Swyburne was pale and pink and dumb like the doll and her husband couldn't rap her with a rock and throw her away.

I don't know.

Anyhow, he used to come and talk to us and he'd talk to Ma a long time after I was in bed. Sometimes I'd wake up and hear them talking. He used to bring me toys until he found out that I could make my own toys and that I liked books.

After that he brought me books. All kinds of books about fairies and Indians and folks in other countries.

Sometimes he and I would talk about the books—especially those I liked. The one I liked most was called *Ten Tales to Inspire Youth.*

That sounds kind of funny but the book was great. It had stories in it all about men. All men. I read all of the stories but I liked the one about the fellow named Orestes who went home from the Trojan War and found his mother had married his father's brother so he killed them. I was always sorry for the women with the whips of flame like forked tongues who used to worry him afterwards. I don't see why the Furies pursued him. They knew he did it because he loved his father so much.

Another story I liked was about Oedipus—a Greek too—who put out his eyes to hurt himself because he killed his father and married his mother by mistake.

But after I read "David and Goliath," I just had to pretend that I was David.

I swiped a half a yard of elastic from Ma and hunted a long time until I found a good forked piece of wood. Then I made a swell slingshot.

The story said that David asked Jehovah (which was God) to let his slingshot shoot good. "Do thou lend thy strength to my arm, Jehovah," he prayed.

I used to say that too just to be like him.

I told Dr. Swyburne I liked these stories.

"Why do you like them?" he asked me.

"Because they are about men," I said.

"Because they are about men! Is that the only reason?"

Then I told him no; that I liked them because the men in the stories were brave and had courage and stuck until they got what they wanted, even if they hurt themselves getting it.

And he laughed and said, to Ma: "Louise, he has the blood, all right!"

And Ma said: "Yes! He is a true Gage. They're brave enough and put their eyes out too. That takes courage all right!"

Ma and I are named Gage, so I stuck out my chest and said: "Ma, which one of us Gages put his eyes out?"

"Me," she said—and she was standing there looking right at me!

I thought she was making fun. So I felt funny.

Dr. Swyburne turned red and said: "I meant the other blood of course. All the Swyburnes are heroes."

I didn't know what he meant. My name is Gage and so is Ma's so he didn't mean me.

Ma threw her head up and looked at him and says: "Oh, are they heroes?" Then she says real quick: "Donald go to bed right now!"

I didn't want to go but I went. I took a long time to take off my clothes and I heard Ma and Dr. Swyburne talking fast like they were fussing.

I couldn't hear exactly what they said but I kept hearing Ma say: "I'm through!"

And I heard Dr. Swyburne say: "You can't be!"

I kind of dozed to sleep. By and by I heard Ma say again: "Well, I'm through!"

And Dr. Swyburne said: "I won't let you be!"

Then I rolled over to think a minute and then go downstairs maybe.

But when I rolled over again, the sun was shining and I had to get up.

Ma never said anything about what happened so I didn't either. She just walked around doing her work fast, holding her head up high like she always does when I make her mad.

So I never said a thing that day.

One day I came home from school. I came in the back way and when I was in the kitchen I could hear a man in the front of the room talking to Ma. I stood still a minute to see if it was Dr. Swyburne though I knew he never comes in the afternoon.

The voice didn't sound like his so I walked in the hall and passed the door. The man had his back to me so I just looked at him a minute and didn't say anything. He had on leather leggings and sort of uniform like soldiers wear. He was stooping over the machine talking to Ma and I couldn't see his face.

Just then I stumbled over the little rug in the hall and he stood up and looked at me.

He was a colored man! Colored just like Ma and me. You see, there aren't any other people in Somerset colored like we are, so I was sort of surprised to see him.

"This is my son, Mr. Frazier," Ma said.

I said pleased to meet you and stepped on Ma's feet. But not on purpose. You know I kind of thought he was going to be named Gage and be some relation to us and stay at our house awhile.

I never saw many colored people—no colored men—and I wanted to see some. When Ma called him Frazier it made my feet slippery so I stubbed my toe.

"Hello, son!" he said nice and quiet.

He didn't talk like Ma and me. He talked slower and softer. I liked him straight off so I grinned and said: "Hello yourself."

"How's the books?" he said then.

I didn't know what he meant at first but I guessed he meant school. So I said: "Books aren't good as the fishin'."

He laughed out loud and said I was all right and said he and I were going to be friends and that while he was in Somerset he was going to come to our house often and see us.

Then he went out. Ma told me he was driving some lady's car. She was visiting Somerset from New York and he would be there a little while.

Gee, I was so glad! I made a fishing rod for him that very afternoon out of a piece of willow I had been saving for a long time.

And one day, he and I went down to the lake and fished. We sat still on top a log that went across a little bay like. I felt kind of excited and couldn't say a word. I just kept looking at him every once in a while and smiled. I did not grin. Ma said I grinned too much.

Pretty soon he said: "What are you going to be when you grow up, son?"

"A colored man," I said. I meant to say some more, but he hollered and laughed so loud that Cato had to run up to see what was doing.

"Sure you'll be a colored man! No way to get out of that! But I mean this: What kind of work are you going to do?"

I had to think a minute. I had to think of all the kinds of work men did. Some of the men in Somerset were farmers. Some kept stores. Some swept the streets. Some were rich and did not do anything at home but they went to the city and had their cars driven to the shop and to meet them at the train.

All the conductors and porters make a lot of scramble to get those men on and off the train, even if they looked as if they could take care of themselves.

So I said to Mr. Frazier: "I want to have an office."

"An office?"

"Yes. In the city so's I can go in to it and have my car meet me when I come to Somerset."

"Fat chance a colored man has!" he said.

"I can too have an office!" I said. He made me sore. "I can have one if I want to! I want to have an office and be a specialist like Dr. Swyburne."

Mr. Frazier dropped his pole and had to swear something awful when he reached for it though it wasn't very far from him.

"Why'd you pick him?" he said and looked at me kind of mad like and before I could think of what to say he said: "Say son, does that guy come up to see your mother?"

"Sure he comes to see us both!" I said.

Mr. Frazier laughed again but not out loud. It made me sore all over. I started to hit him with my pole but I thought about something I'd read once that said even a savage will treat you right in his house—so I didn't hit him. Of course, he wasn't in my house exactly but he was sitting on my own log over my fishing places and that's like being in your own house.

Mr. Frazier laughed to himself again and then all of a sudden he took the pole I had made him out of the piece of willow I had been saving for myself and laid it across his knees and broke it in two. Then he said out loud: "Nigger women," and then threw the pole in the water.

I grabbed my pole right out of the water and slammed it across his face. I never thought of the hook until I hit him, but it did not stick in him. It caught in a tree and I broke the string yanking it out.

He looked at me like he was going to knock me in the water and even though I was scared, I was thinking how I'd let myself fall if he did knock me off—so that I could swim out without getting tangled in the roots under the bank.

But he didn't do it. He looked at me a minute and said: "Sorry, son! Sorry! Not your fault."

Then he put his hand on my hair and brushed it back and sort of lifted it up and said: "Like the rest."

I got up and said I was going home and he came too. I was afraid he would come in but when he got to my gate he said: "So long," and walked right on.

I went on in. Ma was sewing. She jumped up when I came in. "Where is Mr. Frazier?" she asked me. She didn't even say hello to me!

"I hit him," I said.

"You hit him!" she hollered. "You *hit* him! What did you do that for? Are you crazy?"

I told her no. "He said 'nigger women' when I told him that Dr. Swyburne was a friend of ours and came to see us."

Oh Ma looked terrible then. I can't tell you how she did look. Her face sort of slipped around and twisted like the geography says the earth does when the fire inside of it gets too hot.

She never said a word at first. She just sat there. Then she asked me to tell her all about every bit that happened.

I told her. She kept wriggling from side to side like the fire was getting hotter. When I finished, she said: "Poor baby! My baby boy! Not your fault! Not your fault!"

That made me think of Mr. Frazier so I pushed out of her arms and said: "Ma your breast pin hurts my face when you do that!"

She leaned over on the arms of her chair and cried and cried until I cried too.

All that week I'd think of the fire inside of the earth when I looked at Ma. She looked so funny and she kept talking to herself.

On Saturday night we were sitting at the table when I heard a car drive up the road.

"Here's Dr. Swyburne!" I said and I felt so glad I stopped eating.

"He isn't coming here!" Ma said and then she jumped up.

"Sure he's coming," I said. "I know his motor." And I started to get up too.

"You stay where you are!" Ma hollered and she went out and closed the door behind her.

I took another piece of cake and began eating the frosting. I heard Dr. Swyburne come up on the porch.

"Hello, Louise," he said. I could tell he was smiling by his voice.

I couldn't hear what Ma said at first but pretty soon I heard her say: "You can't come here any more!"

That hurt my feelings. I liked Dr. Swyburne. I liked him better than anybody I knew besides Ma.

Ma stayed out a long time and by and by she came in alone and I heard Dr. Swyburne drive away.

She didn't look at me at all. She just leaned back against the door and said: "Dear Jesus! With your help I'll free myself."

I wanted to ask her from what did she want to free herself. It sounded like she was in jail or an animal in a trap in the woods.

I thought about it all during supper but I didn't dare say much. I thought about it and pretended that she was shut up in a prison and I was a time fighter who beat all the keepers and got her out.

Then it came to me that I better get ready to fight to get her out of whatever she was in. I never said anything to her. I carried my air-rifle on my back and my slingshot in my pocket. I wanted to ask her where her enemy was, but she never talked to me about it; so I had to keep quiet too. You know Ma always got mad if I talked about things first. She likes to talk, then I can talk afterwards.

One Sunday she told me she was going for a walk. "Can I go?" I asked her.

"No," she said. "You play around the yard."

Then she put her hat on and stood looking in the mirror at herself for a minute. All of a sudden I heard her say to herself. "All I need is strength to fight out of it."

"Ma'am?" I thought she was talking to me at first.

She stopped and hugged my head like I wish she wouldn't sometimes and then went out.

I stayed still until she got out of the yard. Then I ran and got my rifle and slingshot and followed her.

I crept behind her in the bushes beside the road. I cut across the fields and came out behind the willow patch the way I always do when I am tracking Indians and wild animals.

By and by she came out in the clearing that is behind Dr. Somerset's. They call it Somerset's Grove and it's named for his folks who used to live there—just as the town was.

She sat down so I lay down in the bushes. A sharp rock was sticking in my knee but I was afraid to move for fear she'd hear me and send me home.

By and by I heard someone walking on the grass and I saw Dr. Swyburne coming up. He started talking before he got to her.

"Louise," he said. "Louise! I am not going to give anything up to a nigger."

"Not even a nigger woman whom you took from a nigger?" She lifted her mouth in the senna and manna way.

"Don't say that!" he said. "Don't say that! I wanted a son. I couldn't have taken a woman in my own world—that would have ruined my practice. Elaine couldn't have a child!"

"Yes," Ma said. "It would have ruined you and your profession. What did it do for me? What did it do for Donald?"

"I have told you I will give him the best the world can offer. He is a Swyburne!"

"He is *my* child," Ma hollered. "It isn't his fault he is yours!"

"But I give him everything a father could give his son!"

"He has no name!" Ma said.

"I have too!" I hollered inside of me. "Donald Gage!"

"He has no name," Ma said again, "and neither have I!" And she began to cry.

"He has blood!" said Dr. Swyburne.

"But how did he get it? Oh, I'm through. Stay away from my house and I'll marry one of my men so Donald can be somebody."

"A nigger's son?"

"Don't say that again," Ma hollered and jumped up.

"Do you think I'll give up a woman of mine to a nigger?"

Ma hollered again and hit him right in his face.

He grabbed her wrists and turned the right one, I guess because she fell away from him on that side.

I couldn't stand any more. I snatched out my slingshot and pulled the stone up that was sticking in my knee.

I started to shoot. Then I remembered what David said first, so I shut my eyes and said it: "Do thou, Jehovah (which is God today), lend strength to my arm."

When I opened my eyes Ma had broken away and was running toward the road. Dr. Swyburne was standing still by the tree looking after her like he was going to catch her. His face was turned sideways to me. I looked at his head where his hair was brushed back from the side of his face.

I took aim and let the stone go. I heard him say: "Oh, my God!" I saw blood on his face and I saw him stagger and fall against the tree.

Then I ran too.

When I got home Ma was sitting in her chair with her hat thrown on the floor beside her and her head was lying back.

I walked up to her: "Ma," I said real loud.

She reached out and grabbed me and hugged my head down to her neck like she always does.

The big breast pin scratched my mouth. I opened my mouth to speak and something hot and sharp ran into my tongue.

"Ma! Ma!" I tried to holler. "The pin is sticking in my tongue!"

I don't know what I said though. When I tried to talk again, Ma and Dr. Somerset were looking down at me and I was lying in bed. I tried to say something but I could not say anything. My mouth felt like it was full of hot bread and I could not talk around it.

Dr. Somerset poured something in my mouth and it felt like it was on fire.

"They found Shev Swyburne in my thistle grove this afternoon," he said to Ma.

Ma look up quick. "*Found* him! What do you mean?"

"I mean he was lying on the ground—either fell or was struck and fell. He was dead from a blow on the temple."

I tried to holler but my tongue was too thick.

Ma took hold of each side of her face and held to it, then she just stared at Dr. Somerset. He put a lot of things back in his bag.

Then he sat up and looked at Ma. "Louise," he said, "why is all that thistle down on your skirt?"

Ma looked down. So did I. There was thistle down all over the hem of her dress.

"You don't think I killed him, do you?" she cried, "You don't think *I* did it?" Then she cried something awful.

I tried to get up but I was too dizzy. I crawled across the bed on my stomach and reached out to the chair that had my pants on it. It was hard to do—but I dragged my slingshot out of my pocket, crawled back across the bed and laid it in Dr. Somerset's knees. He looked at me for a minute.

"Are you trying to tell me that you did it, son?" he asked me.

I said yes with my head.

"My God! My God!! His own child!!!"

Dr. Somerset said to Ma: "God isn't dead yet."

Then he patted her on the arm and told her not to tell anybody nothing and they sat down and picked all the thistle down out of the skirt. He took the slingshot and broke it all up and put it all in a paper and carried it downstairs and put it in the stove.

I tried to talk. I wanted to tell him to leave it so I could show my grandchildren what I had used to free Ma like the men do in the books.

I couldn't talk though. My tongue was too thick for my mouth. The next day it burnt worse and things began to float around my eyes and head like pieces of wood in the water.

Sometimes I could see clearly though and once I saw Dr. Somerset talking to another man. Dr. Somerset was saying: "We'll have to operate to save his life. His tongue is poisoned. I am afraid it will take his speech from him."

Ma hollered then: "Thank God! He will not talk! Never! He can't talk! Thank God! Oh God! I thank Thee!" And then she cried like she always does and that time it sounded like she was laughing too.

The other man looked funny and said: "Some of them have no natural feeling of parent for child!"

Dr. Somerset looked at him and said: "You may be fine as a doctor but otherwise you are an awful fool."

Then he told the other man to go out and he began talking to Ma.

"I understand! I understand," he said. "I know all about it. He took you away from somebody and some of these days he might have taken Donald from you. He took Elaine from me once and I told him then God would strip him for it. Now it is all over. Never tell anyone and I will not. The boy knows how to read and write and will be able to live."

So I got a black stump in my mouth. It's shaped like a forked whip.

Some days I pretend I am Orestes with the Furies' whips in my mouth for killing a man.

Some days I pretend I am Oedipus and that I cut it out for killing my own father.

That's what makes me sick all over sometimes.

I killed my own father. But I didn't know it was my father. I was freeing Ma.

Still—I shall never write that on my paper to Ma and Dr. Somerset the way I have to talk to them and tell them when things hurt me.

My father said I was a Swyburne and that was why I liked people to be brave and courageous.

Ma says I am a Gage and that is why I am brave and courageous.

But I am both, so I am a whole lot brave, a whole lot courageous. And I am bearing my Furies and my clipped tongue like a Swyburne and a Gage—'cause I am both of them.

The Pot Maker

Cast

ELIAS JACKSON, the son, "called of God"
MOTHER, Nettie Jackson, Elias' mother
LUCINDA JACKSON, Elias' wife
FATHER, Luke Jackson, Elias' father
LEW FOX, Lucinda's lover

Setting: See first the room. A low ceiling; smoked walls; far more length than breadth. There are two windows and a door at the back of the stage. The door is between the windows. At left and right there are two doors leading to inner rooms. They are lighter than the door at back stage. That leads into the garden and is quite heavy.

You know there is a garden because if you listen carefully you can hear a tapping of bushes against the window and a gentle rustling of leaves and grass. The wind comes up against the house so much awash—like waves against the side of a boat—that you know, too, that there must be a large garden, a large space around the house.

But to come back into the room. It is a very neat room. There are white sash curtains at the window and a red plaid cloth on the table. Geraniums in red flower pots are in each window and even on the table beside the kerosene lamp which is lit there. An old-fashioned wooden clock sits on a shelf in the corner behind the stove at the right. Chairs of various types and degrees of ease are scattered around the table at center.

As the curtain is drawn, see first MOTHER; a plump colored woman of indeterminable age and an indeterminate shade of brown, seated at the table. The FATHER, Luke, whose brown face is curled into a million pleasant wrinkles, sits opposite her at left. LEW stands at the stove facing the two at the table. He must be an over-fat, over-facetious, over-fair, overbearing, over-pleasant, over-confident creature. If he does not make you long to slap him back into a place approaching normal humility, he is the wrong character for the part. You must think as you look at him: "A woman would have to be a base fool to love such a man!"

Then you must relax in your chair as the door at right opens and LUCINDA walks in. "Exactly the woman," you will decide. For at once you can see she is a woman who must have sat down in the mud. It has crept into her eyes. They are dirty. It has filtered through—filtered through her. Her speech is smudged. Every inch of her body, from the twitch of her eyebrow to the twitch of muscles lower down in her body, is soiled. She is of a lighter brown than MOTHER and wears her coarse hair closely ironed to her head. She picks up each foot as if she were loathe to leave the spot it rests on. Thus she crosses the room to the side of ELIAS who is seated at the window, facing the center of the room.

It is hard to describe ELIAS. He is ruggedly ugly, but he is not repulsive. Indeed, you want to stretch out first one hand and then the other to him. Give both hands to him. You want to give both hands to him and he is ruggedly ugly. That is enough.

Argument: When you see ELIAS, he is about to rehearse his first sermon. He has recently been called from the cornfields by God. Called to go immediately and preach and not to dally in any theological school. God summoned him on Monday. This is Wednesday. He is going to preach at the meeting-house on Sunday.

Opportunity, 1927.

SCENE 1

(As the curtain draws back, expectation rests heavily on everyone. MOTHER is poised stiffly on the edge of her chair. Her face and her body say, "Do me proud! You're my son! Do me proud!" FATHER on his side rests easily on his chair; "Make all the mistakes you want. Come off top notch. Come off under the pile. You're my son! My son." That sums them up in general, too. Can you see them? Do you know them?)

Elias: *(rising and walking toward the table)* You all set back kind er in a row like. *(He draws chairs to the far end of the room right)* There, there, Ma here! Pa there! Lew— *(He hesitates and LEW goes to LUCINDA's side and sits down at once. This leaves ELIAS a little uncertain but he goes on)* Now— *(He withdraws a little from them)* Brothers and sisters.

Mother: M-m-m-m, Lias, can't you think of nothin' new to say first? I been hearin' that one since God knows when. Seems like there's somethin' new.

Elias: Well, what'll I say then?

Mother: Oh—"ladies and gent'mun"; somethin' refined like. *(At this point, LEW and LUCINDA seem to get involved in an amused crossing of glances)* But go on then, anything'll be all right. *(The MOTHER stops here and glares at LUCINDA to pay her for forcing her into back water. LUCINDA sees LEW)*

Elias: *(continuing)* Well, Brothers and Sisters! There is a tale I'd like for to tell you all this evening, brothers and sisters; somethin' to cheer your sorrowing hearts in this vale of tears.

Lucinda: What if their hearts ain't happen to be sorrowing?

Father: *(cutting in)* Boun' to be some, chile! Boun' to be! *(The SON flashes thanks to FATHER. He appears to have forgotten the jibe and to be ignorant of the look of approval too. He is a delightful mutual peacemaker)*

Elias: A tale to cheer your sorrowing hearts through this vale of tears.—This here talk is about a pot maker who made pots.

Lucinda: *(laughing to herself—to LEW)* Huh, huh; Lord, ha' mercy.

Mother: *(giving LUCINDA a venomous glance and rising in defense)* Look here, Lias, is that tale in the Bible? You is called of God and He ain't asked you to set nothin' down He ain't writ Himself.

Elias: This is one of them tales like Jesus used to tell the Pharisees when he was goin' round through Galilee with them.

Mother: Jesus ain't never tol' no tales to Pharisees nor run with them either! Onliest thing He ever done was to argue with them when He met them. He gave 'em a good example like.

Elias: Well this'n is somethin' like—wait you all please! Once there was a man who made pots. He lived in a little house with two rooms and all that was in those rooms was pots. Just pots. Pots all made of earthenware. Earthenware. Each one of them had a bottom and a handle just alike. All of them jes' alike. One day the man was talking to them pots—.

Lucinda: *(just loud enough to be disagreeable)* What kinder fool was talking to pots?

Elias: *(ignoring her)* An he says, "Listen you all. You is all alike. Each one of you is got a bottom to set on and a handle. You all is alike now, but you don' have to stay that a way. Do jes' as I tells you and you can turn to be anything you want. Tin pots, iron pots, brass pots, silver pots. Even gold." Then them pots says—

Mother: Lias, who in the name of God ever heard tell of a minister saying pots talked. Them folks ain't goin' to let you do it.

Elias: Ma! Then the pots said, "What we got to do?" And the man, he told them he was goin' to pour something in them. "Don't you all tip over or spill none of the things I put in you. These here rooms is goin' to get dark. Mighty dark. You all is goin' to set here. Each got to set up by hisself. On his own bottom and hold up his handle. You all is goin' to hear rearin' and tearin'. Just set and don't spill on the ground." "Master I got a crack in me," says one of them pots, "I got a crack in me so's I can't hol' nuthin." Then the man took a little dirt and he spit on it and put it on the crack and he patted it—just as gentle like! He never stopped and asked "How'd you get that crack." He didn't do like some folks would have done. He stooped right down and fixed the crack 'cause 'twas in his pot. His own pot. Then he goes out. Them rooms got so dark that a million fireflies couldn't have showed a light in there. "What's in the corner?" says one of the pots. Then they gets scared and rolls over on the ground and spilled.

Lucinda: Uhm. *(She sees only LEW again)*

Elias: *(still ignoring her)* It kept getting darker. Bye 'n bye noises commenced. Sounded like a drove of bees had travelled up long a elephant's trunk and was setting out to sting their way out through the thickest part. "Wah, we's afraid," said some more pots and they spilled right over. For a long time them rooms stayed right dark and the time they was dark they was full of noise and pitchin' and tearin'— but pres'n'y the dark began leaving. The gray day come creepin' in under the door. The pot maker he come in; "Mornin' ya'll, how is you?" he asks. Some of the pots said right cheery, "We's still settin' like you tol' us to set!" Then they looked at their selves and they was all gol'. Some of them kinder had hung their heads but was still settin' up. The pot maker he says, "Never min', you all, you all can be silver. You ain't spilled over." Then some of the pots on the groun' snuk up and tried to stand up and hol' up their heads. "Since you all is so bol' as to try to be what you ain't, you all kin be brass!" An' then he looked at them pots what was laying on the groun' and they all turned to tin. Now sisters and brothers, them pots is people. Is you all. If you'll keep settin' on the truth what God gave you, you'll go be gol'. If you lay down on Him, He is goin' to turn you to tin. There won't be nothin' to you at all. You be as empty as a tin can. . . .

Father: Amen, amen.

Elias: Tain't but just so long that you got to be on this earth in the dark—anyhow. Set up. Set up and hold your head up. Don' lay down on God! Don' lay down on Him! Don' spill on the groun'. No matter how hard the folks wear and tear and worry you. Set up and don' spill the things He give you to keep for Him. They tore Him—but He come into the world Jesus and He went out of it still Jesus. He set hisself up as Jesus and He ain't never laid down. *(Here, LUCINDA yawns loudly and gives a prolonged "Ah-h-h-h!")* Set up to be gol' you all and if you ever feels weak tell God, He won't ask how you got cracked. "Master, I got a crack in me." He'll stoop down and take and heal you. He'll heal you; the pot maker done it and he warn't God. The pot maker he didn't blame the pots for bustin'. He knows that pots can bust and God knows that it wouldn't take but so much anyway to knock any gol' pot over and crack it an' make it tin. . . . That's the reason He's sorry for us and heals us. Ask Him. And set. Set you all. Don't spill on the groun'. Amen. *(There is a silence. The FATHER looks along the floor steadily. ELIAS looks at him. LUCINDA sees LEW. The MOTHER sees her son. Finally ELIAS notes LUCINDA has her hand in LEW's and that they are whispering together. But LEW releases her hand and smiles at ELIAS, rising to his feet at the same time)*

Lew: *(in a tone too nice, too round, too rich to be satisfactory)* Well, well folks! I'll have to go on now. I am congratulating you, sister Nettie, on such a son! He is surely a leadin' light. Leadin' us all straight into Heaven. *(He stops and mouths a laugh)* I'll be seein' you all at the meetin'—good night. *(He bobs up and down as if he were really a toy fool on a string)* Ah—Lucinda—ah—may—I—ask—you—for—a drink of water if—ah—it do not bother you? *(The tone is hollow. There will be no water drunk though they may run the water. LUCINDA smiles and leaves behind him giving a defiant flaunt as she passes ELIAS. This leaves the other three grouped beside the table)*

Father: That is a right smart sermon, 'pears to me. Got some good sense in it.

Mother: But them folks ain't goin' to sit there and hear him go on to tell them pots kin talk. I know that. *(A door bangs within the room in which LUCINDA and LEW have disappeared. LUCINDA comes out, crosses the stage, goes into the room at right. A faint rustling is heard within)*

Mother: *(calling)* 'Cinda, what you doin' in that trunk? Tain't nuthin' you need in there tonight. *(The rustling ceases abruptly—you can almost see LUCINDA's rage pouring in a flood at the door)*

Lucinda: *(from within)* I ain't doin' nothing'— *(She appears at the doorway fastening a string of red beads around her throat)*

Mother: Well, if you ain't doin' nothin', what you doin' with them beads on?

Lucinda: *(flaring)* None of your business.

Mother: Oh, it ain't! Well you jes' walk back in there and rest my best shoes under the side of the bed please, ma'am.

Father: Now Nettie, you women all likes to look—

Mother: Don't name me with that one there!

Elias: Ma, don't carry on with 'Cinda so.

Mother: You ain't nothin' but a turntable! You ain't got sense enough to see that she would jam you down the devil's throat if she got a chance.

Lucinda: I'm goin' long out of here where folks got some sense. *(She starts off without removing the shoes)*

Mother: Tain't whilst to go. I'm goin' callin' myself. Give me my shoes. *(LUCINDA halts at the door. There are no words that can tell you how she looks at her mother-in-law. Words cannot do but so much)*

Lucinda: *(slinging the shoes)* There. *(ELIAS picks them up easily and carries them to his MOTHER. She slips them on, and, catching up a shawl, goes off at back followed by her husband. LUCINDA stamps around the room and digs a pair of old shoes up from somewhere. She slams everything aside that she passes. Finally, she tips one of the geraniums over)*

Elias: *(mildly)* Tain't whilst to carry on so, Lucinda.

Lucinda: Oh, for God's sake, shut up! You and your "tain't whilst to's" make me sick. *(ELIAS says nothing. He merely looks at her)*

Lucinda: That's right! That's right! Stand there and stare at me like some pop-eyed owl. You ain't got sense enough to do anything else. *(ELIAS starts to speak. LUCINDA is warmed up to her subject. What can he say? Even more rapidly)* No you ain't got sense enough to do anything else! Ain't even got sense enough to keep a job! Get a job paying good money! Keep it two weeks and jes' when I'm hoping you'll get a little money ahead so's I could live decent like other women—in my house—You had to go and get called of God to quit and preach!

Elias: *(evenly)* God chose me.

Lucinda: Yas God chose you. He ain't chose you for no preachin'. He chose you for some kinder fool! That's what you are—some kinder fool! Fools can't preach.

Elias: Some do.

Lucinda: Then you must be one of them that does! If you was any kind of man you'd get a decent job and hold it and hold your mouth shut and move me into my own house. Ain't no woman so in love with her man's mother she wants to live five years under the same roof with her like I done. *(ELIAS may have thought of a dozen replies. He makes none. LUCINDA stares at him. Then she laughs aloud. It is a bitter laugh that makes you think of rocks and mud and dirt and edgy weather. It is jagged)* Yes you are some kinder fool. Standing there like a pop-eyed owl— *(there follows the inevitable)* The Lord knows what I ever saw in you!

Elias: *(still evenly)* The Lord does know Lucinda. *(At that LUCINDA falls back into her chair and curses aloud in a singsong manner as if she were chanting a prayer. Then she sits still and stares at him)*

Lucinda: Elias—ain't you never wanted to hit nobody in your life? *(Before he can answer, a shrill whistle is heard outside the window at left. LUCINDA starts nervously and looks at the window. When she sees ELIAS has heard the sound, she tries to act unconcerned)* What kinder bird is that whistlin' at the window? *(She starts toward it. ELIAS puts out a hand and stops her)*

Elias: Tain't whilst to open the window to look out. Can't see nothin' in the dark.

Lucinda: That ain't the side that old well is on, is it? That ain't the window, is it?

Elias: You ought to know! Long as you been livin' here! Five years you just said.

(There is a crackle of bushes outside the window close to the house. A crash. Then a sound of muttering that becomes louder and louder. A subdued splashing. LUCINDA starts to the window but ELIAS gets there first. He puts his back to the wall)

Lucinda: Somebody's fallin' into that well! Look out there!

    Elias: Tain't whilst to.

Lucinda: Tain't whilst to! Oh God—here um calling! Go out there! Tain't whilst to! *(She tries to dart around ELIAS. They struggle. He seizes her wrist, drags her back. She screams and talks all the time they struggle)* Call yourself a Christian! The devil! That's what you is! The devil! Lettin' folks drown! Might be your own mother!

    Elias: Tain't my mother—You know who it is!

Lucinda: How I know? Oh, go out there and save him for God's sake. *(The struggles and splashings are ceasing. A long drawn out "Oh my God" that sounds as if it's coming from every portion of the room, sifts over the stage. LUCINDA cries aloud. It is a tearing, shrieking, mad scream. It is as if someone had torn her soul apart from her body. ELIAS wrenches the door open)* Now Cindy, you was goin' to Lew. Go 'long to him. Go 'long to him. *(He repeats)*

Lucinda: *(trying to fawn at him)* Oh! No! Elias, Oh Master! Ain't you no ways a man? I ain't know that was Lew! I ain't know that was Lew—Oh, yes I did. Lew, Lew. *(She darts past ELIAS as if she has forgotten him. You hear her outside calling)* Lew, Lew.

(Full of mad agony, the screams search the night. But there is no answer. You hear only the sound of the wind. The sound of the wind in the leaves. ELIAS stands listening. All at once there is the same crackling sound outside and a crash and a splash. Once more LUCINDA raises her voice—frightened and choked. He hears the sound of the water. He starts toward the door)

    Elias: Go 'long to Lew. *(He shouts and then sits down)* You both is tin. *(But he raises himself at once and runs back to the door)* God, God, I got a crack in me too! *(He cries and goes out into the darkness. You hear splashing and panting. You hear cries)* 'Cinda, give me your hand! There now! You is 'most out.

(But then you hear another crash. A heavier splashing. Something has given way. One hears the sound of wood splitting. One hears something heavy splashing in the water. One hears only the wind in the leaves. Only the wind in the leaves and the door swings vacant. You stare through the door. Waiting. Expecting to see ELIAS stagger in with LUCINDA in his arms perhaps. But the door swings vacant. You stare—but there is only wind in the leaves. That's all there will be. A crack has been healed. A pot has spilled over on the ground. Some wisps have twisted out)

Curtain

Sterling A. Brown

(1901–1989)

Sterling Allen Brown was born May 1, 1901, in Washington, D.C., to Adelaide Allen, a graduate of Fisk University, and Sterling Nelson Brown, pastor of Lincoln Temple Congregational Church and professor of religion at Howard University. Brown attended Dunbar High School in Washington, D.C., and had the good fortune to be taught by both Angelina Weld Grimké and Jessie Fauset. He graduated in 1922 from Williams College as a Phi Beta Kappa. The next year he earned his M.A. in English from Harvard University. From 1923 to 1926 he taught English at Virginia Seminary College in Lynchburg. He then taught two years at Lincoln University in Missouri and one year at Fisk University before joining the faculty of Howard University in 1929, where he remained until his retirement in 1969 despite an offer to join the all-white faculty of Vassar College in 1945. Over the course of his distinguished career, Brown was involved with the Carnegie Myrdal Study of Race Relations in the United States, the American Folklore Society, the Institute of Jazz Studies, the editorial board of *The Crisis*, the Committee on Negro Studies of the American Council of Learned Societies, and the New Deal Federal Writers' Project, serving as the national editor for *Negro Affairs*.

Brown's first literary recognition came in 1927, when he won first prize in an *Opportunity* contest for his poem, "When de Saints Go Ma'ching Home." This same year he married Daisy Turnball; the couple later adopted one child. From 1926 to 1929, Brown published several poems in *The Crisis, Opportunity, Contempo*, and *Ebony and Topaz*; his first collection of poems, *Southern Road*, was published in 1932. Although Alain Locke declared Brown "The New Negro Folk Poet," he failed to find a publisher for his next volume of poetry, *No Hiding Place*. Brown then focused on academic writing, and he is considered a foundational critic of the African American literary tradition. Some of his major works include his influential essay "Negro Characters as Seen by White Authors," published in the *Journal of Negro Education* (1933); his groundbreaking critical studies, *The Negro in American Fiction* and *Negro Poetry and Drama* (both in 1937); and (with Arthur P. Davis and Ulysses Lee) the classic anthology, *The Negro Caravan* (1941). In 1975 Brown finally published his second poetry collection, *The Last Ride of Wild Bill and Eleven Narratives*. In 1980 Michael Harper compiled *The Collected Poems of Sterling A. Brown*, including many of the poems from the rejected book. Brown died on January 13, 1989, in Takoma Park, Maryland.

See See Rider

MA RAINEY
Recorded in 1924.

See See Rider, see what you done done!
  Lord, Lord, Lord!
You made me love you, now your gal done come.
You made me love you, now your gal done come.

I'm goin' away, baby, I won't be back till fall.
  Lord, Lord, Lord!
Goin' away, baby, won't be back till fall.
If I find me a good man, I won't be back at all.

I'm gonna buy me a pistol just as long as I am tall.
  Lord, Lord, Lord!
Kill my man and catch the Cannon Ball.
If he won't have me, he won't have no gal at all.

See See Rider, where did you stay last night?
  Lord, Lord, Lord!
Your shoes ain't buttoned, clothes don't fit you right.
You didn't come home till the sun was shinin' bright.

Ma Rainey

I

When Ma Rainey
Comes to town,
Folks from anyplace
Miles aroun',
From Cape Girardeau,
Poplar Bluff,
Flocks in to hear
Ma do her stuff;
Comes flivverin' in,[1]
Or ridin' mules,
Or packed in trains,
Picknickin' fools . . .
That's what it's like,

---

1. "Flivver "was slang for an automobile.

Fo' miles on down,
To New Orleans delta
An' Mobile town,
When Ma hits
Anywheres aroun'.

II

Dey comes to hear Ma Rainey from de little river settlements,
From blackbottom cornrows and from lumber camps;
Dey stumble in de hall, jes a-laughin' an' a-cacklin',
Cheerin' lak roarin' water, lak wind in river swamps.

An' some jokers keeps deir laughs a-goin' in de crowded aisles,
An' some folks sits dere waitin' wid deir aches an' miseries,
Till Ma comes out before dem, a-smilin' gold-toofed smiles
An' Long Boy ripples minors on de black an' yellow keys.

III

O Ma Rainey,
Sing yo' song;
Now you's back
Whah you belong,
Git way inside us,
Keep us strong . . .
O Ma Rainey,
Li'l an' low;
Sing us 'bout de hard luck
Roun' our do';
Sing us 'bout de lonesome road
We mus' go . . .

IV

I talked to a fellow, an' the fellow say,
"She jes' catch hold of us, somekindaway.
She sang Backwater Blues one day:

  'It rained fo' days an' de skies was dark as night,
  Trouble taken place in de lowlands at night.

  'Thundered an' lightened an' the storm begin to roll
  Thousan's of people ain't got no place to go.

  'Den I went an' stood upon some high ol' lonesome hill,
  An' looked down on the place where I used to live.'

An' den de folks, dey natchally bowed dey heads an' cried,
Bowed dey heavy heads, shet dey moufs up tight an' cried,
An' Ma lef' de stage, an' followed some de folks outside."

Dere wasn't much more de fellow say:
She jes' 'gits hold of us dataway.

Southern Road, 1932.

Sam Smiley

I

The whites had taught him how to rip
   A Nordic belly with a thrust
Of bayonet, had taught him how
   To transmute Nordic flesh to dust.

And a surprising fact had made
   Belated impress on his mind:
That shrapnel bursts and poison gas
   Were inexplicably color blind.

He picked up, from the difficult
   But striking lessons of the war,
Some truths that he could not forget,
   Though inconceivable before.

And through the lengthy vigils, stuck
   In never-drying stinking mud,
He was held up by dreams of one
   Chockfull of laughter, hot of blood.

II

On the return Sam Smiley cheered
   The dirty steerage with his dance,
Hot-stepping boy! Soon he would see
   The girl who beat all girls in France.

He stopped buckdancing when he reached
   The shanties at his journey's end;
He found his sweetheart in the jail,
   And took white lightning[1] for his friend.

---

1. Illegal liquor; moonshine.

One night the woman whose full voice
　　Had chortled so, was put away
Into a narrow gaping hole,
　　Sam sat beside till break of day.

He had been told what man it was
　　Whose child the girl had had to kill,
Who best knew why her laugh was dumb,
　　Who best knew why her blood was still.

And he remembered France, and how
　　A human life was dunghill cheap,
And so he sent a rich white man
　　His woman's company to keep.

　　　III

The mob was in fine fettle, yet
　　The dogs were stupid-nosed, and day
Was far spent when the men drew round
　　The scrawny woods where Smiley lay.

The oaken leaves drowsed prettily,
　　The moon shone down benignly there;
And big Sam Smiley, King Buckdancer,
　　Buckdanced on the midnight air.

Southern Road, 1932.

Southern Road

Swing dat hammer—hunh—
Steady, bo';
Swing dat hammer—hunh—
Steady, bo';
Ain't no rush, bebby,
Long ways to go.

Burner tore his—hunh—
Black heart away;
Burner tore his—hunh—
Black heart away;
Got me life,[1] bebby,
An' a day.

1. "Got me life" refers to his sentence to life in prison.

Gal's on Fifth Street—hunh—
Son done gone;
Gal's on Fifth Street—hunh—
Son done gone;
Wife's in de ward, bebby,
Babe's not bo'n.

My ole man died—hunh—
Cussin' me;
My ole man died—hunh—
Cussin' me;
Ole lady rocks, bebby,
Huh misery.

Doubleshackled—hunh—
Guard behin';
Doubleshacked—hunh—
Guard behin';
Ball an' chain, bebby,
On my min'.

White man tells me—hunh—
Damn yo' soul;
White man tells me—hunh—
Damn yo' soul;
Got no need, bebby,
To be tole.

Chain gang nevah—hunh—
Let me go;
Chain gang nevah—hunh—
Let me go;
Po' los' boy, bebby,
Evahmo'. . .

Southern Road, 1932.

Strong Men

> The strong men keep coming on.
> —Sandburg

They dragged you from homeland,
They chained you in coffles,
They huddled you spoon-fashion in filthy hatches,
They sold you to give a few gentlemen ease.

They broke you in like oxen,
They scourged you,
They branded you,
They made your women breeders,
They swelled your numbers with bastards. . . .
They taught you the religion they disgraced.

You sang:
  Keep a-inchin' along
  Lak a po' inch worm. . . .

You sang:
  Bye and bye
  I'm gonna lay down dis heaby load. . . .

You sang:
  Walk togedder, chillen,
  Dontcha git weary. . . .
    The strong men keep a-comin' on
    The strong men git stronger.

They point with pride to the roads you built for them,
They ride in comfort over the rails you laid for them.
They put hammers in your hands
And said—Drive so much before sundown.

You sang:
  Ain't no hammah
  In dis lan',
  Strikes lak mine, bebby,
  Strikes lak mine.

They cooped you in their kitchens,
They penned you in their factories,
They gave you the jobs that they were too good for,
They tried to guarantee happiness to themselves
By shunting dirt and misery to you.

You sang:
   Me an' muh baby gonna shine, shine
   Me an' muh baby gonna shine.
     The strong men keep a-comin' on
     The strong men git stronger. . . .

They bought off some of your leaders
You stumbled, as blind men will. . . .
They coaxed you, unwontedly soft-voiced. . . .
You followed a way.
Then laughed as usual.

They heard the laugh and wondered;
Uncomfortable;
Unadmitting a deeper terror. . . .
    The strong men keep a-comin' on
    Gittin' stronger. . . .

What, from the slums
Where they have hemmed you,
What, from the tiny huts
They could not keep from you—
What reaches them
Making them ill at ease, fearful?
Today they shout prohibition at you
"Thou shalt not this"
"Thou shalt not that"
"Reserved for whites only"
You laugh.

One thing they cannot prohibit—
   The strong men . . . coming on
   The strong men gittin' stronger.
   Strong men . . .
   Stronger. . . .

Southern Road, 1932.

Langston Hughes

(1902-1967)

Langston Hughes was a prolific writer and editor who wrote in numerous genres: poetry, short stories, plays, novels, newspaper columns, translations, children's works, autobiographies, and songs. Hughes was one of the most creative and versatile writers of the Harlem Renaissance, and his poem "The Negro Speaks of Rivers" (1921) is arguably the most famous poem of the period.

He was born James Mercer Langston Hughes on February 1, 1902, in Joplin, Missouri, to Carrie Langston and James Nathaniel Hughes. His parents had moved from Oklahoma when his father was denied admission to the bar exam after he studied law by correspondence course. Hughes's parents separated in 1903 when, angered by his inability to find decent work, his father left for Mexico, where he was eventually able to became a lawyer and engineer. Hughes's mother, refusing to go to Mexico, moved from city to city in search of work. Although Hughes went with her on occasion, he spent most of the next twelve years living with his maternal grandmother, Mary Leary Langston, in Lawrence, Kansas. After his grandmother's death in 1915, Hughes was placed with her friend Untie Reed and her husband in Lawrence. He also lived in Lincoln, Illinois, before graduating from high school in Cleveland, Ohio, in 1919. After graduation, he spent a year with his father near Mexico City. In 1921 he enrolled at Columbia University but left after only a year. Between 1923 and 1924 he worked as steward aboard freighters, traveling to the Azores, Africa, and Paris. He jumped ship in Paris and spent several months there working in a nightclub. Hughes wrote throughout his travels and began publishing in *The Crisis* and *The Brownies' Book* under the mentorship of Jessie Fauset. In 1924 he returned to the States, joining his mother in Washington, D.C. He eventually returned to college and graduated in 1929 from Lincoln University in Pennsylvania.

In 1925 when he won the literary contest organized by *Opportunity* magazine, his winning poem, "The Weary Blues," caught the attention of Carl Van Vechten and led to a book contract from Knopf; his first collection, *The Weary Blues*, was published in 1926. The following year Alain Locke introduced him to Charlotte Osgood Mason, a wealthy white patron of African American artists. Mason supported Hughes until a dispute in 1930 involving Zora Neale Hurston ended their relationship. In 1931 Hughes traveled to the American South and West and to Haiti to recover from the split with the woman he and Hurston had called "Godmother." During this time his politics moved farther toward the left and his interest in socialism increased. He published frequently in *New Masses*, a journal associated with the Communist Party. He later visited the Soviet Union to make a movie about American race relations, but the project fell apart.

Hughes's career was prolific and eclectic. In 1937 he served as a reporter covering the Spanish Civil War for the *Afro-American*. Then from 1938 to 1940, he established black theaters in Harlem, Los Angeles, and Chicago. In 1947 Hughes wrote the lyrics for the Broadway musical *Street Scene*. In the 1940s and beyond, Hughes wrote the "Simple" columns for the

Chicago Defender, worked as a visiting professor at Atlanta University, served as poet-in-residence at the University of Chicago's Laboratory School, and lectured in Europe for the U.S. Information Agency. In 1960 Hughes was honored with the Spingarn Medal, the NAACP's highest honor.

Langston Hughes never married and, while there is evidence that he had intimate relationships with men, biographers disagree about his sexual orientation. It is known that Countee Cullen and Alain Locke were both attracted to Hughes in the 1920s, but he did not reciprocate, even when Locke followed him to Paris and offered his house as living quarters if Hughes would attend Howard University. It was to Cullen's home that Hughes immediately went when he returned from Europe in the mid-1920s, their friendship having been formed when Hughes came to New York in 1921. Cullen dedicated "To a Dark Boy" to Hughes when he sent him the poem in 1923, and Hughes sent Cullen the first draft of his signature poem, "The Weary Blues." Hughes split with Cullen soon after he returned, however, for reasons that are unclear. He also formed a close friendship with openly gay artist and writer Richard Bruce Nugent, although they evidently were not lovers, and worked closely with gay writer Wallace Thurman on the groundbreaking issue of *Fire!!* (1926).

Hughes's poetry is best known for its innovative use of jazz and blues rhythms and idioms as well as its skilled adaptation of black street vernacular. Hughes shook up the Du Bois Harlem establishment in 1926 with his manifesto for artistic freedom, "The Negro Artist and the Racial Mountain" (see the essays section). He and Hurston are perhaps the two writers from their peer group who have gained the most critical acclaim in the years since the Harlem Renaissance. They valued African American folk traditions and they collaborated on a play, *Mule Bone* (1931), that attempted to fuse this folk sensibility with the European form of opera. Their falling out over this play is widely cited as one of the death knells for the era they made famous.

Hughes's poetry collections include *Fine Clothes to the Jew* (1927), *Shakespeare in Harlem* (1942), *Montage of a Dream Deferred* (1951), and *The Panther and the Lash* (1967). Among his fiction collections are *Not without Laughter* (1930) and *The Ways of White Folks* (1934). He wrote the following plays: *Mulatto* (1935), *Little Ham* (1935), and *Don't You Want to Be Free* (1936–37). He also wrote two autobiographies: *The Big Sea* (1940) and *I Wonder as I Wander* (1956).

Hughes is also honored for his substantial contributions to histories and anthologies of the Harlem Renaissance, particularly in his work with Arna Bontemps, his closest friend, with whom he collaborated in the writing of Bontemps's landmark *The Harlem Renaissance Remembered* (1972), as well as other books, most notably their anthology, *Poetry of the Negro* (1949). He is the author or editor of more than eighty books and plays and in his lifetime was often labeled "Poet Laureate of the Negro Race." Hughes died in New York. "The Negro Speaks of Rivers" was recited at his funeral service.

The Negro Speaks of Rivers

I've known rivers:
I've known rivers ancient as the world and older than the flow of human blood
    in human veins.

My soul has grown deep like the rivers.

I bathed in the Euphrates when dawns were young.
I built my hut near the Congo and it lulled me to sleep.
I looked upon the Nile and raised the pyramids above it.
I heard the singing of the Mississippi when Abe Lincoln went down to New Orleans,
    and I've seen its muddy bosom turn all golden in the sunset.

I've known rivers:
Ancient, dusky rivers.

My soul has grown deep like the rivers.

The Crisis, June 1921.

Danse Africaine

The low beating of the tom-toms,
The slow beating of the tom-toms,
    Low . . . slow
    Slow . . . low—
    Stirs your blood.
        Dance!
A night-veiled girl
    Whirls softly into a
    Circle of light.
    Whirls softly . . . slowly,
Like a wisp of smoke around the fire—
    And the tom-toms beat,
    And the tom-toms beat,
And the low beating of the tom-toms
    Stirs your blood.

The Crisis, August 1922.

Jazzonia

Oh, silver tree!
Oh, shining rivers of the soul!

In a Harlem cabaret
Six long-headed jazzers play.
A dancing girl whose eyes are bold
Lifts high a dress of silken gold.

Oh, singing tree!
Oh, shining rivers of the soul!

Were Eve's eyes
In the first garden
Just a bit too bold?
Was Cleopatra gorgeous
In a gown of gold?

Oh, shining tree!
Oh, silver rivers of the soul!

In a whirling cabaret
Six long-headed jazzers play.

The Crisis, August 1923.

Song to a Negro Wash-Woman

Oh, wash-woman,
Arms elbow-deep in white suds,
Soul washed clean,
Clothes washed clean,
I have many songs to sing you
Could I but find the words.

Was it four o'clock or six o'clock on a winter afternoon, I saw you wringing out
the last shirt in Miss White Lady's kitchen? Was it four o'clock or six o'clock?
I don't remember.

But I know, at seven one spring morning you were on Vermont Street with a bundle
in your arms going to wash clothes.

And I know I've seen you in the New York subway in the late afternoon coming home
from washing clothes.

Yes, I know you, wash-woman.

‚I know how you send your children to school, and high-school, and even college.
I know how you work to help your man when times are hard.
I know how you build your house up from the washtub and call it home.
And how you raise your churches from white suds for the service of the Holy God.

I've seen you singing, wash-woman. Out in the backyard garden under the apple trees,
   singing, hanging white clothes on long lines in the sunshine.
And I've seen you in church on Sunday morning singing, praising your Jesus because
   some day you're going to sit on the right hand side of the Son of God and forget
   you ever were a wash-woman.
And the aching back and the bundles of clothes will be unremembered then.

Yes, I've seen you singing.

So for you,
O singing wash-woman,
For you, singing little brown woman,
Singing strong black woman,
Singing tall yellow woman,
Arms deep in white suds,
Soul washed clean,
Clothes washed clean,
For you I have
Many songs to sing
Could I but find the words.

The Crisis, January 1925.

Dream Variation

To fling my arms wide
In some place of the sun,
To whirl and to dance
Till the bright day is done.[1]
Then rest at cool evening
Beneath a tall tree
While night comes gently
Dark like me.
That is my dream.
To fling my arms wide

1. This line reads "Till the white day is done" in *The Collected Poems of Langston Hughes,* ed. Arnold Rampersad (New York: Alfred A. Knopf, 1994), 40.

In the face of the sun.
Dance! Whirl! Whirl!
Till the quick day is done.
Rest at pale evening,
A tall, slim tree,
Night coming tenderly
Black like me.

Survey Graphic, March 1925.

Desire

Desire to us
Was like a double death,
Swift dying
Of our mingled breath,
Evaporation
Of an unknown strange perfume
Between us quickly
In a naked
Room.

The Messenger, May 1925.

Poem [2]

(To F. S.)

I loved my friend.
He went away from me.
There's nothing more to say.
The poem ends,
Soft as it began,—
I loved my friend.

The Crisis, May 1925.

Aaron Douglas, "Weary As I Can Be,"
Opportunity, October 1926

The Weary Blues

Droning a drowsy syncopated tune,
Rocking back and forth to a mellow croon,
     I heard a Negro play.
Down on Lenox Avenue the other night
By the pale dull pallor of an old gas light
     He did a lazy sway . . .
     He did a lazy sway . . .
To the tune o' those Weary Blues.
With his ebony hands on each ivory key
He made that poor piano moan with melody.
     O Blues!
Swaying to and fro on his rickety stool
He played that sad raggy tune like a musical fool.
     Sweet Blues!
Coming from a black man's soul.
     O Blues!

In a deep song voice with a melancholy tone
I heard that Negro sing, that old piano moan—
     "Ain't got nobody in all this world,
     Ain't got nobody but ma self.
     I's gwine to quit ma frownin'
     And put ma troubles on the shelf."

Thump, thump, thump, went his foot on the floor.
He played a few chords then he sang some more—
   "I got the Weary Blues
   And I can't be satisfied.
   Got the Weary Blues
   And can't be satisfied—
   I ain't happy no mo'
   And I wish that I had died."
And far into the night he crooned that tune.
The stars went out and so did the moon.
The singer stopped playing and went to bed
While the Weary Blues echoed through his head.
He slept like a rock or a man that's dead.

Opportunity, May 1925.

To Midnight Nan at Leroy's

Strut and wiggle,
   Shameless gal.
Wouldn't no good fellow
   Be your pal?

Hear dat music . . .
   Jungle night.
Hear dat music . . .
   And the moon was white.

Sing your Blues song,
   Pretty Baby.
You want lovin', . . .
   And you don't mean maybe.

Jungle lover . . .
   Night black boy . . .
Two against the moon
   And the moon was joy.

Strut and wiggle,
   Shameless Nan.
Wouldn't no good fellow
   Be your man?

Opportunity, January 1926.

Lullaby

My little dark baby,
My little earth-thing,
My little love-one,
What shall I sing
For your lullaby?
  Stars,
  Stars,
  A necklace of stars
  Winding the night.

My little black baby,
My dark body's baby,
What shall I sing
For your lullaby?
  Moon,
  Moon,
  Great diamond moon,
  Kissing the night.

Oh, little dark baby,
Night black baby,
  Stars, stars,
  Moon,
  Night stars,
  Moon,
For your sleep-song lullaby!

The Crisis, March 1926.

Listen Here Blues

Sweet girls, sweet girls,
Listen here to me.
All you sweet girls,
Listen here to me:
Gin an' whiskey
Kin make you lose yo' 'ginity.

I used to be a good chile,
Lawd, in Sunday School.
Used to be a good chile,—
Always in Sunday School,

Backwater Blues

BESSIE SMITH
Recorded in 1927.

When it rain five days an' de skies turned dark as night
When it rain five days an' de skies turned dark as night
Then trouble taken place in the lowland that night

I woke up this mornin', can't even get outa mah do'
I woke up this mornin', can't even get outa mah do'
That's enough trouble to make a po' girl wonder where she wanta go

Then they rowed a little boat about five miles 'cross the pond
They rowed a little boat about five miles 'cross the pond
I packed all mah clothes, th'owed 'em in, an' they rowed me along

When it thunder an' a-lightnin', an' the wind begin to blow
When it thunder an' a-lightnin', an' the wind begin to blow
An' thousan' people ain' got no place to go

Then I went an' stood up on some high ol' lonesome hill
I went an' stood up on some high ol' lonesome hill
An' looked down on the house where I used to live

Backwater blues done cause me to pack mah things an' go
Backwater blues done cause me to pack mah things an' go
Cause mah house fell down an' I cain' live there no mo'

O-o-o-oom, I cain' move no mo'
O-o-o-oom, I cain' move no mo'
There ain' no place fo' a po' ol' girl to go

Till these licker-headed rounders
Made me everybody's fool.

Good girls, good girls,
Listen here to me.
Oh, you good girls,
Better listen to me:
Don't you fool wid no men cause
They'll bring you misery.

Modern Quarterly, May–July 1926.

Aaron Douglas, "Play de Blues,"
Opportunity, October 1926

Bound No'th Blues

Goin' down de road, Lord,
Goin' down de road.
Down de road, Lord,
Way, way down de road.
Got to find somebody
To help me carry this load.
Road's in front o' me,
Nothin' to do but walk.
Road's in front o' me,
Walk . . . and walk . . . and walk.
I'd like to meet a good friend
To come along an' talk.[1]
Road, road, road, O!
Road, road . . . road . . . road, road!
Road, road, road, O!
On de No'thern road.
These Mississippi towns ain't
Fit fer a hoppin' toad.

1. This is the version that appeared in *Opportunity.* A later version included six additional lines between
"To come along an' talk" and "Road, road, road, O!"

Opportunity, October 1926.

Song for a Dark Girl

Way Down South in Dixie
  (Break the heart of me)
They hung my dark young lover[1]
  To a cross roads tree.

Way Down South in Dixie
  (Bruised body high in air)
I asked the white Lord Jesus
  What was the use of prayer.

Way Down South in Dixie
  (Break the heart of me)
Love is a naked shadow
  On a gnarled and naked tree.

---

1. This line appeared as is in *The Crisis*. It was later changed to "They hung my black young lover."

The Crisis, May 1927.

The Blues I'm Playing

Then began one of the most interesting periods in Mrs. Ellsworth's whole experience in aiding the arts. The period of Oceola. For the Negro girl, as time went on, began to occupy a greater and greater place in Mrs. Ellsworth's interests, to take up more and more of her time, and to use up more and more of her money. Not that Oceola ever asked for money, but Mrs. Ellsworth herself seemed to keep thinking of so much more Oceola needed.

At first it was hard to get Oceola to need anything. Mrs. Ellsworth had the feeling that the girl mistrusted her generosity, and Oceola did—for she had never met anybody interested in pure art before. Just to be given things for *art's sake* seemed suspicious to Oceola.

That first Tuesday, when the colored girl came back at Mrs. Ellsworth's request, she answered the white woman's questions with a why-look in her eyes.

"Don't think I'm being personal, dear," said Mrs. Ellsworth, "but I must know your background in order to help you. Now, tell me . . ."

Oceola wondered why on earth the woman wanted to help her. However, since Mrs. Ellsworth seemed interested in her life's history, she brought it forth so as not to hinder the progress of the afternoon, for she wanted to get back to Harlem by six o'clock.

The Ways of White Folks, 1934.

Born in Mobile in 1903. Yes, ma'am, she was older than she looked. Papa had a band, that is her stepfather. Used to play for all the lodge turn-outs, picnics, dances, barbecues. You could get the best roast pig in the world in Mobile. Her mother used to play the organ in church, and when the deacons bought a piano after the big revival, her mama played that, too. Oceola played by ear for a long while until her mother taught her notes. Oceola played an organ, also, and a cornet.

"My, my," said Mrs. Ellsworth.

"Yes, ma'am," said Oceola. She had played and practiced on lots of instruments in the South before her stepfather died. She always went to band rehearsals with him....

———————

That was some years ago. Eventually art and Mrs. Ellsworth triumphed. Oceola moved out of Harlem. She lived in Gay Street west of Washington Square where she met Genevieve Taggard, and Ernestine Evans, and two or three sculptors, and a cat-painter who was also a protégée of Mrs. Ellsworth. She spent her days practicing, playing for friends of her patron, going to concerts, and reading books about music. She no longer had pupils or rehearsed the choir, but she still loved to play for Harlem house parties— for nothing—now that she no longer needed the money, out of sheer love of jazz. This rather disturbed Mrs. Ellsworth, who still believed in art of the old school, portraits that really and truly looked like people, poems about nature, music that had soul in it, not syncopation. And she felt the dignity of art. Was it in keeping with genius, she wondered, for Oceola to have a studio full of white and colored people every Saturday night (some of them actually drinking gin *from bottles*) and dancing to the most tom-tom-like music she had ever heard coming out of a grand piano? She wished she could lift Oceola up bodily and take her away from all that, for art's sake.

So in the spring, Mrs. Ellsworth organized weekends in the up-state mountains where she had a little lodge and where Oceola could look from the high places at the stars, and fill her soul with the vastness of the eternal, and forget about jazz. Mrs. Ellsworth really began to hate jazz—especially on a grand piano.

If there were a lot of guests at the lodge, as there sometimes were, Mrs. Ellsworth might share the bed with Oceola. Then she would read aloud Tennyson or Browning before turning out the light,[1] aware all the time of the electric strength of that brown-black body beside her, and of the deep drowsy voice asking what the poems were about. And then Mrs. Ellsworth would feel very motherly toward this dark girl whom she had taken under her wing on the wonderful road of art, to nurture and love until she became a great interpreter of the piano. At such times the elderly white woman was glad her late husband's money, so well invested, furnished her with a large surplus to devote to the needs of her protégées, especially to Oceola, the blackest—and most interesting of all.

Why the most interesting?

---

1. Alfred Lord Tennyson (1809–1892) and Robert Browning (1812–1889) were nineteenth-century English romantic poets.

Mrs. Ellsworth didn't know, unless it was that Oceola really was talented, terribly alive, and that she looked like nothing Mrs. Ellsworth had ever been near before. Such a rich velvet black, and such a hard young body! The teacher of the piano raved about her strength.

"She can stand a great career," the teacher said. "She has everything for it."

"Yes," agreed Mrs. Ellsworth, thinking, however, of the Pullman porter at Meharry,[2] "but she must learn to sublimate her soul."

So for two years then, Oceola lived abroad at Mrs. Ellsworth's expense. She studied with Philippe, had the little apartment on the Left Bank,[3] and learned about Debussy's African background.[4] She met many black Algerian and French West Indian students, too, and listened to their interminable arguments ranging from Garvey to Picasso to Spengler to Jean Cocteau,[5] and thought they all must be crazy. Why did they or anybody argue so much about life or art? Oceola merely lived—and loved it. Only the Marxian students seemed sound to her for they, at least, wanted people to have enough to eat. That was important, Oceola thought, remembering, as she did, her own sometimes hungry years. But the rest of the controversies, as far as she could fathom, were based on air.

Oceola hated most artists, too, and the word *art* in French or English. If you wanted to play the piano or paint pictures or write books, go ahead! But why talk so much about it? Montparnasse was worse in that respect than the Village.[6] And as for the cultured Negroes who were always saying art would break down color lines, art could save the race and prevent lynchings! "Bunk!" said Oceola. "My ma and pa were both artists when it came to making music, and the white folks ran them out of town for being dressed up in Alabama. And look at the Jews! Every other artist in the world's a Jew, and still folks hate them."

She thought of Mrs. Ellsworth (dear soul in New York), who never made uncomplimentary remarks about Negroes, but frequently did about Jews. Of little Menuhin she would say, for instance, "He's a *genius*—not a Jew," hating to admit his ancestry.[7]

In Paris, Oceola especially loved the West Indian ball rooms where the black colonials danced the beguin. And she liked the entertainers at Bricktop's. Sometimes late at night there, Oceola would take the piano and beat out a blues for Brick and the assembled guests. In her playing of Negro folk music, Oceola never doctored it up, or filled it full of classical runs, or fancy falsities. In the blues she made the bass notes throb like tomtoms, the trebles cry like little flutes, so deep in the earth and so high in the sky that

2. Pullman porters were African American workers hired to carry suitcases and run errands for the white train passengers.

3. The Left Bank in Paris is an area dominated by artists and intellectuals.

4. Claude Debussy (1862–1918) was an early-twentieth-century French composer.

5. Marcus Garvey (1887–1940), head of the Universal Negro Improvement Association in New York City, a radical black nationalist organization; Pablo Picasso (1881–1973), the Spanish abstract painter and sculptor; Oswald Spengler (1880–1936), the German philosopher; Jean Cocteau (1889–1963), the French modernist writer and surrealist.

6. Montparnasse is an artistic section of Paris; Greenwich Village in New York City is a bohemian section of artists and intellectuals.

7. Yehudi Menuhin (1916–1999) was a Jewish-American violinist.

they understood everything. And when the night club crowd would get up and dance to her blues, and Bricktop would yell, "Hey! Hey!" Oceola felt as happy as if she were performing a Chopin étude for the nicely gloved Oh's and Ah-ers in a Crillon salon.[8]

Music, to Oceola, demanded movement and expression, dancing and living to go with it. She liked to teach, when she had the choir, the singing of those rhythmical Negro spirituals that possessed the power to pull colored folks out of their seats in the amen corner and make them prance and shout in the aisles for Jesus. She never liked those fashionable colored churches where shouting and movement were discouraged and looked down upon, and where New England hymns instead of spirituals were sung. Oceola's background was too well-grounded in Mobile, and Billy Kersands' Minstrels,[9] and the Sanctified churches where religion was a joy, to stare mystically over the top of a grand piano like white folks and imagine that Beethoven had nothing to do with life, or that Schubert's love songs were only sublimations.[10]

Whenever Mrs. Ellsworth came to Paris, she and Oceola spent hours listening to symphonies and string quartets and pianists. Oceola enjoyed concerts but seldom felt, like her patron, that she was floating on clouds of bliss. Mrs. Ellsworth insisted, however, that Oceola's spirit was too moved for words at such times—therefore she understood why the dear child kept quiet. Mrs. Ellsworth herself was often too moved for words, but never by pieces like Ravel's *Bolero* (which Oceola played on the phonograph as a dance record) or any of the compositions of *les Six*.[11]

What Oceola really enjoyed most with Mrs. Ellsworth was not going to concerts, but going for trips on the little river boats in the Seine; or riding out to old chateaux in her patron's hired Renault; or to Versailles, and listening to the aging white lady talk about the romantic history of France, the wars and uprisings, the loves and intrigues of princes and kings and queens, about guillotines and lace handkerchiefs, snuff boxes and daggers. For Mrs. Ellsworth had loved France as a girl, and had made a study of its life and lore. Once she used to sing simple little French songs rather well, too. And she always regretted that her husband never understood the lovely words—or even tried to understand them.

Oceola learned the accompaniments for all the songs Mrs. Ellsworth knew and sometimes they tried them over together. The middle-aged white woman loved to sing when the colored girl played, and she even tried spirituals. Often, when she stayed at the little Paris apartment, Oceola would go into the kitchen and cook something good for late supper, maybe an oyster soup, or fried apples and bacon. And sometimes Oceola had pigs' feet.

8. Frédéric Chopin (1810–1849) was a nineteenth-century Polish composer and pianist.

9. A black minstrel group in vaudeville.

10. German composer Ludwig van Beethoven (1770–1827) and Austrian composer Franz Schubert (1797–1828).

11. Group of six early twentieth-century French composers—Darius Milhaud, Francis Poulenc, Arthur Honegger, Georges Auric, Louis Durey, and Germaine Tailleferre—who reacted against heavy German romantic music popular in their day.

"There's nothing quite so good as a pig's foot," said Oceola, "after playing all day."

"Then you must have pigs' feet," agreed Mrs. Ellsworth.

And all this while Oceola's development at the piano blossomed into perfection. Her tone became a singing wonder and her interpretations warm and individual. She gave a concert in Paris, one in Brussels, and another in Berlin. She got the press notices all pianists crave. She had her picture in lots of European papers. And she came home to New York a year after the stock market crashed and nobody had any money—except folks like Mrs. Ellsworth who had so much it would be hard to ever lose it all.

Oceola's one time Pullman porter, now a coming doctor, was graduating from Meharry that spring. Mrs. Ellsworth saw her dark protégée go South to attend his graduation with tears in her eyes. She thought that by now music would be enough, after all those years under the best teachers, but alas, Oceola was not yet sublimated, even by Philippe. She wanted to see Pete.

Oceola returned North to prepare for her New York concert in the fall. She wrote Mrs. Ellsworth at Bar Harbor that her doctor boyfriend was putting in one more summer on the railroad, then in the autumn he would intern at Atlanta. And Oceola said that he had asked her to marry him. Lord, she was happy!

It was a long time before she heard from Mrs. Ellsworth. When the letter came, it was full of long paragraphs about the beautiful music Oceola had within her power to give the world. Instead, she wanted to marry and be burdened with children! Oh, my dear, my dear!

Oceola, when she read it, thought she had done pretty well knowing Pete this long and not having children. But she wrote back that she didn't see why children and music couldn't go together. Anyway, during the present depression, it was pretty hard for a beginning artist like herself to book a concert tour—so she might just as well be married awhile. Pete, on his last run in from St. Louis, had suggested that they have the wedding Christmas in the South. "And he's impatient, at that. He needs me."

This time Mrs. Ellsworth didn't answer by letter at all. She was back in town in late September. In November, Oceola played at Town Hall. The critics were kind, but they didn't go wild. Mrs. Ellsworth swore it was because of Pete's influence on her protégée.

"But he was in Atlanta," Oceola said.

"His spirit was here," Mrs. Ellsworth insisted. "All the time you were playing on that stage, he was here, the monster! Taking you out of yourself, taking you away from the piano."

"Why, he wasn't," said Oceola. "He was watching an operation in Atlanta."

But from then on, things didn't go well between her and her patron. The white lady grew distinctly cold when she received Oceola in her beautiful drawing room among the jade vases and amber cups worth thousands of dollars. When Oceola would have to wait there for Mrs. Ellsworth, she was afraid to move for fear she might knock something over—that would take ten years of a Harlemite's wages to replace, if broken.

Over the tea cups, the aging Mrs. Ellsworth did not talk any longer about the concert tour she had once thought she might finance for Oceola, if no recognized bureau took it up. Instead, she spoke of that something she believed Oceola's fingers had lost since her return from Europe. And she wondered why any one insisted on living in Harlem.

"I've been away from my own people so long," said the girl, "I want to live right in the middle of them again."

Why, Mrs. Ellsworth wondered farther, did Oceola, at her last concert in a Harlem church, not stick to the classical items listed on the program. Why did she insert one of her own variations on the spirituals, a syncopated variation from the Sanctified Church, that made an old colored lady rise up and cry out from her pew, "Glory to God this evenin'! Yes! Hallelujah! Whooooo!" right at the concert? Which seemed most undignified to Mrs. Ellsworth, and unworthy of the teachings of Philippe.

And furthermore, why was Pete coming up to New York for Thanksgiving? And who had sent him the money to come?

"Me," said Oceola. "He doesn't make anything interning."

"Well," said Mrs. Ellsworth, "I don't think much of him."

But Oceola didn't seem to care what Mrs. Ellsworth thought, for she made no defense.

Thanksgiving evening, in bed together in a Harlem apartment, Pete and Oceola talked about their wedding to come. They would have a big one in a church with lots of music. And Pete would give her a ring. And she would have on a white dress, light and fluffy, not silk. "I hate silk," she said. "I hate expensive things." (She thought of her mother being buried in a cotton dress, for they were all broke when she died. Mother would have been glad about her marriage.) "Pete," Oceola said, hugging him in the dark, "let's live in Atlanta, where there are lots of colored people, like us."

"What about Mrs. Ellsworth?" Pete asked. "She coming down to Atlanta for our wedding?"

"I don't know," said Oceola.

"I hope not, 'cause if she stops at one of them big hotels, I won't have you going to the back door to see her. That's one thing I hate about the South—where there're white people, you have to go to the back door."

"Maybe she can stay with us," said Oceola. "I wouldn't mind."

"I'll be damned," said Pete. "You want to get lynched?"

But it happened that Mrs. Ellsworth didn't care to attend the wedding, anyway. When she saw how love had triumphed over art, she decided she could no longer influence Oceola's life. The period of Oceola was over. She would send checks, occasionally, if the girl needed them, besides, of course, something beautiful for the wedding, but that would be all. These things she told her the week after Thanksgiving.

"And Oceola, my dear, I've decided to spend the whole winter in Europe. I sail on December eighteenth. Christmas—while you are marrying—I shall be in Paris with my precious Antonio Bas. In January, he has an exhibition of oils in Madrid. And in the spring, a new young poet is coming over whom I want to visit Florence, to really know Florence.[12]

12. Florence, Italy, is a city known for its art.

A charming white-haired boy from Omaha whose soul has been crushed in the West. I want to try to help him. He, my dear, is one of the few people who live for their art— and nothing else . . . Ah, such a beautiful life! . . . You will come and play for me once before I sail?"

"Yes, Mrs. Ellsworth," said Oceola, genuinely sorry that the end had come. Why did white folks think you could live on nothing but art? Strange! Too strange! Too strange!

————————

The Persian vases in the music room were filled with long-stemmed lilies that night when Oceola Jones came down from Harlem for the last time to play for Mrs. Dora Ellsworth. Mrs. Ellsworth had on a gown of black velvet, and a collar of pearls about her neck. She was very kind and gentle to Oceola, as one would be to a child who has done a great wrong but doesn't know any better. But to the black girl from Harlem, she looked very cold and white, and her grand piano seemed like the biggest and heaviest in the world—as Oceola sat down to play it with the technique for which Mrs. Ellsworth had paid.

As the rich and aging white woman listened to the great roll of Beethoven sonatas and to the sea and moonlight of the Chopin nocturnes, as she watched the swaying dark strong shoulders of Oceola Jones, she began to reproach the girl aloud for running away from art and music, for burying herself in Atlanta and love—love for a man unworthy of lacing up her boot straps, as Mrs. Ellsworth put it.

"You could shake the stars with your music, Oceola. Depression or no depression, I could make you great. And yet you propose to dig a grave for yourself. Art is bigger than love."

"I believe you, Mrs. Ellsworth," said Oceola, not turning away from the piano. "But being married won't keep me from making tours, or being an artist."

"Yes, it will," said Mrs. Ellsworth. "He'll take all the music out of you."

"No, he won't," said Oceola.

"You don't know, child," said Mrs. Ellsworth, "what men are like."

"Yes, I do," said Oceola simply. And her fingers began to wander slowly up and down the keyboard, flowing into the soft and lazy syncopation of a Negro blues, a blues that deepened and grew into rollicking jazz, then into an earth-throbbing rhythm that shook the lilies in the Persian vases of Mrs. Ellsworth's music room. Louder than the voice of the white woman who cried that Oceola was deserting beauty, deserting her real self, deserting her hope in life, the flood of wild syncopation filled the house, then sank into the slow and singing blues with which it had begun.

The girl at the piano heard the white woman saying, "Is this what I spent thousands of dollars to teach you?"

"No," said Oceola simply. "This is mine. . . . Listen! . . . How sad and gay it is. Blue and happy—laughing and crying. . . . How white like you and black like me. . . . How much like a man. . . . And how like a woman. . . . Warm as Pete's mouth. . . . These are the blues . . . I'm playing."

Mrs. Ellsworth sat very still in her chair looking at the lilies trembling delicately in the priceless Persian vases, while Oceola made the bass notes throb like tom-toms deep in the earth.

O, if I could holler

sang the blues,

Like a mountain jack,
I'd go up on de mountain

sang the blues,

And call my baby back.

"And I," said Mrs. Ellsworth, rising from her chair, "would stand looking at the stars."

Mulatto
A Tragedy of the Deep South

Characters

COLONEL THOMAS NORWOOD, plantation owner, a still vigorous man of about sixty, nervous, refined, quick-tempered, and commanding; a widower who is the father of four living mulatto children by his Negro housekeeper

CORA LEWIS, a brown woman in her forties who has kept the house and been the mistress of Colonel Norwood for some thirty years

WILLIAM LEWIS, the oldest son of Cora Lewis and the Colonel; a fat, easy-going, soft-looking mulatto of twenty-eight; married

SALLIE LEWIS, the seventeen-year-old daughter, very light with sandy hair and freckles, who could pass for white

ROBERT LEWIS, eighteen, the youngest boy; strong and well-built; a light mulatto with ivory-yellow skin and proud thin features like his father's; as tall as the Colonel, with the same gray-blue eyes, but with curly black hair instead of brown; of a fiery, impetuous temper—immature and willful—resenting his blood and the circumstances of his birth

FRED HIGGINS, a close friend of Colonel Norwood; a county politician; fat and elderly, conventionally Southern

SAM, an old Negro retainer, a personal servant of the Colonel

BILLY, the small son of William Lewis; a chubby brown kid about five

TALBOT, the overseer

MOSE, an elderly Negro, chauffeur for Mr. Higgins

Produced in 1935.

Richard Bruce (Nugent), "Drawing for Mulattoes No. 2," *Ebony and Topaz,* 1927

A STOREKEEPER
AN UNDERTAKER
UNDERTAKER'S HELPER, voice off-stage only
THE MOB

ACT ONE

Time: An afternoon in early fall.

The Setting: The living room of the Big House on a Plantation in Georgia. Rear center of the room, a vestibule with double doors leading to the porch; at each side of the doors, a large window with lace curtains and green shades; at left a broad flight of stairs leading to the second floor; near the stairs, downstage, a doorway leading to the dining room and kitchen; opposite, at right of stage, a door to the library. The room is furnished in the long out-dated horsehair and walnut style of the nineties; a crystal chandelier, a large old-fashioned rug, a marble-topped table, upholstered chairs. At the right there is a small cabinet. It is a very clean, but somewhat shabby and rather depressing room, dominated by a large oil painting of NORWOOD'S wife of his youth on the center wall. The windows are raised. The afternoon sunlight streams in.

Action: As the curtain rises, the stage is empty. The door at the right opens and COLONEL NOR-WOOD enters, crossing the stage toward the stairs, his watch in his hand. Looking up, he shouts:

Norwood: Cora! Oh, Cora!

   Cora: (heard above) Yes, Sir, Colonel Tom.

Norwood: I want to know if that child of yours means to leave here this afternoon?

   Cora: (at head of steps now) Yes, sir, she's goin' directly. I's gettin' her ready now, packin' up an' all. 'Course, she wants to tell you goodbye 'fore she leaves.

Norwood: Well, send her down here. Who's going to drive her to the railroad? The train leaves at three—and it's after two now. You ought to know you can't drive ten miles in no time.

   Cora: (above) Her brother's gonna drive her, Bert. He ought to be back here most any time now with the Ford.

Norwood: (stopping on his way back to the library) Ought to be *back* here? Where's he gone?

   Cora: (coming downstairs nervously) Why, he driv' in town 'fore noon, Colonel Tom. Said he were lookin' for some tubes or somethin' 'nother by de mornin' mail for de radio he's been riggin' up out in de shed.

Norwood: Who gave him permission to be driving off in the middle of the morning? I bought that Ford to be used when I gave orders for it to be used, not . . .

   Cora: Yes, sir, Colonel Tom, but . . .

Norwood: But what? *(pausing. Then deliberately)* Cora, if you want that hardheaded yellow son of yours to get along around here, he'd better listen to me. He's no more than any other black buck on this plantation—due to work like the rest of 'em. I don't take such a performance from nobody under me—driving off in the middle of the day to town, after I've told him to bend his back in that cotton. How's Talbot going to keep the rest of those darkies working right if that boy's allowed to set that kind of an example? Just because Bert's your son, and I've been damn fool enough to send him off to school for five or six years, he thinks he has a right to privileges, acting as if he owned this place since he's been back here this summer.

Cora: But, Colonel Tom . . .

Norwood: Yes, I know what you're going to say. I don't give a damn about him! There's no nigger-child of mine, yours, ours—no darkie—going to disobey me. I put him in that field to work, and he'll stay on this plantation till I get ready to let him go. I'll tell Talbot to use the whip on him, too, if he needs it. If it hadn't been that he's yours, he'd-a had a taste of it the other day. Talbot's a damn good overseer, and no saucy, lazy Nigras stay on this plantation and get away with it. *(to CORA)* Go on back upstairs and see about getting Sallie out of here. Another word from you and I won't send your *(sarcastically)* pretty little half-white daughter anywhere, either. Schools for darkies! Huh! If you take that boy of yours for an example, they do 'em more harm than good. He's learned nothing in college but impudence, and he'll stay here on this place and work for me awhile before he gets back to any more schools. *(He starts across the room)*

Cora: Yes, sir, Colonel Tom. *(hesitating)* But he's just young, sir. And he was mighty broke up when you said last week he couldn't go back to de campus. *(COLONEL NORWOOD turns and looks at CORA commandingly. Understanding, she murmurs)* Yes, Sir. *(She starts upstairs, but turns back)* Can't I run and fix you a cool drink, Colonel Tom?

Norwood: No, damn you! Sam'll do it.

Cora: *(sweetly)* Go set down in de cool, then, Colonel. 'Taint good for you to be goin' on this way in de heat. I'll talk to Robert maself soon's he comes in. He don't mean nothing—just smart and young and kinder careless, Colonel Tom, like ma mother said you used to be when you was eighteen.

Norwood: Get on upstairs, Cora. Do I have to speak again? Get on! *(He pulls the cord of the servants' bell)*

Cora: *(on the steps)* Does you still be in the mind to tell Sallie good-bye?

Norwood: Send her down here as I told you. *(impatiently)* Where's Sam? Send him here first. *(fuming)* Looks like he takes his time to answer that bell. You colored folks are running the house to suit yourself nowadays.

Cora: *(coming downstairs again and going toward door under the steps)* I'll get Sam for you.

(CORA exits left. NORWOOD paces nervously across the floor. Goes to the window and looks out down the road. Takes a cigar from his pocket, sits in a chair with it unlighted, scowling. Rises, goes toward servants' bell and rings it again violently as SAM enters, out of breath)

Norwood: What the hell kind of a tortoise race is this? I suppose you were out in the sun somewhere sleeping?

Sam: No, sah, Colonel Norwood. Just tryin' to get Miss Sallie's valises down to de yard so's we can put 'em in de Ford, sah.

Norwood: *(out of patience)* Huh! Darkies waiting on darkies! I can't get service in my own house. Very well. *(loudly)* Bring me some whiskey and soda, and ice in a glass. Is that damn Frigidaire working right? Or is Livonia still too thick-headed to know how to run it? Any ice cubes in the thing?

Sam: Yes, sah, Colonel, yes, sah. *(backing toward door left)* 'Scuse me, please sah, but *(as NORWOOD turns toward library)* Cora say for me to ask you is it all right to bring that big old trunk what you give Sallie down by de front steps. We ain't been able to tote it down them narrer little back steps, sah. Cora say, can we bring it down de front way through here?

Norwood: No other way? *(SAM shakes his head)* Then pack it on through to the back, quick. Don't let me catch you carrying any of Sallie's baggage out of that front door here. You-all'll be wanting to go in and out the front way next. *(turning away, complaining to himself)* Darkies have been getting mighty fresh in this part of the country since the war. The damn Germans should've . . . *(to SAM)* Don't take that trunk out that front door.

Sam: *(evilly, in a cunning voice)* I's seen Robert usin' de front door—when you ain't here, and he comes up from de cabin to see his mammy.

(SALLIE, the daughter, appears at the top of the stairs, but hesitates about coming down)

Norwood: Oh, you have, have you? Let me catch him and I'll break his young neck for him. *(yelling at SAM)* Didn't I tell you some whiskey and soda an hour ago?

(SAM exits left. SALLIE comes shyly down the stairs and approaches her father. She is dressed in a little country-style coat-suit ready for traveling. Her features are Negroid, although her skin is very fair. COLONEL NORWOOD gazes down at her without saying a word as she comes meekly toward him, half-frightened)

Sallie: I just wanted to tell you good-bye, Colonel Norwood, and thank you for letting me go back to school another year, and for letting me work here in the house all summer where mama is. *(NORWOOD says nothing. The girl continues in a strained voice as if making a speech)* You mighty nice to us colored folks certainly, and mama says you the best white man in Georgia. *(Still NORWOOD says nothing. The girl continues)* You been mighty nice to your—I mean to us colored children, letting my sister and me go off to school. The principal says I'm doing pretty well and next year I can go to Normal[1] and learn to be a teacher. *(Raising her eyes)* You reckon I can, Colonel Tom?

---

1. Normal school; a two-year college for training elementary school teachers.

Norwood: Stand up straight and let me see how you look. *(backing away)* Hum-m-m! Getting kinder grown, ain't you? Do they teach you in that school to have good manners, and not be afraid of work, *and to respect white folks?*

Sallie: Yes, sir, I been taking up cooking and sewing, too.

Norwood: Well, that's good. As I recall it, that school turned your sister out a right smart cook. Cora tells me she's got a good job in some big hotel in Chicago. I'm thinking about you going on up North there with her in a year or two. You're getting too old to be around here, and too womanish. *(He puts his hands on her arms as if feeling her flesh)*

Sallie: *(drawing back slightly)* But I want to live down here with mama. I want to teach school in that there empty school house by the Cross Roads what hasn't had a teacher for five years.

(SAM has been standing with the door cracked, overhearing the conversation. He enters with the drink and places it on the table, right. NORWOOD sits down, leaving the girl standing, as SAM pours out a drink)

Norwood: Don't get that into your head, now. There's been no teacher there for years—and there won't be any teacher there, either. Cotton teaches these pickaninnies enough around here. Some of 'em's too smart as it is. The only reason I did have a teacher there once was to get you young ones o' Cora's educated. I gave you all a chance and I hope you appreciate it. *(He takes a long drink)* Don't know why I did it. No other white man in these parts ever did it, as I know of. *(to SAM)* Get out of here! *(SAM exits left)* Guess I couldn't stand to see Cora's kids working around here dumb as the rest of these no good darkies—need a dozen of 'em to chop one row of cotton, or to keep a house clean. Or maybe I didn't want to see Talbot eyeing you gals. *(taking another drink)* Anyhow, I'm glad you and Bertha turned out right well. Yes, hum-m-m! *(straightening up)* You know I tried to do something for those brothers of yours, too, but William's stupid as an ox—good for work, though—and that Robert's just an impudent, hardheaded, yellow young fool. I'm gonna break his damn neck for him if he don't watch out. Or else put Talbot on him.

Sallie: *(suddenly frightened)* Please, sir, don't put the overseer on Bert, Colonel Tom. He was the smartest boy at school, Bert was. On the football team, too. Please, sir, Colonel Tom. Let brother work here in the house, or somewhere else where Talbot can't mistreat him. He ain't used . . .

Norwood: *(rising)* Telling me what to do, heh? *(staring at her sternly)* I'll use the back of my hand across your face if you don't hush. *(He takes another drink. The noise of a Ford is heard outside)* That's Bert now, I reckon. He's to take you to the railroad line, and while you're riding with him, you better put some sense into his head. And tell him I want to see him as soon as he gets back here. *(CORA enters left with a bundle and an umbrella. SAM and WILLIAM come downstairs with a big square trunk, and exit hurriedly, left)*

Sallie: Yes, sir, I'll tell him.

Cora: Colonel Tom, Sallie ain't got much time now. *(to the girl)* Come on, chile. Bert's here. Yo' big brother and Sam and Livonia and everybody's all waiting at de back door to say good-bye. And your baggage is being packed in. *(noise of another car is heard outside)* Who else is that there coming up de drive? *(CORA looks out the window)* Mr. Higgins' car, Colonel Tom. Reckon he's coming to see you . . . Hurry up out o' this front room, Sallie. Here, take these things of your'n *(hands her the bundle and parasol)* while I opens de door for Mr. Higgins. *(in a whisper)* Hurry up, chile! Get out! *(NORWOOD turns toward the front door as CORA goes to open it)*

Sallie: *(shyly to her father)* Good-bye, Colonel Tom.

Norwood: *(his eyes on the front door, scarcely noticing the departing SALLIE, he motions)* Yes, yes, good-bye! Get on now! *(CORA opens the front door as her daughter exits left)* Well, well! Howdy do, Fred. Come in, come in! *(CORA holds the outer door of the vestibule wide as FRED HIGGINS enters with rheumatic dignity, supported on the arm of his chauffeur, MOSE, a very black Negro in a slouchy uniform. CORA closes the door and exits left hurriedly, following SALLIE)*

Norwood: *(smiling)* How's the rheumatiz today? Women or licker or heat must've made it worse—from the looks of your speed!

Higgins: *(testily, sitting down puffing and blowing in a big chair)* I'm in no mood for fooling, Tom, not now. *(to MOSE)* All right. *(The CHAUFFEUR exits front. HIGGINS continues angrily)* Norwood, that damned yellow nigger buck of yours that drives that new Ford tried his best just now to push my car off the road, then got in front of me and blew dust in my face for the last mile coming down to your gate, trying to beat me in here—which he did. Such a deliberate piece of impudence I don't know if I've ever seen out of a nigger before in all the sixty years I've lived in this country. *(The noise of the Ford is heard going out the drive, and the cries of the NEGROES shouting farewells to SALLIE. HIGGINS listens indignantly)* What kind of crazy coons have you got on your place, anyhow? Sounds like a black Baptist picnic to me. *(pointing to the window with his cane)* Tom, listen to that.

Norwood: *(flushing)* I apologize to you, Fred, for each and every one of my darkies. *(SAM enters with more ice and another glass)* Permit me to offer you a drink. I realize I've got to tighten down here.

Higgins: Mose tells me that was Cora's boy in that Ford—and that young black fool is what I was coming here to talk to you about today. That boy! He's not gonna be around here long—not the way he's acting. The white folks in town'll see to that. Knowing he's one of your yard niggers, Norwood, I thought I ought to come and tell you. The white folks at the Junction aren't intending to put up with him much longer. And I don't know what good the jail would do him once he got in there.

Norwood: *(tensely)* What do you mean, Fred—jail? Don't I always take care of the folks on my plantation without any help from the Junction's police force? Talbot can do more with an unruly black buck than your marshal.

Higgins: Warn't lookin' at it that way, Tom. I was thinking how weak the doors to that jail is. They've broke 'em down and lynched four niggers to my memory since it's been built. After what happened this morning, you better keep that yellow young fool out o' town from now on. It might not be safe for him around there—today, nor no other time.

Norwood: What the hell? *(perturbed)* He went in just now to take his sister to the depot. Damn it, I hope no ruffians'll break up my new Ford. What was it, Fred, about this morning?

Higgins: You haven't heard? Why, it's all over town already. He sassed out Miss Gray in the post office over a box of radio tubes that come by mail.

Norwood: He did, heh?

Higgins: Seems like the stuff was sent C.O.D. and got here all smashed up, so he wouldn't take it. Paid his money first before he saw the box was broke. Then wanted the money order back. Seems like the post office can't give money orders back—rule against it. Your nigger started to argue, and the girl at the window—Miss Gray—got scared and yelled for some of the mail clerks. They threw Bert out of the office, that's all. But that's enough. Lucky nothing more didn't happen. *(indignantly)* That Bert needs a damn good beating—talking back to a white woman—and I'd like to give it to him myself, the way he kicked the dust up in my eyes all the way down the road coming out here. He was mad, I reckon. That's one yellow buck don't know his place, Tom, and it's your fault he don't—sending 'em off to be educated.

Norwood: Well, by God, I'll show him. I wish I'd have known it before he left here just now.

Higgins: Well, he's sure got mighty aggravating ways for a buck his color to have. Drives down the main street and don't stop for nobody, white or black. Comes in my store and if he ain't waited on as quick as the white folks are, he walks out and tells the clerk his money's as good as a white man's any day. Said last week standing out on my store front that he wasn't *all* nigger nohow; said his name was Norwood—not Lewis, like the rest of his family—and part of your plantation here would be his when you passed out—and all that kind of stuff, boasting to the walleyed coons listening to him.

Norwood: *(astounded)* Well, I'll be damned!

Higgins: Now, Tom, you know that don't go 'round these parts o' Georgia, nor nowhere else in the South. A darkie's got to keep in his place down here. Ruinous to other niggers hearing that talk, too. All this postwar propaganda on the radio about freedom and democracy—why the niggers think it's meant for them! And that Eleanor Roosevelt,[2] she ought to been muzzled. She's driving our niggers crazy—your boy included! Crazy! Talking about civil rights. Ain't been no race trouble in our country for three years—since the Deekin's lynching—but I'm telling you, Norwood,

2. Eleanor Roosevelt (1884–1962) was the wife of President Franklin Roosevelt and an outspoken advocate for black civil rights.

you better see that that buck of yours goes away from here. I'm speaking on the quiet, but I can see ahead. And what happened this morning about them radio tubes wasn't none too good.

Norwood: (beside himself with rage) A black ape! I—I . . .

Higgins: You been too decent to your darkies, Norwood. That's what's the matter with you. And then the whole county suffers from a lot of impudent bucks who take lessons from your crowd. Folks been kicking about that, too. Guess you know it. Maybe that's the reason you didn't get that nomination for committeeman a few years back.

Norwood: Maybe 'tis, Higgins. *(rising and pacing the room)* God damn niggers! *(furiously)* Everything turns on niggers, niggers, niggers! No wonder Yankees call this the Black Belt! *(He pours a large drink of whiskey)*

Higgins: (soothingly) Well, let's change the subject. Hand me my glass, there, too.

Norwood: Pardon me, Fred. *(He puts ice in his friend's glass and passes him the bottle)*

Higgins: Tom, you get excited too easy for warm weather . . . Don't ever show black folks they got you going, though. I think sometimes that's where you make your mistake. Keep calm, keep calm—and then you command. Best plantation manager I ever had never raised his voice to a nigger—and they were scared to death of him.

Norwood: Have a smoke. *(pushes cigars toward HIGGINS)*

Higgins: You ought've married again, Tom—brought a white woman out here on this damn place o' yours. A woman could help you run things. Women have soft ways, but they can keep things humming. Nothing but blacks in the house—a man gets soft like niggers are inside. *(puffing at cigar)* And living with a colored woman! Of course, I know we all have 'em—I didn't know you could make use of a white girl till I was past twenty. Thought too much o' white women for that—but I've given many a yellow gal a baby in my time. *(long puff at cigar)* But for a man's own house you need a wife, not a black woman.

Norwood: Reckon you're right, Fred, but it's too late to marry again now. *(shrugging his shoulders)* Let's get off of darkies and women for awhile. How's crops? *(sitting down)* How's politics going?

Higgins: Well, I guess you know the Republicans is trying to stir up trouble for us in Washington. I wish the South had more men like Bilbo and Rankin[3] there. But, say, by the way, Lawyer Hotchkiss wants to see us both about that budget money next week. He's got some real Canadian stuff at his office, in his filing case, too—brought back from his vacation last summer. Taste better'n this old mountain juice we get around here. Not meaning to insult your drinks, Tom, but just remarking. I serve the same as you myself, label and all.

Norwood: (laughing) I'll have you know, sir, that this is prewar licker, sir!

---

3. Racist Southern senators.

Higgins: Hum-m-m! Well, it's got me feelin' better'n I did when I come in here—whatever it is. *(puffs at his cigar)* Say, how's your cotton this year?

Norwood: Doin' right well, specially down in the south field. Why not drive out that road when you leave and take a look at it? I'll ride down with you. I want to see Talbot, anyhow.

Higgins: Well, let's be starting. I got to be back at the Junction by four o'clock. Promised to let that boy of mine have the car to drive over to Thomasville for a dance tonight.

Norwood: One more shot before we go. *(He pours out drinks)* The young ones must have their fling, I reckon. When you and I grew up down here it used to be a carriage and the best pair of black horses when you took the ladies out—now it's an automobile. That's a good lookin' new car of yours, too.

Higgins: Right nice.

Norwood: Been thinking about getting a new one myself, but money's been kinder tight this year, and conditions are none too good yet, either. Reckon that's why everybody's so restless. *(He walks toward stairs calling)* Cora! Oh, Cora! . . . If I didn't have a few thousand put away, I'd feel the pinch myself. *(as CORA appears on the stairs)* Bring me my glasses up there by the side of my bed . . . Better whistle for Mose, hadn't I, Higgins? He's probably 'round back with some of his women. *(winking)* You know I got some nice black women in this yard.

Higgins: Oh, no, not Mose. I got my servants trained to stay in their places—right where I want 'em—while they're working for me. Just open the door and tell him to come in here and help me out. *(NORWOOD goes to the door and calls the CHAUFFEUR. MOSE enters and assists his master out to the car. CORA appears with the glasses, goes to the vestibule and gets the COLONEL's hat and cane which she hands him)*

Norwood: *(to CORA)* I want to see that boy o' yours soon as I get back. That won't be long, either. And tell him to put up that Ford of mine and don't touch it again.

Cora: Yes, sir, I'll have him waiting here. *(in a whisper)* It's hot weather, Colonel Tom. Too much of this licker makes your heart upset. It ain't good for you, you know. *(NORWOOD pays her no attention as he exits toward the car. The noise of the departing motor is heard. CORA begins to tidy up the room. She takes a glass from a side table. She picks up a doily that was beneath the glass and looks at it long and lovingly. Suddenly she goes to the door left and calls toward the kitchen)* William, you William! Com'ere, I want to show you something. Make haste, son. *(As CORA goes back toward the table, her eldest son, WILLIAM, enters carrying a five-year-old boy)* Look here at this purty doily yo' sister made this summer while she been here. She done learned all about sewing and making purty things at school. Ain't it nice, son?

William: Sho' is. Sallie takes after you, I reckon. She's a smart little crittur, ma. *(sighs)* De Lawd knows, I was dumb at school. *(to his child)* Get down, Billy, you's too heavy. *(He puts the boy on the floor)* This here sewin's really fine.

Billy: (*running toward the big upholstered chair and jumping up and down on the spring seat*) Gityap! I's a mule driver. Haw! Gee!

Cora: You Billy, get out of that chair 'fore I skins you alive. Get on into de kitchen, sah.

Billy: I'm playin' horsie, grandma. (*jumps up in the chair*) Horsie! Horsie!

Cora: Get! That's de Colonel's favorite chair. If he knows any little darkie's been jumpin' on it, he raise sand.[4] Get on, now.

Billy: Ole Colonel's ma grandpa ain't he? Ain' he ma white grandpa?

William: (*snatching the child out of the chair*) Boy, I'm gonna tan your hide if you don't hush!

Cora: Shs-ss-s! You Billy, hush yo' mouth! Chile, where you hear that? (*to her son*) Some o' you all been talking too much in front o' this chile. (*to the boy*) Honey, go on in de kitchen till yo' daddy come. Get a cookie from 'Vonia and set down on de back porch. (*little BILLY exits left*)

William: Ma, you know it 'twarn't me told him. Bert's the one been goin' all over de plantation since he come back from Atlanta remindin' folks right out we's Colonel Norwood's chilluns.

Cora: (*catching her breath*) Huh!

William: He comes down to my shack tellin' Billy and Marybell they got a white man for grandpa. He's gonna get my chilluns in trouble sho'—like he got himself in trouble when Colonel Tom whipped him.

Cora: Ten or 'leven years ago, warn't it?

William: And Bert's *sho'* in trouble now. Can't go back to that college like he could-a if he'd-a had any sense. You can't fool with white folks—and de Colonel ain't never really liked Bert since that there first time he beat him, either.

Cora: No, he ain't. Leastwise, he ain't understood him. (*musing sadly in a low voice*) Time Bert was 'bout seven, warn't it? Just a little bigger'n yo' Billy.

William: Yes.

Cora: Went runnin' up to Colonel Tom out in de horse stables when de Colonel was showin' off his horses—I 'members so well—to fine white company from town. Lawd, that boy's always been foolish! He went runnin' up and grabbed a-holt de Colonel and yelled right in front o' de white folks' faces, "O, papa, Cora say de dinner's ready, papa!" Ain't never called him papa before, and I don't know where he got it from. And Colonel Tom knocked him right backwards under de horse's feet.

William: And when de company were gone, he beat that boy unmerciful.

Cora: I thought sho' he were gonna kill ma chile that day. And he were mad at me, too, for months. Said I was teaching you chilluns who they pappy were. Up till then Bert had been his favorite little colored child round here.

4. "He will get mad."

William: Sho' had.

Cora: But he never liked him no more. That's why he sent him off to school so soon to stay, winter and summer, all these years. I had to beg and plead to have him home this summer—but I's sorry now I ever got that boy back here again.

William: He's sho' growed more like de Colonel all de time, ain't he? Bert thinks he's a real white man hisself now. Look at de first thing he did when he come home, he ain't seen de Colonel in six years—and Bert sticks out his hand fo' to shake hands with him!

Cora: Lawd! That chile!

William: Just like white folks! And de Colonel turns his back and walks off. Can't blame him. He ain't used to such doings from colored folks. God knows what's got into Bert since he come back. He's acting like a fool—just like he was a boss man round here. Won't even say "Yes, sir" and "No, sir" no more to de white folks. Talbot asked him warn't he gonna work in de field this mornin'. Bert say "No!" and turn and walk away. White man so mad, I could see him nearly foam at de mouth. If he warn't yo' chile, ma, he'd been knocked in de head fo' now.

Cora: You's right.

William: And you can't talk to him. I tried to tell him something the other day, but he just laughed at me, and said we's all just scared niggers on this plantation. Says he ain't no nigger, nohow. He's a Norwood. He's half-white, and he's gonna act like it. *(in amazement at his brother's daring)* And this is Georgia, too!

Cora: I's scared to death for de boy, William. I don't know what to do. De Colonel says he won't send him off to school no mo'. Says he's mo' sassy and impudent now than any nigger he ever seed. Bert never has been like you was, and de girls, quiet and sensible like you knowed you had to be. *(she sits down)* De Colonel say he's gonna make Bert stay here now and work on this plantation like de rest of his niggers. He's gonna show him what color he is. Like that time when he beat him for callin' him "papa." He say he's gwine to teach him his place and make de boy know where he belongs. Seems like me or you can't show him. Colonel Tom has to take him in hand, or these white folks'll kill him around here and then—oh, My God!

William: A nigger's just got to know his place in de South, that's all, ain't he, ma?

Cora: Yes, son. That's all, I reckon.

William: And ma brother's one damn fool nigger. Don't seems like he knows nothin'. He's gonna ruin us all round here. Make it bad for everybody.

Cora: Oh, Lawd, have mercy! *(beginning to cry)* I don't know what to do. De way he's acting up can't go on. Way he's acting to de Colonel can't last. Somethin's gonna happen to ma chile. I had a bad dream last night, too, and I looked out and seed de moon all red with blood. I seed a path o' living blood across this house, I tell you, in my sleep. Oh, Lawd, have mercy! *(sobbing)* Oh, Lawd, help me in ma troubles. *(The noise of the returning Ford is heard outside. CORA looks up, rises, and goes to the window)* There's de chile now, William. Run out to de back door and tell him I wants to see him. Bring him in here where Sam and Livonia and de rest of 'em won't hear everything we's sayin'. I got to talk to ma boy. He's ma baby boy, and he don't know de way.

(Exit WILLIAM through the door left. CORA is wiping her eyes and pulling herself together when the front door is flung open with a bang and ROBERT enters)

Robert: *(running to his mother and hugging her teasingly)* Hello, ma! Your daughter got off, and I've come back to keep you company in the parlor! Bring out the cookies and lemonade. Mister Norwood's here!

Cora: *(beginning to sob anew)* Take yo' hands off me, boy! Why don't you mind? Why don't you mind me?

Robert: *(suddenly serious, backing away)* Why, mama, what's the matter? Did I scare you? Your eyes are all wet! Has somebody been telling you 'bout this morning?

Cora: *(not heeding his words)* Why don't you mind me, son? Ain't I told you and told you not to come in that front door, never? *(suddenly angry)* Will somebody have to beat it into you? What's got wrong with you when you was away at that school? What am I gonna do?

Robert: *(carelessly)* Oh, I knew that the Colonel wasn't here. I passed him and old man Higgins on the road down by the south patch. He wouldn't even look at me when I waved at him. *(half playfully)* Anyhow, isn't this my old man's house? Ain't I his son and heir? *(grandly, strutting around)* Am I not Mr. Norwood, junior?

Cora: *(utterly serious)* I believes you goin' crazy, Bert. I believes you wants to get us all killed or run away or something awful like that. I believes . . . *(WILLIAM enters left)*

William: Where's Bert? He ain't come round back— *(seeing his brother in the room)* How'd you get in here?

Robert: *(grinning)* Houses have front doors.

William: Oh, usin' de front door like de white folks, heh? You gwine do that once too much.

Robert: Yes, like de white folks. What's a front door for, you rabbit-hearted coon?

William: Rabbit-hearted coon's better'n a dead coon any day.

Robert: I wouldn't say so. Besides you and me's only half-coons, anyhow, big boy. And I'm gonna act like my white half, not my black half. Get me, kid?

William: Well, you ain't gonna act like it long here in de middle o' Georgy. And you ain't gonna act like it when de Colonel's around, either.

Robert: Oh, no? My stay down here'll be short and sweet, boy, short and sweet.

The old man won't send me away to college no more—so you think I'm gonna stick around and work in the fields? Like fun? I might stay here awhile and teach some o' you darkies to think like men, maybe—till it gets too much for the old Colonel—but no more bowing down to white folks for me—not Robert Norwood.

Cora: Hush, son!

Robert: Certainly not right on my own old man's plantation—Georgia or no Georgia.

William: (scornfully) I hears you.

Robert: *You* can do it if you want to, but I'm ashamed of you. I've been away from here six years. *(boasting)* I've learned something, seen people in Atlanta, and Richmond, and Washington where the football team went—real colored people who don't have to take off their hats to white folks or let 'em go to bed with their sisters—like that young Higgins boy, asking me what night Sallie was comin' to town. A damn cracker![5] *(to CORA)* 'Scuse me, ma. *(continuing)* Back here in these woods maybe Sam and Livonia and you and mama and everybody's got their places fixed for 'em, but not me. *(seriously)* Nobody's gonna fix a place for me. I'm old man Norwood's son. Nobody fixed a place for him. *(playfully again)* Look at me. I'm a 'fay[6] boy. *(pretends to shake his hair back)* See these gray eyes? I got the right to everything everybody else has. *(punching his brother in the belly)* Don't talk to me, old slavery-time Uncle Tom.

William: (resentfully) I ain't playin', boy. *(pushes younger brother back with some force)* I ain't playin' a-tall.

Cora: All right, chilluns, stop. Stop! And William, you take Billy and go on home. 'Vonia's got to get supper and she don't like no young-uns under her feet in de kitchen. I wants to talk to Bert in here now 'fore Colonel Tom gets back. *(exit WILLIAM left. CORA continues to BERT)* Sit down, child, right here a minute, and listen.

Robert: (sitting down) All right, ma.

Cora: Hard as I's worked and begged and humbled maself to get de Colonel to keep you chilluns in school, you comes home wid yo' head full o' stubbornness and yo' mouth full o' sass for me an' de white folks an' everybody. You know can't no colored boy here talk like you's been doin' to no white folks, let alone to de Colonel and that old devil of a Talbot. They ain't gonna stand fo' yo' sass. Not only you, but I 'spects we's all gwine to pay fo' it, every colored soul on this place. I was scared to death today fo' yo' sister, Sallie, scared de Colonel warn't gwine to let her go back to school, neither, 'count o' yo' doins, but he did, thank Gawd—and then you come near makin' her miss de train. Did she have time to get her ticket and all?

---

5. Derogatory slang for white person.
6. "Ofay"; slang for white.

Robert: Sure! Had to drive like sin to get there with her, though. I didn't mean to be late getting back here for her, ma, but I had a little run-in about them radio tubes in town.

Cora: *(worried)* What's that?

Robert: The tubes was smashed when I got 'em, and I had already made out my money order, so the woman in the post office wouldn't give the three dollars back to me. All I did was explain to her that we could send the tubes back—but she got hot because there were two or three white folks waiting behind me to get stamps, I guess. So she yells at me to move on and not give her any of my "educated nigger talk." So I said, "I'm going to finish showing you these tubes before I move on"—and then she screamed and called the mail clerk working in the back, and told him to throw me out. *(boasting)* He didn't do it by himself, though. Had to call all the white loafers out in the square to get me through that door.

Cora: *(fearfully)* Lawd have mercy!

Robert: Guess if I hadn't-a had the Ford then, they'd've beat me half-to-death, but when I saw how many crackers there was, I jumped in the car and beat it on away.

Cora: Thank God for that!

Robert: Not even a football man *(half-boasting)* like me could tackle the whole Junction. 'Bout a dozen colored guys standing around, too, and not one of 'em would help me—the dumb jiggaboos! They been telling me ever since I been here *(imitating darky talk)* "You can't argue wid whut folks, man. You better stay out o' this Junction. You must ain't got no sense, nigger! You's a fool" . . . Maybe I am a fool, ma—but I didn't want to come back here nohow.

Cora: I's sorry I sent for you.

Robert: Besides you, there ain't nobody in this country but a lot of evil white folks and cowardly niggers. *(earnestly)* I'm no nigger, anyhow, am I ma? I'm half-white. The Colonel's my father—the richest man in the county—and I'm not going to take a lot of stuff from nobody if I do have to stay here, not from the old man either. He thinks I ought to be out there in the sun working, with Talbot standing over me like I belonged in the chain gang. Well, he's got another thought coming! *(stubbornly)* I'm a Norwood—not a field-hand nigger.

Cora: You means you ain't workin' no mo'?

Robert: *(flaring)* No, I'm not going to work in the fields. What did he send me away to school for—just to come back here and be his servant, or pick his hills of cotton?

Cora: He sent you away to de school because *I* asked him and begged him, and got down on my knees to him, that's why. *(quietly)* And now I just wants to make you see some sense, if you can. I knows, honey, you reads in de books and de papers, and you knows a lot more'n I do. But, chile, you's in Georgy—and I don't see how it is you don't know where you's at. This ain't up North—and even up yonder where we hears it's so fine, yo' sister has to pass for white to get along good.

Robert: (bitterly) I know it.

Cora: She ain't workin' in no hotel kitchen like de Colonel thinks. She's in a office typewriting. And Sallie's studyin' de typewriter, too, at de school, but yo' pappy don't know it. I knows we ain't s'posed to study nothin but cookin' and hard workin' here in Georgy. That's all I ever done, or knowed about. I been workin' on this very place all ma life—even 'fore I come to live in this Big House. When de Colonel's wife died, I come here, and borned you chilluns. And de Colonel's been real good to me in his way. Let you all sleep in this house with me when you was little, and sent you all off to school when you growed up. Ain't no white man in this county done that with his cullud chilluns before, far as I can know. But you—Robert, be awful, awful careful! When de Colonel comes back, in a few minutes, he wants to talk to you. Talk right to him, boy. Talk like you was colored, 'cause you ain't white.

Robert: (angrily) And I'm not black, either mama. Look at me, mama. *(rising and throwing up his arms)* Don't I look like my father? Ain't I as light as he is? Ain't my eyes gray like his eyes are? *(The noise of a car is heard outside)* Ain't this our house?

Cora: That's him now. *(agitated)* Hurry, chile, and let's we get out of this room. Come on through yonder to the kitchen. *(She starts toward the door left)* And I'll tell him you're here.

Robert: I don't want to run into the kitchen. Isn't this our house? *(As CORA crosses hurriedly left, ROBERT goes toward the front door)* The Ford is parked out in front, anyway.

Cora: (at the door left to the rear of the house) Robert! Robert! *(As ROBERT nears the front door, COLONEL NORWOOD enters, almost runs into the boy, stops at the threshold and stares unbelievingly at his son. CORA backs up against the door left)*

Norwood: Get out of here! *(He points toward the door to rear of the house where CORA is standing)*

Robert: (half-smiling) Didn't you want to talk to me?

Norwood: Get out of here!

Robert: Not that way. *(The COLONEL raises his cane to strike the boy. CORA screams. ROBERT draws himself up to his full height, taller than the old man and looking very much like him, pale and proud. The man and the boy face each other. NORWOOD does not strike)*

Norwood: (in a hoarse whisper) Get out of here. *(His hand is trembling as he points)*

Cora: Robert! Come on, son, come on! Oh, my God, come on. *(opening the door left)*

Robert: Not that way, ma. *(ROBERT walks proudly out the front door. NORWOOD, in an impotent rage, crosses the room to a small cabinet right, opens it nervously with a key from his pocket, takes out a pistol, and starts toward the front door. CORA overtakes him, seizes his arm, stops him)*

Cora: He's our son, Tom. *(She sinks slowly to her knees, holding his body)* Remember, he's our son.

Curtain

ACT TWO

Scene One

Time: After supper. Sunset.

Setting: The same.

Action: As the curtain rises, the stage is empty. Through the windows the late afternoon sun makes two bright paths toward the footlights. SAM, carrying a tray bearing a whiskey bottle and a bowl of ice, enters left and crosses toward the library. He stoops at the door right, listens a moment, knocks, then opens the door and goes in. In a moment SAM returns. As he leaves the library, he is heard replying to a request of NORWOOD's.

Sam: Yes, sah, Colonel! Sho' will, sah! Right away, sah! Yes, sah, I'll tell him. *(He closes the door and crosses the stage muttering to himself)* Six o'clock. Most nigh that now. Better tell Cora to get that boy right in here. Can't nobody else do nothin' with that fool Bert but Cora. *(He exits left. Can be heard calling)* Cora! You, Cora . . .

(Again the stage is empty. Off stage, outside, the bark of a dog is heard, the sound of Negroes singing down the road, the cry of a child. The breeze moves the shadows of leaves and tree limbs across the sunlit paths from the windows. The door left opens and CORA enters, followed by ROBERT)

Cora: *(softly to ROBERT behind her in the dining room)* It's all right, son. He ain't come out yet, but it's nearly six and that's when he said he wanted you, but I was afraid maybe you was gonna be late. I sent for you to come up here to de house and eat supper with me in de kitchen. Where'd you eat yo' vittals at, chile?

Robert: Down at Willie's house, ma. After the old man tried to hit me you still want me to hang around and eat up here?

Cora: I wanted you to be here on time, honey, that's all. *(She is very nervous)* I kinder likes to have you eat with me sometimes, too, but you ain't et up here more'n once this summer. But this evenin' I just wanted you to be here when de Colonel sent word for you, cause we's done had enough trouble today.

Robert: He's not here on time, himself, is he?

Cora: He's in de library. Sam couldn't get him to eat no supper tonight, and I ain't seen him a-tall.

Robert: Maybe he wants to see *me* in the library, then.

   Cora: You know he don't 'low no colored folks in there 'mongst his books and things 'cept Sam. Some o' his white friends goes in there, but none o' us.

Robert: Maybe he wants to see me in there, though.

   Cora: Can't you never talk sense, Robert? This ain't no time for foolin' and jokin'. Nearly thirty years in this house and I ain't never been in there myself, not once, 'mongst de Colonel's papers. *(The clock strikes six)* Stand over yonder and wait till he comes out. I's gwine on upstairs now, so's he can talk to you. And don't aggravate him no mo' fo' God's sake. Agree to whatever he say. I's scared fo' you, chile, de way you been actin',' and de fool tricks you done today, and de trouble about de post office besides. Don't aggravate him. Fo' yo' sake, honey, 'cause I loves you—and fo' all de po' colored folks on this place what has such a hard time when his humors get on him—agree to whatever he say, will you, Bert?

Robert: All right, ma. *(voice rising)* But he better not start to hit me again.

   Cora: Shs-ss-s! He'll hear you. He's right in there.

Robert: *(sullenly)* This was the day I ought to have started back to school—like my sister. I stayed my summer out here, didn't I? Why didn't he keep his promise to me? You said if I came home I could go back to college again.

   Cora: Shs-ss-s! He'll be here now. Don't say nothin', chile. I's done all I could.

Robert: All right, ma.

   Cora: *(approaching the stairs)* I'll be in ma room, honey, where I can hear you when you goes out. I'll come down to de back door and see you 'fore you goes back to de shack. Don't aggravate him, chile.

(She ascends the stairs. The boy sits down sullenly, left, and stares at the door opposite from which his father must enter. The clock strikes the quarter after six. The shadows of the window curtains have lengthened on the carpet. The sunshine has deepened to a pale orange, and the light paths grow less distinct across the floor. The boy sits up straight in his chair. He looks at the library door. It opens. NORWOOD enters. He is bent and pale. He looks across the room and sees the boy. Suddenly he straightens up. The old commanding look comes into his face. He strides directly across the room toward his son. The boy, half afraid, half defiant, yet sure of himself, rises. Now that ROBERT is standing, the white man turns, goes back to a chair near the table, right, and seats himself. He takes out a cigar, cuts off the end and lights it, and in a voice of mixed condescension and contempt, he speaks to his son. ROBERT remains standing near the chair)

Norwood: I don't want to have to beat you another time as I did when you were a child. The next time I might not be able to control myself. I might kill you if I touched you again. I been runnin' this plantation for thirty-five years, and I never had to beat a Nigra as old as you are. I never had to beat one of Cora's children either but you. The rest of 'em had sense 'nough to keep out of my sight, and to speak to me like they should. . . . I don't have any trouble with my colored folks. Never have trouble. They do what I say, or what Mr. Talbot says, and that's all there is to it. I give 'em a chance.

If they turn in crops they get paid. If they're workin' for wages, they get paid. If they want to spend their money on licker, or buy an old car, or fix up their cabins, they can. Do what they choose long as they know their places and it don't hinder their work. And to Cora's young ones I give all the chances any colored folks ever had in these parts. More'n many a white child's had. I sent you all off to school. Let Bertha go on up North when she got grown and educated. Intend to let Sallie do the same. Give your brother William that house he's living in when he got married, pay him for his work, help him out if he needs it. None of my darkies suffer. Sent you to college. Would have kept on, would have sent you back today, but I don't intend to pay for no darky, or white boy either if I had one, that acts the way you've been acting. And certainly for no black fool. Now I want to know what's wrong with you? I don't usually talk about what I'm going to do with anybody on this place. It's my habit to tell people *what to do,* not discuss it with 'em. But I want to know what's the matter with you—whether you're crazy or not. In that case, you'll have to be locked up. And if you aren't, you'll have to change your ways a damn sight or it won't be safe for you here, and you know it—venting your impudence on white women, parking the car in front of my door, driving like mad through the Junction, and going everywhere, just as you please. Now, I'm going to let you talk to me, but I want you to talk right.

Robert: *(still standing)* What do you mean, "talk right?"

Norwood: I mean talk like a nigger should to a white man.

Robert: Oh! But I'm not a nigger, Colonel Tom. I'm your son.

Norwood: *(testily)* You're Cora's boy.

Robert: Women don't have children by themselves.

Norwood: Nigger women don't know the fathers. You're a bastard.

(ROBERT clenches his fist. NORWOOD turns toward the drawer where the pistol is, takes it out, and lays it on the table. The wind blows the lace curtains at the windows, and sweeps the shadows of falling leaves across the paths of sunlight on the floor)

Robert: I've heard that before. I've heard it from Negroes, and I've heard it from white folks. Now I hear it from you. *(slowly)* You're talking about my mother.

Norwood: I'm talking about Cora, yes. Her children are bastards.

Robert: *(quickly)* And you're their father. *(angrily)* How come I look like you, if you're not my father?

Norwood: Don't shout at me, boy. I can hear you. *(half-smiling)* How come your skin is yellow and your elbows rusty? How come they threw you out of the post office today for talking to a white woman? How come you're the crazy young buck you are?

Robert: They had no right to throw me out. I asked for my money back when I saw the broken tubes. Just as you had no right to raise that cane today when I was standing at the door of this house where *you* live, while *I* have to sleep in a shack down the road with the field hands. *(slowly)* But my mother sleeps with you.

Norwood: You don't like it?

Robert: No, I don't like it.

Norwood: What can you do about it?

Robert: *(after a pause)* I'd like to kill all the white men in the world.

Norwood: *(starting)* Niggers like you are hung to trees.

Robert: I'm not a nigger.

Norwood: You don't like your own race? *(ROBERT is silent)* Yet you don't like white folks either?

Robert: *(defiantly)* You think I ought to?

Norwood: You evidently don't like me.

Robert: *(boyishly)* I used to like you, when I first knew you were my father, when I was a little kid, before that time you beat me under the feet of your horses. *(slowly)* I liked you until then.

Norwood: *(a little pleased)* So you did, heh? *(fingering his pistol)* A pickaninny calling me "papa." I should've broken your young neck for that first time. I should've broken your head for you today, too—since I didn't then.

Robert: *(laughing scornfully)* You should've broken my head?

Norwood: Should've gotten rid of you before this. But you was Cora's child. I tried to help you. *(aggrieved)* I treated you decent, schooled you. Paid for it. But tonight you'll get the hell off this place and stay off. Get the hell out of this county. *(suddenly furious)* Get out of this state. Don't let me lay eyes on you again. Get out of here now. Talbot and the storekeeper are coming up here this evening to talk cotton with me. I'll tell Talbot to see that you go. That's all. *(NORWOOD motions toward the door, left)* Tell Sam to come in here when you go out. Tell him to make a light here.

Robert: *(impudently)* Ring for Sam—I'm not going through the kitchen. *(He starts toward the front door)* I'm not your servant. You're not going to tell me what to do. You're not going to have Talbot run me off the place like a field hand you don't want to use any more.

Norwood: *(springing between his son and the front door, pistol in hand)* You black bastard! *(ROBERT goes toward him calmly, grasps his father's arm and twists it until the gun falls to the floor. The older man bends backward in startled fury and pain)* Don't you dare put your . . .

Robert: *(laughing)* Why don't you shoot, papa? *(louder)* Why don't you shoot?

Norwood: *(gasping as be struggles, fighting back)* . . . black . . . hands . . . on . . . you . . .

Robert: *(hysterically, as he takes his father by the throat)* Why don't you shoot, papa? *(NORWOOD's hands claw the air helplessly. ROBERT chokes the struggling while man until his body grows limp)* Why don't you shoot! *(laughing)* Why don't you shoot? Huh? Why?

(CORA appears at the top of the stairs, hearing the commotion. She screams)

Cora: Oh, my God! *(She rushes down. ROBERT drops the body of his father at her feet in a path of flame from the setting sun. CORA starts and stares in horror)*

Robert: *(wildly)* Why didn't he shoot, mama? He didn't want *me* to live. Why didn't he shoot? *(laughing)* He was the boss. Telling me what to do. Why didn't he shoot, then? He was the white man.

Cora: *(falling on the body)* Colonel Tom! Colonel Tom! Tom! Tom! *(gazes across the corpse at her son)* He's yo' father, Bert.

Robert: He's dead. The white man's dead. My father's dead. *(laughing)* I'm living.

Cora: Tom! Tom! Tom!

Robert: Niggers are living. He's dead. *(picks up the pistol)* This is what he wanted to kill me with, but he's dead. I can use it now. Use it on all the white men in the world, because they'll be coming looking for me now. *(stuffs the pistol into his shirt)* They'll want me now.

Cora: *(rising and running toward her boy)* Quick, chile, out that way *(pointing toward the front door)* so they won't see you in de kitchen. Make for de swamp, honey. Cross de fields fo' de swamp. Go de crick way.[7] In runnin' water, dogs can't smell no tracks. Hurry, chile!

Robert: Yes, mama. I can go out the front way now, easy. But if I see they gonna get me before I can reach the swamp, I'm coming back here, mama, and *(proudly)* let them take me out of my father's house—if they can. *(pats the gun under his shirt)* They're not going to string me up to some roadside tree for the crackers to laugh at.

Cora: *(moaning aloud)* Oh, O-o-o! Hurry! Hurry, chile!

Robert: I'm going, ma. *(He opens the door. The sunset streams in like a river of blood)*

Cora: Run, chile!

Robert: Not out of my father's house. *(He exits slowly, tall and straight against the sun)*

Cora: Fo' God's sake, hurry, chile! *(glancing down the road)* Lawd have mercy! There's Talbot and de storekeeper in de drive. They sees my boy! *(moaning)* They sees ma boy. *(relieved)* But thank God, they's passin' him! *(CORA backs up against the wall in the vestibule. She stands as if petrified as TALBOT and the STOREKEEPER enter)*

Talbot: Hello, Cora. What's the matter with you? Where's that damn fool boy o' your'n goin', coming out the front door like he owned the house? What's the matter with you, woman? Can't you talk? Where's Norwood? Let's have some light in this dark place. *(He reaches behind the door and turns on the lights. CORA remains backed up against the wall, looking out into the twilight, watching ROBERT as he goes across the field)* Good God, Jim! Look at this! *(The TWO WHITE MEN stop in horror before the sight of NORWOOD's body on the floor)*

---

7. "Go by way of the creek."

Storekeeper: He's blue in the face. *(bends over the body)* That nigger we saw walking out the door! *(rising excitedly)* That nigger bastard of Cora's . . . *(stooping over the body again)* Why the Colonel's dead!

Talbot: That nigger! *(rushes toward the door)* He's running toward the swamp now . . . We'll get him . . . Telephone down there, in the library. Telephone the sheriff. Get men, white men, after that nigger.

(STOREKEEPER rushes into the library. He can be heard talking excitedly on the phone)

Storekeeper: Sheriff! Sheriff! Is this the sheriff? I'm calling from Norwood's plantation. That nigger, Bert, has just killed Norwood—and run, headed for the swamp. Notify the gas station at the crossroads! Tell the boys at the sawmill to head him off at the creek. Warn everybody to be on the lookout. Call your deputies! Yes! Yes! Spread a dragnet. Get out the dogs. Meanwhile we'll start after him. *(He slams the phone down and comes back into the room)* Cora, where's Norwood's car? In the barn? *(CORA does not answer)*

Talbot: Talk, you black bitch!

(She remains silent. TALBOT runs, yelling and talking, out into the yard, followed by the STOREKEEPER. Sounds of excited shouting outside, and the roar of a motor rushing down the drive. In the sky the twilight deepens into early night. CORA stands looking into the darkness)

Cora: My boy can't get to de swamp now. They's telephoned the white folks down that way. So he'll come back home now. Maybe he'll turn into de crick and follow de branch home directly. *(protectively)* But they shan't get him. I'll make a place for to hide him. I'll make a place upstairs down under de floor, under ma bed. In a minute ma boy'll be runnin' from de white folks with their hounds and their ropes and their guns and everything they uses to kill po' colored folks with. *(distressed)* Ma boy'll be out there runnin'. *(turning to the body on the floor)* Colonel Tom, you hear me? Our boy, out there runnin'. *(fiercely)* You said he was ma boy—ma bastard boy. I heard you . . . but he's yours too . . . but yonder in de dark runnin'—runnin' from yo' people, from white people. *(pleadingly)* Why don't you get up and stop 'em? He's *your* boy. His eyes is gray—like your eyes. He's tall like you's tall. He's proud like you's proud. And he's runnin'—runnin' from po' white trash what ain't worth de little finger o' nobody what's got your blood in 'em, Tom. *(demandingly)* Why don't you get up from there and stop 'em, Colonel Tom? What's that you say? He ain't your chile? He's ma bastard chile? My yellow bastard chile? *(proudly)* Yes, he's mine. But don't call him that. Don't you touch him. Don't you put your white hands on him. You's beat him enough, and cussed him enough. Don't you touch him now. He *is* ma boy, and no white folks gonna touch him now. That's finished. I'm gonna make a place for him upstairs under ma bed. *(backs away from the body toward the stairs)* He's ma chile. Don't you come in ma bedroom while he's up there. Don't you come to my bed no mo'. I calls you to help me now, and you just lays there. I calls you for to wake up, and you just lays there. Whenever you called me, in de night, I woke up. When you called for me to love, I always reached out ma arms fo' you. I borned you five chilluns and now one of 'em is out yonder in de dark runnin' from yo' people. Our youngest boy out yonder in de dark runnin'. *(accusingly)* He's runnin' from you, too. You said he warn't your'n—he's just Cora's po' little yellow bastard. But he *is* your'n, Colonel Tom. *(sadly)* And he's runnin' from you. You are out yonder in de dark *(points toward the door)* runnin' our chile, with de hounds and de gun in yo' hand, and Talbot's followin' 'hind you with a rope to hang Robert with. *(confidently)* I been sleepin' with you too long, Colonel Tom, not to know that this ain't you layin' down there with yo' eyes shut on de floor. You can't fool me—you ain't never been so still like this before—you's out yonder runnin' ma boy. *(scornfully)* Colonel Thomas Norwood, runnin' ma boy through de fields in de dark, runnin' ma poor little helpless Bert through de fields in de dark to lynch him. . . . Damn you, Colonel Norwood! *(backing slowly up the stairs, staring at the rigid body below her)* Damn you, Thomas Norwood! God damn you!

Curtain

Scene Two

Time: One hour later. Night.

Setting: The same.

Action: As the curtain rises, the UNDERTAKER is talking to SAM at the outer door. All through this act the approaching cries of the man hunt are heard.

Undertaker: Reckon there won't be no orders to bring his corpse back out here, Sam. None of us ain't seen Talbot or Mr. Higgins, but I'm sure they'll be having the funeral in town. The coroner told us to bring the body into the Junction. Ain't nothin' but niggers left out here now.

Sam: (very frightened) Yes, sah! Yes, sah! You's right, sah! Nothin' but us niggers, sah!

Undertaker: The Colonel didn't have no relatives far as you know, did he, Sam?

Sam: No, sah. Ain't had none. No, sah! You's right, sah!

Undertaker: Well, you got everything o' his locked up around here, ain't you? Too bad there ain't no white folks about to look after the Colonel's stuff, but every white man that's able to walks out with the posse. They'll have that young nigger swingin' before ten.

Sam: (trembling) Yes, sah, yes, sah! I 'spects so. Yes, sah!

Undertaker: Say, where's that woman the Colonel's been living with—where's that black housekeeper, Cora, that murderin' bastard's mother?

Sam: She here, sah! She's up in her room.

Richard Bruce (Nugent), "Drawing for Mulattoes No. 4," *Ebony and Topaz,* 1927

Undertaker: (*curiously*) I'd like to see how she looks. Get her down here. Say, how about a little drink before we start that ride back to town, for me and my partner out there with the body?

Sam: Cora got de keys to all de licker, sah!

Undertaker: Well, get her down here then, double quick! (*SAM goes up the stairs. The UNDERTAKER leans in the front doorway talking to his partner outside in the wagon*) Bad business, a white man having saucy nigger children on his hands, and his black woman living in his own house.

Voice Outside: Damn right, Charlie.

Undertaker: Norwood didn't have a gang o' yellow gals, though, like Higgins and some o' these other big bugs. Just this one bitch far's I know, livin' with him damn near like a wife. Didn't even have much company out here. And they tell me ain't been a white woman stayed here overnight since his wife died when I was a baby. (*SAM's shuffle is heard on the stairs*) Here comes a drink, I reckon, boy. You needn't get down off the ambulance. I'll have Sam bring it out there to you. (*SAM descends followed by CORA who comes down the stairs. She says nothing. The UNDERTAKER looks up grinning at CORA*) Well, so you're the Cora that's got these educated nigger children? Hum-m! Well, I guess you'll see one of 'em swinging full of bullet holes when you wake up in the morning. They'll probably hang him to that tree down here by the Colonel's gate—'cause they tell me he strutted right out the front gate past that tree after the murder. Or maybe they'll burn him. How'd you like to see him swinging there roasted in the morning when you wake up, girlie?

Cora: (*calmly*) Is that all you wanted to say to me?

Undertaker: Don't get smart! Maybe you think there's nobody to boss you now. We gonna have a little drink before we go. Get out a bottle of rye.

Cora: I takes ma orders from Colonel Norwood, sir.

Undertaker: Well, you'll take no more orders from him. He's dead out there in my wagon—so get along and get the bottle.

Cora: He's out yonder with de mob, not in your wagon.

Undertaker: I tell you he's in my wagon!

Cora: He's out there with de mob.

Undertaker: God damn! (*to his partner outside*) I believe this black woman's gone crazy in here. (*to CORA*) Get the keys out for that licker, and be quick about it! (*CORA does not move. SAM looks from one to the other, frightened*)

Voice Outside: Aw, to hell with the licker, Charlie. Come on, let's start back to town. We want to get in on some of that excitement, too. They should've found that nigger by now—and I want to see 'em drag him out here.

Undertaker: All right, Jim. (*to CORA and SAM*) Don't you all go to bed until you see that bonfire. You niggers are getting beside yourselves around Polk County. We'll burn a few more of you if you don't be careful. (*He exits, and the noise of the dead-wagon going down the road is heard*)

Sam: Oh, Lawd, hab mercy on me! I prays, Lawd hab mercy! O, ma Lawd, ma Lawd, ma Lawd! Cora, is you a fool? *Is* you a fool? Why didn't you give de mens de licker, riled as these white folks is? In ma old age is I gonna be burnt by de crackers? Lawd, is I sinned? Lawd, what has I done? *(suddenly stops moaning and becomes schemingly calm)* I don't have to stay here tonight, does I? I done locked up de Colonel's library, and he can't be wantin' nothin'. No, ma Lawd, he won't want nothin' now. He's with Jesus—or with de devil, one. *(to CORA)* I's gwine on away from here. Sam's gwine in town to his chilluns' house, and I ain't gwine by no road either. I gwine through de holler where I don't have to pass no white folks.

Cora: Yes, Samuel, you go on. De Colonel can get his own drinks when he comes back tonight.

Sam: *(bucking his eyes in astonishment at CORA)* Lawd God Jesus!

(He bolts out of the room as fast as his old legs will carry him. CORA comes down stairs, looks for a long moment out into the darkness, then closes the front door and draws the blinds. She looks down at the spot where the COLONEL's body has lain)

Cora: All de colored folks are runnin' from you tonight. Po' Colonel Tom, you too old now to be out with de mob. You got no business goin', but you had to go, I reckon. I 'members that time they hung Luke Jordon, you sent yo' dogs out to hunt him. The next day you killed all de dogs. You were kinder softhearted. Said you didn't like that kind of sport. Told me in bed one night you could hear them dogs howlin' in yo' sleep. But de time they burnt de courthouse when that po' little cullud boy was locked up in it 'cause they said he hugged a white girl, you was with 'em again. Said you had to go help 'em. Now you's out chasin' ma boy. *(As she stands at the window, she sees a passing figure)* There goes yo' other woman, Colonel Tom, Livonia is runnin' from you too, now. She would've wanted you last night. Been wantin' you again ever since she got old and fat and you stopped layin' with her and put her in the kitchen to cook. Don't think I don't know, Colonel Tom. Don't think I don't remember them nights when you used to sleep in that cabin down by de spring. I knew 'Vonia was there with you. I ain't no fool, Colonel Tom. But she ain't bore you no chilluns. I'm de one that bore 'em. *(musing)* White mens, and colored womens, and little bastard chilluns—that's de old way of de South—but it's ending now. Three of your yellow brothers yo' father had by Aunt Sallie Deal—what had to come and do your laundry to make her livin'—you got colored relatives scattered all over this county. Them de ways o' de South—mixtries, mixtries.[8] *(WILLIAM enters left, silently, as his mother talks. She is sitting in a chair now. Without looking up)* Is that you, William?

William: Yes, ma, it's me.

Cora: Is you runnin' from him, too?

8. "Mixed race" or "mysteries"; it's not clear which.

William: (hesitatingly) Well, ma, you see . . . don't you think kinder . . . well, I reckon I ought to take Libby and ma babies on down to de church house with Reverend Martin and them, or else get 'long to town if I can hitch up them mules. They's scared to be out here, my wife and her ma. All de folks done gone from de houses down yonder by de branch, and you can hear de hounds a bayin' off yonder by de swamp, and cars is tearin' up that road, and de white folks is yellin' and hollerin' and carryin' on somethin' terrible over toward de brook. I done told Robert 'bout his foolishness. They's gonna hang him sure. Don't you think you better be comin' with us, ma? That is, do you want to? 'Course we can go by ourselves, and maybe you wants to stay here and take care o' de big house. I don't want to leave you, ma, but I . . . I . . .

Cora: Yo' brother'll be back, son, then I won't be by myself.

William: (bewildered by his mother's sureness) I thought Bert went . . . I thought he run . . . I thought . . .

Cora: No, honey. He went, but they ain't gonna get him out there. I sees him comin' back here now, to be with me. I's gwine to guard him 'till he can get away.

William: Then de white folks'll come here, too.

Cora: Yes, de Colonel'll come back here sure. (The deep baying of the hounds is heard at a distance through the night) Colonel Tom will come after his son.

William: My God, ma! Come with us to town.

Cora: Go on, William, go on! Don't wait for them to get back. You never was much like neither one o' them—neither de Colonel or Bert—you's mo' like de field hands. Too much o' ma blood in you, I guess. You never liked Bert much, neither, and you always was afraid of de Colonel. Go on, son, and hide yo' wife and her ma and your chilluns. Ain't nothin' gonna hurt you. You never did go against nobody. Neither did I, till tonight. Tried to live right and not hurt a soul, white or colored. (addressing space) I tried to live right, Lawd. (angrily) Tried to live right, Lawd. (throws out her arms resentfully as if to say, "and this is what you give me") What's de matter, Lawd, you ain't with me?

(The hounds are heard howling again)

William: I'm gone, ma. (He exits fearfully as his mother talks)

Cora: (bending over the spot on the floor where the COLONEL has lain. She calls) Colonel Tom! Colonel Tom! Colonel Tom! Look! Bertha and Sallie and William and Bert, all your chilluns, runnin' from you, and you layin' on de floor there, dead! (pointing) Out yonder with the mob, dead. And when you come home upstairs in my bed on top of my body, dead. (goes to the window, returns, sits down, and begins to speak as if remembering a far-off dream) Colonel Thomas Norwood! I'm just poor Cora Lewis, Colonel Norwood. Little black Cora Lewis, Colonel Norwood. I'm just fifteen years old. Thirty years ago, you put your hands on me to feel my breasts, and you say, "You a pretty little piece of flesh, ain't you? Black and sweet, ain't you?" And I lift up ma face, and you pull me to you, and we laid down under the trees that night and I wonder if your wife'll know when you go back up the road into the big house. And I wonder if my mama'll know it, when I go back to our cabin. Mama said she nursed you when you was a baby, just like she nursed me. And I loved you in the dark, down there under that tree by de gate, afraid of you and proud of you, feelin' your gray eyes lookin' at me in de dark. Then I cried and cried and told ma mother about it, but she didn't take it hard like I thought she'd take it. She said fine white mens like de young Colonel always took good care o' their colored womens. She said it was better than marryin' some black field hand and workin' all your life in de cotton and cane. Better even than havin' a job like ma had, takin' care o' de white chilluns. Takin' care o' you, Colonel Tom. *(As CORA speaks the sound of the approaching mob gradually grows louder and louder. Auto horns, the howling of dogs, the far-off shouts of men, full of malignant force and power, increase in volume)* And I was happy because I liked you, 'cause you was tall and proud, 'cause you said I was sweet to you and called me purty. And when yo' wife died—de Mrs. Norwood *(scornfully)* that never bore you any chilluns, the pale beautiful Mrs. Norwood that was like a slender pine tree in de winter frost . . . I knowed you wanted me. I was full with child by you then—William, it was—our first boy. And ma mammy said, go up there and keep de house for Colonel Tom, sweep de floors and make de beds, and by and by, you won't have to sweep de floors and make no beds. And what ma mammy said was right. It all come true. Sam and Rufus and 'Vonia and Lucy did de waitin' on you and me, and de washin' and de cleanin' and de cookin'. And all I did was a little sewin' now and then, and a little preservin' in de summer and a little makin' of pies and sweet cakes and things you like to eat on Christmas. And de years went by. And I was always ready for you when you come to me in de night. And we had them chilluns, your chilluns and mine, Tom Norwood, all of 'em! William, born dark like me, dumb like me, and then Baby John what died; then Bertha, white and smart like you; and then Bert with your eyes and your ways and your temper, and mighty nigh your color; then Sallie, nearly white, too, and smart, and purty. But Bert was yo' chile! He was always yo' child. . . . Good-looking, and kind, and headstrong, and strange, and stubborn, and proud like you, and de one I could love most 'cause he needed de most lovin'. And he wanted to call you "papa," and I tried to teach him no, but he did it anyhow and *(sternly)* you beat him, Colonel Thomas Norwood. And he growed up with de beatin' in his heart, and your eyes in his head, and your ways, and your pride. And this summer he looked like you that time I first knowed you down by de road under them trees, young and fiery and proud. There was no touchin' Bert, just like there was no touchin' you. I could only love him, like I loved you. I could only love him. But I couldn't talk to him, because he hated you. He had your ways—and you beat him! After you beat that chile, then you died, Colonel Norwood. You died here in this house, and you been living dead a long time. You lived dead. *(Her voice rises above the nearing sounds of the mob)* And when I said this evenin', "Get up! Why don't you help me?" you'd done been dead a long time—a long time before you laid down on this floor, here, with the breath choked out o' you—and Bert standin' over you living, living, living. That's why you hated him. And you want to kill him. Always, you wanted to kill him. Out there with de hounds and de torches and de cars and de guns, you want to kill ma boy. But you won't kill him! He's comin' home first. He's comin' home to me. He's comin' home! *(Outside the noise is tremendous now, the lights of autos flash on the window curtains, there are shouts and cries. CORA sits, tense, in the middle of the room)* He's comin' home!

A Man's Voice: *(outside)* He's somewhere on this lot.

Another Voice: Don't shoot, men. We want to get him alive.

Voice: Close in on him. He must be in them bushes by the house.

First Voice: Porch! Porch! Porch! There he is yonder—running to the door!

(Suddenly shots are heard. The door bursts open and ROBERT enters, firing back into the darkness. The shots are returned by the mob, breaking the windows. Flares, lights, voices, curses, screams)

Voices: Nigger! Nigger! Nigger! Get the nigger!

(CORA rushes toward the door and bolts it after her son's entrance)

Cora: *(leaning against the door)* I was waiting for you, honey. Yo' hiding place is all ready, upstairs, under ma bed, under de floor. I sawed a place there fo' you. They can't find you there. Hurry—before yo' father comes.

Robert: *(panting)* No time to hide, ma. They're at the door now. They'll be coming up the back way, too. *(sounds of knocking and the breaking of glass)* They'll be coming in the windows. They'll be coming in everywhere. And only one bullet left, ma. It's for me.

Cora: Yes, it's fo' you, chile. Save it. Go upstairs in mama's room. Lay on ma bed and rest.

Robert: *(going slowly toward the stairs with the pistol in his hand)* Goodnight, ma. I'm awful tired of running, ma. They been chasing me for hours.

Cora: Goodnight, son.

(CORA follows him to the foot of the steps. The door begins to give at the forcing of the mob. As ROBERT disappears above, it bursts open. A great crowd of white men pour into the room with guns, ropes, clubs, flashlights, and knives. CORA turns on the stairs, facing them quietly. TALBOT, the leader of the mob, stops)

Talbot: Be careful, men. He's armed. *(to CORA)* Where is that yellow bastard of yours—upstairs?

Cora: Yes, he's going to sleep. Be quiet, you all. Wait. *(she bars the way with outspread arms)*

Talbot: (harshly) Wait, hell! Come on, boys, let's go! *(A single shot is heard upstairs)* What's that?

Cora: (calmly) My boy . . . is gone . . . to sleep!

(TALBOT and some of the men rush up the stairway, CORA makes a final gesture of love toward the room above. Yelling and shouting, through all the doors and windows, a great crowd pours into the room. The roar of the mob fills the house, the whole night, the whole world. Suddenly TALBOT returns at the top of the steps and a hush falls over the crowd)

Talbot: Too late, men. We're just a little too late.

(A sigh of disappointment rises from the mob. TALBOT comes down the stairs, walks up to CORA and slaps her once across the face. She does not move. It is as though no human hand can touch her again)

Curtain

Gwendolyn B. Bennett

(1902–1981)

One of the most important movers and shakers of the Harlem Renaissance, Gwendolyn Bennett was a talented painter, poet, essayist, and editor. Her distinguished painting career was overshadowed by her literary activity; she remains best known for her poetry, especially "Hatred" and "Heritage," and for her editorial work at *Opportunity* magazine.

She was born on July 8, 1902, in Giddings, Texas, to Mayme Bennett and Joshua Robin, who became teachers on a Nevada Indian reservation. The family moved to Washington, D.C., when Gwendolyn was a small child; shortly afterwards her parents divorced. At age seven, she was kidnapped by her law student father and taken to Harrisburg, Pennsylvania, and then Brooklyn, New York, where she attended high school from 1918 to 1921. She did not see her mother again until 1924. Bennett studied fine arts at Columbia University and graduated from the Pratt Institute in 1924, at which time she became an assistant professor of fine art at Howard University in Washington, D.C. Bennett played an important role in the Harlem Renaissance Civic Club dinner of March 21, 1924, for which she wrote and recited the poem "To Usward." She won a Delta Sigma Theta Sorority scholarship to Paris where she studied art from 1925 to 1926 and met Ernest Hemingway and Henri Matisse. In 1927 she won another scholarship to study art at the Barnes Foundation.

Bennett's poems and artwork appeared in *The Crisis, Opportunity, Palms,* and other journals from 1923 to 1934, and her poems were included in the major anthologies of her day: *The New Negro* (1925), *Caroling Dusk* (1927), and *Ebony and Topaz* (1927). Of equal importance was Bennett's role as an editor and columnist. She wrote the "Ebony Flute" arts column for *Opportunity* (1926–28) and served as its assistant editor while continuing her duties as a professor at Howard. She also was one of the editors of *Fire!!*, an experimental journal that survived only one issue in 1926. It was in *Fire!!* that Bennett published one of her two short stories, "Wedding Day." "Tokens" appeared in *Ebony and Topaz* a year later and is reprinted here for the first time.

After her marriage to Alfred Jackson in 1928, Bennett's career changed markedly. She had been fired from Howard the previous year because Jackson was a medical student and faculty were not allowed to date students; after his graduation they moved South to Tennessee and then Florida. The couple moved to Hemstead, Long Island, in 1932.

When her husband died in 1936, Bennett moved to Harlem. Here she joined the Harlem Artists Guild and helped direct the Harlem Community Art Center with friend and sculptor Augusta Savage from 1938 to 1941. She was suspended for political reasons, accused of having Communist Party affiliations. Briefly serving at the Jefferson School and the George Washington Carver School during World War II, Bennett became secretary for the Consumers Union until her retirement in 1968. Among her students were the influential African American painters Jacob Lawrence and Romare Bearden. She and her second husband, Richard Crosscup, whom she married in 1940, then ran an antiques shop in Kutztown, Pennsylvania, where she died.

Gwendolyn Bennett, "The Pipes of Pan," cover of *The Crisis,* March 1924

Heritage

I want to see the slim palm-trees,
Pulling at the clouds
With little pointed fingers. . . .

I want to see lithe Negro girls
Etched dark against the sky
While sunset lingers.

I want to hear the silent sands,
Singing to the moon
Before the Sphinx-still face. . . .

I want to hear the chanting
Around a heathen fire
Of a strange black race.

I want to breathe the Lotus flow'r,
Sighing to the stars
With tendrils drinking at the Nile. . . .

I want to feel the surging
Of my sad people's soul,
Hidden by a minstrel-smile.

Opportunity, December 1923.

To a Dark Girl

I love you for your brownness
And the rounded darkness of your breast.
I love you for the breaking sadness in your voice
And shadows where your wayward eye-lids rest.

Something of old forgotten queens
Lurks in the lithe abandon of your walk
And something of the shackled slave
Sobs in the rhythm of your talk.

Oh, little brown girl, born for sorrow's mate,
Keep all you have of queenliness,
Forgetting that you once were slave,
And let your full lips laugh at Fate!

Negro Poets and Their Poems, 1923.

Hatred

I shall hate you
Like a dart of singing steel
Shot through still air
At even-tide,
Or solemnly
As pines are sober
When they stand etched
Against the sky.
Hating you shall be a game
Played with cool hands
And slim fingers.
Your heart will yearn
For the lonely splendor
Of the pine tree
While rekindled fires
In my eyes
Shall wound you like swift arrows.
Memory will lay its hands
Upon your breast
And you will understand
My hatred.

Opportunity , June 1926.

Advice

You were a sophist,
Pale and quite remote,
As you bade me
Write poems—
Brown poems
Of dark words
And prehistoric rhythms . . .
Your pallor stifled my poesy
But I remembered a tapestry
That I would some day weave
Of dim purples and fine reds
And blues
Like night and death—
The keen precision of your words
Wove a silver thread
Through the dusk softness
Of my dream-stuff. . . .

Caroling Dusk, 1927.

Fantasy

I sailed in my dreams to the Land of Night
Where you were the dusk-eyed queen,
And there in the pallor of moon-veiled light
The loveliest things were seen . . .

A slim-necked peacock sauntered there
In a garden of lavender hues,
And you were strange with your purple hair
As you sat in your amethyst chair
With your feet in your hyacinth shoes.

Oh, the moon gave a bluish light
Through the trees in the land of dreams and night.
I stood behind a bush of yellow-green
And whistled a song to the dark-haired queen . . .

Caroling Dusk, 1927.

Richard Bruce (Nugent),
"Wedding Day," *Fire!!*
November 1926

Wedding Day

His name was Paul Watson and as he shambled down rue Pigalle he might have been any other Negro of enormous height and size. But as I have said, his name was Paul Watson. Passing him on the street, you might not have known or cared who he was, but any one of the residents about the great Montmartre district of Paris could have told you who he was as well as many interesting bits of his personal history.

He had come to Paris in the days before colored jazz bands were the style. Back home he had been a prize fighter. In the days when Joe Gans was in his glory Paul was following the ring, too. He didn't have that fine way about him that Gans had and for that reason luck seemed to go against him. When he was in the ring he was like a mad bull, especially if his opponent was a white man. In those days there wasn't any sympathy or nicety about the ring and so pretty soon all the ring masters got down on Paul and he found it pretty hard to get a bout with anyone. Then it was that he worked his way across the Atlantic Ocean on a big liner—in the days before colored jazz bands were the style in Paris.

Things flowed along smoothly for the first few years with Paul's working here and there in the unfrequented places of Paris. On the side he used to give boxing lessons to aspiring youths or gymnastic young women. At that time he was working so steadily that he had little chance to find out what was going on around Paris. Pretty soon, however, he grew to be known among the trainers and managers began to fix up bouts for him. After one or two successful bouts a little fame began to come into being for him. So it was that after one of the prize-fights, a colored fellow came to his dressing room to congratulate him on his success as well as invite him to go to Montmartre to meet "the boys."

Paul had a way about him and seemed to get on with the colored fellows who lived in Montmartre and when the first Negro jazz band played in a tiny Parisian cafe Paul was among them playing the banjo. Those first years were without event so far as Paul was concerned. The members of that first band often say now that they wonder how it was that nothing happened during those first seven years, for it was generally known how great was Paul's hatred for American white people. I suppose the tranquility in the light of what happened afterwards was due to the fact that the cafe in which they worked was one in which mostly French people drank and danced and then too, that was before there were so many Americans visiting Paris. However, everyone had heard Paul speak of his intense hatred of white folks. It only took two Benedictines[1] to make him start talking about what he would do to the first "Yank" that called him "nigger." But the seven years came to an end and Paul Watson went to work in a larger cafe with a larger band, patronized almost solely by Americans.

---

1. A kind of liqueur.

Fire!!, November 1926.

I've heard almost every Negro in Montmartre tell about the night that a drunken Kentuckian came into the cafe where Paul was playing and said:

"Look heah, Bruther, what you all doin' ovah heah?"

"None ya bizness. And looka here, I ain't your brother, see?"

"Jack, do you heah that nigger talkin' lak that tah me?"

As he said this, he turned to speak to his companion. I have often wished that I had been there to have seen the thing myself. Every tale I have heard about it was different and yet there was something of truth in each of them. Perhaps the nearest one can come to the truth is by saying that Paul beat up about four full-sized white men that night besides doing a great deal of damage to the furniture about the cafe. I couldn't tell you just what did happen. Some of the fellows say that Paul seized the nearest table and mowed down men right and left, others say he took a bottle, then again the story runs that a chair was the instrument of his fury. At any rate, that started Paul Watson on his siege against the American white person who brings his native prejudices into the life of Paris.

It is a verity that Paul was the "black terror." The last syllable of the word, nigger, never passed the lips of a white man without the quick reflex action of Paul's arm and fist to the speaker's jaw. He paid for more glassware and cafe furnishings in the course of the next few years than is easily imaginable. And yet, there was something likable about Paul. Perhaps that's the reason that he stood in so well with the policemen of the neighborhood. Always some divine power seemed to intervene in his behalf and he was excused after the payment of a small fine with advice about his future conduct. Finally, there came the night when in a frenzy he shot the two American sailors.

They had not died from the wounds he had given them; hence his sentence had not been one of death but rather a long term of imprisonment. It was a pitiable sight to see Paul sitting in the corner of his cell with his great body hunched almost double. He seldom talked and when he did his words were interspersed with oaths about the lowness of "crackers."[2] Then the World War came.[3]

It seems strange that anything so horrible as that wholesale slaughter could bring about any good and yet there was something of a smoothing quality about even its baseness. There has never been such equality before or since such as that which the World War brought. Rich men fought by the side of paupers; poets swapped yams with dry-goods salesmen, while Jews and Christians ate corned beef out of the same tin. Along with the general leveling influence came France's pardon of her prisoners in order that they might enter the army. Paul Watson became free and a French soldier. Because he was strong and had innate daring in his heart he was placed in the aerial squad and cited many times for bravery. The close of the war gave him his place in French society as a hero. With only a memory of the war and an ugly scar on his left cheek he took up his old life.

2. Derogatory slang for white people.
3. World War I (1914–1918).

His firm resolutions about American white people still remained intact and many chance encounters that followed the war are told from lip to lip proving that the war and his previous imprisonment had changed him little. He was the same Paul Watson to Montmartre as he shambled up rue Pigalle.

Rue Pigalle in the early evening has a sombre beauty—gray as are most Paris streets and other-worldish. To those who know the district it is the Harlem of Paris and rue Pigalle is its dusky Seventh Avenue. Most of the colored musicians that furnish Parisians and their visitors with entertainment live somewhere in the neighborhood of rue Pigalle. Some time during every day each of these musicians makes a point of passing through rue Pigalle. Little wonder that almost any day will find Paul Watson going his shuffling way up the same street.

He reached the corner of rue de la Bruyère and with sure instinct his feet stopped. Without half thinking he turned into "the Pit." Its full name is the Flea Pit. If you should ask one of the musicians why it was so called, he would answer you to the effect that it was called "the pit" because all the "fleas" hang out there. If you did not get the full import of this explanation, he would go further and say that there were always "spades"[4] in the pit and they were as thick as fleas. Unless you could understand this latter attempt at clarity you could not fully grasp what the Flea Pit means to the Negro musicians in Montmartre. It is a tiny cafe of the genus that is called *bistro* in France. Here the fiddle players, saxophone blowers, drum-beaters and ivory ticklers gather at four in the afternoon for a porto or a game of billiards. Here the cabaret entertainers and supper musicians meet at one o'clock at night or thereafter for a whiskey and soda, or more billiards. Occasional sandwiches and a "quiet game" also play their parts in the popularity of the place. After a season or two it becomes a settled fact just what time you may catch so-and-so at the famous "Pit."

The musicians were very fond of Paul and took particular delight in teasing him. He was one of the chosen few that all of the musicians conceded as being "regular." It was the pet joke of the habitues of the cafe that Paul never bothered with girls. They always said that he could beat up ten men but was scared to death of one woman.

"Say fellow, when ya goin' a get hooked up?"

"Can't say, Bo. Ain't so much on skirts."

"Man alive, ya don't know what you're missin'—somebody little and cute telling ya sweet things in your ear. Paris is full of women folks."

"I ain't much on 'em all the same. Then too, they're all white."

"What's it to ya? This ain't America."

"Can't help that. Get this—I'm collud, see? I ain't got nothing for no white meat to do. If a woman eva called me nigger I'd have to kill her, that's all!"

"You for it, son. I can't give you a thing on this Mr. Jefferson Lawd way of lookin' at women."

"Oh, tain't that. I guess they're all right for those that wants 'em. Not me!"

---

4. Vulgar slang for black people.

"Oh you ain't so forty.[5] You'll fall like all the other spades I've ever seen. Your kind falls hardest."

And so Paul went his way—alone. He smoked and drank with the fellows and sat for hours in the Montmartre cafes and never knew the companionship of a woman. Then one night after his work he was walking along the street in his queer shuffling way when a woman stepped up to his side.

"Voulez-vous?"[6]

"Naw, gowan away from here."

"Oh, you speak English, don't you?"

"You an 'merican woman?"

"Used to be 'fore I went on the stage and got stranded over here."

"Well, get away from here. I don't like your kind!"

"Aw, Buddy, don't say that. I ain't prejudiced like some fool women."

"You don't know who I am, do you? I'm Paul Watson and I hate American white folks, see?"

He pushed her aside and went on walking alone. He hadn't gone far when she caught up to him and said with sobs in her voice:—

"Oh, Lordy, please don't hate me 'cause I was born white and an American. I ain't got a sou[7] to my name and all the men pass me by 'cause I ain't spruced up. Now you come along and won't look at me 'cause I'm white."

Paul strode along with her clinging to his arm. He tried to shake her off several times but there was no use. She clung all the more desperately to him. He looked down at her frail body shaken with sobs, and something caught at his heart. Before he knew what he was doing he had said:—

"Naw, I ain't that mean. I'll get you some grub. Quit your cryin'. Don't like seein' women folks cry."

It was the talk of Montmartre. Paul Watson takes a woman to Gavarnni's every night for dinner. He comes to the Flea Pit less frequently, thus giving the other musicians plenty of opportunity to discuss him.

"How times do change. Paul, the woman-hater, has a Jane now."

"You ain't said nothing, fella. That ain't all. She's white and an 'merican too."

"That's the way with these spades. They beat up all the white men they can lay their hands on but as soon as a gang of golden hair with blue eyes rubs up close to them they forget all they ever said about hatin' white folks."

"Guess he thinks that skirt's gone on him. Dumb fool!"

"Don' be no chineeman. That old gag don' fit for Paul. He cain't understand it no more'n we can. Says he jess can't help himself, every time she looks up into his eyes and asks him does he love her. They sure are happy together. Paul's goin' to marry her, too. At first

---

5. "You're not so tough."

6. Literally, "Do you want?" She is propositioning him.

7. A French coin of low value.

she kept saying that she didn't want to get married 'cause she wasn't the marrying kind and all that talk. Paul jus' laid down the law to her and told her he never would live with no woman without being married to her. Then she began to tell him all about her past life. He told her he didn't care nothing about what she used to be jus' so long as they loved each other now. Guess they'll make it."

"Yeah, Paul told me the same tale last night. He's sure gone on her all right."

"They're gettin' tied up next Sunday. So glad it's not me. Don't trust these American dames. Me for the Frenchies."

"She ain't so worse for looks, Bud. Now that he's been furnishing the green for the rags."[8]

"Yeah, but I don't see no reason for the wedding bells. She was right—she ain't the marrying kind."

. . . and so Montmartre talked. In every cafe where the Negro musicians congregated Paul Watson was the topic for conversation. He had suddenly fallen from his place as bronze God to almost less than the dust.

The morning sun made queer patterns on Paul's sleeping face. He grimaced several times in his slumber, then finally half-opened his eyes. After a succession of dream-laden blinks he gave a great yawn, and rubbing his eyes, looked at the open window through which the sun shone brightly. His first conscious thought was that this was the bride's day and that bright sunshine prophesied happiness for the bride throughout her married life. His first impulse was to settle back into the covers and think drowsily about Mary and the queer twists life brings about, as is the wont of most bridegrooms on their last morning of bachelorhood. He put this impulse aside in favor of dressing quickly and rushing downstairs to telephone Mary to say "happy wedding day" to her.

One huge foot slipped into a worn bedroom slipper and then the other dragged painfully out of the warm bed were the courageous beginnings of his bridal toilette. With a look of triumph he put on his new gray suit that he had ordered from an English tailor. He carefully pulled a taffeta tie into place beneath his chin, noting as he looked at his face in the mirror that the scar he had received in the army was very ugly—funny, marrying an ugly man like him.

French telephones are such human faults. After trying for about fifteen minutes to get Central 32.01 he decided that he might as well walk around to Mary's hotel to give his greeting as to stand there in the lobby of his own, wasting his time. He debated this in his mind a great deal. They were to be married at four o'clock. It was eleven now and it did seem a shame not to let her have a minute or two by herself. As he went walking down the street towards her hotel he laughed to think of how one always cogitates over doing something and finally does the thing he wanted to in the beginning anyway.

Mud on his nice gray suit that the English tailor had made for him. Damn—gray suit—what did he have a gray suit on for, anyway. Folks with black faces shouldn't wear gray suits. Gawd, but it was funny that time when he beat up that cracker at the Periquet. Fool

8. "Now that he's been paying for her clothes."

couldn't shut his mouth he was so surprised. Crackers—damn 'em—he was one nigger that wasn't 'fraid of 'em. Wouldn't he have a hell of a time if he went back to America where black was black. Wasn't white nowhere, black wasn't. What was that thought he was trying to get ahold of—bumping around in his head—something he started to think about but couldn't remember it somehow.

The shrill whistle that is typical of the French subway pierced its way into his thoughts. Subway—why was he in the subway—he didn't want to go any place. He heard doors slamming and saw the blue uniforms of the conductors swinging on the cars as the trains began to pull out of the station. With one or two strides he reached the last coach as it began to move up the platform. A bit out of breath he stood inside the train and looking down at what he had in his hand he saw that it was a tiny pink ticket. A first class ticket in a second class coach. The idea set him to laughing. Everyone in the car turned and eyed him, but that did not bother him. Wonder what stop he'd get off—funny how these French said descend when they meant get off—funny he couldn't pick up French—been here so long. First class ticket in a second class coach!—that was one on him. Wedding day today, and that damn letter from Mary. How'd she say it now, "just couldn't go through with it," white women just don't marry colored men, and she was a street woman, too. Why couldn't she have told him flat that she was just getting back on her feet at his expense. Funny that first class ticket he bought, wish he could see Mary— him a-going there to wish her "happy wedding day," too. Wonder what that French woman was looking at him so hard for? Guess it was the mud.

Tokens

High on the bluff of Saint Cloud stands the Merlin Hospital, immaculate sentinel of Seraigne . . . Seraigne with its crazy houses and aimless streets, scrambling at the foot of Saint Cloud's immense immutability. Row on row the bricks of the hospital take dispassion- ate account of lives lost or found. It is always as though the gay, little town of Seraigne were thumbing its nose at Saint Cloud with its famous Merlin Hospital where life is held in a test-tube, a thing to be caught or lost by a drop or two of this or a pellet of that. And past the rustic stupidity of Seraigne's gaiety lies the wanton unconcern of the Seine. The Seine . . . mute river of sorrows . . . grim concealer of forgotten secrets . . . endlessly flowing . . . touching the edges of life . . . moving purposefully along with a grey disdain for the empty, foolish gaiety of Seraigne or the benign dignity of Merlin Hos- pital, high on the warm cliffs of Saint Cloud.

A trim nurse had drawn Jenks Barnett's chair out onto one of the balconies that over- looked the Seine. Listlessly, aimlessly he turned his thoughts to first one aspect and then

Ebony and Topaz, 1927.

another of the Seine, Merlin Hospital, the cliffs of Saint Cloud, Seraigne . . . over and again . . . the Seine, Merlin Hospital, the cliffs . . . of . . . Saint . . . Cloud . . . silly, little Seraigne. It was a better way—that Seine business. Just swallow up life and sorrow and sadness . . . don't bother about the poor fools who are neither dead nor alive . . . just hanging on to the merest threads of existence . . . coughing out one's heart and yet somehow still keeping heart. Purposeless thoughts these as one just [as] purposelessly fingers the blanket that covers one's emaciated, almost lifeless legs. But the Seine goes on, and Seraigne continues to be happy, and the pain in one's chest grows no easier.

It so happened that at this particular time there were a number of colored patients at the Merlin Hospital. Most of them were musicians who had remained in Paris after the World War.[1] Two of them had come to London and thence to Paris with Will Marion Cook in the Negro entertainer's heyday.[2] Jenks was one of these. He had been a singer in those days. His voice was now spoken of in the hushed tones one uses when speaking of the dead. He had cherished great plans for himself in those days and no one dared hope otherwise, so rare was his voice in range and quality. That was all changed now. . . .

Merlin Hospital had won nation-wide fame as a haven for patients suffering from tuberculosis. An able staff of doctors and nurses administered daily hope of recovery to broken bodies or perhaps kindly, though inadequate, solace to those whose cases were hopeless. Jenks Barnett had been there five weeks. His case was one of the hopeless ones. The tale of his being there did not take long in the telling. Shortly after the success of Cook's orchestra with its inimitable "singing trombonist" Tollie had come— Tollie Saunders with her golden voice and lush laughter. From the very first she and Jenks had hit it off well together. It was not long before he was inextricably enmeshed in the wonder of her voice and the warm sweetness of her body. Dinner at Les Acacias . . . for Tollie . . . a hat for her lovely head . . . that dress in Chanel's window . . . she wanted one of those large opal rings . . . long nights of madness under the charm of her flute-sweet voice. His work began to suffer. Soon he was dismissed from the orchestra. Singing *soirées*[3] didn't pay too well. And then one day before the pinch of poverty came Tollie had left him, taking with her all the pretty things he had given her . . . leaving no farewell . . . her chance had come to sing in an American production and she had gone. No word of their plan to startle the singing world with their combined talents; no hint of regret that she was leaving . . . just gone. Three nights on a gorgeous drunk and he had awakened to find himself in a dingy, damp Parisian jail with a terrific pain in his back . . . eighteen days in which he moved from one prison-house to another . . . sunshine and air again when his friends had finally found him and arranged for his release . . . sunshine lasts but a short time in Paris . . . endless days of splashing through the Paris rain in search of a job . . . always that pain between his shoulder-blades . . . then night upon night of

1. World War I (1914–1918).

2. Will Marion Cook (1869–1944) coauthored a Broadway musical with poet Paul Laurence Dunbar (1872–1906) in 1889, *Clorindy*.

3. French for "evenings"; i.e., parties at night.

blowing a trombone in a stuffy little *Boîte de Nuit*[4] during which time he forgot the pain in his back . . . and drink . . . incessant drink . . . one more drink with the fellows . . . and after the job cards and more drink. One came to Merlin after one had been to the American Hospital. One came to Merlin after one had been to every other hospital round about Paris. It does not take long to become accustomed to the turning knife in one's chest. It is good for a hopeless cause to watch the uncurbed forgetfulness of the Seine.

Spring had sent ahead its perfume this day. It was as though the early March air were powdered with the pollen of many unborn flowers. A haze settled itself in the air and on the breast of the river. Jenks forgot for a moment the relentless ache in his bosom and breathed deeply in sheer satisfaction. In the very midst of this gesture of aliveness the tool of death, lodged in his lung, gave a wrench. A hacking cough rose in his throat and then seemed to become stuck there. His great, gaunt frame was shaken in a paroxysm of pain. The fit of stifled coughing over, his head fell back upon the pillow. A nurse hurried to his side. "Guess you'd better go in now. I told you not to move around."

With quick, efficient hands she tucked the cover more closely about his legs, lowered the back of the invalid chair in which he was sitting, and pushed him carefully back into the hospital. As his chair was rolled through the ward it was as though he were running the gamut of scorn. Jenks was not a favorite at the hospital by any stretch of the imagination. Few of the patients there had escaped the lash of his tongue. Sour at life and the raw deal it had left him, he now turned his attention to venting his spume on those about him. Nurses, doctors, orderlies, fellow-patients, persistent friends . . . all shared alike the blasphemy of his words. Even Bill Jackson, the one friend who continued to brave the sting of his vile tongue, was not spared. Bill had known him and loved him before Tollie came. It was in this memory that he wrapped himself when Jenks was most unbearable. He accused Bill of stealing his money when he asked him to bring him something from the city. . . . There had been many who had tried to make Jenks' last days easier but one by one they had begun to stay away until now there was only Bill left. Little wonder the other patients in the hospital heaped invective upon him as he passed.

So thin he was as he lay beneath the covers of the bed that his knees and chest made scarcely perceptible mounds in the smooth whiteness of the bed. The brown of his face had taken on the color of dried mud. Great seams folded themselves in his cheeks. There he lay, the rotting hulk of what he had once been. He had sent for Bill. . . . these waiting moments were so long!

"Hi there, Jenks" . . . it was Bill's cheery voice . . . "thought you'd be outside."

"Can't go out no more. Nearly kicked off the other day."

"Thas all right . . . you'll come around all right."

"For God sakes cut it out. I know I'm done for. You know it, too, damn it all."

"Come on now, fella, be your age. You can't last long if you get yourself all worked up. Take it easy."

---

4. French for a nightclub.

"Oh I get so damned sick of the whole business I wish I would hurry up and die. But whose business is that but mine . . . got somethin' to tell you."

"Shoot."

"See I'm dyin' . . . get me. They keep stickin' that needle in me but I know damn well I'm dyin'. Now what I want you to do is this . . . I wrote a letter to Tollie when I first came here . . . it's in her picture in my suitcase . . . you know that silver frame. Well when I die I want you to give it to her, if it's a thousand years from now . . . just a token of the time when we were in love. Don't forget it. Then you remember that French kid that used to be on the ward downstairs . . . she always liked that radium clock of mine. She's been transferred to the Gerboux Sanitarium . . . almost well now. I think they said she would be out in a year. Good kid . . . used to climb up here every afternoon . . . stairs sort of wore her out, too. Give her my clock and tell her I hope she lives to be well and strong 'cause I never'll make it. God, she was an angel if ever there was one . . . used to sit there on that chair where you're sittin' now and just look at me and say how she wished she could die in my place 'cause I was such a big man . . . and could sing so . . . I believe she'd like to have something to remember me by. And, Bill, you take . . . that . . . mmmghgmmmm . . . mmm. . . ."

That strangling cough rose in his throat. His eyes, always cruel, seemed to look out softly at Bill. A nurse hurried swiftly into the room and injected a hypodermic needle into his arm. A tremor went through his body. His eyelids half closed . . . he slept.

The days dragged out in one week after another. Jenks lingered on like the days. Outside the Seine flowed endlessly on unhindered and free. It was all so futile and strange . . . waiting this way.

June had laid her warm mouth upon the face of the earth. With soft languor the sun slid tenderly over the cliffs of Saint Cloud . . . even tenderly over the grey bricks of Merlin Hospital. Jenks had raged so about not being allowed to lie on the balcony that at last the hospital authorities had relented . . . there was such a short time left for him anyway . . . he might as well have what he wanted . . . this was the first day that had been warm enough. As he lay there he looked out across the cliffs, past the little town of Seraigne, out past the Seine . . . on . . . on . . . immune to life . . . conversant with death . . . on to the great simplicities. He got to thinking of when he was a boy . . . the songs he used to sing . . . he almost thought he'd try to sing now . . . what did it matter if he got another coughing spell . . . but then the nurses would all be in a flurry. Nice to be out here once more looking at the Seine and the world where people lived and breathed.

Bill sighed as he placed the little clock on the mantlepiece. Funny world, this! The French girl had died in late May. He had better not tell Jenks . . . it might upset him. No-o-ope better just keep the clock here. Funny how the first kind thing Jenks had done for anybody since Tollie left him should be done for a person who was dead.

High on the bluff of Saint Cloud stands the Merlin Hospital, immaculate sentinel of Seraigne . . . with its crazy houses and aimless streets, scrambling at the foot of Saint Cloud's immense immutability. Row upon row the bricks of the hospital take dispassionate account of lives lost or found.

Wallace Thurman

(1902–1934)

Journalist, editor, novelist, story writer, playwright, screenwriter, and prime mover of the young generation challenging the "Talented Tenth" establishment of the Harlem Renaissance, Wallace Thurman was born August 16, 1902, in Salt Lake City, Utah, to Beulah and Oscar Thurman. His parents separated and his mother had several subsequent husbands. Nevertheless, his maternal grandmother, Emma Jackson (Ma Jack), was a constant in his life. Upon graduating from high school, he initially attended the University of Utah but transferred to the University of Southern California in 1922. He did not graduate but Thurman was a voracious reader familiar with Shakespeare, Nietzsche, Baudelaire, Flaubert, Freud, Ibsen, and many others. While in Los Angeles, he wrote "Inklings," a column in a local black newspaper; worked in the post office; and founded and edited *The Outlet*, but the magazine failed after six months. After unsuccessfully trying to inaugurate a West Coast version of the Harlem Renaissance, he left for Harlem in 1925.

He worked as a reporter and editor for Theophilus Lewis's *The Looking Glass* and was later hired as managing editor for A. Philip Randolph and Chandler Owen's *The Messenger,* where he was responsible for publishing Langston Hughes's first short stories. In 1926 he left the magazine to become circulation editor of the white religious magazine *The World Tomorrow*. That same year the first and only issue of *Fire!!* was published under Thurman's editorship and with the collaboration of Langston Hughes, Zora Neale Hurston, Aaron Douglas, John P. Davis, Richard Bruce Nugent, and Gwendolyn Bennett. The magazine had been conceived by Hughes and Nugent as an independent alternative to the Harlem establishment periodicals, *Opportunity*, *The Crisis*, and *The Messenger*. They, along with Hurston, Bennett, Douglas, and Davis, unanimously elected Thurman as its editor, and he shouldered the substantial production cost. Despite the failure of *Fire!!*, it was a landmark publication of the Harlem Renaissance, and Thurman helped to launch another new radical magazine, *Harlem: A Forum of Negro Life*, which also produced only one issue.

The next year, in 1929, he was hired as a reader for Macaulay's Publishing, making him the only black reader at a major New York publishing house. This was also the year that his play, *Harlem: A Melodrama of Negro Life*, written with white freelance writer William Jourdan Rapp, made it to Broadway and his first novel, *The Blacker the Berry*, was published, both meeting with popular success and considerable critical attention. *Harlem* was based on Thurman's short story, "Cordelia the Crude," published in *Fire!!,* and the source of controversy among the Harlem intelligentsia for its bold portrayal of a prostitute: noted African American literary critic Benjamin Brawley and W.E.B. Du Bois found both the play and the journal offensive and alarming. To younger writers like Hughes, Nugent, Helene Johnson, Rudolph Fisher, Bennett, and Dorothy West, however, Thurman's impact on the Harlem scene was deeply appreciated as a fresh approach to black working-class life. Thurman and Rapp collaborated on a second play, *Jeremiah the Magnificent*, whose subject was Marcus Garvey, but it failed to secure a producer. They began a third play, *Black Cinderella*, but it was never completed.

Thurman's next novel, *Infants of the Spring* (1932), created another firestorm, for it satirized leading figures of the Renaissance, including his own crowd. It is notable for its inclusion of veiled gay characters, particularly one based on openly gay writer Richard Bruce Nugent. This novel and his *Blacker the Berry* are the first novels to portray African American gay themes, and Thurman's decision to include a story with gay characters in *Fire!!* places him among the most significant early sources of this important subject. Thurman was widely considered to be gay himself, despite his six-month marriage to Louise Thompson in 1928. He was known to have white male lovers in the 1920s and his closest friend was Nugent.

He published one other novel, *The Interne* (1932), coauthored with white writer Abraham Furman. Thurman wrote these novels while still working at Macaulay's, but in 1934 he left for a lucrative position as a screenwriter for an independent production company. He wrote two film scripts that were later produced, but after only a few months he returned to New York in ill health. After collapsing at a reunion party with his Harlem friends, he was hospitalized at City Hospital on Welfare Island. He died a few months later at the age of thirty-two, diagnosed with tuberculosis. Nella Larsen's brother-in-law, the Rev. William Lloyd Imes, read the obituary, calling Thurman "priceless." Dorothy West lamented his passing as a fatal blow to the Harlem Renaissance: "He was our leader, and when he died, it all died with him."

The Last Citadel

There is an old brick house in Harlem
Way up Fifth Avenue;
With a long green yard and windows barred
It stands silent, salient,
Unconquered by the surrounding black horde.

Opportunity, April 1926.

God's Edict

Let the wind-rolled waves tell the tale of the sea,
And the talkative pines tell the tale of the tree;
Let the motored purr of an automobile
Tell the hum-drum tale of power and steel.
Let the blithesome chirp tell the tale of the bird,
And sad, low sounds tell the tale of the herd;
Then enthrone man on the dunce's stool
And let his tale be the tale of a fool.

Opportunity , July 1926.

Richard Bruce (Nugent), "Cordelia the Crude," *Fire!!* November 1926

Cordelia the Crude

Physically, if not mentally, Cordelia was a potential prostitute, meaning that although she had not yet realized the moral import of her wanton promiscuity nor become mercenary, she had, nevertheless, become quite blasé and bountiful in the matter of bestowing sexual favors upon persuasive and likely young men. Yet, despite her seeming lack of discrimination, Cordelia was quite particular about the type of male to whom she submitted, for numbers do not necessarily denote a lack of taste, and Cordelia had discovered after several months of active observation that one could find the qualities one admires or reacts positively to in a varied hodge-podge of outwardly different individuals.

The scene of Cordelia's activities was the Roosevelt Motion Picture Theatre on Seventh Avenue near 145th Street. Thrice weekly the program changed, and thrice weekly Cordelia would plunk down the necessary twenty-five cents evening admission fee, and saunter gaily into the foul-smelling depths of her favorite cinema shrine. The Roosevelt Theatre presented all of the latest pictures, also, twice weekly, treated its audiences to a vaudeville bill, then too, one could always have the most delightful physical contacts . . . hmm. . . .

Cordelia had not consciously chosen this locale nor had there been any conscious effort upon her part to take advantage of the extra opportunities afforded for physical pleasure. It had just happened that the Roosevelt Theatre was more close to her home than any other neighborhood picture palace, and it had also just happened that Cordelia had become almost immediately initiated into the ways of a Harlem theatre chippie[1] soon after her discovery of the theatre itself.

It is the custom of certain men and boys who frequent these places to idle up and down the aisle until some female is seen sitting alone, to slouch down into a seat beside her, to touch her foot or else press her leg in such a way that it can be construed as accidental if necessary, and then, if the female is wise or else shows signs of willingness to become wise, to make more obvious approaches until, if successful, the approached female will soon be chatting with her baiter about the picture being shown, lolling in his arms, and helping to formulate plans for an after-theatre rendezvous. Cordelia had, you see, shown a willingness to become wise upon her second visit to the Roosevelt. In a short while she had even learned how to squelch the bloated, lewd faced Jews and eager middle-aged Negroes who might approach as well as how to inveigle the likeable little yellow or brown half men, embryo avenue sweetbacks,[2] with their well modeled heads, stickily plastered hair, flaming cravats, silken or broadcloth shirts, dirty underwear, low cut vests, form fitting coats, bell-bottom trousers and shiny shoes with metal cornered heels

1. Slang for prostitute.
2. Budding male prostitutes of Seventh Avenue, Harlem's main thoroughfare.

Fire!!, November 1926.

clicking with a brave, brazen rhythm upon the bare concrete floor as their owners angled and searched for prey.

Cordelia, sixteen years old, matronly mature, was an undisciplined, half literate product of rustic South Carolina, and had come to Harlem very much against her will with her parents and her six brothers and sisters. Against her will because she had not been at all anxious to leave the lackadaisical life of the little corn pone settlement where she had been born, to go trooping into the unknown vastness of New York, for she had been in love, passionately in love with one John Stokes who raised pigs, and who, like his father before him, found the raising of pigs so profitable that he could not even consider leaving Lintonville. Cordelia had blankly informed her parents that she would not go with them when they decided to be lured to New York by an older son who had remained there after the demobilization of the war time troops. She had even threatened to run away with John until they should be gone, but of course John could not leave his pigs, and John's mother was not very keen on having Cordelia for a daughter-in-law—those Joneses have bad mixed blood in 'em—so Cordelia had had to join the Gotham bound caravan[3] and leave her lover to his succulent porkers.

However, the mere moving to Harlem had not doused the rebellious flame. Upon arriving Cordelia had not only refused to go to school and refused to hold even the most easily held job, but had also victoriously defied her harassed parents so frequently when it came to matters of discipline that she soon found herself with a mesmerizing lack of home restraint, for the stress of trying to maintain themselves and their family in the new environment was far too much of a task for Mr. and Mrs. Jones to attend to facilely and at the same time try to control a recalcitrant child. So, when Cordelia had refused either to work or to attend school, Mrs. Jones herself had gone out for day's work,[4] leaving Cordelia at home to take care of their five room railroad flat, the front room of which was rented out to a couple "living together," and to see that the younger children, all of whom were of school age, made their four trips daily between home and the nearby public school—as well as see that they had their greasy, if slim, food rations and an occasional change of clothing. Thus Cordelia's days were full—and so were her nights. The only difference being that the days belonged to the folks at home while the nights (since the folks were too tired or too sleepy to know or care when she came in or went out) belonged to her and to—well—whosoever will, let them come.

Cordelia had been playing this hectic, entrancing game for six months and was widely known among a certain group of young men and girls on the avenue as a fus' class chippie when she and I happened to enter the theatre simultaneously. She had clumped down the aisle before me, her open galoshes swishing noisily, her two arms busy wriggling themselves free from the torn sleeve lining of a shoddy imitation fur coat that one of her mother's wash clients had sent to her. She was of medium height and build, with overly developed legs and bust, and had a clear, keen light brown complexion. Her too slick,

3. Gotham is a common name for New York City.
4. Domestic service.

too naturally bobbed hair, mussed by the removing of a tight, black turban was of an undecided nature, i.e., it was undecided whether to be kinky or to be kind, and her body, as she sauntered along in the partial light had such a conscious sway of invitation that unthinkingly I followed, slid into the same row of seats and sat down beside her.

Naturally she had noticed my pursuit, and thinking that I was eager to play the game, let me know immediately that she was wise, and not the least bit averse to spooning[5] with me during the evening's performance. Interested, and, I might as well confess, intrigued physically, I too became wise, and played up to her with all the fervor, or so I thought, of an old timer, but Cordelia soon remarked that I was different from mos' of des' sheiks,[6] and when pressed for an explanation brazenly told me in a slightly scandalized and patronizing tone that I had not even felt her legs . . . !

At one o'clock in the morning we strolled through the snowy bleakness of one hundred and forty-fourth street between Lenox and Fifth Avenues to the walk-up tenement flat in which she lived, and after stamping the snow from our feet, pushed through the double outside doors, and followed the dismal hallway to the rear of the building where we began the tedious climbing of the crooked, creaking, inconveniently narrow stairway. Cordelia had informed me earlier in the evening that she lived on the top floor—four flights up east side rear—and on our way we rested at each floor and at each half way landing, rested long enough to mingle the snowy dampness of our respective coats, and to hug clumsily while our lips met in an animal kiss.

Finally only another half flight remained, and instead of proceeding as was usual after our amorous demonstration I abruptly drew away from her, opened my overcoat, plunged my hand into my pants pocket, and drew out two crumpled one dollar bills which I handed to her, and then, while she stared at me foolishly, I muttered good-night, confusedly pecked her on her cold brown cheek, and darted down into the creaking darkness.

Six months later I was taking two friends of mine, lately from the provinces, to a Saturday night house-rent party[7] in a well known whore house on one hundred and thirty-fourth street near Lenox Avenue. The place as we entered seemed to be a chaotic riot of raucous noise and clashing color all rhythmically merging in the red, smoke filled room. And there I saw Cordelia savagely careening in a drunken abortion of the Charleston and surrounded by a perspiring circle of handclapping enthusiasts. Finally fatigued, she whirled into an abrupt finish, and stopped so that she stared directly into my face, but being dizzy from the calisthenic turns and the cauterizing liquor she doubted that her eyes recognized someone out of the past, and, visibly trying to sober herself, languidly began to dance a slow drag with a lean hipped pimply faced yellow man who had walked between her and me. At last he released her, and seeing that she was about to

5. Making out.
6. "Most of these sheiks," i.e., operators.
7. A rent party was one where guests paid an entrance fee, used by the tenants to help pay the rent that month.

leave the room I rushed forward calling Cordelia?—as if I was not yet sure who it was. Stopping in the doorway, she turned to see who had called, and finally recognizing me said simply, without the least trace of emotion,—'Lo kid. . . .

And without another word turned her back and walked into the hall to where she joined four girls standing there. Still eager to speak, I followed and heard one of the girls ask: Who's the dicty[8] kid? . . .

And Cordelia answered: The guy who gimme ma' firs' two bucks. . . .

Emma Lou

More acutely than ever before Emma Lou began to feel that her luscious black complexion was somewhat of a liability, and that her marked color variation from the other people in her environment was a decided curse. Not that she minded being black, being a Negro necessitated having a colored skin, but she did mind being too black. She couldn't understand why such should be the case, couldn't comprehend the cruelty of the natal attenders who had allowed her to be dipped, as it were, in indigo ink when there were so many more pleasing colors on nature's palette. Biologically, it wasn't necessary either; her mother was quite fair, so was her mother's mother, and her mother's brother, and her mother's brother's son; but then none of them had had a black man for a father. Why *had* her mother married a black man? Surely there had been some eligible brown-skin men around. She didn't particularly desire to have had a "high yaller"[1] father, but for her sake certainly some more happy medium could have been found.

She wasn't the only person who regretted her darkness either. It was an acquired family characteristic, this moaning and grieving over the color of her skin. Everything possible had been done to alleviate the unhappy condition, every suggested agent had been employed, but her skin, despite bleachings, scourgings, and powderings, had remained black—fast black—as nature had planned and effected.

She should have been born a boy, then color of skin wouldn't have mattered so much, for wasn't her mother always saying that a black boy could get along, but that a black girl would never know anything but sorrow and disappointment? But she wasn't a boy; she was a girl, and color did matter, mattered so much that she would rather have missed receiving her high school diploma than have to sit as she now sat, the only odd and conspicuous figure on the auditorium platform of the Boise high school. Why had she allowed them to place her in the center of the first row, and why had they

8. Dicty is slang for stuck up or high-class.
1. A term connoting light-colored skin.

The Blacker the Berry, 1929.

insisted upon her dressing entirely in white so that surrounded as she was by similarly attired pale-faced fellow graduates she resembled, not at all remotely, that comic
picture her Uncle Joe had hung in his bedroom? The picture wherein the black, kinky
head of a little red-lipped pickaninny[2] lay like a fly in a pan of milk amid a white expanse
of bedclothes.

But of course she couldn't have worn blue or black when the call was for the wearing of white, even if white was not complementary to her complexion. She would have
been odd-looking anyway no matter what she wore and she would also have been conspicuous, for not only was she the only dark-skinned person on the platform, she was
also the only Negro pupil in the entire school, and had been for the past four years. Well,
thank goodness, the principal would soon be through with his monotonous farewell
address, and she and the other members of her class would advance to the platform center as their names were called and receive the documents which would signify their uncon-
ditional release from public school.

As she thought of these things, Emma Lou glanced at those who sat to the right and
to the left of her. She envied them their obvious elation, yet felt a strange sense of superiority because of her immunity for the moment from an ephemeral mob emotion. Get
a diploma?—What did it mean to her? College? Perhaps. A job?—Perhaps again. She was
going to have a high school diploma, but it would mean nothing to her whatsoever. The
tragedy of her life was that she was too black. Her face and not a slender roll of ribbon-
bound parchment was to be her future identification tag in society. High school diploma
indeed! What she needed was an efficient bleaching agent, a magic cream that would
remove this unwelcome black mask from her face and make her more like her fellow
men.

"Emma Lou Morgan."

She came to with a start. The principal had called her name and stood smiling down
at her benevolently. Some one—she knew it was her Cousin Buddie, stupid imp—
applauded, very faintly, very provokingly. Some one else snickered.

"Emma Lou Morgan."

The principal had called her name again, more sharply than before and his smile was
less benevolent. The girl who sat to the left of her nudged her. There was nothing else
for her to do but to get out of that anchoring chair and march forward to receive her
diploma. But why did the people in the audience have to stare so? Didn't they all know
that Emma Lou Morgan was Boise high school's only nigger student? Didn't they all know—
but what was the use. She had to go get that diploma, so summoning her most insou-
ciant manner, she advanced to the platform center, brought every muscle of her lithe limbs
into play, haughtily extended her shiny black arm to receive the proffered diploma, bowed
a chilly thanks, then holding her arms stiffly at her sides, insolently returned to her seat
in that forboding white line, insolently returned once more to splotch its pale purity and
to mock it with her dark, outlandish difference.

2. A derogatory term for a black child.

———

Emma Lou had been born in a semi-white world, totally surrounded by an all-white one, and those few dark elements that had forced their way in had either been shooed away or else greeted with derisive laughter. It was the custom always of those with whom she came into most frequent contact to ridicule or revile any black person or object. A black cat was a harbinger of bad luck, black crape was the insignia of mourning, and black people were either evil niggers with poisonous blue gums or else typical vaudeville darkies. It seemed as if the people in her world never went halfway in their recognition or reception of things black, for these things seemed always to call forth only the most extreme emotional reactions. They never provoked mere smiles or mere melancholy, rather they were the signal either for boisterous guffaws or pain-induced and tear-attended grief.

Emma Lou had been becoming increasingly aware of this for a long time, but her immature mind had never completely grasped its full, and to her, tragic significance. First there had been the case of her father, old black Jim Morgan they called him, and Emma Lou had often wondered why it was that he of all the people she heard discussed by her family should always be referred to as if his very blackness condemned him to receive no respect from his fellow men.

She had also begun to wonder if it was because of his blackness that he had never been in evidence as far as she knew. Inquiries netted very unsatisfactory answers. "Your father is no good." "He left your mother, deserted her shortly after you were born." And these statements were always prefixed or followed by some epithet such as "dirty black no-gooder" or "durn his onery black hide." There was in fact only one member of the family who did not speak of her father in this manner, and it was her Uncle Joe, who was also the only person in the family to whom she really felt akin, because he alone never seemed to regret, to bemoan, or to ridicule her blackness of skin. It was her grandmother who did all the regretting, her mother who did the bemoaning, her Cousin Buddie and her playmates, both white and colored, who did the ridiculing.

Emma Lou's maternal grandparents, Samuel and Maria Lightfoot, were both mulatto products of slave-day promiscuity between male masters and female chattel. Neither had been slaves, their own parents having been granted their freedom because of their rather close connections with the white branch of the family tree. These freedmen had migrated into Kansas with their children, and when these children had grown up they in turn had joined the westward-ho parade of that current era, and finally settled in Boise, Idaho. . . .

———

Summer vacation was nearly over and it had not yet been decided what to do with Emma Lou now that she had graduated from high school. She herself gave no help nor offered any suggestions. As it was, she really did not care what became of her. After all it didn't seem to matter. There was no place in the world for a girl as black as she anyway. Her grandmother had assured her that she would never find a husband worth a dime, and her mother had said again and again, "Oh, if you had only been a boy!" until Emma Lou had often wondered why it was that people were not able to effect a change of sex or at least a change of complexion.

It was her Uncle Joe who finally prevailed upon her mother to send her to the University of Southern California in Los Angeles. There, he reasoned, she would find a larger and more intelligent social circle. In a city the size of Los Angeles there were Negroes of every class, color, and social position. Let Emma Lou go there where she would not be as far away from home as if she were to go to some eastern college.

Jane and Maria, while not agreeing entirely with what Joe said, were nevertheless glad that at last something which seemed adequate and sensible could be done for Emma Lou. She was to take the four year college course, receive a bachelor degree in education, then go South to teach. That, they thought, was a promising future, and for once in the eighteen years of Emma Lou's life every one was satisfied in some measure. Even Emma Lou grew elated over the prospects of the trip. Her Uncle Joe's insistence upon the differences of social contacts in larger cities intrigued her. Perhaps he was right after all in continually reasserting to them that as long as one was a Negro, one's specific color had little to do with one's life. Salvation depended upon the individual. And he also told Emma Lou, during one of their usual private talks, that it was only in small cities one encountered stupid color prejudice such as she had encountered among the blue vein circle in her home town.

"People in large cities," he had said, "are broad. They do not have time to think of petty things. The people in Boise are fifty years behind the times, but you will find that Los Angeles is one of the world's greatest and most modern cities, and you will be happy there."

On arriving in Los Angeles, Emma Lou was so busy observing the colored inhabitants that she had little time to pay attention to other things. Palm trees and wild geraniums were pleasant to behold, and such strange phenomena as pepper trees and century plants had to be admired. They were very obvious and they were also strange and beautiful, but they impinged upon only a small corner of Emma Lou's consciousness. She was minutely aware of them, necessarily took them in while passing, viewing the totality without pondering over or lingering to praise their stylistic details. They were, in this instance, exquisite theatrical props, rendered insignificant by a more strange and a more beautiful human pageant. For to Emma Lou, who, in all her life, had never seen over five hundred Negroes, the spectacle presented by a community containing over fifty thousand, was sufficient to make relatively commonplace many more important and charming things than the far famed natural scenery of Southern California.

She had arrived in Los Angeles a week before registration day at the university, and had spent her time in being shown and seeing the city. But whenever these sightseeing excursions took her away from the sections where Negroes lived, she immediately lost all interest in what she was being shown. The Pacific Ocean in itself did not cause her heart beat to quicken, nor did the roaring of its waves find an emotional echo within her. But on coming upon Bruce's Beach for colored people near Redondo, or the little strip of sandied shore they had appropriated for themselves at Santa Monica, the Pacific

Ocean became an intriguing something to contemplate as a background for their activities. Everything was interesting as it was patronized, reflected through, or acquired by Negroes.

Her Uncle Joe had been right. Here, in the colored social circles of Los Angeles, Emma Lou was certain that she would find many suitable companions, intelligent, broad-minded people of all complexions, intermixing and being too occupied otherwise to worry about either their own skin color or the skin color of those around them. Her Uncle Joe had said that Negroes were Negroes whether they happened to be yellow, brown, or black, and a conscious effort to eliminate the darker elements would neither prove nor solve anything. There was nothing quite so silly as the creed of the blue veins: "Whiter and whiter, every generation. The nearer white you are the more white people will respect you. Therefore all light Negroes marry light Negroes. Continue to do so generation after generation, and eventually white people will accept this racially bastard aristocracy, thus enabling those Negroes who really matter to escape the social and economic inferiority of the American Negro."

Such had been the credo of her grandmother and of her mother and of their small circle of friends in Boise. But Boise was a provincial town, given to the molding of provincial people with provincial minds. Boise was a backwoods town out of the main stream of modern thought and progress. Its people were cramped and narrow, their intellectual concepts stereotyped and static. Los Angeles was a happy contrast in all respects.

On registration day, Emma Lou rushed out to the campus of the University of Southern California one hour before the registrar's office was scheduled to open. She spent the time roaming around, familiarizing herself with the layout of the campus and learning the names of the various buildings, some old and vineclad, others new and shiny in the sun, and watching the crowds of laughing students, rushing to and fro, greeting one another and talking over their plans for the coming school year. But her main reason for such an early arrival on the campus had been to find some of her fellow Negro students. She had heard that there were to be quite a number enrolled, but in all her hour's stroll she saw not one, and finally somewhat disheartened she got into the line stretched out in front of the registrar's office, and, for the moment, became engrossed in becoming a college freshman.

All the while, though, she kept searching for a colored face, but it was not until she had been duly signed up as a student and sent in search of her advisor that she saw one. Then three colored girls had sauntered into the room where she was having a conference with her advisor, sauntered in, arms interlocked, greeted her advisor, then sauntered out again. Emma Lou had wanted to rush after them—to introduce herself, but of course it had been impossible under the circumstances. She had immediately taken a liking to all three, each of whom was what is known in the parlance of the black belt as high brown, with modishly-shingled bobbed hair and well formed bodies, fashionably attired in flashy sport garments. From then on Emma Lou paid little attention to the business of choosing subjects and class hours, so little attention in fact that the advisor thought her exceptionally tractable and somewhat dumb. But she liked students to come that way. It made the task of being advisor easy. One just made out the program to suit oneself, and had no tedious explanations to make as to why the student could not have such and such a subject at such and such an hour, and why such and such a professor's class was already full.

After her program had been made out, Emma Lou was directed to the bursar's office to pay her fees. While going down the stairs she almost bumped into two dark-brown-skinned boys, obviously brothers if not twins, arguing as to where they should go next. One insisted that they should go back to the registrar's office. The other was being equally insistent that they should go to the gymnasium and make an appointment for their required physical examination. Emma Lou boldly stopped when she saw them, hoping they would speak, but they merely glanced up at her and continued their argument, bringing cards and pamphlets out of their pockets for reference and guidance. Emma Lou wanted to introduce herself to them, but she was too bashful to do so. She wasn't yet used to going to school with other Negro students, and she wasn't exactly certain how one went about becoming acquainted. But she finally decided that she had better let the advances come from the others, especially if they were men. There was nothing forward about her, and since she was a stranger it was no more than right that the old-timers should make her welcome. Still, if these had been girls . . . , but they weren't, so she continued her way down the stairs.

In the bursar's office, she was somewhat overjoyed at first to find that she had fallen into line behind another colored girl who turned around immediately, and, after saying hello, announced in a loud, harsh voice:

"My feet are sure some tired!"

Emma Lou was so taken aback that she couldn't answer. People in college didn't talk that way. But meanwhile the girl was continuing:

"Ain't this registration a mess?"

Two white girls who had fallen into line behind Emma Lou snickered. Emma Lou answered by shaking her head. The girl continued:

"I've been standin' in line and climbin' stairs and talkin' and a-signin' till I'm just 'bout done for."

"It is tiresome," Emma Lou returned softly, hoping the girl would take a hint and lower her own strident voice. But she didn't.

"Tiresome ain't no name for it," she declared more loudly than ever before, then, "Is you a new student?"

"I am," answered Emma Lou, putting much emphasis on the "I am."

She wanted the white people who were listening to know that she knew her grammar if this other person didn't. "Is you," indeed! If this girl was a specimen of the Negro students with whom she was to associate, she most certainly did not want to meet another one. But it couldn't be possible that all of them—those three girls and those two boys for instance—were like this girl. Emma Lou was unable to imagine how such a person had ever gotten out of high school. Where on earth could she have gone to high school? Surely not in the North. Then she must be a southerner. That's what she was, a southerner—Emma Lou curled her lips a little—no wonder the colored people in Boise spoke as they did about southern Negroes and wished that they would stay South. Imagine any one preparing to enter college saying "Is you," and, to make it worse, right before all these white people, these staring white people, so eager and ready to laugh. Emma Lou's face burned.

"Two mo', then I goes in my sock."[3]

Emma Lou was almost at the place where she was ready to take even this statement literally, and was on the verge of leaving the line. Supposing this creature did "go in her sock!" God forbid!

"Wonder where all the spades[4] keep themselves? I ain't seen but two 'sides you."

"I really do not know," Emma Lou returned precisely and chillily. She had no intentions of becoming friendly with this sort of person. Why she would be ashamed even to be seen on the street with her, dressed as she was in a red-striped sport suit, a white hat, and white shoes and stockings. Didn't she know that black people had to be careful about the colors they affected?

The girl had finally reached the bursar's window and was paying her fees, and loudly differing with the cashier about the total amount due.

"I tell you it ain't that much," she shouted through the window bars. "I figured it up myself before I left home."

The cashier obligingly turned to her adding machine and once more obtained the same total. When shown this, the girl merely grinned, examined the list closely, and said:

"I'm gonna' pay it, but I still think you're wrong."

Finally she moved away from the window, but not before she had turned to Emma Lou and said,

"You're next," and then proceeded to wait until Emma Lou had finished.

Emma Lou vainly sought some way to escape, but was unable to do so, and had no choice but to walk with the girl to the registrar's office where they had their cards stamped in return for the bursar's receipt. This done, they went onto the campus together. Hazel Mason was the girl's name. Emma Lou had fully expected it to be either Hyacinth or Geranium. Hazel was from Texas, Prairie Valley, Texas, and she told Emma Lou that her father, having become quite wealthy when oil had been found on his farm lands, had been enabled to realize two life ambitions—obtain a Packard touring car and send his only daughter to a "fust-class" white school.

Emma Lou had planned to loiter around the campus. She was still eager to become acquainted with the colored members of the student body, and this encounter with the

---

3. Two more people in line ahead of her would be served and then she would "pull money out of her sock" to pay the registration fee, a country phrase. The character is not really going to pull money out of her sock; it is just a figure of speech.

4. A derogatory or vulgar reference to black people. Here it is used as a term of familiarity and is not meant to be derogatory.

crass and vulgar Hazel Mason had only made her the more eager. She resented being approached by any one so flagrantly inferior, any one so noticeably a typical southern darky, who had no business obtruding into the more refined scheme of things. Emma Lou planned to lose her unwelcome companion somewhere on the campus so that she could continue unhindered her quest for agreeable acquaintants.

But Hazel was as anxious to meet some one as was Emma Lou, and having found her was not going to let her get away without a struggle. She, too, was new to this environment and in a way was more lonely and eager for the companionship of her own kind than Emma Lou, for never before had she come into such close contact with so many whites. Her life had been spent only among Negroes. Her fellow pupils and teachers in school had always been colored, and as she confessed to Emma Lou, she couldn't get used "to all these white folks."

"Honey, I was just achin' to see a black face," she had said, and, though Emma Lou was experiencing the same ache, she found herself unable to sympathize with the other girl, for Emma Lou classified Hazel as a barbarian who had most certainly not come from a family of best people. No doubt her mother had been a washerwoman. No doubt she had innumerable relatives and friends all as ignorant and as ugly as she. There was no sense in any one having a face as ugly as Hazel's, and Emma Lou thanked her stars that though she was black, her skin was not rough and pimply, nor was her hair kinky, nor were her nostrils completely flattened out until they seemed to spread all over her face. No wonder people were prejudiced against dark skinned people when they were so ugly, so haphazard in their dress, and so boisterously mannered as was this present specimen. She herself was black, but nevertheless she had come from a good family, and she could easily take her place in a society of the right sort of people.

The two strolled along the lawn-bordered gravel path which led to a vine-covered building at the end of the campus. Hazel never ceased talking. She kept shouting at Emma Lou, shouting all sorts of personal intimacies as if she were desirous of the whole world hearing them. There was no necessity for her to talk so loudly, no necessity for her to afford every one on the crowded campus the chance to stare and laugh at them as they passed. Emma Lou had never before been so humiliated and so embarrassed. She felt that she must get away from her offensive companion. What did she care if she had to hurt her feelings to do so. The more insulting she could be now, the less friendly she would have to be in the future.

"Good-by," she said abruptly, "I must go home." With which she turned away and walked rapidly in the opposite direction. She had only gone a few steps when she was aware of the fact that the girl was following her. She quickened her pace, but the girl caught up with her and grabbing hold of Emma Lou's arm, shouted,

"Whoa there, Sally."[5]

It seemed to Emma Lou as if every one on the campus was viewing and enjoying this minstrel-like performance. Angrily she tried to jerk away, but the girl held fast.

5. A reference to telling a horse to slow down, a country phrase.

"Gal, you sure walk fast. I'm going your way. Come on, let me drive you home in my buggy."

And still holding on to Emma Lou's arm, she led the way to the side street where the students parked their cars. Emma Lou was powerless to resist. The girl didn't give her a chance, for she held tight, then immediately resumed the monologue which Emma Lou's attempted leave-taking had interrupted. They reached the street, Hazel still talking loudly, and making elaborate gestures with her free hand.

"Here we are," she shouted, and releasing Emma Lou's arm, salaamed[6] before a sport model Stutz roadster. "Oscar,"[7] she continued, "meet the new girl friend. Pleased to meetcha, says he. Climb aboard."

And Emma Lou had climbed aboard, perplexed, chagrined, thoroughly angry, and disgusted. What was this little black fool doing with a Stutz roadster? And of course, it would be painted red—Negroes always bedecked themselves and their belongings in ridiculously unbecoming colors and ornaments. It seemed to be a part of their primitive heritage which they did not seem to have sense enough to forget and deny. Black girl—white hat—red and white striped sport suit—white shoes and stockings—red roadster. The picture was complete. All Hazel needed to complete her circus-like appearance, thought Emma Lou, was to have some purple feathers stuck in her hat.

Still talking, the girl unlocked and proceeded to start the car. As she was backing it out of the narrow parking space, Emma Lou heard a chorus of semi-suppressed giggles from a neighboring automobile. In her anger she had failed to notice that there were people in the car parked next to the Stutz. But as Hazel expertly swung her machine around, Emma Lou caught a glimpse of them. They were all colored and they were all staring at her and at Hazel. She thought she recognized one of the girls as being one of the group she had seen earlier that morning, and she did recognize the two brothers she had passed on the stairs. And as the roadster sped away, their laughter echoed in her ears, although she hadn't actually heard it. But she had seen the strain in their faces, and she knew that as soon as she and Hazel were out of sight, they would give free rein to their suppressed mirth.

Although Emma Lou had finished registering, she returned to the university campus on the following morning in order to continue her quest for collegiate companions without the alarming and unwelcome presence of Hazel Mason. She didn't know whether to be sorry for the girl and try to help her or to be disgusted and avoid her. She didn't want to be intimately associated with any such vulgar person. It would damage her own position, cause her to be classified with some one who was in a class by herself, for Emma Lou was certain that there was not, and could not be, any one else in the university just like Hazel. But despite her vulgarity, the girl was not all bad. Her good nature was infectious, and Emma Lou had surmised from her monologue on the day before how utterly unselfish a person she could be and was. All of her store of the world's goods were at

6. Bowed ceremoniously with arms extended in front of her.
7. Oscar is the name Hazel has given to her car.

hand to be used and enjoyed by her friends. There was not, as she had said, "a selfish bone in her body." But even that did not alter the disgusting fact that she was not one who would be welcome by the "right sort of people." Her flamboyant style of dress, her loud voice, her raucous laughter, and her flagrant disregard or ignorance of English grammar seemed inexcusable to Emma Lou, who was unable to understand how such a person could stray so far from the environment in which she rightfully belonged to enter a first class university. Now Hazel, according to Emma Lou, was the type of Negro who should go to a Negro college. There were plenty of them in the South whose standard of scholarship was not beyond her ability. And then, in one of those schools, her darky-like clownishness would not have to be paraded in front of white people, thereby causing discomfort and embarrassment to others of her race, more civilized and circumspect than she.

The problem irritated Emma Lou. She didn't see why it had to be. She had looked forward so anxiously, and so happily to her introductory days on the campus, and now her first experience with one of her fellow colored students had been an unpleasant one. But she didn't intend to let that make her unhappy. She was determined to return to the campus alone, seek out other companions, see whether they accepted or ignored the offending Hazel, and govern herself accordingly.

It was early and there were few people on the campus. The grass was still wet from a heavy overnight dew, and the sun had not yet dispelled the coolness of the early morning. Emma Lou's dress was of thin material and she shivered as she walked or stood in the shade. She had no school business to attend to; there was nothing for her to do but to walk aimlessly about the campus.

In another hour, Emma Lou was pleased to see that the campus walks were becoming crowded, and that the side streets surrounding the campus were now heavy with student traffic. Things were beginning to awaken. Emma Lou became jubilant and walked with jaunty step from path to path, from building to building. It then occurred to her that she had been told that there were more Negro students enrolled in the School of Pharmacy than in any other department of the university, so finding the Pharmacy building she began to wander through its crowded hallways.

Almost immediately, she saw a group of five Negro students, three boys and two girls, standing near a water fountain. She was both excited and perplexed, excited over the fact that she was so close to those she wished to find, and perplexed because she did not know how to approach them. Had there been only one person standing there, the matter would have been comparatively easy. She could have approached with a smile and said, "Good morning." The person would have returned her greeting and it would then have been a simple matter to get acquainted.

But five people in one bunch, all known to one another and all chatting intimately together!—it would seem too much like an intrusion to go bursting into their gathering—too forward and too vulgar. Then, there was nothing she could say after having said "good morning." One just didn't break into a group of five and say, "I'm Emma Lou Morgan, a new student, and I want to make friends with you." No, she couldn't do that. She would just smile as she passed, smile graciously and friendly. They would know that she was a stranger, and her smile would assure them that she was anxious to make friends, anxious to become a welcome addition to their group.

One of the group of five had sighted Emma Lou as soon as she had sighted them:

"Who's this?" queried Helen Wheaton, a senior in the College of Law.

"Some new 'pick,'[8] I guess," answered Bob Armstrong, who was Helen's fiancé and a senior in the School of Architecture.

"I bet she's going to take Pharmacy," whispered Amos Blaine.

"She's hottentot[9] enough to take something," mumbled Tommy Brown. "Thank God, she won't be in any of our classes, eh Amos?"

Emma Lou was almost abreast of them now. They lowered their voices, and made a pretense of mumbled conversation among themselves. Only Verne Davis looked directly at her and it was she alone who returned Emma Lou's smile.

"Whatcha grinnin' at?" Bob chided Verne as Emma Lou passed out of earshot.

"At the little frosh, of course. She grinned at me. I couldn't stare at her without returning it."

"I don't see how anybody could even look at her without grinning."

"Oh, she's not so bad," said Verne.

"Well, she's bad enough."

"That makes two of them."

"Two of what, Amos?"

"Hottentots, Bob."

"Good grief," exclaimed Tommy, "why don't you recruit some good-looking co-eds out here?"

"We don't choose them," Helen returned.

"I'm going out to the Southern Branch where the sight of my fellow female students won't give me dyspepsia."

"Ta-ta, Amos," said Verne, "and you needn't bother to sit in my car any more if you think us so terrible." She and Helen walked away, leaving the boys to discuss the sad days which had fallen upon the campus.

Emma Lou, of course, knew nothing of all this. She had gone her way rejoicing. One of the students had noticed her, had returned her smile. This getting acquainted was going to be an easy matter after all. It was just necessary that she exercise a little patience. One couldn't expect people to fall all over one without some preliminary advances. True, she was a stranger, but she would show them in good time that she was worthy of their attention, that she was a good fellow and a well-bred individual quite prepared to be accepted by the best people.

She strolled out on to campus again trying to find more prospective acquaintances. The sun was warm now, the grass dry, and the campus overcrowded. There was an infec-

---

8. "Pick" is short for pickaninny, a derogatory reference to black children from the South.

9. Hottentot is a derisive word for an African.

tious germ of youth and gladness abroad to which Emma Lou could not remain immune. Already she was certain that she felt the presence of that vague something known as "college spirit." It seemed to enter into her, to make her jubilant and set her every nerve tingling. This was no time for sobriety. It was the time for youth's blood to run hot, the time for love and sport and wholesome fun.

Then Emma Lou saw a solitary Negro girl seated on a stone bench. It did not take her a second to decide what to do. Here was her chance. She would make friends with this girl and should she happen to be a new student, they could become friends and together find their way into the inner circle of those colored students who really mattered.

Emma Lou was essentially a snob. She had absorbed this trait from the very people who had sought to exclude her from their presence. All of her life she had heard talk of "the right sort of people," and of "the people who really mattered," and from these phrases she had formed a mental image of those to whom they applied. Hazel Mason most certainly could not be included in either of these categories. Hazel was just a vulgar little nigger from down South. It was her kind, who, when they came North, made it hard for the colored people already resident there. It was her kind who knew nothing of the social niceties or the polite conventions. In their own home they had been used only to coarse work and coarser manners. And they had been forbidden the chance to have intimate contact in schools and in public with white people from whom they might absorb some semblance of culture. When they did come North and get a chance to go to white schools, white theaters, and white libraries, they were too unused to them to appreciate what they were getting, and could be expected to continue their old way of life in an environment where such a way was decidedly out of place.

Emma Lou was determined to become associated only with those people who really mattered, northerners like herself or superior southerners, if there were any, who were different from whites only in so far as skin color was concerned. . . .

Arna
Bontemps

(1902–1973)

Arnaud Wendell Bontemps was born on October 13, 1902, in Alexandria, Louisiana, to Maria Carolina Pembroke, a former schoolteacher, and Paul Bismark Bontemps, a brick mason. When Bontemps was three, his family moved to Los Angeles to avoid the racism of the South. Bontemps's mother died when he was twelve. From 1917 to 1920 Bontemps was enrolled by his father in San Fernando Academy, a predominantly white boarding school run by the Seventh-Day Adventist Church. In 1923 he graduated from Pacific Union College, also run by the church.

In 1924 he began teaching at the Seventh-Day Adventist Harlem Academy in New York. That same year, at the age of twenty-one, Bontemps published his first poem, "Hope," in *The Crisis*. He quickly developed a literary reputation, winning three important poetry prizes: Pushkin Awards from *Opportunity* for "Golgotha Is a Mountain" (1926) and "The Return" (1927) and first prize in the 1927 poetry contest sponsored by *The Crisis* for his poem "Nocturne at Bethesda."

Bontemps married Alberta Johnson in 1926; the couple had six children. Although Bontemps was enjoying literary success, his literary pursuits created conflict with his superiors at Harlem Academy. In fact, after the publication of his first novel, *God Sends Sunday* (1931), church officials transferred him against his will to another Adventist school, Oakwood Junior College in Huntsville, Alabama. In 1932 he won a prize from *Opportunity* for his short story "A Summer Tragedy." This same year he published his first children's book, *Popo and Fina*, which he cowrote with Langston Hughes. His second children's book, *You Can't Pet a Possum*, came out in 1934, which was also his last year at Oakwood Junior College. He took a teaching assignment at Shiloh Academy in Chicago, working there from 1935 to 1937. While there he published his second and most respected novel, *Black Thunder* (1936). He next went to work for the Illinois Writers' Project, part of the Works Progress Administration. There he met white writer Jack Conroy, with whom he later frequently collaborated. In 1939 his novel *Drums at Dusk* was published and the play *St. Louis Woman* was written; this was a musical adaption of his first novel, which he revised with the assistance of Countee Cullen. Johnny Mercer and Harold Arlen wrote the music and lyrics.

In 1943 Bontemps earned his master's degree in library science from the University of Chicago. He then became librarian at Fisk University in Nashville, where he remained until 1965. In 1966 Bontemps taught courses at the University of Illinois–Chicago Circle and in 1969 he became a lecturer and curator of the James Weldon Johnson Collection at Yale University. He remained at Yale until 1971, at which time he returned to Nashville. He died on June 4, 1973, of a heart attack.

Bontemps was an important chronicler of the Harlem Renaissance, and the author or editor of thirty-three books. Among his most significant other works are a collection of poetry, *Personals* (1963), *The Fast Sooner Hound* (1942), written with Jack Conroy, *The Story of the Negro* (1948), for which he won the Jane Addams Children's Book Award, and *Chariot in the*

Sky (1951). His important anthologies include *The Poetry of the Negro, 1746–1949* (1949), with Langston Hughes; *The Book of Negro Folklore* (1958), with Hughes; and *American Negro Poetry* (1963).

Golgotha Is a Mountain

Golgotha is a mountain, a purple mound
Almost out of sight.
One night they hanged two thieves there,
And another man.
Some women wept heavily that night;
Their tears are flowing still. They have made a river;
Once it covered me.
Then the people went away and left Golgotha
Deserted.
Oh, I've seen many mountains:
Pale purple mountains melting in the evening mists and blurring on the borders of
    the sky.

I climbed old Shasta[1] and chilled my hands in its summer snows.
I rested in the shadow of Popocatepetl[2] and it whispered to me of daring prowess.
I looked upon the Pyrenees[3] and felt the zest of warm exotic nights.
I slept at the foot of Fujiyama[4] and dreamed of legend and of death.
And I've seen other mountains rising from the wistful moors like the breasts of a
    slender maiden.
Who knows the mystery of mountains!
Some of them are awful, others are just lonely.
. . . .

Italy has its Rome and California has San Francisco,
All covered with mountains.
Some think these mountains grew
Like ant hills
Or sand dunes.
That might be so—
I wonder what started them all!
Babylon is a mountain
And so is Nineveh,[5]
With grass growing on them;
Palaces and hanging gardens started them.

1. A mountain in northern California.
2. A volcano in Mexico much loved by the people.
3. A large mountain range between France and Spain.
4. The most famous and best-loved mountain in Japan.
5. Babylon and Nineveh are cities mentioned in the Bible.

I wonder what is under the hills
In Mexico
And Japan!
There are mountains in Africa too.
Treasure is buried there:
Gold and precious stones
And moulded glory.
Lush grass is growing there
Sinking before the wind.
Black men are bowing.
Naked in that grass
Digging with their fingers.
I am one of them:
Those mountains should be ours.
It would be great
To touch the pieces of glory with our hands.
These mute unhappy hills,
Bowed down with broken backs,
Speak often one to another:
"A day is as a year," they cry,
"And a thousand years as one day."
We watched the caravan
That bore our queen to the courts of Solomon;[6]
And when the first slave traders came
We bowed our heads.
"Oh, Brothers, it is not long!
Dust shall yet devour the stones
But we shall be here when they are gone."
Mountains are rising all around me.
Some are so small they are not seen;
Others are large.
All of them get big in time and people forget
What started them at first.
Oh the world is covered with mountains!
Beneath each one there is something buried:
Some pile of wreckage that started it there.
Mountains are lonely and some are awful.

. . . .

One day I will crumble.
They'll cover my heap with dirt and that will make a mountain.
I think it will be Golgotha.

Opportunity, May 1926.

6. This is a reference to the biblical queen of Sheba.

Length of Moon

Then the golden hour
Will tick its last
And the flame will go down in the flower.

A briefer length of moon
Will mark the sea-line and the yellow dune.

Then we may think of this, yet
There will be something forgotten
And something we should forget.

It will be like all things we know:
A stone will fail; a rose is sure to go.

It will be quiet then and we may stay
Long at the picket gate, —
But there will be less to say.

Fire!!, November 1926.

Nocturne at Bethesda

I thought I saw an angel flying low,
I thought I saw the flicker of a wing
Above the mulberry trees, but not again.
Bethesda sleeps. This ancient pool that healed
A host of bearded Jews does not awake.

This pool that once the angels troubled does not move.
No angel stirs it now, no Saviour comes
With healing in His hands to raise the sick
And bid the lame man leap upon the ground.

The golden days are gone. Why do we wait
So long upon the marble steps, blood
Falling from our open wounds? and why
Do our black faces search the empty sky?
Is there something we have forgotten? some precious thing
We have lost, wandering in strange lands?

There was a day, I remember now,
I beat my breast and cried, "Wash me God,
Wash me with a wave of wind upon
The barley; O quiet One, draw near, draw near!

Walk upon the hills with lovely feet
And in the waterfall stand and speak.

"Dip white hands in the lily pool and mourn
Upon the harps still hanging in the trees
Near Babylon along the river's edge,
But oh, remember me, I pray, before
The summer goes and rose leaves lose their red."

The old terror takes my heart, the fear
Of quiet waters and of faint twilights.
There will be better days when I am gone
And healing pools where I cannot be healed.
Fragrant stars will gleam forever and ever
Above the place where I lie desolate.

Yet I hope, still I long to live.
And if there can be returning after death
I shall come back. But it will not be here;
If you want me you must search for me
Beneath the palms of Africa. Or if
I am not there then you may call to me
Across the shining dunes; perhaps I shall
Be following a desert caravan.

I may pass through centuries of death
With quiet eyes, but I'll remember still
A jungle tree with burning scarlet birds.
There is something I have forgotten, some precious thing.
I shall be seeking ornaments of ivory.
I shall be dying for a jungle fruit.

You do not hear, Bethesda.
O still green water in a stagnant pool!
Love abandoned you and me alike.
There was a day you held a rich full moon
Upon your heart and listened to the words
Of men now dead and saw the angels fly.
There is a simple story on your face;
Years have wrinkled you. I know, Bethesda!
You are sad. It is the same with me.

The Crisis, December 1926.

Charles Cullen, *The Black Christ,* 1929

A Black Man Talks of Reaping

I have sown beside all waters in my day.
I planted deep, within my heart the fear
That wind or fowl would take the grain away.
I planted safe against this stark, lean year.

I scattered seed enough to plant the land
In rows from Canada to Mexico
But for my reaping only what the hand
Can hold at once is all that I can show.

Yet what I sowed and what the orchard yields
My brother's sons are gathering stalk and root,
Small wonder then my children glean in fields
They have not sown, and feed on bitter fruit.

Caroling Dusk, 1927.

God Give to Men

God give the yellow man
An easy breeze at blossom time.
Grant his eager, slanting eyes to cover
Every land and dream
Of afterwhile.

Give blue-eyed men their swivel chairs
To whirl in tall buildings.
Allow them many ships at sea,
And on land, soldiers
And policemen.

For black man, God,
No need to bother more
But only fill afresh his meed
Of laughter,
His cup of tears.

God suffer little men
The taste of soul's desire.

Caroling Dusk, 1927.

The Return

1

Once more, listening to the wind and rain,
Once more, you and I, and above the hurting sound
Of these comes back the throbbing of remembered rain,
Treasured rain falling on dark ground.
Once more, huddling birds upon the leaves
And summer trembling on a withered vine.
And once more, returning out of pain,
The friendly ghost that was your love and mine.

2

Darkness brings the jungle to our room:
The throb of rain is the throb of muffled drums.
Darkness hangs our room with pendulums
Of vine and in the gathering gloom
Our walls recede into a denseness of
Surrounding trees. This is a night of love
Retained from those lost nights our fathers slept
In huts; this is a night that must not die.
Let us keep the dance of rain our fathers kept
And tread our dreams beneath the jungle sky.

3

And now the downpour ceases.
Let us go back once more upon the glimmering leaves
And as the throbbing of the drums increases
Shake the grass and dripping boughs of trees.
A dry wind stirs the palm; the old tree grieves.

Time has charged the years: the old days have returned.

Let us dance by metal waters burned
With gold of moon, let us dance
With naked feet beneath the young spice trees.
What was that light, that radiance
On your face?—something I saw when first
You passed beneath the jungle tapestries?

A moment we pause to quench our thirst
Kneeling at the water's edge, the gleam
Upon your face is plain; you have wanted this.
Let us go back and search the tangled dream
And as the muffled drum-beats throb and miss

Remember again how early darkness comes
To dreams and silence to the drums.

Let us go back into the dusk again,
Slow and sad-like following the track
Of blowing leaves and cool white rain
Into the old gray dream, let us go back.
Our walls close about us, we lie and listen
To the noise of the street, the storm and the driven birds.
A question shapes your lips; your eyes glisten
Retaining tears, but there are no more words.

Ebony and Topaz, 1927.

A Summer Tragedy

Old Jeff Patton, the black share farmer, fumbled with his bow tie. His fingers trembled, and the high, stiff collar pinched his throat. A fellow loses his hand for such vanities after thirty or forty years of simple life. Once a year, or maybe twice if there's a wedding among his kin-folks, he may spruce up; but generally fancy clothes do nothing but adorn the wall of the big room and feed the moths. That had been Jeff Patton's experience. He had not worn his stiff-bosomed shirt more than a dozen times in all his married life. His swallowtailed coat lay on the bed beside him, freshly brushed and pressed, but it was as full of holes as the overalls in which he worked on week days. The moths had used it badly. Jeff twisted his mouth into a hideous toothless grimace as he contended with the obstinate bow. He stamped his good foot and decided to give up the struggle.

"Jennie," he called.

"What's that, Jeff?" His wife's shrunken voice came out of the adjoining room like an echo. It was hardly bigger than a whisper.

"I reckon you'll have to he'p me wid this heah bow tie, baby," he said meekly. "Dog if I can hitch it up."

Her answer was not strong enough to reach him, but presently the old woman came to the door, feeling her way with a stick. She had a wasted, dead-leaf appearance. Her body, as scrawny and gnarled as a stringbean, seemed less than nothing in the ocean of frayed and faded petticoats that surrounded her. These hung an inch or two above the tops of her heavy, unlaced shoes and showed little grotesque piles where the stockings had fallen down from her negligible legs.

"You oughta could do a heap mo' wid a thing like that 'n me—beingst as you got yo' good sight."

Opportunity, June 1933.

"Looks like I oughta could," he admitted. "But ma fingers is gone democrat on me.[1] I get all mixed up in the looking glass an' can't tell whicha way to twist the devilish thing."

Jennie sat on the side of the bed and old Jeff Patton got down on one knee while she tied the bow knot. It was a slow and painful ordeal for each of them in this position. Jeff's bones cracked, his knee ached, and it was only after a half dozen attempts that Jennie worked a semblance of a bow into the tie.

"I got to dress maself now," the old woman whispered. "These is ma old shoes an' stockings, and I ain't so much as unwrapped ma dress."

"Well, don't worry 'bout me no mo', baby," Jeff said. "That 'bout finishes me. All I gotta do now is slip on that old coat 'n ves' an' I'll be fixed to leave."

Jennie disappeared again through the dim passage into the shed room. Being blind was no handicap to her in that black hole. Jeff heard the cane placed against the wall beside the door and knew that his wife was on easy ground. He put on his coat, took a battered top hat from the bed post, and hobbled to the front door. He was ready to travel. As soon as Jennie could get on her Sunday shoes and her old black silk dress, they would start.

Outside the tiny log house the day was warm and mellow with sunshine. A host of wasps was humming with busy excitement in the trunk of a dead sycamore. Gray squirrels were searching through the grass for hickory nuts and blue jays were in the trees, hopping from branch to branch. Pine woods stretched away to the left like a black sea. Among them were scattered scores of log houses like Jeff's, houses of black share farmers. Cows and pigs wandered freely among the trees. There was no danger of loss. Each farmer knew his own stock and knew his neighbor's as well as he knew his neighbor's children.

Down the slope to the right were the cultivated acres on which the colored folks worked. They extended to the river, more than two miles away, and they were today green with the unmade cotton crop. A tiny thread of a road, which passed directly in front of Jeff's place, ran through these green fields like a pencil mark.

Jeff, standing outside the door with his absurd hat in his left hand, surveyed the wide scene tenderly. He had been forty-five years on these acres. He loved them with the unexplained affection that others have for the countries to which they belong.

The sun was hot on his head, his collar still pinched his throat, and the Sunday clothes were intolerably hot. Jeff transferred the hat to his right hand and began fanning with it. Suddenly the whisper that was Jennie's voice came out of the shed room.

"You can bring the car round front whilst you's waitin'," it said feebly. There was a tired pause; then it added, "I'll soon be fixed to go."

"A'right, baby," Jeff answered. "I'll get it in a minute."

But he didn't move. A thought struck him that made his mouth fall open. The mention of the car brought to his mind, with new intensity, the trip he and Jennie were about to take. Fear came into his eyes; excitement took his breath. Lord, Jesus!

---

1. That is, they have minds of their own.

"Jeff . . . Oh Jeff," the old woman's whisper called.

He awakened with a jolt. "Hunh, baby?"

"What you doin'?"

"Nuthin. Jes studyin'. I jes been turnin' things round 'n round in ma mind."

"You could be gettin' the car," she said.

"Oh yes, right away, baby."

He started round to the shed, limping heavily on his bad leg. There were three frizzly chickens in the yard. All his other chickens had been killed or stolen recently. But the frizzly chickens had been saved somehow. That was fortunate indeed, for these curious creatures had a way of devouring "poison" from the yard and in that way protecting against conjure and bad luck and spells. But even the frizzly chickens seemed now to be in a stupor. Jeff thought they had some ailment; he expected all three of them to die shortly.

The shed in which the old model-T Ford stood was only a grass roof held up by four corner poles. It had been built by tremulous hands at a time when the little rattle-trap car had been regarded as a peculiar treasure. And, miraculously, despite wind and downpour, it still stood.

Jeff adjusted the crank and put his weight on it. The engine came to life with a sputter and bang that rattled the old car from radiator to tail light. Jeff hopped into the seat and put his foot on the accelerator. The sputtering and banging increased. The rattling became more violent. That was good. It was good banging, good sputtering and rattling, and it meant that the aged car was still in running condition. She could be depended on for this trip.

Again Jeff's thought halted as if paralyzed. The suggestion of the trip fell into the machinery of his mind like a wrench. He felt dazed and weak. He swung the car out into the yard, made a half turn, and drove around to the front door. When he took his hands off the wheel, he noticed that he was trembling violently. He cut off the motor and climbed to the ground to wait for Jennie.

A few moments later she was at the window, her voice rattling against the pane like a broken shutter.

"I'm ready, Jeff."

He did not answer, but limped into the house and took her by the arm. He led her slowly through the big room, down the step, and across the yard.

"You reckon I'd oughta lock the do'?" he asked softly.

They stopped and Jennie weighed the question. Finally she shook her head.

"Ne' mind the do'," she said. "I don't see no cause to lock up things."

"You right," Jeff agreed. "No cause to lock up."

Jeff opened the door and helped his wife into the car. A quick shudder passed over him. Jesus! Again he trembled.

"How come you shaking so?" Jennie whispered.

"I don't know," he said.

"You mus' be scairt, Jeff."

"No, baby, I ain't scairt."

He slammed the door after her and went around to crank up again. The motor started easily. Jeff wished that it had not been so responsive. He would have liked a few more minutes in which to turn things around in his head. As it was, with Jennie chiding him about being afraid, he had to keep going. He swung the car into the little pencilmark road and started off toward the river, driving very slowly, very cautiously.

Chugging across the green countryside, the small, battered Ford seemed tiny indeed. Jeff felt a familiar excitement, a thrill, as they came down the first slope to the immense levels on which the cotton was growing. He could not help reflecting that the crops were good. He knew what that meant, too; he had made forty-five of them with his own hands. It was true that he had worn out nearly a dozen mules, but that was the fault of old man Stevenson, the owner of the land. Major Stevenson had the odd notion that one mule was all a share farmer needed to work a thirty-acre plot. It was an expensive notion, the way it killed mules from overwork, but the old man held to it. Jeff thought it killed a good many share farmers as well as mules, but he had no sympathy for them. He had always been strong, and he had been taught to have no patience with weakness in men. Women or children might be tolerated if they were puny, but a weak man was a curse. Of course, his own children—

Jeff's thought halted there. He and Jennie never mentioned their dead children any more. And naturally he did not wish to dwell upon them in his mind. Before he knew it, some remark would slip out of his mouth and that would make Jennie feel blue. Perhaps she would cry. A woman like Jennie could not easily throw off the grief that comes from losing five grown children within two years. Even Jeff was still staggered by the blow. His memory had not been much good recently. He frequently talked to himself. And, although he had kept it a secret, he knew that his courage had left him. He was terrified by the least unfamiliar sound at night. He was reluctant to venture far from home in the daytime. And that habit of trembling when he felt fearful was now far beyond his control. Sometimes he became afraid and trembled without knowing what had frightened him. The feeling would just come over him like a chill.

The car rattled slowly over the dusty road. Jennie sat erect and silent, with a little absurd hat pinned to her hair. Her useless eyes seemed very large and very white in their deep sockets. Suddenly Jeff heard her voice, and he inclined his head to catch the words.

"Is we passed Delia Moore's house yet?" she asked.

"Not yet," he said.

"You must be drivin' mighty slow, Jeff."

"We jes as well take our time, baby."

There was a pause. A little puff of steam was coming out of the radiator of the car. Heat wavered above the hood. Delia Moore's house was nearly half a mile away. After a moment Jennie spoke again.

"You ain't really scairt, is you, Jeff?"

"Nah, baby, I ain't scairt."

"You know how we agreed—we gotta keep on goin'."

Jewels of perspiration appeared on Jeff's forehead. His eyes rounded, blinked, became fixed on the road.

"I don't know," he said with a shiver. "I reckon it's the only thing to do."

"Hm."

A flock of guinea fowls, pecking in the road, were scattered by the passing car. Some of them took to their wings; others hid under bushes. A blue jay, swaying on a leafy twig, was annoying a roadside squirrel. Jeff held an even speed till he came near Delia's place. Then he slowed down noticeably.

Delia's house was really no house at all, but an abandoned store building converted into a dwelling. It sat near a crossroads, beneath a single black cedar tree. There Delia, a catlike old creature of Jennie's age, lived alone. She had been there more years than anybody could remember, and long ago had won the disfavor of such women as Jennie. For in her young days Delia had been gayer, yellower, and saucier than seemed proper in those parts. Her ways with menfolks had been dark and suspicious. And the fact that she had had as many husbands as children did not help her reputation.

"Yonder's old Delia," Jeff said as they passed.

"What she doin'?"

"Jes sittin' in the do'," he said.

"She see us?"

"Hm," Jeff said. "Musta did."

That relieved Jennie. It strengthened her to know that her old enemy had seen her pass in her best clothes. That would give the old she-devil something to chew her gums and fret about, Jennie thought. Wouldn't she have a fit if she didn't find out? Old evil Delia! This would be just the thing for her. It would pay her back for being so evil. It would also pay her, Jennie thought, for the way she used to grin at Jeff—long ago when her teeth were good.

The road became smooth and red, and Jeff could tell by the smell of the air that they were nearing the river. He could see the rise where the road turned and ran along parallel to the stream. The car chugged on monotonously. After a long silent spell, Jennie leaned against Jeff and spoke.

"How many bale o' cotton you think we got standin'?" she said.

Jeff wrinkled his forehead as he calculated.

"'Bout twenty-five, I reckon."

"How many you make las' year?"

"Twenty-eight," he said. "How come you ask that?"

"I's jes thinkin'," Jennie said quietly.

"It don't make a speck o' diffence though," Jeff reflected. "If we get much or if we get little, we still gonna be in debt to old man Stevenson when he gets through counting up agin us. It's took us a long time to learn that."

Jennie was not listening to these words. She had fallen into a trance-like meditation. Her lips twitched. She chewed her gums and rubbed her old gnarled hands nervously.

Suddenly, she leaned forward, buried her face in the nervous hands, and burst into tears. She cried aloud in a dry, cracked voice that suggested the rattle of fodder on dead stalks. She cried aloud like a child, for she had never learned to suppress a genuine sob. Her slight old frame shook heavily and seemed hardly able to sustain such violent grief.

"What's the matter, baby?" Jeff asked awkwardly. "Why you cryin' like all that?"

"I's jes thinkin'," she said.

"So you the one what's scairt now, hunh?"

"I ain't scairt, Jeff. I's jes thinkin' 'bout leavin' eve'thing like this—eve'thing we been used to. It's right sad-like."

Jeff did not answer, and presently Jennie buried her face again and continued crying.

The sun was almost overhead. It beat down furiously on the dusty wagon path road, on the parched roadside grass, and the tiny battered car. Jeff's hands, gripping the wheel, became wet with perspiration; his forehead sparkled. Jeff's lips parted and his mouth shaped a hideous grimace. His face suggested the face of a man being burned. But the torture passed and his expression softened again.

"You mustn't cry, baby," he said to his wife. "We gotta be strong. We can't break down."

Jennie waited a few seconds, then said, "You reckon we oughta do it, Jeff? You reckon we oughta go 'head an' do it really?"

Jeff's voice choked; his eyes blurred. He was terrified to hear Jennie say the thing that had been in his mind all morning. She had egged him on when he had wanted more than anything in the world to wait, to reconsider, to think things over a little longer. Now *she* was getting cold feet. Actually, there was no need of thinking the question through again. It would only end in making the same painful decision once more. Jeff knew that. There was no need of fooling around longer.

"We jes as well to do like we planned," he said. "They ain't nuthin else for us now— it's the bes' thing."

Jeff thought of the handicaps, the near impossibility, of making another crop with his leg bothering him more and more each week. Then there was always the chance that he would have another stroke, like the one that had made him lame. Another one might kill him. The least it could do would be to leave him helpless. Jeff gasped . . . Lord, Jesus! He could not bear to think of being helpless, like a baby, on Jennie's hands. Frail, blind Jennie.

The little pounding motor of the car worked harder and harder. The puff of steam from the cracked radiator became larger. Jeff realized that they were climbing a little rise. A moment later the road turned abruptly and he looked down upon the face of the river.

"Jeff."

"Hunh?"

"Is that the water I hear?"

"Hm. Tha's it."

"Well, which way you goin' now?"

"Down this-a way," he answered. "The road runs 'longside o' the water a lil piece."

She waited a while calmly. Then she said, "Drive faster."

"A'right, baby," Jeff said.

The water roared in the bed of the river. It was fifty or sixty feet below the level of the road. Between the road and the water there was a long smooth slope, sharply inclined. The slope was dry; the clay had been hardened by prolonged summer heat. The water below, roaring in a narrow channel, was noisy and wild.

"Jeff."

"Hunh?"

"How far you goin'?"

"Jes a lil piece down the road."

"You ain't scairt is you, Jeff?"

"Nah, baby," he said trembling. "I ain't scairt."

"Remember how we planned it, Jeff. We gotta do it like we said. Bravelike."

"Hm."

Jeff's brain darkened. Things suddenly seemed unreal, like figures in a dream. Thoughts swam in his mind foolishly, hysterically, like little blind fish in a pool within a dense cave. They rushed, crossed one another, jostled, collided, retreated, and rushed again. Jeff soon became dizzy. He shuddered violently and turned to his wife.

"Jennie, I can't do it. I can't." His voice broke pitifully.

She did not appear to be listening. All the grief had gone from her face. She sat erect, her unseeing eyes wide open, strained and frightful. Her glossy black skin had become dull. She seemed as thin and as sharp and bony as a starved bird. Now, having suffered and endured the sadness of tearing herself away from beloved things, she showed no anguish. She was absorbed with her own thoughts, and she didn't even hear Jeff's voice shouting in her ear.

Jeff said nothing more. For an instant there was light in his cavernous brain. That chamber was, for less than a second, peopled by characters he knew and loved. They were simple, healthy creatures, and they behaved in a manner that he could understand. They had quality. But since he had already taken leave of them long ago, the remembrance did not break his heart again. Young Jeff Patton was among them, the Jeff Patton of fifty years ago who went down to New Orleans with a crowd of country boys to the Mardi Gras doings. The gay young crowd—boys with candy-striped shirts and rouged brown girls in noisy silks—was like a picture in his head. Yet it did not make him sad. On that very trip Slim Burns had killed Joe Beasley—the crowd had been broken up. Since then Jeff Patton's world had been the Greenbrier Plantation. If there had been other Mardi Gras carnivals, he had not heard of them. Since then there had been no time; the years had fallen on him like waves. Now he was old, worn out. Another paralytic stroke like the one he had already suffered would put him on his back for keeps. In that condition, with a frail blind woman to look after him, he would be worse off than if he were dead.

Suddenly Jeff's hands became steady. He actually felt brave. He slowed down the motor of the car and carefully pulled off the road. Below, the water of the stream boomed, a soft thunder in the deep channel. Jeff ran the car onto the clay slope, pointed it directly toward the stream, and put his foot heavily on the accelerator. The little car leaped furiously down the steep incline toward the water. The movement was nearly as swift and direct as a fall. The two old black folks, sitting quietly side by side, showed no excitement. In another instant the car hit the water and dropped immediately out of sight.

A little later it lodged in the mud of a shallow place. One wheel of the crushed and upturned little Ford became visible above the rushing water.

Countee Cullen

(1903-1946)

Countee Cullen was one of the most honored poets of the Harlem Renaissance, winning every major prize of his era. He has come to symbolize the essence of what W.E.B. Du Bois meant by the term the "Talented Tenth," the most talented ten percent of the African American community, as well as the conservative aesthetics of lyric poetry. Born Countee Porter on May 30, 1903, to Elizabeth Lucas in Louisville, Kentucky, Countee was given over to the care of his paternal grandmother, Elizabeth Porter, after his father disappeared and raised in Baltimore, then Harlem. Although his mother stayed in contact with Cullen throughout his life, he never lived with her; he remained with his grandmother until her death in 1918. At age thirteen he was adopted by Reverend Frederick A. Cullen, founder and pastor of the Salem Methodist Episcopal Church of Harlem and his wife, Carolyn. He attended the predominantly white public school, De Witt Clinton High School. Upon his graduation in 1922, he enrolled in New York University and graduated Phi Beta Kappa in 1925.

While attending N.Y.U., Cullen began publishing in national journals: *Opportunity*, *The Crisis*, *Bookman*, *Poetry*, and *American Mercury*. He also won prizes in the American undergraduate Witter Bynner Poetry Contests and in the contests run by *The Crisis* and *Opportunity*. In fact, by his senior year in college, Cullen had secured a contract from Harper and Brothers to publish his first poetry collection, *Color* (1925). The success of the volume led Alain Locke to include several of his poems in the landmark anthology *The New Negro* (1925) and established him as a major figure of the Harlem Renaissance. In 1926 Cullen graduated with an M.A. in English from Harvard and became the assistant editor of *Opportunity*, a position he held until 1928. The year 1927 was a banner one for Cullen as he received the first literature award from the William Harmon Foundation and published two volumes of poetry, *Copper Sun* and *The Ballad of the Brown Girl*, and edited *Caroling Dusk*, a touchstone African American poetry anthology. The following year Cullen received a Guggenheim Fellowship to study in Paris, a city to which he would return several times after 1930. This same year he married Nina Yolande Du Bois, daughter of W.E.B. Du Bois, in an elaborate wedding attended by one thousand of the "Talented Tenth." Two months after the wedding, Cullen left for France with his close companion Harold Jackman and without his bride. The couple formalized the divorce the same year. He was married a second time, to Ida Mae Robertson in 1940. Despite these two marriages, it is commonly agreed that Cullen was probably bisexual and that his closest relationship was with Harold Jackman, to whom he dedicated his most famous poem, "Heritage." Jackman was his lifelong confidant and companion.

By 1929, with the publication of *The Black Christ*, illustrated by his brother Charles, Cullen's career was in decline; reviewers commented on his lack of development, though he continued to be heralded by the era's artistic leaders. His only novel, *One Way to Heaven* (1932), was poorly received. Cullen worked with Harry Hamilton to adapt the novel into a play, but it was never professionally produced. In 1934 he began teaching French and later creative writing at Frederick Douglass Junior High School in New York, where he remained until his death at age forty-two from uremic poisoning.

Cullen's other works include a translation of Euripides, *The Medea and Some Poems* (1935) and two collections of children's stories, *The Lost Zoo* (1940) and *My Lives and How I Lost Them* (1942). Cullen collaborated with Arna Bontemps on the dramatization of Bontemps's novel *God Sends Sunday* into the play *St. Louis Woman*, but he died two and a half months before it was performed. *On These I Stand: An Anthology of the Best Poems of Countee Cullen* (1947), a collection Cullen had arranged, was published posthumously.

Heritage

(*For Harold Jackman*)[1]

What is Africa to me:
Copper sun or scarlet sea,
Jungle star or jungle track,
Strong bronzed men, or regal black
Women from whose loins I sprang
When the birds of Eden sang?
One three centuries removed
From the scenes his fathers loved,
Spicy grove, cinnamon tree,
What is Africa to me?

So I lie, who all day long
Want no sound except the song
Sung by wild barbaric birds
Goading massive jungle herds,
Juggernauts of flesh that pass
Trampling tall defiant grass
Where young forest lovers lie,
Plighting troth beneath the sky.
So I lie, who always hear,
Though I cram against my ear
Both my thumbs, and keep them there,
Great drums throbbing through the air.
So I lie, whose fount of pride,
Dear distress, and joy allied,
Is my somber flesh and skin,
With the dark blood dammed within
Like great pulsing tides of wine

---

1. Harold Jackman was the person to whom Cullen was closest.

That, I fear, must burst the fine
Channels of the chafing net
Where they surge and foam and fret.

Africa? A book one thumbs
Listlessly, till slumber comes.
Unremembered are her bats
Circling through the night, her cats
Crouching in the river reeds,
Stalking gentle flesh that feeds
By the river brink; no more
Does the bugle-throated roar
Cry that monarch claws have leapt
From the scabbards where they slept.
Silver snakes that once a year
Doff the lovely coats you wear,
Seek no covert in your fear
Lest a mortal eye should see;
What's your nakedness to me?
Here no leprous flowers rear
Fierce corollas in the air;
Here no bodies sleek and wet,
Dripping mingled rain and sweat,
Tread the savage measures of
Jungle boys and girls in love.
What is last year's snow to me,
Last year's anything? The tree
Budding yearly must forget
How its past arose or set—
Bough and blossom, flower, fruit,
Even what shy bird with mute
Wonder at her travail there,
Meekly labored in its hair.
One three centuries removed
From the scenes his fathers loved,
Spicy grove, cinnamon tree,
What is Africa to me?

So I lie, who find no peace
Night or day, no slight release
From the unremittent beat
Made by cruel padded feet
Walking through my body's street.
Up and down they go, and back,
Treading out a jungle track.
So I lie, who never quite
Safely sleep from rain at night—
I can never rest at all
When the rain begins to fall;
Like a soul gone mad with pain

I must match its weird refrain;
Ever must I twist and squirm,
Writhing like a baited worm,
While its primal measures drip
Through my body, crying, "Strip!
Doff this new exuberance.
Come and dance the Lover's Dance!"
In an old remembered way
Rain works on me night and day.

Quaint, outlandish heathen gods
Black men fashion out of rods,
Clay, and brittle bits of stone,
In a likeness like their own,
My conversion came high-priced;
I belong to Jesus Christ,
Preacher of humility;
Heathen gods are naught to me.

Father, Son, and Holy Ghost,
So I make an idle boast;
Jesus of the twice-turned cheek,
Lamb of God, although I speak
With my mouth thus, in my heart
Do I play a double part.
Ever at Thy glowing altar
Must my heart grow sick and falter,
Wishing He I served were black,
Thinking then it would not lack
Precedent of pain to guide it,
Let who would or might deride it;
Surely then this flesh would know
Yours had borne a kindred woe.
Lord, I fashion dark gods, too,
Daring even to give You
Dark despairing features where,
Crowned with dark rebellious hair,
Patience wavers just so much as
Mortal grief compels, while touches
Quick and hot, of anger, rise
To smitten cheek and weary eyes.
Lord, forgive me if my need
Sometimes shapes a human creed.

All day long and all night through,
One thing only must I do:
Quench my pride and cool my blood,
Lest I perish in the flood.
Lest a hidden ember set
Timber that I thought was wet

Burning like the dryest flax,
Melting like the merest wax,
Lest the grave restore its dead.
Not yet has my heart or head
In the least way realized
They and I are civilized.

Color, 1925.

Sacrament

She gave her body for my meat,
    Her soul to be my wine,
And prayed that I be made complete
    In sunlight and starshine.

With such abandoned grace she gave
    Of all that passion taught her,
She never knew her tidal wave
    Cast bread on stagnant water.

Color, 1925.

Tableau

   (For Donald Duff)

Locked arm in arm they cross the way,
    The black boy and the white,
The golden splendor of the day,
    The sable pride of night.

From lowered blinds the dark folk stare,
    And here the fair folk talk,
Indignant that these two should dare
    In unison to walk.

Oblivious to look and word
    They pass, and see no wonder
That lightning brilliant as a sword
    Should blaze the path of thunder.

Color, 1925. The dedication appears in *Color,* but not in the March 25, 1924, issue of *Survey Graphic.*

Yet Do I Marvel

I doubt not God is good, well-meaning, kind,
And did He stoop to quibble could tell why
The little buried mole continues blind,
Why flesh that mirrors Him must some day die,
Make plain the reason tortured Tantalus[1]
Is baited by the fickle fruit, declare
If merely brute caprice dooms Sisyphus[2]
To struggle up a never-ending stair.
Inscrutable His ways are, and immune
To catechism by a mind too strewn
With petty cares to slightly understand
What awful brain compels His awful hand.
Yet do I marvel at this curious thing:
To make a poet black, and bid him sing!

1. A figure in Greek myth who, after death, could not drink water because the pool in which he was placed retreated whenever he tried to reach it; nor could he eat the fruit of the tree overhead, because its branches moved away whenever he tried to reach it.

2. Another figure of Greek myth; his fate after death was to roll a huge rock uphill only to have it roll back upon him endlessly.

Color, 1925.

From the Dark Tower

We shall not always plant while others reap
The golden increment of bursting fruit,
Nor always countenance, abject and mute,
That lesser men should hold their brothers cheap;
Not everlastingly while others sleep
Shall we beguile their limbs with mellow flute,
Not always bend to some more subtle brute;
We were not made eternally to weep.

The night whose sable breast relieves the stark,
White stars is no less lovely being dark,
And there are buds that cannot bloom at all
In light, but crumple, piteous, and fall;
So in the dark we hide the heart that bleeds,
And wait, and tend our agonizing seeds.

Fire!! November 1926. "From the Dark Tower" was also the title of Cullen's column in *Opportunity* in which he wrote editorials and book reviews.

Friendless Blues

MERCEDES GILBERT
Recorded in 1926.

Feel so low down an' sad Lawd,
Feel so low down an' sad Lawd,
Lost everything I ever had.

Ain't got no friend nowhere Lawd,
Ain't got no friend nowhere Lawd,
All by myself no one to care.

I met a man in my own home town,
In my own home town.
I met a man in my own home town,
Coaxed me away now he has thrown me down.
I want to see that Indian River shore,
Indian River shore.
I want to see that Indian River shore,
If I get back I'll never leave no more.

When I was home the door was never closed,
door was never closed.
When I was home the door was never closed.
Where my home is now the good Lawd only knows.
'Member the time when I was young and gay,
when I was young and gay,
'Member the time when I was young and gay,
Had many friends hanging 'round me ev'ry day.

Money's all gone I'm so far from home,
I'm so far from home.
Money's all gone I'm so far from home,
far from home.
I just sit here all alone and cry an' moan,
cry an' moan.

Harlem men won't treat no gal right,
won't treat no gal right.
Harlem men won't treat no gal right,
no gal right.
They make you work all day and fight all night,
fight all night.

Colored Blues Singer

Some weep to find the Golden Pear
Feeds maggots at the core,
And some grow cold as ice, and bear
Them prouder than before.

But you go singing like the sea
Whose lover turns to land;
You make your grief a melody
And take it by the hand.

Such songs the mellow-bosomed maids
Of Africa intone
For lovers dead in hidden glades,
Slow rotting flesh and bone.

Such keenings tremble from the kraal,[1]
Where sullen-browed abides
The second wife whose dark tears fail
To draw him to her sides.

Somewhere Jeritza[2] breaks her heart
On symbols Verdi[3] wrote;
You tear the strings of your soul apart,
Blood dripping note by note.

---

1. This Dutch term has multiple meanings, any or all of which the poet may be invoking. A kraal is an enclosure for cattle in southern Africa; it is also a village of South African natives, usually surrounded by a stockade having a central space for livestock.

2. Maria Jeritza (1887–1982) was an Austrian soprano of the opera.

3. Giuseppe Verdi (1813–1901) was an Italian composer who wrote scores for several famous operas.

Copper Sun, 1927.

To Certain Critics

Then call me traitor if you must,
Shout treason and default!
Say I betray a sacred trust
Aching beyond this vault.
I'll bear your censure as your praise,
For never shall the clan
Confine my singing to its ways
Beyond the ways of man.

No racial option narrows grief.
Pain is no patriot,
And sorrow plaits her dismal leaf
For all as lief as not.
With blind sheep groping every hill,
Searching an oriflamme,[1]
How shall the shepherd heart then thrill
To only the darker lamb?

1. Any banner or standard, especially one that serves as a rallying point or symbol.

Ebony and Topaz, 1927.

Little Sonnet to Little Friends

Let not the proud of heart condemn
Me that I mould my ways to hers,
Groping for healing in a hem
No wind of passion ever stirs;
Nor let them sweetly pity me
When I am out of sound and sight;
They waste their time and energy;
No mares encumber me at night.

Always a trifle fond and strange,
And some have said a bit bizarre,
Say, "Here's the sun," I would not change
It for my dead and burnt-out star.
Shine as it will, I have no doubt
Some day the sun, too, may go out.

The Black Christ, 1929.

Frequently publishing under the name Aquah Laluah, Gladys May Casely Hayford was an African woman born on May 11, 1904, to prominent West African parents in Axim, the Gold Coast (Ghana). Her mother, Adelaide Smith Casely Hayford, was a distinguished educator who visited the United States, participated in social welfare and peace activities, and founded the Girls' Vocational and Industrial School in Freetown, Sierra Leone. Her father was a prominent Gold Coast lawyer and leader in the Pan-African movement. Gladys was their only child. She was educated in England and Wales, attending college at Colwyn Bay. Frail in health and slightly lame in one leg, Hayford was drawn to a rather bohemian existence during her youth. A talented musician, visual artist, and writer, she resisted her mother's wishes that she take over the Freetown school where she taught African folklore and literature.

Gladys May Casely Hayford

(a k a Aquah Laluah)

(1904–1950)

Hayford secured an invitation from Columbia University to become a student there in 1929 after sending some of her poetry and received an invitation from Radcliffe as well upon the publication of three of her poems in *The Atlantic Monthly*. She never made it to either institution, however, since she lacked the money to complete her journey to New York. Nevertheless, she continued to be published in the United States by *The Messenger*, *Opportunity*, and Cullen's *Caroling Dusk* (1927). Hayford joined an African jazz troupe in Berlin and fell in love with one of its male members. But twice hospitalized for emotional breakdowns in Europe, Hayford returned to Africa for good in late 1932, marrying a Freetown man in 1936. Estranged from her husband, who evidently abused her, she left Freetown for Accra in 1939; there her son, Kobe, was born. Hayford died of cholera at the age of forty-six.

Rainy Season Love Song

Out of the tense awed darkness, my Frangepani[1] comes:
Whilst the blades of Heaven flash round her, and the roll of thunder drums,
My young heart leaps and dances, with exquisite joy and pain,
As, storms within and storms without, I meet my love in the rain.

"The rain is in love with you darling; it's kissing you everywhere,
Rain pattering over your small brown feet, rain in your curly hair;
Rain in the vale that your twin breasts make, as in delicate mounds they rise;
I hope there is rain in your heart, Frangepani, as rain half fills your eyes."

Into my hands she cometh, and the lightning of my desire
Flashes and leaps about her, more subtle than Heaven's fire;
"The lightning's in love with you darling; it is loving you so much
That its warm electricity in you pulses wherever I may touch.
When I kiss your lips and your eyes, and your hands like twin flowers apart,
I know there is lightning, Frangepani, deep in the depths of your heart."

The thunder rumbles about us, and I feel its triumphant note
As your warm arms steal around me, and I kiss your dusky throat;
"The thunder's in love with you darling; it hides its power in your breast,
And I feel it stealing o'er me as I lie in your arms at rest.
I sometimes wonder, beloved, when I drink from life's proffered bowl,
Whether there's thunder hidden in the innermost parts of your soul."

Out of my arms she stealeth, and I am left alone with the night,
Void of all sounds save peace, the first faint glimmer of light.
Into some quiet, hushed stillness my Frangepani goes.
Is there peace within like the peace without? Only the darkness knows.

1. A kind of fragrant flower.

Caroling Dusk, 1927.

The Serving Girl

The calabash wherein she served my food
Was smooth and polished as sandalwood;
Fish, as white as the foam of the sea,
Peppered, and golden fried for me.
She brought palm wine that carelessly slips
From the sleeping palm tree's honeyed lips.
But who can guess, or even surmise,
The countless things she served with her eyes?

Caroling Dusk, 1927.

Lullaby

Close your sleepy eyes, or the pale moonlight will steal you,
Else in the mystic silence, the moon will turn you white.
Then you won't see the sunshine, nor smell the open roses,
Nor love your Mammy anymore, whose skin is dark as night.
You will only love the shadows, and the foam upon the billows,
The shadow of the vulture's wings, the call of mystery,
The hooting of the night owl, and the howling of the jackal,
The sighing of the evil winds, the call of mystery.
Wherever moonlight stretches her arms across the heavens,
You will follow, always follow, till you become instead,
A shade in human draperies, with palm fronds for your pillow,
In place of Mammy's bibini,[1] asleep on his wee bed.

1. "Bibini" is Fanti, a language of the Ivory Coast in West Africa, for baby boy.

The Crisis, March 1929.

The Palm Wine Seller

Akosua selling palm wine
In the broiling heat;
Akosua selling palm wine
Down our street.

Frothing calabashes
Filled unto the brim,
Boatmen quaffing palm wine
In toil's interim.

Tossing off their palm wine,
Boatmen deem her fair;
Through the haze of palm wine,
Note her jet-black hair.

Roundness of her bosom,
Brilliance of her eyes,
Lips that form a cupid's bow,
Whereon love's dew lies.

Velvet gleam of shoulder,
Arch of bare black feet,
Soft caressing hands,
These her charms complete.

Thus illusioned boatmen
Dwell on 'Kosua's charms,
Blind to fallen bosom,
Knotted thin black arms.

Lips creased in by wrinkles,
Eyes dimmed with the years,
Feet whose arch was altered,
Treading vales of tears.

Hair whose roots life's madness
Knotted and turned wild.
On her heart a load of care,
On her back, a child.

Akosua selling palm wine
In the broiling heat;
Akosua selling palm wine
Down our street.

Opportunity, February 1930.

(William) Waring Cuney

(1906–1976)

Although Waring Cuney is frequently overlooked, he made considerable contributions to the Harlem Renaissance. He is best known for "No Images," which won first prize in the 1926 *Opportunity* poetry contest. William Waring and his twin brother, Norris Wright (who became a printer and published the last poetry collection of Georgia Douglas Johnson), were born on May 6, 1906, to the distinguished mixed-race family of Madge Louise Baker and Norris Cuney II in Washington, D.C. Cuney was educated in the public schools, including Dunbar High School, where Angelina Weld Grimké taught. He studied briefly at Howard University, but graduated from Lincoln University in Pennsylvania; he and Langston Hughes are sometimes referred to as among "the Lincoln University poets." He later studied at the New England Conservatory of Music in Boston and continued voice training in Rome. Although Cuney never performed professionally, some of his lyrics were used by performers such as Josh White, who recorded some of Cuney's protest songs on the popular Depression-era album *Southern Exposure*. Burl Ives also recorded a number of his lyrics. Cuney's poetry was frequently published in anthologies, including Countee Cullen's *Caroling Dusk* (1927) and *The Book of American Negro Poetry* (1922 and 1931), edited by James Weldon Johnson. His work was also included in the first and only issue of *Fire!!* (November 1926).

Cuney served in the South Pacific during World War II as a technical sergeant and earned the Asiatic Pacific Theater Ribbon and three Bronze Stars. After the war, Cuney returned to the Bronx, New York, where he studied music at Columbia University. In the 1950s his poetry, along with that of Hughes, was translated into German and published in Germany. Cuney's poetry was also translated into Dutch and included in an anthology of African American poetry. Although Cuney self-published several broadsides after the war, it was not until 1960 that his first collection of poems, *Puzzles*, was published, but only in Holland. In 1973, a second volume, *Storefront Church*, was published in London. Cuney withdrew from the black literary community in 1962. Much of his biography remains obscure and many of his poems, though anthologized and recorded, have not been collected.

No Images

She does not know
Her beauty,
She thinks her brown body
Has no glory.

If she could dance
Naked,
Under palm trees
And I see her image in the river
She would know.

But there are no palm trees
On the street,
And dish water gives back no images.

Opportunity, June 1926.

Dust

Dust,

Through which
Proud blood
Once flowed.

Dust,

Where a civilization
Flourished.

Dust,
The Valley of the Nile.
Dust.

You proud ones, proud of the skill
With which you play this game—Civilization;
Do not forget that it is a very old game.
Men used to play it on the banks
Of the Tigris and the Euphrates[1]
When the world was a wilderness.

There is a circle around China
Where once a wall stood.
Carthage is a heap of ashes.[2]
And Rome knew the pomp and glory
You know now.

1. Large rivers in southwest Asia that flow through Turkey, Syria, and Iraq.
2. An ancient city-state in North Africa.

The Coliseum tells a story[3]
The Woolworth Building may repeat.[4]

Dust,
Pharaohs and their armies sleep there.

Dust,
Shall it stir again?

Will Pharaohs rise and rule
And their armies march once more?

Civilization continually shifts
Upon the places of the earth.

3. The Roman Coliseum, where Christians and others were forced to fight wild animals or other men for the amusement of the spectators.
4. Frank Winfield Woolworth (1852–1919) was an American businessman who founded the Woolworth department store chain. The Woolworth Building was a famous structure in Chicago, at one time its tallest building.

Caroling Dusk, 1927.

The Radical

Men never know
What they are doing.
They always make a muddle
Of their affairs;
They always tie their affairs
Into a knot
They cannot untie.
Then I come in
Uninvited.

They do not ask me in;
I am the radical,
The bomb thrower,
I untie the knot
That they have made,
And they never thank me.

Caroling Dusk, 1927.

Richard Bruce Nugent

(a k a Richard Bruce)

(1906–1987)

Richard Bruce Nugent, also known as Bruce Nugent and Richard Bruce, was born on July 2, 1906, to Pauline Minerva Bruce and Richard Henry Nugent, a prominent Washington, D.C. family. His parents were art enthusiasts and encouraged their son's exposure to the arts. Nugent's younger brother, Gary Lambert Nugent, became a successful jazz dancer. Bruce Nugent attended Dunbar High School where Angelina Weld Grimké was teaching, but the family moved to New York City after his father's death. Nugent was thirteen at the time. In New York, Nugent worked a variety of odd jobs including bellhop and errand boy, but he eventually decided to become an artist and informed his mother that he would no longer seek employment. His mother responded to this decision by sending him to his grandmother in Washington, D.C., but there, at the home of lifelong friend Georgia Douglas Johnson, Nugent met Langston Hughes in 1925 and become enthralled with the New Negro Movement. He returned to New York with his new friend Hughes and immediately became a favorite among such young artists as Zora Neale Hurston, Wallace Thurman, Countee Cullen, and Aaron Douglas.

Nugent's first published poem, "Shadow," appeared in a 1925 issue of *Opportunity*. Two years later the poem was reprinted in Cullen's *Caroling Dusk* (1927). Nugent also contributed his story "Sahdji" to Alain Locke's landmark anthology, *The New Negro* (1925). Although this is veiled by its heterosexual subject, Nugent's story is considered by some to be the earliest gay prose text written by an African American due to its allusion to the love of a male warrior for his chief's son. With Locke's encouragement, Nugent collaborated with African American composer William Grant Still, who wrote the musical score, to adapt the story into a one-act play, *Sahdji, an African Ballet*. The play was included in Locke and Montgomery Gregory's *Plays of Negro Life* (1927) and in 1932 it was performed at the Eastman School of Music in Rochester, New York. Because of the notoriety he garnered from his openly gay lifestyle in Harlem and D.C., his pursuit of homosexual themes in his writing, and his erotic drawings and poetry, Nugent often assumed the pseudonym Richard Bruce to accommodate his parents, who wanted the family protected from gossip.

In 1926 Nugent joined several members of the younger set in founding a new literary journal, *Fire!!,* that only lasted for one issue. Thurman, Hughes, and Hurston were editors, John P. Davis was business manager, and Nugent was the distributor. Nugent also contributed two drawings and his best-known story, "Smoke, Lilies, and Jade!" to the magazine. The story is frequently described as the most explicit homoerotic prose text of the Harlem Renaissance. Shortly after the demise of the magazine, Nugent began touring with DuBose Heyward's play *Porgy* and was with the cast for several years. In 1928 he coedited and contributed to close friend Thurman's new magazine, *Harlem: A Forum of Negro Life*. However, this journal lasted only one issue as well. Nugent also contributed to Dorothy West's short-lived *Challenge* and *New Challenge* and to *Trend*, a poetry magazine. While his works are few in number, Nugent published important artwork and groundbreaking pieces in *Fire!!*, *Opportunity*, *The Crisis*, and *Ebony and Topaz* (1927).

During the Depression, Nugent, like many writers, worked for the Federal Arts Project and the Federal Theatre. In the early 1930s the Harmon Foundation exhibited his artwork. In 1960 Nugent and Romare Bearden cofounded the Harlem Cultural Council, a community-based group of artist-activists. Although Nugent was married (in 1952) to Grace Marr, a nurse, for seventeen years until her death, he identified himself as gay his entire life. He embraced the gay and lesbian movement of the 1960s and 1970s and appeared in the 1984 documentary *Before Stonewall* defending gay rights. The gay themes in his creative work, along with his central social role in the Harlem Renaissance itself, and his efforts in its later preservation, have secured for Bruce Nugent a place in the history of the movement. Nugent died in New York City in 1987.

Shadow

Silhouette

On the face of the moon

Am I.

A dark shadow in the light.

A silhouette am I
On the face of the moon
Lacking color
Or vivid brightness
But defined all the clearer
Because
I am dark,
Black on the face of the moon.

A shadow am I
Growing in the light,
Not understood as is the day,
But more easily seen
Because
I am a shadow in the light.

Opportunity, October 1925. Published under the name R. Bruce Nugent.

Aaron Douglas, "Sahdji," *The New Negro,* 1925

Sahdji

That one now . . . that's a sketch of a little African girl . . . delightfully black . . . I made it while I was passing through East Africa . . . her name was Sahdji . . . wife of Konombju . . . chieftan . . . of only a small tribe . . . Warpuri was the area of his sovereign domain . . . but to get back to Sahdji . . . with her beautiful dark body . . . rosy black . . . graceful as the tongues of flame she loved to dance around . . . and pretty . . . small features . . . large liquid eyes . . . over-full sensuous lips . . . she knew how to dance too . . . better than any . . .

Sahdji was proud . . . she was the favorite wife . . . as such she had privileges . . . she did love Konombju . . .

Mrabo . . . son of Konombju, loved Sahdji . . . his father . . . fifty-nine . . . too old for her . . . fifty-nine and eighteen . . . he could wait . . . he loved his father . . . but . . . maybe death . . . his father was getting old . . .

Numbo idolized Mrabo . . . Numbo was a young buck . . . would do anything to make Mrabo happy . . .

one day Sahdji felt restless . . . why . . . it was not unusual for Konombju to lead the hunt . . . even at his age . . . Sahdji jangled her bracelets . . . it was so still and warm . . . she'd wait at the door . . . standing there . . . shifting . . . a blurred silhouette against the brown of the hut . . . she waited . . . waited. . .

maybe . . .

she saw the long stream of natives in the distance . . . she looked for Konombju . . . what was that burden they carried . . . why were they so solemn . . . where was Konombju . . .

the column reached her door . . . placed their burden at her feet . . . Konombju . . . an arrow in his back . . . just accident . . . *Goare go shuioa go elui ruri*—(when men die they depart forever)—they hadn't seen him fall . . . hunting, one watches the hunt . . . a stray arrow . . . Konombju at her feet . . .

preparations for the funeral feast . . . the seven wives of Konombju went to the new chief's hut . . . Mrabo . . . one . . . two . . . three . . . he counted . . . no Sahdji . . . six . . . seven . . . no Sahdji . . .

the funeral procession filed past the door . . . and Mrabo . . . Mrabo went to . . . the drums beat their boom . . . boom . . . deep pulsing heart-quivering boom . . . and the reeds added their weird dirge . . . the procession moved on . . . on to Konombju's hut . . . boom . . . b-o-o-m . . .

there from the doorway stepped Sahdji . . . painted in the funeral red . . . the flames from the ground are already catching the branches . . . slowly to the funeral drums she swayed . . . danced . . . leading Konombju to his grave . . . her grave . . . their grave . . .

The New Negro, 1925. Published under the name R. Bruce Nugent.

they laid the body in the funeral hut . . . *Goa shoa motho go sale motho*—(when a man dies a man remains)—Sahdji danced slowly . . . sadly . . . looked at Mrabo and smiled . . . slowly triumphantly . . . and to the wails of the wives . . . boom-boom of the drums . . . gave herself again to Konombju . . . the grass-strewn couch of Konombju . . .

Mrabo stood unflinching . . . but Numbo, silly Numbo had made an old . . . old man of Mrabo.

Smoke, Lilies, and Jade!

He wanted to do something . . . to write or draw . . . or something . . . but it was so comfortable to lay there on the bed . . . his shoes off . . . and think . . . think of everything . . . short disconnected thoughts to wonder. . . to remember . . . to think and smoke . . . why wasn't he worried that he had no money . . . he had five cents . . . but he had been hungry . . . he was hungry and still . . . all he wanted to do was . . . lay there comfortably smoking . . . think . . . wishing he were writing . . . or drawing . . . or something . . . something about the things he felt and thought . . . but what did he think . . . he remembered how his mother had awakened him one night . . . ages ago . . . six years ago . . . Alex . . . he had always wondered at the strangeness of it . . . she had seemed so . . . so . . . so just the same . . . Alex . . . I think your father is dead . . . and it hadn't seemed so strange . . . yet . . . one's mother didn't say that . . . didn't wake one at midnight every night to say . . . feel him . . . put your hand on his . . . then whisper with a catch in her voice . . . I'm afraid . . . she don't wake Lam . . . yet it hadn't seemed as it should have seemed . . . even when he had felt his father's cool wet forehead . . . it hadn't been tragic . . . or weird . . . not at all as one should feel when one's father had died . . . even his reply of . . . yes he is dead . . . had been commonplace . . . hadn't been dramatic . . . there had been no tears . . . no sobs . . . not even a sorrow . . . and yet he must have realized that one's father couldn't smile . . . or sing anymore . . . after he had died . . . every one remembered his father's voice . . . it had been a lush voice . . . a promise . . . then that dressing together . . . his mother and himself . . . in the bathroom . . . why was the bathroom always the warmest room in the house in the winter . . . as they had put on their clothes . . . his mother had been telling him what he must do . . . and cried softly . . . and that had made him cry too but you mustn't cry Alex . . . remember you have to be a little man now . . . and that was all . . . didn't other wives and sons cry more for their dead than that . . . anyway people never cried for beautiful sunsets . . . or music . . . and those were the things that hurt . . . the things to sympathize with . . . then out into the snow and dark of the morning . . . first to the undertaker's . . . no first to Uncle Frank's

Fire!! November 1926. Published under the name Richard Bruce.

. . . why did Aunt Lula have to act like that . . . to ask again and again . . . but when did he die . . . when did he die . . . I just can't believe it . . . poor Minerva . . . then out into the snow and dark again . . . how had his mother expected him to find the night bell at the undertaker's . . . he was the most sensible of them tho . . . all he said was . . . what . . . Harry Francis . . . too bad . . . tell mamma I'll be there first thing in the morning . . . then down the deserted streets again . . . to grandmother's . . . it was growing light now . . . it must be terrible to die in daylight . . . grandpa had been sweeping the snow off the yard . . . he had been glad of that because . . . well he could tell him better than he could grandma . . . grandpa father's dead . . . and he hadn't acted strange either . . . books lied . . . he had just looked at Alex a moment then continued sweeping . . . all he said was . . . what time did he die . . . she'll want to know . . . then passing thru the lonesome street toward home . . . Mr. Minnie Grant was closing a window and spied him . . . hallow Alex and how's your father this mornin' . . . dead . . . get out . . . tch tch tch an' I was just around there with a cup a' custard yesterday . . . Alex puffed contentedly on his cigarette . . . he was hungry and comfortable . . . and he had an ivory holder inlaid with red jade and green . . . funny how the smoke seemed to climb up that ray of sunlight . . . went up the slant just like imagination . . . was imagination blue . . . or was it because he had spent his last five cents and couldn't worry . . . anyway it was to lay there and wonder . . . and remember . . . why was he so different from other people . . . the only things he remembered of his father's funeral were the crowded church and the ride in the hack . . . so many people there in the church . . . and ladies with tears in their eyes . . . and on their cheeks . . . and some men too . . . why did people cry . . . vanity that was the reason . . . yet they weren't exactly hypocrites . . . but . . . it had made him furious . . . all these people crying . . . it wasn't THEIR father . . . and he wasn't crying . . . couldn't cry for sorrow although he had loved his father more than . . . than . . . it had made him so angry that tears had come into his eyes . . . and he had been ashamed of his mother . . . crying into a handkerchief . . . so ashamed that tears had run down his cheeks and he had frowned . . . and someone . . . a woman . . . had said . . . look at that poor little dear . . . Alex is just like his father . . . and the tears had run fast . . . because he *wasn't* like his father . . . he couldn't sing . . . he didn't want to sing . . . he didn't want to sing . . . Alex blew a cloud of smoke . . . blue smoke . . . when they had taken his father from the vault three weeks later . . . he had grown beautiful . . . his nose had become perfect and clear . . . his [hair] turned jet black and silky and glossy . . . and his skin was a transparent green . . . like the sea only not so deep . . . and where it was drawn over the cheekbones a pale beautiful red appeared . . . like a blush . . . why hadn't his father looked like that always . . . but no . . . to have sung would have broken the wondrous repose of those lips and maybe that was his beauty . . . maybe it was wrong to think thoughts like these . . . but they were nice and pleasant and comfortable . . . when one was smoking a cigarette thru an ivory holder . . . inlaid with red jade and green . . .

he wondered why he couldn't find work . . . a job . . . when he had first come to New York he had . . . and he had only been fourteen then—was it because he was nineteen now that he felt so idle . . . and contented . . . or because he was an artist . . . but was he an artist . . . was one an artist before one became known . . . of course he was an artist . . . and strangely enough so were all his friends . . . he should be ashamed that he didn't work . . . but . . . was it five years in New York . . . or the fact that he was an artist . . . when his mother said she couldn't understand him . . . why did he vaguely pity her instead of being ashamed . . . he should be . . . his mother and all his relatives said so . . . his brother was three years younger than he and yet he had already been away from home a year . . . on the stage . . . making thirty-five dollars a week . . . had three suits of clothes and many clothes and was going to help his mother . . . while he . . . Alex . . . was content to lay and smoke and meet friends at night . . . to argue and read Wilde . . . Freud . . . Boccacio and Schnitzler . . . to attend Gurdjieff meetings and know things[1] . . . Why did they scoff at him for knowing such people as Carl . . . Mencken . . . Toomer . . . Hughes . . . Cullen . . . Wood . . . Cabell[2] . . . oh the whole lot of them . . . was it because it seemed so incongruous to him that he . . . who was so little known . . . should call by first names people they would like to know . . . were they jealous . . . no mothers aren't jealous of their sons . . . they are proud of them why then . . . when these friends accepted him and liked him . . . no matter how he dressed . . . why did mother ask . . . and you went looking like that . . . Langston was a fine fellow . . . he knew there was something in Alex . . . and so did Rene Borgia . . . and Zora and Clement and Miguel[3] . . . and . . . and . . . and all of them . . . if he went to see mother she would ask . . . how do you feel Alex with nothing in your pockets . . . I don't see how you can be satisfied . . . Really you are a mystery to me . . . I'm sure I don't know . . . none of my brothers were lazy and shiftless . . . I can never remember the time when they weren't sending money home and when your father was your age he was supporting a family . . . where you get your nerve I don't know . . . just because you tried to write one or two little poems that no one understands . . . you seem to think the world owes you a living . . . you should see by now how much is thought of them . . . you can't sell any of them . . . and you won't do anything to make

---

1. Oscar Wilde (1854–1900) was a gay Irish writer who was put on trial in England for obscenity; Sigmund Freud (1856–1939) was an Austrian psychoanalyst who pioneered theories of sexual repression and the unconscious mind; Giovanni Boccaccio (1313–1375) was an Italian poet; Arthur Schnitzler (1862–1931) was an Austrian dramatist and novelist; Georgi Gurdjieff was a Russian mystic who established the Institute for the Harmonious Development of Man, near Fountainbleau, France. Gurdjieff was a popular spiritual leader among Greenwich Village and Harlem Renaissance artists, especially Jean Toomer, who dedicated his life to teaching Gurdjieff's doctrines.

2. Carl Van Vechten (1880–1964) was a white writer, photographer, and power broker in the Harlem Renaissance, who mentored several black writers; H. L. Mencken (1880–1956) was an irreverent white editor, satirist, and critic of the 1920s; Jean Toomer (1894–1967) was the author of *Cane* (1923) and a Gurdjieff disciple; Langston Hughes (1902–1967) was a poet and a good friend of Nugent's; Countee Cullen (1903–1946) was a poet of the Harlem Renaissance; Clement Wood was a white writer who published the novel *Nigger* (1923); James Branch Cabell (1879–1958) was a white American author.

3. Langston Hughes; Alexander Woollcott (1887–1943) was a well-known theatre critic and member of the Algonquin Round Table; Rene Borgia was the poet laureate of Venezuela and a close friend of Nugent's; Zora Neale Hurston (1891–1960), the Harlem Renaissance novelist; Clement Wood; Miguel Covarrubias (1904–1957) was a Mexican artist and illustrator who came to New York in 1923 and became a well-known illustrator of Harlem life.

money . . . wake up Alex . . . I don't know what will become of you . . .

it was hard to believe in one's self after that . . . did Wilde's parents or Shelley's or Goya's talk to them like that[4] . . . but it was depressing to think in that vein . . . Alex stretched and yawned . . . Max had died . . . Margaret had died . . . so had Sonia . . . Cynthia . . . Juan-Jose and Harry . . . all people he had loved . . . loved one by one and together . . . and all had died . . . he never loved a person long before they died . . . in truth he was tragic . . . that was a lovely appellation . . . The Tragic Genius . . . think to go through life known as the Tragic Genius . . . romantic . . . but it was more or less true . . . Alex turned over and blew another cloud of smoke . . . was all life like that . . . smoke . . . blue smoke from an ivory holder . . . he wished he were in New Bedford[5] . . . New Bedford was a nice place . . . snug little houses set complacently behind protecting lawns . . . half open windows showing prim interiors from behind waving cool curtains . . . inviting . . . like precise courtesans winking from behind lace fans . . . and trees . . . many trees casting lacy patterns of shade on the sun dipped sidewalks . . . small stores . . . naively proud of their pseudo grandeur . . . banks . . . called institutions for saving . . . all naive . . . that was it . . . New Bedford was naive . . . after the sophistication of New York it would fan one like a refreshing breeze . . . and yet he had returned to New York . . . and sophistication . . . was he sophisticated . . . no because he was seldom bored . . . seldom bored by anything . . . and weren't the sophisticated continually suffering from ennui[6] . . . on the contrary . . . he was amused . . . amused by the artificiality of sophistication and naiveté alike . . . but maybe that in itself was the essence of sophistication or . . . was it cynicism . . . or were the two identical . . . he blew a cloud of smoke . . . it was growing dark now . . . and the smoke no longer had a ladder to climb . . . but soon the moon would rise and then he would clothe the silver moon in blue smoke garments . . . truly smoke was like imagination . . .

Alex sat up . . . pulled on his shoes and went out . . . it was a beautiful night . . . and so large . . . the dusky blue hung like a curtain in an immense arched doorway . . . fastened with silver tacks . . . to wander in the night was wonderful . . . myriads of inquisitive lights . . . curiously prying into the dark . . . and fading unsatisfied . . . he passed a woman . . . she was not beautiful . . . and he was sad because she did not weep that she would never be beautiful . . . was it Wilde who had said . . . a cigarette is the most perfect pleasure because it leaves one unsatisfied . . . the breeze gave to him a perfume stolen from some wandering lady of the evening . . . it pleased him . . . why was it that men wouldn't use perfumes . . . they should . . . each and every one of them liked perfumes . . . the man who denied that was a liar . . . or a coward . . . but if ever he were to voice that thought or express it . . . he would be misunderstood . . . it made him feel tragic and great . . . but maybe it would be nicer to be understood . . . but no . . . no great artist

---

4. Oscar Wilde; Percy Bysshe Shelley (1792–1822) was a British nineteenth-century romantic poet known for his scandalous love life; Francisco de Goya (1746–1828) was a Spanish painter.

5. New Bedford, Massachusetts; a small New England fishing village.

6. French for boredom.

is . . . then again . . . neither were fools . . . they were strangely akin these two . . . Alex thought of a sketch he would make . . . a personality sketch of Fania[7] . . . straight classic features tinted proud purple . . . sensuous fine lips . . . gilded for truth . . . eyes . . . half opened and lids colored mysterious green . . . hair black and straight . . . drawn sternly mockingly back from the false puritanical forehead . . . maybe he would make Edith too[8] . . . skin a blue . . . infinite like night . . . and eyes . . . slant and grey . . . very complacent like a cat's . . . Mona Lisa lips[9] . . . red and seductive as . . . as pomegranate juice . . . in truth it was fine to be young and hungry and an artist . . . to blow blue smoke from an ivory holder . . .

here was the cafeteria . . . it was almost as tho it had journeyed to meet him . . . the night was so blue . . . how does blue feel . . . or red or gold or any other color . . . if colors could be heard he would paint most wondrous tunes . . . symphonious . . . think . . . the dulcet tones of a blue like night . . . of a red like pomegranate juice . . . like Edith's lips . . . of the fairy tones to be heard in a sunset . . . like rubies shaken in a crystal cup . . . of the symphony of Fania . . . and silver . . . and gold . . . he had heard the sound of gold but they weren't the sounds he wanted to catch . . . no . . . they must be liquid . . . not so staccato but flowing variations of the same one caliber . . . there was no one in the cafe as yet . . . he sat and waited . . . that was a clever idea he had had about the color [of] music . . . but after all he was a monstrous clever fellow . . . Jurgen had said that[10] . . . funny how characters in a book said the things one wanted to say . . . he would like to know Jurgen . . . how does one go about getting an introduction to the characters in a book . . . go up to the brown cover of the book and knock gently . . . and say hello . . . then timidly . . . is Duke Jurgen there . . . or . . . no because if he entered the book in the beginning Jurgen would only be a pawn broker . . . and one didn't enter a book in the center . . . but what foolishness . . . Alex lit a cigarette . . . but Cabell was a master to have written Jurgen . . . and an artist . . . and a poet . . . Alex blew a cloud of smoke . . . a few lines of one of Langston's poems came to describe Jurgen . . . .

> Somewhat like Ariel
> Somewhat like Puck
> Somewhat like a gutter boy
> Who loves to play in muck.
> Somewhat like Bacchus
> Somewhat like Pan
> And a way with women
> Like a sailor man. . . .

Langston must have known Jurgen . . . suppose Jurgen had met people like Tonio

---

7. Fania Marinoff (1887–1971) was married to Carl Van Vechten and was an actress.

8. Edith Wilson (1906–1981) was an African American singer who appeared in Broadway shows, including *Blackbirds of 1926*.

9. The *Mona Lisa* is a well-known portrait of an Italian woman by Renaissance artist, mathematician, scientist, and sculptor Leonardo da Vinci (1452–1519).

10. Duke Jurgen is a fictional character in a James Branch Cabell novel.

Kroeger[11] . . . what a vagrant thought . . . Kroeger . . . Kroeger . . . Kroeger . . . why here
was Rene . . . Alex had almost gone to sleep . . . Alex blew a cone of smoke as he took
Rene's hand . . . it was nice to have friends like Rene . . . so comfortable . . . Rene was
speaking . . . Borgia joined them . . . and de Diego Padro[12] . . . their talk veered to Cabell
. . . James Branch Cabell . . . beautiful . . . marvelous . . . Rene had an enchanting accent
. . . said sank for thank and souse for south . . . but they couldn't know Cabell's greatness . . . Alex searched the smoke for expression . . . he . . . he . . . well he has created
a phantasy mire . . . that's it . . . from clear rich imagery . . . life and silver sands . . . that's
nice . . . and silver sands . . . imagine lilies growing in such a mire . . . when they close
at night their gilded underside would close and protect . . . but that's not it at all . . . his
thoughts just carried and mingled like . . . like odors . . . suggested but never definite
. . . Rene was leaving . . . they all were leaving . . . Alex sauntered slowly back . . . the houses
all looked sleepy . . . funny . . . made him feel like writing poetry . . . and about death
too . . . an elevated crashed by overhead scattering all his thoughts with its noise[13] . . .
making them spread . . . in circles . . . then larger circles . . . just like a splash in a calm pool
. . . what had he been thinking . . . of . . . a poem about death . . . but he no longer felt
that urge . . . just walk and think and wonder . . . think and remember and smoke . . .
blow smoke that mixed with his thoughts and the night . . . he would like to live in a large
white palace . . . to wear a long black cape . . . very full and lined with vermillion . . .
to have many cushions and to lie there among them . . . talking to his friends . . . lie there
in a yellow silk shirt and black velvet trousers . . . like music-review artists talking and
pouring strange liquors from curiously beautiful bottles . . . bottles with long slender
necks . . . he climbed the noisy stairs of the odorous tenement . . . smelled of fish . . .
of stale fried fish and dirty milk bottles . . . he rather liked it . . . he liked the acrid smell
of horse manure too . . . strong . . . thoughts . . . yes to lie back among strangely fashioned cushions and sip eastern wines and talk . . . Alex threw himself on the bed . . . removed
his shoes . . . stretched and relaxed . . . yes and have music waft softly in the darkened
and incensed room . . . he blew a cloud of smoke . . . oh the joy of being an artist and
of blowing blue smoke thru an ivory holder inlaid with red jade and green . . .

the street was so long and narrow . . . so long and narrow . . . and blue . . . in the distance it reached the stars . . . and if he walked long enough . . . far enough . . . he could
reach the stars too . . . the narrow blue was so empty . . . quiet . . . Alex walked music
. . . it was so nice to walk in the blue after a party . . . Zora had shone again . . . her stories
. . . she always shone . . . and Monty was glad[14] . . . everyone was glad when Zora shone

11. Fictional hero of a Thomas Mann story.

12. An unknown member of Nugent's social circle.

13. An elevated subway train.

14. Possibly, though not likely, T. Montgomery Gregory (1887–1971), African American writer, educator, and coeditor of *Plays of Negro Life* (1927), which included Nugent's play *Sahdji*. Gregory lived in Wash-ington, D.C., and Atlanta, however, and may not have had the apartment in Greenwich Village alluded to here.

. . . he was glad he had gone to Monty's party . . . Monty had a nice place in the village[15] . . . nice lights . . . and friends and wine . . . mother would be scandalized that he could think of going to a party . . . without a copper to his name . . . but then mother had never been to Monty's . . . and mother had never seen the street seem long and narrow and blue . . . Alex walked music . . . the click of his heels kept time with a tune in his mind . . . he glanced into a lighted cafe window . . . inside were people sipping coffee . . . men . . . why [did] they sit there in the loud light . . . didn't they know that outside the street . . . the narrow blue street met the stars . . . that if they walked long enough . . . far enough . . . Alex walked and the click of his heels sounded . . . and had an echo . . . sound being tossed back and forth . . . someone was approaching . . . and their echoes mingled . . . and gave the sound of castanets . . . Alex liked the sound of the approaching man's footsteps . . . he walked music also . . . he knew the beauty of the narrow blue . . . Alex knew that by the way their echoes mingled . . . he wished he could speak . . . but strangers don't speak at four o'clock in the morning . . . at least if they did he couldn't imagine what would be said . . . maybe . . . pardon me but are you walking toward the stars . . . yes, sir, and if you walk long enough . . . then may I walk with you I want to reach the stars too . . . perdone me senor tiene vd. fosforo[16] . . . Alex was glad he had been addressed in Spanish . . . to have been asked for a match in English . . . or to have been addressed in English at all . . . would have been blasphemy just then . . . Alex handed him a match . . . he glanced at his companion apprehensively in the match glow . . . he was afraid that his appearance would shatter the blue thoughts . . . and stars . . . ah . . . his face was a perfect complement to his voice . . . and the echo of their steps mingled . . . they walked in silence the castanets of their heels clicking perfect accompaniment . . . the stranger inhaled deeply and with a nod of content and a smile . . . blew a cloud of smoke . . . Alex felt like singing . . . the stranger knew the magic of blue smoke also . . . they continued in silence . . . the castanets of their heels clicking rhythmically . . . Alex turned in his doorway . . . up the stairs and the stranger waited for him to light the room . . . no need for words . . . they had always known each other . . . as they undressed by the pale blue dawn . . . Alex knew he had never seen a more perfect human being . . . his body was all symmetry and music . . . and Alex called him Beauty[17] . . . long they lay . . . blowing smoke and exchanging thoughts . . . and Alex swallowed with difficulty . . . he felt a glow of tremor . . . and they talked . . . and . . . slept . . .

Alex wondered more and more why he liked Adrian so . . . he liked many people . . . Wallie . . . Zora . . . Clement . . . Gloria . . . Langston . . . John . . . Gwenny[18] . . . oh many

15. Greenwich Village.

16. Spanish for "Excuse me, sir; do you have a match?"

17. This figure is thought to be a composite of Miguel Covarrubias (Mexican), Countee Cullen's close friend Harold Jackman (African American), the 1920s movie star Rudolph Valentino, and Langston Hughes. When Nugent met Hughes, they walked all night together, engrossed in their newfound friendship.

18. Wallace Thurman (1902–1934) roomed with Nugent and was the editor of *Fire!!;* Zora Neale Hurston; Clement Wood; Langston Hughes; possibly John Wesley Work, Jr. (1901–1981), African American composer and educator at Fisk University in Nashville; Gwendolyn Bennett (1902–1981), Harlem Renaissance poet, artist, and essayist.

people and they were friends . . . but Beauty . . . it was different . . . once Alex had admired Beauty's strength . . . and Beauty's eyes had grown soft . . . and he had said . . . I like you more than anyone Dulce[19] . . . Adrian always called him Dulce . . . and Alex had become confused . . . was it that he was so susceptible to beauty that Alex liked Adrian so much . . . but no . . . he knew other people who were beautiful . . . Fania and Gloria . . . Monty and Bunny[20] . . . but he was never confused before them . . . while Beauty . . . Beauty could make him believe in Buddha . . . or imps . . . and no one else could do that . . . that is no one but Melva[21] . . . but then he was in love with Melva . . . and that explained that . . . he would like Beauty to know Melva . . . they were both so perfect . . . such complements . . . yes he would like Beauty to know Melva because he was in love with both . . . there he had thought it . . . actually dared to think it . . . but Beauty must never know . . . Beauty couldn't understand . . . indeed Alex couldn't understand . . . and it had pained him . . . almost physically . . . and tired his mind . . . Beauty . . . Beauty was in the air . . . the smoke . . . Beauty . . . Melva . . . Beauty . . . Melva . . . Alex slept . . . and dreamed . . .

he was in a field . . . a field of blue smoke and black poppies . . . and red calla lilies . . . he was searching . . . on his hands and knees . . . searching . . . among black poppies and red calla lilies . . . he was searching . . . pushed aside poppy stems . . . he saw two strong white legs . . . dancer's legs . . . the contours pleased him . . . his eyes wandered . . . on past the muscular hocks to the firm white thighs . . . the rounded buttocks . . . then the lithe narrow waist . . . strong torso and broad deep chest . . . the heavy shoulders . . . the graceful neck . . . squared chin and quizzical lips . . . grecian nose with its temperamental nostrils . . . the brown eyes looking at him . . . like . . . Monty looked at Zora . . . his hair curly black and all tousled . . . and it was Beauty . . . and Beauty smiled and looked at him and smiled . . . said I'll wait Alex . . . and Alex became confused and continued his search . . . on his hands and knees . . . pushing aside poppy stems and lily stems . . . a poppy . . . a black poppy . . . a lily . . . a red lily . . . and when he looked back he could no longer see Beauty . . . Alex continued his search . . . thru poppies . . . lilies . . . poppies and red calla lilies . . . and suddenly he saw . . . two small feet . . . olive-ivory . . . two well turned legs curving gracefully from slender ankles . . . and the contours soothed him . . . he followed them . . . past the narrow hips to the tiny waist . . . the fragile yet firm breasts . . . the graceful slender throat . . . the soft rounded chin . . . slightly parting lips . . . and straight little nose with its slightly flaring nostrils . . . the black eyes with lights in them . . . looking at him . . . the forehead and straight cut black hair . . . and it was Melva . . . and she looked at him and smiled and said . . . I'll wait Alex . . . and Alex became confused and kissed her . . . became confused and continued his search . . . on his hands and knees . . . pushed a poppy stem . . . a black-poppy stem . . . pushed aside a lily stem . . . a red lily stem . . . a poppy . . . a lily . . . and suddenly he

19. Spanish for "sweet," a term of endearment.
20. Fania Marinoff; the others are unknown members of Nugent's social circle.
21. An unknown friend of Nugent's.

stood erect . . . exultant . . . and in his hand he held . . . an ivory holder inlaid with red jade . . . and green . . .

and Alex awoke . . . Beauty's hair tickled his nose . . . Beauty was smiling in his sleep . . . half his face stained flush color by the sun . . . the other half in shadow . . . blue shadow . . . his eyelashes casting cobwebby blue shadows on his cheek . . . his lips were so beautiful . . . quizzical . . . Alex wondered why he always thought of that passage from Wilde's *Salome* when he looked at Beauty's lips[22] . . . I would kiss your lips . . . he WOULD like to kiss Beauty's lips . . . Alex flushed warm . . . with shame . . . or was it shame . . . he reached across Beauty for a cigarette . . . Beauty's cheek felt cool to his arm . . . his hair felt soft . . . Alex lay smoking . . . such a dream . . . red calla lilies . . . red calla lilies . . . and . . . what could it all mean . . . did dreams have meanings . . . Fania said . . . and black poppies . . . thousands . . . millions . . . Alex put out his cigarette . . . closed his eyes . . . he mustn't see Beauty yet . . . speak to him . . . his lips were too hot . . . dry . . . the palms of his hands too cool and moist . . . thru his half closed eyes he could see Beauty . . . propped . . . cheek in hand . . . on one elbow . . . looking at him . . . lips smiling quizzically . . . he wished Beauty wouldn't look so hard . . . Alex was finding it difficult to breathe . . . breathe normally . . . why MUST Beauty look so long . . . and smile that way . . . his face seemed nearer . . . it was . . . Alex could feel Beauty's hair upon his forehead . . . breathe normally . . . could feel Beauty's breath upon his nostrils and lips . . . and it was clean and faintly colored with tobacco . . . breathe normally Alex . . . Beauty's lips were nearer . . . Alex closed his eyes . . . how did one act . . . his pulse was hammering . . . from wrist to fingertip . . . Beauty's lips touched his . . . his temples throbbed . . . throbbed . . . his pulse hammered from wrist to fingertip . . . Beauty's breath came short now . . . softly staccato . . . breathe normally Alex . . . you are asleep . . . Beauty's lips touched his . . . breathe normally . . . and pressed hard . . . hard and cool . . . his body trembled . . . breathe normally Alex . . . Beauty's lips pressed hard . . . hard and cool . . . how much pressure does it take to waken one . . . Alex sighed . . . moved softly . . . how does one act . . . Beauty's hair barely touched him now . . . his breath was faint on . . . Alex's nostrils . . . and lips . . . Alex stretched and opened his eyes . . . Beauty was looking at him propped on one elbow . . . cheek in his palm . . . Beauty spoke . . . scratch my head please Dulce . . . Alex was breathing normally now . . . propped against the bedhead . . . Beauty's head in his lap . . . Beauty spoke . . . I wonder why I like to look at some things Dulce . . . things like smoke and cats . . . and . . . you . . . Alex's pulse no longer hammered from wrist to fingertip . . . wrist to fingertip . . . the rose dusk had become blue night . . . and soon . . . soon they would go out into the blue . . .

---

23. Oscar Wilde's play, *Salome,* which shared the playbill with Willis Richardson's *The Chip Woman's Fortune* when both plays were produced in New York in 1923. *Salome,* written in the late nineteenth century, was deemed obscene by the British government and never produced there.

Sahdji, an African Ballet

Characters

KONOMBJU, an Azandé Chieftain
MRABO, heir of Konombju
SAHDJI, favorite wife of Konombju
THE SEVEN OTHER WIVES OF KONOMBJU
THE MEDICINE MAN
DANCING WOMEN, attendants of the Medicine Man
THREE COUNSELLORS, aged attendants of Konombju
THE CHANTER, the interpreter of the Ballet

Scene: Ancestral Central Africa; a hunting feast of the Azandé tribe. An open clearing, near the dense forest to the left, where trunks of trees and vines weave a dense pattern in scarlet, yellow, and green on the black of the shadowy depths of the jungle. At right centre is a chief's hut, with bamboo side curtains, its one doorway framed in lashed bamboo, and one bamboo latticed window. An elliptical shield leans against the doorpost,—a brilliantly decorated clay jug stands on the bare ground under the window. Early morning—just after dawn. The tribe is preparing for a hunt.

Curtain rises on scene as described. The women are grouped before the chief's hut; the MEDICINE MAN and attendants are grouped at left centre, and at extreme left, completing the half-circle, is KONOMBJU with his THREE COUNSELLORS. The CHANTER, an enormous black man, is discernable at the extreme left, who stands stationary throughout the ballet. A ceremonial blanket falls from his left shoulder, in rippling folds to the ground. His right arm, free of the robe, is striped above and below the elbow with curious metal bands of white and gilt metal, and he grasps an enormous spear. A glistening bush of silver hair bristles all over his head. From time to time, making only gestures with his spear, he chants in a booming singsong voice, the African proverbial sayings which are indicated for his rôle. All other action is dance pantomime.

The tom-toms have been beaten for several minutes, at a rapid pace, before the curtain rises, and are on the stage manipulated by three men, straddling their drums in back centre. As the curtain rises, the drumming slows down somewhat, and in the foreground six or eight bucks, dressed in warriors' garb, some with spears and some with bows and arrows, are dancing—it being the time of the feast before the hunt. There is the thud-thud of bare feet on the bare ground, beating in a rhythm separate from that of the tom-toms and the accompanying gourd-rattles. Gradually as the dance slows down, and the circle of the dancers closes in in an ever contracting circle, a chant picks up from the male voices.

CHANT

God of the thousand-flamed fire,
God of the lights and shadows
Many-tongued fire,
In the heart of the jungle,
In the middle of the forest,
In the center of the hearth-fire,

Plays of Negro Life, 1927.

> Thou of many places,
> Visit upon us the light of your shining,
> Visit upon us your shadows to hide us
> So that we see and be not seen
> So that we conquer
> And to you,—for your trouble
> Your care for your children,
> We feast on our first kill.
> To you, and you only.

At the end of the Hunting Chant, the women raise their arms in salute to the warriors, and SAHDJI appears at the doorway of the chief's hut, standing motionless.

The Chanter: Be silent, tree! Don't listen to the noise of hatchets!

SAHDJI glances quickly in the direction of KONOMBJU, and re-enters the hut. The MEDICINE MAN comes forward to charm the King's spear, while the dancing attendants bring his shield to him from the doorway. They prostrate themselves as they deliver the shield to the MEDICINE MAN, who gives it to the chief. The women attendants then begin to dance in flattery to the chief a Victory Chant for the success of the hunt:

> CHANT

> Sharper than spears
> Are the eyes of the hunter,—
> Stronger than shields
> Is the strength of his sinews,—
> And when he has killed,
> He has slain in his bosom,
> Fear and the gods of mischance.

> Only the tiger conquers the tiger,
> Only the lion's kin stalks down
> The king of the forest.
> Hail to the man possessed of the might
> Of the jungle, the thousand-fold
> Might of the jungle!

> Hail to the man possessed of the might
> Hail to the hunter of hunters!
> Empty handed he goes to his forest,
> Heavy with spoils he returns to his women;
> Lean and sly are his early out-goings,
> Fat are his feats at the home-coming.

As their chant nears its end, SAHDJI appears again in the doorway, her robe laid aside, smeared in red ochre and clad only in a girdle. As she is noticed, a shudder of horror spreads over the crowd, the wives of KONOMBJU leave in dignified affront, the dancing women stare, and the COUNSELLORS cloak their faces.

The Chanter: There is blood in the dregs.

SAHDJI moves undaunted toward the chief, and begins to hum the Victory Chant, slowly beginning to dance it. She dances the same figures as the dancing women, only more gracefully. The dancing attendants, recovering from their astonishment, weave her an accompaniment, and the tom-toms and the chant merge into a minor variant of the Victory Chant. Body bent forward from the waist, head thrown high and arms extended tautly behind her, she dances in unison with the tom-tom beat till the chant and the drumming abruptly stop and leave her in a supplicant posture before KONOMBJU. Flattered, he makes a gesture of defiant approval.

The Chanter: The flames from the ground are already catching the branches.

KONOMBJU rises before the COUNSELLORS have uncloaked their faces; his stir moves them to rise and begin preparations for the hunt. The dancing women grimace and shrug their shoulders discreetly. A warmer gold begins to appliqué the clearing, throwing into sharper relief the crescent of young bucks and the half-moon of the MEDICINE MAN and women. With an imperious gesture, KONOMBJU, ignoring the prostrate SAHDJI, commands the warriors to the hunt. Four bucks, with shields and spears, go off left, the COUNSELLORS salute, KONOMBJU exits followed by the remaining warriors.

The Chanter: A man does not use one finger to take out an arrow.

SAHDJI slowly rises to her feet, and with her head high, walks to the hut. The dancing women assume the familiarity that they dared not show in the chief's presence and smirk at her. She ignores them. They turn to the MEDICINE MAN in chagrin. He motions them off back center, and going up to the COUNSELLORS, for a minute they cluster in conference; they yawn behind the flattened palms of their hands, then make a gesture of warding off evil, and exit.

The Chanter: Death is at the end of the cloak.

SAHDJI, after a long pause, peers furtively from the doorway, makes a gesture of impatience and re-enters the hut. After a little, a lithe bronze figure, dressed for the hunt, with shield and lance comes from the left, stealthily scans the scene, and crosses to the hut, resting his shield and spear under the bamboo window. It is MRABO, nephew of KONOMBJU—a royal leopard skin is about his shoulders. SAHDJI's form appears at the window and her hand waves through the bamboo bars. MRABO, up to this time self-possessed, starts and rather hastily rushes into the hut. After a moment, he re-enters and starts to take his spear and shield inside. He hesitates, beckons an attendant, gives him his spear, and takes from him a short side-sword, which he buckles on and re-enters.

The Chanter: You can daub yourself with ochre, but not with kingship.

NUMBO, MRABO's attendant, can be seen on skirmish watch, first one side of the hut, then the other. His friendliness is indicated by his evident concern to screen the lovers from intruders.

The Chanter: The fig tree does not call the birds.

The curtain is lowered to indicate a passage of time, but lifts on the same scene. As it lifts, the CHANTER exclaims solemnly—

The Chanter: Time is no longer than a rope.

It is now sunset. The lights have been shifted to cast a sunset pattern of mauve and orange. The shadows run in the opposite direction from the previous scene, and a glow is seen through the background of the forest.
    MRABO comes out of the hut, followed by SAHDJI, who hands him his shield. They linger a moment, and MRABO then suddenly makes off centre stage, behind the hut. SAHDJI gazes after him, and then enters the hut.

The Chanter: The little fountain ahead makes one very thirsty.

SAHDJI peeps furtively out of the doorway . . . then with light steps, skips into the clearing. With improvised dance steps she gathers twigs and fragments of wood, and builds a fire, fanning the embers with her hands and breath. In the midst of the ceremony—

The Chanter: God's fire is never quenched.

SAHDJI pays no attention but concentrates in hypnotic gaze on the glowing flames, which mount higher and higher and cast long graceful shadows. Then she begins the Fire Dance, in, around and behind the fire, leaping with graceful bounds over the blaze, as graceful and capricious as the tongues of the flames she dances about. Throughout, her dance keeps the rhythm of the fire, and as the flames die down, her movements become slower and slower, until as the fire flares, her dance becomes intermittent, and as the flames fail and flicker out in one last spurt, SAHDJI sinks to the ground.

The Chanter: Darkness has eaten her own child.

The forest that was fantastically alive with red gleams and yellow flares and quivering shadows is now veiled in purple silence. Out of the sepulchral darkness, the booming voice of the CHANTER is heard—

The Chanter: Darkness gossips about no one. *(a pause)* One link only sounds because of
          another! *(a longer pause, and then in a voice of foreboding—)* Watcher of the
          moon, beware of darkness!

An evening breeze, after the short stillness, begins to stir the foliage. Gradually, with intervals of silence as if varied with the wind, distant but approaching drum-beats are heard, and then wails in chorus. SAHDJI quickly rises and lights a flare torch. She is in evident terror and alarm.

The Chanter: It is nothing—we shall meet near the oxhide. The tread and the dull chant
          come nearer and nearer.

          Goare go shinoa
          Go elui ruri
          Goare go shinoa
          Go elui ruri

The CHANTER makes his first decided movement as he hears the Death Chant, clashes his spear against the metal boss of his shield, and then drops the spear point to the ground. In a rumbling voice, he echoes the chant—

> Go elui ruri—Go elui ruri—
> When a man dies, he departs forever.

The other wives file in from behind the hut, extreme right, and dishevel their hair as they enter, softly wailing, and in evident alarm. SAHDJI, startled by them, commences to dishevel her hair, but then rearranges it, facing the forest clearing.

With rhythmic funeral tread, black shadows are seen between the tree trunks, and a streaming file of natives slowly comes through the underbrush, bearing a burden swung between shoulder poles. SAHDJI waits swaying softly, and as she recognizes the situation retreats backward to her doorway. The body-bearers file in; already some of the men are smeared with ash-colored ochre. KONOMBJU's shield is being carried behind the bearers. SAHDJI, perceiving it, stops her ears with her hands, while the wives break out in loud, rhythmic wails. The bearers place the body at SAHDJI's feet, as the MEDICINE MAN, rushing on, prostrates himself over the body. With grave hocus-pocus, he crawls around the body, sniffs, listens, chafes the hands, which drop with a thud on the ground as he releases them, beats on the ground with his wand,— threatens the bearers, who flee to a safe distance, and then as he realizes the situation smears his face with white ochre from his pouch and snaps his wand ceremonially in two. At the crackling sound, the whole assembly break out in hysterical wails, and in the first lull the CHANTER speaks.

The Chanter: It is not hunger, the chooser of servants, but spears, the slayers of princes.

MRABO comes forward, glances quickly at SAHDJI, who casts her gaze to the ground, and approaches the MEDICINE MAN. They glare at one another for a moment then MRABO adjusts his leopard skin with an air of authority and the MEDICINE MAN prostrates himself in obeisance. Fumbling for the king's sceptre, he finds it in the girdle of the corpse and hands it to MRABO. SAHDJI jangles her bracelets.

The Chanter: (lifting his spear, and in a fresh tone of voice) When a man dies, a man remains.
Always build a fence round the king's word.

As if listening to some supernatural voice from another direction, MRABO stretches his height, takes on full composure, and grips his sceptre with an air of authority. He orders the MEDICINE MAN to prepare the body for the funeral ceremonies. The elder wives of KONOMBJU have smeared themselves with white ochre and put on mourning dress—they re-enter in pairs and singly from right and left of hut. MRABO takes his stand in the doorway of KONOMBJU's hut. The women wail before the body and then, with obeisance before MRABO, file past him into the hut.

The Chanter: We are wandering in the belly of a bullock.

SAHDJI alone has not shown signs of grief, but gazes at MRABO, who avoids her gaze. Slowly the warrior-bucks, dressed for the funeral rites, file on stage and take up gradually the heavy sway and stomp of the Death Dance. It has the same arm movement of the homage of the women, but a leg movement stomp (beating the ground with the sole of the foot) that is more and more terrific as it mounts to a crescendo in the unison of the dancing.

SAHDJI, as if for the first time awake to the terror of the situation, flees, as the CHANTER says—

The Chanter: Those who pick berries in the same wood do not love each other.

The Death Dance reaches an orgiastic climax around the grass-strewn couch which the MEDICINE MAN and his attendants have made for KONOMBJU, and is subsiding as SAHDJI re-enters, dressed for bridal ceremony in red ochre instead of the white ochre of the funeral rites. Again there is astonishment on all sides, registered differently—but especially by the elders, who cloak their faces. MRABO starts to cloak his face, but is restrained by curiosity.

The Chanter: They say that an ant once made an errand boy of an elephant.

Swaying slowly to the boom of the off-stage funeral drums, SAHDJI, with a dagger and a pot of ointment, approaches the body of KONOMBJU, ignoring the outstretched wand of the MEDICINE MAN. The crowd shivers at the sacrilege; turn their backs. The elders appeal to MRABO with gestures, but he stands hypnotically transfixed, his eyes on SAHDJI. She places the dagger in KONOMBJU's hand, and anoints the body with the ointment. Over her and around her, warriors and attendants erect a four-cornered canopy of native cloth supported at the corners by four long spears, and lean KONOMBJU's shields at the two corners and over the body. The MEDICINE MAN comes on with the Death Figure, which he installs at the head of the chief. Attendants bring the food vessels, which are placed beside the body, and then the death mask is erected on KONOMBJU's spear point. This is the signal for MRABO to approach the bier— the drums beat a march rhythm in anticipation, but he approaches reluctantly and with evident dread. Seeing his dismay, the elders try to persuade SAHDJI to leave the bier, but she takes the dagger from KONOMBJU's hand, and turns the point toward her own bosom. As they sense the import of the gesture, they shrink back, and MRABO turns his back on the scene in grief. The women are amazed and strain forward. The men recoil.

The Chanter: A word can never turn back, only a finger can.

The drum music becomes fainter—MRABO, with a sudden start, decides to leave the scene, and commands the wives, and then the warriors to leave. They exit slowly right and back centre. He then goes into the hut with his Counsellors, who glance furtively at the bier in passing it. Only the MEDICINE MAN hesitates. MRABO turns back with a threatening gesture, which he suddenly breaks off as the MEDICINE MAN in turn raises his wand. There is derision and triumph on the MEDICINE MAN's face. Both exit separately; the MEDICINE MAN extreme left into the forest, MRABO into the hut. (after a pause in the silence)

The Chanter: It is nothing—we shall meet near the oxhide. *(and after another pause)* Water is never tired of flowing.

SAHDJI gradually detaches herself from the couch. With slow graceful bendings from the waist, she begins to dance. Reverential gestures and oblivious abandon alternate as she is torn between her loyalty to the vow of death and her desire for life. The slow, stately steps of the funeral march give way time and again to the sheer love of rhythm and dance. She whirls, turns, writhes around the death couch, until suddenly her whirling brings her face to face with the death mask. She shrinks from it in superstitious horror,—then gradually recovering herself, approaches and swiftly touches it, hastening away before harm can befall her. Again she comes forward and touches it, and cowers at her own daring.

At the first touching of the mask, the CHANTER has turned away from the front face he has maintained throughout, and cast his spear point to the ground. At the interval after the second touch, he chants—

The Chanter: When man is silent, God speaks.

SAHDJI, becoming bold, snatches the mask from the pole, places it on the ground and mockingly dances around it. She then replaces it on the spear, and in wilder and wilder gestures before it, hurls insult after insult upon it. Finally completely fatigued, she has retreated backward to a position directly in front of the canopy couch, and throws herself backward over the body. Reaching for the dagger, she lifts it as MRABO, who has apparently been watching the scene, appears suddenly in the doorway in arrested posture of striding toward the couch. He recoils as he sees the up-lifted dagger, and covers his face with his shield, as SAHDJI plunges it into her bosom and turns in her death throes upon the body of KONOMBJU. Quick curtain, just as the CHANTER says—

The Chanter: All clouds have lightning. Darkness has eaten her own child.

Curtain

Dorothy West

(1907–1998)

Dorothy West was born June 2, 1907, in Boston, the only child of Rachel Pease and Isaac Christopher West. Her father, an ex-slave from Virginia, was known as "the Black Banana King" for his wholesale fruit business. Her father's prosperity enabled her to attend Girls' Latin School and spend summer vacations at Oak Bluffs on Martha's Vineyard. By the age of fifteen, West was already publishing stories in *The Boston Post*. She graduated from Girls' Latin School in 1923 and began course work at Boston University and the Columbia University School of Journalism. In 1926 West and her cousin, poet Helene Johnson, moved to New York City to participate in the Harlem Renaissance. The same year she won second place, tied with Zora Neale Hurston, in a contest sponsored by *Opportunity* for her first important short story "The Typewriter." Later included in *The Best Short Stories of 1926,* edited by Edward O'Brien, it remains her best-known short story.

West and her cousin were the youngest of the Harlem bohemian set (before Mae Cowdery came to town a few years later). She socialized with the editors of *Fire!!,* becoming good friends with Hurston and Wallace Thurman. She supplemented her writing income with bit theater parts and work as a welfare relief investigator in Harlem and then for the Works Progress Administration. In 1932 she joined a group of African Americans, including Langston Hughes, traveling to the Soviet Union to complete a film about race relations, but the film was never made. In 1934 West founded the important magazine *Challenge* and served as its editor in an attempt to revive the Renaissance. In 1937 the last issue of *Challenge* was published and West founded *New Challenge* the same year with her friend Marian Minus as coeditor and Richard Wright as associate editor, but it failed after one issue.

West's more than sixty short stories, written from 1926 to 1960, were published in *Opportunity, The Saturday Evening Quill,* and *The New York Daily News,* which published twenty-six of the stories. She began writing for *The Vineyard Gazette* after moving to Martha's Vineyard in 1947 to care for an ailing aunt. She neither married nor had children and very little is known about her personal life. Her acclaimed novel *The Living Is Easy* was published in 1948. West gained renewed critical attention with its 1982 reprint. In the 1980s West's essays in *The Vineyard Gazette* caught the attention of Jacqueline Kennedy Onassis, a Doubleday editor and summer resident of Martha's Vineyard. Onassis convinced West to finish her novel *The Wedding,* which she had laid aside during the Black Power era due to its focus on social class and color differences within the black community. In 1995 Doubleday published not only *The Wedding* but also a collection of short stories, *The Richer the Poorer.* "The Black Dress" is reprinted here for the first time. West died a few years later at age ninety-one; she was the last surviving member of the Harlem Renaissance.

The Typewriter

It occurred to him, as he eased past the bulging knees of an Irish wash lady and forced an apologetic passage down the aisle of the crowded car, that more than anything in all the world he wanted not to go home. He began to wish passionately that he had never been born, that he had never been married, that he had never been the means of life's coming into the world. He knew quite suddenly that he hated his flat and his family and his friends. And most of all the incessant thing that would "clatter clatter" until every nerve screamed aloud, and the words of the evening paper danced crazily before him, and the insane desire to crush and kill set his fingers twitching.

He shuffled down the street, an abject little man of fifty-odd years, in an ageless overcoat that flapped in the wind. He was cold, and he hated the North, and particularly Boston, and saw suddenly a barefoot pickaninny[1] sitting on a fence in the hot, Southern sun with a piece of steaming corn bread and a piece of fried salt pork in either grimy hand.

He was tired, and he wanted his supper, but he didn't want the beans, and frankfurters, and light bread that Net would undoubtedly have. That Net had had every Monday night since that regrettable moment fifteen years before when he had told her—innocently—that such a supper tasted "right nice. Kinda change from what we always has."

He mounted the four brick steps leading to his door and pulled at the bell, but there was no answering ring. It was broken again, and in a mental flash he saw himself with a multitude of tools and a box of matches shivering in the vestibule after supper. He began to pound lustily on the door and wondered vaguely if his hand would bleed if he smashed the glass. He hated the sight of blood. It sickened him.

Some one was running down the stairs. Daisy probably. Millie would be at that infernal thing, pounding, pounding. . . . He entered. The chill of the house swept him. His child was wrapped in a coat. She whispered solemnly, "Poppa, Miz Hicks an' Miz Berry's orful mad. They gointa move if they can't get more heat. The furnace's birnt out all day. Mama couldn't fix it." He said hurriedly, "I'll go right down. I'll go right down." He hoped Mrs. Hicks wouldn't pull open her door and glare at him. She was large and domineering, and her husband was a bully. If her husband ever struck him it would kill him. He hated life but he didn't want to die. He was afraid of God, and in his wildest flights of fancy, couldn't imagine himself an angel. He went softly down the stairs.

He began to shake the furnace fiercely. And he shook into it every wrong, mumbling softly under his breath. He began to think back over his uneventful years, and it came to him as rather a shock that he had never sworn in all his life. He wondered uneasily if he dared say "damn." It was taken for granted that a man swore when he tended a stubborn furnace. And his strongest interjection was "Great balls of fire!"

---

1. A derogatory term for black child; it is not used in a derogatory sense here but merely indictes the Southern setting for this character's memory of his youth.

The cellar began to warm, and he took off his inadequate overcoat that was streaked with dirt. Well, Net would have to clean that. He'd be damned—! It frightened him and thrilled him. He wanted suddenly to rush upstairs and tell Mrs. Hicks if she didn't like the way he was running things, she could get out. But he heaped another shovelful of coal on the fire and sighed. He would never be able to get away from himself and the routine of years.

He thought of that eager Negro lad of seventeen who had come North to seek his fortune. He had walked jauntily down Boylston Street, and even his own kind had laughed at the incongruity of him. But he had thrown up his head and promised himself: "You'll have an office here some day. With plate-glass windows and a real mahogany desk." But, though he didn't know it then, he was not the progressive type.[2] And he became successively, in the years, bell boy, porter, waiter, cook, and finally janitor in a down town office building.

He had married Net when he was thirty-three and a waiter. He had married her partly because—though he might not have admitted it—there was no one to eat the expensive delicacies the generous cook gave him every night to bring home. And partly because he dared hope there might be a son to fulfill his dreams. But Millie had come, and after her twin girls who had died within two weeks, then Daisy, and it was tacitly understood that Net was done with child-bearing.

Life, though flowing monotonously, had flowed peacefully enough until that sucker of sanity became a sitting-room fixture. Intuitively at the very first he had felt its undesirability. He had suggested hesitatingly that they couldn't afford it. Three dollars: food and fuel. Times were hard, and the twenty dollars apiece the respective husbands of Miz Hicks and Miz Berry irregularly paid was only five dollars more than the thirty-five a month he paid his own Hebraic landlord. And the Lord knew his salary was little enough. At which point Net spoke her piece, her voice rising shrill. "God knows I never complain 'bout nothin'. Ain't no other woman got less than me. I bin wearin' this same dress here five years an' I'll wear it another five. But I don't want nothin'. I ain't never wanted nothin'. An' when I does as', it's only for my children. You're a poor sort of father if you can't give that child jes' three dollars a month to rent that typewriter. Ain't 'nother girl in school ain't got one. An' mos' of 'ems bought an' paid for. You know yourself how Millie is. She wouldn't as' me for it till she had to. An' I ain't going to disappoint her. She's goin' to get that typewriter Saturday, mark my words."

On a Monday then it had been installed. And in the months that followed, night after night he listened to the murderous "tack, tack, tack" that was like a vampire slowly drinking his blood. If only he could escape. Bar a door against the sound of it. But tied hand and foot by the economic fact that "Lord knows we can't afford to have fires burnin' an' lights lit all over the flat. You'all gotta set in one room. An' when y'get tired of settin' y' c'n go to bed. Gas bill was somep'n scandalous last month."

He heaped a final shovelful of coal on the fire and watched the first blue flames. Then,

2. The type to succeed, to progress upward in his jobs.

his overcoat under his arm, he mounted the cellar stairs. Mrs. Hicks was standing in her kitchen door, arms akimbo. "It's warmin'," she volunteered.

"Yeh," he was conscious of his grime-streaked face and hands, "it's warmin'. I'm sorry 'bout all day."

She folded her arms across her ample bosom. "Tending a furnace ain't a woman's work. I don't blame your wife none 'tall."

Unsuspecting he was grateful. "Yeh, it's pretty hard for a woman. I always look after it 'fore I goes to work, but some days it jes' ac's up."

"Y'oughta have a janitor, that's what y'ought," she flung at him. "The same cullud man that tends them apartments would be willin'. Mr. Taylor has him. It takes a man to run a furnace, and when the man's away all day—"

"I know," he interrupted, embarrassed and hurt, "I know. Tha's right, Miz Hicks tha's right. But I ain't in a position to make no improvements. Times is hard."

She surveyed him critically. "Your wife called down 'bout three times while you was in the cellar. I reckon she wants you for supper."

"Thanks," he mumbled and escaped up the back stairs.

He hung up his overcoat in the closet, telling himself, a little lamely, that it wouldn't take him more'n a minute to clean it up himself after supper. After all Net was tired and prob'ly worried what with Miz Hicks and all. And he hated men who made slaves of their women folk. Good old Net.

He tidied up in the bathroom, washing his face and hands carefully and cleanly so as to leave no—or very little—stain on the roller towel. It was hard enough for Net, God knew.

He entered the kitchen. The last spirals of steam were rising from his supper. One thing about Net she served a full plate. He smiled appreciatively at her unresponsive back, bent over the kitchen sink. There was no one could bake beans just like Net's. And no one who could find a market with frankfurters quite so fat.

He sank down at his place. "Evenin', hon."

He saw her back stiffen. "If your supper's cold, 'tain't my fault. I called and called."

He said hastily, "It's fine, Net, fine. Piping."

She was the usual tired housewife. "Y'oughta et your supper 'fore you fooled with that furnace. I ain't bothered 'bout them niggers. I got all my dishes washed 'cept yours. An' I hate to mess up my kitchen after I once get it straightened up."

He was humble. "I'll give that old furnace an extra lookin' after in the mornin'. It'll las' all day to-morrow, hon."

"An' on top of that," she continued, unheeding him and giving a final wrench to her dish towel, "that confounded bell don't ring. An'—"

"I'll fix it after supper," he interposed hastily.

She hung up her dish towel and came to stand before him looming large and yellow. "An' that old Miz Berry, she claim she was expectin' comp'ny. An' she knows they must 'a' come an' gone while she was in her kitchen an' couldn't be at her winder to watch for 'em. Old liar," she brushed back a lock of naturally straight hair. "She wasn't expectin' nobody."

"Well, you know how some folks are—"

"Fools! Half the world," was her vehement answer. "I'm goin' in the front room an' set down a spell. I bin on my feet all day. Leave them dishes on the table. God knows I'm tired, but I'll come back an' wash 'em." But they both knew, of course, that he, very clumsily, would.

At precisely quarter past nine when he, strained at last to the breaking point, uttering an inhuman, strangled cry, flung down his paper, clutched at his throat and sprang to his feet, Millie's surprised young voice, shocking him to normalcy, heralded the first of that series of great moments that every humble little middle-class man eventually experiences.

"What's the matter, poppa? You sick? I wanted you to help me."

He drew out his handkerchief and wiped his hot hands. "I declare I must 'a' fallen asleep an' had a nightmare. No, I ain't sick. What you want, hon?"

"Dictate me a letter, poppa. I c'n do sixty words a minute.—You know, like a business letter. You know, like those men in your building dictate to their stenographers. Don't you hear 'em sometimes?"

"Oh, sure, I know, hon. Poppa'll help you. Sure. I hear that Mr. Browning—Sure."

Net rose. "Guess I'll put this child to bed. Come on now, Daisy, without no fuss.—Then I'll run up to pa's. He ain't bin well all week."

When the door closed behind them, he crossed to his daughter, conjured the image of Mr. Browning in the process of dictating, so arranged himself, and coughed importantly.

"Well, Millie—"

"Oh, poppa, is that what you'd call your stenographer?" she teased. "And anyway pretend I'm really one—and you're really my boss, and this letter's real important."

A light crept into his dull eyes. Vigor through his thin blood. In a brief moment the weight of years fell from him like a cloak. Tired, bent, little old man that he was, he smiled, straightened, tapped impressively against his teeth with a toil-stained finger, and became that enviable emblem of American life: a business man.

"You be Miz Hicks, huh, honey? Course we can't both use the same name. I'll be J. Lucius Jones. J. Lucius. All them real big doin' men use their middle names. Jus' kinda looks big doin', doncha think, hon? Looks like money, huh? J. Lucius." He uttered a sound that was like the proud cluck of a strutting hen. "J. Lucius." It rolled like oil from his tongue.

His daughter twisted impatiently. "Now, poppa—I mean Mr. Jones, sir—please begin. I am ready for dictation, sir."

He was in that office on Boylston Street, looking with visioning eyes through its plate-glass windows, tapping with impatient fingers on its real mahogany desk.

"Ah—Beaker Brothers, Park Square Building, Boston, Mass. Ah—Gentlemen: In reply to yours at the seventh instant I would state—"

Every night thereafter in the weeks that followed, with Daisy packed off to bed, and

Net "gone up to pa's" or nodding inobtrusively in her corner there was the chameleon change of a Court Street janitor to J. Lucius Jones, dealer in stocks and bonds. He would stand, posturing importantly, flicking imaginary dust from his coat lapel, or, his hands locked behind his back, he would stride up and down, earnestly and seriously debating the advisability of buying copper with the market in such a fluctuating state. Once a week, too, he stopped in at Jerry's, and after a preliminary purchase of cheap cigars, bought the latest trade papers, mumbling an embarrassed explanation: "I got a little money. Think I'll invest it in reliable stock."

The letters Millie typed and subsequently discarded, he rummaged for later, and under cover of writing to his brother in the South, laboriously with a great many fancy flourishes, signed each neatly typed sheet with the exalted J. Lucius Jones.

Later, when he mustered the courage he suggested tentatively to Millie that it might be fun—just fun, of course! —to answer his letters. One night—he laughed a good deal louder and longer than necessary—he'd be J. Lucius Jones, and the next night—here he swallowed hard and looked a little frightened—Rockefeller or Vanderbilt or Morgan[3]—just for fun, y'understand! To which Millie gave consent. It mattered little to her one way or the other. It was practice, and that was what she needed. Very soon now she'd be in the hundred class. Then maybe she could get a job!

He was growing very careful of his English. Occasionally—and must be admitted, ashamedly—he made surreptitious ventures into the dictionary. He had to, of course. J. Lucius Jones would never say "Y'got to" when he meant "It is expedient." And, old brain though he was, he learned quickly and easily, juggling words with amazing facility.

Eventually he bought stamps and envelopes—long, important looking envelopes—and stammered apologetically to Millie, "Honey, poppa thought it'd help you if you learned to type envelopes too. Reckon you'll have to do that, too, when y'get a job. Poor old man," he swallowed painfully, "came round selling these envelopes. You know how 'tis. So I had to buy 'em." Which was satisfactory to Millie. If she saw through her father, she gave no sign. After all, it was practice, and Mr. Hennessey had said that—though not in just those words.

He had got in the habit of carrying those self-addressed envelopes in his inner pocket where they bulged impressively. And occasionally he would take them out—on the car usually—and smile upon them. This one might be from J. P. Morgan. This one from Henry Ford.[4] And a million-dollar deal involved in each. That narrow, little spinster, who, upon his sitting down, had drawn herself away from his contact, was shunning J. Lucius Jones![5]

Once, led by some sudden, strange impulse, as an outgoing car rumbled up out of the subway, he got out a letter, darted a quick, shamed glance about him, dropped it in

3. John D. Rockefeller, Cornelius Vanderbilt, J. P. Morgan—all millionaires of the time.
4. The car manufacturer.
5. Most likely a white woman who shrinks at the prospect of touching a black man.

an adjacent box, and swung aboard the car, feeling, dazedly, as if he had committed a crime. And the next night he sat in the sitting-room quite on edge until Net said suddenly, "Look here, a real important letter come today for you, pa. Here 'tis. What you s'pose it says," and he reached out a hand that trembled. He made brief explanation. "Advertisement, hon. Thassal."

They came quite frequently after that, and despite the fact the he knew them by heart, he read them slowly and carefully, rustling the sheet, making inaudible, intelligent comments. He was, in these moments, pathetically earnest.

Monday, as he went about his janitor's duties, he composed in his mind the final letter from J. P. Morgan that would consummate a big business deal. For days now letters had passed between them. J. P. had been at first frankly uninterested. He had written tersely and briefly. He wrote glowingly of the advantages of a pact between them. Daringly he argued in terms of billions. And at last J. P. had written his next letter would be decisive. Which next letter, this Monday, as he trailed about the office building, was writing itself on his brain.

That night Millie opened the door for him. Her plain face was transformed. "Poppa— poppa, I got a job! Twelve dollars a week to start with! Isn't that *swell!*"

He was genuinely pleased. "Honey, I'm glad. Right glad," and went up the stairs, unsuspecting.

He ate his supper hastily, went down into the cellar to see about his fire, returned and carefully tidied up, informing his reflection in the bathroom mirror, "Well, J. Lucius, you c'n expect that final letter any day now."

He entered the sitting-room. The phonograph was playing. Daisy was singing lustily. Strange. Net was talking animatedly to Millie, busy with needle and thread over a neat, little frock. His wild glance darted to the table. The pretty, little centerpiece, the bowl and wax flowers all neatly arranged; the typewriter gone from its accustomed place. It seemed an hour before he could speak. He felt himself trembling. Went hot and cold.

"Millie—your typewriter's—gone!"

She made a deft little in and out movement with her needle. "It's the eighth, you know. When the man came to-day for the money, I sent it back. I won't need it no more—now! —the money's on the mantelpiece, poppa."

"Yeh," he muttered. "All right."

He sank down in his chair, fumbled for the paper, found it.

Net said, "Your poppa wants to read. Stop your noise, Daisy."

She obediently stopped both her noise and the phonograph, took up her book, and became absorbed. Millie went on with her sewing in placid anticipation of the morrow. Net immediately began to nod, gave a curious snort, slept.

Silence. That crowded in on him, engulfed him. That blurred his vision, dulled his brain. Vast, white, impenetrable. . . . His ears strained for the old, familiar sound. And silence beat upon them. . . . The words of the evening paper jumbled together. He read: J. P. Morgan goes—

It burst upon him. Blinded him. His hands groped for the bulge beneath his coat. Why this—this was the end! The end of those great moments—the end of everything! Bewildering pain tore through him. He clutched at his heart and felt, almost, the jagged edges drive into his hand. A lethargy swept down upon him. He could not move, nor utter a sound. He could not pray, nor curse.

Against the wall of that silence J. Lucius Jones crashed and died.

The Black Dress

They sent me word that morning that old Mr. Johnson had died in the night. It was not really a surprise to me. I knew he had been lingering for weeks.

That was my chiefest reason for writing to Margaret. Deep in his heart old Johnson, her father, loved her very much. It would not be so hard for him to go with her hand in his. Margaret I knew had forgiven him his early injustice. I felt she would be glad to brighten his last pain-black days. They would not be many. He could not live beyond the year, and it was Christmas week when I wrote her to come.

I did not mention her father's hopeless illness. I simply asked her, for old time's sake, to come and hang up her stocking with mine, as we had done when we were very young.

Her acceptance came in a day or two. She was between shows and husbands. It would be good to see me again after twelve long years. Did I still have dimples? Would I find her changed? For better, for worse?

I wondered. Margaret and I had been like sisters all our growing years. I suppose she loved me more than she loved anyone else. She had only an impatient tolerance for her bigoted father. But the years had probably softened this into something nearer affection. After all, he was her only living relative.

To my knowledge she never wrote him. Nor did she write me. Occasionally I would get a telegram of extravagant endearment, and very often a generous check. My babies, who had never seen her, spoke of her as Aunt Margaret.

I wrote her regularly. She had always seemed hard to the home folks, but I felt I understood her. She was not hard. She was simply unsentimental. She had one goal, the stage. She had to fight the whole community, beginning with her father, to make them accept the theatre as a legitimate profession. The fight with her father had been long and bitter. The neighbors had taken his side. Naturally that did something to her spirit. When she left home at eighteen, it was not a girl but a bitter woman who said good-by to me, the only one to bid her good-by and God-speed.

I hoped the years had taken the edge off her bitterness. I always mentioned her father in my letters. Toward the last I would say he sent love. For old Johnson did love Margaret.

Opportunity, May 1934.

And I am sure, on the lonely nights, he wished very much he could unsay the things that had sent her from him. Well, while there is life, it is not too late. At least he could say he was sorry he had said them. That was in my mind, knowing the time, his time, was so short, when I wrote to Margaret.

The hospital called me the morning of Christmas eve. They asked me the address of old Johnson's nearest of kin. I gave them Margaret's before I realized she would be in town that evening. After I hung up I hoped she had already left. For I could tell her more tenderly than a cold telegram.

Someone rang my bell. It was the boy with the tree my husband had bought on his way to work. The children were wild. And when I saw their excited faces, I suddenly and selfishly decided that I could not bring death into my house to mar the happiest day of their year.

No, Margaret must wait until tomorrow evening to be told. I would tell her after the last tired child had been tucked into bed. In the meantime I would make some arrangements with an undertaker.

I knew this was the most wicked thing I would ever do in my life. But, oh, she would understand when we stood and smiled down at the sleeping children that it would have been cruel to spoil their day with our grown-up grief.

Early that evening a taxi rolled up. A woman got out. I flew downstairs to open my door with words of gay greeting or solemn condolence ready on my lips. Margaret's dear familiar face was radiant. She did not know. I held her fast in my arms.

I shall never forget our happy evening. She was like a sprite, never still. She fell in love with small Margaret. Once she said fiercely to the shining faces, "Be happy. Let nothing stand in the way of your being happy." I thought, How hard her beautiful face is. It is only I who know she is not hard.

We were tired at last. Sentimentally we were going to sleep together. My husband was banished to a cot in the dining room, and sometime during the night he would fill our stockings.

Margaret and I were in my room together. She opened her bag to fetch out the stocking. On the top lay a black dress, looking as if it had been stuffed in hastily. I caught my breath sharply. She followed my glance.

She said indifferently, "This went in at the last moment. It'll have to be pressed before I wear it."

My throat went dry. For the first time in my life I was going to sleep with a stranger.

Born Helen Johnson in Boston on July 7, 1907, Helene Johnson was an only child whose mother, Ella Benson, worked as a domestic in Cambridge; her father, William Johnson, was unknown to her. She was told her father was of Greek origin and that he lived in Chicago, but she never met him. Raised in part by her maternal aunts in Oak Bluffs, Martha's Vineyard, an African American resort community, she lived for a time with her cousin, fiction writer Dorothy West, with whom she traveled to New York in the mid-1920s. It was one of these aunts who gave her the name "Helene." Educated in Oak Bluffs and Boston, Johnson attended Boston University before traveling to Harlem in the winter of 1926. She studied journalism at Columbia University, as did West.

Helene Johnson

(1907–1995)

She had already gained critical attention with the publication of her prize-winning poems in *Opportunity* beginning in 1925. Her work also appeared in William Stanley Braithwaite's *Anthology of Magazine Verse for 1926* and in the only issue of *Fire!!* (November 1926) as well as in *The Messenger* and a special issue of *Palms* edited by Countee Cullen. A rising young star of the Harlem Renaissance movement, Johnson reached the zenith of her fame in May 1927 when her poem "Bottled," a work with innovative poetic slang and unorthodox rhythms, appeared in *Vanity Fair*. These were all impressive achievements for a young African American woman experimenting with erotic themes and the use of street vernacular, a new form mastered by Langston Hughes but eschewed, for a variety of reasons, by women poets. Eight of Johnson's poems appeared in Countee Cullen's influential anthology, *Caroling Dusk* (1927). Her work was also published in James Weldon Johnson's *The Book of American Negro Poetry* in 1931.

Because Helene Johnson's poetry appears in every major periodical and anthology of the Harlem Renaissance from 1925 through her final publications in *Challenge* (1934) and *New Challenge* (1937), and because much of her poetry is both innovative and thematically relevant beyond her time, she is one of the movement's most important poets despite her short time in the public eye. Dividing her time between New York and Boston after 1929, Johnson married William Warner Hubbell III, a motorman, in 1933, and had a daughter in 1940. She was later divorced. According to her obituary in *The New York Times*, Helene Johnson continued to write a poem a day for the rest of her life, but she stopped publishing after 1937. She addressed this silence in an interview published in 1992: "It's very difficult for a poor person to be that fastened. They have to eat. In order to eat, you have to be fastened, and tightly." Helene Johnson died in Manhattan at the age of eighty-nine.

EBONY and TOPAZ

A COLLECTANEA

Charles Cullen, cover of *Ebony and Topaz*, 1927

My Race

Ah, my race,
Hungry race,
Throbbing and young—
—Ah, my race,
Wonder race,
Sobbing with song—
Ah, my race,
Laughing race,
Careless in mirth—
Ah, my veiled
Unformed race,
Fumbling in birth.

Opportunity, July 1925.

Magalu

Summer comes.
The ziczac hovers
'Round the greedy-mouthed crocodile.
A vulture bears away a foolish jackal.
The flamingo is a dash of pink
Against dark green mangroves,
Her slender legs rivalling her slim neck.
The laughing lake gurgles delicious music in its throat
And lulls to sleep the lazy lizard,
A nebulous being on a sun-scorched rock.
In such a place,
In this pulsing, riotous gasp of color,
I met Magalu, dark as a tree at night,
Eager-lipped, listening to a man with a white collar
And a small black book with a cross on it.
Oh Magalu, come! Take my hand and I will read you poetry,
Chromatic words,
Seraphic symphonies,
Fill up your throat with laughter and your heart with song.
Do not let him lure you from your laughing waters,
Lulling lakes, lissome winds.
Would you sell the colors of your sunset and the fragrance
Of your flowers, and the passionate wonder of your forest
For a creed that will not let you dance?

Opportunity, July 1926.

The Road

Ah, little road, all whirry in the breeze,
A leaping clay hill lost among the trees,
The bleeding note of rapture-streaming thrush
Caught in a drowsy hush
And stretched out in a single, singing line of dusky song.
Ah, little road, brown as my race is brown,
Your trodden beauty like our trodden pride,
Dust of the dust, they must not bruise you down.
Rise to one brimming golden, spilling cry!

Opportunity, July 1926.

Mother

Soft hair faintly white where the angels touch it;
Pale candles flaming in her eyes
Hallowing her vision of Christ;
And yet I know
She would break each Commandment
Against her heart,
And bury them pointed and jagged in her soul—
That I may smile.

Opportunity, September 1926.

Bottled

Upstairs on the third floor
Of the 135th Street library
In Harlem, I saw a little
Bottle of sand, brown sand,
Just like the kids make pies
Out of down at the beach.
But the label said: "This
Sand was taken from the Sahara desert."
Imagine that! The Sahara desert!
Some bozo's been all the way to Africa to get some sand.

And yesterday on Seventh Avenue
I saw a darky dressed fit to kill

In yellow gloves and swallowtail coat
And swirling a cane. And everyone
Was laughing at him. Me too,
At first, till I saw his face
When he stopped to hear a
Organ grinder grind out some jazz.
Boy! You should a seen that darky's face!
It just shone. Gee, he was happy!
And he began to dance. No
Charleston or Black Bottom for him.[1]
No sir. He danced just as dignified
And slow. No, not slow either.
Dignified and *proud!* You couldn't
Call it slow, not with all the
Cuttin' up he did. You would a died to see him.

The crowd kept yellin' but he didn't hear,
Just kept on dancin' and twirlin' that cane
And yellin' out loud every once in a while.
I know the crowd thought he was coo-coo.
But say, I was where I could see his face,
And somehow, I could see him dancin' in a jungle,
A real honest-to-cripe jungle, and he wouldn't have on them
Trick clothes—those yaller shoes and yaller gloves
And swallowtail coat. He wouldn't have on nothing.
And he wouldn't be carrying no cane.
He'd be carrying a spear with a sharp fine point
Like the bayonets we had "over there."[2]
And the end of it would be dipped in some kind of
Hoo-doo poison. And he'd be dancin' black and naked and gleaming.
And he'd have rings in his ears and on his nose
And bracelets and necklaces of elephants' teeth.
Gee, I bet he'd be beautiful then all right.
No one would laugh at him then, I bet.
Say! That man that took that sand from the Sahara desert
And put it in a little bottle on a shelf in the library,
That's what they done to this shine, ain't it? Bottled him.
Trick shoes, trick coat, trick cane, trick everything—all glass—
But inside—
Gee, that poor shine!

1. The Charleston and the Black Bottom were popular dances of the 1920s.
2. African American soldiers fought in France during World War I in the U.S. Army.

Vanity Fair, May 1927.

Poem

Little brown boy,
Slim, dark, big-eyed,
Crooning love songs to your banjo
Down at the Lafayette[1]—
Gee, boy, I love the way you hold your head,
High sort of and a bit to one side,
Like a prince, a jazz prince. And I love
Your eyes flashing, and your hands,
And your patent-leathered feet,
And your shoulders jerking the jig-wa.[2]
And I love your teeth flashing,
And the way your hair shines in the spotlight
Like it was the real stuff.
Gee, brown boy, I loves you all over.
I'm glad I'm a jig.[3] I'm glad I can
Understand your dancin' and your
Singin', and feel all the happiness
And joy and don't care in you.
Gee, boy, when you sing, I can close my ears
And hear tom-toms just as plain.
Listen to me, will you, what do I know
About tom-toms? But I like the word, sort of,
Don't you? It belongs to us.
Gee, boy, I love the way you hold your head,
And the way you sing, and dance,
And everything.
Say, I think you're wonderful. You're
Allright with me,
You are.

1. The Lafayette Theater in Harlem.

2. A popular dance of the time.

3. Slang for African American; when used by white people, it was a term of insult, but here, it's recast as a term of pride.

Caroling Dusk, 1927.

Sonnet to a Negro in Harlem

You are disdainful and magnificent—
Your perfect body and your pompous gait,
Your dark eyes flashing solemnly with hate;
Small wonder that you are incompetent
To imitate those whom you so despise—
Your shoulders towering high above the throng,
Your head thrown back in rich, barbaric song,
Palm trees and mangoes stretched before your eyes.
Let others toil and sweat for labor's sake
And wring from grasping hands their meed of gold.
Why urge ahead your supercilious feet?
Scorn will efface each footprint that you make.
I love your laughter, arrogant and bold.
You are too splendid for this city street!

Opportunity, July 1927.

Mae V. Cowdery

(1909–1953)

Born in Philadelphia on January 10, 1909, Mae Virginia Cowdery was the only child of a social worker mother, who was an assistant director of the Bureau for Colored Children, and a postal worker/caterer father, Lemuel Cowdery. She attended the Philadelphia High School for Girls (of which Jessie Fauset was an alumna). While she was still a high school senior, she published three poems in *Black Opals* (1927), a Philadelphia journal, and won first prize in a poetry contest run by *The Crisis* for "Longings." That same year, 1927, she won the Krigwa Poetry Prize for "Lamps." She published an impressionist short story, "Lai-Li," in *Black Opals* the following year, reminiscent of Richard Bruce Nugent's "Sahdji," which had appeared in *The New Negro* (1925). She published "Dusk" in Charles S. Johnson's *Ebony and Topaz* (1927); the poem recalls Angelina Weld Grimké's poem of the same name, which was published in *Caroling Dusk* (1927). Both pieces suggest Cowdery read and admired the work of these writers, though we can only speculate.

After graduation, Cowdery came to New York in 1927 to attend the Pratt Institute, although the school records show no evidence of her attendance until 1931. She frequented the cabarets of Harlem and Greenwich Village, where she lived. A photograph of her published by *The Crisis* in 1928 reveals a young woman of unusual beauty, style, and originality, with a bow tie, tailored jacket, and very short hair. Widely published in the late twenties in *The Crisis*, Cowdery was one of the few women of the Harlem Renaissance to bring out a volume of her own work, *We Lift Our Voices and Other Poems* (1936) with a foreword by William Stanley Braithwaite, who termed her "a fugitive poet," perhaps because of her unconventional love poetry addressed to women. Cowdery's poetry was inspired by Edna St. Vincent Millay, whom she may have known during her years in the Village. It is startlingly homoerotic. Hers are among the first identifiably lesbian texts of the twentieth century. Her poetry from the early thirties suggests Cowdery had a daughter, but no mention is made of a marriage or children in the scanty biographical material about her.

In spite of winning honors at an early age and receiving encouragement from Langston Hughes (with whom she corresponded between 1926 and 1936), Alain Locke, Benjamin Brawley, and others, Cowdery fell into obscurity after 1936. Jessie Fauset's brother, Arthur Huff Fauset, who knew her in Philadelphia, called her "a flame that burned out rapidly . . . a flash in the pan with great potential who just wouldn't settle down." Critic Richard Long, who met her in the early 1950s, observed: "She seemed a bright intelligence made bored and restless by her surroundings." Mae Cowdery took her own life at the age of forty-four.

Prove It on Me Blues

MA RAINEY
Recorded in 1928.

Went out last night, had a great big fight,
Everything seemed to go wrong;
I looked up, to my surprise,
The gal I was with was gone.

Where she went, I don't know,
I mean to follow everywhere she goes;
Folks said I'm crooked, I didn't know where she took it,
I want the whole world to know.

They say I do it, ain't nobody caught me,
Sure got to prove it on me;
Went out last night with a crowd of my friends,
They must've been women, 'cause I don't like no men.

It's true I wear a collar and a tie,
Make the wind blow all the while;
They say I do it, ain't nobody caught me,
They sure got to prove it on me.

Say I do it, ain't nobody caught me,
Sure got to prove it on me;
I went out last night with a crowd of my friends,
They must've been women, 'cause I don't like no men.

Wear my clothes just like a fan,
Talk to the gals just like any old man;
'Cause they say I do it, ain't nobody caught me,
Sure got to prove it on me.

Dusk

Like you
Letting down your
Purple-shadowed hair
To hide the rose and gold
Of your loveliness
And your eyes peeping thru
Like beacon lights
In the gathering darkness.

Ebony and Topaz, 1927.

Heritage

It is a blessed heritage
To wear pain,
A bright smile on our lips.
Our dark fathers gave us
The gift of shedding sorrow
In a song.

We Lift Our Voices, 1936.

Insatiate

If my love were meat and bread
And sweet cool wine to drink,
They would not be enough,
For I must have a finer table spread
To sate my entity.

If her lips were rubies red,
Her eyes two sapphires blue,
Her fingers ten sticks of white jade,
Coral tipped . . . and her hair of purple hue
Hung down in a silken shawl . . .
They would not be enough
To fill the coffers of my need.

If her thoughts were arrows
Ever speeding true
Into the core of my mind,
And her voice round notes of melody
No nightingale or lark
Could ever hope to sing . . .
Not even these would be enough
To keep my constancy.

But if my love did whisper
Her song into another's ear
Or place the tip of one pink nail
Upon another's hand,
Then would I forever be
A willing prisoner . . .
Chained to her side by uncertainty!

We Lift Our Voices, 1936.

Poem . . . for a Lover

I would give you
The blue-violet dreams
Of clouds . . . forgotten
And left to grow old
In the sky.

I would give you
The dew-drenched hope
Of flowers . . . forgotten
By a long dead lover
And left in a garden to die.

But you have no need
Of my meagre gifts
With your gay little songs
And lips . . . redder
Than bitter-sweet berries
Left on a leafless bush
By the frost . . .

We Lift Our Voices, 1936.

BIBLIOGRAPHY

Baker, Houston. *Afro-American Poetics: Revisions of Harlem and the Black Aesthetic.* Madison: University of Wisconsin Press, 1996.

———. *Modernism and the Harlem Renaissance.* Chicago: University of Chicago Press, 1987.

Beam, Joseph, ed. *In the Life: A Black Gay Anthology.* Boston: Alyson Publishers, 1986.

Bell, Bernard. *The Afro-American Novel and Its Tradition.* Amherst: University of Massachusetts Press, 1987.

———. "W.E.B. Du Bois's Struggle to Reconcile Folk Art and High Art." In *Critical Essays on W.E.B. Du Bois,* edited by William L. Andrews, 106–122. Boston: Hall, 1985.

Bone, Robert A. *The Negro Novel in America.* New Haven: Yale University Press, 1965.

Bontemps, Arna, ed. *The Harlem Renaissance Remembered.* New York: Dodd, Mead, 1972.

Brades, Susan Ferleger. *Rhapsodies in Black: Art of the Harlem Renaissance.* Berkeley: University of California Press, 1997.

Brown, Sterling, Arthur P. Davis, and Ulysses Lee, eds. *The Negro Caravan.* New York: Dryden Press, 1941.

Butler, Judith. "Passing, Queering: Nella Larsen's Psychoanalytic Challenge." In *Female Subjects in Black and White: Race, Psychoanalysis, Feminism,* edited by Elizabeth Abel, Barbara Christian, and Helene Moglen. Berkeley: University of California Press, 1997.

Carby, Hazel. *Reconstructing Womanhood: The Emergence of the Afro-American Woman Novelist.* New York: Oxford University Press, 1987.

Chauncey, George. *Gay New York: Gender, Urban Culture, and the Making of the Gay Male World, 1890–1940.* New York: Basic Books, 1994.

Christian, Barbara. *Black Women Novelists: The Development of a Tradition, 1892–1976.* Westport, Conn.: Greenwood Press, 1980.

Cobb, Michael. "Insolent Racing, Rough Narrative: The Harlem Renaissance's Impolite Queers." *Callaloo* 23, no. 1 (winter 2000): 328–351.

Cooke, Michael. *Afro-American Literature in the Twentieth Century: The Achievement of Intimacy.* New Haven: Yale University Press, 1984.

Cullen, Countee, ed. *Caroling Dusk: An Anthology of Verse by Negro Poets.* New York: Harper & Bros., 1927.

Davis, Angela. *Blues Legacies and Black Feminism.* New York: Random House, 1998.

Davis, Arthur P. *From the Dark Tower: Afro-American Writers, 1900–1960.* Washington, D.C.: Howard University Press, 1974.

Davis, Thadious M. *Nella Larsen: Novelist of the Harlem Renaissance.* Baton Rouge: Louisiana State University Press, 1994.

Duberman, Martin, ed. *Queer Representations: Reading Lives, Reading Cultures.* New York: New York University Press, 1997.

Faderman, Lillian. *Odd Girls and Twilight Lovers: A History of Lesbian Life in Twentieth-Century America.* New York: Columbia University Press, 1991.

Gates, Henry Louis, Jr. "The Black Man's Burden." In *Fear of a Queer Planet: Queer Politics and Social Theory,* edited by Michael Warner. Minneapolis: University of Minnesota Press, 1993.

———, and Nellie Y. McKay, eds. *The Norton Anthology of African American Literature.* New York: W.W. Norton, 1997.

Giles, Freda Scott. "Willis Richardson and Eulalie Spence: Dramatic Voices of the Harlem Renaissance." *American Drama* 5, no. 2 (1996): 1–22.

Harris, Trudier, and Thadious M. Davis, eds. *Afro-American Writers from the Harlem Renaissance to 1940.* Vol. 51 of *Dictionary of Literary Biography.* Detroit: Gale, 1987.

Harrison, Daphne Duval. *Black Pearls: Blues Queens of the 1920s.* New Brunswick: Rutgers University Press, 1988.

Hatch, James V., and Leo Hamalian, eds. *Lost Plays of the Harlem Renaissance: 1920–1940.* Detroit: Wayne State University Press, 1996.

Hawkeswood, William. *One of the Children: Gay Black Men in Harlem.* Berkeley: University of California Press, 1996.

Heibling, Mark. *The Harlem Renaissance: The One and the Many.* Westport, Conn.: Greenwood Press, 1999.

Hemenway, Robert E. *Zora Neale Hurston: A Literary Biography.* Champaign-Urbana: University of Illinois Press, 1977.

Hill, Patricia Liggins, et al. *Call and Response: The Riverside Anthology of the African American Literary Tradition.* Boston: Houghton Mifflin, 1998.

Honey, Maureen, ed. *Shadowed Dreams: Women's Poetry of the Harlem Renaissance.* New Brunswick: Rutgers University Press, 1989.

Huggins, Nathan. *Harlem Renaissance.* New York: Oxford University Press, 1971.

———, ed. *Voices from the Harlem Renaissance.* New York: Oxford University Press, 1976.

Hull, Gloria. *Color, Sex, and Poetry: Three Women Writers of the Harlem Renaissance.* Bloomington: Indiana University Press, 1987.

———, ed. *Give Us Each Day: The Diary of Alice Dunbar-Nelson.* New York: W.W. Norton, 1984.

Hutchinson, George. *The Harlem Renaissance in Black and White.* Cambridge: Harvard University Press, 1996.

Johnson, Charles S., ed. *Ebony and Topaz: A Collectanea.* New York: NUL, 1927.

Johnson, James Weldon, ed. *The Book of American Negro Poetry.* New York: Harcourt, Brace & Company, 1922 and 1931.

Kellner, Bruce, ed. *The Harlem Renaissance: An Annotated Bibliography.* Westport, Conn.: Greenwood Press, 1984.

Kerlin, Robert T., ed. *Negro Poets and Their Poems.* Washington, D.C.: Associated Publishers, 1923.

Kramer, Victor. *The Harlem Renaissance Re-Examined.* New York: AMS, 1987.

Lewis, David Levering, ed. *When Harlem Was in Vogue.* New York: Alfred A. Knopf, 1981.

———. *The Portable Harlem Renaissance Reader.* New York: Viking, 1994.

Locke, Alain. *The New Negro: Voices of the Harlem Renaissance.* New York: Albert and Charles Boni, 1925.

Locke, Alain, and Montgomery Gregory, eds. *Plays of Negro Life.* New York: Harper & Bros., 1927.

Martin, Tony. *Literary Garveyism: Garvey, Black Arts, and the Harlem Renaissance.* Dover, Mass.: Majority Press, 1983.

McDowell, Deborah. *The Changing Same: Black Women's Literature, Criticism, and Theory.* Bloomington: Indiana University Press, 1995.

Miller, Jeanne Marie A. "Georgia Douglas Johnson and May Miller: Forgotten Playwrights of the New Negro Renaissance." *College Language Association Journal* 33, no. 4 (1990): 349–366.

Mitchell, Angelyn, ed. *Within the Circle: An Anthology of African American Literary Criticism from the Harlem Renaissance.* Durham: Duke University Press, 1994.

Nelson, Emmanuel. *Critical Essays: Gay and Lesbian Writers of Color.* New York: Haworth Press, 1993.

Perkins, Kathy A. *Black Female Playwrights: An Anthology of Plays before 1950.* Bloomington: Indiana University Press, 1989.

Rampersad, Arnold. Introduction to *The New Negro: Voices of the Harlem Renaissance,* edited by Alain Locke. New York: Atheneum, 1992.

———. *The Life of Langston Hughes.* New York: Oxford University Press, 1986.

Richardson, Willis, ed. *Plays and Pageants from the Life of the Negro.* Great Neck, N.Y.: Core Collection Books, 1930.

Roses, Lorraine, and Ruth Randolph, eds. *The Harlem Renaissance and Beyond: Literary Biographies of 100 Black Women Writers 1900–1945.* Cambridge: Harvard University Press, 1990.

———. *Harlem's Glory: Black Women Writing, 1900–1950.* Cambridge: Harvard University Press, 1996.

Schockley, Ann Allen. "Afro-American Women Writers: The New Negro Movement, 1924–1933." In *Rereading Modernism: New Directions in Feminist Criticism,* edited by Lisa Rado, 123–135. New York: Garland, 1994.

Scott, Freida. "Black Drama and the Harlem Renaissance." *Theatre-Journal* 37, no. 4 (1984): 426–439.

Singh, Amritjit. *The Novels of the Harlem Renaissance.* University Park: Pennsylvania State University Press, 1976.

———, William Shiver, and Stanley Brodwin, eds. *The Harlem Renaissance: Revaluations.* New York: Garland, 1989.

Smith, Barbara. *The Truth That Never Hurts: Writings on Race, Gender, and Freedom.* New Brunswick: Rutgers University Press, 1998.

Spencer, Jon Michael. "The Black Church and the Harlem Renaissance." *African American Review* 30, no. 3 (1996): 453–460.

———. *The New Negroes and Their Music: The Success of the Harlem Renaissance.* Knoxville: University of Tennessee Press, 1997.

Sullivan, Megan. "Folk Plays, Home Girls, and Back Talk: Georgia Douglas Johnson and Women of the Harlem Renaissance." *College Language Association Journal* 38, no. 4 (1995): 404–419.

Tate, Claudia, ed. *Georgia Douglas Johnson: The Selected Works.* New York: G.K. Hall, 1997.

Thurman, Wallace, ed. *Fire!!* (November 1926). Reprint, Westport, Conn.: Negro Universities Press, 1970.

Wall, Cheryl. *Women of the Harlem Renaissance.* Bloomington: Indiana University Press, 1995.

Watson, Steven. *The Harlem Renaissance: Hub of African-American Culture, 1920–1930.* New York: Pantheon Books, 1995.

Weinberg, Jonathan. "'Boy Crazy': Carl Van Vechten's Queer Collection." *The Yale Journal of Criticism* 7, no. 2 (1994): 25–49.

Wilson, Sondra Kathryn, ed. *"The Crisis" Reader: Stories, Poetry, and Essays from the N.A.A.C.P.'s "Crisis Magazine."* New York: Modern Library, 1999.

———. *"The Opportunity" Reader: Stories, Poetry, and Essays from the Urban League's "Opportunity Magazine."* New York: Modern Library, 1999.

Wintz, Cary D., *Black Culture and the Harlem Renaissance.* Houston: Rice University Press, 1988.

———, ed. *Black Writers Interpret the Harlem Renaissance.* New York: Garland, 1996.

———, ed. *The Emergence of the Harlem Renaissance.* New York: Garland, 1996.

———, ed. *Remembering the Harlem Renaissance.* New York: Garland, 1996.

Woods, Gregory. "Gay Re-Readings of the Harlem Renaissance Poets." In *Critical Essays: Gay and Lesbian Writers of Color,* edited by Emmanual Nelson, 127–142. New York: Haworth, 1993.

Worth, Robert F. "Nigger Heaven and the Harlem Renaissance." *African-American Review* 29, no. 3 (1995): 461–473.

Young, Mary E. "Anita Scott Coleman: A Neglected Harlem Renaissance Writer." *College Language Association Journal* 40, no. 3 (1997): 271–287.

CREDITS

All material from *Opportunity* and *Ebony and Topaz* (1927), ed. Charles S. Johnson, is reprinted by permission of the National Urban League. This includes "Heritage," "Hatred," "Tokens," by Gwendolyn B. Bennett; *The Pot Maker,* by Marita O. Bonner; "A Summer Tragedy," "Golgotha Is a Mountain," "The Return," by Arna Bontemps; "Black Faces," "Wash Day," "Definition," by Anita Scott Coleman; "Dusk," by Mae Cowdery; "To Certain Critics," by Countee Cullen; "No Images," by (William) Waring Cuney; "Problems Facing Negro Young Women," by Marion Vera Cuthbert; "The Black Finger," "Dusk," by Angelina Weld Grimké; "The Palm Wine Seller," by Gladys May Casely Hayford; "To Midnight Nan at Leroy's," "Bound No'th Blues," "The Weary Blues," "Dream Variation," by Langston Hughes; "Spunk," by Zora Neale Hurston, "The Black Runner," by Georgia Douglas Johnson; "Mother," "My Race," "Magalu," "Sonnet to a Negro in Harlem," "The Road," by Helene Johnson; "Fog," *'Cruiter,* by John F. Matheus; "A Point of View," by Brenda Ray Moryck; "Shadow," by Richard Bruce Nugent; "The Negro-Art Hokum," by George Schuyler; "Letter to My Sister," by Anne Spencer; "The Last Citadel," "God's Edict," by Wallace Thurman; "The Voodoo's Revenge," by Eric Walrond; "The Typewriter," "The Black Dress," by Dorothy West. Illustrations by Aaron Douglas, "Play de Blues," "Weary As I Can Be"; Charles Cullen, cover of *Ebony and Topaz;* Richard Bruce Nugent, Drawings for Mulattoes No. 2 and No. 4 from *Ebony and Topaz.*

All material from *The Crisis* is reprinted by permission of the National Association for the Advancement of Colored People. The editors wish to thank The Crisis Publishing Company, Incorporated, the magazine of the National Association for the Advancement of Colored People, for authorizing the use of these works. This includes "On Being Young—A Woman—and Colored," "One Boy's Story," by Marita O. Bonner; "Nocturne at Bethesda," by Arna Bontemps; "Negro Laughter," "Two Old Women A-Shopping Go!" by Anita Scott Coleman; *On the Fields of France,* by Joseph Seamon Cotter, Jr.; "Criteria of Negro Art," by W.E.B. Du Bois; "Violets," "The Proletariat Speaks," by Alice Dunbar-Nelson; "Impressions of the Second Pan-African Congress," "Oriflamme," "Mary Elizabeth," "Here's April," by Jessie Redmon Fauset; "Song for a Dark Girl," "Danse Africaine," "Jazzonia," "Lullaby," "Poem [2]," "The Negro Speaks of Rivers," by Langston Hughes; "Lullaby," by Gladys May Casely Hayford; "Motherhood," "Escape," "Wishes," by Georgia Douglas Johnson; "In Haiti Is Riot of Color—" by John F. Matheus; "Exodus," "The Bronze Legacy," "The Bird in the Cage," by Effie Lee Newsome; *Undertow,* by Eulalie Spence; "White Things," "Grapes: Still-Life," by Anne Spencer; "Song of the Son," by Jean Toomer. Illustrations by Gwendolyn B. Bennett, "Pipes of Pan"; Aaron Douglas, Krigwa poster; Louise Latimer, "Blowing Bubbles"; Vivian Schuyler, "Lift Every Voice," "The Library Hour," "Drawing from Life"; Laura Wheeler (Waring), "Wishes," "Spring," "Woman Playing Harp," "The Veil of Spring," "The Strength of Africa," "Africa in America."

Cafe, by William H. Johnson (ca. 1939–1940). Reproduced by permission of the Smithsonian American Art Museum, Gift of the Harmon Foundation.

All other material is in the public domain.

INDEX OF WRITERS AND ARTISTS

ABOUT THE EDITORS

Maureen Honey (Ph.D., Michigan State University) is professor of English and Women's Studies at the University of Nebraska–Lincoln. She is the author of numerous articles and books, including *Bitter Fruit: African American Women in World War II* (University of Missouri Press, 1999), *Shadowed Dreams: Women's Poetry of the Harlem Renaissance* (Rutgers University Press, 1989), *Breaking the Ties That Bind: Popular Stories of the New Woman, 1915–1930* (University of Oklahoma Press, 1992), and *Creating Rosie the Riveter: Class, Gender, and Propaganda during World War II* (University of Massachusetts Press, 1984).

Venetria K. Patton (Ph.D., University of California–Riverside) is the Coordinator of African American and African Studies and an associate professor of English and Women's Studies at the University of Nebraska–Lincoln. Her book, *Women in Chains: The Legacy of Slavery in Black Women's Fiction* (2000), was published by SUNY Press. She is currently working on an essay collection on black women's slave narratives and a book tentatively entitled *The Making and Unmaking of Whiteness and Blackness: An Analysis of Racial Tropes in American Literature.*